TECHNOLOGY OF OBJECT-ORIENTED LANGUAGES AND SYSTEMS TOOLS 13

Proceedings of the thirteenth International Conference

TOOLS EUROPE '94 VERSAILLES, FRANCE

Editors: Boris Magnusson, Bertrand Meyer, Jean-Marc Nerson, Jean-François Perrot

Prentice Hall

New York London Toronto Sydney Tokyo Singapore

First published 1994 by
Prentice Hall International (UK) Limited
Campus 400, Maylands Avenue
Hemel Hempstead
Hertfordshire, HP2 7EZ
A division of
Simon & Schuster International Group

Printed and bound in Great Britain by
Redwood Books, Trowbridge, Wiltshire

Library of Congress Cataloging-in-Publication Data

Available from the publisher

British Library Cataloguing in Publication Data

A catalogue record for this book is available from the British Library

ISBN 0-13-350539-1 (pbk)

1 2 3 4 5 98 97 96 95 94

CONTENTS

PREFACE

For its fifth anniversary, TOOLS Europe is showing how much object technology has matured far it has spread.

The TOOLS 13 program consists of almost forty high quality articles authored by contributors originating from about fifteen different countries. It covers such topics as user interfaces, simulation, lessons learned from the practice of O-O analysis and design methods, real time and database issues, business and financial applications, and two particularly hot subjects : reuse and metrics.

The accompanying tutorial programs covers a wide range of areas, from Ada9X to frameworks, teaching object-orientation, multimedia, library design, comparison and assessment of languages and methods, software development issues and object-oriented databases.

A major innovation is the inclusion of three special tracks devoted to the major object-oriented languages : Eiffel in Action, Smalltalk World and C++ and Objects.

This is for TOOLS the opportunity to combine breadth and depth : addressing the special needs of the Eiffel, Smalltalk and C++ communities, and encouraging them to share their perspectives and debate their experiences with the hope that they will enrich each other. This is in line with the major objective of TOOLS : serving as the meeting point for practitioners and researchers, users and developers, managers and engineers, clients and suppliers of object technology.

Particular thanks are due to the program co-chairs (Boris Magnusson and Jean-François Perrot) as well as to the chairs of the specialized programs (Eric Mahe and Marc Goldberg for C++ and Objects, Jean Bezivin and Mario Wolczco for Smalltalk World, Richard Wiener for Eiffel in Action).

Many thanks also to the reviewers, the contributors, and the enthusiastic exhibitors and sponsors. The organization committee under the leadership of Madeleine Fonlupt was a tremendous help.

We hope that you will enjoy TOOLS 13 as much as we enjoyed putting it together.

Jean-Marc Nerson

Bertrand Meyer

PROGRAM COMMITTEE

Program Co-Chairs:

Boris Magnusson, Lund University (Sweden)
Jean-François Perrot, Université Paris VI (France)

TOOLS Conference

Pierre America
Philips Research Laboratories

Bruce Anderson
University of Essex

François Bancilhon
O2 Technology

Matthias Bücker
Ciba Geigy AG

David M. Butler
Limit Point Systems

Françoise Carré
Matra Espace

Eduardo Casais
Forschungszentrum Informatik Karlsruhe

Bernard Coulange
Verilog

Elspeth Cusack
British Telecom

Paul Dubois
Lawrence Livermore National Laboratory

Bjorn Freeman-Benson
Aarhus University

Annick Fron
AFC Europe

Jean-Marc Geib
University of Lille

Ivar Jacobson
Objective Systems

Bruce E. Krell
Krell Inc.

Stein Krogdahl
University of Oslo

Chris Laffra
IBM TJ. Watson Research Center

Ole Lehrmann Madsen
University of Aarhus

Dino Mandrioli
Politecnico di Milano

Marc Nanard
LIRM

Oscar Nierstrasz
University of Geneva

Walter G. Olthoff
University of Kaiserslautern

Rob Pooley
University of Edinburgh

Roger Rousseau
University of Nice Sophia Antipolis

Jean Claude Royer
University of Nantes

Kees Smedema
Philips Medical Systems

Dave Thomas
Object Technology International

Jean Vaucher
CRIM, Montreal

Kim Waldén
ENEA Data AB

Anthony I. Wasserman
Interactive Development Environments

Roberto Zicari
University of Frankfurt

C++ and Objects

Isabelle Cacheux
Geomath International

Marc Goldberg (program co-chair)
Rational

Nasser Ketani
CR2A

Eric Mahé (program co-chair)
Sun Microsystems France

Thuy Nguyen
Matra Datavision

Eiffel in Action

Richard Wiener (program chair)
JOOP

Smalltalk World

Jean-Bézivin (program co-chair)
University of Nantes

Mario Wolczcko (program co-chair)
Sun Microsystems

INVITED LECTURES

Roger Osmond

Bytex Corporation
4 Technology Drive
Westborough, MA 01581-01760
USA
e-mail: rfo@bytex.com

Large project experience

Industry leader Roger Osmond will discuss how object-oriented techniques helped turn the tables around at Bytex Corporation (Boston, Massachussetts) and share his experience of dos and don'ts.

Keynote: François Allard
Simulation Facilities Section
ESA/ESTEC/WGS
Keplerlaan 1
2200 AG Noordwijk
The Netherlands
e-mail: francois@wgs.estec.esa.nl

Abstract: Object-Oriented Programming at the European Space Agency

The European Space Agency has been pursuing for several years now the development of software based on object-oriented techniques. The proposed address will describe first the past, present and foreseen efforts at ESA in terms of object-oriented environments, tools and applications. The domains of application, the nature of the tools and the nature of the encountered difficulties or benefits will be mentioned.

Furthermore, ESA has tried to develop some tools or applications in what can be considered the border of applicability of object-oriented programming: real-time simulation of dynamic systems, virtual reality, operational software.

The result of these efforts can provide a number of interesting lessons which will be mentioned. The presentation will thus continue with some reflections about object orientation. In particular there seems to be limits to the approach which can be felt both from the technical (in particular design and validation) and the "enterprise culture" points of view. In this respect a distinction will be made between "mathematical" (i.e. based on a pre-defined mathematical analysis) and pre-mathematical software (based on a more qualitative description).

At the same time, the number of requests and efforts for new application domains, tools and environments is increasing. This creates the need to define guidelines,influence the definition of software life-cycle standards (like ESA's PSS-05 standard) and address issues implied by using such software in an operational context: of particular importance here are the problems linked to verification and validation.

Finally, the address will conclude with some ideas and issues about the future of object-oriented programming in general and at ESA in particular. It will be argued that this future is the definition of software systems with "emergent" properties or computation characteristics.

Bertrand Meyer

Interactive Software Engineering
270 Storke Road, Suite 7
Goleta, CA 83117
USA
e-mail: bertrand@eiffel.com

Uses and Misuses of Inheritance

Bertrand Meyer, author of the best-seller *Object-Oriented Software Construction*, will discuss one of the most tricky questions in the field: how to use inheritance, and how not to misuse it.

SUBMITTED ARTICLES

USER INTERFACES, GRAPHICS AND SIMULATION

Rollit: An Application Builder

Solange Karsenty and Chris Weikart
Digital Equipment Corporation, Paris Research Laboratory
85 Avenue Victor Hugo, 92500 Rueil-Malmaison, France
{karsenty,weikart}@prl.dec.com

Abstract

Contemporary user interface development systems greatly simplify creation of traditional *dialogue* user interface made of buttons or menus, but they do not support the construction and manipulation of application-specific graphical objects. This article describes Rollit, a *domain-specific*, interactive, application builder developed at the DEC Paris Research Laboratory. The goal of this system is to automatically generate, as a result of direct manipulation, the domain-specific user interface and its run-time behavior as well as the traditional dialogue user interface. Application programmers construct complex objects from standard components, define the interactions between those objects and attach behaviors to them. A constraint-based inference system facilitates the definition of geometrical constraints between objects. Our run-time system kernel supports standard operations on those objects, such as creation and deletion, cut and paste, grouping, save and load. This article describes our system, illustrates its usefulness through applications built within our environment, and shows how it reduces the effort required to develop such applications.

1 Introduction

In the domain of user interface development systems, interactive user interface builders have moved from research prototypes to available products in less than a decade. Such tools support user interface design as a separate task and facilitate prototyping and user testing. Today's builders use direct manipulation techniques to assemble toolkit components and create the user interface layout. However, these builders only deal with the part of the user interface that uses interactors such as menus and buttons assembled in dialogues. Still missing is the application-specific component, which must be implemented by conventional programming.

User interface development tools often reach their limits when the task is to build the application-specific user interface. This interface is a window or "black box", where the developer must deal with input and output at all levels of abstraction through conventional programming. This part of the user interface is application dependent, since it is closely related to the application's semantics. Here, user interaction requires a fine grained control which breaks the usual separation between application and user interface. As an example, the application-specific user interface of a circuit editor is composed of circuits, while the traditional dialogue user interface is made of buttons and menus to open and save files, or define parameters. When the user manipulates the circuits, the application maintains a context that depends on the semantics of the different circuit components.

Thus, the application-specific user interface represents a more complex problem than the traditional dialogue user interface. We see two significant differences. First, the dialogue user interface is made of "universal" widgets available in common toolkits. The application-specific user interface, on the other hand, is application dependent; what is needed, then, is a way to define the widgets themselves (circuits components, for example). Second, application-specific data is highly dynamic and responds to a specific run-time behavior – objects will typically be created, deleted and modified by the end user. In

From TOOLS EUROPE '94 (Technology of Object-Oriented Languages and Systems).

contrast, menus and buttons are usually static.

In summary, the creation of the complete application interface requires: (1) specification of the presentation part, (2) specification of its run-time behavior, and (3) support for the management of the application data structures. Some tools deal with (1) or (2), while (3) is often provided by specialized libraries. But so far we know of no user interface development systems explicitly providing all three. The goal of our work is to increase the functionality of user interface builders by providing high-level tools addressing all three aspects of the problem. We dramatically decrease the amount of work needed to develop a complete application by providing complete support for the management of application data.

This article is organized as follows: we first review existing tools, then present Rollit examples that illustrate the construction of an application from a user's point of view. Finally, we describe Rollit, and conclude with lessons learned.

2 Related Work

In this section we review tools that provide support for the application-specific user interface, which reflects the data that is managed by the application. Several systems manage application data with a mapping to an intermediate representation. This is flexible for existing applications but the mapping can become expensive and complicated.

Humanoid [Szekely90] allows the mapping of application data to a widget tree, therefore application data remains external to the system. Serpent [Bass91] also uses this approach. It manages an active database that contains shared data between the interface and the functional core. A declarative language, Slang, is used to describe the data mapped to the presentation layer. Another language, Saddle, is used to describe the database itself. This database contains templates that are instantiated at run-time, with the possibility to describe behavior when an instance is created or deleted.

Rollit directly manages application data and its user interface. This frees us from the limitations of a fixed set of widgets, and allows us to create more original applications. In this sense, our work is similar to Demo [Wolber91] or Peridot [Myers88], since we can create new widgets by direct manipulation. Peridot, which relies on knowledge inferencing techniques, concentrates on demonstrating the behavior of such interactors. Lapidary [Myers89] concentrates on the graphical creation of widgets, and allows creating new types of widgets. Trip3 [Miyashita92] is a system that concentrates on inferring relationships by generalization from example objects that are drawn with a graphical editor. None of these systems provide explicit support for run-time management of application data and abstractions for the creation of a complete graphical application.

Ibuild [Vlissides92] is a user interface builder based on Unidraw [Vlissides89], a collection of classes that facilitates the creation of graphical editors. The type of graphical editors created with Unidraw are a subset of our targeted applications. In addition to standard widgets, Ibuild provides support for building new objects through a purely graphical editor. However, these objects are not "first class" and must be accessed through a specific interface in order to extract useful data. Ibuild generates basic object classes that can be used by the developer to create a complete application.

SX/Tools [Kuhme92] is a system that provides support for the creation of application-specific objects. It concentrates on the design of the user interface – presentation and behavior – by providing explicit support for creating application-specific objects. So-called "direct composition" means that every object is responsible (provides methods) for its own design as well as its behavior. A graphical editor provides "toolboxes" of prototype objects which can be instantiated and customized using these design methods. The developer writes scripts to describe their behavior but SX/Tools requires writing additional code in order to manage application objects. The task of mapping application data to graphical objects is left to the developer.

3 A Tour With Examples

In this section, we briefly describe Rollit's graphical editor, **FunBuild**, which is used to build the domain-specific application objects. Then we show examples that illustrate a variety of applications built with

Rollit.

FunBuild provides a set of primitive objects organized in a palette. The developer or graphic designer uses FunBuild to construct the layout of graphical objects and specify their attributes. The system kernel includes a set of predefined graphical objects such as rectangles, circles, ellipses, lines, polylines, texts and images. These are used to build *composite* objects that can be added to the palette and/or saved as source code object classes. Composite objects are organized as a hierarchy that corresponds to, for example, a circuit with subcomponents.

FunBuild allows the specification of geometrical constraints between objects and within objects. Geometrical constraints are applied between object *handles*. Handles are placed on corners and midpoints of graphical shapes. New handles can be created interactively by clicking on the objects themselves. Geometrical constraints include connectors, aligners, enclosers, spacers, repulsers and attractors. Constraints are established interactively by direct manipulation. FunBuild uses a constraint inference system that proposes possible constraints and lets the user choose and apply them. Funbuild also provides relations that apply to object attributes. A relation is a constraint which is satisfied upon explicit request, while geometrical constraints are always satisfied. For example, objects can be automatically popped up or hidden by defining relations that apply to their visibility. This kind of relation can be triggered by a mouse click.

Our first example, a circuit editor, was created in less than an hour. FunBuild was used to design the circuit building blocks, *i.e.* the different gates available in the circuit editor tool palette. These gates are made of polygons, user-defined handles (input and output connectors) and labels. For each gate, FunBuild generates files that describe their structure, attributes, behavior and constraints. These objects can then be used directly in the final application.

This application is built on an application framework, with a runtime-configurable dialogue interface, which allows access to a panoply of application services such as cut, copy and paste of application objects. It also provides a set of predefined behaviors that allow circuits to be created, selected, moved and resized by direct manipulation. Circuits can be connected with wires: a wire is created by a click and drag action.

Figure 1 shows the construction of the application objects. An AND gate object is being modified under FunBuild (top window). After we edit and save the new description, we can immediately see the effect by creating a new instance of this gate under the running application. The circuit editor need not be recompiled or rerun because the saved object is interpreted at run-time. The interpreter is part of Rollit's library, linked with the application. In this example, existing gates remain unmodified by default; in future versions Rollit will also have the capability of updating all existing instances based on the new prototype. When the user deletes a gate in the final application, the connected wires are also deleted: such behavior is also specified within FunBuild.

Figure 2 shows the final circuit editor. It provides multiple views of the circuits and allows editing of subcomponents. In the figure, the user is editing the gate label in the top right view.

The second example is a navigation tool for the Digital Paris Research Laboratory (Figure 3). FunBuild was used to draw the maps and create the navigation paths: visibility relations were defined under FunBuild in order to allow navigation through the maps. In this example, the library is a component of the global map that is linked to another more detailed map of the library. When the user clicks on the library icon, the application opens another view on the library map. This kind of run-time behavior is directly defined under the graphical editor by creating a relation between the icon and the map. In addition, our application objects have not only a visual appearance, but they can also produce sound. In this case, the feature allows us to play vocal on-line help.

FunBuild can also be used to build arbitrary widgets such as a slider, as demonstrated in a videotape [Karsenty93]. Finally, the last example is an iconic shell. FunBuild was used to build different types of icons (files, directories, executables). Each icon contains a drawing, a bitmap, and a text label for the file or directory name. Operations such as selection (see Figure 4), moving and copying of files are inherited from standard behaviors.

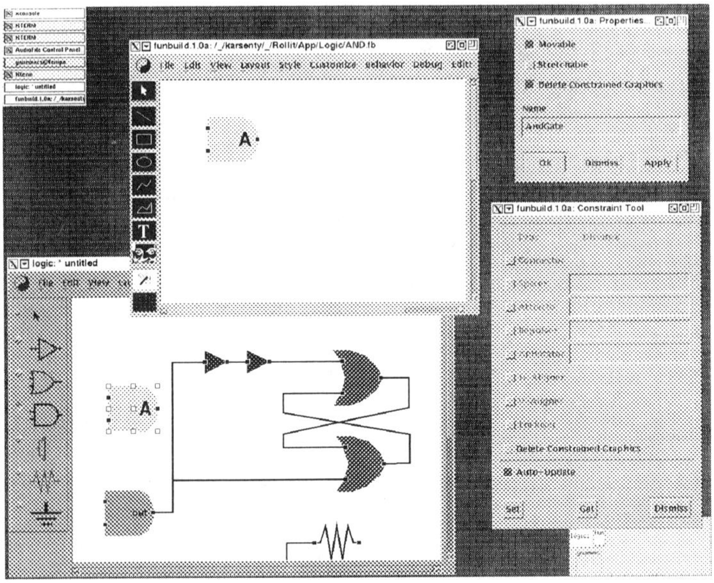

Figure 1: FunBuild: building an AND gate application object (top window) and testing it in the final application (bottom window)

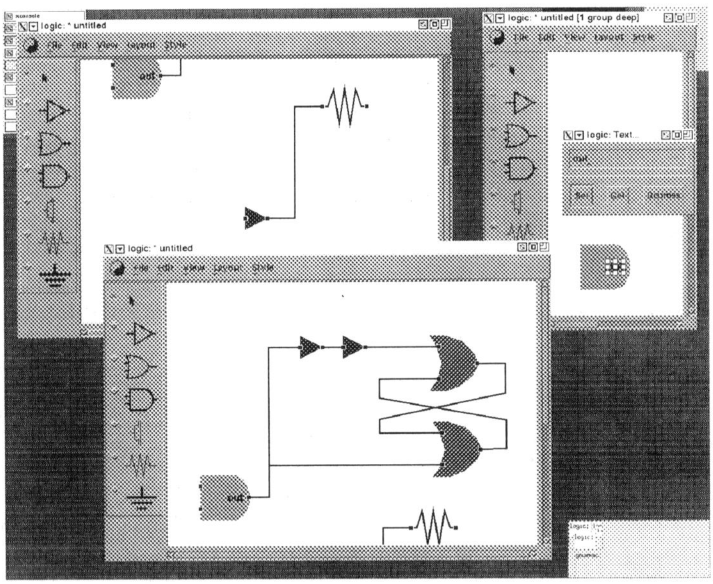

Figure 2: The circuit editor

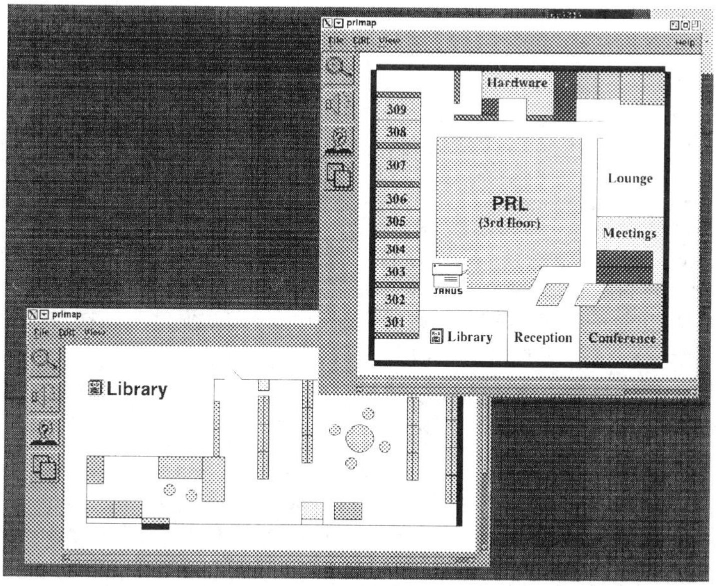

Figure 3: The PRL navigator

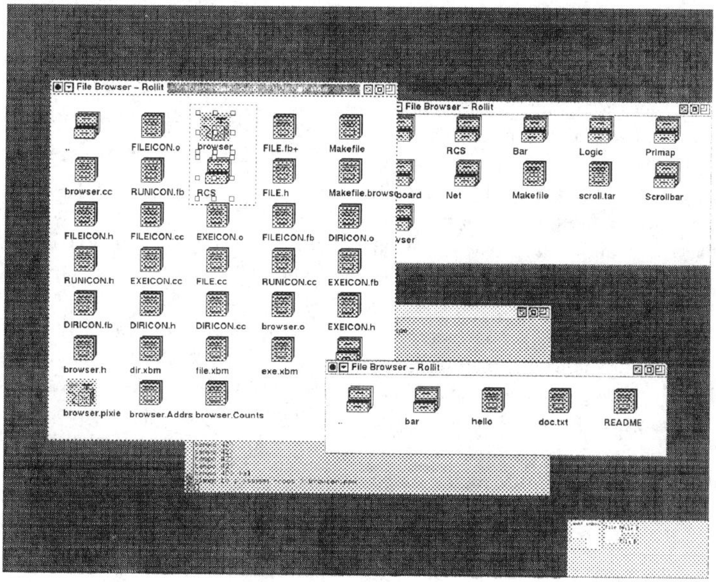

Figure 4: The iconic shell

4 Rollit

In this section, we describe the different components of the **Rollit** system. Rollit combines an interactive editor for generating application object classes and an application framework that uses these classes (see Figure 5). Rollit applications are either directly built on top of the kernel (such as the iconic shell), or within the application framework (such as the circuit editor and the PRL navigator). The editor FunBuild is itself an application built with Rollit and the application framework.

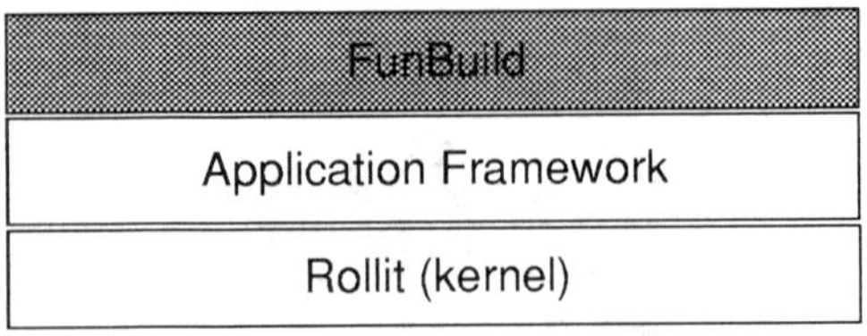

Figure 5: Rollit architecture

4.1 The Kernel

Rollit's kernel provides the generic data structure used and generated by FunBuild. This data structure is a graph where vertices are graphical objects and edges are constraints or relations between vertices. Both vertices and edges are "first class" objects. As an example, Figure 6 shows a graphical object with its corresponding data structure. The top of the figure is what the user manipulates: two graphical objects, a circle and a rectangle that are aligned horizontally, with an arrow between them, and text annotations. The bottom represents the data structure composed of five graphical objects or vertices (the arrow, the circle, the rectangle and two texts) and five constraints or edges: c1 and c2 that connect both arrow endpoints to the circle and rectangle, a1 and a2 that maintain the texts annotating the circle and rectangle, and h1 that maintains the circle and rectangle horizontally aligned.

The graph is recursive, that is, a vertex can itself be a graph. This characteristic allows us to create *composite* objects that can be visualized and manipulated as single entities. For example, a circuit is made of recursive components: logical blocks have

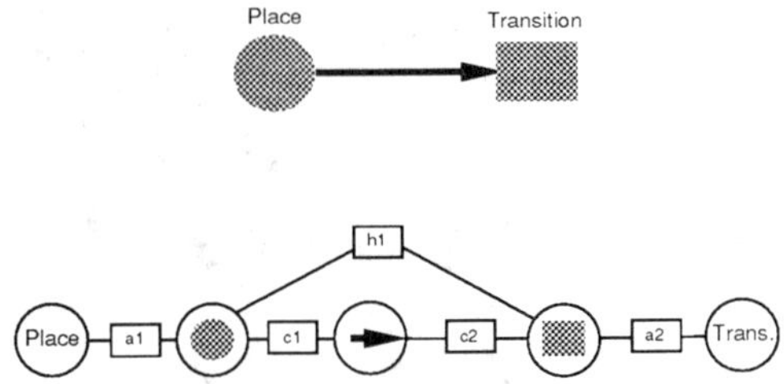

Figure 6: Graphical object (top) and its associated data structure (bottom: circles are vertices and boxes are edges)

input and output connectors, and each block or subcomponent is recursively made of gates with input and output connectors. The navigation tool uses this feature to create the navigation path: the library is a subcomponent of the global composite map.

Customizable editors such as Edge [Newberry90] or TGE [Karrer90] also use a graph to represent the application data, but it is directly mapped to graphics; in contrast, vertices are our only graphical objects. Hence, the *graphical* arrow in the figure corresponds to a vertex in the graph while it would corresponds to an arc in Edge or TGE. While TGE focuses on the graphical representation of graphs, we are aiming at arbitrary graphical representations. Our targeted applications are therefore more diverse.

Rollit's kernel also includes a constraint solver, a constraint inference system, and a set of behaviors that are discussed in the following sections. The types of graphical objects that can be created with Rollit determine a class of applications domains: graphical applications that manage objects such as complex diagrams, graphs, trees, circuits (CAD tools), networks, hypermedia data and arbitrary widgets. Such applications require graphics, possibly images and sound and have specific constraints to govern the behavior of the graphical objects.

4.2 The Front End: FunBuild

FunBuild stands for **Fun**ctional core **Build**er, in reference to the semantic part of an interactive application [Bass91]. FunBuild is a sophisticated graphical editor that uses the application support provided by Rollit: data management operations, viewing operations, persistency and constraints. FunBuild allows access to most kernel features. FunBuild functions include:

- Multi-selection;
- Creation and deletion of objects and constraints;
- Drawing aids (constraint inference system, grid);
- Setting of object attributes;
- Specification of run-time behavior (constraints, reactivity to user input);
- Cut, copy and paste;
- Grouping: composite object;
- Persistency;
- PostScript output;
- Zooming and multi-view.

Composites, or groups, are edited through multiple views of subcomponents without ungrouping the composite itself. This feature is fundamental since composites – like other objects – can have their attributes modified and constraints can be applied to them. Ungrouping a composite in order to edit its components would loose these attributes and constraints.

4.3 Constraints

Geometrical constraints are applied with FunBuild through a powerful constraint inferencing system: **Rockit**. Rockit identifies the possible graphical constraints between objects in a scene and allows the designer to quickly and easily select and apply the desired constraints. The inferred constraints are presented to the user by sonic and graphical feedback. As the user manipulates the object, the object *gravitates* towards the most likely constraint scenario. Rockit makes it easy to try other likely scenarios by simply clicking a mouse button, causing the system to cycle through the other possibilities. The Rockit system has been presented in detail in [Karsenty92b] and the use of auditory feedback within FunBuild in [Karsenty92a, Karsenty93].

Geometrical constraints are solved in real-time while the user manipulates objects in the scene. Therefore,

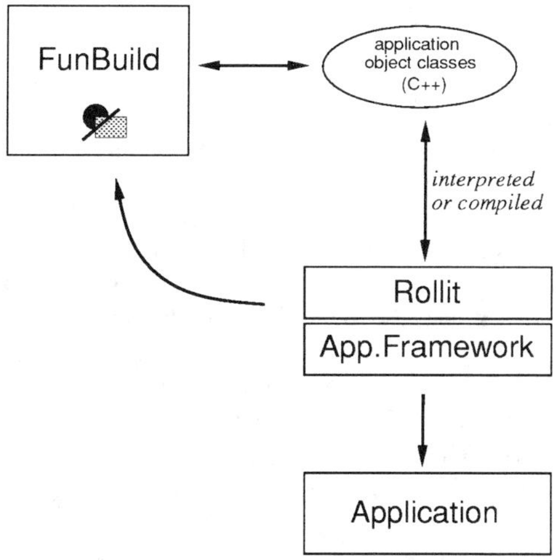

Figure 7: Rollit's development process: FunBuild is used to generate application object classes. These object classes can be used by the application framework based on Rollit. They can be modified with FunBuild while specializing the final application. The final application is either a standalone executable or an executable that interprets the generated object classes.

the user cannot create over-constrained situations where the system would have no solution: Rockit only proposes constraints that are compatible with the current constraint system. Since constraints are satisfied for every mouse move, we need a very efficient constraint solver. Our solver builds a three-level recursive constraint hierarchy: the algorithm satisfies constraints that apply first within the selected (or dragged) object(s), then between the selected object(s) and other objects, finally between remaining objects. This algorithm runs recursively on components of composite objects.

Our implementation is inspired by Alien [Cournarie91] which is based on the technique of local propagation. The solver is completely independent of the constraints: all it needs to know is whether a constraint is satisfied, and how to ask a constraint to satisfy itself. Therefore a constraint can be of any nature; in particular, it is not necessarily geometrical.

4.4 Generating the Final Application

When saving objects, FunBuild generates C++ code, which is either interpreted or compiled in the final application. The choice between compiling and interpreting gives us a flexible scheme: as long as the application is under development, the generated classes are interpreted at run-time. This allows the developer to edit these classes and have immediate feedback, because the application does not need to be recompiled. However, when the application is released, this code can be compiled with the rest of the application. Figure 7 illustrates the development process of an application.

Below is a simplified version of a generated *AndGate* class for the circuit editor. The user gives a class name with FunBuild, and FunBuild generates three files. The first file contains the class declaration, which contains an accessor for a text output label named *outlabel*:

```
/*** AndGate.h -  class declaration ***/
class AndGate : public RiGraphic {
  public:
    AndGate (RiGraphic *parent, POINT* pos);
    RiText * Outlabel();
};
```

The second file contains the corresponding class constructor:

```
/*** AndGate.cc -  class constructor ***/
AndGate :: AndGate (RiGraphic *p) :
           RiGraphic(){
#ifdef COMPILED
#include "AndGate.fb"
#else
  LoadFile ("AndGate.fb");
#endif
  if (p) p->AddChild (this);
}
```

The third file contains the body of the class constructor:

```
/*** file AndGate.fb ***/
COLOR* col2 = new COLOR ("black");
COLOR* col3 = new COLOR (62913,60816,0);
ENV* env4 = new GENV (col2, ...)
RiEllipse* go0 = new RiEllipse (149,78,
                                209,158);
RiGraphic* var1 = new RiGraphic (*go0,*env4);
var1->Stretchable (FALSE);
this->AddChild (var1);
[ .... ]
this->Stretchable (FALSE);
this->DelConstrainedGraphic (TRUE);
this->ClassName ("AndGate");
this->NewHandle (*new POINT(119,98));
this->NewHandle (*new POINT(119,138));
this->NewHandle (*new POINT(209,118));
```

These are method calls to construct an *AndGate* object: graphical appearance, geometrical and non-geometrical constraints, attributes, handles, run-time behavior. Depending on the COMPILED flag in the class constructor (*AndGate.cc*), this file is either compiled or interpreted in the class constructor.

None of the generated files are to be edited by hand. Customization is achieved by deriving new classes from the generated base class. The developer can regenerate the base class with FunBuild without loosing modifications added in the derived class. This is how application code is connected to Rollit objects.

Compiling insures good performance. It also has the advantage that the application is a standalone executable. On the other hand the interpreter, which is always part of the generated application, can prove useful in the final application. For example, in the circuit editor, one could allow the end-user to modify and save the circuit components themselves. This is a powerful means of end-user customization. We have deliberately chosen not to create another language for persistent objects, and we see this as an advantage: C++ is both the programming language and the format (a subset thereof) for persistent objects.

Applications often need to access components of composite objects from within the application. FunBuild allows naming object components. In the example above, a label for the output connector was given the name *outlabel* under FunBuild. Rollit generates an accessor for this label.

4.5 Customizing the Application

A fundamental aspect of Rollit is application customization. Part of it is done within FunBuild and part of it by writing additional code.

Pre-conditions

Creation and deletion of objects and constraints is

controlled by pre-conditions that the developer can overload by writing additional code in the application. As shown by Gieskens [Gieskens92], the use of pre-conditions at run-time provides a fine-grained control over the user interface behavior. Let us consider again the circuit editor and assume that we have specified the circuit components. We now want to specify that a wire can only connect an input connector to an output connector. This condition can be verified by overloading the creation pre-condition in the wire class. If the condition is not met, the creation of the line is canceled. Adding this pre-condition requires writing ten lines of additional source code.

Default pre-conditions can be specified under FunBuild by setting object attributes. For example, if there is a constraint between graphical objects *A* and *B*, the deletion of *A* can cause the deletion of *B*. The circuit editor uses this mechanism to automatically delete the connected wires when a gate is deleted. Constraint deletion also uses this mechanism. Deleting a constraint can trigger the deletion of constrained objects.

Behaviors

In addition to pre-conditions, the customization of the dynamic aspect of the interaction at run-time is achieved by *behaviors*. A behavior is a first class object that filters input events and encapsulates common sequences of actions. Behaviors are associated to graphical objects and to windows by a mechanism called registration. A graphical object or window can register an arbitrary number of behaviors; a behavior can be shared among several objects or windows. Rollit includes a large set of behaviors that can be composed in order to create new ones. Default behaviors for windows allow the manipulation of the global selection or the creation of an object. For example, the user can click and drag a bounding box to select several objects at once, or click and drag a shape whose position and size are used to create an instance of a class. Behaviors for objects are of two types: behaviors for object handles and behaviors for the objects themselves. Default handle behaviors allow moving, resizing and duplicating objects. Default object behaviors allow selecting them. For example, in the iconic shell, the icon copy and move behaviors were specialized to also perform the actual system operations.

4.6 The Application Framework

The last component of Rollit is the application framework, which allows the creation of complete applications. The application framework provides an application skeleton that constructs a tool palette and set of menus. The tool palette is automatically built from a set of objects classes defined under FunBuild and the menus provide access to Rollit services. All the examples cited above were built within this framework, including FunBuild itself. Rollit's kernel is completely independent from the application framework, therefore Rollit users are not limited to building applications based on this framework. They can instead use a traditional user interface builder or just a conventional toolkit in combination with Rollit.

This framework allows rapid construction of graphical editors that can be easily modified. Behaviors are automatically associated to each element in the tool palette, and they can be customized too. For example, in the circuit editor, wire creation was modified in order to create the constraints that connect both ends to the gates. When the user selects a tool, the application enters a mode where objects are created by a click and drag action.

5 Status and Implementation

Rollit's kernel is built on top of the Xtv toolkit [Beaudouin90], while the application framework uses the Motif [OSF90] toolkit in addition to Rollit. It is entirely developed in C++ and runs on mips DECStations (Ultrix) and DEC Alpha workstations (OSF/1). Rollit has been released as a research prototype to users inside the company who use it for various application domains. We are building applications ourselves, and have done some measurements in order to estimate the time and code savings. A basic net editor, built without the application framework, required one hour of work and represents around 50 lines of additional source code that implement the semantic checking of interconnections. An application based on the framework, such as the circuit editor, represents 200 lines of code. We estimate that the same application, built with a traditional toolkit and interface builder, would require around 2000 lines of code. The navigator (*i.e.* the maps and the navigation path) was almost entirely specified under FunBuild. Since the application is mostly retrieving information in real time from the local network (e.g. the state of a printer), it consists of a set of system calls to standard Unix commands.

6 Lessons Learned

Rollit focuses on the graphical description of objects, as well as on support for management and manipulation of application data objects and interaction between these objects. The combination of constraint, pre-condition, and behavior objects provides a rich basis for the description of run-time behavior. In other words, we support the presentation of the application as well as its semantics. We have found that four design rules were crucial to the success of the system: open design (collaboration with other tools), applicability (covering a significant range of applications), usability, performance and scaling.

Open Design
Rollit could be used to create a custom toolkit and solve the problem of building the entire application interface (dialogue and domain-specific); however we chose to design Rollit as one component of a user interface development environment (UIDE). In particular, considering the numerous traditional user interface builders based on standard toolkits, we have maintained a clean separation between the kernel and the application framework. Our system can collaborate with other tools, unlike many systems that require the complete application be built within the same environment. We have also developed applications that are based solely on Rollit's kernel.

Applicability
We have illustrated a variety of application domains through several examples. So far, we have been able to design applications in areas such as information display, circuit design, educational software, hypermedia, and graphical editors. Rollit has recently been released to developers working in the domains of telecommunications, scientific visualization and visual programming.

Usability
We conducted user testing during the iterative design and development stages of the graphical editor. We submitted tasks to several users with various levels of expertise, and we videotaped each session. This immediatly revealed inconsistencies, such as the vocabulary for menus and dialogues, as well as functionality conflicts leading to the wrong goal. Thanks to this feedback, the final result is an intuitive and consistent specialized graphical editor. The inferencing system, Rockit, which allows the designer to place constraints while dragging the objects in the scene, makes it very easy to build basic objects. Furthermore, FunBuild provides direct manipulation access to most Rollit functions.

Performance and Scaling
Rollit objects are lightweight. Therefore the system scales very well in size and response time for data structures made of hundreds of objects. We are working with hardware designers on a schematic editor that would deal with large schematics containing over a thousand objects. The typical size of a standalone application generated with Rollit is one megabyte for a kernel-based application and four megabytes for a Motif (application framework) application (stripped RISC binaries).

7 Future Work

We are currently continuing the exploration of direct manipulation techniques for the specification of run-time behavior. The interactive editor is our testbed for the specification of these dynamic aspects. We intend to provide support for creation of arbitrary relations on object attributes. The current mechanism for defining relations lacks abstraction. The developer must write code in order to create new types of relations. We are also working on automating the creation of constraints in the final application. This can be achieved by example. An example demonstrates constraints that exist between certain classes of objects. These constraints can automatically be created when the end-user create objects. For instance, if an example shows two boxes that are aligned, the final application will systematically align a new box with the closest one.

8 Conclusion

We have described a system that addresses the problem of building the complete application user interface. Rollit complements traditional user interface builders because it is centered around the domain-specific user interface. Rollit is fully implemented and includes a sophisticated graphical editor for the design of application objects but also explicit support for application: display, management, and run-time behavior of application data. In addition, Rollit facilitates defining the semantics of the application. Our experience with the system shows a reduction of the development time for a significant category of applications.

Acknowledgements

We thank Michel Beaudouin-Lafon for his contribution and numerous discussions on this work. Michel Gangnet, Henry Levy, and Peter Van Roy have helped improve the readability of this article. James Landay has provided the initial design of Rockit.

References

[Beaudouin90] Michel Beaudouin-Lafon, Yves Berteaud, and Stéphane Chatty. Creating Direct Manipulation Applications with Xtv. In *Proc. European X Window System Conference EX'90*, pages 148–155, November 1990.

[Bass91] Len Bass and Joëlle Coutaz. *Developing Software for the User Interface*. Addison Wesley, 1991.

[Cournarie91]
Eric Cournarie and Michel Beaudouin-Lafon. Alien: a prototype-based constraint system. In *Second Eurographics Workshop on Object Oriented Graphics*, pages 93–114, June 1991.

[Gieskens92] Daniel F. Gieskens and James D. Foley. Controlling User Interface Objects through Pre- and Postconditions. In *CHI'92 Proceedings, Human Factors in Computing Systems*, pages 189–194. Addison Wesley, 1992.

[Karsenty92a] Solange Karsenty, James A. Landay, and Chris Weikart. Audio Cues for Graphic Design. In *Human Factors in Computing Systems, CHI'92 Posters and Short Talks Proceedings*, pages 77–78, Monterey, CA, May 1992. ACM Press, Addison Wesley.

[Karsenty92b] Solange Karsenty, James A. Landay, and Chris Weikart. Inferring Graphical Constraints with Rockit. In *People and Computers VII: Proceedings of HCI'92*, University of York, U.K., September 1992. Cambridge University Press. Also as Research Report 17, Digital Equipment Corporation, Paris Research Laboratory.

[Karsenty93] Solange Karsenty, James A. Landay, and Chris Weikart. Inferring Graphical Constraints With Rockit. In *Human Factors in Computing Systems, Proceedings of InterCHI'93 (Formal Video Program)*, page 531, Amsterdam, April 1993. ACM Press, Addison Wesley.

[Karrer90] Anthony Karrer and Walt Scacchi. Requirements for an Extensible Object–Oriented Tree/Graph Editor. In *Proc. ACM SIGGRAPH Symposium on User Interface Software and Technology*, pages 84–91, October 1990.

[Kuhme92] Thomas Kühme and Matthias Schneider-Hufschmidt. SX/Tools - An Open Design Environment for Adaptable Multimedia User Interfaces. In *Eurographics'92 Proceedings, Volume 11 (3)*, pages 94–105, Cambridge, September 1992.

[Miyashita92] Ken Miyashita, Satoshi Matsuoka, Shin Takahashi, Akinori Yonezawa, and Tomihisa Kamada. Declarative Programming of Graphical Interface by Visual Examples. In *Proceedings of ACM Symposium on User Interface Software Technology, UIST'92*, pages 107–116, Monterey, CA, May 1992. ACM Press.

[Myers88] Brad A. Myers. *Creating User Interfaces by Demonstration*. Academic Press, 1988.

[Myers89] Brad A. Myers, Brad Vander Zanden, and Roger B. Dannenberg. Creating Graphical Interactive Objects by Demonstration. In *Proceedings of ACM Symposium on User Interface*

Software Technology, pages 95–104, November 1989.

[Newberry90] Frances Newberry Paulisch and Walter F. Tichy. EDGE: An Extensible Graph Editor. *Software Practice and Experience*, 20(S1):63–88, June 1990.

[OSF90] OSF, editor. *OSF/Motif Programmer's Reference*. Prentice Hall, 1990.

[Szekely90] Pedro Szekely. Template–Based mapping of application data to interactive display. In *Proceedings ACM SIGGRAPH Symposium on User Interface Software and Technology*, pages 1–9, Snowbird, October 1990.

[Vlissides89] John M. Vlissides and Mark A. Linton. Unidraw: A Framework for Building Domain-Specific Graphical Editors. Technical Report CSL–TR–89–380, Stanford University, July 1989.

[Vlissides92] John Vlissides, Steve Tang, and Charles Brauer. *Ibuild User's Guide*. Stanford University, September 1992.

[Wolber91] David Wolber and Gene Fisher. A Demonstrational Technique for Developing Interfaces with Dynamically Created Objects. In *Proceedings of ACM Symposium on User Interface Software Technology*, pages 221–230, November 1991.

A Motif Widget to Display, Animate and Edit Graphics

D. Muller **L. Mariaux** **A. Nicolas**

Centre de Génie Electrique de Lyon – URA CNRS 829
Ecole Centrale de Lyon
BP 163 – 69131 ECULLY - Cedex
e-mail: muller,mariaux,nicolas@trotek.ec-lyon.fr

Abstract – Since OSF/Motif is lacking any tool in the domain of graphics, we developed a new widget providing high level primitives for anyone who needs interactive or animated graphics.

This widget is able to display various classes of objects, which are internally defined using the same kind of object-orientedness as the X toolkit uses to define the concept of a widget.

This paper will discuss our motivations for defining a new type of object, rather than using standard widgets or gadgets or creating new ones. We will also describe the way we implemented this concept of an object, and give some examples showing how application programs make use of it.

Background

The COLOS group – where COLOS stands for "COnceptional Learning Of Science" – was founded in 1988 with major support from Hewlett Packard. It is based on the ideas of Zvonko Fazarinc [Gerard 88] , a former HP senior scientist. Our major goal is to use the potential of modern computer technology for a better and more direct approach towards presentation and understanding of basic concepts in science and technology [Fazarinc 90].

The project currently consists of ten groups from universities of seven European countries [Härtel 93], working in the same hardware and software environment on the new generation of fast RISC-workstations using industrial standards like X-windows and Motif.

This paper will present a contribution to that project. The *XcEdgar* widget – where *Edgar* stands for Editable Graphics Area – is intended to be a tool providing an easy way to display any graphics for Motif-based portable applications. Although *Edgar* is still under development, objects like polylines, polygons, rectangles, circles, pixmaps and text are already available. All these objects may be created, drawn, moved, resized, rotated or destroyed, interactively as well as programmatically, without any low-level X11 calls.

About the object-orientedness of the X toolkit

The X toolkit – better known as *Xt* [Nye 90] – introduces an object-oriented programming method obtained by using plain C, but conforming to a given philosophy. Since we used that same philosophy to program the objects our widget knows about, we will first introduce the kind of object-orientedness that may be obtained by such a programming method.

Since most object-oriented languages use *encapsulated objects inheriting* behavior from *classes* where *methods* are defined allowing the objects to send *messages*, let us define all these terms while showing how *Xt* implements the corresponding concept.

1) Objects:

An object is generally defined as "a block of private data associated with a collection of procedures that can access that data" [Cox 87].

From TOOLS EUROPE '94 (Technology of Object-Oriented Languages and Systems).

When implemented using plain C, such an object might simply be defined as a structure containing the so-called *instance variables,* whereas the *object-id* becomes simply a pointer to that structure.

The objects *Xt* introduces are called *widgets.* All widgets inherit from the most basic object named *Core.* In fact, a widget is intended to be essentially a graphical object, which results in the instance structure of the Core object containing information like position, size, X-window-id, *etc.* Most objects the final user of a Motif application sees on the screen – like buttons, frames, menus, lists, *etc.* are the visible part of underlying widgets. As a consequence, widgets are only poor candidates for abstract object implementation, which would have all of these window management-related instance variables as part of their data structure, without using them.

Xt introduces also simpler objects known as *gadgets.* Gadgets do not have their own associated window, thus they have a smaller instance structure. But just like widgets, the gadgets are intended to be *visible* objects. To achieve that, all the processes of visualizing a gadget and keeping its image up-to-date are delegated to its parent. As an example, the items of popup – or pulldown – menus are typically pushbutton gadgets. Like widgets, gadgets are not intended to be used to implement abstract objects, and their structure is tightly coupled with some methods of their container widgets.

2) Messages:

The process of sending a message to an object may be easily understood as applying a procedure to that object. Using plain C this results simply in a function call passing the object-id as an argument.

3) Encapsulation:

Encapsulation means that the only way to access or to modify one object's associated data is to use the given object's procedures – or *methods.*

To achieve this goal *Xt* provides a way to access *(XtGetValues)* or to modify *(XtSetValues)* any instance variable of any widget or gadget, but it provides also a mechanism to hide the instance structure from the application programmer, so as not to tempt him to get around the above functions by accessing the widget structure members directly.

This mechanism relies on a widget private header file where the instance structure is defined, whereas the application programmer only has access to a public header file defining the widget type to be a pointer to an opaque structure.

The private header file could, for example, define a widget structure like:

```
typedef struct _XcEdgarRec {
            . . .
            list of instance variables
            . . .
} XcEdgarRec;
```

whereas the public header file would completely hide the structure contents from the application program by simply specifying:

```
typedef struct
            _XcEdgarRec *          XcEdgarWidget;
```

4) Classes:

When speaking about a number we use to say it is of *type* int, or of *type* float or double. When speaking about things like objects or widgets, we say instead that they are of *class* PushButton, or Frame or *Edgar.* Implementing the concept of a class in C also results in creating a structure containing the so-called class variables. Class variables consist of data common to all instances of one class of objects, and accessible by any one of them.

Any *Xt* class structure contains, for example, information like a pointer to its superclass, the size of the instance record, and several pointers to functions allowing instance data access.

5) Methods:

As defined above, the methods are the functions allowing manipulation of the instance data. To understand how *Xt* implements this concept, we have to examine separately the methods intended to be called by the toolkit and the methods to be called by the user code.

Since any new widget may define its own new instance variables, it seems obvious that all of that data cannot be known by the toolkit. On the other hand, we already introduced some functions *Xt* provides to manipulate that data *(cf. XtSetValues* and *XtGetValues).* To achieve this, every object class has to provide a set of methods allowing the toolkit to access its data in a predefined manner. Some of these methods correspond typically to object-oriented considerations like *initialize, set_values, get_values* and *destroy*, whereas others are more closely related to the widget's visualization like *resize, expose* and *query_geometry.*

Since the application program has no direct access to the widget's instance structure, the only way to manipulate that data is to call a set of public C functions the widget provides. As an example, if a *Circle* widget would have two instance variables: *center* and *radius,* these would be accessed and modified using the *Xt* standard procedures, but public functions like *CircleGetPerimeter* and *CircleGetArea* could be provided.

6) Inheritance:

Inheritance is a powerful feature of many object-oriented systems. It allows new classes to be created that have most or all of the characteristics of an existing class but with a few additional or different features. *Xt* implements this mechanism by simply including the components of the class and instance record from each of the widget's superclasses in the new widget's class and instance data structure.

Since the *Edgar* widget inherits from *Core, Composite, Constraint, XmManager* and *XmDrawingArea,* its instance record is defined as:

```
typedef struct _XcEdgarRec {
        CorePart                core;
        CompositePart           composite;
        ConstraintPart          constraint;
        XmManagerPart           manager;
        XmDrawingAreaPart       drawing_area;
        XcEdgarPart             edgar;
} XcEdgarRec;
```

whereas its class record declaration is:

```
typedef struct _XcEdgarClassRec {
        CoreClassPart           core_class;
        CompositeClassPart      composite_class;
        ConstraintClassPart     constraint_class;
        XmManagerClassPart      manager_class;
        XmDrawingAreaClassPart  drawing_area_class;
        XcEdgarClassPart        edgar_class;
} XcEdgarClassRec;
```

Structure of the Edgar objects

The *Edgar* widget is specified to be a drawing area able to display things like polylines, circles, rectangles, polygons, strings *etc.,* but also more complicated ones like pixmaps and subwidgets. X low-level access has to be transparent, particularly concerning the color management. It has to offer defaults for every parameter like color, linewidth, linestyle, *etc.* in order to allow the user to have a result with minimum effort (assume one function call). It has to provide functions to manipulate the objects, like creation, destruction, translation, rotation, deformation *etc.* All these functions have to be accessible by direct user interaction as well as by using a programmatic interface, and *Edgar* has to be designed to be easily used as the drawing area of pixel-oriented or line-oriented graphic editors. Finally, it has to be kept in mind that the *Edgar* widget is to be used in highly interactive Computer Aided Education applications using animation to aid intuitive understanding of complex phenomena. As such, the functions *Edgar* provides must be as fast as possible to allow their use for animated graphics.

The above set of specifications duties shows clearly that our widget has to be able to display various *classes* of *objects.* The use of *Edgar* as a display for animated graphics requires that those objects be neither widgets nor gadgets, since their display and management would then be performed by many *Xt* functions, which, though powerful, ar not optimized in terms of speed. This impelled us to introduce our own concept of *Edgar objects* and *Edgar object classes.*

1) Edgar objects:

All the *Edgar* objects share a common part which could be compared to the *CorePart* of the widgets:

```
typedef struct _XcGraphObject {
        struct _XcGraphObject *             previous;
        struct _XcGraphObject *             next;
        struct _XcGraphObject *             group;
        struct _XcGraphObjectClass *        class;
        String                              name;
        Coordinates                         origin;
        Boolean                             active;
        Boolean                             movable;
        . . .
} XcGraphObject;
```

The instance record shows first two pointers, *previous* and *next*, allowing *Edgar* to manage the objects using chained lists,

Editors or even non-interactive displays may want to group a list of objects, to be able for example to move them all together. *Edgar* provides a special object to group other objects. If an object is part of a group, the *group* structure member points to that group's instance record.

Finally, an object's instance record has to provide the object's *name*, a pointer to the *class* the object belongs to, information on how to display it and a set of flags storing the object's state and properties.

2) Edgar object classes:

The *Edgar* object classes are instances of an object named *XcGraphObjectClass*.

```
typedef struct _XcGraphObjectClass {
        String                          name;
        Atom *                          name_id;
        XcGraphObjectActions *          actions;
        Cardinal                        num_resources;
        XcGraphObjectResourceList       resources;
        . . .
} XcGraphObjectClass
```

Such a class stores its name first as a string and second as an atom for faster comparison. The class record contains also a pointer to the list of *methods* the class has to provide. These methods are either *object-oriented* or *visualization-oriented* (see *The object actions* below). Finally, every object class has an associated list of resources like color, linewidth and linestyle for a polyline object.

3) Object actions:

Every object class has to provide a set of methods allowing manipulation of the object instances. Pointers to these methods are stored for each object class in a record named *XcGraphObjectActions:*

```
typedef struct {
    XcCreateProc                 create;
    XcDestroyProc                destroy;
    . . .
    XcDrawProc                   draw;
    XcEraseProc                  erase;
    XcMoveAndResizeProc          move_resize;
    . . .
    XcResizeSelectProc           resize_select;
    XcResizeSelectionMovedProc resize_selection_moved;
    XcResizeUnSelectProc         resize_unselect;
} XcGraphObjectActions;
```

Some of these actions are more directly related to the object management, like *create* or *destroy*. Such methods have to handle the dynamic allocation of all the object's instance variables.

Another set of methods allow manipulation of the object's visualization, like *draw*, *erase* and *move_resize*. All of the above functions allow a programmatic access to the object.

Finally, methods have to be provided to be called during user interaction. An example of such methods is given by *resize_select*, which is called when the user selects an object for resizing; *resize_selection_moved*, which is repeatedly called while the user drags the mouse to allow the interactive update of the object's view; and *resize_unselect*, which is called when the user releases the mouse button to end the interactive resize process.

In fact, up to thirty-eight functions are needed to fully describe the behavior of an object that can be manipulated programmatically as well as interactively, some of which are hidden from the outer world, but internally used by higher level actions like the ones described above.

4) Object resources:

An object class also provides a pointer to a list of resources. Such a resource is of type *XcGraphObjectResource:*

```
typedef struct _XcGraphObjectResource {
        Atom *                          name;
        XcGraphObjectResourceClass *    type;
        Cardinal                        offset;
} XcGraphObjectResource, *XcGraphObjectResourceList;
```

where *name* is the private name of that resource of the object class. The disk object class has, for example, two resources describing its color, named *Color* and *Border_color*. The *offset* member indicates how to find the corresponding resource inside the object instance record.

In fact, the *XcGraphObjectResource* record describes the structure of an *instance* of a resource whose member *type* points to the resource's *class*. Presently, *Edgar* defines up to twenty-five resource classes, such as *xcPixelResourceClass* for all color resources, *xcLineWidthResourceClass* and *xcLineStyleResourceClass* which should be self-explanatory, and many others related to integers, floats or coordinates, polygon fill style, strings or font characteristics.

The resource class record is named *XcGraphObjectResourceClass:*

```
typedef struct {
      Atom *                       name;
      Cardinal                     size;
      XcObjectConverterProc        convert_from_string;
      XcGetInteractiveProc         get_interactive;
} XcGraphObjectResourceClass;
```

and contains the resource class name, the size of the associated resource, and two pointers to converters. The first one is a function able to translate a string to a value of the corresponding resource, like for example the string "blue" into a Pixel value, or the string "3.141592" into a float of value pi.

The second converter is intended to be used by editors. Like the previous one it is a function returning a value of the given resource. But this time the returned value is expected to be given interactively by the end-user. An interactive function returning a color, could for example ask the user to pick any color from the screen or from a displayed colormap, or to type-in the color's name, *etc.*

IMPLEMENTED EDGAR OBJECTS

1) Polyline:

A polyline instance is defined by at least two points. Since memory space is dynamically allocated the number of points is limited only by the amount of available memory. A polyline may be moved, rescaled and rotated. It is also possible to add or to remove points from inside a polyline, and to modify the coordinates of an existing point. Polylines may be displayed either with lines connecting the vertices, or with any other *Edgar* object used to mark the vertices, or by combining these two modes.

Polylines are good candidates to display curves, grids, axes and fast enough to be used in animated graphics.

2) Polygon:

A polygon is in principle an object whose boundary is supposed to be a closed polyline. In fact, if the specified boundary is not closed, *Edgar* closes it automatically. A polygon behaves exactly like a polyline, with the only difference being that it has a background color while the polyline does not.

3) Circle, Disk:

A circle is defined by a center and a radius. It may be moved, rescaled and even rotated, but will ever remain mathematically circular with respect to the *Edgar* coordinate system. If the X and Y scales are not identical the circle may appear elliptical on the screen. As expected, rotation makes sense only if the rotation center is not identical to the circle's center.

A disk is a filled circle.

4) Rectangle, Tile:

A rectangle is defined by its width and height and by the angle it makes with the horizontal. A rectangle may be moved, rescaled and rotated, and its width/height ratio modified. Even if resized after having been rotated, it does not shear and remains a rectangle with right angles.

A tile is a filled rectangle.

5) Text:

A text is defined by its string and by its font. It may be moved, rescaled and rotated, although the rotation does not affect yet the text direction. If rescaled, a new font is automatically recomputed to fit the required dimension.

Since the process of recomputing a font is quite time-comsuming and incompatible with animation (it can take up to one second to get a new font from disk), the text object posseses a boolean instance variable to disable resizing. It is also possible for several text objects to be considered as font clients, sharing the font of a text object known as the font server. Font clients may not be rescaled directly, but their size changes if the font server is resized.

6) Pixmap:

A pixmap is a pixel image. A pixmap may be moved easily, and even rescaled and rotated. But since rescaling and rotation are done using complex filtering algorithms, they are unfit for animation purposes.

7) Group:

The group is a special object able to group together any number of other *Edgar* objects including another group. A group is defined by the ordered list of its component objects. Objects may be added to or removed from the list. Group motion, rescaling or rotation results in all group members being similarly moved, rescaled or rotated.

Still-to-be-implemented objects

1) Ellipse:

The generic arc of an ellipse is defined by its two axes, its starting angle and its aperture angle.

2) Subwidget:

An *Edgar* object to encapsulate any standard widget.

Applications using Edgar

1) rectif:

rectif is an application computing in real time the analytical waveform equations to show any current – or voltage – waveform appearing in a single-phase bridge rectifier with a resistive, inductive and back-electromotive load. Up to 250 first-year students use this application every year [Muller 93].

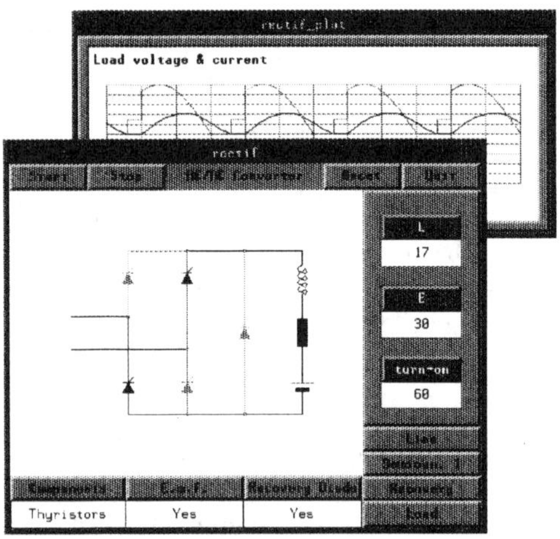

Fig. 1. A typical screen layout of the *rectif* application.

As shown in Fig.1 the *rectif* application uses several *Edgar* widgets as non-interactive displays. The application main window uses an *Edgar* widget to display the circuit where the current path is shown using red color. During the simulation process this window is constantly updated, producing an animated display showing the current flow. This aids in intuitive understanding of the semiconductor switching sequences.

The voltage or current waveforms are also displayed using *Edgar* widgets and animated by scrolling from right to left while time passes. The instant corresponding to the displayed current path is arbitrarily taken as being at the stripchart left border.

2) sched:

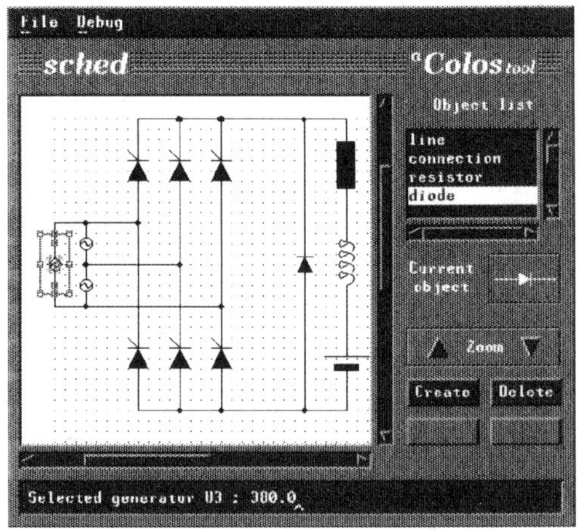

Figure 2: The *sched* application showing a typical circuit layout

The *sched* application (see fig.2) is a generic line-oriented schematic editor coupled with various databases. One of these allows the interactive definition of any electrical circuit, which can be analyzed and solved by a resolution module. *sched* uses an *Edgar* widget in interactive mode to create the circuit layout by positioning the given components using a predefined grid.

After the user positions one terminal of the chosen component by clicking the mouse near a gridpoint, the component is drawn using rubberband while dragging the mouse. Once the mouse button is released the second terminal snaps onto the nearest grid point.

This application uses also *Edgar* features to zoom in or out, and to pan the displayed sub-window over the whole workspace. Finally, one may notice that the small window showing the current object is also an *Edgar* widget used as a non-interactive display.

3) mWave:

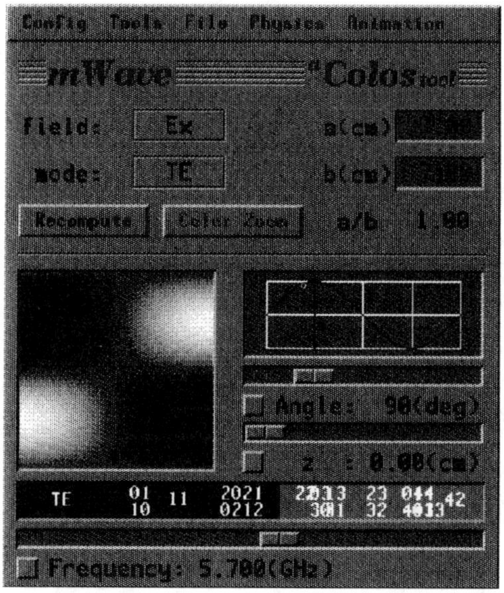

Figure 3: The *mWave* application showing the amplitude of the electric field for mode TE32 propagating in a wave-guide of 7 by 7cm cross-section

mWave is a package solving in real time the analytical field equations to show the electric or the magnetic field – for either TE or TM modes – inside an infinitely long wave-guide of circular or rectangular cross-section [Muller 93].

Since the field values are computed at each individual pixel, the main window of that application is not an *Edgar* widget. However, the phase display showing a sine wave and the frequency display showing the mode cutoff frequencies are *Edgar* widgets.

No other widgets would have easily allowed to obtain the required behavior for those two displays, where the cursor on the phase display and the separation line indicating the cutoff frequency move with the slider located below them, which is under interactive control of the end user.

Conclusion

One main goal of the COLOS project members is to use the power offered by modern computer technology to provide students a highly interactive environment for intuitive understanding of complex phenomena by intensive use of animation.

Since OSF/Motif is lacking any tool in the domain of graphics an even more animated graphics, we developed a new widget named *Edgar* conforming to the Motif standard, and providing high level primitives for static, animated or interactive graphics.

Despite the fact that the set of specifications for *Edgar* was quite heavy for a unique widget, the choice of using an object-oriented programming style allowed us to fulfill most commonly accepted requirements of software quality [Meyer 88]:

1) Modularity:

The use of the concept of *Edgar* objects resulted in a highly modular package. Every *Edgar* object is a well-defined separate module fulfilling a predefined set of tasks. This modularity makes it easy to develop a new object without having to modify any of the existing code, except adding the name of the new object to the list of existing ones. Modularity also significantly improved team efficiency since every individual may be assigned to program a given object, which requires no interaction at all with the rest of the team.

2) Reusability:

Another significant advantage of modularity is an appreciable gain of reusability. By defining well the tasks of the methods, it becomes easy, for example, to use an already existing method for a new object. The *disk* and *circle* objects, the *rectangle* and the *tile*, the *polygon* and the *polyline* share some methods, while other methods are common to all objects except the *group* and the *pixmap*.

References

[Cox 87] B.J. Cox, "Object Oriented Programming – An Evolutionary Approach", Addison-Wesley Publishing Company, Reading, April 1987.

[Fazarinc 90] Z. Fazarinc, "Computer simulation in physics", IEEE Potentials, April 1990, pp. 30-33.

[Gerard 88] B. Gerard, "Extraordinary people," Measure (Hewlett-Packard internal magazine), July-August 1988, pp. 8-10.

[Härtel 93] H. Härtel, "The Project COLOS – COnceptual Learning Of Science – Objectives, Background and First Results," COLOS project internal paper, Kiel, January 1993

[Meyer 88] B. Meyer, "Object-Oriented Software Construction," Prentice-Hall, New-York, 1988.

[Muller 93] D. Muller, L. Mariaux, A. Nicolas, "A computer aided education environment used in teaching the single-phase bridge rectifier," European Association for Education in Electrical and Information Engineering (EAEEIE) annual conference, Prague, Czech Republic, Sept.8–10, 1993.

[Muller 93] D. Muller, L. Nicolas, A. Nicolas, "A C.A.E. package for an intuitive approach to microwaves," Compumag conference on the Computation of Electromagnetic Fields, Miami, Florida, Oct.31–Nov.4, 1993.

[Nye 90] A. Nye, T. O'Reilly, "X Toolkit Intrinsics Programming Manual – OSF/Motif Edition," O'Reilly & Associates Inc., Sebastopol CA, 1990.

An Object-Oriented Approach to manage Multimedia Documents

M. P. Papa, S. Giurleo, G. Rizzo, A. Forti, G. Corrente, G. Molaro

Bull HN Sud S.p.A. - Area R&D "Electronic Document Management"
Nucleo Industriale Pianodardine - 83030 Prata P.U. (Avellino) - ITALY
Tel. +39-825-764240 Fax +39-825-764230 Email m.papa@bsav.bull.it

Abstract

In this paper we describe some aspects and issues related with the development of an Object-Oriented Multimedia Information System for an Office Environment which is being developed in the R&D laboratories of Bull HN Sud. The system provides integrated facilities for creating, filing, retrieving and browsing multimedia objects. This article is not an overview of the complete system but it makes a particular emphasis on some Object-Oriented features of the project. An Object-Oriented model of multimedia documents is presented which is based on concepts of Document Conceptual Structure and Document Type that both are very useful in the process of efficient information retrieval. Moreover, we discuss some design and implementation issues concerning the visual programming experience and the use of the Object-Oriented DBMS technology.

1. Introduction

The project we are going to describe is called OOCM (Object Oriented Content Management) and deals with design and implementation of a multimedia document management system.

Multimedia documents in OOCM are collection of objects of different types such as text, images, voice, graphics and traditional formatted data. The development of the system is based on a distributed architecture working on a client-server paradigm. Functionalities such as creation, modification and presentation of multimedia information are accessible to the user from the client workstation. Documents are stored in large-capacity storage devices like optical disks and jukeboxes of optical disks residing at the server workstation.

From TOOLS EUROPE '94 (Technology of Object-Oriented Languages and Systems).

An Object Oriented DBMS and an Information Retrieval Engine provide efficient filing and retrieval management. Hypermedia capabilities are provided as well, therefore user may also navigate links among documents.

The structure of multimedia documents is more complex than objects usually managed in Form Processing Systems [Gehani 82] or Information Retrieval Systems [Salton 83]. It is very difficult to support different operations (such as editing, presentation and retrieval) on such kinds of data in an homogeneous way and to present different data to the user by an uniform interface.

Several research studies have been made in the past ten years on this subject ([Tsichritzis 85], [Christodoulakis 86], [Thanos 90], etc), many considerations have been done and important results have been achieved. A fundamental idea on which is based the Multos Esprit Project ([Bertino 87], [Thanos 90]) is that it is useful to have several structural descriptions of a multimedia document in order to support different operations. The Multos document model uses the Office Document Architecture (ODA)[1] to specify document presentation information [Ecma 85]. The logical and layout structure of ODA support operations of editing, formatting, presentation and exchanging. The logical structure determines how logical components, that is, syntactic components such as sections and paragraphs, are related to the document content portions; the layout structure determines how layout components, such as pages, frames and blocks, are arranged on an output device at presentation time. For many operations, such as query specification by content and document creation, instead, it is important to see a document in terms of its conceptual components. A

[1]ODA is an international standard defined by ISO, ECMA and CCITT

conceptual component is a document component used for some specific purpose.

The second chapter of this paper presents concepts and structure of multimedia documents implemented in our system by means of an Object-Oriented model. All the capabilities of our system are based on this model.

The fact that object-oriented models are more adequate than relational models to describe multimedia information is largely proved ([Christodoulakis 86], [Horak 84], [Nierstrasz 85]). In [Gibbs 85] is explored the relevance of the conceptual modelling area to the design of office information systems. The ability of semantic data models to specify constructs that correspond directly to real world entities is referred as an object-oriented approach. Object-Oriented models combine the advantages of data languages, such as abstraction and information hiding, with the support of procedures (methods) to form an object-oriented programming environment that is combined with a data base management system. Object-Oriented models are also very appropriate tools for clearly describing data and their interrelationships in a complex environment such as the multimedia database environment. They emphasize a clear object interface approach in which the objects are well identified and the methods that are applicable to them are completely known by a user at any point in time. The procedure is more one of adapting the model to the world than the world to the model.

Furthermore, Object Oriented Data Base Management Systems technology currently represents a concrete way to better manage multimedia objects ([Waterworth 91], [Bertino 91], [Bertino 92], [Atkinson 89]). An ODBMS is defined as a DBMS that directly supports a model based on the Object-Oriented paradigm. ODBMSs support fundamental features required from multimedia document management applications such as:

- filing of heterogeneous data in a unique database with uniform access methods and query process on different kinds of data;
- management of large repositories of unformatted data such as text data, images, voice which traditional DBMS are not able to handle;
- management of composite objects (composite objects are objects defined as *parts of* other objects which means that there is an aggregation relation among objects);
- automation of large amounts of data with tight and complex interconnections and of data model that frequently changes over the time (such as Hypermedia, CAD and CASE systems);
- storing of reusable classes in order to increase productivity;
- integration in a unique data base of data description and methods implementing the object behaviour.

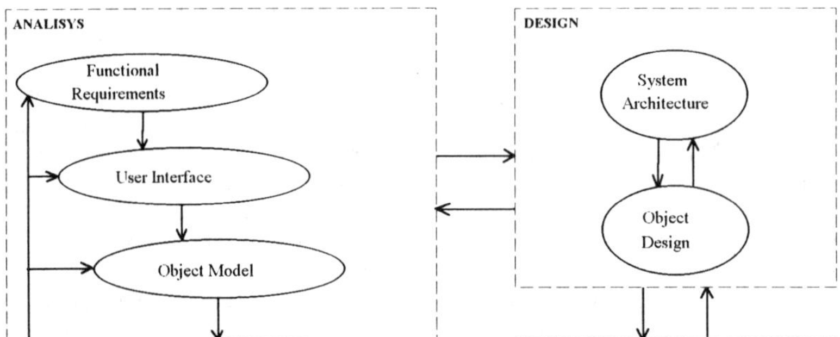

- Figure 1 - Software life cycle

In the third chapter, devoted to some design and implementation aspects of our system, we synthesize the architecture of the system and we talk about the status of the implementation.

The whole development of the project has been guided by the OMT (Object Modelling Technique) methodology [Rumbaugh 91] by which we was inspired in order to establish the steps of the software life cycle and to fix output products for each step. Figure 1 represents phases and activities that we are following during our work.

Dashed lines circumscribe the set of activities related to a specific phase of the methodology. Bold words specify phases and ellipses indicate activities. Arrows represent the iteration process among phases and among activities within phases.

We have experimented the use of a known OMT case tool which is also a C++ code generator.

2. The Object Model of Multimedia Documents

2.1 How we see the Document

The multimedia document is the main information unit managed by our system. Electronic form of documents may be created in different ways. Multimedia documents may be interactively generated in a given station using an application that is external to our system. Alternatively, documents may be in a paper form. A scanner device and OCR capability are used for extracting information from the document. Moreover, they may be created by an application, which is proprietary of our system, specialized to deal with a certain kind of data. Finally, we might have a document which is a combination of portions arrived from all these different sources. This hetereogeneous environment, unfortunately, means that the system has to deal in a different way with each type of data.

The document model represents the unifying concept which gives the possibility to integrate different kinds of data and manage them in a homogeneous way.

Document in our system exists in term of its ***Content Portions*** and of the following abstractions:

- ***Profile***
- ***Conceptual Structure***
- ***Miniature***
- ***Fasttalk***

Abstractions are known to the user and may assist him in many occasions, such as in the retrieval session to identify the appropriate document.

Profile is a set of attributes that characterizes the document and is used mainly for retrieval purposes. Examples of attributes are name, creation data, author, etc. They consist of formatted data as booleans, integers, reals and strings.

Conceptual Structure describes the document content in terms of its conceptual components. A conceptual component indicates a portion of a document having a particular meaning for the user and which can be used for some specific purpose. Examples are the address in a letter or the title, authors and abstract in a technical report. For many operations, such as query specification by content and document creation, it is important to see a document in terms of its conceptual components. In the paragraph 2.2 a clear description of the conceptual structure is done.

Miniatures are realistic visual abstractions of the document, which are displayed for the user during browsing. Miniature can be a reduced image of a meaningful page of the document.

Fasttalk is created manually by the user. It contains a short (one to two seconds of talk) description of the document's content, or an excerpt of the document. Fasttalk, like miniatures, help the user during retrieval. On the basis of what the user sees and hears, he can decide if the document is one of the ones he wants retrieved. A similar idea was already experimented in a research prototype developed some years ago at University of Toronto ([Tsichritzis 85], [Christodoulakis 86]).

Profile's attributes and text historically represent the only active components during the retrieval process of multimedia documents [Bertino 87]. In fact, Data Base Management Systems and Information Retrieval technologies make available techniques for access methods definition and query processing aspects concerning attribute and text data respectively. A research activity has been done in the past years on document retrieval based on image content so that images contained in documents become active components in the formulation of queries and, therefore, in accessing documents ([Conti 90], [Costantopoulos 90], [Rabitti 87]).

In our system we assume to use document abstractions in order to improve the retrieval process and to provide the user with an help in query formulation and refining. However, we basically offer features of attributes and text searching; in addition, we give the possibility to formulate mixed queries on components of the documents conceptual structure; moreover, image (miniatures) and voice (fasttalk) data participate to the activity of user query refining.

2.2 The Conceptual Document Model

As we said above, one of the important ideas adopted in our model is the description of the document in terms of its Conceptual Structure. This concept was firstly introduced in the document management field by the Multos project [Rabitti 90] [Meghini 91]. Examples of conceptual components are sections, chapters, paragraphs of a book. The Conceptual Structure is basically a hierarchical structure composed of a root object, intermediate objects composed of one or more other objects, and leaf objects. We repeat here that the conceptual structure is important for query specification since conceptual components are more meaningful to the user than ODA logical and layout components.

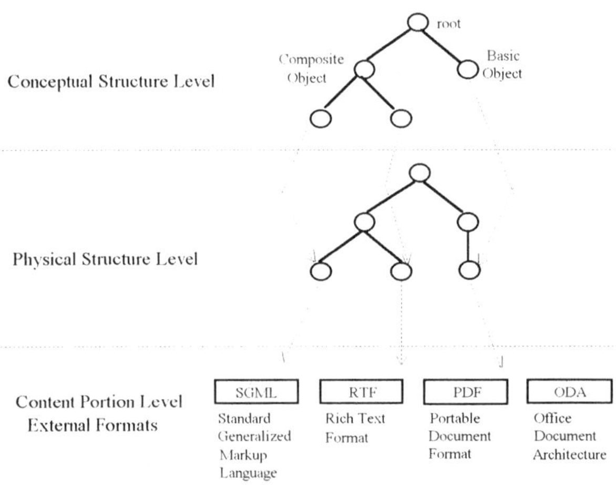

- Figure 2 - OOCM Document Model vs External World

From what concerns operations such as creation, editing and presentation of multimedia content portions we leave these tasks to the applications that are able to handle them. This means that we have to deal with a complex environment of different formats (such as ODA [Ecma 85], PDF [Bienz 93], RTF [Microsoft 92]), external to the system, in order to control the addressing mechanism between the conceptual structure and the content portions. In figure 2 we describe this situation.

Basically, we assume to impose a conceptual structure on the content portions of the document, so the conceptual components have to address one or more blocks of data at the ***Content Portion Level***. Because we have to do with different internal formats of Content Portions we need to introduce an intermediate level, called ***Physical Structure Level***, which represents an indirect addressing mechanism from the ***Conceptual Structure level*** to the Content Portion level. This intermediate level acts as a filter of different formats, so that they are transparent to the higher level which works on the same way always, independently from the different kinds of data which is pointing to.

Consequently, our system, on one hand, allows users to impose a Conceptual Structure on content portions created by different external applications and, on the other hand, it is able to interpret external formats, like ODA and SGML, that already contain information on the semantics of the content.

As it is easy to understand, the heart of our model is the ***Document Conceptual Structure***, which we are going to define using an object-oriented data model.

The graph of figure 3 represents a typical document of our system with objects of the conceptual level, modeling the document conceptual structure, objects of the physical level, mapping the conceptual structure to the content portions, and objects of the hypertextual dimension, providing a linking mechanism among conceptual objects of the same or different documents.

Objects have a unique identifier. Objects may have a set of attributes and methods associated with them. An object may be composed of other objects. For example a *Document Conceptual Root* object may be composed of more *Basic Conceptual Objects*. The composition of more complex objects from more elementary ones forms an aggregation hierarchy.

Aggregation is a particular association with *is part-of* semantics. A generic example of association is represented by the hypertext link among conceptual objects of different documents (or of the same document). Hypertextual links are carried out in our system by autonomous objects (called *link*) which give more emphasis to the association itself. A link connects two objects of association is represented by the hypertext link among conceptual objects of different documents (or of the same document). Hypertextual links are carried out in our system by autonomous objects (called *link*) which give more emphasis to the association itself. A link connects two objects of conceptual structure using the concept of hot area (or *anchor*) of the document content.

In figure 3 simple arrows represent the *is part of* association and double arrows represent other kind of associations.

Viceversa, a BPO is always connected to one and only one BCO.

The set of BPO maps the whole document without intersections (each elementary part of the document content, that is to say a character of a text or a pixel of a bitmap or a frame of a sound, belongs to one and only one BPO).

As example, Figures 4 and 5 describe two instances of the Conceptual and Physical Structure in two different moments of the document life.

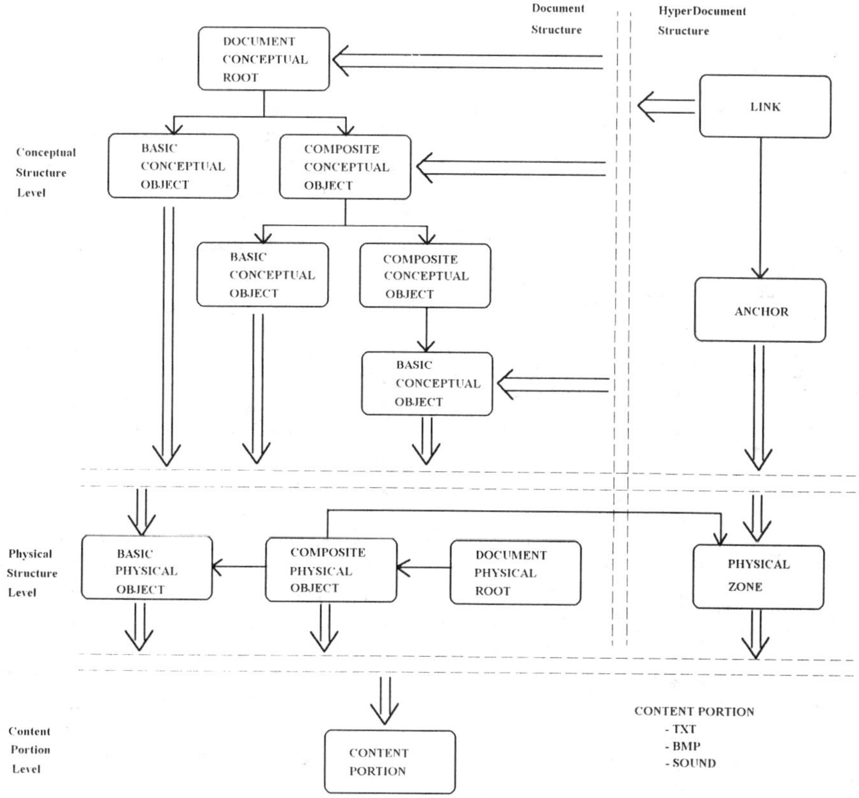

- Figure 3 - General relationships among objects

A ***Basic Conceptual Object (BCO)*** may refer to a unique or more content portions. For example, if each Content Portion represents a physical page, a paragraph that starts in a physical page and ends in the middle of an other physical page, refers to at least two Content Portions (see figure 5). A ***Basic Physical Object (BPO)*** refers always to a unique Content Portion or to a part of a Content Portion. Consequently the Basic Conceptual Object may refer to one or more Basic Physical Object.

Physical Zones, instead, do not cover the entire document content and may have intersections. They are introduced in order to map anchors of the Hypertext Level on the Content Portion Level.

A ***Composite Physical Object (CPO)*** identifies a physical storage unit, such as a file, or a physical presentation unit, such as a page, which may be decomposed in directly addressable components. The Composite Physical Object may not contain other CPOs but it is composed of at least one BPO.

The Content Portion objects are in a one to one connection with the file of contents.

The physical structure serves the conceptual structure as a pointing mechanism towards the content. From the conceptual structure, only the BCOs (leaves) point to the BPOs. From the physical structure only the BPOs point to the actual content.

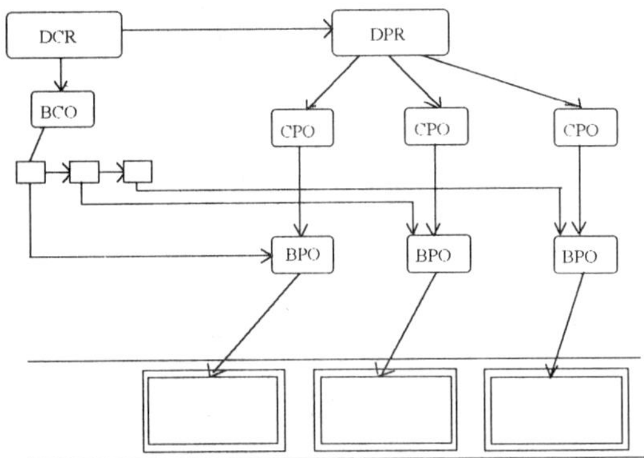

- Figure 4 - Default document structure

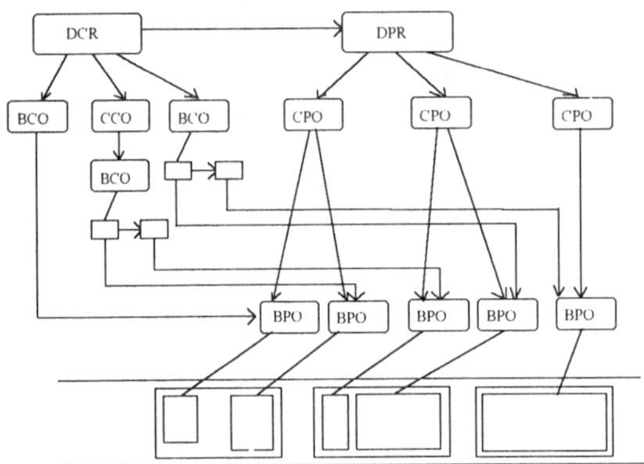

- Figure 5 - Document structure at a certain point of time

Objects we have talked about so far may be organized in classes through *instance-of* relationships. So, we consider the following classes:

Conceptual Structure Level
- ***Document Conceptual Root***
- ***Composite Conceptual Object***
- ***Basic Conceptual Object***

Physical Structure Level
- ***Document Physical Root***
- ***Composite Physical Object***
- ***Basic Physical Object***
- ***Physical Zone***

Hypertext Dimension
- ***Link***
- ***Anchor***

Content Portion Level
- ***Content Portion***

Classes may be organized into superclasses through an *is a* or generalization hierarchy. In figure 6 is represented the generalization hierarchy of Conceptual, Physical and Hypertext Levels. The *Linkable Object* class is superclass of *Basic Conceptual Object* and *Composite Conceptual Object* classes. A class may be subclass of more classes (for example the class *DCR* is subclass of the class *CCO* and of *Linkable Object*). A class has a set of common attributes for all instances of the class itself. All subclasses of such class inherit these attributes. Methods that are applicable to the objects of a certain class are also applicable to the objects that are instances of its subclasses. Figure 6 synthesizes the inheritance hierarchies existing among the specified classes.

Figure 6 shows two new superclasses for the Hypertext level: Hyper Object and Linkable Object. The Linkable Object is an abstract class; instances of its inherited subclasses may be source and/or destination point of a link. Hyper Object is an abstract class as well.

Hyper Object*, *Linkable Object*, *Link and ***Anchor*** classes allow to model the Hypermedia data base. Components of multimedia documents (*Document Conceptual Roots, Composite Conceptual Objects, Basic Conceptual Objects*) are *nodes* (*Linkable Objects*) of that data base; *links* specify two *anchors* located in two different linkable objects in order to allow navigation from *source node* to *destination node* of the data base itself.

Figure 6 introduces the following specialization classes:
- subclasses of Basic Physical Object: **BPO_TXT, BPO_BMP, BPO_SND;**
- subclasses of Physical Zone: **PZ_TXT, PZ_BMP, PZ_SND.**

In figure 7 are represented the aggregation hierarchies for objects of our model. Aggregation is the *part-of* relationship in which objects representing the components of something are associated with an object representing the entire assembly.

Arrows in figure 7 indicate the triggering operation. For triggering we intend the automatic propagation of an operation to a graph of objects when this operation is applied to an object of the graph.

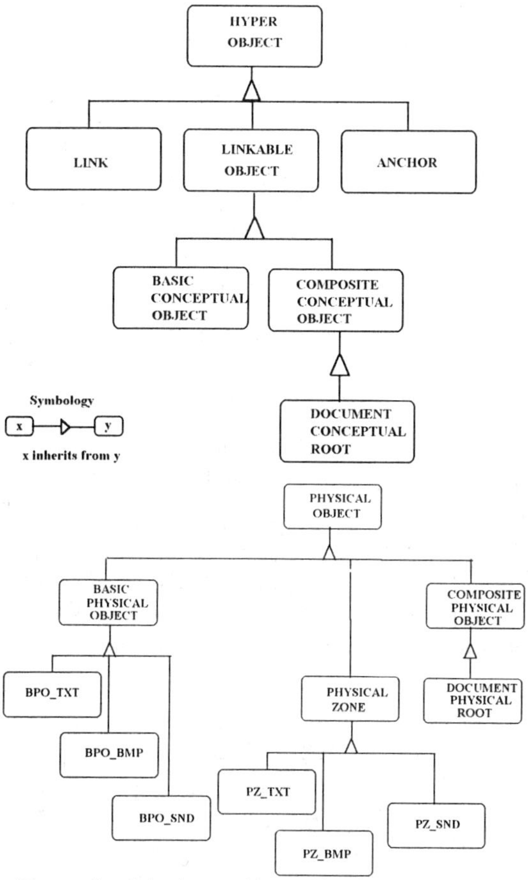

- Figure 6 - Inheritance hierarchies for objects of the document model

Numbers at the ends of association lines in the object diagrams indicate multiplicity. They specify how many instances of one class may relate to a single instance of an associated class.

2.3 Document Type Management

In the previous paragraph is described the object model for the Conceptual Structure of the document: the focus was on conceptual objects, such as DCR, CCO and BCO, and on objects of the physical level, such as DPR, CPO and BPO, which realize the interface level between conceptual and content portion levels. We did not give yet a particular meaning to Conceptual Structure objects, we only said that a retrieval process based on conceptual objects, besides attributes and text, may be very effective. Authors of the current paper believe that an office filing and retrieval system providing the expressed feature is very useful to the end-user; on the other end, existing literature ([Thanos 90] [Meghini 91]) and research work currently going on [Meghini 93] about related subjects encourage this belief.

It is possible to introduce ***component types*** (such as the type address, date, abstract, chapter, etc.) and ***document types*** (such as letter, report, manual) within this model. Type is in our model a central concept, because it represents a structured approach to office documents. It is assumed that is necessary to focus on a regularity of office documents and this is expressed by the type concept. Whether such regularity exists always is subject to debate; not always there is a way of constraining office knowledge to be formatted. Types impose structure on documents in the same way that formatted data impose structure on knowledge. The user is not left free to create documents with any structure he wants. The guidance to the use of predefined document types can be considered constraining by some people; in many cases it may result extremely convenient.

The *component/document type* concept rises because several similar documents (and similar components inside documents) exist in an office environment. The similarity consists in the same *Conceptual Structure* and, in some extreme cases, in the same printed words (this is the case of forms). So the use of predefined types serves mainly to include similar documents in predefined classes. An important reason being that the structure specified within the type can be used to build efficient access methods and may help in query formulation.

An example of a structure of a *component type* is Address which can be defined as the aggregation of the component types Street, City and Country; while an example of a structure of a *document type* is Letter which can be defined as the aggregation of the component shown in figure 8.

The fact that document and each component of it may be expressed in terms of its contained components and that order of components may be specified is a determinant factor for automatic generation of the document conceptual structure at capture time. The automatic extraction of conceptual structures is a key market requirement, because end-users do not want to be bored with a manual structuring process.

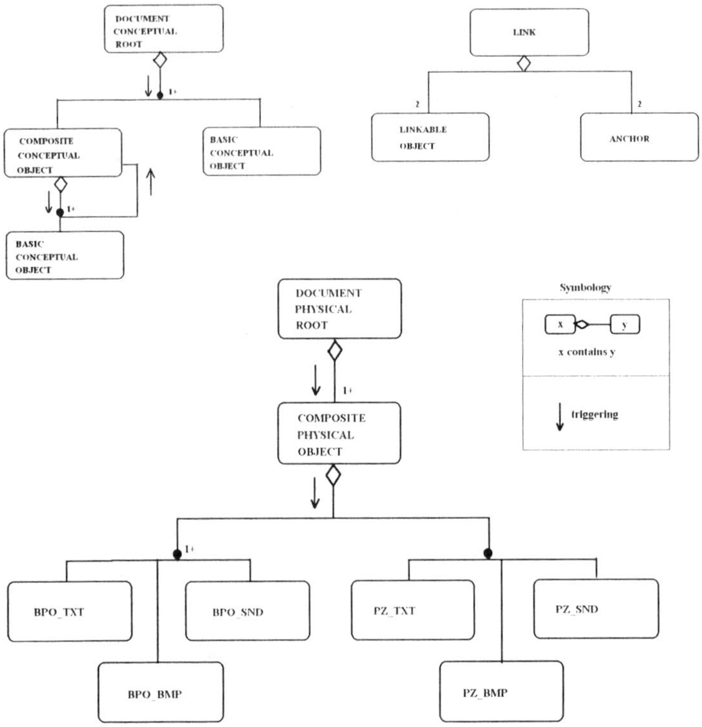

- Figure 7 - Aggregation hierarchies for objects of the document model

Multimedia document structures tend to differ greatly from instance to instance. If a document type is defined as the complete structure of all the documents belonging to that type, conceptual document types would be obtained which match only one or a few document instances, thus loosing the advantages of type definition in document access and retrieval. For this reason, the concept of a *weak document type* is introduced into the conceptual document model. A weak type only partially specifies the structure of its instances. This concept was firstly introduced by [Rabitti 90].

Therefore, a weak document type is the specification of the types of the conceptual components that a set of documents have in common. Documents are the instances of document types. An instance of a weak type may have a more complex and detailed structure than that specified in the definition of the type. Let's think, by example, to a Book document type where it is not possible to specify a priory the number of chapters (see figure 10), which will be clear only when an instance is created. In figure 8 an other example is done where the type of a component, Letter Body, in the type Letter definition is not specified. In the definition of component types, therefore, it is necessary to introduce particular constructors (such as choice, alternative, cycle, etc.) and a class of objects which we call *bud*.

So, while in the previous paragraph we described our Object-Oriented model for structures of document instances, here we are going to present the Object-Oriented model for structures of document types, which represent in our system the means to define document instances (for this reason we call document type structures also *metastructures*).

Document instances and types are both defined as structures of connected components. The main difference is that the type structure may contain alternative, cycle and choice constructors that only at instance definition time are solved in a fixed structure.

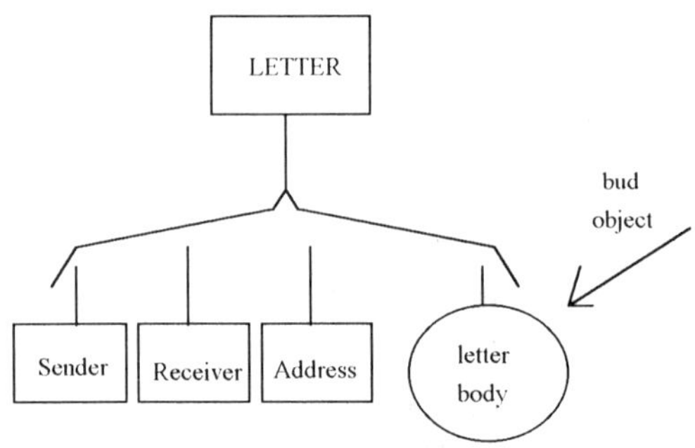

- Figure 8 - The metastructure for the generic type Letter

Classes of document type structures are characterized by their position inside the metastructure tree (such as root node, composite node and leaf node), and by the particular constructor they implement (such as choice, cycle, etc). In figure 9 the inheritance hierarchy for such classes is represented.

The class *MetaStructure Object* is an abstract class which has attributes and methods common to all other classes. Its inherited classes are:

- *CLO_Type* which is an abstract class which defines methods and attributes of composite objects;
- *BLO_Type* is the class of leaf objects;
- *bud Object* is the class of objects which structure is not specified in the type definition.

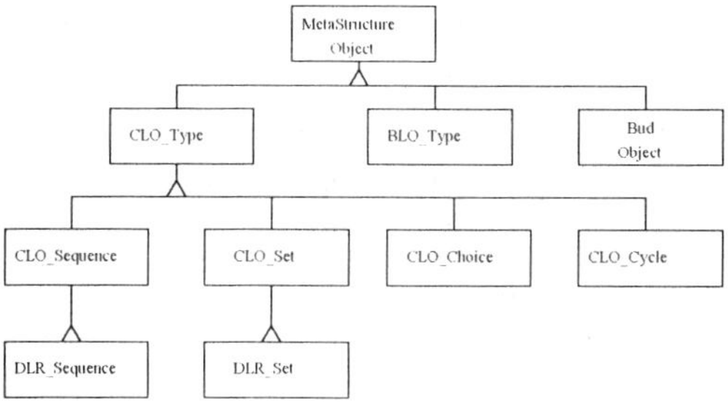

- Figure 9 - Inheritance hierarchy for objects of the document type structure

Each of the classes *CLO_Sequence*, *CLO_Set*, *CLO_Choice*, *CLO_Cycle* implement a mechanism of *composition* or of *substitution* of metastructure objects. For composition it is intended the fact that user decisions concern children objects of the object in question; in the substitution, instead, user decides the object (or objects) that needs to have the control in place of the object in question in the instance structure.

The singled out constructors are the followings:
- *SEQUENCE* is a composition mechanism which does not leave freedom to users because the order of children objects is completely defined;
- *SET* is a composition mechanism where the metastructure object specifies a set of children which have to be ordered by the user;
- *CYCLE* is a substitution mechanism that describes and object on which a number of iterations may be made;
- *CHOICE* is a substitution mechanism which describes a list of objects from which the user must select one.

In figure 10 it is possible to examine two examples of type structures that contain some of these constructors.

3. Design and implementation issues

A first prototype of the system has been developed which implements the object model of multimedia documents presented in the last chapter. The Gemstone ODBMS provides the physical implementation of the object model including objects and methods in a unique physical representation. The prototype is based on a client-server architecture as shown in figure 11. Client stations are IBM PCs with DOS/Windows 3.1 O.S. and the server station is a DPX 20/RISC 6000 with AIX O.S.

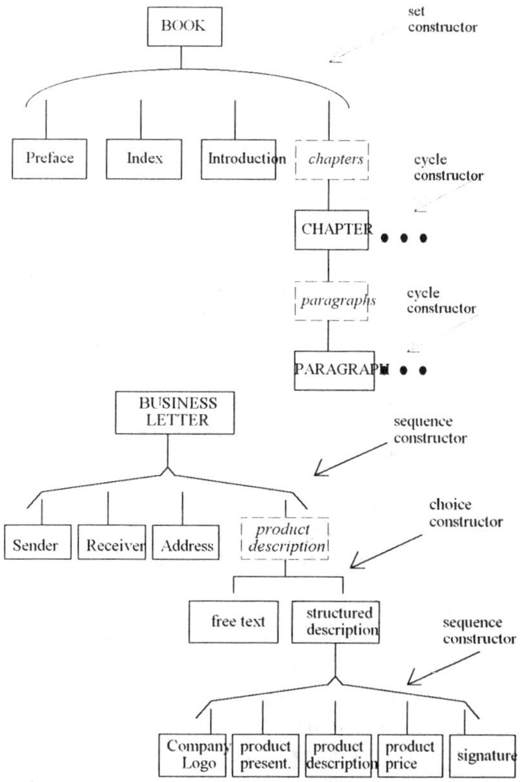

- Figure 10 - The metastructures for types BOOK and BUSINESS LETTER

The system architecture is devided in subsystems. The decomposition of system in subsystems is organized as a sequence of horizontal levels and vertical partitions and the interaction between levels is of type client-server. Each subsystem is composed of a module or a set of modules, and each module is a set of classes. Thus, we provide a complete class library for each module of the system. The representation in layers of the system architecture reduces system complexity emphasizing information hiding.

Currently working prototype concerns with the implementation of a particular user agent, called Document Manager, which gives the possibility to capture document content portions and to create and manipulate the conceptual structure of the document at the client workstation, to archive documents into the server station and, finally, to retrieve them. Figure 12 presents the most relevant part of the Doc Manager user interface.

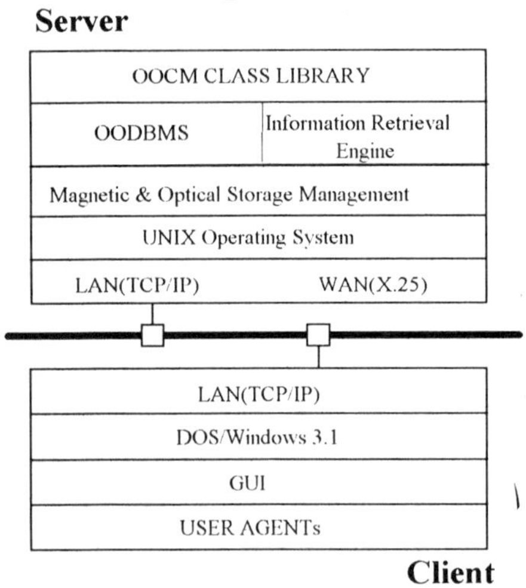

- Figure 11 - General architecture of OOCM

The user may see two views of the document, physical (Content Portions) and conceptual (Conceptual Components), by means of a *splitter window* devided in a Physical Viewer and in a Conceptual Viewer. Physical Viewer shows miniatures of the Content Portions and Conceptual Viewer shows objects of the Conceptual Structure. User creates a new conceptual object by a drag operation on miniatures.

The implementation of this prototype has been completely done in C++ programming language using the Microsoft 7.0 compiler on the client station and Bull BOSX C++ Compiler on the server station. The user interface has been developed by the Visual C++/MFC 2.0.

We do not describe in details the whole system architecture, but we want to spend still few words expressing some considerations on the visual programming experience and on using the ODBMS.

In the Visual C++ programming environment, offered by Microsoft, the skeleton of an application is developed starting from a basic framework, the MFC 2.0 library. The fundamental elements of an MFC 2.0 application design are the following classes:

- ***CDocument*** which incapsulates and handles data related to a specific application,
- ***CView*** which manages document data viewing and user-application interfacing.

More than one view may be associated to an instance of a class CDocument; an example are physical and conceptual views of the OOCM document in the splitter window of the Document Manager.

Visual C++ supplies the following set of tools that facilitates application development:

- ***AppWizard*** which automatically generates the minimal skeleton of the application,
- ***AppStudio*** that is a handler of user interface resources, a type of dialogue editor,
- ***Class Wizard*** which enables user to define a message handler and join it to a message_id for each object of the application. It creates the message map for each class and handles the correct routing of messages. Windows applications are, in fact, *message driven*: each user action generates messages that are dispatched to the windows of the application and managed by the corresponding *message handler*.
- ***Browser*** which allows direct accessing and consulting of the currently open project classes, because a repository of classes is supplied.

In summary, during our programming experience, we verified the following advantages:

- Visual C++ supplies free features to user-interface management, such as the scrolling operation,
- code is organized in a real object-oriented fashion: the environment transparently generates, for each class defined by ClassWizard, a header file and an implementation file (splitting between data and functions),
- ClassWizard and Browser help user in extending and refining code: ClassWizard allows automatic code generation of a new class offering an user-friendly interface for the specification of inheritance and aggregation associations respect to already existing classes; Browser, instead, enables user to directly access a specific portion of the class code in order to modify it.

The process development in such a type of environment results clearly improved in terms of increasing of productivity, reducing of code lines number and abatement of working time.

Obviously, programmers discover all these advantages only after they have been achieved a good comprehension of the offered mechanisms and tools. A bad use of existing tools may cause trivial errors that are difficult to localize.

The main advantage we derived in using the ODBMS is the possibility to work in a homogeneous object-oriented environment: we designed in the analysis phase an object model of the document conceptual structure which we implemented at the client workstation, in an object-oriented programming language and we translated, at the server workstation, in a GemStone physical schema.

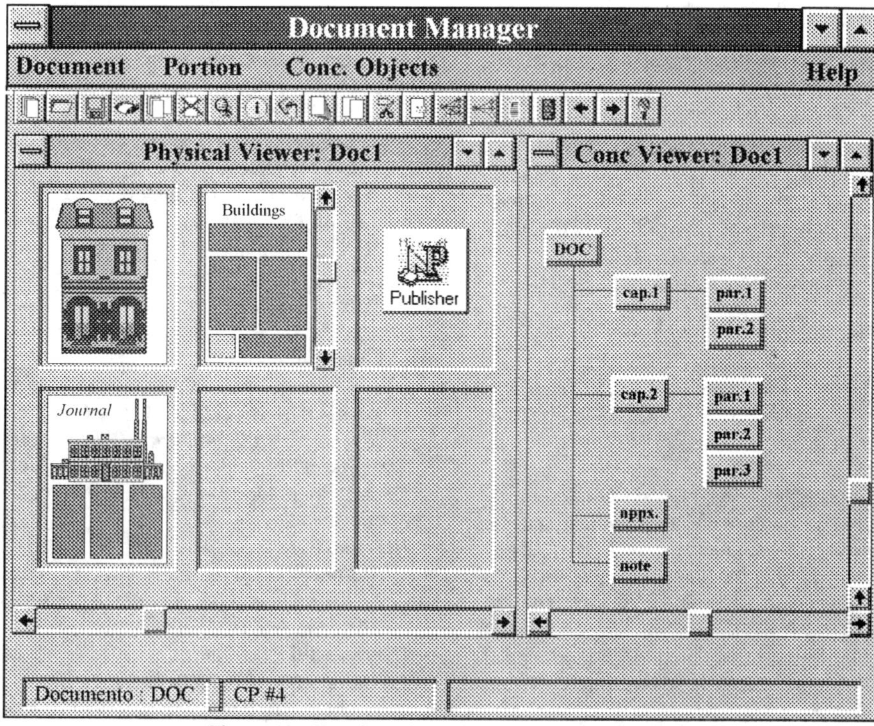

- Figure 12 - User interface of the Document Manager

The ODBMS we have used is **GemStone**, by Servio Corporation. The native language of GemStone is OPAL, derived from SmallTalk, but we developed our application using the C++ class library interface. Unfortunately, this choice made some restrictions on the features supplied by the ODBMS, for example we could not store into the data base methods associated with data (data bases having this property are called *active*), which assure the independence of the data base from applications.

The architectural choice we have made in our prototype is to concentrate on the client station the creation and manipulation of objects of the Document Conceptual Structure (we call this set of operations *authoring environment*) in order to avoid frequent accesses to the ODBMS residing at the server station. We devote to the server operations such as filing, retrieving, hypertextual navigation, integration with the Information Retrieval Engine and user-queries resolution.

As it is clear from the above description, the Document Model is a complex interconnection of objects: we deal with tree structures (conceptual and physical structures) and with transversal links among objects of these tree structures (hypertextual links and connections among conceptual and physical structures). In addition, objects of this structure can be achieved both in a navigational way and by a query approach. For that reason we appreciated very much the Gemstone feature of managing **composite objects**, that is to say the ability to define objects in terms of other objects and to easy implement the triggering mechanisms. Furthermore, Gemstone offers control mechanisms to assure integrity and consistency of composite objects. Unfortunately, Gemstone does not establish additional semantics to composite objects, so it does not supply management of locking, authorizations and physical clustering.

An other limitation of GemStone is on the **authorization** mechanism which is user oriented rather than object oriented: it allows to fix permissions on repositories of objects (*segments*) instead of on single objects. Features like **versions** and **long transactions** management are not supported.

Finally, Gemstone supplies objects **query** management only based on attributes of type long, double, char, char* or on object id, but it does not allow to insert user-defined methods in the queries.

4. Concluding Remarks

In this paper we have presented issues related to the development of a multimedia information system for an office environment.

We have, firstly, introduced the system describing the exact nature of the OOCM document and the way the system communicates with the outside world. We said that document content may be captured in several different ways, that OOCM superimposes a Conceptual Structure on content portions and it introduces an interface level, called Physical Structure, which is able to filter different external file formats.

We have described an object-oriented model for multimedia documents based on concepts of *Document Conceptual Structure* and *Document Type*. Document retrieval in this environment is based on attributes, on content, and Conceptual Objects.

A first prototype of the system has been developed which allows to capture contents, to create and manipulate Conceptual Structures, to file documents into an ODBMS residing on the server station, and, finally, to retrieve them. The prototype has been implemented in C++ on a client-server architecture.

We have discussed some implementation results concerning the use of the object-oriented DBMS technology and the Visual C++ programming experience.

Acknowledgements

Other people participated to the activity of prototyping of this project: M. Ferrise, D. Vitale, P. Guarente, P. Russo, G. Amendola, M. Martiello. We thank all of them for their contributions.

We are grateful also to Gennaro Ragucci, manager of the multimedia area in the site of Avellino, for its encouragements and suggestions.

Many thanks to the top management of Bull Italia and Bull HN Sud because it really believes that our research efforts are important to achieve high quality professionals that are the key factors for any effort in high technology.

References

[Atkinson 89]
M. Atkinson, F. Bancilhon, D. DeWitt, K. Dittrich, D. Maier, S. Zdonik-*The Object-Oriented Database System Manifesto-In Proceedings of the first International Conference on Deductive and Object-Oriented Databases, Kyoto, Japan, December 1989.*

[Bertino 87]
E. Bertino, S. Gibbs, F. Rabitti, C. Thanos-*The design of a multimedia office filing system*-Appeared in "Rivista d'informatica", n. 3, 1987

[Bertino 89]
E. Bertino-*Problematiche nel progetto di sistemi di gestione di basi di dati per il supporto di applicazioni CAD*-Appeared in "Rivista di informatica", n.1, 1989

[Bertino 91]
E. Bertino-*Sistemi di gestione di basi di dati orientate agli oggetti*-Appeared in "Rivista di informatica", n.4, 1991

[Bertino 92]
E. Bertino, L. D. Martino-*Sistemi di basi di dati orientate agli oggetti Concetti e architetture*-Published by Addison Wesley Masson, 1992

[Bienz 93]
T.Bienz, R. Cohn-*Portable Document Format Reference Manual*-Edited by Adobe Systems Incorporated-Published by Addison Wesley, 1993

[Christodoulakis 84]
S. Christodoulakis, J. Vanderbroek, J. Li, T. Li, S. Wan, Y. Wang, M. P. Papa and E. Bertino-*Development of a Multimedia Information System for an Office Environment*-Proceedings of the tenth International Conference on "Very Large Data Bases", Singapore, August 1984

[Christodoulakis 85]

S. Christodoulakis-*Office Filing*-Appeared in "Office Automation" edited by Springer-Verlag Berlin Heidelberg, 1985

[Christodoulakis 86]
S. Christodoulakis, M. Theodoridou, F. Ho, M. P. Papa and A. Pathria-*Multimedia Document Presentation, Information Extraction, and Document Formation in MINOS: A Model and a System*-Appeared in "ACM Transactions on Office Information Systems", Vol. 4, No. 4, October 1986

[Conti 90]
P. Conti and F. Rabitti-*Image Retrieval by Semantic Content*-Appeared in "Multimedia Office Filing The Multos Approach" published by North-Holland Amsterdam- New York- Oxford-Tokyo 1990

[Costantopoulos 90]
P. Costantopoulos, Y. Drakopoulos and Y. Yeorgaroudakis-*Multimedia Document Retrieval by Pictorial Content*-Appeared in "Multimedia Office Filing The Multos Approach" edited by North-Holland Amsterdam- New York- Oxford-Tokyo 1990

[Ecma 85]
Ecma Tc-29-*Office Document Architecture*-Standard Ecma-101, Sept. 1985

[Gehani 82]
Gehani, N.-*The potential of forms in office automation*-Appeared in IEEE Transactions on Communication, January 1982

[Gibbs 85]
S. Gibbs-*Conceptual Modelling and Office Information Systems*-Appeared in "Office Automation" edited by D. Tsichritzis, Springer-Verlag, 1985

[Horak 84]
W. Horak, G. Kronert-*An Object-Oriented Office Document Architecture Model for Processing and Interchange of Documents*-Proceedings of ACM SIGOA conference 1984

[Meghini 91]
C. Meghini, F. Rabitti, C. Thanos-*Conceptual Modeling of Multimedia Documents*-Appeared in "Computer" of IEEE Computer Society, October 1991

[Meghini 93]
C. Meghini, F. Sebastiani, U. Straccia, C. Thanos-*A Model of Information Retrieval based on a Terminological Logic*-Proceedings of the Sixteenth Annual International ACM SIGIR Conference on Research and Development in Information Retrieval, Pittsburgh,PA USA, June 1993

[Microsoft 92]
GC0165: Rich Text Format (RTF) Specification Microsoft Product Support Services Application Note, June 1992

[Thanos 90]
Multimedia Office Filing The Multos Approach-Edited by C. Thanos-North-Holland-Amsterdam-New York-Oxford-Tokyo, 1990

[Nierstrasz 85]
O. M. Nierstrasz-*An Object Oriented Systems*-Appeared in "Office Automation" edited by D. Tsichritzis, Springer-Verlag, 1985

[Papa 85]
M. P. Papa, S. Christodoulakis, M. Theodoridou-*Multimedia Document Presentation and Communication*-Proceedings of the AICA Conference, Firenze, September 1985

[Papa 90]
M. P. Papa-*L'utilizzo di ipermedia per gestire i dati multimeniali di un courseware basati sul modello object-oriented*-Proceedings of Didamatica Conference, Catania, Maggio 1990

[Rabitti 87]
F. Rabitti, P. Stanchev-*Graphical Image Retrieval from Large Image Databases*-Proceedings of AICA conference, Trento, settember 1987

[Rabitti 90]
F. Rabitti-*The Multos Document Model*-Appeared in "Multimedia Office Filing The Multos Approach" edited by North-Holland Amsterdam-New York- Oxford-Tokyo, 1990

[Rumbaugh 91]
J. Rumbaugh, M. Blaha, W. Premerlani, F. Eddy, W. Lorensen-*Object-Oriented Modeling and Design*-Published by Prentice Hall, 1991

[Tsichritzis 81]
D. Tsichritzis-*Omega Alpha*-Technical Report of the Computer Systems Research Group, University of Toronto, 1981

[Tsichritzis 85]
D. Tsichritzis, S. Christodoulakis, A. Lee and J. Vanderbroek-*A Multimedia Filing System*-Appeared in "Office Automation" edited by Springer-Verlag Berlin Heidelberg, 1985

[Salton 83]
G. Salton, M. J. McGill-*Introduction to Modern Information Retrieval*-McGraw-Hill Publishing Company, 1983

[Waterworth 91]
MULTIMEDIA Tecnologia e applicazioni-edited by A. Waterworth-published by Muzzio Nuovo Millennio, 1991

Putting Icons into (Con–) Text

Wolfgang Weck

Institute for Scientific Computing
ETH Zürich
CH-8092 Zürich
e-mail: Weck@inf.ethz.ch

Abstract

Using icons as handles to objects allows for a new simple design paradigm for user interfaces. The key is a concept that inherits icons from graphical user interfaces and the interpretation of sequential text from traditional text interfaces. The basic tool is the object oriented text model. It is shown what power lies in the introduction of icons into text as well as how icons can be used in a better way, if being seen in some context. An implementation of the concept and some application examples are described.

Introduction

The world of user interfaces splits into two paradigms: Text based and graphical user interfaces. It is a tradition to consider these two paradigms as completely different. But, modern text editing systems have already proven that this is not true. At least, text systems based on text attributed with fonts, size, color etc. and supporting a pointing device like a mouse for input, have many aspects of a graphical user interface. Still, the basic data structure is text.

An important concept from the graphical user interface area is the abstraction of entities through small atomic objects on the screen, called icons. In this paper we want to discuss the idea of a hybrid user interface, whose basic data structure is text but that also features icons as an abstraction mechanism. The idea is of striking simplicity. It turns out that both the paradigm for the user and the implementation are simple. Nevertheless, there is no application of this concept nor any reference in literature known to the author.

Our concept for user interface design emerged directly from the need for an abstraction of complex objects and the possibility to use a modern object oriented text model. The need rises in scientific computation systems, where results of different kinds and sizes need to be manipulated by, and represented to, the user. The way to solve these problems was suggested by the extensible text models of [Weinand-88, Calder-90, Szyperski-92].

The rest of the paper is organized as follows: We begin with a short discussion of terminology, to separate those aspects of *text* and *icon* which are important in the following sections. Afterwards we give a historical introduction to the idea of viewing icons as objects that are floating within a text environment. The third section gives some application examples. In the three sections following thereafter we show how our paradigm extends the facilities of both the traditional text oriented user interface paradigm and the traditional graphical user interface model. The seventh section describes conceptually an abstract class *Icon*, being the essence of our paradigm. Finally, we briefly discuss our implementation within the Oberon environment [Reiser-91, WiGu-92].

From TOOLS EUROPE '94 (Technology of Object-Oriented Languages and Systems).

Terminology

Though the concepts of texts and icons are well known in isolation, we briefly recall them to separate the aspects this paper is based on from those that we consider irrelevant in our context.

Icons are known from graphical user interfaces. In most cases they have a very specific role. They serve to abstract coarse objects, like files, processes, etc. We adopt this idea on a very abstract level. An icon represents some object in a compact form. In other words, icons are identifiers. Since only graphical operations are available in these interfaces, one normally associates with the term icon the notion of specific gestures like clicking on an icon, or dragging and dropping icons. In our context, this is of little interest. We claim that the interpretation of gestures is a feature independent of the interpretation of icons within context.

Text has two important aspects. First, it has visual character. It is used to represent documents, etc. From this view of text, many applications for text editing and preparation have emerged. The text produced by such tools is intended to be read by humans. Second, text may be used to direct the computer's operations. In this form it is intended to be read by the computer. Only in recent time it has been recognized that these are just two aspects of text. In modern text based user interfaces any piece of text in any document might be interpreted as a command or as data to be processed by a command. In the following, we postulate an environment of that kind. We assume that there are reasonable possibilities available to manipulate text and to select it for interpretation later on.

From Object Oriented Text Models to Icons Floating in Texts

The object oriented programming technique has significantly inspired advances in editor design. Especially, an increasing number of extensible text editors has become available. A frequently adopted scheme for extending texts is the interpretation of text as a sequence of (extensible) objects. One very common and simple extension of such objects are attributed characters. Other extensions are graphs, tables, and sometimes entire paragraphs, pages, and other structural entities [Vetterli-91, Szyperski-92]. We do not want to go into details of the different existing possibilities to implement this model. For our considerations, the important part of the concept is the facility to extend some basic class of elements, floating within text. We will call that basic class *text elements*.

However, most of the realized text elements are designed to be printed and to be read by humans. In other words: The main purpose of the object oriented text model as stated above, is document preparation for desktop publishing. Nevertheless, text elements were also employed to design user interfaces. Doing so, text is the environment, and the text elements are interface objects like slide bars, buttons, etc. that are acted upon by the user. One possible application for this is rapid design of dialog masks: With a normal text editor the mask can be composed out of several elements in combination with plain text as description. This entire document can be stored and displayed with a different view, allowing only manipulation of the contents of the individual text elements, not of the text itself. The latter view thus forms a mask for user input. In general, this can be seen as implementing a graphical user interface as described in [Linton-89, Mili-92] within a text environment. Text elements might also be used to implement hypertext [Conklin-87].

In this paper we want to focus on another aspect of text: Due to its sequential character, it can be read and subjected to a parsing mechanism that tries to interpret the text in some way. In itself, this aspect of text is very common: Many of the systems in use today operate with input of commands in a command line. The input text is interpreted by a so-called command interpreter. In the area of scientific computing, text is a very important carrier, not only for commands, but also for data; i.e., parameters and results are represented textually.

Without going into implementation details, it should be mentioned that modern systems allow not only to interpret typed text, but also text that is already visible on the screen.

Examples are the upcoming user interfaces for symbolic algebra systems, so-called worksheets, featuring a text editor combined with some mechanism to issue a command that interprets some part of the text and changes the contents of the worksheet appropriately. Note that at this point a very strong interaction of text editing and text interpretation becomes apparent.

This situation suggests the combination of the two issues described above: Text as subjected to parsing and interpretation may contain extensible text elements that are also interpreted in some specific way. Or, in other words, special parsers can be constructed, that are able to analyse text containing text elements besides characters. In the following, we will call these objects *icons*. Since this name is associated with several different concepts, we want to emphasize those concepts which are important in the context of this paper.

We consider an icon as an atomic object within a user interface that refers directly to some object. Thus, it is an identifier for (or a handle to) an object. This is the most important property. Concerning the icon's appearance, the important concept is atomicity; i.e., an icon is a token not to be composed of several units, as, for example, a name is composed of separable characters. Minor issues are the presentation of the icon to the user and the kind of object to be identified through the icon. Especially, we consider it an orthogonal issue whether the object has methods to interpret certain gestures, e.g. clicking of a mouse button in the objects visual area.

Application Examples

Before reflecting the applications of icons within text more theoretically, we want to present some practical examples, where the concept explained above is being used. It is natural that the biggest effect of icons within text is gained when they are part of some expression, i.e., text being parsed and analysed as input to some operation. Thus, one of the first applications of the concept has been a matrix calculation tool box, where matrices are abstracted by icons. Scientists often operate with matrices of extreme size. Stating, say, the product of two 100 × 100 matrices is much easier if the matrices are single relatively small objects, as opposed to each being given as a hundred lines of one hundred numbers each. Since the icons representing huge matrices are still of reasonable size and the environment of the entire expression is just text, it is easy to put a statement of the following kind in any document:

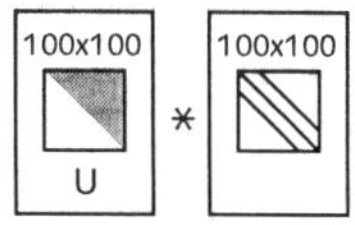

Figure 1: Product of two 100 × 100 matrices

When appearing in an interactive environment instead of on paper, it is easy to view the full data associated with each of the icons, or to evaluate the entire expression. Note that the shape of the matrix icons above gives extra information about the objects represented by them. It is obvious that one matrix is in upper triangular form whereas the other one is a band matrix.

A matrix icon might contain a describing caption too, but this is optional and has no meaning to the system. The purpose of such a caption is to give some optional extra information to the user only. Captions are not used to identify objects. Several icons might contain the same caption (or even none at all) while still refering to different objects. Further, since captions are not names to be parsed and analysed they need not to satisfy specific syntax rules but are simply sequences of characters.

More general, icons are used to abstract subexpressions in our current computer algebra interface project. There, the use of icons is not restricted to certain types of objects, like matrices, but arbitrary symbolic expressions can be folded into one icon. These icons in turn are used to form new expressions, which might also be abstracted by icons again.

Another application that has been realized is the interface for a text searching system. The result of a text search query is a set of text positions. Quite often, these sets are of respectable size and the user's intention is not to view all matches found, but to refine his or her query, using previous results. Thus, the search engine itself interprets expressions, including references to earlier results [Fawcett-89]. In a new interface to this system we used icons to abstract result sets. Expressions for refining queries are simply composed of plain text and such icons (Figures 2 and 3).

"cat" *Match* within docs Definition

Figure 2: Expression denoting reduction of the set of all occurrences of "cat" to the set of those within text regions labeled "Definition".

"icon" *Match* near "text" *Match*

Figure 3: Results in the set of occurrences of "icon" where a occurrence of "text" is close. (Notably, when searching the Oxford English Dictionary this set is empty.)

In the previous example, the expressions are to be evaluated by a special object: a text searching engine. Thus, initiation of such an evaluation can be seen as sending the message *Evaluate* and the expression to the search engine object. As a matter of fact, the text search engine understands several messages beside *Evaluate*; e.g. *Search*, *Replace*, and *Stop*. An icon representing such an object displays a menu, from which the method to be activated can be selected (Figure 4).

OED
OED.Lookup ↑
PATFace.Search ↑
PATFace.Evaluate ↑
PATFace.Replace ↑
PATFace.Stop
SearchEngine

Figure 4: Icon representing the text search engine for the OED

A completely different application is the use of primitive icons as delimiters, e.g. in script-like texts. Consider a text that is to be interpreted as a sequence of calls of commands with parameters. It is then necessary to determine the start points of new commands. Traditionally, one simply defines a special character that marks the beginning of every command. This character might also be a control character, such as *carriage return*. Unfortunately, if parameters of the commands can possibly contain any character, this will lead to conflicts. Thus, it is advantageous to use an object of a unique class in this place. In our example application there exist so-called *Activators* that mark text positions as start of executable and parameterised commands. Furthermore, we have introduced *Slots*, which are placeholders to be filled with a textual copy of the most recent text selection. Both *Activators* and *Slots* are very primitive icons, since when being parsed only their class is of interest (Figure 5).

↳Write.Print MyPrinter [1] ↳System.DeleteFiles [1]

Figure 5: Example for script containing activator and slot icons

In the following sections we want to discuss the more principal impact of our suggested concept and compare it to the existing paradigms of text based user interfaces as well as to graphical user interfaces already making use of icons as abstractions for some kinds of objects.

Icons are Identifiers: Getting Rid of Named Variables

To allow manipulation of objects, the user must be able to refer to these objects. Doing so is easy if a simple and concise textual representation exists. Tools to show and edit text are widely available. But this approach fails for objects having a too large textual representation or none at all.

Examples of these are the objects being used in mathematical software: In numerical applications there are matrices and vectors that are occasionally much too large to comprehend when only available as plain text. In symbolic computation one deals with sets of equations and expressions which again may be very large. Another example might be the result of a query in an information retrieval system: As a result to a query one gets a set of entry points to the database, which itself is a possible parameter for refining operations. One more example of a similar kind is produced by some DNA sequence matching systems when searching for similar sequences in a database. The result of such a process is a collection of matches, which themselves are complex data records. Again, the possibility to refer to previously generated results is of greater interest than viewing the full information associated with them immediately.

More theoretically: The user will activate commands. This is conceptually very close to procedure or method calls. The problem we are dealing with is the mechanism of parameter passing. This has traditionally been solved by employing exactly the same mechanism as in programming languages: Abstraction of objects by assigning them to a named variable or, from another point of view, binding them to a name. This mechanism works well in the area of programming, where a very limited scope for the validity of such bindings is defined. Even better is the case where there are possibilities for static checks of certain properties, e.g., type compatibility, without executing the program. When manipulating data within a user interface however, the process is of an interactive nature and the scope for name bindings is the entire session. We claim that this combination of name binding and interactive computation has many disadvantages.

Assigning a value to a variable, or binding a value to some name, represents an agreement between the computer and its user. Both agree that a specific name shall denote the

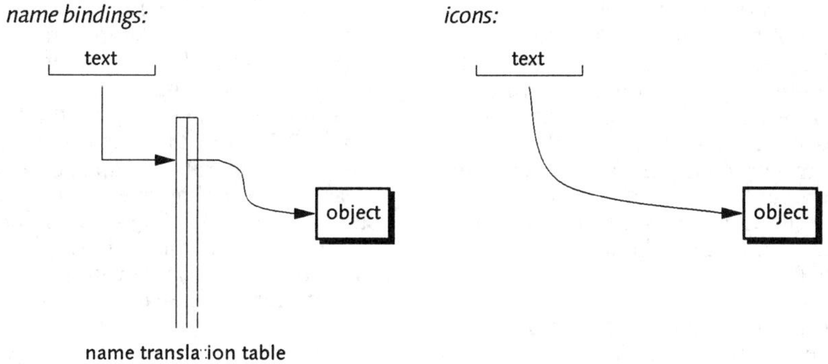

Figure 6: Illustration of the referencing mechanisms of name bindings and icons

corresponding object (see Figure 6). Since it has an effective memory, the computer will stick to this agreement. Not so the user, who has to remember the same mapping as the computer, but in his or her head. Besides the fact that this just takes mental capacity of the user, the risk of forgetting is much too high. Often enough, one has some difficulty remembering a name one has introduced some time ago – especially, when a distracting phone call happened in the mean time. This can normally be overcome by searching the history of the session. However, this process is tedious. But even worse, one may accidentally assign a new value to some variable, the original value of which is still needed. This may mean loss of data and – still worse – continuation of computation based on wrong assumptions. In the latter case, wrong results are produced without notice.

These few examples should demonstrate that the introduction of hidden state, i.e., of a name translation table which has to be synchronized between the computer and the memory of the user, is a bad concept. Icons can easily be used to eliminate such a name translation table, since their reference mechanism is direct without additional (hidden) information. Further, in contrast to names, the reference mechanism and the appearance of icons are not coupled. Thus, one has more choices for the representation. There need not be a unique name involved at all, since the user might recognize an icon by other attributes, e.g. the context in which it has been placed. (Note that the possibility to position icons within text allows the user to keep arbitrary comments close to it. Searching for an icon could then be done by means of text search in these comments. Here text becomes the context for the human – not for the machine.)

We would like to point out that our remark above does not represent a principal objection against the usage of names, as long as there exists a clear bounded scope. A piece of text containing a sequence of statements to be executed in one step like a procedure (e.g. by activation of an interpreter command) might use named variables as well as icons. Whereas the latter would represent input values, the former could be viewed as local variables of a procedure. The name bindings are valid exactly during the execution of the script. Hence, all output values have to be bound to icons instead of names. This paradigm of *atomic script interpretation* has already been implemented in our matrix computation system.

Icons as Unique Extensions of the Character Set

From another point of view introducing icons into text is equivalent to extending the character set in a very specific way. The speciality about this is that the various extensions of different components will not interfere. This is in contrast to assigning some special meaning to a specific character code. The latter does not guarantee the independence of different extensions: Two extensions that are not aware of each other might use the same code for different purposes. In contrast, classes are unique for the entire system. Hence, for an object, the property of belonging to a specific class is a unique characteristic.

As an application, one may consider a command that is intended to accept arbitrary text as a parameter, including special characters, control characters, etc. A special case of this are wrapper commands, i.e. commands whose parameter text contain other commands, together with their parameters. Having no independence of extensions in this case, conflicts can not be avoided. The need for such commands, can be seen from the fairly complicated quoting and escaping rules of most existing text command based user interfaces. Consider the *sh* command in Unix as an example. These rules could be simplified by using icons for unique and interference free delimiters.

Surrounding Text is Context: Extending the Flexibility of Icons

In this section we want to approach our suggested concept from the opposite direction and compare our view of icons to the traditional paradigm of graphical user interfaces, i.e. we want to show how context can contribute to the idea of icons. We claim that in interfaces made up by icons placed on a two dimensional plane, the possibilities to operate with these icons are very limited since there is very few context. Consider icons representing mathematical expressions. Suppose you want to add two such expressions. The only way to do this is to select both icons and activate a summation command. (Whether the latter is represented by an icon or can be activated from a menu or in any other way does not make any difference here.) For summation, multiplication, and any other commutative operation this works perfectly. But, consider a non-commutative operation, like subtraction or division. To execute such an operation it is essential to distinguish the first and the second operator. When execution of a command means to drag the icons representing the parameters into another icon representing the operation, this is hard to do. The same holds if the parameters have to be selected and the operation is activated afterwards. The only solution that does not introduce modes or hidden states would be to mark selections differently to explicitly show their order. We feel that this concept is not easy to comprehend for the user. It is hard to imagine such a system with a growing number of selection levels. In contrast, an expression like the following is very readable:

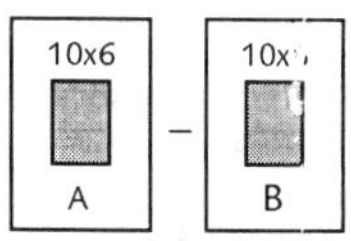

Figure 7: Difference of two matrices

A further aspect here is that the operation within a graphical user interface is completely documentation free, i.e., it does not document what actions have been taken. In contrast to this, text augmented with icons has some similarities with hypertext [Conklin-87]. The icons serve to establish the links from text to the objects they are representing. One can compose expressions or program statements and put them into any document. Upon receipt of such a document, it is easy to use part of it as input directly, e.g., to verify the computation that has been done. Still, the hypertext paradigm does not build on the ability to parse and interpret part of texts. Text elements within a hypertext interpret certain gestures but are not used by a text interpreter.

Another advantage of having the concepts of textual interfaces merged into those of graphical interfaces, is that it is sometimes much easier to give a part of a parameter in textual form. Since we do not restrain ourselves to represent every entity by an icon, it is up to the user to mix plain text and icons. For illustration the following example expression from matrix calculation may serve:

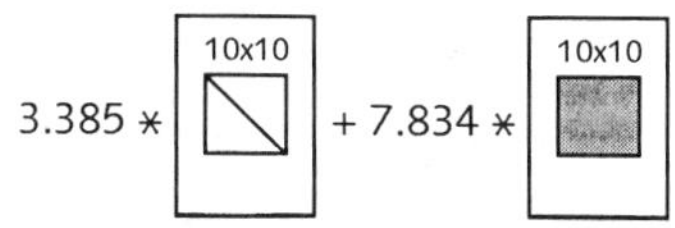

Figure 8: Expression mixing text and icons

The Class Icon

As our central point we want to suggest the addition of a new abstract class *Icon* to the system. This class is an extension of the more abstract text elements, mentioned above. It is itself extended to specific concrete classes, as needed for specific applications. In the following, we will focus on the properties of the class *Icon*.

Instances of class *Icon* have a twofold purpose. First, as any text element, an icon must have a method to draw itself on the screen. Second, it must export a reference to the object it represents, called the *referenced object* in the following. Normally, the appearance of an icon on the screen depends on the class of the object being represented; sometimes, even on the particular instance of that class. Hence, the method for drawing the icon has to be abstract in the class *Icon*. Subclasses of *Icon* implement the individual display mechanism as well as a method to reference objects of a specific class (or extensions thereof).

Postulating that all objects are derived from a basic class *Object*, the reference mechanism could be the same for all instances of *Icon* and therefore it might as well be implemented in the base class *Icon* itself. But, we feel that defining individual typed references in each subclass of *Icon* leads to a cleaner design.

Remembering that the instances of class *Icon* and its subclasses will be part of texts that can not only be edited by the user and interpreted by a specific interpreter, but also be stored into and loaded from files, we expect icons to store their referenced object with the text. Hence, additional methods for file reading and writing are required. These methods depend heavily on the class of the referenced object. This is another argument for subclassing *Icon* for each class of referenced objects. Alternatively, the referenced objects themselves would have to provide load and store methods, and the icon objects would simply forward the corresponding messages.

To be able to implement the text editing functions, a method to copy an icon is also needed. When implementing the copy method, it has to be decided whether the entire pair of icon and referenced object is to be copied (deep copy), or only the instance variables of the icon, including the reference, are replicated (shallow copy). In class *Icon* no preparations are taken for either way, since the decision really should be left to the concrete application. With icons representing huge amounts of data (e.g. large matrices) or complicated dynamic data structures, deep copy may be too expensive. Furthermore, some applications may even rely on all copies of an icon referring to the same object. On the other hand, there are many applications where deep copy is essential, since each copy needs to be changeable individually.

More formally, the class *Icon* could be defined as follows:

```
Icon = CLASS (Texts.Element)
    CopyFrom (source: Icon);
    Draw (p: Port; fnt: Fonts.Font; col: INTEGER);
    Load (VAR r: Files.Rider);
    Store (VAR r: Files.Rider)
END;
```

Note that the draw method also receives the attributes of the text element, such as font and color, just as a character would. This allows to adapt the representation to the surrounding text. Since we do not want to associate icons with little pictures (picked from a library or designed with an editor) only, we intentionally included a draw method allowing arbitrary drawings on the screen. This more flexible approach allows for very specialized representations giving additional information about the associated value.

All these methods are abstract, i.e., they have to be implemented in every concrete subclass. Since we assume that an interpreter of text is aware of the subclasses of *Icon* used to identify objects it can process, we can leave the specification of the reference mechanism to the subclasses; that is, no abstract method in the class *Icon* is required for this. All the methods defined here provide the interface of an icon to the text system of its environment. They are already needed for text elements in general. Thus, the class *Icon* as defined above serves only to distinguish icons from other text elements.

So far we have excluded methods to interpret gestures such as mouse clicks executed on an icon. We stated above that this aspect of icons is not related to the aspect of being interpretable as part of text. In our existing implementation however, we have introduced additional abstract methods into the base class to standardize the behavior of two frequently needed operations. First, for icons representing a value, preparations are taken to show and edit some textual or graphical representation in a separate viewer. One might view that as *opening the icon*. Second, it is possible to assign an operation to an icon, that is executed when clicking on it. This can be seen as *activating the icon*. For more details, we refer to the section on implementation issues later in this paper.

We also want to introduce two partially abstract classes, both extending class *Icon*. Both of them define part of the appearance of the icon on screen, but leave all the other methods abstract. The simpler class of the two is called *DefaultIcons*. Its instances appear as little boxes containing two character strings, one giving a caption (or comment) describing the object represented by the icon and the other hinting at its class.

The second extension class, called *MenuIcons*, arose from the wish to abstract the concept of the method call in object oriented programming, which is in our context roughly a command call with an implicit parameter. Similar to *DefaultIcons*, *MenuIcons* appear as boxes containing strings stating caption and kind. Additionally, a menu is displayed, from which the method to be activated can be selected.

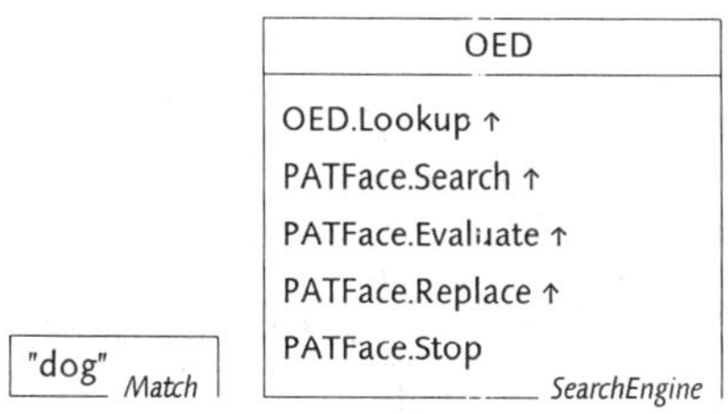

Figure 9: A *DefaultIcon* and a *MenuIcon* as used within the interface for text searching.

A problem arises when combining the shallow copy strategy with the store and load mechanism of texts: Consider an icon in a text referring to some object. Upon inserting another copy of this icon into the same text, two icons having a reference to the same object each are found within one text. After store and a subsequent load of the text, the two icons will refer to two separate objects, if that situation is not taken care of. The case becomes more difficult, when references to one object exist in different text documents simultaneously. After a store and reload of one of the documents the uniqueness of the reference is lost.

Though it may cause conceptual difficulties, in practice we did not yet encounter an application where the combination of shallow copy, support for load and store, and sensitivity to the distinction between similar objects existed. A practical solution of the problem however is still considered to be an open problem. It would require some sort of unique global object identification. The possibility of sending text files containing icons and referenced objects to other machines makes this problem even harder.

An Implementation

The concept discussed in the previous sections has been implemented in the *Oberon System* [Reiser-91, WiGu-92], using the editor and application framework *Write* described in [Szyperski-92]. The latter fulfils the need for a flexible and extensible editor. It supports so-called *Elems*, which are extensible objects floating in text. We created a new extension of these, called *Icons*, implementing the class *Icon* described earlier. Each concrete class is an extension of this and has to implement the reference mechanism on its own. An interpreter, being expected to work with icons of such a class, has to be aware of the concrete extension to be able to retrieve the referenced objects.

The implemented class *Icon* is slightly more complex than the theoretical one outlined above. This has several reasons. To begin with, we have slightly extended the power of icons by introducing two methods for standard interpretation of gestures. Oberon features a three button mouse, so there is more than one possible mouse click on an icon that can be interpreted. We currently support two gestures. One to *open* the icon, and another one to *activate* it. The first feature allows to get a (possibly editable) view of the complete data represented by the icon. This view together with the associated model can be passed back to the icon, to allow update of the original data to the edited version. (Methods *Externalize* and *Internalize*.) The parameters of these two methods are display frames that are directly used within a viewer. Additionally, a caption is passed that is used to name the new viewer and that might be edited too.

The activation of an icon is simply the call of a special method, whose behavior depends on the concrete extension. (Method *Op*.)

Further additional effort was spent to make icons independent from their graphical environment. This comes from the observation that the representations of the icons became more and more elaborate. Furthermore, since icons might appear in any

```
TYPE
   Icon = POINTER TO IconDesc
   IconDesc = RECORD (Texts.ElemDesc) END;

PROCEDURE (i: Icon) Identify (VAR module, procedure: ARRAY OF CHAR);
PROCEDURE (i: Icon) CopyFrom (source: Icon);
PROCEDURE (i: Icon) GetDim (textPos, unit, indent: LONGINT; fnt: Fonts.Font; VAR voff, w, h: LONGINT);
PROCEDURE (i: Icon) Draw (p: DrawPort; fnt: Fonts.Font; col: INTEGER);
PROCEDURE (i: Icon) Externalize (VAR caption, menu: ARRAY OF CHAR; VAR f: Display.Frame);
PROCEDURE (i: Icon) Internalize (caption: ARRAY OF CHAR; f: Display.Frame);
PROCEDURE (i: Icon) Store (VAR r: Files.Rider);
PROCEDURE (i: Icon) Load (VAR r: Files.Rider);
PROCEDURE (i: Icon) Op;
```

Figure 10: Interface definition of the abstract class Icon

text document in any place, a representation not only on the screen, but also on paper is desired. On the other hand, the programmer of a concrete extension of *Icon* will not want to do his work twice, i.e. program separate drawing routines for display and printer. Thus, we introduced a special helper class, called *Port*, to abstract the real output device (Method *Draw*).

Since the actual size of an icon depends on the data it represents, there has to be a way to obtain the size of the icon before drawing it. This is essential for the layout algorithm to be able to generate a reasonable text layout. (Method *GetDim*).

For storing in a file or for generating a copy of an icon, it is not sufficient to externalize or replicate all the data; but one also needs a way to identify the concrete class to be able to allocate a new instance. In particular for filing, a persistent representation is needed. Thus, it is the duty of the programmer of an extension to provide an allocating procedure. Any icon object has to implement a method giving the name (module name and procedure name) of its corresponding allocation procedure. (Method *Identify*.)

To summarize, Figure 10 gives a reproduction of the complete definition of the class *Icon* in Oberon-2 [Mössenböck-91]. The methods *CopyFrom*, *Store* and *Load* have the behavior as hinted by their names and described in the conceptual section.

Several extensions of this abstract class have been implemented and used in many different applications. Figure 11 gives an overview of the classes mentioned in this paper and their embedding into the Oberon environment. *MenuIcons* and *DefaultIcons* themselves are partially abstract. They basically implement the drawing methods, whereas the reference mechanism is still abstract. Most of the icon classes shown in Figure 11 have been mentioned in the section on application examples.

Conclusion

The idea to use icons in a textual context as explained in this paper has several advantages. Conceptually it inherits from the pure text based user interface paradigm as well as from the graphical user interface paradigm. We pointed out how the new concept contributes to improve on both paradigms. Figure 12 shall illustrate this fact.

In spite of its simplicity, the concept appears to be new in literature as well as in application. There is no other reference known to the author describing the combination of extensible objects floating in text with the property of text being interpretable.

We introduced a class for icons being able to be parsed as part of a text. This class exports only abstract methods and might be identical to the base class of extensible objects in an object oriented text model (*Elems* in [Szyperski-92] or *Glyphs* in [Calder-90]). The

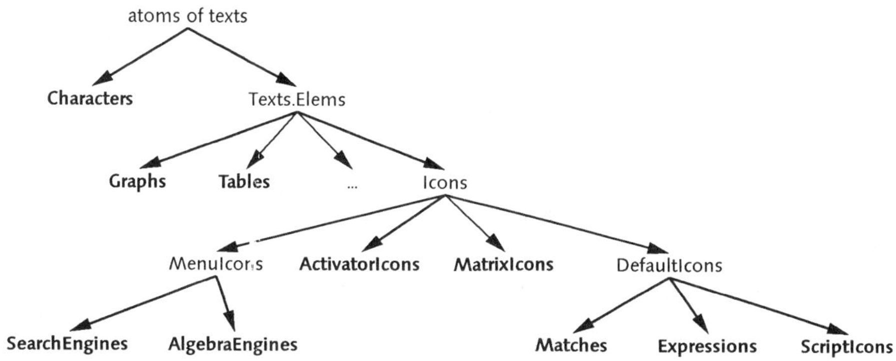

Figure 11: Class hierarchy of the implementation in Oberon (concrete classes in bold face)

implementation of the reference mechanism can be left to the concrete extensions. However, we suggest to include additional abstract methods for gesture interpretation into the icon base class, though this is not related to the identifier property of icons.

Our implementation within the Oberon environment has already been used for a variety of applications, mainly in the area of scientific computing. Examples are interfaces for a matrix calculation tool, a text data base system, and DNA sequence matching algorithms. Especially the class *DefaultIcon* turned out to be very useful in construction ofboth user interface prototypes as well as test beds for new modules offering only a programming interface. In the area of

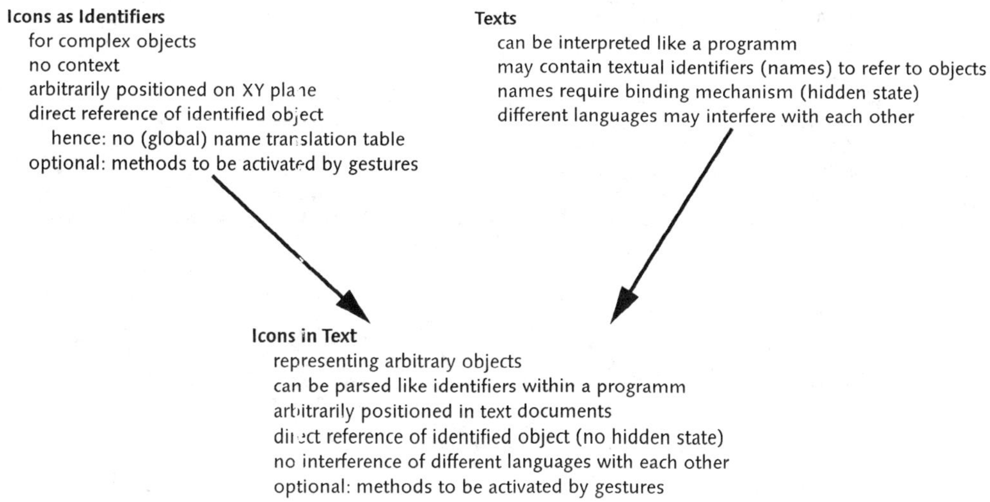

Figure 12: Overview over the concepts of Icons in Text

scientific computing it is important to keep the overhead for the design of simple user interfaces as low as possible, since quite often the time spent to program an algorithm for a test exceeds the time of its productive use. Thus, being able to create usable ad hoc interfaces is a major advantage.

The simplicity of our idea leads to an equally simple and straightforward implementation – given the right environment, i.e., an object oriented text model. We believe that the concept can easily be reimplemented within environments other than the Oberon system. Even implementing the entire text model together with the proper extension should be a possible way of integrating the concept into commercial user interfaces. We want to point out that our implementation of the abstract classes *Icon* and *DefaultIcon*, which are already useful for many applications, consists of less than 500 lines of source code

Acknowledgements

The first who applied my paradigm while programming user interfaces were Rolf Eberhardt and Walter Schmidli. I want to thank them for their helpful feedback. I wish to thank Marc Brandis, Dominik Gruntz, Philipp Heuberger, Cuno Pfister, Clemens Szyperski and Stefan Vorkötter who read earlier versions of this paper and made many valuable comments. Finally, I thank Prof. G.H.Gonnet for confronting me with the problems in scientific computing and his support of my research.

References

[Calder-90] P. R. Calder, M. A. Linton, *Glyphs: Flyweight Objects for User Interfaces*, Proc. ACM Symp. on User Interface Software and Technology (UIST), 1990.

[Conklin-87] J. Conklin, Hypertext: *An Introduction and Survey*, IEEE Computer, Sept. 1987.

[Fawcett-89] H. Fawcett, *PAT 3.3 Users.Guide*, University of Waterloo, Centre for the New Oxford English Dictionary, 1989.

[Linton-89] M. A. Linton, J. M. Vlissides, P. Calder, *Composing User Interfaces with InterViews*, IEEE Computer, Febr. 1989.

[Mili-92] H. Mili, A. E. El Wahidi, Y. Intrator, *Building a Graphical Interface for a Reuse-Oriented CASE Tool*, Proc. Tools 8, Prentice Hall, 1992.

[Mössenböck-91] H. Mössenböck, *The Programming Language Oberon-2*, Struct. Programming, 12:4, 1991.

[Reiser-91] M. Reiser, *The Oberon System - User's Guide and Programmer's Manual*, Addison-Wesley, Reading, MA. 1991.

[Szyperski-92] C. A. Szyperski, *Write-ing Applications: Designing an Extensible Text-Editor as an Application Framework*, Proceedings of the Seventh International Conference on Technology of Object-Oriented Languages and Systems, TOOLS EUROPE '92, Dortmund, Germany Prentice-Hall, Englewood Cliffs, NJ, 1992.

[Vetterli-91] Ch. Vetterli, *OPUS: Entwurf und Realisierung eines erweiterbaren, objectorientierten Dokumentenverarbeitungssystems*, PhD Thesis. Diss. No. 9456, ETH Zürich, 1991.

[Weinand-88] A. Weinand, E. Gama, R. Marty, *ET++ - An object-oriented application framework in C++*, Proc. OOPSLA '88, San Diego, CA, 1988.

[WiGu-92] N. Wirth, J. Gutknecht, *Project Oberon. The Design of an Operating System and Compiler*, Addison-Wesley, Reading, MA, 1992.

ANALYSIS AND MODELING

Derived Metaclasses in SOM

Scott Danforth
Ira Forman
IBM Object Technology Products

Abstract

This paper describes SOM's solution to "metaclass incompatibility," a problem that can occur when an object-oriented programming (OOP) model allows specialized class functionality to be defined using metaclasses. Although restrictions imposed by various OOP models avoid this problem (e.g., by not supporting classes as objects, or supporting only single inheritance), SOM's approach is unique in that it imposes no such restrictions. As a result, SOM allows programmers to package and compose solutions in ways that are unavailable in other models.

Introduction

In SOM (IBM's System Object Model), a class is a run-time object that has a class referred to as a metaclass. Metaclasses in SOM can be named, which allows properties of classes to be factored and reused. While this provides programmers with increased design capabilities, it also raises issues related to how class designers choose metaclasses, and whether their choices might be inconsistent with the requirements of a given class. These issues were raised and discussed by Graube [Gra89], but, in practice, have remained largely unresolved. This paper describes SOM's solution to the problem.

We begin with a short overview of SOM. We then expain the problem of metaclass incompatibility and illustrate why this is an issue for SOM and other object models that support metaclasses. Finally, we show how SOM resolves this issue by dynamically deriving new metaclasses when this is called for.

SOM Overview

SOM supports the definition and use of language-neutral object-oriented systems [SOM93]. Although OOP languages also provide for construction of object-oriented systems, SOM does so in a way that is independent of programming languages by providing a runtime application programming interface (API) to SOM objects that is based on simple procedure calls.

SOM's objective is not to replace existing programming languages, but to support OOP by allowing applications written in all of these languages to use common binary class libraries, and to allow class implementors to extend and replace these libraries without breaking existing application binaries.

A SOM class library is distributed as a dynamic link library (DLL) that can be replaced without requiring recompilation of applications that use its classes (as long as the new library doesn't require changes in the applications' source code). Binary software packaging technology is now common in the case of procedure libraries. Most modern operating systems support some form of dynamic linkage for use of shared procedure code libraries, but SOM is unique in that it extends this capability to OOP class libraries. This is essential if system-provided OOP class libraries are to be used by software vendors, because end-users do not have access to application source or the compilers necessary for regenerating executables when new releases of a system library are installed. The benefits of object-oriented programming for

From TOOLS EUROPE '94 (Technology of Object-Oriented Languages and Systems).

software development are widely accepted, but SOM is the only system-level framework that allows binary packaging of language-neutral OOP class libraries.

Language neutrality and support for backwards binary compatibility are two reasons why SOM was chosen for building the OS/2 Workplace Shell [Min92, Orf92, IBM92]. The result is that OS/2 application developers can use powerful, full-function OOP technology to build applications by subclassing Workplace Shell classes, knowing that major enhancements and modifications of the Workplace Shell class hierarchy will not invalidate their application binaries.

SOM need not be used to implement all of the objects and classes important to an application framework. Many objects created and used by a class library may be strictly internal to that library's implementation -- with no need for being accessed from multiple languages or applications. Perhaps these "internal" objects will be SOM objects (in those cases where SOM class libraries provide useful functionality), or perhaps they will be objects provided by some other class library (e.g., a Smalltalk, Eiffel, or C++ class library), depending on the programming language that is used. Only classes intended to be backwards binary compatible across application and language boundaries (or useful to non-OOP languages) need to be SOM classes. Also, the implementation of SOM classes may make use of non-SOM classes. For example, C++ objects might be used as instance variables when C++ is used to implement a class of SOM objects.

SOM Terminology

A *SOM Object* is a run-time entity with a specific set of *methods* and *instance variables*. The methods (which correspond to virtual functions in C++) are used by a programmer to request behavior from the object. The instance variables encode the object's state, and are used by the object's implementation to support method execution. When a method is invoked on an object, the object is said to be the *receiver* or *target* of the method call.

An object's *implementation* determines the procedures that execute its methods (such procedures are therefore called *method procedures*) and determines the types and overall structural layout of the object's instance variables. The method procedures and instance variables that implement an object are *encapsulated* -- not directly available to an object's user. Instead, an object's user is given access to the object through an *interface*.

An *object type* represents a specific interface through which an object's methods may be invoked. By declaring an object type for a procedure argument or local variable, a programmer chooses the interface used for accessing the corresponding object. OMG's CORBA Interface Definition Language (IDL) is used to define SOM object interfaces [OMG93, SOM93], and the SOM language bindings allow programmers to use these interface names when typing variables.

In SOM, as in most approaches to OOP, *classes* define the implementation of objects. Every SOM object is an instance of some, specific SOM class. Because a class determines the methods available on its instances, all the objects of a given class support the same interface. The process of class definition in SOM therefore starts with an IDL definition of the interface that its objects will support, and the name of this interface is then given to the class as well. As result, a class name in SOM is always a type name (even though the things named are different -- a type is an object interface, a class is an object implementation).

Subclassing is the well-known OOP technique for incrementally deriving new classes by inheriting, extending, and modifying existing object implementations. The classes from which a new class is derived are called its *parent classes*. Through subclassing, a derived class in SOM inherits all of its parents methods. Furthermore, by default, it inherits its parents' method procedures and instance variables. As usual, subclasses can *override* inherited methods by defining new method procedures, and can introduce new methods and instance variables. In the event that a method is inherited from multiple parents (which may support the method with different method procedures), SOM provides ways for resolving ambiguities. SOM's multiple inheritance model is based on graph inheritance [Sny86], and the instance variables introduced by a class's ancestors in this event are only inherited once.

In SOM, classes are themselves objects. That is, classes in SOM have their own methods and interfaces, and are themselves implemented by other classes. The term *class object* is used when referring to an object that is a class. The terms, *class methods* and *class variables* are used to distinguish between the methods and state variables of a class object and those that it defines for its instances.

A class whose instances are classes is called a *metaclass*. Thus, in SOM, the methods of a class are defined by a metaclass. In SOM, a class's methods include those that implement inheritance from the class's parents. As a result, SOM programmers that define metaclasses can actually modify the default semantics of inheritance provided by the SOM kernel.

SOM objects that are not classes are called *proper objects*; SOM classes that are not metaclasses are called *proper classes*.

SOM Kernel Classes

The SOM kernel DLL contains two primitive classes that are the basis for all subsequent classes:

- SOMObject -- the root ancestor for all SOM classes, and
- SOMClass -- the common ancestor of all SOM metaclasses.

All SOM objects are an instance of a SOM class, and all SOM classes are ultimately derived by subclassing from SOMObject. Thus, all SOM objects (namely, all proper objects, all proper classes, and all metaclasses) can execute the methods introduced by SOMObject. In a similar manner, all SOM classes are an instance of a SOM metaclass, and all SOM metaclasses are ultimately derived from SOMClass. Thus, all classes can execute the methods introduced by SOMClass. Because they are classes, both SOMObject and SOMClass are instances of SOMClass.

In addition to SOMObject and SOMClass, the SOM kernel includes the class, SOMClassMgr, which implements a runtime class registry. This allows dynamically loading and unloading DLLs that define SOM classes. When the SOM runtime environment is created, the above three classes and a class manager (i.e., a proper object that is an instance of SOMClassMgr) are created. The relationships between these four objects are illustrated in Figure 1. Note the use of two object relationships in this figure: the instance relationship, and the subclass relationship

An important difference between SOM and OOP models without class objects is the occurrence of an instance relationship between objects. This provides an additional dimension of design when defining classes, and can be of equal importance to the inheritance relationship. Figure 2 provides a more elaborate example of some possible SOM objects and relationships enabled by the ability to define named metaclasses and use these when sub-

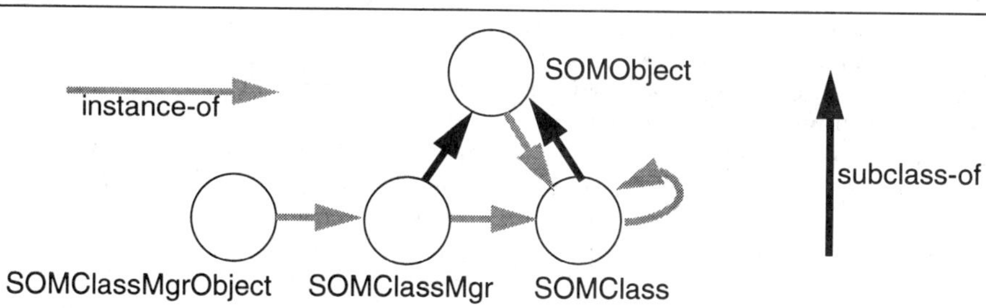

Figure 1 -- Relationships between the SOM Kernel Objects

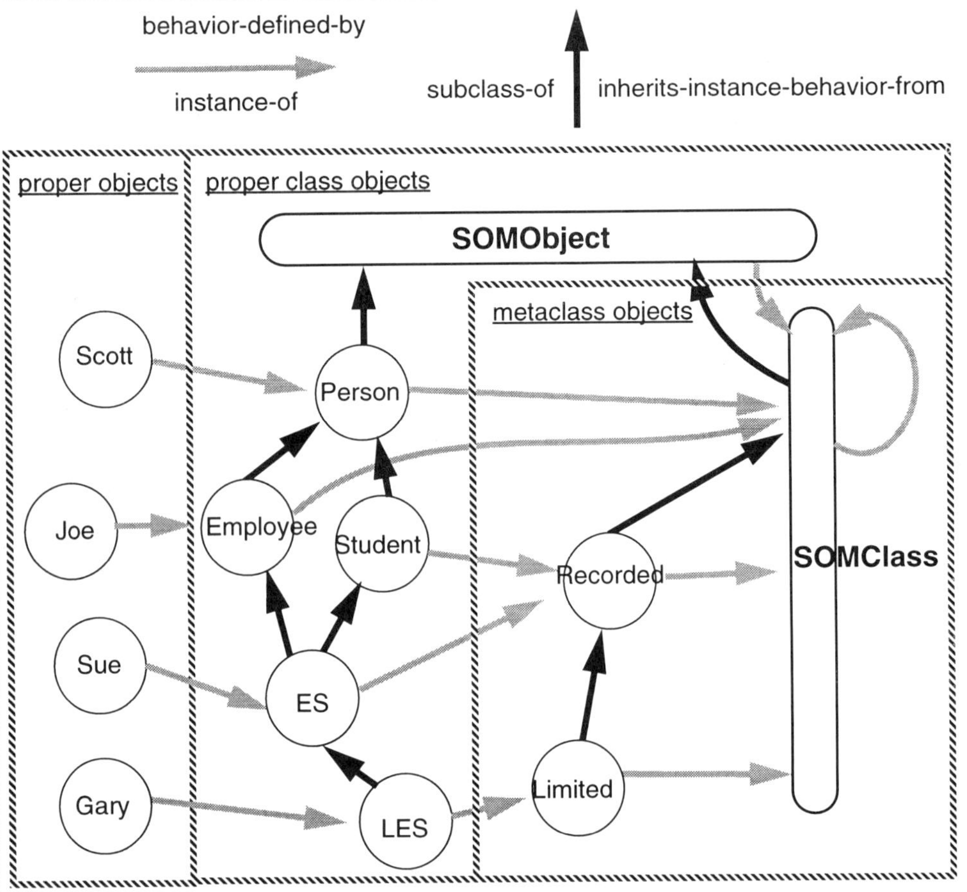

Figure 2 —Example Objects, Classes and Metaclasses in SOM

classing. This figure explicitly distinguishes the three categories of SOM objects, and illustrates the use of metaclasses besides SOMClass. In this example, the object named Recorded is a metaclass whose purpose is to define the implementation of classes that keep an explicit list of their instances (sometimes called a class extent). The metaclass Limited defines the implementation of classes that limit their extent to a certain cardinality. As suggested by the arrow labels in Figure 2, the instance relationship can be characterized as the "behavior-defined-by" relationship, whereas the subclass relationship can be viewed as the "inherits-instance-behavior-from" relationship.

The Fundamental Guarantee of OOP

We believe the following guarantee is necessary for a system to be considered an OOP system. This guarantee enables the construction of generic code by OOP programmers, which is an important capability of OOP. Often this guarantee is referred to as "polymorphism."

> If the class **A** is an ancestor of the class **B**, then any code that can be proven to execute without method resolution errors on any

instance of class **A** must also execute without method resolution errors on any instance of class **B**.

There are, of course, many conflicting models of what OOP is, and what polymorphism means. But, we believe that the above guarantee, illustrated in Figure 3, lies at the heart of all of these.

Supporting Explicit Metaclasses

We believe SOM is the only OOP system to make this guarantee while also allowing programmers to define named metaclasses and to explicitly use arbitrary metaclasses when subclassing. To illustrate why this is an interesting problem, we begin with a few essential details about how subclassing is done in SOM.

In SOM, a new class is declared by indicating (among other things):

- its parent classes, and (optionally)
- a metaclass.

When the class object is created at runtime, it is constructed as an immediate subclass of the indicated parents. Furthermore, if a metaclass is indicated in the class declaration, the new class will be constructed either as an instance of the indicated metaclass or as an instance of some class derived from the indicated metaclass.

Why isn't a class always an instance of the metaclass indicated in its declaration? The answer is that SOM allows class declarations such as illustrated by the following example, while also supporting the fundamental guarantee referred to above.

In this example, IDL is used to declare a metaclass named Recorded, and two proper classes named A and B.

```
interface Recorded: SOMClass
{ readonly attribute sequence <SOMObject>
     extent;
};
interface A : SOMObject
{ implementation { metaclass = Recorded; };
};

interface B : A
{ implementation { metaclass = SOMClass; };
}
```

This IDL is illustrated in Figure 4. The metaclass Recorded introduces an attribute that results in the definition of a class variable for storing a class extent, and a _get_extent class method for accessing this extent. Both A and B inherit the method somGetClass introduced by SOMObject, whose purpose is to return the class of an object. As a result, the procedure Proc illustrated in Figure 4 is typesafe (it can be proven to execute without method resolution errors on an instance of A). Figure 4 shows what would happen if SOM allowed B's class to be SOMClass, the metaclass explicitly indicated in B's declaration. The result would be a

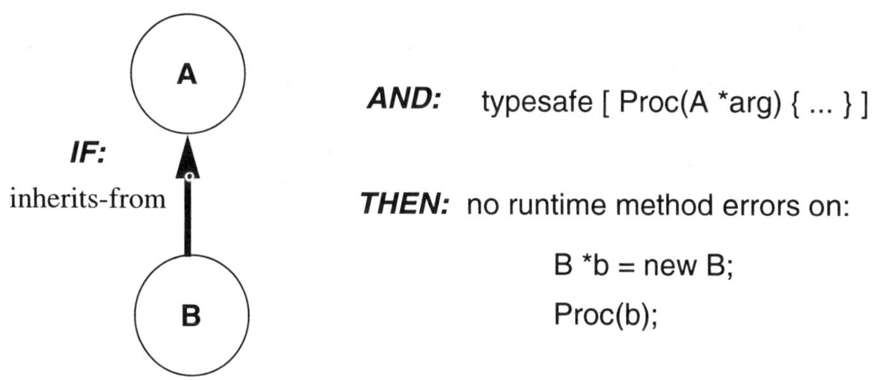

Figure 3 —The Fundamental Guarantee of OOP Systems

In SOM, unlike in this diagram, B's class will not be SOMClass

```
// This procedure is typesafe
   Proc(A *arg)
   {
   arg->somGetClass()->_get_extent();
   }

// Yet, this code gives a method error
    B *b = new B;
    Proc(b);
```

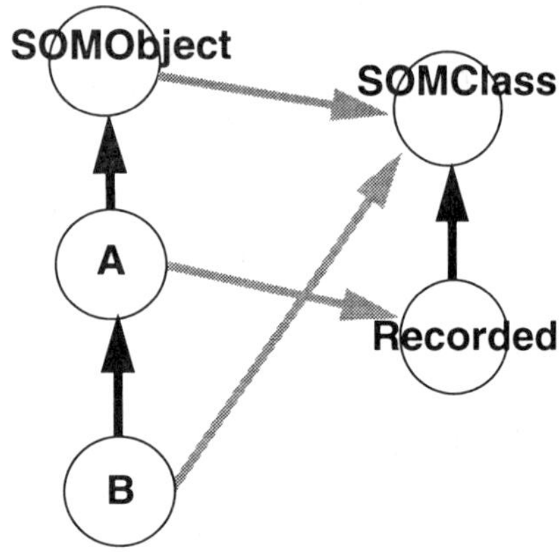

Figure 4 — The Metaclass Compatibility Problem

failure of the fundamental OOP guarantee when Proc is applied to an instance of B (because SOMClass does not define the _get_extent method for its instances). This kind of situation was first addressed by Nicolas Graube [Gra89], who characterized the problem in terms of *metaclass compatibility.* Put simply, SOMClass is not compatible with the requirements placed on B's class by the fundamental guarantee of OOP.

However, SOM will not construct class hierarchies with metaclass incompatibilities. Instead, SOM will automatically build new metaclasses that are compatible with their requirements, dynamically subclassing from existing metaclasses whenever this is necessary. In the example of Figure 4, it is not actually necessary to build a new metaclass, since Recorded satisfies all the requirements appropriate to this example. So, here, SOM will simply use Recorded as the class of B.

An example in which derivation of a new metaclass is necessary is provided by Figure 5. Here, a new class C is derived using multiple inheritance from two other classes, A and B, whose classes are, respectively, MA and MB. The question here: What should be the class of C? The solution must guarantee that C (i.e., the class object itself) has the interfaces of both the A and B class objects. In OOP, as illustrated in Figure 6, we know how to guarantee this. We simply derive the class of C (named DMC, for

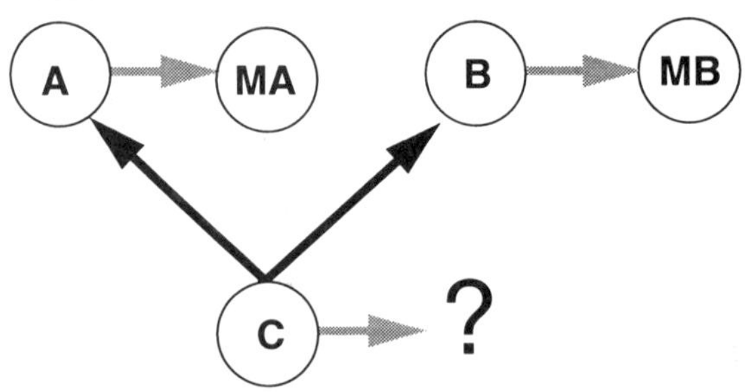

Figure 5 -- Of what class should C be an instance ?

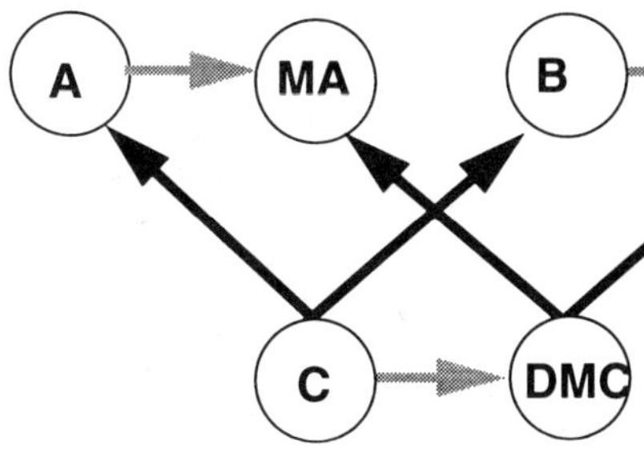

Figure 6 — The solution: C's metaclass must be derived from A's and B's metaclasses

"Derived Metaclass") from the classes of C's parents. Figure 6 thus illustrates the fundamentals of SOM's approach to derived metaclasses. Of course, a general solution must deal with any number of parents and an explicit metaclass (when one is indicated).

Figure 7 presents the general case using IDL, and illustrates the resulting SOM-derived metaclass. This shows how SOM uses multiple inheritance to derive a new metaclass whose instance's interfaces are compatible with both (1) the requirements indicated by the programmer that uses subclassing to derive a new class and (2) the requirements implied by the need to support the newly-defined class as a polymorphic object.

It is interesting to note the conditions under which the problem solved by derived meta-

```
Interface C : P1, P2, ..., PN
{
  implementation { metaclass = MC; };
};
```

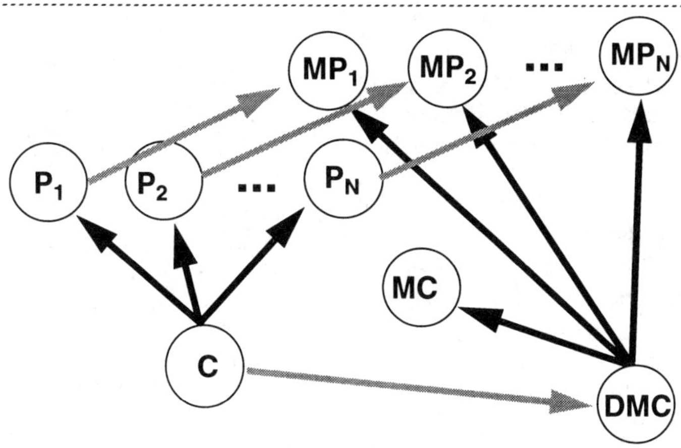

Figure 7— A General Solution for Interface Compatibility

classes can arise. Metaclass incompatibility (intuitively characterized as the absence of required class methods or class variables) can arise in the case of single inheritance models that allow explicit metaclasses and it can arise in the case of multiple inheritance models that allow either explicit or implicit (unnamed) metaclasses. Smalltalk has implicit metaclasses but doesn't support multiple inheritance. C++ allows multiple inheritance but doesn't allow metaclasses. Thus, neither of these object models needs to worry about metaclass compatibility. On the other hand, object models such as ObjVLisp [Bri87] and CLOS [Bob88] can encounter the problem [Gra89]. None of these systems provide the benefits offered by dynamic creation of metaclasses as described in this paper.

Dealing with Object State

The approach illustrated in Figure 7 guarantees metaclass compatibility by assuring the existence of the necessary interfaces and class variables. But there is more to OOP than method signatures. In particular, objects have state, and this state must be initialized. Simply guaranteeing compatible interfaces is not enough.

In SOM, a class' state includes:

- an instance method table (introduced by SOMClass)
- a variety of other class variables (often introduced by subclasses of SOMClass -- i.e., other metaclasses)

And, of course, a class' state must be initialized before the class is used. The SOM API provides methods whose purpose is to provide for initialization (and uninitialization):

SOMObject::somInit	misc variable init.
SOMClass::somInitMIClass	load method table
SOMClass::somClassReady	register class
SOMObject::somUninit	free storage

In general, a metaclass designer overrides each of these methods to perform class-specific initialization (or uninitialization). And, each of the resulting method procedures used by a metaclass implementation normally makes parent method calls to cooperatively invoke similar functionality implemented by the parents of the metaclass. To correctly initialize (uninitialize) all the variables containing a class's state, then, a derived metaclass in SOM overrides the above methods with code that makes the necessary parent method calls on all of its metaclass parents. This assures that all appropriate initialization code is executed.

With the approach illustrated in Figure 7, It is possible that a derived metaclass might be included among the parents of some other derived metaclass. Because a derived metaclass introduces no new methods or class variables, it is sufficient to compute a "frontier" of nonderived metaclasses (above which are no derived metaclasses, and below which are all derived metaclasses). Calls for the above methods can then be made to the classes on this frontier, from which parent method calls will proceed.

SOM classes themselves can be used to package the necessary initialization calls to non-derived frontier classes. This is done by using an additional derived metaclass parent with an explicit metaclass. The IDL for these two classes follows and is illustrated in Figure 8. The explicit metaclass introduces, as a class variable, the nonderived frontier referred to above.

```
Interface MSOMParentDerived : SOMClass
{ readonly attribute sequence <SOMClass>
      nonDerivedFrontier;
}
Interface SOMParentDerived : SOMClass
{ implementation {
      metaclass = MSOMParentDerived;
      somInit: override;
      somInitMIClass: override;
      somClassReady: override;
      somUninit: override; }
};
```

A final solution utilizing SOMParentDerived for supporting initialization/uninitialization of class object state is depicted in Figure 9. What is the class of the derived metaclass, DMC, in Figure 9? The answer is that the solution we have described is recursively employed to determine the class of DMC. This must be done before DMC itself can be created, of course, since DMC is an instance of its class. SOMClass is ultimately reached by this recursion, which guarantees termination. Often this hap-

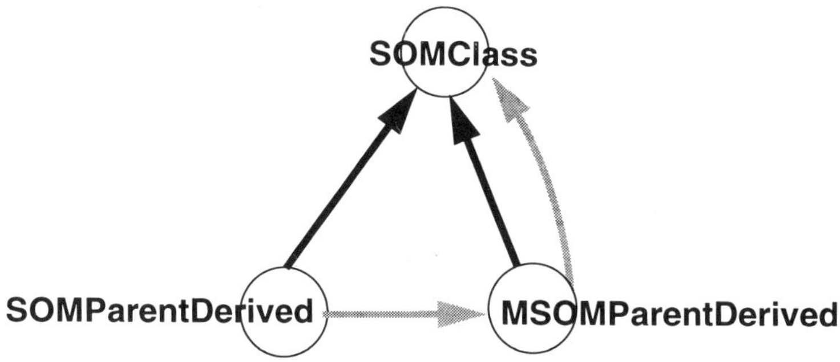

Figure 8— Using Classes to Package a Solution to Initialization and Uninitialization

pens in a single step (e.g., in the case where SOMClass is the class of MC and MP_1 ... MP_N), by using MSOMParentDerived as the class of DMC, but the answer in general depends on the classes of MC and MP_1 ... MP_N.

Conclusion

SOM allows and encourages the definition and explicit use of named metaclasses. By using explicit metaclasses, programmers that perform subclassing can not only effect the behavior of class instances (by choosing the parents of class), but they can also affect the behavior of class objects themselves (by explicitly indicating a metaclass when declaring a class). Furthermore, because the essential behavior of a class is that it defines the behavior of its instances, metaclasses offer useful ways of influencing instance behavior as well.

While allowing unrestricted access to this functionality, SOM is unique in that it relieves programmers of the responsibility for avoiding metaclass incompatibility when defining a new class. At first glance, this might seem to be merely a useful (though important) convenience. But, in fact, it is essential, because SOM is predicated on backwards binary compatibility with respect to changes in class implementations.

A programmer might, at one point in time, know the classes of all the ancestor classes of a new subclass (and so on, recursively), and, as result, be able to explicitly derive an appropriate class for the new subclass using the approach we have described above. But, we doubt that a system based on requiring this would ever be successful. And, in any case, SOM must guarantee that a class implementation will continue to execute and function correctly when any of its ancestor class's implementations are changed (which includes specifying different parents, or different metaclasses). Thus, requiring a static solution (either on the part of a programmer or a compiler) is not acceptable in SOM.

Instead, derived metaclasses allow SOM to make the necessary guarantees. A SOM programmer need never worry about the problem of metaclass incompatibility. SOM does this for the programmer automatically, at runtime, as class objects are being constructed. As a result, explicit metaclasses in SOM can be used by class implementors to simply "add in" whatever behavior is desired for a new class. SOM automatically handles anything else that might be needed due to the requirements of ancestor classes.

One way to view the overall use of derived metaclasses in SOM is that it provides a useful way of automatically combining small pieces of functionality packaged using SOM classes into a large number of different configurations. Software reuse is one promise of OOP technology, and it has been gratifying to find that many useful kinds of functionality are automatically composed in this way. Examples include aspects important to the implementation of DSOM (a SOM class framework allowing

SOM Semantics for a Class Specification

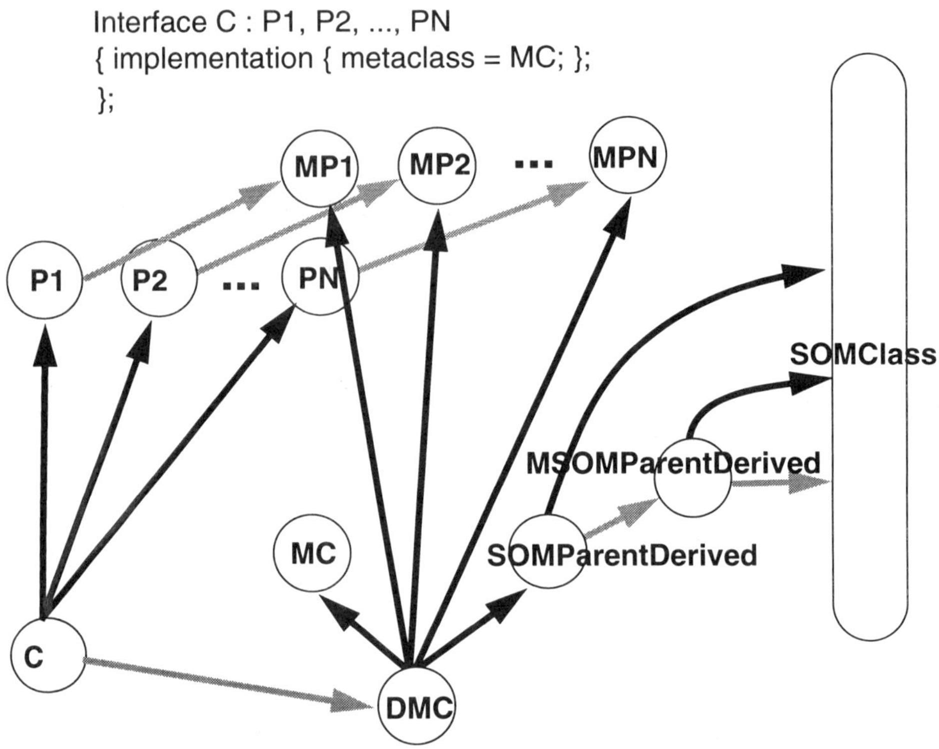

Figure 9 — Final Solution

transparent distribution of objects [SOM93]), Replication (a SOM class framework providing single-copy serializability for distributed, replicated objects [SOM93]), and "before/after" metaclasses [For93]. Another example is provided by the metaclass cooperation framework, described in the following section.

Derived metaclasses in SOM thus support an important dimension of design for OOP based on use of the instance relationship for automatic composition and reuse of classes. SOM therefore allows using OOP to solve application problems in ways that are difficult to address in systems where explicit use of the instance relationship between objects is restricted or simply unavailable.

Further Work

Derived metaclasses do not solve all the problems encountered by SOM metaclass programmers. In particular, the dynamic behavior of different metaclasses combined into a derived metaclass may result in "interference" between these metaclasses. This problem does not manifest itself as a failure of polymorphism (the problem identified by [Gra89] and addressed in this paper), but as an operational conflict between different metaclasses' behavior. For example, this problem could arise when two unrelated metaclasses are combined into a derived metaclass, and each wants a different method procedure to execute when a new object is created. If the two metaclasses both use their somInitMIClass code to override the object creation method, then the last override to execute will "win," interfering with the other metaclass, whose method procedure will not execute.

The question is how to associate a multiplicity of method procedures with a single method. When method procedures are contributed by classes related by inheritance, parent method calls serve this purpose. But, the metaclasses combined into derived metaclasses are not related by inheritance.

To address this problem, SOM uses derived metaclasses to implement a "metaclass cooperation framework." This provides a programming model in which metaclasses achieve their objectives cooperatively by combining different method procedures into a "cooperation chain." Interference (when it would otherwise occur) is prevented by identifying conflicting requests concerning the ordering of method procedures in this chain. This maximizes the opportunity for cooperation between metaclasses (since, for most purposes, ordering doesn't matter) and guarantees that metaclasses will never mysteriously cease to operate correctly as a result of interference with other metaclasses.

Many interesting comparisons can be drawn between this work and the independently-developed techniques that are appropriate for use within CLOS [Kic91]. The SOM metaclass cooperation framework is the topic of a separate paper currently under development.

Summary

SOM-derived metaclasses (metaclasses created automatically by SOM in order to support classes as polymorphic objects) provide essential support for the definition and use of metaclasses in SOM. Our experience has shown that SOM-derived metaclasses provide a sound and extremely flexible foundation for development and use of higher-level metaclass protocols. The derived metaclass structures automatically constructed by SOM are often quite complex, spanning many "meta-levels" in order to guarantee that all the right interfaces are supported on all the right levels.

References

[Bob88] D. G. Bobrow and G. Kiczales, "The Common Lisp Object System Metaobject Kernel: A Status Report," ACM Conference on Lisp and Functional Programming, July, 1988.

[Bri87] J.-P. Briot and P. Cointe, "A Uniform Model for Object-Oriented Languages Using the Class Abstraction," IJCAI Vol. 1, August, 1987.

[For93] Ira Forman, Scott Danforth and Hari Madduri, "Composition of Before/After Metaclasses in SOM," submitted to TOOLS Europe 94.

[Kic91] G. Kiczales, J. des Rivieres, and D. G. Bobrow, *The Art of the Metaobject Protocol*, MIT Press, Cambridge MA, 1991.

[Gra89] Nicolas Graube, "Metaclass Compatibility," OOPSLA Conference Proceedings, 1989.

[IBM92] *OS/2 Version 2.0 Volume 4: Application Development,* IBM Doc. GG24-3774-00, 1992.

[Min92] Mark Minasi, et al., *Inside OS/2 2.0*, New Riders Publishing, 1992.

[Orf92] Robert Orfali, and Dan Harkey, *Client/Server Programming with OS/2 2.0*, Van Nostrand Reinhold, 1992.

[OMG93] *The Common Object Request Broker: Architecture and Specification,* Revision 1.1, Object Management Group and X/Open, 1993.

[SOM93] *SOMObjects Developer ToolKit, Users Guide*, IBM, June, 1993.

[Sny86] Alan Snyder, "Encapsulation and Inheritance in OOP Languages," OOPSLA Conference Proceedings, 1986.

Practical Experiences with OMT

Ed Doesburg
Doré Eijkman
Anneke Kleppe
Jos Warmer

PTT Research
P.O. Box 421
2260 AK Leidschendam
The Netherlands

This paper describes the experiences with using object orientation and OMT within PTT Research, part of the Royal PTT Nederland NV. It describes a number of projects that were done with OMT followed by what we learned in the process of applying the technique.
Some of the conclusions we come to are typical for OMT, others apply to object orientation in general. Both positive and negative aspects are pointed out and suggestions are given for improvement.

1 Introduction

This paper describes the introduction of the Object Modeling Technique ([RBP+91]) at PTT Research. PTT Research is a part of the Royal PTT Nederland NV. Starting with a small pilot project in 1992, OMT is now used in more than five software development projects. One of these projects involves an investment of roughly forty man-years, which, to our standards, is a very large project.
The following sections will state in detail why we chose OMT as object oriented modeling and design technique and how we have used the technique in various ways in different projects.

From TOOLS EUROPE '94 (Technology of Object-Oriented Languages and Systems).

The emphasis of this paper lies on what we have learned through our experiences about OMT and object orientation in general. We give suggestions on improvement of the method and on the pragmatics of the method. Section 6 gives information on the results of our efforts to promote object orientation and OMT within the Royal PTT Nederland NV.

2 Why OMT

This section describes the very pragmatic manner in which we decided to use OMT as an introduction to object orientation. In January 1992 we decided in PTT Research to look seriously at object orientation. Because there was little experience (only one person) with using object oriented techniques in systems development, we planned on doing a pilot project to learn and evaluate an object oriented method. To choose this method we decided to make a selection based on an evaluation done earlier by a different group within PTT Research. Besides that, we studied the literature with evaluations of object oriented methods, e.g. [ABC+91] and [dCF92]. So we did not study all methods available, but only those recommended by others.
Our criteria for making a choice were dictated by the demands of our organization. In general we work on relatively small projects, on very different platforms, in many application domains. Furthermore, part of the work done at PTT Research does not go beyond the analysis phase. Our criteria were:

1. The method should be a truely object oriented method, e.g. it should at least support the concepts identity, classification, polymorphism and inheritance.
2. The method should be suitable for projects of moderate size (with an average of 5 project-members).
3. The method should be independent of any programming language.
4. Tools should be available to support the method.
5. The method should at least account for the specification phase of the system development life-cycle.
6. The method should support specification of parts of the system at different levels of detail.

The methods we examined and rejected were: Booch ([Boo90]), Buhr ([Buh91]), HOOD ([HOO90]), Objectory ([Jac92]), OOA/OOD ([CY91]), and RDD ([WBWW90]). The Booch method emphasizes the design phase instead of the analysis phase which is our major target for a system development method. The Buhr and the HOOD method are both based on one programming language (ADA). Besides, the HOOD method does not support inheritance. Objectory was rejected because at the time the method (with tool) was very expensive. For a pilot project the investment was simply too high. OOA/OOD was still somewhat vague in it's description of how to perform the steps in the design part of the method. RDD is also a design method and uses some very complicated notations for the collaboration models.
The final choice was made for OMT because this method supports all phases of the life-cycle. Another reason was that next to the object model two other models are made with established techniques.
We realize that since the time of this evaluation new methods have appeared, e.g. Fusion ([CAB+93)] and Martin and Odell [OM93]. that may or may not better apply to our criteria. Until now we have not evaluated any of them, but we plan on doing that in the near future.

3 Projects

In this section we will describe projects in which object orientation techniques were used within PTT Research for the last two years. They will be described in the order in which they were done, so the process in which we learned object orientation and OMT can be understood.

3.1 The start: Brutus and OO-Brutus

As stated in the previous section, we started with a small pilot project. However, the pilot project should have a real follow-up project if it succeeded. At the time the Brutus project was looking for a method to use in their system development.
Brutus is a large project, concerning about forty man-years over a period of four years. It has to build a tool for telecommunication networks, which evaluates the performance of proposed networks. The average number of people working in the project is more than twenty, from three different departments within PTT Research. Our department performs all system development. The other two departments develop algorithms and models that must be incorporated into the system. Brutus is planned to deliver a usable version of the system at the end of each year.
We were convinced that traditional methods like structured analysis and design were not suited to solve the problem tackled by Brutus.
The modeling method used should at least help with two problems:

- communication between the system developers and the other departments, and
- item communication between the developers themselves.

Because object orientation seemed to be the most promising method, we decided that there would be a pilot project for the evaluation of an object oriented method, that could be used in the Brutus project. The pilot was called 'OO-Brutus'. If the pilot proved successful, the method would be used for all aspects of the system development in Brutus. OO-Brutus used the application domain of Brutus as it's domain. In OO-Brutus we did only part of the analysis phase, but it became clear quickly that the object-model was a perfect aid for communication between the people with different backgrounds from the three departments. Therefore the Brutus project, that evaluated the results of the pilot, decided halfway 1992 to go for OMT. The actual development effort for Brutus started in January 1993. The implementation is done in C++ on powerful Unix workstations, because the efficiency demands for the different models are extremely high. Within Brutus the object model is used extensively. The data flow notation for the functional model is used only for the high level description of the functional model. For the lower levels of abstraction it is much easier to write the functional models in a notation that is more appropriate to the specific domain. In this case mathematical formulas and algorithms in pseudo-code are used.

3.2 The follow-up: Binnenhuis and AMS II

Because of the successful pilot, we decided to use OMT in another project, Binnenhuis, in the second half of 1992. This project, which delivered a running application at the end of 1992, was done completely with OMT. Implementation took place with C++ on a PC, running MS-Windows. The goal was to develop a system for the planning and evaluation of mobile indoor telecommunication systems.

This project was the first in which we used OMT for every phase of the system development. Therefore we needed considerably more time for the analysis and design phases. But to our surprise we could shorten the implementation phase so much that the complete project ended only two weeks over schedule. The learning time for OMT has been counted as part of the analysis and design phases. In the Binnenhuis project OMT was used in a very pragmatic way. Any part of the method that did not fit our needs was either changed or not used. For example scenarios were used in a different way from what OMT describes. We also found that there were no tools available that supported the notations in a usable way. We had to use a simple drawing tool (idraw) to draw all models. To save time, a few scripts were made to generate C++ code from structured English.

We also introduced the use of OMT in a completely different kind of project, AMS II. AMS II is an application for supporting the Customer Problem Service in locating errors in the ISDN local loop. The main function of AMS is to generate a diagnosis on a suspect local loop by correlating several information resources. The aim of the project was to specify in general terms the requirements for the application. The resulting specification consists of an object model and corresponding data dictionary, a high level description of the functional model, and the system design. After some hesitation (why do it in a way that is different from the way we are used to), the project members and the people who authorized the project became enthusiast about the clarity that the OMT models provided.

3.3 Start of 1993

Our experiences in the projects mentioned above were very positive. The analysis models of OMT give everyone concerned a very clear view of the system. Since January 1993 a growing number of projects is using OMT for the specification and/or implementation of their systems.

In the first half year of 1993 a small (330 hours) project, Inzicht, started in which a prototype environment was created. This environment is used by data modelers of PTT Telecom, to create data models and show the possibilities of alternative data models. The system was developed on a PC using Smalltalk/V Windows. Some object models were created during analysis and design before the implementation took place. During implementation we found that evolution of a Smalltalk application is very easy. We developed three different versions of the application within nine weeks, to give the users the opportunity to get involved in the final product. As a result, numerous changes were made to the application.

As of now, the OMT object models of Inzicht are not up to date. Many classes from the final application are missing. However, the classes present in the OMT object model still provide the basic architecture of the current implementation. It is difficult to keep the OMT models up to date in a rapidly evolving application. They should be kept up to date, because the source code is not good enough for documentation purposes. This is the same problem as with conventional systems development: the documentation is always behind. But in contrast to models from conventional methods, the OMT models, although not complete, still are correct.

3.4 "Object Orientation and OMT" course

Early 1993 we developed a two day introductory course on "Object Orientation and OMT". This course focusses on the object oriented concepts and on building the three OMT models from the analysis phase. This course was given five times during 1993 to about sixty PTT Research employees from different departments. Thus educating about 15 % of our research population.

3.5 Two simulation projects

During 1993 the POTS project was set up to introduce more of our researchers to OMT and Smalltalk. POTS stands for Plain Old Telephone System. In this system a network configuration of telephones, telephone exchanges and lines can be specified and establishing connections between two telephones can be simulated. When a connection is established the user sees which exchanges and lines are part of a connection. The system is currently under implementation in Smalltalk/Visualworks on SUN workstations.
The project DFP-SIM is building a simulator of the Distributed Functional Plane for the Intelligent Network (IN) architecture.
The aim of IN is to provide more flexible call control architectures for quicker and cheaper introduction of new services and features in the public switched telephone networks. DFP-SIM will create an environment in which new services can be simulated before they are implemented in the actual network and new IN-functions can be added for rapid evaluation purposes. The development of the object models in the analysis phase took 3 man-months. The system is currently under implementation in Smalltalk/Visualworks on SUN workstations.
Other areas in which our advice is asked for are using OMT in signalling, and using object oriented concepts and methods in the general area of telecommunication architectures.

Table 1 gives facts and figures of some aspects of the different projects mentioned before. This should give the reader a better idea of the projects.

4 Opinions on OMT

In this section we want to state the positive and negative aspects of OMT that we experienced using this method in the projects described in section 3. We also give indications on how we solved the negative aspects. The remarks in this section reflect the opinion of quite a number of members from the projects mentioned in the previous section. The background of the project members lies within very different, mostly technical, disciplines: technical engineering, physics, mathematics, computer science, chemistry, linguistics, etc.

4.1 Positive remarks

Most of the positive points mentioned here are valid for the analysis phase from OMT.

- The strongest point of OMT is the object model.
  The object model is the part of OMT that is best understood and it is the most enveloped part of OMT. It is very useful for the understanding of the problem domain, and it is an important aid in the discussion about the system and the problem domain.6

- After a short introduction all project members could easily read and communicate about the models.
  The introduction consisted of two parts, at first the global introduction to object orientation and at second an introduction to OMT, where the main topic was the reading of the three OMT models.
  Because the objects in the models relate to objects in the 'real' world, the project members found the models easy to read and understand. Even the project members not familiar with any other notation formalism, experienced no problems with the reading of the object model.

Table 1: (Numbers of) OMT items used in projects at PTT Research

	OO-Brutus	Brutus	Binnenhuis	AMS-II	DFP-SIM	POST	Inzicht
DD items	64	280	23	91	42	13	20
classes	32	130	43	49	58	13	20
link objects	4	0	0	5	1	4	0
inheritance	2	26	2	2	9	3	13
aggregation	11	35	9	9	11	2	0
association	19	142	33	61	56	18	6
sheets	3	21	7	9	9	3	3
scenario's	1	8	31	0	11	4	0
event traces	1	0	0	0	20	4	0
STD	2	3	3	0	6	2	0
DFD	1	0	7	1	0	1	0
phases	A	ADI	ADI	A	ADI	ADI	ADI
current phase	finished	D/I	finished	finished	I	I	finished
language	n.a	C++	C++	n.a	Smalltalk	Smalltalk	Smalltalk
OMT tools	idraw	OMTool	idraw	texcad	OMTool	OMTool	OMTool
members	3	23	3	4	3	4	2

Legend:
DD items = number of items in the data dictionary
STD = state transition diagram
DFD = data flow diagram
A = analysis phase
D = design phase
I = implementation phase
'members' stands for number of project members.

- The sequence of steps to compose the object model are quite clear and easy to follow to most people.
  When people new to OMT used it for the first time, we saw that the steps suggested by the method were followed strictly. After they had seen what the steps are and what the result of the steps are, they selected the steps that were useful for them and made their own changes to the method. Of course the concepts of the models were maintained.

- The basic concepts of OMT give a lot of expressive power.
  Looking at the concepts used in the projects (see appendix A), one can see that mainly the basic concepts of OMT are used, and that the advanced concepts are rarely used.
  This contributes to the readability of the models. With the basic concepts one already has a powerful formalism to specify the problem domain.
  This is also a reason that people can easily read OMT models and use OMT. You can easily start with only the basic concepts and gradually use the more advanced concepts when needed.

- The analysis phase of the method itself is independent of the programming language used.
  One does not need to know which programming language to use until the design phase. This is of course a condition on every analysis method. But in general it is very difficult to analyze a problem without the programming language and it's way of solving problems in

mind. In OMT, in the analysis phase, one can really forget about constraints that the programming language puts on the solution.

- The three different models view the system from completely different points of view.
  The three models of OMT describe three different aspects of the system: the static , dynamic and functional view. These different views make it possible to look at completely different aspects of a system, and every view contributes to a better understanding of the system as a whole. Moreover, here is a defined connection between the three models.
  Depending on the system you want to specify, one model can be more important that the other models. The object model is always the most important model in OMT, but the level of detail can vary, depending on the system built. The dynamic and functional behavior of the system make the dynamic model or the functional model of more or less importance Sometimes one of the two is not needed at all. In a few projects we didn't make a functional model. So OMT provides a very flexible way to specify a system.
  The different, connected views of the models can not be found in any single traditional analysis and design method. With these methods, you generally focus on only one aspect of a system.

- The specification can be worked out to any desired level of detail. OMT does not prescribe a certain level of detail for the specification.

  The specification and implementation of a software system is, when using object orientation, a highly iterative process. This means that one can start at a global level and specify the systems task at that level. After that you can stay at that level, or you can specify it in more detail, until you reach the desired level of detail.
  The level of detail doesn't have to be the same for each part of the system. The same holds for the start of the implementation. An object class does not have to be specified in detail before the implementation of an object class can start.
  What is important however, is that the project members are aware of the level of detail on which the specification is made, so they can communicate at the same level and understand each other.

4.2 Negative remarks

- The relation between the three models is not always clear.

  The relation between the concept 'operation' in the object model, the concepts 'event', 'action' and 'activity' in the dynamic model and the concept 'process' in the functional model is not clear. Also, the notation used in the functional model does not make clear which object performs a process.

- Some of the definitions of basic concepts are not clear.
  The definitions of 'operation' and 'event' in the dynamic model are not clear. In [RBP$^+$91] four or five different descriptions of 'event' can be found. Building a dynamic model is difficult without a clear definition of both concepts.

- The steps to build a dynamic model in the analysis phase are not practical.
  For the dynamic model the steps were difficult to follow in practice. The definition and identification of events and states are unclear. Activity and action are defined well, but they are difficult to identify.
  The steps for constructing the functional model do not help very much. Taking the input and output of the system as a basis does not suffice for highly interactive systems.

- The functional model of OMT is useless in the analysis phase.
  There are at least two fundamental problems with the functional model provided by OMT.

  - The goal of the functional model in the analysis phase should be to describe **what** the system operations do. The OMT functional model describes **how** operations are performed and therefore it does not fit in the analysis phase.

- A data flow diagram is about **data**. In an object oriented system (as for example described by OMT) there is no data, there are only objects. This means that the basic concept of data flow diagrams is not suitable within an object oriented description of a system.

In the projects we did, the notation of the functional model indeed did not fit its purpose. It was much easier to use a notation that was more appropriate for the specific domain. We used for example mathematical formulas and algorithms in pseudo-code.
Also, the majority of the functional models wre used only in the design phase.

- The design stage is not clear
In the analysis phase OMT provides a good description of the steps one should follow. In the design phase OMT only describes some rather vague steps to follow. They are more 'rules of thumb' than a design methodology.

Furthermore, the results of the design phase are not specified exact enough.The models should be specified in more detail, but it is unclear which details are to be specified and how detailed they should be. So you don't know what to do, neither where to stop.

4.3 Suggestions for improvement of OMT

To solve the problems we had with OMT, we came to the following suggestions. Our problems were mainly with the dynamic model, so these suggestions are mainly on improving the dynamic modeling. We found the functional model too weak to try and fix it. We used other notations instead.

- Use the following additional steps for construction of the models.

  - After constructing the object model according to the steps in the book try to identify the operations for the objects.
  In brainstorm sessions identify the responsibilities of the objects, just like the method RDD prescribes, see [WBWW90]. After that, make the scenarios and use them to find any missing operations.
  - Use the operations as the basis for the construction of the state transition diagram.

- Make more extensive use of the concept of 'scenario'.
We have used scenario's extensively to model the communication between objects in the system. In many cases the scenario's were worked out in such detail that they acted as a replacement for the functional model as well.
For example the Objectory method [Jac92] uses the concept of use-case's as the most important aspect of the system development. One could easily borrow some of the ideas from Objectory's use-case's to expand the use of scenario's in OMT.

- Do not use the distinction between internal and external events.
In the dynamic model the user is also seen as an object, although it is not seen as one in the object model. In this way the distinction between internal and external events cannot be made.

- Redefine the terms 'operation' and 'event'.
This is done to make the relation between de dynamic and the object model more explicit.
An operation is:
  - a transformation of a value, or
  - an access to information held by an object (attribute or relation).

  An event is:
  - a message between two objects in the dynamic model

- Use a different notation for the functional model.
The use of other notations as pseudocode, mathematical formulea and anything the users are familiar with is strongly recommended. In a number of cases we used the scenario's to describe the systems operations in detail. So the scenario's were our functional model and they form the basis for the dynamic model.

The 'operational model' as it is defined in Fusion ([CAB+93]) seems a much better method to describe the functional aspects of a system during analysis.

- Define the result of the design phase as the complete interface for each object class. This contains for each class:

  - all attributes, including the type and possible values.
  - all operations, including the complete signature and a clear description of the effect of the operation. Preferably in the form of the pre- and post-conditions.

The class descriptions are most effectively written in a textual format in the chosen implementation language. Writing down the complete interface of each class in the graphical object model from OMT results in huge class boxes and unreadable models.

5 General opinions on Object Orientation

In the previous sections we stated our experiences and opinions on OMT. Some of our experiences cannot be contributed to the method used (OMT), but is related to object oriented development in general. In this section we will state, what we think as general observations on object orientation. As in the previous section, the remarks are grouped into positive and negative ones.

5.1 Positive remarks

- Discussions around the object model help to clarify the understanding of the problem.
  The object model is the most important model in the discussion about the problem domain. Again because the objects and their behavior relate to objects in the 'real' world, the project members can easily check whether the correct objects are identified, whether there are objects missing, and whether the behavior of an object is correct.

- The delimitation of the system becomes clearer.
  The selection of object classes from all possible candidates caused a lot of discussion on the actual boundaries and the operation of the system. The need to make choices contributed to a better understanding and delimitation of the system.

- More time is needed in the analysis and design phases, but much less in the implementation phase.
  Because in the analysis phase the problem domain is specified, and not just the system that must be built, the analysis phase takes more time than used in traditional analysis methods. This has the effect that more time is spent in understanding the problem and the problem domain.
  However, the time 'lost' in the analysis phase is 'won' in the implementation phase, at least when you use an object oriented language. The implementation phase taken much less time than in a traditional system development method. All our implementations use an object oriented language, so we don't know whether this holds if a traditional procedural language is used.

- The development of a system is a seamless process.
  Going from analysis to design is very easy. In fact this is so easy that is causes problems for the management of the project. See the next section on negative remarks for a description of these problems. After the design is done, implementation is straightforward, as is clear from the speed in which it took place in several projects.

5.2 Negative remarks

- The distinction between the phases of the project is not clear.
  For the Brutus project, which is rather large, this is felt as a real problem. This feeling existed mainly among the project members. The project leader himself did not experience this as a problem, probably because he has a better overview of the whole process. However, problems of the project members become a problem for the project leader, so he is concerned about it.
  We think that the main cause for this problem is the iterative way of specification and

development. When using a traditional method to develop a software system, each phase delivers a well defined product. In OMT the products of the analysis and the design phase are actually the same.Both products exist of the three models, only the level of detail is different. In practice it is difficult to state where the analysis stops and where the design starts.

- Lack of metrics to relate the progress of the project to.
This point is probably just a matter of time. If more projects are executed using object oriented methods, these metrics will be coll-ected. But at the moment we just use the traditional rules and our 'traditional' experie-nce.
The collection of metrics for object oriented projects is an important subject for further attention and study.

- The supporting tools are not mature yet.
As stated in [CY91] a tool is essential for a method to get accepted and used. For OMT we looked at three tools, Paradigm Plus, Objectmaker and OMTool. At the time (1992) the versions of Paradigm Plus (1.0.2) and Objectmaker (2.0) we used, were not stable enough, or would not startup, and were diffi-cult to use. OMTool is reasonable stable and easy to use, but is very limited in its possibili-ties. The only model that is really supported is the object model, the other models are supp-orted, but in a rather rudimentary form. The correspondence between the three models is not supported by the tool.
The event trace, which is a very valuable notation form for the construction of a dynamic model, is not supported by any of the tools. This is really a great lack. Therefore we have to use other tools to make these traces.
For most of the projects we did, we used OMTool, because there was, and still is, no better tool available. For other projects we did not use a case tool but a simple drawing tool instead. (See table 1 for a complete list.)
There is also the question about the functionality needed from CASE tools for object oriented development. Current products tend to follow the tools for the traditional methods. Because of the seamless process in object orientation CASE tool could integrate all phases in a much easier way. This is clear-ly a problem for further research.

- System developers tend to be sceptical about new ways to build systems.
As with every new analysis or development method, people are sceptical to use it. The method must first prove it self, and then, if it is really better than the method used, people are willing to use it. This holds for object orientation as well as for OMT.

6 Related work and future developments

Within the Royal PTT Nederland NV the inter-est in object oriented techniques is growing. The implications of using these techniques are not yet fully clear but the possible benefits are becoming more and more apparent. In the fol-lowing we will indicate how object orientation is slowly being put to use in this large company.
To further introduce and promote the use of object orientation within the Royal PTT Nederland NV we have established a knowledge center on object orientation called OO-Center within PTT Research.
The members of the OO-Center give informa-tion and advice to projects that are using object oriented techniques concerning various topics like tools and languages, or how to use OMT. The in house OMT course which was mentioned before was developed within the scope of the OO-Center.
In 1994 a project will start which will examine the possibilities to increase the efficiency of a department of PTT Telecom by introducing object oriented techniques. This department is concerned with development and maintenance of large technical applications, for instance, an application that is continuously measuring the amount of telecommunication traffic between the exchanges in the Dutch telecommunications network.
More ongoing work is done within the TRIAS project. This project started at the end of 1992 and will probably be running until 1995. The aim of the TRIAS project is to introduce within PTT Telecom a three-layer-model for designing

business aware applications. The three-layer-model is based on the Bellcore OSCA architecture. Keywords in both the TRIAS architecture as well as in the OSCA architecture are building blocks and contracts between these building blocks. A building block is a special kind of object. A contract states the external interface of a building block.
Currently [1] an effort is made to derive guidelines for developing building blocks and for specifying the contracts. The introduction of the three-layer-model will very likely proceed in a stepwise manner. First the method currently in use will be extended. Apart from that a new method will be selected, which will probably be one of the more or less established object oriented development methods. When some experience is gained with working with building blocks this new method will be introduced. OMT is an important candidate for this new method.
Interest in object orientation is also growing in the other part of the Royal PTT Nederland NV, PTT Post. Currently we are investigating how to introduce object oriented techniques into the postal business. Not only the maturity of the object oriented techniques but also the specific applications where object orientation will be most successful are taken into account. The consequences of introduction, e.g. in the form of investments in training and/or equipment are considered. Advice is given on changes in procedures and the consequences of these changes for the organization.

7 Conclusions

Using OMT in software development projects of various size and impact on the organization has proven to be very successful. The clearness of the models and the actions to be undertaken in the analysis phase is a strong asset of the method. The object model is a good means to clarify and understand the application that is to be implemented. The guidelines in the analysis phase are very supportive for beginners.

[1] At the time this paper was submitted, which is october 1993.

Still the method has it's problems. We trust that it will be developed further. In fact Michael Blaha and Frederick Eddy stated at the ECOOP '92 conference that they were working on a completely different functional model. We are also very interested in new methods that are being developed. We hope they will combine the positive aspects and mend the negative aspects of the 'old' methods.
The tools also need further development. Very often we meet people who are enthusiast about the method but will not use it because of the limited tool support provided.
Also further work has to be done in the area of metrics and project management. Our experience is that most projects using object oriented techniques stay small whether they tackle a complicated problem or not. The need for metrics and different forms of management are not that great for the individual projects, but they are very much needed for the average manager that accords the projects. In other words if object orientation is to be accepted on a large scale, metrics and different forms of project management are a necessity.

8 Acknowledgements

This paper would not have been possible without the contributions of many people. First and foremost we like to acknowledge the work of all project members of the projects described in this paper. Our knowledge and experience has gained much from interacting with these critical but open minded colleagues. Next we like to thank all participants of our 'Object Orientation with OMT' course for their eagerness to learn and their enthusiasm about object oriented analysis and design. Bert Hilberink, Harry Fluks and Ronald Janmaat own our gratitude for their thoughtful comments on earlier versions of this paper.

References

[ABC+91] P. Arnold, S. Bodoff, D. Coleman, H. Gilchrist, and F. Hayes. An evaluation of five object-oriented development methods. Technical Report HPL-91-52, Information Management Laboratory, HP Laboratories Bristol, juni 1991.

[Boo90] G. Booch. *Object Oriented Design with Applications.* Benjamin/Cunnings, 1990.

[Buh91] R.J.A. Buhr. *Practical Visual Techniques in System Design: with Applications to Ada.* Prentice Hall, 1991.

[CAB+93] D. Coleman, P. Arnold, S. Bodoff, C. Dollin, H. Gilchrist, F. Hayes, and P. Jeremaes. *Object-Oriented Development: the Fusion Method.* Prentice Hall, first edition, 1993.

[CY91] P. Coad and E. Yourdon. *Object-Oriented Analysis.* Yourdon Press, Prentice Hall Building, New Jersey, second edition, 1991.

[dCF92] Dennis de Champeaux and Penelope Faure. A comparative study of object-oriented analysis methods. *Journal of object-oriented programming*, April 1992.

[HOO90] HOOD Technical Group. *HOOD reference manual*, October 1990.

[Jac92] Ivar Jacobsen. *Object-Oriented Software Engineering.* Addison-Wesley, first edition, 1992.

[OM93] J. Odell and J. Martin. *Object-Oriented Analysis and Design.* Prentice Hall, first edition, 1993.

[RBP+91] J. Rumbaugh, M. Blaha, W. Premerlani, F. Eddy, and W. Lorensen. *Object-Oriented Modeling and Design.* Prentice Hall, Englewood Cliffs, New Jersey, 1991.

[WBWW90] R. Wirfs-Brock, B. Wilkerson, and L. Wiener. *Designing Object-Oriented Software.* Prentice Hall, Englewood Cliffs, New Jersey, 1990.

A Concepts used in the projects

Table 2: concepts of the object model

	OOB	Brut	bin	AMS	dfp	pots	inzicht
class	+	+	+	+	+	+	+
inheritance	+	+	+	+	+	+	+
aggregation	+	+	+	+	+	+	-
association	+	+	+	+	+	+	+
qualified association	-	-	-	-	-	-	-
multiplicity	+	+	+	+	+	+	+
ordering	-	+	-	-	-	+	-
link attribute	-	-	-	-	-	-	-
ternary association	-	-	+	+	-	+	+
instances	-	-	-	-	-	-	-
abstract operation	-	-	-	-	-	-	+
link class	+	-	-	+	+	+	-
multiple inheritance	-	-	-	-	-	-	-
overlapping subclasses	-	-	-	-	-	-	-
class attributes/operations	-	-	+	+	-	-	+
derived attributes	+	-	-	-	-	-	-
propagation of operations	-	-	-	-	-	-	-
derived class	-	-	-	-	-	-	-
derived association	-	-	-	-	-	-	-
constraint between associations	+	-	-	-	+	-	-
constraint on objects	-	-	-	-	-	-	+

Table 3: concepts of the dynamic model

	OOb	Brut	bin	AMS	dfp	pots	inzicht
event	+	-	+	-	+	+	-
event attribute	-	-	-	-	+	+	-
initial/final states	+	-	+	-	+	-	-
event action	-	-	-	-	+	+	-
output event on transition	-	-	+	-	+	+	-
event guard	-	-	+	-	+	+	-
action in state	-	-	-	-	-	-	-
activity in state	+	-	+	-	+	+	-
state generalization	-	-	-	-	+	-	-
concurrent states	-	-	+	-	-	-	-
control splitting/synchronization	-	-	-	-	-	-	-

B Equipment used

The following tools were used:

	tool	version	system
OO-Brutus	idraw	unkhown	SUN/OS
Brutus	OMTool C++ SparcCompiler tools.h++ DataViews DVXDesigner	1.2 3.0.1 5.0 9.1a 2.0D	SUN/OS SUN/OS SUN/OS SUN/OS SUN/OS
Binnenhuis	idraw Borland C++ C++Views	unknown 3.1 2.0	SUN/OS MS Windows 3.1 MS Windows 3.1
AMS-II	texcad	unknown	MS Windows 3.1
DFP-SIM	OMTool ObjectWorks/Smalltalk Visualworks	1.2.1 4.1 1.0	MS Windows SUN/OS SUN/OS
POTS	OMTool ObjectWorks/Smalltalk Visualworks	1.2 4.1 1.0	SUN/OS SUN/OS SUN/OS
Inzicht	OMTool Smalltalk/V Windows	1.2 2.0	SUN/OS MS Windows 3.1

Specifying and Validating Requirements: The VENUS System

Aphrodite Tsalgatidou, Dimitris Gouscos, Constantin Halatsis

Department of Informatics, University of Athens, TYPA Buildings, Panepistimioupolis, Ilisia, GR-157 71 Athens, GREECE
email: {afrodite, gouscos, halatsis} @ di.uoa.ariadne-t.gr

Abstract

Requirements specification and validation is recognized as a crucial part of the information systems' development process. This paper presents the VENUS integrated environment for requirements engineering. The underlying conceptual framework of VENUS combines the entity-relationship, object-oriented and rule-based paradigms for data and behaviour modelling. VENUS tools enable systems analysts to formulate, analyse and validate requirements specifications which can be automatically mapped either to a C++ prototype or to the model of Rule-Based Nets (RBNs), a variant of Predicate-Transition Nets. RBNs constitute an executable model of requirements specifications and can be studied by analytical PN algorithms, animated and validated against test cases. The VENUS environment, therefore, provides an integrated, complete and formal, yet user-friendly, framework for requirements engineering. A VENUS prototype has been implemented so far, and work is still in progress towards (i) full-scale development and (ii) mapping of executable requirements specifications to design and implementation structures.

1. Introduction

The importance of requirements specifications in the information systems development process is not a recently identified need [Endres 75]. It has been earlier realised that incorrect requirements specifications result in the most serious errors in the information systems development process, because the cost to fix them increases as development progresses [Boehm 75]. However, there is still a lack of methods and tools to focus on the capture and validation of requirements specifications and the efforts reported in [Reubenstein 91], [Zave 91] and [Fickas 93] are among the few exceptions that can be found in this area. The large number of existing methodologies for systems analysis and design produce inherently static specifications. Furthermore, CASE tools play a passive rather than an active role in requirements specifications. In order to validate the captured requirements, developers try to derive system behaviour from static descriptions. What is needed is an approach and a set of tools that enables developers to obtain a 'working' model of a system at the early requirements phase, so that its behaviour can be better understood and appreciated. This may be achieved if the produced requirements specifications are executable. An executable specification is a formal model of the system which can simulate the system's behaviour when executed by a suitable interpreter. Thus, such a specification can be thought of as a prototype of a proposed information system and therefore it should be comprehensible, modifiable, easy to check for internal consistency and free from bias towards specific implementation strategies.

To this end, this paper presents the VENUS system which is an integrated environment offering a number of tools to support the requirements engineering process. The tools offered by VENUS assist a system analyst to elicitate, specify, analyse and validate executable requirements specifications within an object-oriented framework. Petri nets [Murata 89] are used as the underlying formalism for expressing object-oriented requirements specifications in a graphical manner. Animation and execution are some of the mechanisms used by VENUS for

From TOOLS EUROPE '94 (Technology of Object-Oriented Languages and Systems).

validating object-oriented executable requirements specifications.

The object-oriented approach has been found appropriate for developing requirements specifications in the VENUS system for the following reasons:

- it enables the uniform modelling of various real world objects in a direct and natural way, concealing any specific details inside them;
- it allows to model dynamic behaviour and interaction of objects in a high-level language, making specifications easy to comprehend by non-programmers;
- it provides useful abstractions, such as generalisation, aggregation and specialization, which facilitate extensions of the model and incorporation of new sorts of information and also result in compact and robust requirements specifications;
- it provides executable specifications which can be used for prototyping and validation purposes and for implementation of the final system in an object-oriented language.

The rest of the paper is organised as follows: the next section discusses work related to this approach; section 3 presents the VENUS environment; section 4 describes the stepwise construction of requirements specifications expressed in the Object-oriented Rule-based Model (ORM) and its translation to a C++ prototype; section 5 shows the mapping of ORM to the graphical Petri net-based RBN model and gives a formal definition of RBNs; in section 6 the validation of ORM is discussed and finally in section 7 the conclusions are presented.

2. Related work

The development of VENUS relates to work on object-oriented development as well as in the areas of formal methods, executable specifications and testing, Petri nets and graphical animation.

The object-oriented approach has been used in systems analysis and development and examples may be found in [Booch 92], [Coad 91], [Coleman 92], [Rumbaugh 91] and [van Baelen 92]. Furthermore, examples of the use of rules in requirements specifications may be found in [D'Haenens 90] and [Loucopoulos 91]. The VENUS approach demostrates the combination of both the object-oriented and the rule-based paradigms within a uniform framework integrating all system aspects.

Formal software development methods like Z [Spivey 87], OBJ [Goguen 87], VDM [Jones 86] and its extensions [Dürr 92] receive much attention in academic environments, but have yet to be used in large-scale industrial projects. The main reason for this, apart from their strong need for computerized support tools, is that their strict mathematical background is not easily understood by the majority of systems analysts and end-users, thus making difficult the construction and validation of formal speficications [Plat 92]. Based on the premise that the entire information systems development process, and requirements engineering in particular, should be undertaken in a framework that does not compromise user-friendliness for formality, the VENUS approach uses formal notations mapped to graphical models, thus attempting to come up with formally correct, yet easily understandable, requirements specifications.

The importance of constructing executable specifications has been realised by researchers and developers within the software engineering community and a number of executable system models, executable specification languages and tools contributing in this direction have appeared lately. For example PAISLey [Zave 91] is a language designed for real-time distributed systems and uses an operational approach for building a requirements specification, emphasizing the definition of processes as the building blocks of the system. VENUS differs from PAISLey in the sense that requirements specifications are object-oriented and objects, rather than processes, are the basic building blocks of the system model.

In the line of thought of [Kemmener 85], where it is stated that executable requirements specifications must be tested early in the development process to ensure that the specified system can be implemented and operate in an effective and efficient manner, VENUS enables systems analysts to test specifications right after requirements capture and well before design. Again like the proposal of [Kemmener 85], the VENUS environment offers two sorts of testing tools: (i) a rapid prototyping tool (C++ code generator) and (ii) a symbolic execution tool.

Symbolic execution in VENUS is accomplished by means of graphical animation and Petri nets. Animation, on the one hand, has proven to be a valuable validation technique; results reported in [Finkelstein 92], [Dahler 87] and [Shand 88] are among the many examples in this area. On the other hand, Petri nets constitute a powerful formalism [Murata 89] and have been used as a modelling tool in various applications. For example, in [Lakos 93] a language for object-oriented Petri nets (LOOPN) is used for modelling a door controller protocol. Other examples may be found in [Brinkkemper 90] and [Kappel 91], where extensions of Petri nets are used to reconcile the informal requirements engineering process to the more strictly-defined system development activities. The expressive power of Petri nets has lead to the development of many analysis and animation tools like PROD [PROD 93], Cabernet [Pezzé 92], UltraSAN [Obal 93], POSES [POSES 92] etc. The majority of these tools, however, trade advanced functionality for treatment of specific classes of Petri nets, whereas a generic and customizable PN meta-tool would be of great practical value. VENUS introduces a rule-based extension of Petri nets for modelling and animating object-oriented requirements specifications for validation purposes, and offers a custom-made graphical editor/animator.

3. The VENUS environment

The VENUS environment is depicted in fig. 1. This figure shows the tools provided by VENUS as well as their input and output models. The usual sequence of steps that may be followed by an analyst during the requirements development process is also shown in this figure. The tools provided by the VENUS environment are:

- A syntax-directed textual editor for constructing textual Entity-Relationship Models (ERMs).
- A graphical editor for constructing graphical ERMs.
- A mapping tool which takes as input ERM specifications and produces specifications of an Object-oriented Static Model (OSM). OSM specifications are static since they are produced from static ERM specifications, thus OSM must be extended to incorporate the dynamic behaviour of the identified object classes; this is accomplished with the use of the next tool.
- A syntax-directed textual editor for adding dynamic aspects to OSM specifications and producing specifications of the Object-oriented Rule-based Model (ORM).
- A C++ generator, which takes as input ORM specifications and produces executable specifications in C++.
- A mapping tool which takes as input ORM specifications and produces specifications of the RBN model.
- A graphical editor/animator for the RBN model. This tool may be used to edit and animate graphical RBN specifications.

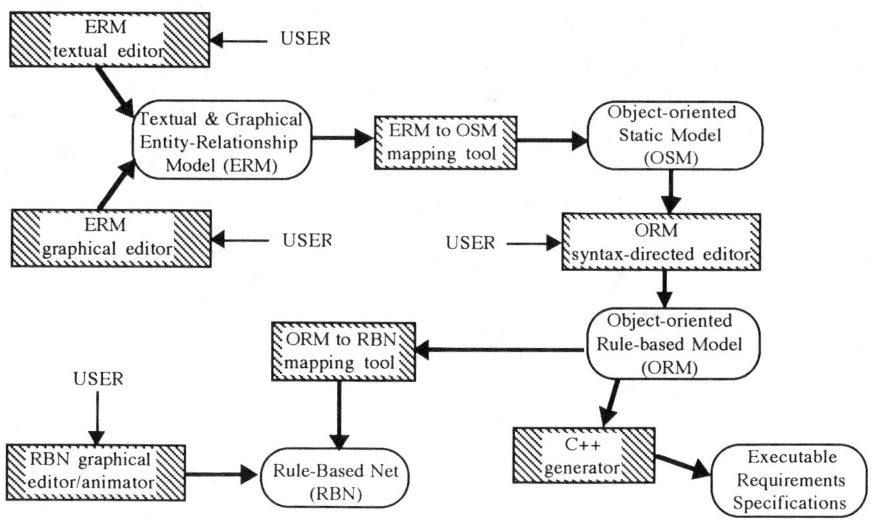

Fig. 1 The VENUS environment

Depending on the analyst's preferences and experience, the development of specifications may start at different stages of the VENUS development process. Furthermore, VENUS architecture allows more than one analysts to cooperate during the development process with each one of them being involved in a different stage.

In the following section we mainly concentrate on the object-oriented development of requirements.

4. The Object-oriented Rule-based Model (ORM)

Requirements specifications are formulated in an Object-oriented Rule-based Model (ORM) which contains the static and dynamic aspects of the various identified object classes. The behaviour of object classes is expressed in terms of Rules which are grouped in Behaviour Units (BUs). More specifically, the hierarchy of object classes may be constructed

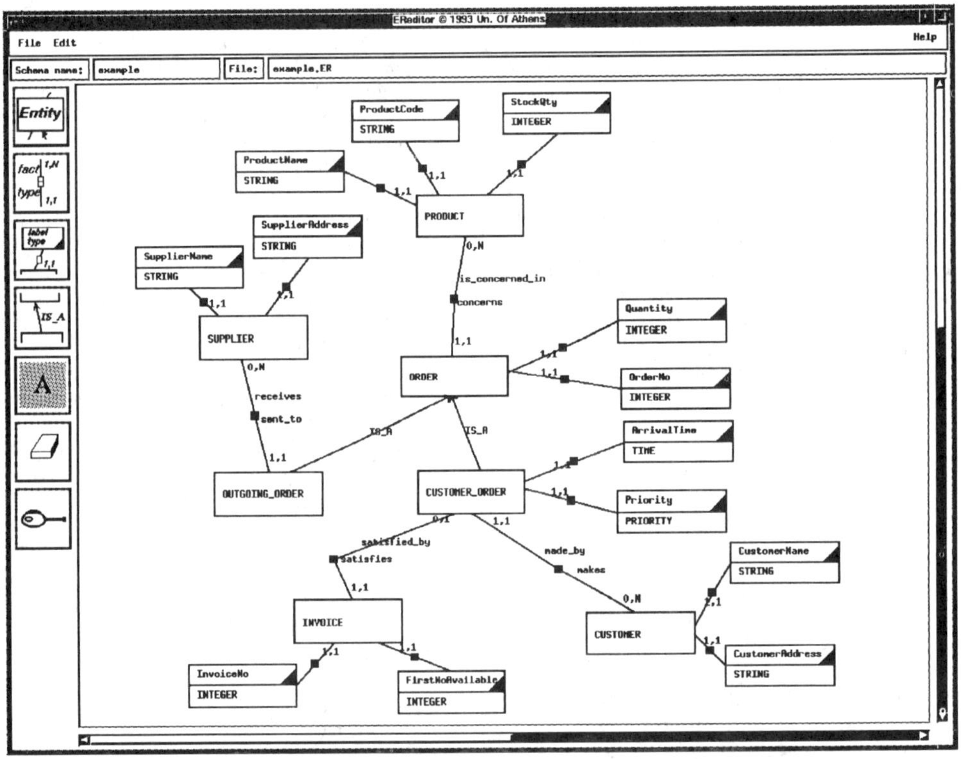

Fig. 2 An example of an ERM

by first forming a binary Entity-Relationship Model (ERM) enriched with inheritance on the basis of a linguistic approach [Tsalgatidou 91]. Figure 2 shows an example of such a model.

The produced ERM is mapped to an Object-oriented Static Model (OSM) [Gouscos 92]. As is obvious, OSM contains only the specifications of the static system aspects. Therefore, OSM is subsequently enhanced so as to include the dynamic system aspects and any new object classes that may be needed. The ORM syntax-directed editor is used to incorporate these enhancements to OSM and produce the Object-oriented Rule-based Model (ORM). Fig. 3 contains part of the ORM which resulted from the ERM of figure 2. More specifically, fig. 3 shows the ORM specification which resulted from the mapping of the CUSTOMER_ORDER entity type of fig. 2 into the corresponding object class of OSM and from subsequent enhancement of this class with its dynamic aspects.

ORM models the dynamic aspects of object classes in their behavioural part using the concepts of *behaviour units (BUs), signals* and *rules*. The static and behavioural parts of ORM complement each other, in the sense that the static part specifies only the structural aspects of data without specifying any operations on them, while the behavioural part presupposes the existence of object classes and specifies their behaviour in terms of BUs, signals and dynamic rules.

The concept of *BUs* is used to partition the behaviour of an object class. Each BU belongs to one class of the object-oriented model and is associated with a specific triggering signal type. The receipt of individual signals of this type activates the behaviour described in this BU. A BU may be either *class BU* or *instance BU* and has the following general structure:

```
class | instance BU <BU_name>
triggered by <signal> (<signal_parameters>)
  <BU body>
end BU <BU_name>
```

The body of a BU is a set of dynamic rules having the form

```
[IF <preconditions> THEN] <actions>
```

The *preconditions* of a rule are expressed by a boolean formula and have to be satisfied before the *actions* described in its *THEN part* can be executed. The receipt of a triggering signal by a BU activates all the dynamic rules of that BU. The preconditions of rules of the same BU are mutually exclusive, so that exactly one of the rules will always fire. Actions in the *THEN* part of a rule may modify/create/delete object instances and/or produce some *signals* sent to other BUs or to the external environment of the modelled system. A rule belongs to exactly one BU and a BU belongs to exactly one class; therefore the dynamic behaviour of each object class is modelled as a collection of rules grouped in the BUs specified for that class and triggered by specific signals.

ORM supports simple inheritance of both static and dynamic aspects as follows:

- object classes inherit all the static properties of their superclasses and may introduce new ones
- object classes also inherit the BUs of their superclasses without any changes and/or redefine (some of) them by changing (some of) their existing rules or by adding new ones; they may also introduce new BUs describing behaviour not specified by their superclasses.

For each rule R, the rule model provides a*highest acceptor class* field (hac(R)) containing the name of the class where rule R is defined and a *lowest acceptor classes* field (lac(R)) containing the names of the lowest subclasses of hac(R) that still inherit rule R.

The dynamic behaviour of an information system is modelled as a sequence of firings of rules, grouped in BUs and triggered by specific signals. All the rules of a BU are triggered by the same signal. The firing of each rule, may result in the activation of other BUs by generating appropriate signals. The interaction of an information system with its external environment is modelled by the receipt or sending of signals. Thus, signals serve as the means of communication between the various parts of an information system and between the system and its external environment. More information about ORM may be found in [Tsalgatidou 93].

The dynamic behaviour of a system modelled in this way can be demonstrated and checked by executing the system specifications. For this purpose VENUS offers a C++ generator tool, currently under development, which is used for transforming ORM specifications to C++ executable specifications. Appendix A depicts part of the executable specifications which are produced by applying the C++ generator tool to the ORM specifications of figure 3. In this way, developers can validate the captured requirements by executing the specifications and running test cases.

Apart from C++ executable specifications a graphical representation of ORM, accompanied with graphical animation and execution facilities and supported by formal tools, would provide greater help to its analysis and validation. Furthermore, the validation process would be even more facilitated by presenting the system's dynamic behaviour at different levels of abstraction. To this end,

Petri nets are used in the VENUS environment as an underlying formalism to graphically represent the ORM model in a number of abstraction levels and to validate it by means of graphical animation and formal validation tools. The Petri net model used in VENUS is called Rule Based Net (RBN) and derived from ORM specifications using the ORM to RBN mapping tool (see fig. 1). In the following section we give a formal definition of the RBN model and we explain how ORM is mapped to RBN.

```
object class CUSTOMER_ORDER subclass of ORDER
instance properties
    name ArrivalTime card 1,1 domain TIME
    name Priority card 1,1 domain PRIORITY
    name Customer card 1,1
        domain OBJECTID of CUSTOMER
    name Invoice card 0,1
        domain OBJECTID of INVOICE
end instance properties
class behaviour
    class BU
        CUSTOMER_ORDER.ProcessOrdersOnHold
    triggered by ProcessOrdersOnHold(Product)
        rule R1 hac CUSTOMER_ORDER
            lac {CUSTOMER_ORDER}
        begin
            execute NotifyOrders
                (signal.Product,OnHold) ;
        end
    end BU CUSTOMER_ORDER.ProcessOrdersOnHold
end class behaviour
instance behaviour
    instance BU CUSTOMER_ORDER.ProcessNow
    triggered by ProcessNow( )
        rule R1 hac CUSTOMER_ORDER
            lac {CUSTOMER_ORDER}
        begin
            if self.Quantity > self.Product.StockQuantity
            then
                execute SetPriority(OnHold) ;
                NoShipment(self.OrderNo) -> EXT ENV ;
        end
        rule R2 hac CUSTOMER_ORDER
            lac {CUSTOMER_ORDER}
        begin
            if self.Quantity <=
            self.Product.StockQuantity then
                execute SetPriority(Processed) ;
                IssueInvoice(self.ObjectId) -> INVOICE ;
                DecreaseStock(self.Quantity) ->
                    self.Product ;
        end
    end BU CUSTOMER_ORDER.ProcessNow
end instance behaviour
class procedures
    procedure NotifyOrders
        (Product card 1,1 domain OBJECTID of
        PRODUCT,
        Priority card 1,1 domain PRIORITY)
    begin
        for each Customer_Order where
        (Customer_Order.Product = signal.Product) and
        (Customer_Order.Priority = signal.Priority) do
            ProcessNow( ) -> Customer_Order ;
    end
end class procedures
instance procedures
    procedure SetPriority
        (NewPriority card 1,1 domain PRIORITY)
    begin
        self.Priority := NewPriority ;
    end
end instance procedures
end object class CUSTOMER_ORDER
```

Fig. 3 An ORM specification

5. The Rule-Based Net (RBN) Model

A Rule-Based Net is a Petri net-based model used for graphical representation of ORM specifications. RBNs resemble Predicate-Transition (PrT) nets [Genrich 81] augmented with additional information. Basically, an RBN contains inscribed places, inscribed transitions as well as inscribed arcs connecting places and transitions. An RBN also contains an underlying structure defining information used in the various inscriptions.

Analysts may interactively produce RBNs at different levels of abstraction using the ORM to RBN mapping tool. At the highest abstraction level, a 'context RBN' is produced which contains only one transition for the behaviour of the entire modelled system, as well as input and output places for the signals sent to and from the external environment (see fig. 4(a)). Places are inscribed with signal names and parameters of the corresponding signals. A 'high-level RBN' is formed in the next abstraction level by decomposing the unique transition of the 'context RBN' to one transition for each object class of ORM as well as to places for the signals exchanged between object classes (see fig. 4(b)). Subsequently, each 'object class transition' of the 'high-level RBN' may be further decomposed into other transitions and places, representing the BUs contained in the corresponding object class and the signals exchanged between these BUs. In this 'medium-level RBN', transitions model BUs and are inscribed with BU names, whereas places are again inscribed with the names and parameters of the corresponding signals (see fig. 4(c)). Each 'BU transition' may be further decomposed into one transition for each rule contained in the corresponding BU and inscribed with the rule name. By following these steps for all the object classes the 'low-level RBN' is constructed which is the last but one abstraction level of RBN for the whole ORM (see fig. 4(d)). At the final step, the 'body' of each rule (namely the *hac, lac, preconditions* and *actions* of each rule) is introduced into the corresponding rule transition thus producing a 'detailed RBN' (see fig. 5(a)). This 'detailed RBN' is always accompanied by its structure Σ (see fig. 5(b)).

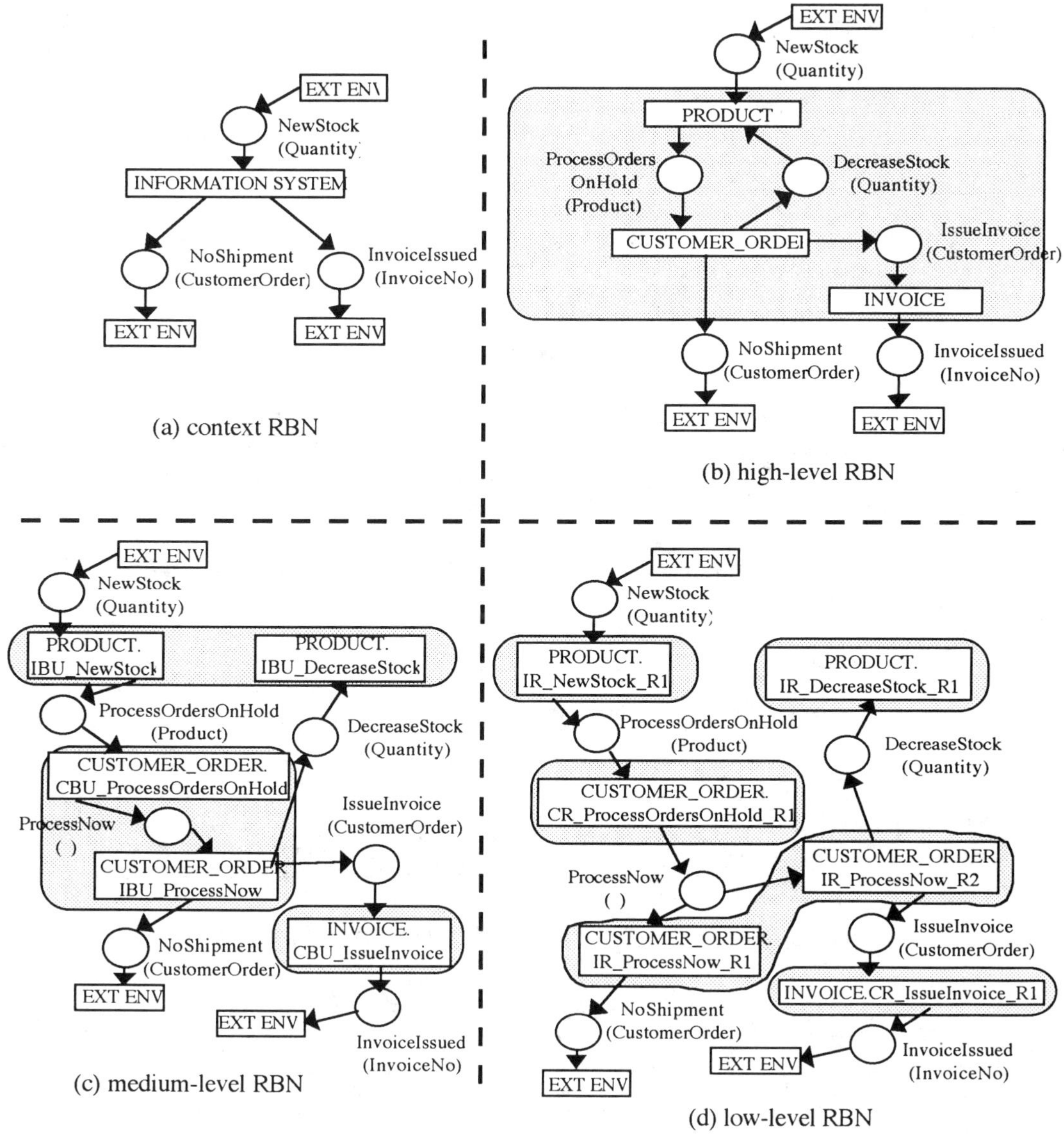

Fig. 4 Abstraction levels of the RBN corresponding to the behavioural component of an ORM partly depicted in fig. 3

A transition may produce more than one signals of the same type during one firing, as a result of the execution of the actions of the corresponding rule. The number of produced signals of a given signal type denotes the multiplicity of the corresponding output arc.

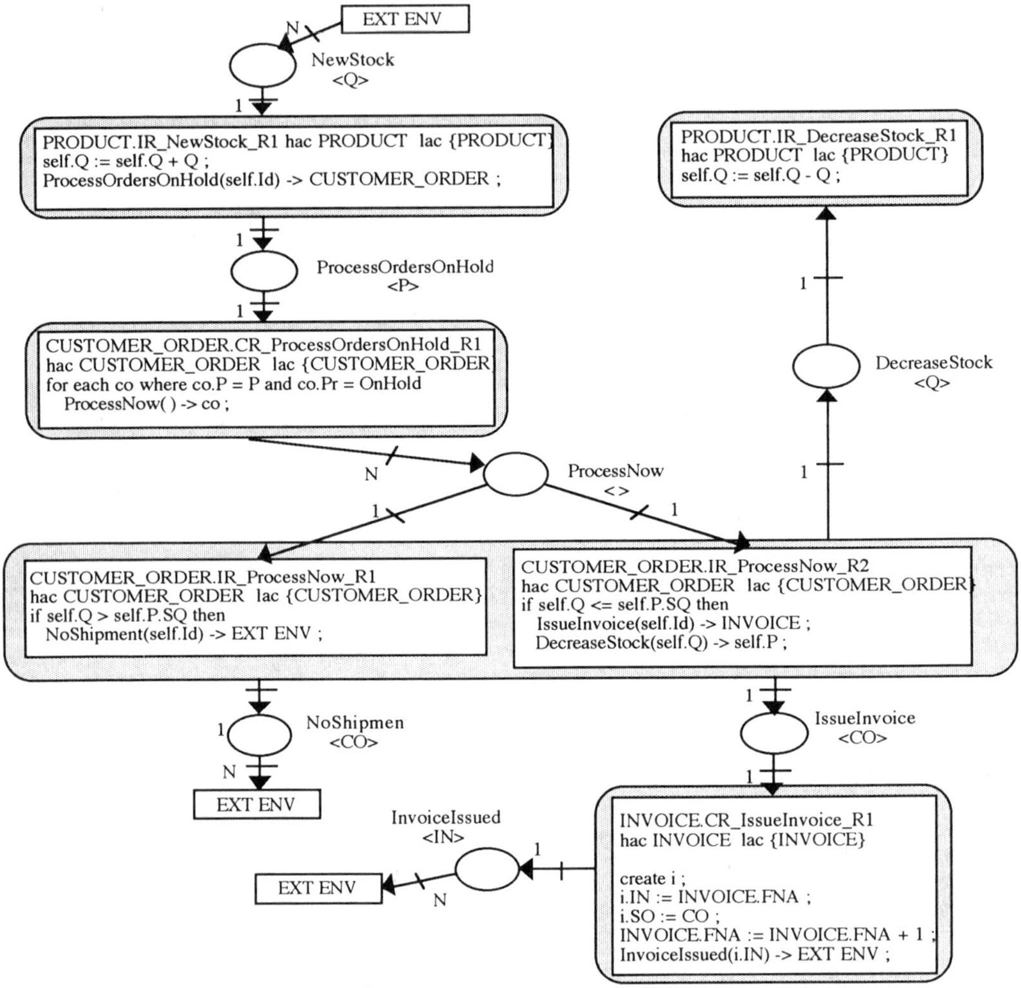

Fig. 5(a) Detailed RBN corresponding to the behavioral component of an ORM partly depicted in fig. 3

Thus, arcs are inscribed with an integer multiplicity. An arc from a place to a transition has always multiplicity equal to one, since a rule requires exactly one signal in order to execute. In the graphical representation of RBN, signal instances are depicted as tokens. If a signal has no parameters, the corresponding token is represented graphically by an anonymous bullet; otherwise, the token is represented as a tuple of signal parameter values.

A 'detailed RBN' is formally defined as a tuple

$$R=\langle P,T,F,K,N,\Sigma,sig,insc,hac,lac,M_0\rangle$$

where

- P is a non-empty set of RBN places;
- T is a non-empty set of RBN transitions;
- $F \subseteq (P \times T) \cup (T \times P)$, with $F \neq \emptyset$, is a set whose elements are the RBN arcs;
- $K : P \rightarrow \{1,2, ..., INF\}$ is a function that maps each place of P to an integer number denoting the capacity of this place, i.e. the number of tokens that this place can hold; the value INF is used for some places with infinite capacity;

- $N : F \rightarrow N_{def} \cup N_{undef}$ is a function that maps each arc of F to an integer number denoting the multiplicity of this arc, i.e., the number of tokens transferred across this arc, each time the transition at the one end of the arc fires; the two multiplicity domains are defined as

  $N_{def} = \{ 1,2, \dots \}$, and

  $N_{undef} = \{ N_1, N_2, \dots \}$

  with $N_i \in N_{def}$
- Σ is the underlying structure of an RBN and has the form

  $\Sigma = \langle D^{val}, D^{obj}, D^{sig} \rangle$

  where D^{val} denotes the domain of signal parameters and of object instance properties, D^{obj} denotes the domain of objects of the RBN, and D^{sig} denotes the signal domain of the RBN (see fig. 5(b)).
- D^{val} represents the value domain of the RBN; D^{val} is a non-empty set of tuples of the form

  <IndivType, Relations, Operations, Values>

  Each of these tuples describes a specific type of values that may appear in the signal types that label the places and arcs of the RBN, or in the properties of (the instances of) object classes.
- D^{obj} represents the object domain of the RBN, i.e. the collection of the object classes of the application. D^{obj} is a non-empty set of tuples of the form

  <ClassName, SuperClassName, Properties>

  For each object class of the object domain of the RBN, the set D^{obj} contains a corresponding tuple with the above three fields.
- D^{sig} represents the signal domain of an RBN; it is a non-empty set of signal types, i.e., a non-empty set of tuples of the form

  <SignalName, SignalParameters>

  Each of these tuples describes a specific type of signals that may appear as tokens in the RBN places.
- sig : $P \rightarrow D^{sig}$ is a function that maps each place of the RBN to a signal type from the signal domain of the RBN
- insc is a function which maps each transition of T to a dynamic rule

1. Value classes (component D^{val})

```
{ < OBJECTID, OBJECT, {=}, { }, predefined > ,
  < STRING, OBJECT, { }, { }, predefined > ,
  < INTEGER, OBJECT, { >, <= }, { +, - }, predefined
>,
  < PRIORITY, OBJECT, { = }, { },
    {OnHold,Immediate, Processed } > ,
  <TIME, OBJECT, { }, { }, predefined> }
```

2. Object classes (component D^{obj})

```
{ < OBJECT, OBJECT, { } ,
    { < ObjectId, (1,1), OBJECTID, all > } > ,
  < PRODUCT, OBJECT, { } ,
    { < ProductName, (1,1), STRING, all > ,
      < ProductCode, (1,1), STRING, all > ,
      < StockQuantity, (1,1), INTEGER, [0-...] > ,
      < OrderedIn, (0,N), OBJECTID of ORDER, all > }
>,
  < SUPPLIER, OBJECT, { } ,
    { < SupplierName, (1,1), STRING, all > ,
      < SupplierAddress, (1,N), STRING, all > ,
      < PendingOrders, (0,N), OBJECTID of
        OUTGOING_ORDER, all > } > ,
  < CUSTOMER, OBJECT, { } ,
    { < CustomerName, (1,1), STRING, all > ,
      < CustomerAddress, (1,N), STRING, all > ,
      < OrdersMade, (0,N), OBJECTID of
        CUSTOMER_ORDER, all > } > ,
  < ORDER, OBJECT, { } ,
    { < OrderNo, (1,1), INTEGER, [1-...] > ,
      < Quantity, (1,1), INTEGER, [1-...] > ,
      < Product, (1,1), OBJECTID of PRODUCT, all >
  }> ,
  < CUSTOMER_ORDER, ORDER, { } ,
    { < ArrivalTime, (1,1), TIME, all > ,
      < Priority, (1,1), PRIORITY, all > ,
      < Customer, (1,1), OBJECTID of CUSTOMER,
        all > ,
      < Invoice, (0,1) OBJECTID of INVOICE, all > }
  > ,
  < OUTGOING_ORDER, ORDER, { } ,
    { < Supplier, (1,1), OBJECTID of SUPPLIER, all >
  }> ,
  < INVOICE, OBJECT,
    { < FirstNoAvailable, (1,1), INTEGER, [1-...] > } ,
    { < InvoiceNo, (1,1), INTEGER, [1-...] > } > }
```

3. Signal types (component D^{sig})

```
{ < NewStock ,
    { < Quantity, (1,1), INTEGER, [1-...] > } ,
    { EXT ENV }, PRODUCT > ,
  < ProcessOrdersOnHold,
    { Product, (1,1), OBJECTID of PRODUCT, all > } ,
    { PRODUCT }, CUSTOMER_ORDER > ,
  < ProcessNow,
    { } ,
    { CUSTOMER_ORDER }, CUSTOMER_ORDER > ,
  < NoShipment,
    { < CustomerOrder, (1,1), OBJECTID of
        CUSTOMER_ORDER, all > } ,
    { CUSTOMER_ORDER }, EXT ENV > ,
  < DecreaseStock,
    { < Quantity, (1,1), INTEGER, all > } ,
    { CUSTOMER_ORDER }, PRODUCT > ,
  < IssueInvoice,
    { < CustomerOrder, (1,1), OBJECTID of
        CUSTOMER_ORDER, all > } ,
    { CUSTOMER_ORDER }, INVOICE > ,
  < InvoiceIssued,
    { < InvoiceNo, (1,1), INTEGER, [1-...] > } ,
    { INVOICE }, EXT ENV > }
```

Fig. 5(b) The structure Σ of the RBN of fig. 5(a)

- hac is an element-valued function that relates each transition t of T to an object class called highest acceptor class of transition t - hac(t) - which is the object class where the rule inscribed in transition t has been originally defined
- lac is a set-valued function that relates each transition t of T to some object classes called lower acceptor classes of t - lac(t) - which are the lowest classes in the object schema that inherit the rule inscribed in transition t
- M_0 is an initial marking that assigns token to places.

Thus, an RBN is a simple formal model showing *control flow* within a system and at the same time hiding, in the corresponding transitions, information about *what* is happening in the system. One of the advantages of using RBNs for modelling the dynamic behaviour of systems is that their graphical representation facilitates validation, as well as analytical study of system behaviour by exploiting certain properties of the nets; this is the topic of the next section.

6. Validation of RBN specifications

Validation of user requirements, i.e. elimination of ambiguity, inconsistency and incompleteness is a difficult process. Requirements specifications are valid if they are *deterministic*, *complete*, *consistent* and *correct*, and all these features can be ensured for RBN specifications. First of all, RBN specifications can be considered deterministic when the behaviour of the system model is always predictable; this follows from the premise that information systems are considered to behave deterministically, i.e., to produce a given result under given conditions. Secondly, RBN specifications can be considered complete if there is always something happening, whenever a signal arrives. Thirdly, RBN specifications can be considered consistent when there are no transitions with the same triggering signal and the same preconditions but with contradictory actions. Finally, RBN specifications are considered correct when they describe the behaviour that end-users expect of their system.

One way of validating ORM requirements specifications is by executing the corresponding C++ prototype whose generation was discussed in section 4. ORM requirements specifications can also be validated through analytical study and animation of the constructed RBN model. The executability of the RBN formalism and its potential for graphical animation provide invaluable help during the validation process. Animation has proven to be a valuable validation tool, and the results of using early animation show that it is a very promising means for reducing errors during requirements modelling and for ensuring that the intended system behaviour has been properly captured and modelled. Although animation provides remarkable assistance in the case of small systems, larger applications necessitate tools which can automatically detect contradictions, inconsistencies and redundancies in the model. The formal foundation of RBNs offers a sound basis for the development of such tools. A number of algorithms have been developed for proving various properties of a PrT net, like safeness, reachability, etc. [Murata 89], and since the RBN model is a variant of PrT nets and it can be automatically mapped to a specialised PrT net [Tsalgatidou 93] certain properties of the modelled system can be checked by exploiting PrT-net verification algorithms. For RBNs, the problem of proving that the system model can perform certain operations is reduced to the problem of proving that certain net markings are reachable from a given initial marking.

The above analysis motivates our current effort on developing the VENUS integrated environment for specification of object-oriented rule-based requirements, their mapping to RBN specifications and animation and formal validation of RBNs. VENUS is being developed on Sun SPARC workstations running BSD Unix, X11R5 and OSF/Motif, in ANSI C++ and Prolog. The RBN graphical editor/animator uses graphical animation to validate RBN models in terms of determinism, completeness, consistency and correctness. A systems analyst dealing with small-scale applications may use this tool to 'run' realistic scenarios and 'what-if' cases for validation purposes. Missing and dead transitions and circular structures are easily detected, and this feedback is used for interactively redesigning the specifications. RBN specifications for large systems can be automatically validated by applying formal validation algorithms, currently under development.

7. Conclusions

The VENUS approach combines both the object-oriented and rule-based paradigms within a uniform framework, integrating all aspects of information systems. Two important advantages are that the final requirements specifications still represent explicitly application domain policy in terms of dynamic rules, and that the mapping of ORM schemas to C++ executable specifications and to the RBN model for validation purposes is formally defined and automated.

RBNs are validated through graphical animation, offering the advantages of rapid prototyping. In this way, requirements analysis can come up with easily modifiable, modular, clear, concise, compact and executable requirements specifications at the very early stages of system development. The sound foundation of RBNs makes this formalism a very good candidate notation for requirements specifications by allowing the use of formal validation tools and, subsequently, the mapping of requirements specifications to design and implementation structures (currently under development).

Two other interesting features of the RBN model are the ability to represent the dynamic behaviour of a system in different levels of abstraction and formality and the modelling of the behaviour of one object class in a single transition of a 'high-level RBN'. This latter feature is compliant to the so-called 'localisation principle' suggesting to describe each object in isolation from the others [Rolland 92], since all the rules and signals related to one object are localised in a corresponding 'high-level RBN' transition instead of being spread out in a huge RBN for the entire system, as is the case in classical behaviour models.

Although work on VENUS is still in progress, the current version of the system already demonstrates a number of capabilities that can be used to bridge the gap between informal and formal specifications. The analyst is responsible for communicating with the end-user and entering the required information in the system. VENUS supports the analyst by offering tools (graphical and syntax-directed editors, C++ generator, RBN graphical editor/animator) to construct and validate requirements specifications, and provides specific support for evolutionary construction of requirements, using the facilities of the underlying system to ensure that each change is carried out in a consistent way thoughout the requirements specification process.

The viability of this approach is currently under testing by using it into two real world applications: the modelling of office-related activities in a public organisation and in a university department. The early construction of a 'working' user requirements model seems to facilitate a lot the process of its validation and the results are very promising.

We believe that the work described in this paper contributes to the development of systems that satisfy the initial user requirements and that are flexible enough to incorporate and reflect any future changes. Future work will focus on the construction of a full-scale prototype that can be tested on real-world applications and on the development of algorithms for mapping RBN specifications to design and implementation structures.

Acknowledgements

The authors would like to thank Phoebus Vilanakis and Thanos Avdis for their contribution in the VENUS development.

References

[Boehm 75] B.W. Boehm et al, "Some Experiences with Automated Aids to the Design of Large-Scale Reliable Software", *IEEE Transactions on Software Engineering*, vol.1, no.2, February 1975.

[Booch 92] G. Booch, *Object-Oriented Design and Applications*, 2nd edition, Addison-Wesley, 1992.

[Brinkkemper 90] S. Brinkkemper & A.H.M. ter Hofstede, "The Conceptual Task Model: a Specification Technique between Requirements Engineering and Program Development", *Proceedings of CAiSE '90*, LNCS, vol.436, Springer-Verlag, 1990, pp.228-250.

[Coad 91] P. Coad & E. Yourdon, *Object-Oriented Analysis*, Prentice-Hall Int., 1991.

[Coleman 92] D. Coleman, F. Hayes & S. Bear, "Introducing Objectcharts or How to Use Objectcharts in Object-Oriented Design", *IEEE Transactions on Software*

Engineering, vol.18, no.1, January 1992, pp.9-18.

[Dahler 87] J. Dahler et al, "A Graphical Tool for the Design and Prototyping of Distributed Systems", *ACM SIGSOFT,* vol.12, no.3, 1987, pp. 25-36.

[D'Haenens 90] I. D'Haenens, F. van Assche, E. Halpin & B. Karakostas, "Experiences with Rule-Based Dynamic Modelling", in [Sol 91], pp.231-239.

[Dürr 92] E. Durr & J. van Katwijk, "VDM++ A Formal Specification Language for Object-Oriented Designs", *Proceedings of the 7th Internatinal Conference TOOLS EUROPE '92,* Dortmund, Germany, 1992, Prentice-Hall, pp.63-77.

[Endres 75] A. Endres, "An Analysis of Errors and their Causes in System Programs", *IEEE Transactions on Software Engineering,* vol.1, no.6, June 1975, pp.140-149.

[Fickas 93] S. Fickas & A. Finkelstein (eds.), *Proceedings of IEEE International Symposium on Requirements Engineering*, San Diego, California, 4-6 Jan. 1993, IEEE Computer Soc. Press.

[Finkelstein 92] A. Finkelstein & J. Kramer, "TARA: Tool-Assisted Requirements Analysis", in [Loucopoulos 92], pp. 413-432.

[Genrich 81] H.J. Genrich & K. Lautenbach, "System Modelling with High-Level Petri Nets", *Theoretical Computer Science*, vol. 13, 1981, pp. 109-136.

[Goguen 82] J. Goguen & J. Meseguer, "Rapid Prototyping in the OBJ Executable Specification Language", *ACM SIGSOFT Software Engineering Notes*, vol.7, no.5, 1982, p.75.

[Gouscos 92] D. Gouscos & A. Tsalgatidou, "The ERM, ORM and RBN Models", Technical Report, Dept. of Informatics, University of Athens, May 1992.

[Jones 86] C.B. Jones, *Systematic Software Development Using VDM*, Prentice-Hall, 1986.

[Kappel 91] G. Kappel & M. Schrefl, "Using an Object-Oriented Diagram Technique for the Design of Information Systems", in [Sol 91], pp.97-129.

[Kemmener 85] R.A. Kemmener, "Testing Formal Specifications to Detect Design Errors", IEEE Transactions on Software Engineering, vol.11, no.1, January 1985, pp.32-43.

[Lakos 93] C.A. Lakos & C.D. Keen, "Modelling a Door Controller Protocol in LOOPN", *Proceedings of the 10th Internatinal Conference TOOLS EUROPE '93,* Versailles, France, 1993, Prentice-Hall, pp.31-44.

[Loucopoulos 91] P. Loucopoulos, P. Mc Brien, F. Schumacker, C. Theodoulidis, V. Kopanas & B. Wangler, "Integrating Database Technology, Rule-Based Systems and Temporal Reasoning for Effective Information Systems: The TEMPORA Paradigm", *Information Systems,* vol.1, no.1, April 1991.

[Loucopoulos 92] P. Loucopoulos & R. Zicari (eds.), *Conceptual Modeling, Databases and CASE,* John Wiley & Sons, 1992.

[Murata 89] T. Murata, "Petri Nets: Properties, Analysis and Applications", *Proceedings of the IEEE,* vol.77, no.4, April 1989.

[Obal 93] W.D. Obal II & W.H. Sanders, "Importance Sampling Simulation in UltraSAN", *Simulation*, vol.61, no.5, November 1993.

[Pezzé 92] M. Pezzé & C. Ghezzi, "Cabernet: A Customizable Environment for the Specification and Analysis of Real-Time Systems", Dipartimento di Elettronica e dell' Informazione, Politecnico di Milano, September 1992.

[Plat 92] N. Plat, J. van Katwijk & H. Toetenel, "Application and Benefits of Formal Methods in Software Development", *Software Engineering Journal*, vol.7, no.5, September 1992, pp.335-346.

[POSES 92] *Das Programmsystem POSES*, Gesellschaft für Prozeßautomation & Consulting mbH Chemnitz, August 1992.

[PROD 93], *PROD User's Guide*, Helsinki University of Technology, Digital Systems Laboratory, January 1993.

[Reubenstein 91] H.B. Reubenstein & R.C. Waters, "The Requirements Apprentice: Automated Assistance for Requirements Acquisition", *IEEE Transactions on Software Engineering,* vol., no.3, March 1991, pp. 226-240.

[Rolland 92] C. Rolland, "Trends and Perspectives in Conceptual Modelling", in [Loucopoulos 92], pp. 27-48.

[Rumbaugh 91] J. Rumbaugh, M. Blaha, W. Premerlani, F. Eddy & W. Lorensen, *Object-Oriented Modelling and Design*, Prentice-Hall, 1991.

[Shand 88] J. Shand et al, "An Enviroment for the Execution and Graphical Animation of JSD Specifications", in *Procs. of*

International Workshop of KBS in S/W Engineering, UMIST, Manchester, 1988.

[Sol 91] H.G. Sol & K.M. van Hee (eds.), *Dynamic Modelling*, North-Holland, 1991.

[Spivey 87] M. Spivey, *The Z Notation: A Reference Manual*, Oxford University Computing Laboratory Programming Research Group, 1987.

[Tsalgatidou 91] A. Tsalgatidou & P. Loucopoulos, "An Object-Oriented Rule-Based Approach to the Dynamic Modelling of Information Systems", in [Sol 91], pp.131-147.

[Tsalgatidou 93] A. Tsalgatidou, D. Gouscos & C. Halatsis, "Rule-Based Behaviour Modelling of Information Systems", *Proceedings of the 26th Hawaiian Conference on Systems Sciences (HICSS-26)*, vol.IV, January 1993, IEEE Computer Society Press, pp. 409-418.

[van Baelen 92] S. van Baelen, J. Lewi, E. Steegmans & H. van Riel, "EROOS: An Entity-Relationship Based O O Specification Method", *Proceedings. of the 7th International Conference TOOLS EUROPE '92*, Prentice-Hall, 1992, pp.103-118.

[Zave 91] P. Zave, "An Insider's Evaluation of PAISLey", *IEEE Transactions on Software Engineering*, vol.17, no.3, March 1991, pp. 212-225.

A. Appendix

```
/***********************************\
* CUSTOMER ORDER: CLASS DEFINITION *
\***********************************/

class META_CUSTOMER_ORDER:
public META_ORDER
{
/* CLASS BEHAVIOUR */
public:
void CBU_ProcessOrdersOnHold (OBJECTID Product) ;
/* CLASS BEHAVIOUR RULES */
protected:
void CR_ProcessOrdersOnHold_R1
    (OBJECTID Product) ;
/* CLASS PROCEDURES */
private:
void CP_NotifyOrders
    (OBJECTID Product, PRIORITY Priority) ;
/* INSTANCE RETRIEVAL MECHANISM */
public:
OBJECTID Create (CUSTOMER_ORDER &Obj) ;
void Update (CUSTOMER_ORDER &Obj) ;
void Delete (OBJECTID ObjId) ;
void Retrieve
    (OBJECTID ObjId, CUSTOMER_ORDER &Obj) ;
void RetrieveFirst (CUSTOMER_ORDER &Obj) ;
void RetrieveNext (CUSTOMER_ORDER &Obj) ;
};

class CUSTOMER_ORDER: public ORDER
{
/* CUSTOMER_ORDER: CLASS-PART DEFINITION */
public:
static META_CUSTOMER_ORDER C ;
/* INSTANCE PROPERTIES */
TIME ArrivalTime ;
PRIORITY Priority ;
OBJECTID Customer ;
OBJECTID Invoice ;
/* INSTANCE BEHAVIOUR */
void IBU_ProcessNow (void) ;
/* INSTANCE BEHAVIOUR RULES */
protected:
void IR_ProcessNow_R1 (void) ;
void IR_ProcessNow_R2 (void) ;
/* INSTANCE PROCEDURES */
private:
void IP_Set_Priority (PRIORITY Priority) ;
};

/**************************************\
* CUSTOMER ORDER: CLASS-PART METHODS *
\**************************************/

void META_CUSTOMER_ORDER::
    CBU_ProcessOrdersOnHold (OBJECTID Product)
{
CR_ProcessOrdersOnHold_R1(Product) ;
}

void META_CUSTOMER_ORDER::
    CR_ProcessOrdersOnHold_R1 (OBJECTID Product)
{
CP_NotifyOrders(Product, OnHold) ;
}

void META_CUSTOMER_ORDER::CP_NotifyOrders
    (OBJECTID Product, PRIORITY Priority)
{
CUSTOMER_ORDER CustOrder ;
PRODUCT Prod ;

CUSTOMER_ORDER::C.RetrieveFirst(CustOrder) ;
while (CustOrder.ObjectId)
{
if ((CustOrder.Product == Product) &&
    (CustOrder.Priotity == Priority))
{
PRODUCT::C.Retrieve(Product,Prod) ;
Prod.IP_SetPriority(Immediate) ;
CustOrder.IBU_ProcessNow() ;
}
CUSTOMER_ORDER::C.RetrieveNext(CustOrder) ;
}
}

/*****************************************\
* CUSTOMER ORDER: INSTANCE-PART METHODS *
\*****************************************/

void CUSTOMER_ORDER::IBU_ProcessNow (void)
{
IR_ProcessNow_R1 () ;
IR_ProcessNow_R2 () ;
}

void CUSTOMER_ORDER::IR_ProcessNow_R1 (void)
{
PRODUCT Prod ;

PRODUCT::C.Retrieve (this -> Product, Prod) ;
if (this -> Quantity > Prod.StockQty)
{
IP_SetPriority(OnHold) ;
EXT_ENV_NoShipment(this -> OrderNo) ;
}
}

void CUSTOMER_ORDER::IR_ProcessNow_R2 (void)
{
PRODUCT Prod ;

PRODUCT::C.Retrieve (this -> Product, Prod) ;
if (this -> Quantity <= Prod.StockQty)
{
IP_SetPriority(Processed) ;
INVOICE::C.IssueInvoice(this -> ObjectId) ;
Prod.DecreaseStock(this -> Quantity) ;
}
}

void CUSTOMER_ORDER::IP_SetPriority
    (PRIORITY Priority)
{
this -> Priority = Priotity ;
C.Update(*this) ;
}
```

Attribute: A Semantic and Seamless Construct

Amândio Vaz Velho
Rogerio Carapuça

INESC/IST
Rua Alves Redol 9, Apartado 10105, 1017 Lisboa, Codex, PORTUGAL
Phone: + 351.1.3100000 - Fax: + 351.1.525843 - E_mail: avv@eniac.inesc.pt

Abstract

Association has been considered an essential concept in the context of object-oriented (OO) modeling. An association represents a semantic relationship among instances of classes. The main advantages of using associations are simplicity and informality which are critical in early stages of domain analysis. However, in an OO context, the use of associations brings about some important drawbacks. Indeed, associations violate encapsulation, abstraction and extendibility. This paper shows how the concept of attribute, understood as instance variable in OO programming languages, can be semantically enriched in such a way that it becomes as expressive as the notion of association, without having its drawbacks. The paper also shows that attributes provide a good support for a seamless development process. Indeed, it can be used throughout the development life cycle, as a unifying concept able to model, either analysis/ design issues as multiplicity of relationships, or implementation issues such as instance variable types. Moreover, attributes reduce the semantic overloading among types of relationships, have a formal definition and allow a well-defined integration with the dynamic model. The paper advocates that an ideal method would have to capitalize on the advantages of both concepts (association, attribute).

1 - Introduction

A common approach to analysis and design is the use of different views or schemes, each of which capturing different real-world aspects. Static or structural views provide abstract models describing the different entities that can be identified as well as the relationships among them. Static views have been explored for a long time in the semantic data model community [Hull87, Peckham88]. Most of the object-oriented analysis and design methods (OOADMs) blend object orientation with data modeling techniques and, thus, also include a static view [Shlaer88, Booch91, Coad91, Martin92, Rumbaugh91].

From TOOLS EUROPE '94 (Technology of Object-Oriented Languages and Systems).

Association is an essential concept where static modeling is concerned. An Association represents a semantic relationship among instances of classes (a horse runs in a race; in each race there is a given number of horses taking part). James Rumbaugh et al. with their Object Modeling Technique (OMT), have been pushing the concept of association in the object-oriented community for a long time [Rumbaugh87, Rumbaugh91, Rumbaugh92]. The OMT association concept has been so successful that it was adopted by the recent version of the Booch Method [Booch93]. Several OOADMs feature concepts equivalent to the OMT association. For a survey of notations used by those methods see [Fowler92].

Authors who support associations advocate that they should be considered as semantic constructs of similar weight to classes and inheritance [Rumbaugh87]. They advocate that associations abstract interactions among classes in a natural way, without having to specify a particular implementation. Associations avoid that such interactions are buried in the attributes (instance variables) and operation (methods) of the classes. According to Rumbaugh, associations are even more important than inheritance in the context of system modeling [Rumbaugh92].

Thus, the basic concepts of an *association-object* model (e.g. an object model extended with associations) are the following: class, attribute, operation, specialization and association. This is the case of OMT object model.

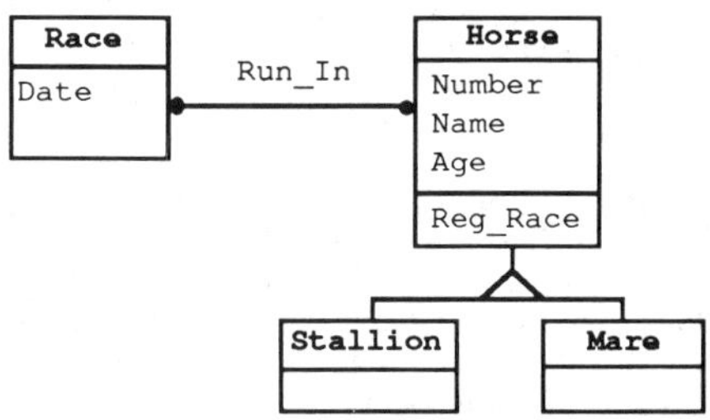

Figure 1 - OMT Object Model

Figure 1 depicts in the OMT notation a small fragment of a race of horses object model. This example was adopted from [Rumbaugh92]. To facilitate the comparison between attributes and associations, the same example will be used in this paper. We have introduced some simplifications as well as some "nuances" that maybe are not much common in races of horses (we apologize to the race addicts).

Classes model real-world entities (`Horse`, `Race`), specialization models inheritance among classes (`Stallion`, `Mare`) and associations model structural information shared by real-world entities (`Run_In`). Classes are constituted by attributes and operations. Attributes model entity-valued properties (`Date`, `Number`, `Name`, `Age`) and operations model events that may occur during the entities' lifetime (`Reg_Race`). A black dot on one of the extremes of an association indicates a multiplicity of many. The absence of a black dot, not exemplified in figure 1, indicates a multiplicity of one.

Associations are certainly more abstract than object-oriented programming languages (OOPLs) attributes. Associations abstract the structural interaction among classes through a semantic concept. On contrary, with OOPLs attributes, issues concerned with the semantics of the interaction among classes, such as multiplicity for instance, are specified and ensured in an ad hoc way. However, associations have some basic weaknesses. Indeed, associations break some of the object-oriented principles, namely encapsulation, abstraction and extendibility. Let us explain why we support this thesis.

The object-oriented paradigm understands the world constituted by objects, which are abstract representations of real-world entities. Objects are classified in classes and interact by messages. Every thing concerned with an entity should be encapsulated inside an object, namely through variables representing its internal state (attributes) and operations. Classes can be extended by inheritance what makes them reusable software packages [Meyer88, Wegner90, Booch91].

An association is something that is external to classes but concerns with objects, namely with objects' structure. Thus, associations are a breakdown in encapsulation of classes.

An association is also a breakdown in abstraction. The world is constituted by entities, which have structural and behavioral properties. Such properties belong to the entities and, therefore, are not at the same level as the entities themselves[1]. The association-object model understand the world constituted by entities, exhibiting state and behavior, and associations. Associations would introduce virtual entities in the models. Those virtual entities do not really exist. They are mostly introduced to play a factorization role, spreading the relationships among entities. This introduces a semantic gap between the real-world and the models and, therefore, the resulting models are less abstract.

Associations considered of similar weight to classes, endanger extendibility and, therefore, reusability because reusability is technically achieved, not only but also, through extendibility [Meyer87]. The inheritance issue has been deeply studied for classes [Cardelli84, Stein89, Cook89]. Associations can not be dealt with exactly the same way as classes. Therefore, to achieve extendibility either for classes as well as for associations two different inheritance mechanisms would be needed. It could be easy if the inheritance issue is considered in an informal and less accurate way. However, if the issue would be considered in an accurate way, the resulting object model would be much more complex. We could ask for instance, what does polymorphism means for associations? Indeed, OOADMs which adopt an association object-model don't allow the specialization of associations [Coad91] or don't provide a formal and complete semantics for that issue [Martin92].

Let us sum up the ideas developed so far. Associations certainly have more semantics than OOPLs attributes but they penalize encapsulation, abstraction, extendibility and reusability. On the other hand, OOPLs attribute is a semantically poor construct but it conforms with the object-oriented principles.

One way to preserve both, semantics and conformance to the object-oriented principles, would be to enrich semantically the concept of attribute, making it as expressive as associations. This is the approach adopted by SOM (Semantic Object Model) and that will be described in the rest of this paper. SOM is an OOADM, which has been developing at INESC. Its main goal is to provide a method, which combines within a single model and language the constructs of OOPLs and the constructs of OOADM. See [Velho93] for a SOM general presentation.

Figures 2a-2b are SOM models of a fragment of a horses' racetrack universe. SOM features a graphical language (G-SOM) and a textual language (T-SOM). T-SOM syntax was inspired in Eiffel [Meyer92].

[1] Of course, two users can see the same situation in different ways. Thus, a *Marriage*, for example, can be a property for user *a* (*Bride*) and an entity for user *b* (*Priest*). However, this issue has to do with the way as concepts are used during modeling and not with the concepts themselves. We are talking about concepts.

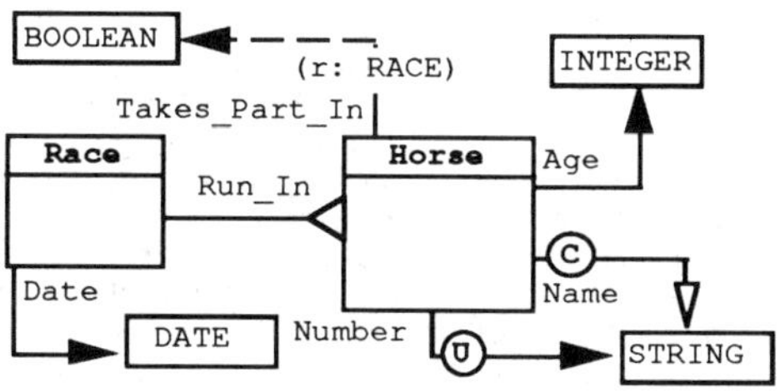

Figure 2.a - SOM Object Model: G-SOM

```
CLASS Horse
  INTERFACE
    Number, Name, Age,
    Takes_Part_In -> PUBLIC;
    Run_In -> RACE;
    Birth, Dead, BirthDay,
    Reg_Race, Fall_Ill  -> RACES_MANAGER
  ATTRIBUTES
    Number, Name OPTIONAL: STRING;
    Age: INTEGER;
    Run_In OPTIONAL: RELATION SET[RACE];
    Takes_Part_In (r: RACE): BOOLEAN
      Do Result := Not (Run_In = Void)
            and then (Run_In.Has(r)) End
  EVENTS
    *Birth (nu, na: STRING)
      Do Number := nu; Name := na;
         Age := 0; Run_In := Void
    End;

    BirthDay Do Age := Age + 1 End;

    Reg_Race (r: RACE)
      Require Age >= 3; Not Run_In.Has(r)
      Do Run_In.Put(r)
      Ensure Run_In.Has(r) End;

    Fall_Ill (rec_date: DATE)
      Do
        For Each r In Run_In Do
          If r.Date <= rec_date
            Then Run_In.Remove(r)
    End;

    ++Dead

  LIFE CYCLE
    Birth ->
    (BirthDay | Reg_Race | Fall_Ill) ->
    Dead
  INVARIANT
    Age >= 0; Unique(Number); Constant(Name)
END - - Class Horse
```

Figure 2.b - SOM Object Model: T-SOM

In G-SOM (figure 2.a), classes are depicted by boxes and attributes by polygonal lines with special symbols at the extremes (triangles, arrows, etc.). Those symbols have to do with multiplicity. They will be explained later. In T-SOM (figure 2.b), attributes are declared in a dedicated section, called Attributes as well.

Figures 2a-2b will be commented with more detail bellow. For now we would like to stress that SOM models all static relationships through attributes no matter if they involve basic classes as `Integer` and `String` or semantically meaningful classes as `Race`. Indeed, `Run_In` is an attribute of `Horse` just as `Number`, `Name`, `Age` and `Takes_Part_In` are.

The semantics of attributes includes the basic semantics of OOPLs instance variables, which is concerned with implementation issues. However, SOM enriches the semantics of OOPLs instances variables, in order to make attributes able to deal with more abstract issues as, for instances, the optional versus mandatory issue and the multiplicity issue.

For example, figures 2.a-2.b declare the attribute `Run_In` as being a collection of objects in which elements are held through a `Set`. However, `Run_In` is also declared an optional attribute, what means that its value can be void. In G-SOM, the symbol of a mandatory attribute is drawn filled and the symbol of an optional attribute is drawn unfilled. In T-SOM, the name of an optional attribute is followed by the keyword Optional. The multiplicity of the relationship between the set of `Horse` instances and the set of `Race` instances, defined by the attribute `Run_In`, is declared as many-many. This is the meaning of the keyword Relation, which, in figure 2.b, goes before the `Run_In` type (`Set[Race]`).

Attributes are as expressive as associations but, since they are internal to classes, they do not break encapsulation. Besides, they directly correspond to the real word understanding as constituted by entities that encapsulate structural and behavioral properties. Hence, they do not introduce any aberration in real-world understanding and, therefore, yield highly abstract models. We should also stress that attributes allow to deal with the specialization of relationships simply by using the inheritance mechanism defined for classes. Indeed, as it will be shown later, specialization of relationships can be featured simply by attribute rewriting.

We also believe that attributes contribute to a seamless development process. The main feature of a seamless development process is the use of the same concepts and notations throughout the development life cycle [Nerson92]. This has been recognized as a great advantage with particular effects on system traceability and understandability [Meyer91]. We believe that a method can only be efficient as far as a seamless development process is concerned if it features concepts (and notations) rich enough from a semantic point of view to capture analysis as well as design and implementation issues. The semantics of SOM attributes is able to capture issues that range from multiplicity until data structures and update. Therefore, they can be used as a uniform concept from analysis up to implementation, whatever it is the specific development process that is adopted.

Attributes also have other advantages: they reduce the semantic overloading among types of relationships, have a formal definition and allow a well-defined integration with the dynamic model. These, and other advantages will be explained later.

Although associations have the above discussed drawbacks, they really are simple and informal. These are critical requirement in early stages of domain analysis. Besides, associations are well understood by object-oriented software developers who come from the Entity-Relationship [Chen76] school. These are association's strengths, which are not featured by attributes. In our opinion an ideal method would have to capitalize on the advantages of both concepts (association, attribute). This could be achieved by allowing a software developer to start with an association based model or an attribute based model and, in the former case, to convert an early association based model that achieves simplicity, into an attribute based model which would retain object-oriented strengths.

The rest of this paper is structured as follows: Section 2 presents the concept of class as understood by SOM. Section 3 formalizes the raw attribute semantics. It is close to the semantics of instance variables in OOPLs. Sections 4-7 describe the way SOM enriches this raw semantics up to its notion of attribute. Sections 8-9 illustrates how SOM deals with specialization of relationships and non-binary attributes. Throughout section 4-9, the paper compares the way attributes and associations deal with the brought up data modeling issues. Those comparisons will mainly refer to OMT associations because they probably are the most well-known in the object modeling community. Finally, section 10 sums up our conclusions. This paper does not include a complete and accurate treatment of all issues related with attributes. To complement this paper's descriptions interested readers are invited to see [Velho92].

2 - SOM Basic Object Model

A *class* defines a set of features shared by some objects. Those objects are said to be class *instances*. Among the main features defined by a class are the attributes, the events, one life cycle and the invariants. *Attributes* define static relationships with other objects. *Events* occur during an objects' lifetime and change the value of the attributes. The *life cycle* states a temporal pattern for the occurrence of events. *Invariants* define assertions on the values of the attributes, which must always hold throughout the objects' lifetime. This notion of class is basically the same as that of Oblog [Sernadas91].

Let us exemplify this using class `Horse`. Class `Horse` was declared, in G-SOM, in figure 2-a and, in T-SOM, in figure 2.b. `Number`, `Name`, `Age`, `Takes_Part_In` and `Run_In` are attributes of `Horse`. They represent relationships with the classes `Integer`, `String`, `Boolean` and `Race`. `Takes_Part_In` is a derived attribute. Derived attributes are simply functions, which may have parameters. `Takes_Part_In` has value true, whenever the target horse is registered in the race indicated by the parameter. In G-SOM, derived attributes are depicted by dashed lines. T-SOM adopts the Eiffel syntax for functions.

`Birth`, `BirthDay`, `Reg_Race`, `Fall_Ill` and `Dead` are events of `Horse`. `Birth` is a *creation event*, i. e., only after its occurrence instances of `Horse` are actually created, and `Dead` is a *destruction event*, i. e., after its occurrence, nothing else may happen to instances of `Horse`.

Events are specified by a set of pre conditions, a body and a set of post conditions. A *pre condition* is a state assertion that must hold in order that an event is allowed to occur. The *body* is composed by a set of *statements*, which specify how an event changes the value of the attributes. A *post condition* is a state assertion that must hold after an event occurrence.

Event `Reg_Race` models the registration of a horse in a given race. Event `Fall_Ill` considers that a horse has fallen ill and will be in recovery until a given date (`rec_date`). Therefore, if the horse is registered in a race scheduled to a date before the recovery date, the respective registration is canceled. The pre conditions of `Reg_Race` (`Require`) impose that only adult horses, it means older than 3, may be target of a `Reg_Race` event and that a horse may not be registered in a race in which it is presently registered. The body of `Reg_Race` (`Do`) specifies its effect as being that determined by the occurrence of the event `Put` on the object linked to the attribute `Run_In`. The post condition of `Reg_Race` (`Ensure`) specifies that after a horse has been registered in a given race, the race must belong to the value of the attribute `Run_In`.

The life cycle is expressed as a regular expression, which alphabet is the set of event types. The life cycle of class `Horse` states that between the creation and the destruction events, any number of occurrences of the events `BirthDay`, `Reg_Race`, and `Fall_Ill`, are allowed. This is the default life cycle and, in accordance with the SOM rules, could have been omitted.

The invariants of class `Horse` state that a horse can not have a negative age. Moreover, they state that the attribute `Number` is a key for the set of instances of `Horse` and the value of the attribute `Name` may not be changed throughout the lifetime of the instances of Horse. This explains the 'U' and the 'C' drawn on the polygonal lines, which in figure 2-a depict the attributes `Number` and `Name`.

Besides attributes, events, life cycle and invariants, the definition of a class also includes an interface. The *interface* of a class defines the set of attributes and events, together designated by *services*, that instances of other types may lookup or call. SOM, following Eiffel, features a *selective export* mechanism allowing a class to exhibit different interfaces (protocols) for objects belonging to different types. In T-SOM the interface is declared in a dedicated section. According to the section Interface of class `Horse`, the attributes `Number`, `Name`, `Age` and `Takes_Part_In` are *public*. This means that any object may lookup their value. On the other hand, the value of the attribute `Run_In` may only be looked up by instances of the class `Race`. The events may only be called by `Races_Manager`. `Races_Manager` would be a stand alone object. This means class `Races_Manager` would have a single instance. This object would take the responsibility by the system's interface.

3 - Raw Semantics

This section presents the precise and basic understanding SOM has about the concept of attribute. This precedes the description of the way as SOM enriches the concept of attribute, which will be done in the next sections. The definition presented bellow is very similar of that used in OOPLs for instance variables. Indeed, as we have said, the raw attribute semantics is very close to that of instance variables. Initially only binary attributes will be considered. Afterwards, we will show how the notions introduced about binary attributes are extended to non-binary attributes. This section also introduces the concepts of value and extension of an attribute in a formal way. Those concepts are essential for reasoning about attributes in an abstract way.

3.1 - Attributes, Fields and References

A *binary attribute* is a triple $<c_d, att, c_t>$, being: c_d the class where the attribute is declared, called the *domain class*; *att* an identifier, called the *name* of the attribute; c_t a class, called the *type* of the attribute. Each one of the instances of a class c_d has one *field* for each one of the attributes of c_d. The value of a field is always a *reference* that can be *void* or *linked*. If the value of a field corresponding to an attribute $<c_d, att, c_t>$ is a linked reference, such reference must be linked to an instance of c_t.

It is important to keep in mind that the value of a field is always a reference. Thus, the value of a field corresponding to the attribute `<Horse, Run_In, SET[RACE]>` (attribute `Run_In` of class `Horse`) is not a set of references linked to objects of type `Race` but a reference to an object of the type `SET[RACE]`.

3.2 - Values and Extensions

To finish this section, let us introduce a couple of basic concepts. These concepts are necessary in order to define the notions which enrich the semantics of the attributes. Such basic concepts are those of extension of a class, collection, value of an attribute and extension of an attribute.

The *extension of a class c*, denoted by *Ext(c)*, is a set whose elements are the instances of *c*.

Due to space limitations we can not formally introduce the concept of collection. Collections are repositories of objects.

A *collection* is a generic class, e. g. a class with a type parameter, which inherits from a specific pre-defined deferred class[1]. That deferred class defines the semantics of the services that must be supported by all repositories of objects.

The class `SET[RACE]`, which is the type of the attribute `Run_In` of the class `Horse`, would be an example of a collection. Among those services supported by all collections, are the events `Put` and `Remove`. `Put` includes an object into a collection and `Remove` does the opposite. `Put` is used in the event `Reg_Race` and `Remove` is used in the event `Fall_Ill`. `Has` is another service that is supported by all collections. `Has` is a boolean derived attribute, which verifies if a given object belongs to the value of a given collection attribute. By collection attribute we mean an attribute whose type is a collection. `Has` is used in the definition of the attribute `Takes_Part_In` and in the pre and post conditions of the event `Reg_Race`. Collection attributes may be involved in iteration statements (`ForEach...In...Do...End`). Those statements call a given set of services on all the objects which belong to a given collection. The event `Fall_Ill` includes an example.

So far, the concept of value of an attribute has not been introduced yet. Actually, we have only introduced the concept of value of a field corresponding to an attribute. The concept of value of a field corresponding to an attribute is based on the concept of reference. A reference is an implementation concept and, therefore, does not allow an abstract reasoning. The

[1] Such as in Eiffel, deferred classes are those which don't provide a full implementation for all services.

concepts of value of an attribute and of extension of an attribute, which are next introduced, allow to forget references and to understand the value of an attribute as an object or as a set of objects. Moreover, they allow to abstract the relationship underlying to an attribute as a mathematical relation. The definitions follow:

Let us consider an attribute $<c_d, att, c_t>$, an object $b \in Ext(c_d)$ and $f_{att}(b)$ the value of the field of b corresponding to *att*. The *value* of *att* for *b*, denoted by $V_{att}(b)$, is defined as follows:

(i) If $f_{att}(b)$ is a void reference then, $V_{att}(b) = \Phi$[1];

(ii) If c_t is not a collection and $f_{att}(b)$ is not a void reference then, $V_{att}(b)$ is a set. Its single element is the object linked to $f_{att}(b)$;

(iii) If c_t is a collection, e. g. c_t has the form $C[X]$, then,

$V_{att}(b) = \{x \in Ext(X) : (v\_att(b), x)=true\}$[2]

where $(v\_att(b), x)$ stands for the value of the evaluation of $att.has(x)$ at the object linked to $f_{att}(b)$.

Let us consider an attribute $<c_d, att, c_t>$. The *extension* of *att*, denoted by $Ext(att)$, is a mathematical relation $Ext(att){:}X*Y$[3], such that:

(i) $X=Ext(c_d)$;

(ii) If c_t is not a collection then, $Y=Ext(c_t)$;

(iii) If c_t is a collection with the form $C[T]$ then, $Y=Ext(T)$;

(iv) $Ext(att) =$

$$\{(x,y) \mid (x \in Ext(c_d)) \wedge (y \in V_{att}(x))\}.$$

The concepts of value and extension of an attribute will allow that various concepts, which transform an attribute from a pointer into a semantic construct, could have a formal definition. Section 4-7 are dedicated to those concepts. Besides simple and well-know concepts, such as those of single-valued and multi-value attribute, the notions of inverse attribute, dependent attribute and category of attribute are introduced. The concept of inverse attribute allows information concerning a relationship to be seen from any one of the participating entities. The concept of dependent attribute allows to model the notion of "attribute of a relationship". SOM considers that each attribute belongs to a given category. Each one of the categories supported in SOM has a semantics that corresponds to a kind of relationship, which very often occurs in the real-world.

4 - Single-Valued, Multi-Valued, Mandatory and Optional Attributes

Concepts dealt with in this section are simple and well-known concepts, which are normally supported by semantic data models. OOADMs that adopt data modeling techniques also feature them. This section simply provides a formal definition for those concepts. Those definitions are based on the concept of extension of an attribute. The definitions follow:

An attribute $<c_d, att, c_t>$ is *single-valued if* during the whole lifetime of the instances of c_d, $Ext(att)$ is always a function. This means that:

$$\forall x \in Ext(c_d) \mid (\exists\, y_1 : (x, y_1) \in Ext(att)) \Rightarrow (\nexists\, y_2 : ((x, y_2) \in Ext(att)) \wedge (y_1 \neq y_2))$$

Otherwise $<c_d, att, c_t>$ is *multi-valued.*

A single-value attribute is simply an attribute which type is not a collection and, therefore, its value is constituted by, at most, a single object. Multi-valued attributes are those which type is a collection. In class `Horse` declared in figures 2.a-2.b, `Run_In` is the only multi-valued attribute. The other attributes are single-valued.

An attribute $<c_d, att, c_t>$ is *mandatory* if during the whole lifetime of the instances of c_d, $Ext(att)$ is always a total mathematical relation on c_d. This means that:

$$\forall x \in Ext(c_d) \mid (\exists\, y : (x, y) \in Ext(att))$$

Otherwise $<c_d, att, c_t>$ is *optional.*

Basically a mandatory attribute is that whose value may not be the empty set. In class `Horse`, `Run_In` and `Name` are optional attributes. The others are mandatory attributes. Readers should observe that to say that an attribute is mandatory is not the same as to require that the value of a field which corresponds to it, may not be a void reference. This would be enough for single-valued

---

[1] Φ stands for the empty set.

[2] In formulas like this one, the symbols '/' and ':' should be read as 'it holds' and 'such that', respectively.

[3] A mathematical relation *rel* between two sets *X* and *Y*, denoted by $rel{:}X*Y$, is a sub-set of the cartesian product X*Y. Thus, each element of *rel* is a tuple (x,y) such that: $x \in X$ and $y \in Y$.

attributes but won't for multi-valued attributes. Methods which do not distinguish between value of a field and value of an attribute would not be able to deal with this issue.

In methods that support the concept of association, the mandatory versus optional issue is dealt by multiplicity constraints. A mandatory attribute corresponds to a multiplicity 1-many or 1-1 and an optional attribute corresponds to a multiplicity 0-any or 0-1. However, multiplicity only applies to associations and not to entity-valued properties. Therefore, such methods are not able to support optional entity-valued properties, such as, for example, the attribute `Name` of `Horse`. SOM does not have that drawback because it deals, in the same way, with entity-valued properties and relationships among classes which model real-world concepts (semantic classes). SOM uses the concept of attribute to model either entity-valued properties or relationships among semantic classes.

5 - Inverse Attributes

Two attributes $<f_d, ftt, f_t>$ and $<g_d, gtt, g_t>$ are said to be *inverse* if during the whole lifetime of the instances of f_d and of the instances of g_d, *Ext(ftt)* and *Ext(gtt)* are always inverse relations. This means that:

$$((x,y) \in Ext(ftt)) \Leftrightarrow ((y,x) \in Ext(gtt))$$

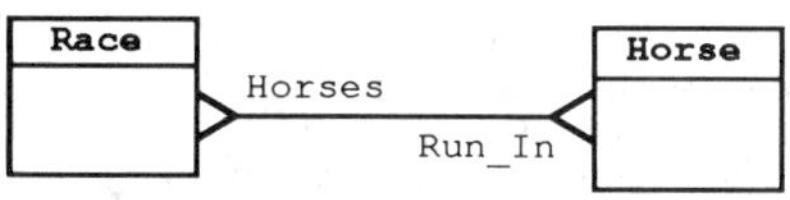

Figure 3.a: Inverse Attributes: G-SOM

```
CLASS Race
  ATTRIBUTES
    Horses OPTIONAL: RELATION LIST[HORSE]
      <-> Run_In; ...
END - - Class Horse
```

Figure 3.b: Inverse Attributes: T-SOM

In figures 3.a-3.b, class `Race` is declared as having an attribute `Horses`. Attribute `Horses` is inverse of the attribute `Run_In` of class `Horse`. In G-SOM, inverse attributes are drawn on the extremes of the same polygonal line. In T-SOM after the type of an attribute we may (optionally) put the symbol '<->' followed by the name of its inverse attribute. Declaring `Horses` and `Run_In` inverse, means that whenever the value of one of them is updated, on some instance of its domain class, the values of the inverse attribute on some instances of the respective domain class, are automatically updated. This is done in order to keep inverse the respective extensions. For example, when the event `Run_In.put(r)` occurs on an instance of `Horse` linked to an attribute `h`, the event `r.Horses.put(h)` will also occur.

In SOM multiplicity and type are independent issues. Indeed, in figure 3.b `Horses` is declared as being a relation whose type is `LIST[HORSE]`. On the other hand, In figure 2.b `Run_In` was declared as being a relation whose type is `SET[RACE]`. As will be explained later, relation is the category of the attributes `Horses` and `Run_In`. The extension of a relation attribute is a many-many mathematical relation.

This approach is not always followed. For instance, [Rumbaugh87] reports an object-oriented programming system called DSM, which support a concept called relation. DSM relations allow to model one-many and many-many relationships. However, DSM users may not choose the data structure used to store the objects. Such data structure is determined by the system implementation (a fully indexed lockup table). While separating the multiplicity issue from the data structure issue, the SOM solution gives more versatility to the software developers. There are not any special reason (even performance) to forbid that relations might be supported by sets, lists or hash tables for instance. Moreover, the semantics of an attribute is also determined by its type where important issues such as the order, for example, may be considered.

However, there are situations in which a software developer needs a collection attribute, but he or she does not care about the data structure used to hold the objects. To correspond to those situations, SOM allows that software developers could specify the multiplicity of a collection attribute and partially omit the type information. In this case, the type is assumed to be a default type used in SOM to support collections. The services available in such type are only the services shared by all collection (`Put`, `Remove`, `Has`, etc.). The data structure actually used depends on the SOM implementation. Thus, in figure 3.b attribute Horses could have been declared in the following way:

```
Horses OPTIONAL:
       RELATION [HORSE]
```

In this case the type of `Horses` would be the SOM default type for collections.

Inverse attributes represent a limited breakdown in the encapsulation of classes. Indeed, for declaring the attribute `gtt` inverse of the attribute `ftt` it is necessary to refer to `gtt` in the text of the domain class of `ftt`. However, SOM demands that `gtt` be exported to the domain class of `ftt`. Inverse attributes can be understood as a window through which it has obtained permission to break the encapsulation.

This is what happens in reality. For instance, a married woman knows that her husband has a Wife attribute and a married man knows that his wife has a Husband attribute. The basic point is that often the knowledge about a relationship is shared by the participating entities. This should not be hidden but, on the contrary, should be stressed in the models.

6 - Dependent Attributes

SOM models all static relationships with attributes. However, relationships also can have attributes [Chen76]. A relationship's attribute is supported in SOM by the notion of dependent attribute. This section illustrates the main features of dependent attribute.

Attributes considered so far are said to be *non-dependent attributes*. As it was defined above, for each one of the non dependent attributes of a given class, corresponds to a field in each one of the objects belonging to the class extension.

A *dependent attribute* is defined, not for the instances of a given domain class, but, for the objects belonging to the value of some multi-valued attribute. Therefore, each one of the instances of a class c_d has one field for each one of the objects belonging to the value of each one of the dependent attributes of c_d. The multi-valued attribute of which a dependent attribute depends, is said to be its *owner attribute*. An owner attribute may itself be a dependent attribute.

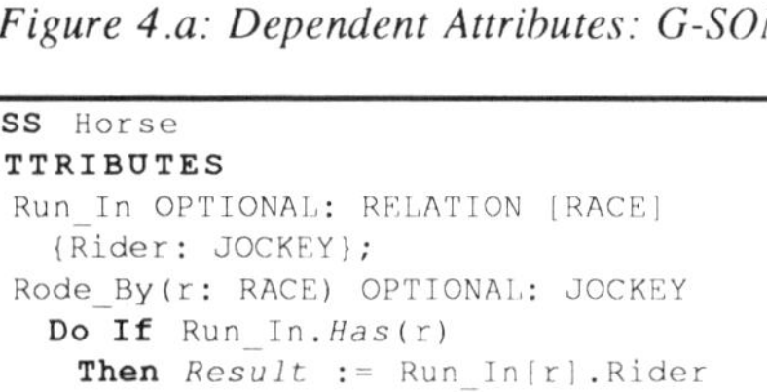

Figure 4.a: Dependent Attributes: G-SOM

```
CLASS Horse
  ATTRIBUTES
    Run_In OPTIONAL: RELATION [RACE]
      {Rider: JOCKEY};
    Rode_By(r: RACE) OPTIONAL: JOCKEY
      Do If Run_In.Has(r)
        Then Result := Run_In[r].Rider
        Else Result := Void; ...
END - - Class Horse
```

Figure 4.b: Dependent Attributes: T-SOM

Figures 4.a-4.b exemplify dependent attributes. They consider that, for each one of the races in which a horse takes part in, it is held information about the jockey who has ridden the horse. Rider is defined as a dependent attribute, which owner attribute is the attribute Run_In. In G-SOM, dependent attributes obey to rules similar to those used for non-dependent attributes. However, instead of being drawn on the borders of the rectangle which corresponds to the domain class, they are drawn on the borders of an anonymous rectangle linked to the polygonal line of the owner attribute through a knot. In T-SOM, dependent attributes are introduced after their owner attributes. Besides, the set of dependent attributes which depend on a given owner attribute is delimited by parentheses. Through the attribute Rider, each one of the instances of Horse holds a set of Jockey references, as many as the number of Race instances that belong to the value of the attribute Run_In.

Figure 4.b also introduces a derived attribute called Rode_By. This attribute gives the jockey who has ridden the target horse in a specific race. That race is given as parameter. This attribute was introduced only to exemplify the notation used to access one of the values which corresponds to a dependent attribute. The difference from non-dependent attribute is that before the common dot notation is applied, a specific value on the extension of the owner attribute (Run_In[r]) must be fixed.

Readers should ask why Rider was defined as a dependent attribute on the attribute Run_In of Horse and was not defined as a dependent attribute on the attribute Horses of Race. Indeed Horses and Run_In are inverse attributes. Actually, SOM provides special syntactical and semantic support for dependent attributes whose owner attributes are inverse. Eventually, those dependent attributes can have the same name. Due to space limitations these features will not be introduced in this paper.

OMT features the concept of link attribute and the concept of qualifier. OMT calls links to the elements (values) of an association. A link attribute is a value attached to each link in an association. A qualifier is a special case of a link attribute that is unique within the links of a given association attached to a single object. The semantics of dependent attributes are almost the same as the semantics of link attributes. As much as we have understood the OMT concepts, the main difference between OMT link attributes and SOM dependent attributes, is the following: OMT supports the concept of link attribute but does not support the concept of link association, in other words, a link attribute whose type is not a basic type but a semantic class. To achieve that in OMT, it would be necessary to convert an association into a class. However, those classes are not exactly equal to "normal" classes. They have implicit object references to the classes in the association. Therefore, to support this in a formal way, a parallel type system would be needed. We can ask, for example, what is the syntax and the semantics of creation events defined on association classes or what are the conformance rules for association classes. Because SOM does not distinguish attributes from associations, SOM does not have to deal with these problems.

7 - Attributes Category

Research on semantic data models brought to information modeling several constructs, which try to abstractly capture the semantics of some patterns of relationship among real-world entities, which very often occur. Models like RM/T [Codd79] feature a very rich set of constructs. One of the advantages of those constructs is the reduction of the semantic overlapping among relationship types [Kent79]. This means that two different patterns of relationship among real-world entities are not modeled through the same concept but, instead, the modeling method provides specific concepts for each of them.

Regarding the way as relationships are dealt with, the approach of association-object models can be considered a retreat, when compared with what semantic data models feature. Indeed, different kinds of relationship are modeled by the same concept, association for example. The differences among them are stated through multiplicity constraints. For instance, in OMT one-one, one-many and many-many relationships, either mandatory as well as optional, are all modeled with the concept of association.

SOM, trying to reach a minimal semantic overlapping among relationship types, such as in the semantic data models, features the notion of category of an attribute. SOM supports several categories of attributes. Each one of them defines a particular combination of the single-valued and the multi-valued issue, the optional and the mandatory issue, the multiplicity issue and the inverse attribute issue. Such combinations correspond to specific patterns of relationship among real-world entities, which very often occur.

This section describes the SOM categories of attributes. The categories of attributes supported in SOM are the following: designator, association, relation, double designator, aggregate and component. Only relation applies to non-binary attributes. Binary relations, which are many-many multi-valued attributes, have already been informal introduced. Hence, this section won't bring up this category. On its hand, non-binary relations will be considered in a later section.

Figure 5.a will be used in order to exemplify the concepts introduced in this section. Figure 5.a extends figure 4.a with additional details. The figure considers that each race is run at a single track and that each track hosts many races in a given day. Class `Race_Day` groups together all the races at a track on a single day. Figure 5.a considers that among the various kind of races, there are the claiming races. After a horse has been registered in a claiming race and before the race run, any registered owner can put in a bid - called a *claim* - to buy the horse at the conclusion of the race. We have also considered that a race can optionally have doping control. With exception of the doping issue the other issues considered in figure 5.a were adopted from the example used in [Rumbaugh92].

7.1 - Designators and Associations

A *designator* is a binary and single-valued attribute, either mandatory or optional. The multiplicity of its extension is many-one during the whole lifetime of the instances of its domain class.

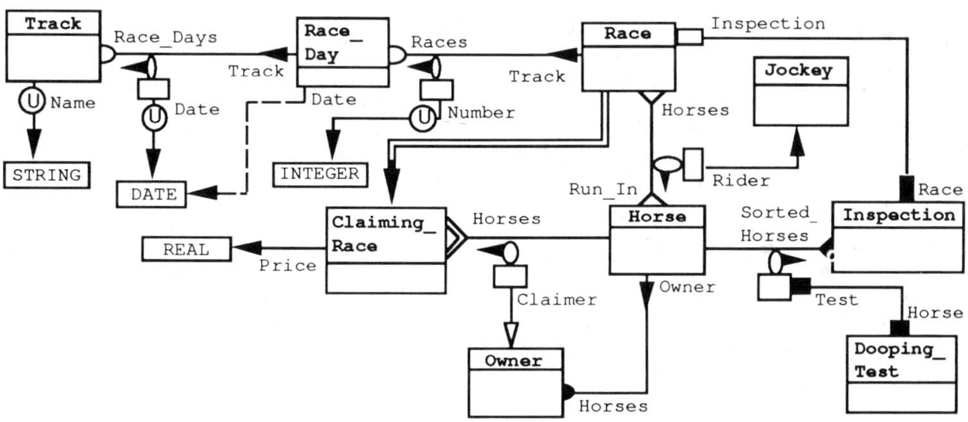

Figure 5.a - Categories of Attributes: G-SOM

Single-valued attributes were defined as being those which extension is a function. As every function respects a many-one multiplicity constraint[1], we can simply say that a designator is a single valued attribute on which no multiplicity constraint is imposed.

An *association* is a binary and multi-valued attribute, $<c_d, att, T[X]>$, either mandatory or optional The multiplicity of its extension is one-many during the whole lifetime of the instances of its domain class. This means that:

$$\forall y \in X \,/\, (\exists\, x_1 \in c_d : (x_1, y) \in Ext(att)) \Rightarrow$$
$$(\nexists\, x_2 \in c_d : ((x_2, y) \in Ext(att)) \wedge (x_1 \neq x_2))$$

```
CLASS Race_Day
  ATTRIBUTES
    Track: TRACK <-> Race_Days;
    Date: DATE
      Do Track.Race_Days[Self].Date End;
    Races OPTIONAL: ASSOCIATION [RACE]
      {Number: INTEGER}; _
    INVARIANTS
      Unique ([Number]) From Races;
      For Each r In Races
        Is Races[r].Number > 0 End; ...
END - - Class Race Day
```

Figure 5.b - Designators and Associations

All the single-valued attributes we have seen so far are designators. Figures 5.a and 5.b includes other examples of designators as well as examples of associations. Figure 5.b is a T-SOM fragment of the class `Race_Day`. In G-SOM designators are depicted by arrows. The arrow is drawn close to the type class, if the attribute does not have inverse; close to the domain class, if the attribute has inverse. The symbol of association is a ellipse drawn close to the domain class. In T-SOM, the category of an attribute is generally indicated anticipating its type by a specific keyword (`Association`, `D_Desg`, `Aggregate`, `Component`, `Relation`). SOM considers that by default single-valued attributes are designators. Thus no keyword exists for designators. The attributes of `Race_Day`, `Track`, `Date` and the dependent attribute `Number`, are designators. `Date` is a derived attribute which gives the date which corresponds to a given race day.

The invariants of figure 5.b exemplify again the notation used to access dependent attributes, already explained in section 6. They also show how the *`Unique`* expression may be applied to the extension of an attribute. In this expression, `Number` is delimited by parentheses because it is a dependent attribute. In figure 2.b it was seen how *`Unique`* is applied to the extension of a class.

For each one of the categories of attributes, SOM states an inverse attribute validity rule and an inverse attribute semantic rule. Those rules apply whenever an inverse attribute has been declared. *Inverse attribute validity rules* restrict the type and the category of the inverse attribute. *Inverse attribute semantic rules* give the statements that occur on the objects which belong to the value of an attribute. This is done in order to keep as inverse relations the extension of the attribute and the extension of its inverse attribute, whenever a statement that can change the attribute extension occurs.

The specific *inverse attribute validity rule* which holds *for designators* is the following.

Let us consider two attributes $<fa, ftt, ft>$ and $<ga, gtt, gt>$, being *ftt* a designator. For *gtt* be inverse of *ftt* it must respect the following assertions:

(i) *gtt* must be an association;

(ii) *ga* must be equal to *ft*;

(iii) *gt* must be equal to *X[fa]*, being *X* a collection type.

We will exemplify inverse attribute semantic rules when aggregates and components are introduced.

7.2 - Double Designators, Aggregates and Components

The three categories introduced in this section impose one-one multiplicity constraints.

A *double designator* is a binary and single-valued attribute, either mandatory or optional. The multiplicity of its extension is one-one during the whole lifetime of the instances of its domain class. The attribute must hold the following constraint: (i) if the attribute is mandatory and an inverse has been declared then, the inverse attribute must be mandatory as well; (ii) if the attribute is optional and an inverse has been declared, the inverse attribute must be optional as well.

An *aggregate* is a binary, single-valued and mandatory attribute. The multiplicity of its extension is one-one during the whole lifetime of the instances of its domain class. The attribute must hold the following constraint: if an inverse attribute has been declared then, such inverse attribute, which is said to be a *component*, must be optional.

Aggregates and components model the part-of semantics. That semantics is featured by the relationship between a race and a doping

[1]The function definition can be understood as being the same as that of many-one multiplicity constraint.

inspection done on it. There is a one-one relationship between a race and an inspection. Moreover, every inspection is obligatorily linked to a race but it is not obligatory that a race has a doping inspection.

```
CLASS Inspection
  ATTRIBUTES
    Race: AGGREGATION RACE <-> Inspection;
    Sorted_Horses: RELATION [HORSE]
      {Test: D_DESG DOPING_TEST}; _
    INVARIANTS
      For Each h In Sorted_Horses
        Is h.Takes_Part_In(Race) End; ...
END - - Class Inspection
```

Figure 5.c - Aggregates and Double Designators: T-SOM

In figure 5.a a doping inspection is modeled by the class `Inspection`. A T-SOM fragment of class `Inspection` is presented in figure 5.c. Class `Inspection` has an aggregate attribute `Race`, which type is the class `Race`. On the other hand, Class `Race` (figure 5.a) has a component attribute `Inspection`, which type is the class `Inspection`. The attributes `Race` and `Inspection` are inverse. In G-SOM, aggregates and components share the same symbol, a lengthened rectangle. The symbol is drawn filled for aggregates and not filled for components. Besides `Race`, class `Inspection` has other two attributes, namely `Sorted_Horses` and `Test`. `Test` is a dependent attribute. For each horse that was sorted to be checked in a given race, `Test` gives the respective doping test. `Test` is a mandatory double designator. Indeed, every sorted horse must do a doping test and every test must has been done by a sorted horse. Besides, there is a one-one relationship between the sorted horses and the doping tests[1]. The invariant of class `Inspection` (figure 5.c) imposes that every horse sorted to be checked must takes part in the race which the inspection says respect.

Readers could think that, since either double designator as well as aggregates and components model one-one relationships a single concept should be enough. The big difference among those categories is in the inverse attribute semantic rule. When an inverse attribute has been declared the effect of a destruction event, for instance, is not the same in all the three cases. When an object that has a double designator attribute is deleted, the object that is the value of that attribute is deleted as well. For aggregates and components the rule is a little different.

The *inverse attribute semantic rule for aggregates and components* is the following:

Let us consider two attributes *<fa, ftt, ft>* and *<ga, gtt, gt>*, being *ftt* an aggregate or a component and, therefore, *gtt* a component or an aggregate, respectively. Be de_{fa} a destruction event of *fa* and de_{ga} the anonymous destruction event of *ga*[2]. Be exp_{ft} an expression whose type conforms with *ft*. Let us denote by *(i, [I])*, the assertion that states that whenever the statement *i* occurs it has the effect of the sequence of statements *I*. Then, the following assertion hold:

(i) *(ftt := exp_{ft} ,*
[ftt.gtt := Void; ftt := exp_{ft} ;
***If** ftt /= Void **Then** ftt.gtt := Current]);*

(ii) *If ftt is an aggregate then,*
(de_{fa}, [ftt.gtt := Void; de_{fa}]);

(iii) *If ftt is a component then,*
*(de_{fa}, [**If** ftt /= Void **Then** ftt.de_{ga};*
de_{fa}]).

The second and the third assertions basically say that when an aggregate is deleted the inverse component is set to void. On the other hand, when a component is deleted the inverse aggregate is deleted as well.

An important characteristic of SOM attributes is its formal definition. This allows to achieve a well-defined integration with the dynamic model. The definitions of SOM categories of attributes include static or structural issues, as for example the multiplicity. However, it is also specified what dynamic effects are implied by those structural issues. This is not featured by the well-known OOADM nowadays available (neither they claim to feature a formal definition). For example, methods such as those from Booch, Coad and Yourdon, Martin and Odell and Rumbaugh, for example, all feature concepts equivalent to aggregates and inverse attributes, eventually with different names. However, as far as we have realized, neither of them specify something like an inverse attribute semantic rule for aggregates. The consequences of such situation are obvious. Basically, software developers would have to state pieces of the semantics of some constructs in an ad hoc way.

---

[1] Actually, as `Test` is a dependent attribute, the one-one relationship is not between all doping tests whenever done and all horses that have ever done a doping test. The one-one relationship is only between all doping tests done in a given race and all horses that have done a doping test in that race.

[2] SOM considers that every class has a pre-defined anonymous destruction event. Obviously, this event can not be called by user defined classes. Its effect consists on the simple destruction of the target instance.

7.3 - Why Those?

It would be a good question to ask why SOM features those categories of attributes that were described and not others with a different semantics. Of course, we can not provide a scientific answer for this question. What we can say is that in the experimental systems we have developed with SOM, we have found evidences showing that those categories are highly orthogonal as well as complete. By orthogonal we mean that their semantics does not overlap. By complete we mean they are virtually able to model, in an acceptable way from the abstraction point of view, all kinds of relationship we have found in data modeling problems. However, our experience seems to show that the extension of the semantics of certain categories in order to make them able to model non-binary cases would be useful.

8 - Relationships Specialization

SOM features a specialization mechanism based on the concept of *phase*. Phases are intended for modeling roles in a semantically meaningful way. SOM considers that roles can be assumed and discarded in a dynamic way. In this section we only want to exemplify how the specialization of relationships is understood in SOM.

In figure 5.a `Claiming_Race` is considered a specialization of `Race` or, in the SOM terminology, a phase of `Race`. For every horse that takes part in a race, class `Race` holds the information of the horse's jockey, through the dependent attribute `Rider`. For claiming races, besides the jockey, it is necessary to know the claim that was put in, if any. In SOM, this is supported by the rewriting of the attribute `Horses` of `Race` in phase `Claiming_Race`. In this particular case, the rewriting consists on the extension of one additional dependent attribute. This is the meaning of the double trace used in the symbol (triangle) of the attribute `Horses` in phase `Claiming_Race`.

We basically want to show that, in SOM, the specialization of relationships is supported by rewriting facilities. Therefore, the specialization of relationships does not introduce a particularly new issue. All the available knowledge about services rewriting and classes conformance rules [Cook89] applies to the specialization of relationships as well. However, methods that deal with this issue through the transformation of the relationships into classes, which afterwards are specialized, can not fully apply this knowledge because relationship classes are not equal to "normal" classes.

9 - Non-Binary Relations

Relation is the only category of attribute that may be non-binary. In the current stage of our work we have taken this decision because the majority of the non-binary attributes have the relation semantics. Besides, we have gotten problems in specifying precisely the semantics of non-binary attributes of the other categories. Supporting non binary attributes of any category would make SOM much more complex. This section lightly explains and exemplifies the semantics of non-binary relations.

Suppose we want to model stakes. This could be done by a ternary relation among a gamble, a horse and a race. Indeed, we could introduce in class `Gamble` an attribute `Stakes`, which would be a ternary relation with classes `Horse` and `Race`. `Horse` and `Race` are said to be the *argument classes* of the relation. A dependent attribute `Fee`, would hold the stake fee. Figure 6 includes a G-SOM representation of class Gamble. Due to simplification reasons, inverse attributes were not considered.

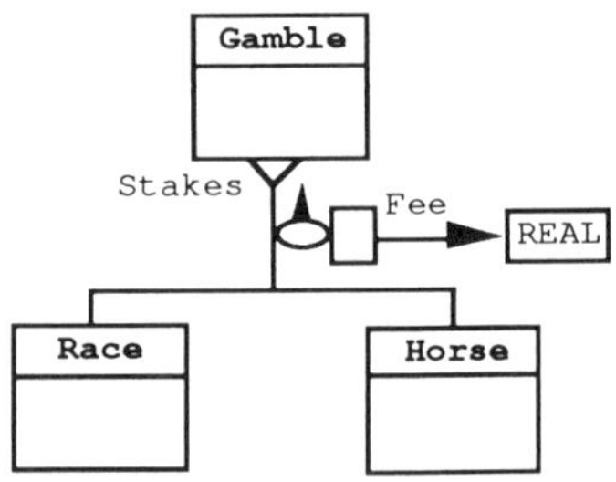

Figure 6 - Non-binary attributes: G-SOM

SOM considers that for each non-binary attribute there is automatically defined a class, which is said to be a *relation class*. Such class has a set of designators, called *argument designators*, as many as the argument classes of the relation. Each argument designator has as type the corresponding argument class. A unique constraint and a constant constraint are defined on the set of all argument designators. The type of a non-binary relation is a collection and the type of the elements of that collection is the respective relation class.

Thus, For each one of the instances of `Gamble` the value of the attribute `Stakes` would be constituted by a collection of unique and immutable pairs of objects, one of type `Race` and the other of type `Horse`. SOM provides special syntactical support to deal with non-binary attribute, namely to include new elements in their value in an easy way.

The semantics of SOM non-binary relations is very close of the semantics of Martin and Odell relations. However, in SOM the relation is the attribute, which value is a set of relation class instances. In the Martin and Odell method, the relation is the relation class extension.

10 - Conclusions

During the previous sections it was shown how the concept of attribute can be semantically enriched, in such a way that it becomes as expressive as the concept of association without, however, having the drawbacks of association. The ideas in this paper are refinements of well-known concepts. The contribution of the work is that these ideas have been integrated in a novel way. Let us sums up the main strengths of attribute and of association.

The main strengths of attribute are the following: Conformance with the OO principles, namely encapsulation and abstraction; full preservation of the OO advantages, namely extendibility and reusability; minimal semantic overlapping among types of relationships; formal definition; good support for a seamless development process; well-defined integration with the dynamic model.

On its hand, the main strengths of association are the following: good support for the beginning of domain analysis due to simplicity and informality; language independence; similarity with extended Entity-Relationship models.

We have already commented on the weaknesses of association. Let we now comment on the weaknesses of attribute.

The main point against attribute could be that, from a given point of view, attribute includes too much semantics and formality and, therefore, would not be suitable for the beginning of domain analysis. Addicts of associations could say that when software developers are trying to discover what are the main concepts of the problem domain, it could be enough to say, for example, that there is an association between classes a and b. At this stage, the majority of semantics included in the attribute concept, would be unnecessary. Hence, it is possible to consider that attribute is not suitable for the beginning of analysis. Attribute would be more suitable for detailed analysis, design and implementation.

With exception of the type information, attribute does not include more semantics than association. The point is that the notions related with attribute feature a formal definition while the notions related with association does not. We would say that the 'excess of semantics' point can also be applied to association itself. At a given moment even the multiplicity issue can be superfluous.

We think the answer for this issue can be tool support, which would allow to increment detail in a coherent way. For example, it should be possible, to start saying that an attribute is multi-valued, afterwards to say that its multiplicity is one-may and, in another time, to say that the attribute is of type List. We have been building a development environment for SOM with that philosophy. This environment includes a compiler, which transforms SOM specification in C++ classes that are supported by an object-oriented database. ONTOS [Ontologic92] has been presently used.

An other point against attribute could be the fact that, association, such as it is supported in OMT for example, is a language independent construct. During the detailed design and the implementation phases, association can be syntactically and semantically transformed into constructs of a specific programming language. On its turn, attribute is embedded in the SOM languages. Therefore, if a C++ user, for example, would want to use the SOM concept of attribute he or she would have to learn a new language.

This could be true for T-SOM but wouldn't be for G-SOM. In the present stage SOM is not a production-quality method. Therefore, we have been developing the SOM concepts using a syntax that is close to the syntax of a specific OOPL, in the case Eiffel. However, it is perfectly possible to image the SOM concepts smoothly embedded, from the syntactical point of view, in a different programming language. Hence, instead of T-SOM, we can image a C++-SOM version or a Smalltalk-SOM version.

Graphical notation also deserves a comment. The OMT graphical notation for associations adopts one of the many dialects that have been used for extended Entity-Relationship (ER) models. The SOM notation can be considered a break with that style. In the ER dialects, in an association between classes a and b, the multiplicity constraints on the a instances are drawn close to the b symbol. SOM introduces a graphical symbol for each one of the attribute categories. However, this symbol is drawn close to the attribute's domain class. We think the SOM style is more object-oriented because what concerns with a given class is drawn close to that class. However, we recognize that the style of SOM can be a problem for those who have been using ER dialects for a long time.

As we have already said an ideal method would have to capitalize on the advantages of both concepts (association, attribute). We will dedicate more attention to this aspect in the future.

References

Booch, G (1991), *Object Oriented Design with Applications*, Addison Wesley.

Booch, G (1993), *Object Oriented Analysis and Design with Applications*, Addison Wesley.

Cardelli, L (1984), A Semantics of Multiple Inheritance, Semantics of Data Types, *LNCS 173*, Spring-Verlag, pp. 51-68.

Chen, P (1976), The Entity-Relationship Model: Towards an Unified View od Data, *ACM TODS*, 1:1, pp. 9-36.

Coad, P & Yourdon, E, (1991) *Object Oriented Analysis*, (2nd Edition), Yourdon Press, Englewood Cliffs, N.J.

Codd, E (1979), Extending the Database Relational Model to Capture More Meaning, *ACM Trans. on Database Systems*, Vol. 4, Nº 4, Dece., pp. 397-434.

Cook, W (1989), A Proposal for Making Eiffel Type-safe, *Proc. ECOOP'89*, Nottingham, England, July 10-14, Cambridge University Press, pp. 57-70.

Fowler, M (1992), *A Comparison of Object-Oriented Analysis and Design Methods*, Tutorial Notes, OOPSLA-92 Conference on Object-Oriented Programming Systems, Languages, and Applications, Vancouver, British Columbia, Canada.

Hull, R & King, R (1987), Semantic Database Modeling: Survey, Applications, and Research Issues, *ACM Computing Surveys*, Vol. 19, Nº 3, pp. 201-260.

Kent, W (1979), Limitations of Record-based Information Models, *ACM Transactions on Database Systems*, Vol. 4, Nº 1, pp. 107-131.

Martin J & Odell J (1992), *Object Oriented Analysis and Design*, Prentice Hall, Englewood Cliffs, N.J.

Meyer, B (1987), Reusability: The Case for Object-Oriented Design, *IEEE Software*, Vol. 4, Nº 2, pp. 50-64.

Meyer, B (1988), *Object-oriented Software Construction*, Prentice-Hall Internacional.

Meyer, B (1991), Design by Contract, *Advances in Object-Oriented Software Engineering*, Mandrioli, D & Meyer, B, Prentice Hall, Englewood Cliffs, N.J, pp. 1-50.

Meyer, B (1992), *Eiffel The Language*, Prentice Hall, Object-Oriented Series.

Nerson, J.-N. (1992), Applying Object-Oriented Analysis and Design, In: *Communication of ACM*, Vol. 35, Nº 9, September 1992.

Peckham, J & Maryanski, F (1988), Semantic Data Models, *ACM Computing Surveys*, Vol. 20, Nº 3, pp. 153-189.

Ontologic (1992), *ONTOS Reference Manual*, ONTOS Inc.

Rumbaugh, J (1987), Relations as Semantic Constructs in an Object-Oriented Language, *Proceedings of the Conference On Object-Oriented Programming Systems, Languages and Applications-87*, SIGPLAN NOTICES, Vol. 22, Nº 12, pp. 466, 481.

Rumbaugh, J, Blaha, M, Permerlani, W, Eddy, F & Lorensen, W (1991), *Object-Oriented Modelling and Design*, Prentice-Hall.

Rumbaugh, J (1992), Horsing around with associations, *Journal of Object-Oriented Programming*, Modeling & Design, February, pp. 49-53.

Sernadas , A & Ehrich, H.-D, What is an Object After All (1991), in Meersman, R, Kent, W & Khosla, S, *Object Oriented Databases: Analysis, Design and Construction (DS-4)*, North-Holland.

Shlaer, S & Mellor, S (1988), *Object Oriented System Analysis: Modeling the World in Data*, Yourdon Press, Englewood Cliffs, N.J.

Stein, L, Lieberman, H & Ungar, D (1989), A Shared View of Sharing: The Treaty of Orlando, in Kim, W & Lochovsky, F, *Object-Oriented Concepts, Databases, and Applications*, Addisom-Wesley, pp. 31-48.

Velho, A, (1992), *Attributes in SOM*, (in Portuguese) INESC Technical Report.

Velho, A & Carapuça, R (1993) From Enity-Relationship Models to Role-Attribute Models, *Proceedings of the 12ª International Conference on Entity-Relationship Approach*, Arlington, Dallas, USA, December, 1993, E/R Institute, pp. 253-264.

Wegner, P (1990), Concepts and Paradigms of Object-Oriented Programming, *ACM SIGPLAN, OOPS Messenger*, Vol. 1, Nº 1.

REAL TIME AND DATABASES

Index Configurations in Object-Oriented Databases*

Sunil Choenni[1,3] Elisa Bertino[2] Henk M. Blanken[1] Thiel Chang[3]

[1]University of Twente
P.O.B. 217, 7500 AE Enschede,
The Netherlands

[2]University of Milan
Via Comelico 39-41, 20135 Milan,
Italy

[3]G.A.K.
P.O.B. 8300, 1005 CA Amsterdam,
The Netherlands

Abstract

An operation in object-oriented databases gives rise to the processing of a path. An index configuration aims to accelerate the processing of such a path. This may be achieved by splitting a path into subpaths and allocating the most beneficial index to each subpath. We address the following problem: 'given an object-oriented logical schema, a workload defined on the schema and some other database characteristics (such as the page size, etc.), determine the optimal set of index configurations; this is the one with the lowest costs in processing the workload'. The idea of our approach is to determine a number of *non-overlapping* paths, since several operations will lead to several paths, and to select the optimal index configuration for each path.

1 Introduction

Object-oriented data models are based on the following fundamental concepts. A real world entity is represented by an object. Each object is uniquely identified by an object identifier (*oid*) which is supposed to be generated by the database system. An object has associated a state and a behaviour. The state of the object is defined by the value of its attributes. The value of an attribute can be either an atomic object, such as an integer, a string, etc., or a non-atomic object; a non-atomic object in turn consists of a set of attributes. Therefore, objects can be built in terms of other objects giving rise to nested objects. The behaviour of an object is specified by a set of methods which operate on the object state.

Objects with the same attributes and behaviour are grouped in classes. The set of attributes in the class define the object structure. Each attribute has a value which falls in a pre-defined domain. The domain can be either an atomic class or a non-atomic class. In this way a relation between two classes C and C', in which C' is the domain of an attribute of class C, can be established which is called a part-of relationship between the two classes. Since the class C' has on his turn part-of relationships with the classes of its attributes and so on, the definition of a class C results into a tree with C as root. This is called an aggregation hierarchy. The attributes of class C' in the aggregation hierarchy will be called *nested* attributes of C. An example of an aggregation hierarchy is given in Figure 1. Multi-valued attributes are marked by '+'. Table 1 introduces some abbreviations which will be used in the rest of the paper.

Classes can be ordered in inheritance hierarchies. The inheritance hierarchy gives the possibility to define a class, called subclass, as a specialization of another existing class, called superclass. A subclass inherits the attributes and methods of its superclass and may have additional attributes and methods. In Figure 1 the classes Vehicle, Truck and Bus form an inheritance hierarchy.

*This research has been partially supported by the Dutch Organization for Scientific Research (NWO) while the first author was visiting the University of Genova for three months.

From TOOLS EUROPE '94 (Technology of Object-Oriented Languages and Systems).

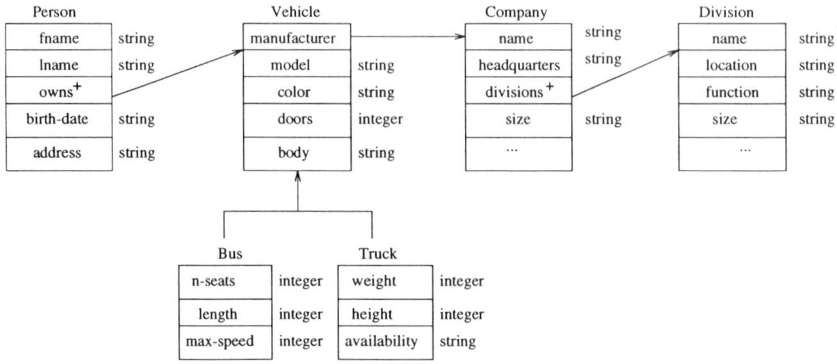

Figure 1: Example of an object-oriented logical schema

Per	=	*Person*	*Veh*	=	*Vehicle*
Div	=	*Division*	*Comp*	=	*Company*
man	=	*manufacturer*	*divs*	=	*divisions*

Table 1: Used abbreviations

To be viable, not only the concepts have to be supported by an architecture that directly implements them but querying and maintaining the database should require an acceptable amount of time. This may be established by two techniques which differ fundamentally. One way is to place the objects efficiently on disks such that fetching the objects requires a minimal number of page accesses. Clustering objects belonging to different classes and storing them on the same page is a topic belonging to this field [Tsangaris 92].

Another technique to accelerate database operations is by constructing efficient access structures on a database given a certain physical implementation of the database. The allocation of indices on attributes belongs to this field. In this paper we study how to utilize this technique under certain assumptions. We assume that a page contains objects of only one class and only forward references between objects exists. Super- and subclasses of an inheritance hierarchy are stored in separate tables. Furthermore, we assume that attributes do not have NULL values. Figure 2 contains some instances of Figure 1.

A database operation in an object-oriented data model against a nested predicate leads to the processing of a path. Consider a database operation against the aggregation hierarchy of Figure 1: 'Retrieve the persons who own a bus manufactured by the company Fiat'. To process this query we have to walk through the classes *Per*, *Bus* and *Comp*, resulting in the path *Per.owns.man.namec*. Evaluating this path in a naive way by taking an object of the class *Per*, checking which vehicle he owns and in the case he owns a bus checking if this is manufactured by the Fiat company may be very expensive. Therefore, several indexing techniques [Bertino 90, Bertino 92c, Bertino 92d, Kemper 90, Kim 89, Maier 86, Valduriez 87] and caching techniques [Kato 92] have been proposed to accelerate the processing of such paths.

In this paper we address the following problem: 'given an object-oriented logical schema, a number of database operations on the schema (workload) and some other database characteristics (such as the number of objects in each class, page size, etc.) determine the optimal set of index configurations; this is the one with the lowest costs in processing the workload'. To tackle the problem we determine a number of *non-overlapping* paths. Operations which lead to paths which overlap each other will be unified to a single path. Then each path P will be split into a proper set of subpaths and on each of the subpaths the most beneficial index will be allocated. The set of indexed subpaths will be called an *index configuration* of P.

For the moment we consider a limited number of indexing techniques: simple index, inherited index, nested inherited-index, multi-index, and multi-inherited index and the possibility of not indexing a (sub)path. We note, however, that the principles of the approach will remain the same adding more indexing techniques.

Comparable research has been reported in

[Kemper 90, Bertino 92a, Choenni 94a] which differs from this work on the following important points. In [Kemper 90] an indexing technique, called access support relation, is proposed. Then the authors suggest that a path may be split into several subpaths and different access support relations may be allocated to each subpath, which is similar to the notion of index configuration (except that in their work they propose a single indexing technique while we consider several indexing techniques). However, no algorithm is proposed in [Kemper 90] for determining the splitting of the path.

The remaining two papers address the problem with regard to operations leading to the same path. As a consequence predicates could be evaluated only against the last attribute of a path. Furthermore, the case of not indexing a subpath has not been taken into account in [Choenni 94a].

The indexing techniques chosen in this paper deal with inheritance as well as with nested objects while the techniques in [Bertino 92a] deal only with nested objects.

The remainder of this paper is organized as follows: Section 2 summarizes the main principles of the indexing techniques considered in the paper and how they can be used in processing database operations. Section 3 is devoted to the workload model. Section 4 is devoted to the notion of index configuration and the basics to develop an algorithm for the selection of optimal index configurations. In Section 5 the algorithm is presented. Section 6 concludes the paper.

2 Indexing techniques

To make the paper self-contained we briefly discuss the main principles of the indexing techniques which we consider. These are the simple index, multi-index, inherited index, multi-inherited index and nested inherited index. Before starting this discussion we recall some preliminary definitions in the next section adopted from [Bertino 89, Kim 89].

2.1 Preliminary definitions

A database operation gives rise to the processing of a path of the form $P_{1,n} = C_1.A_1.A_2.....A_n$. The following gives a formal definition of a path.

Definition 2.1 Given an aggregation hierarchy H, a path $P_{1,n} = C_1.A_1.A_2.....A_n$ in which

- Class C_l appears at most once in the path
- C_1 is a class in H
- A_1 is an attribute of C_1
- A_l is an attribute of C_l in H, such that C_l is the domain of attribute A_{l-1} of class C_{l-1}, $1 < l \leq n$. □

Some notions related to definition 2.1 follow. The length of a path $P_{1,n}$ is equal to the number of classes along the path. The classes along a path are denoted collectively by $class(P_{1,n})$. The scope of a path $P_{1,n}$ consists of all the classes in $class(P_{1,n})$ and their subclasses and is denoted by $scope(P_{1,n})$. A subclass z of a class C_l is denoted as $C_{l,z}$. Note, the second subscript does not imply an order of the subclasses. It is only meant to distinguish the classes by labeling them. In the case a class does not have an inheritance hierarchy or when it is clear that we mean the root class at the highest level we omit the second subscript. The set of subclasses in an inheritance hierarchy rooted at class $C_{l,z}$ together with the root class is denoted as $C^*_{l,z}$. Furthermore the attribute A_n is called the *ending attribute* and C_1 is called the *starting class*.

Example 2.1 Consider the path $P_{Per,namec} = Per.owns.man.namec$ in the aggregation hierarchy of Figure 1. It is clear the classes involved with path $P_{Per,namec}$ are Per, Veh and $Comp$. Therefore, $class(P_{Per,namec}) = (Per, Veh, Comp)$. Since Vehicle has two subclasses Bus and Truck and the other classes in $class(P_{Per,namec})$ do not have subclasses $scope(P_{Per,namec}) = (Per, Veh, Bus, Truck, Comp)$. □

2.2 Index organizations

We discuss the main principles of the index organizations considered in this paper. The indices are supposed to be organized as B^+-trees and the leaf nodes are chained. The non-leaf node records contain pairs (attribute value, pointer). The pointer contains the physical address of the next-level index node. The leaf nodes contain the index records. The information stored in an index record differs per indexing technique as will

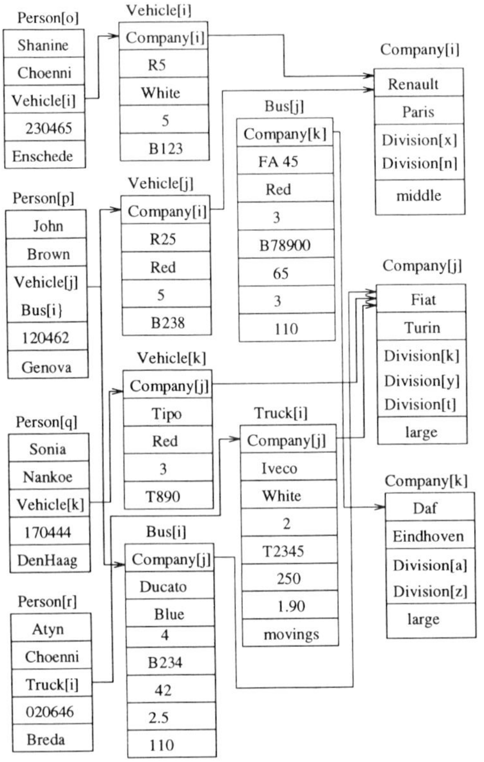

Figure 2: Some objects belonging to schema 1.

be shown.

Simple index (SIX) A simple index is an index on an attribute of a single class. With each value v of the indexed attribute the *oids* of the objects are associated which have v as value for the indexed attribute. Considering Figure 2, an index on the attribute *color* of the class *Veh* results into the pairs (White, {Vehicle[i]}) and (Red, {Vehicle[j]), Vehicle[k]}). Note, Vehicle[i], Vehicle[j] and Vehicle[k] are *oids*.

Inherited index (IIX) An inherited index is an index on an attribute of all classes in a class inheritance-hierarchy rooted at a particular class. This organization is also known as class hierarchy index [Kim 89]. Allocating an IIX on the attribute *color* of the class *Veh* considering Figure 2 again results into the pairs (White, {Vehicle[i]}, {Truck[i]}), (Red, {Vehicle[j], Vehicle[k]}, {Bus[j]}) and (Blue, {Bus[i]}).

Multi-index (MX) A multi-index allocates an index on each class in the scope of a path. The indexed attributes are the ones specified in the path. Suppose we have a path $P_{1,n} = C_1.A_1.A_2.....A_n$ and a class $C_l \in scope(P_{1,n})$ such that A_l is an attribute of C_l, then an index on A_l associates with each value v of A_l the *oids* of the objects of C_l having v as value for attribute A_l. Considering the path $P_{Per,namec} = Per.owns.man.namec$ and the figures 1 and 2 an index on this path results into an index on *namec* of the class *Comp*, an index on *man* of the classes *Veh*, *Bus* and *Truck* and an index on the attribute *owns* of the class *Per*. Thus, we achieve the following pairs for the index on *namec* (Fiat, {Company[j]}), (Renault, {Company[i]}) and (Daf, {Company[k]}). An index on the attribute *man* of the classes *Veh*, *Bus* and *Truck* results into entries into three indexes, namely (Company[i], {Vehicle[i], Vehicle[j]}) and (Company[j], {Vehicle[k]}) respectively (Company[j], {Bus[i]}) and (Company[k], {Bus[j]}) respectively (Company[j], {Truck[i]}. Finally an index on the attribute *owns* of the class *Per* looks as follows (Vehicle[i], {Person[o]}), (Vehicle[j], {Person[p]}), (Vehicle[k], {Person[q]}), (Truck[i], {Person[r]}) and (Bus[i], {Person[p]}).

Multi-inherited index (MIX) An MIX organization may be regarded as a combination of the last two index organizations. A multi-inherited index differs from a multi-index in the sense that a multi-inherited index allocates an index on all classes $\in class(P_{1,n})$ while the multi-index allocates an index on all classes $\in scope(P_{1,n})$. Furthermore, if a class $C_l \in class(P_{1,n})$ forms an inheritance hierarchy then an index on attribute A_l associates with each value v of A_l the *oids* of the objects of C_l and of its subclasses which have v as value for A_l (implying an inherited index). Considering $P_{Per,namec} = Per.owns.man.namec$ and the figures 1 and 2 again a multi-inherited index on the path results into an index on *namec* of the class *Comp*, (Fiat, {Company[j]}), (Renault, {Company[i]}) and (Daf, {Company[k]}), an index on *man* of the class *Veh* and its subclasses, (Company[i], {Vehicle[i], Vehicle [j]}), (Company[j], {Vehicle[k]}, {Bus[i]}, {Truck[i]})

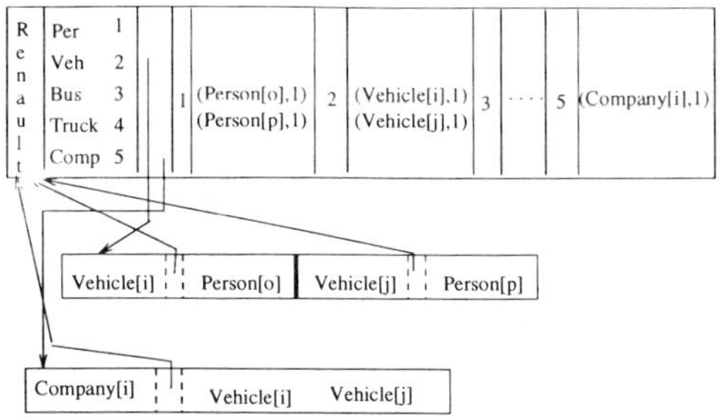

Figure 3: Example of a nested inherited index on the path *Per.owns.man.namec*

and (Company[k], {Bus[j]}) and an index on the attribute *owns* of the class *Per*, (Vehicle[i], {Person[o]}), (Vehicle[j], {Person[p]}), (Vehicle[k], {Person[q]}), (Truck[i], {Person[r]}) and (Bus[i], {Person[p]}).

Nested inherited-index (NIX) In this organization two kinds of indices can be distinguished, a primary and an auxiliary index. The primary index associates with each value v of the ending attribute A_n of a path $P_{1,n}$ all the objects of the classes in the scope of $P_{1,n}$ possessing this value. Therefore, the primary index is inverted with respect to the values of A_n and is used for queries. Logically a NIX on $P_{Per,namec}$ contains the following entries: (Fiat, {Company[j]}, {Vehicle[k]}, {Bus[i]}, {Truck[i]}, {Person[p], Person[q], Person[r]}), (Renault, {Company[i]}, {Vehicle[i], Vehicle[j]}, {Person[o], Person[p]}) and (Daf, {Company[k]}, {Bus[j]})

The auxiliary index associates with the *oid* of an object $O_{l,z}$ the list of *oids* of the (aggregation) parents of $O_{l,z}$. An auxiliary index aims to accelerate the maintenance of the primary index. Furthermore, it may accelerate the processing of some queries [Choenni 94b]. An example of a NIX index record on the path $P_{Per,namec}$ with regard to the key value Renault is given in Figure 3. The first field contains a value (Renault) of the indexed attribute *namec* (called key value). In the second field all the classes of the scope of $P_{Per,namec}$ are listed and the addresses of the classes in the primary index record. When an index record occupies more than one page this can be useful.

If an attribute A_l, such as *owns*, is a multi-valued attribute the objects of the classes rooted at $C_{l,1}$ which hold the key value for the ending attribute A_n are stored as pairs (*oid*, numchild) in which *oid* identifies the object and numchild is the number of children which holds the key value for the nested attribute. If A_l is a single valued attribute it is sufficient to store the *oid* of the object which holds the key value for A_n since the value of numchild will be one. The value of numchild is used to determine whether an object should be deleted from the primary index or not. If the value of numchild becomes zero the object should be deleted.

Each class, except the first class and its subclasses (since they do not have parents), is connected with an auxiliary index record by the third field of the primary index record. An auxiliary index record consists of a sequence of 3-tuples. For an object $O_{l,z}$ the 3-tuple contains the *oid* of the object in the first field. The second field connects the auxiliary record with the primary index records. The last field is a list of *oids* of the parents of $O_{l,z}$ in the aggregation hierarchy. Note, for a class $C_{l,z}$ there are as many 3-tuples as the number of objects in the class.

For a more detailed description concerning the organization we refer to [Bertino 92c].

2.3 Database operations

We illustrate how the several indexing techniques can be used in processing retrievals, insertions and deletions. For ease of presentation, we use examples to describe the operations. Formal algorithms and mathematical cost models for these operations can be found in [Bertino 92c, Choenni 94a, Choenni 94b]. Since a SIX and an IIX are special cases of an MX respectively an MIX we will not consider them in further discussion explicitly.

Retrievals Suppose we have the query 'retrieve the persons who own a vehicle manufactured by Renault'. This implies that the path $P_{Per,namec} = Per.owns.man.namec$ should be processed. If an MX is allocated to the path then the following index look ups are required to solve the query. First, we access the index on *namec* with key value Renault resulting into Company[i]. Then we access the index on *man* for the classes *Veh*, *Bus* and *Truck* with key value Company[i]. This results into the *oids* Vehicle[i] and Vehicle[j] since there are no index records for *man* for the classes *Bus* and *Truck* with key value Company[i]. Finally, the index on *owns* corresponding to class *Per* with values Vehicle[i] and Vehicle[j] is accessed resulting into Person[o] and Person[p]. So, to solve the query using an MX 5 index look ups are required.

Processing the query assuming that an MIX is allocated to $P_{Per,namec}$ is quite similar with the situation that an MX is allocated. The difference is that an IIX is allocated to the attribute *man*. This means that we can retrieve in one index look up the vehicles, busses and trucks which are manufactured by Company[i]. So, to solve the query we require 3 index look ups.

It should be clear that solving the query when a NIX is allocated to the path requires 1 index look up. We have to retrieve the primary record with key value Renault.

Deletions Consider the operation 'delete Vehicle[i]' and the path $P_{Per,namec}$. Suppose that an MX is allocated to $P_{Per,namec}$. The deletion of Vehicle[i] means that the MX should be updated. The following actions should be performed. The index on *man* for the class *Veh* with key value Company[i], which is determined from the object Vehicle[i], should be accessed. Vehicle[i] has to be deleted from this index record. Then the index record corresponding to the index on *owns* for class *Per* with key Vehicle[i] has to be discarded. Since the class *Per* does not have subclasses the index update has been completed. Note, if *Per* would have had subclasses then the records corresponding to the index on *owns* for these subclasses with key value Vehicle[i] should be discarded as well.

In the case an MIX is allocated to $P_{Per,namec}$ a similar reasoning holds.

In the case a NIX is allocated to $P_{Per,namec}$ the overall effect of the delete operation on the index should be that Vehicle[i] and all objects referencing Vehicle[i] (this is Person[o]) should be discarded from the primary record with key value Renault. Moreover, the 3-tuples for Vehicle[i] and Person[o] should be discarded as well. Finally, Vehicle[i] should be discarded as parent of Company[i] from its 3-tuple.

Therefore, the following actions are involved in updating the NIX due to the deletion of Vehicle[i]. First the value of *man* for Vehicle[i] is determined, which is Company[i]. Then the auxiliary index with key value Company[i] is accessed; the 3-tuple of Company[i] is modified by deleting Vehicle[i] and the pointer to the primary record is determined (in this case the one with key value Renault). In the primary record the address of the class *Veh* is determined to delete Vehicle[i] from the lists of *oids* and the pointer to the auxiliary record for class *Veh*. The auxiliary record for class *Veh* is accessed and the 3-tuple of Vehicle[i] is retrieved. The *oids* of the Vehicle[i] parents are determined. In this case this is Person[o]. Then the 3-tuple of Vehicle[i] is removed. In the primary record we determine where the *oids* of the class *Per* are stored. Then we delete Person[o].

Insertions Assuming that an MX is allocated to $P_{Per,namec}$ let us study the effect of inserting Vehicle[i] referencing to Company[i] on the index. To keep the index on *man* for the class *Veh* up to date we should retrieve the index record with key value Company[i] and Vehicle[i] should be added to the record. Note, if an MIX is allocated to the path the same action should be performed.

Suppose that a NIX is allocated to the path. The effect of the insertion is that Vehicle[i] should be added to the primary record with key value Renault, and to the parent list of Company[i]. Therefore, the following actions are performed. The auxiliary index record is accessed with key value Company[i], Vehicle[i] is added to the 3-tuple as parent and the pointer to the primary record is determined. Then, in the primary record the address of the class *Veh* is determined and Vehicle[i] is added to the list of *oids*.

3 Workload model

Each operation implies the processing of a path. The operations of a workload will lead to different paths. These paths may overlap each other totally or partially. In the case paths are overlapping each others they will be unified to a single path.

Let $(\alpha_{l,z}, \beta_{l,z}, \gamma_{l,z})$, $1 \leq l \leq n$, $1 \leq z \leq nc_l$ represent the frequency of queries against an attribute A_n of a path with respect to $C_{l,z}$, the frequency of insertions and deletions on $C_{l,z}$ respectively. In practice database administrators may predict these frequencies very well.

To determine the workload on the unified path

Class	$LD_{named}(P_{Per,named})$	$LD_{named}(P_{Comp,named})$	$LD_{divs}(P_{Veh,divs})$
Per	(0.3, 0.1, 0.1)	(−, −, −)	(−, −, −)
Veh	(0.3, 0.0, 0.05)	(−, −, −)	(0.2, 0.0, 0.15)
Bus	(0.05, 0.05, 0.1)	(−, −, −)	(0.3, 0.0, 0.0)
Truck	(0.0, 0.1, 0.0)	(−, −, −)	(0.2, 0.1, 0.0)
Comp	(0.1, 0.1, 0.1)	(0.4, 0.1, 0.3)	(0.4, 0.0, 0.25)
Div	(0.2, 0.2, 0.1)	(0.0, 0.1, 0.0)	(−, −, −)

Table 2: Workload characteristics belonging to the paths $P_{Per,named}$, $P_{Comp,named}$ and $P_{Veh,divs}$.

Class	$LD_{named}(P_{Per,named})$	$LD_{divs}(P_{Per,named})$
Per	(0.3, 0.1, 0.1)	(−, −, −)
Veh	(0.3, 0.0, 0.05)	(0.2, 0.0, 0.15)
Bus	(0.05, 0.05, 0.1)	(0.3, 0.0, 0.0)
Truck	(0.0, 0.1, 0.0)	(0.2, 0.1, 0.0)
Comp	(0.5, 0.2, 0.4)	(0.4, 0.0, 0.25)
Div	(0.2, 0.3, 0.1)	(−, −, −)

Table 3: Workload characteristics belonging to the *unified* path $P_{Per,named}$.

we may discern two situations. First, if two paths have the same ending attribute then the load in the unified path with regard to class $C_{l,z}$ is $\{(\alpha^1_{l,z} + \alpha^2_{l,z}, \beta^1_{l,z} + \beta^2_{l,z}, \gamma^1_{l,z} + \gamma^2_{l,z}\}$, in which $(\alpha^1_{l,z}, \beta^1_{l,z}, \gamma^1_{l,z})$ and $(\alpha^2_{l,z}, \beta^2_{l,z}, \gamma^2_{l,z})$ represent the frequency of queries against the ending attribute, the frequency of insertions and deletions in $C_{l,z}$ due to the first respectively the second path.

Second, if the paths do not have the same ending attribute the workload on the unified path is the union of the workloads defined on the separated paths.

In the following, the load distribution on a path $P_{1,n} = C_1.A_1.A_2...A_n$ against attribute A_n is denoted by $LD_{A_n}(P_{1,n}) = \{(\alpha_{1,1}, \beta_{1,1}, \gamma_{1,1}), ..., (\alpha_{1,nc_1}, \beta_{1,nc_1}, \gamma_{1,nc_1}), ..., (\alpha_{n,1}, \beta_{n,1}, \gamma_{n,1}), ..., (\alpha_{n,nc_n}, \beta_{n,nc_n}, \gamma_{n,nc_n})\}$.

Example 3.1 Consider the paths $P_{Per,named}$ = *Per.owns.man.divs.named*, $P_{Comp,named}$ = *Comp.divs.named* and $P_{Veh,divs}$ = *Veh.man.divs* with their belonging workload as given in Table 2. Then, the unified path of the three paths is equal to $P_{Per,named}$. However, the workload on the path becomes as in Table 3. □

In example 3.1 the load is distributed against two attributes *divs* and *named*. In the following we call these attributes *load relevant* attributes.

The workload on a subpath of a unified path $P'_{1,n}$ depends on the starting class of the subpath and on the attributes against which queries are evaluated. In the case a subpath $S_{g,p} = C_g.A_g.A_{g+1}...A_p$ includes attributes (not coincident with the ending attribute) against which queries are evaluated we determine the workload against these attributes and the ending attribute of the subpath. In the following we will call these attributes *subpath relevant*.

Suppose we have the subpath $S_{Veh,named}$ of an unified path $P_{Per,named}$ with workload characteristics as in Table 3. Then, the subpath relevant attributes of subpath $S_{Veh,named}$ are *divs* and *named* since these attributes are load relevant and are included in the subpath $S_{Veh,named}$.

The workload on a subpath can be determined in the following way. We determine the load on the subpath due to each subpath relevant attribute separately. We distinguish two cases.

If the starting class of a subpath $S_{g,p}$ is equal to the starting class of its superpath $P'_{1,n}$ the load distribution against a subpath relevant attribute A_l will remain the same for the involved classes (the ones in the scope of $S_{g,l}$). Otherwise, the load on $S_{g,p}$ against A_l ($LD_{A_l}(S_{g,p})$) is $\{(\alpha_{g,1} + \sum_{i=1}^{g-1}\sum_{j=1}^{nc_i}\alpha_{i,j}, \beta_{g,1}, \gamma_{g,1}), (\alpha_{g,2}, \beta_{g,2}, \gamma_{g,2}), ...(\alpha_{l,nc_l}, \beta_{l,nc_l}, \gamma_{l,nc_l})\}$ since processing of queries against A_l with regard to a class in *scope*$(C_1.A_1...A_{g-1})$ entails a processing of $C_g.A_g...A_l$ as well. Note, $\alpha_{i,j}$, $1 \leq i < l$, $1 \leq j \leq nc_i$, represents the frequency of queries against A_l with respect to class $C_{i,j}$. In the same way the load against against all subpath relevant attributes can be determined.

We should determine also the load against all load relevant attributes for which hold that the position of the load relevant attribute is greater than the position of the ending attribute A_p of subpath $S_{g,p}$. This can be achieved in the same way as described above. Example 3.2 illustrates these techniques.

Example 3.2 Let us consider the unified path $P_{Per,named}$ and its workload as in Table 3. We illustrate how the load distributions of the subpaths $S_{Per,divs}$, $S_{Veh,divs}$ and $S_{Veh,named}$ can be determined.

Since $S_{Per,divs}$ has the same starting class as $P_{Per,named}$ the distribution on $S_{Per,divs}$ due to the load against *divs* is equal to $LD_{divs}(P_{Per,named})$, which is $(Veh, Bus, Truck, Comp) = \{(0.2, 0.0, 0.15), (0.3, 0.0, 0.0), (0.2, 0.1, 0.0), (0.4, 0.0, 0.25)\}$.

Since, the position of the load relevant attribute *named* is greater than the position of *divs* we have to determine the distribution on $S_{Per,divs}$ due to the load against *named*. This is $(Per, Veh, Bus, Truck, Comp) = \{(0.3, 0.1, 0.1), (0.3, 0.0, 0.05), (0.05, 0.05, 0.1), (0.0, 0.1, 0.0), (0.5, 0.2, 0.4)\}$.

Note that it is not allowed to take the sum of the corresponding attributes, e.g., it is not correct to say that the load due to queries against attribute *divs* with respect to *Comp* is $0.5+0.4 = 0.9$ since we will lose information. To process a query against the attribute *named* we determine the divisions which satisfy to the predicate against *named*. This results into a set of *oids* of objects in class *Div*. Then for each of these *oid* we determine the companies having such a division. So, for the queries against *named* we have to realize that we should access in general a set of key values on the index allocated to *divs* while for the queries against *divs* we should access one key value on the index allocated to *divs*.

To determine the load on the class *Veh* for the subpath $S_{Veh,divs}$ against attribute *divs* we compute first the load on *Veh* due to the evaluation of queries against the load relevant attribute *named* which has a greater position than *divs*. The load on *Veh* due to evaluations against *named* is $(0.3 + 0.3, 0.0, 0.05)$. The rationale behind this can be understood by considering how the path $P_{Per,named}$ is processed using an index. As it has been discussed already we determine the *oids* of the objects of class *Div* which satisfy to the predicate against *named*. Then these *oids* serves as input to determine the companies which have such divisions, and so on. Suppose that the path $P_{Per,named}$ is divided into three subpaths $S_{Per,owns}$, $S_{Veh,divs}$ and $S_{Div,named}$ and we have to process a query against attribute *named* with respect to class *Per* with frequency 0.3. Then, we process the subpath $S_{Div,named}$ first, resulting into a set of *oids* with serves as for $S_{Veh,divs}$. The processing of $S_{Veh,divs}$ results on its turn into a set of *oids* which serves as input for $S_{Per,owns}$. It should be clear that not only the subpath $S_{Per,owns}$ should be walked through with a frequency of 0.3 but also the subpaths $S_{Veh,divs}$ and $S_{Div,named}$. Furthermore, since the frequency of queries with respect to *Veh* against *named* is 0.3 this means that the subpath $S_{Veh,divs}$ should be walked through with a frequency of 0.6.

It should be clear that the frequencies of insertions and deletions do not have to be propagated.

According Table 3 the load on *Veh* due to evaluations against *divs* is $(0.2, 0.0, 0.15)$. So, the total load against *divs* with respect to class *Veh* for subpath $S_{Veh,divs}$ is $(0.6, 0.0, 0.05)$ due to the attribute *named* and $(0.2, 0.0, 0.15)$ due to the attribute *divs*. To get the total load of the remainder classes in the scope of $S_{Veh,divs}$ against *divs* a similar reasoning holds. In Table 4 the results are presented.

To compute the load for subpath $S_{Veh,named}$ one should notice that there are two subpath relevant attributes *divs* and the ending attribute *named*. So, the load for $S_{Veh,named}$ concerns against these attributes. It should be clear that the load against *divs* will remain the same as in the column $LD_{divs}(P_{Per,named})$. For the load against *named* we have to realize that the frequency of class *Per* should be propagated to class *Veh* since the processing of a query with respect to *Per* against *named* means that the subpath $S_{Veh,named}$ should be walked through as well. The load distribution is given in Table 4. □

4 Index configurations

Since each indexing technique has its own advantages and disadvantages it may be sensible to split a path into subpaths and to make a trade-off between the available indexing techniques, on basis of the operations defined on each subpath, in indexing each subpath.

Let $S_{g,k} = C_g.A_g.A_{g+1}...A_k$ be a subpath. Then the subpath $S_{k+1,w} = C_{k+1}.A_{k+1}.A_{k+2}...A_w$, $w \geq k+1$ is called the successive subpath of $S_{g,k}$ and $S_{g,k}$ is called the preceding subpath of $S_{k+1,w}$.

(Sub)Class	$LD_{named}(S_{Veh,divs})$	$LD_{divs}(S_{Veh,divs})$	$LD_{divs}(S_{Veh,named})$	$LD_{named}(S_{Veh,named})$
Per	$(-,-,-)$	$(-,-,-)$	$(-,-,-)$	$(-,-,-)$
Veh	$(0.6, 0.0, 0.05)$	$(0.2, 0.0, 0.15)$	$(0.2, 0.0, 0.15)$	$(0.6, 0.0, 0.05)$
Bus	$(0.05, 0.05, 0.1)$	$(0.3, 0.0, 0.0)$	$(0.3, 0.0, 0.0)$	$(0.05, 0.05, 0.1)$
$Truck$	$(0.0, 0.1, 0.0)$	$(0.2, 0.1, 0.0)$	$(0.2, 0.1, 0.0)$	$(0.0, 0.1, 0.0)$
$Comp$	$(0.5, 0.2, 0.4)$	$(0.4, 0.0, 0.25)$	$(0.4, 0.0, 0.25)$	$(0.5, 0.2, 0.4)$
Div	$(-,-,-)$	$(-,-,-)$	$(-,-,-)$	$(0.2, 0.3, 0.1)$

Table 4: Load distributions for some subpaths of the path $P_{Per,named}$.

This brings us to the subject of index configuration.

Definition 4.1 An index configuration of degree m for path $P_{1,n} = C_1.A_1.A_2...A_n$ $(n \geq 1)$, $IC_m(P_{1,n})$ is defined as a sequence of pairs $\{T_1, T_2, ..., T_m\}$ $m \leq n$. A pair T_i has the form $(S_{k,k+l_i}, X_i)$ in which

- $S_{k,k+l_i} = C_k.A_k.A_{k+1}.....A_{k+l_i}$ $(k \geq i,\ l_i \geq 0)$ is a subpath with length $l_i + 1$. Class $C_k \in class(P_{1,n})$ is the starting class of the subpath and attribute A_{k+l_i} is the ending attribute of the subpath.
- X_i is the index organization allocated to subpath S_i. In the case no index is allocated this is denoted by θ.
- the T_i's are ordered such that the subpath corresponding to T_{i+1} is the successive subpath of the subpath corresponding to T_i. □

Example 4.1 Consider the path $P_{Per,namec}$ = *Per.owns.man.namec*. Index configurations of degrees 1, 2 and 3 are $IC_1(P_{Per,namec})$ = $\{(Per.owns.man.namec$, MIX$)\}$, $IC_2(P_{Per,namec})$ = $\{(Per.owns$, SIX$)$, $(Veh.man.namec$, NIX$)\}$ respectively $IC_3(P_{Per,namec})$ = $\{(Per.owns, \theta)$, $(Veh.div$, IIX$)$, $(Comp.namec, \theta)$ $\}$. □

4.1 Searching cost of indices

The processing cost of a query using indices is determined by the retrieval costs of the index records required for locating the objects on disk which satisfy to the query and the costs to retrieve these objects. We concentrate on the retrieval cost of the indices required for locating the objects on disk. We call this the *searching* cost.

The following proposition determines the searching costs involved in processing queries with regard to the starting class of a path $P_{1,n}$ having an index configuration of degree $m > 1$. It says that the searching cost for a query against the ending attribute with regard to the starting class of $P_{1,n}$ is equal to the sum of the searching cost on each subpath. The proof of the proposition and its corollary can be found in [Choenni 94b].

Proposition 4.1 Let $P_{1,n} = C_1.A_1.A_2...A_n$, $(n \geq 1)$, be a path with configuration $IC_m(P_{1,n}) = \{T_1, T_2, ..., T_m\}$, $1 < m \leq n$, $X_i \in \{MX, MIX, NIX, \theta\}$ and $C(i)$ is the starting class of the subpath belonging to T_i. Then, the searching cost for a query with respect to class $C(1)$ against the ending attribute A_n of $P_{1,n}$, $CR_{IC_m(P_{1,n})}(C(1)) = \sum_{i=1}^{m} CR_{X_i}(C(i))$, in which $CR_{X_i}(C(i))$ represents the searching cost on the subpath corresponding to T_i of the objects of class $C(i)$ which satisfy to the predicate against the ending attribute A_n.

Corollary 4.1 The searching cost for a query against the ending attribute A_n with respect to a class $C_{l,z}$ in the scope of the subpath belonging to T_g such that $T_g \in IC_m(P_{1,n})$ and $m > 1$ can be expressed as $CR_{IC_m(P_{1,n})}(C_{l,z}) = CR_{X_g}(C_{l,z}) + \sum_{i=g+1}^{m} CR_{X_i}(C(i))$.

Until now we have studied how to determine the searching cost for a query against the ending attribute of a path. The searching cost for a query against an *arbitrary* attribute can be achieved by considering the arbitrary attribute as the ending attribute and applying corollary 4.1. The following example illustrates this.

Example 4.2 Consider $P_{1,n}$ with configuration $\{T_1, T_2, ..., T_m\}$, the subpaths $C_q.A_q.A_{q+1}...A_z$ belonging T_p and $C_h.A_h...A_k$ belonging to T_g $(g < p)$. Suppose we want compute the searching cost for a query against attribute A_x with respect to class $C_{l,z}$ which is in the scope of $C_h.A_h...A_k$.

In determining the searching cost we replace $C_q.A_q.A_{q+1}...A_z$ by $C_q.A_q.A_r...A_x$. We determine the cost with regard to class $C_{q,1}$ against the attribute A_x resulting into $CR_{X_p}(C_{q,1})$. Then we compute for each subpath belonging to $T_{g+1},...,T_{p-1}$ the searching cost against their ending attributes with regard to their starting classes since these subpaths should be walked through in processing the query. Let say that the costs are $\sum_{i=g+1}^{p-1} CR_{X_i}(C(i))$. Finally we compute the cost against the ending attribute of the subpath belonging to T_g with regard to class $C_{l,z}$ resulting into $CR_{X_g}(C_{l,z})$. The sum of $CR_{X_p}(C_{q,1})$, $\sum_{i=g+1}^{p-1} CR_{X_i}(C(i))$ and $CR_{X_g}(C_{l,z})$ is the cost required to find the *oids* of the objects of $C_{l,z}$ which satisfy to the query. □

4.2 Maintenance cost of a subpath

The maintenance cost on a path depends whether the path is indexed or not. In the case a path has been indexed then the maintenance cost of an index record, due to a deletion, also depends on the indices allocated to the previous class and its subclasses (Section 2.3).

Consider the pairs $T_i = (S_{k,t}, X_i)$ and $T_{i+1} = (S_{t+1,w}, X_{i+1})$ in which X_i, $X_{i+1} \in \{MX, MIX, NIX\}$. Note, $S_{k,t} = C_k.A_k.A_{k+1}...A_t$ and $S_{t+1,w} = C_{t+1}.A_{t+1}.A_{t+2}...A_w$.

Then, independently of X_i the attribute A_t will be inverted. Since the domain of A_t are the *oids* of the objects belonging to class $C^*_{t+1,1}$ these *oids* will be the key values in the index records. So, the index records have the form $\{(o^{nr}_{t+1,z},...),(o^{nr1}_{t+1,z},...),...\}$, in which $o^{nr}_{t+1,z}$ is an *oid* of an object in class $C_{t+1,z}$.

A deletion of an object of class $C_{t+1,j}$, let say $o^{nr1}_{t+1,j}$ implies that the index on $S_{t+1,w}$ should be updated. The cost of this action is expressed by $CD_{X_{i+1}}(C_{t+1,j})$. Furthermore, the index on $S_{k,t}$ should be updated also. This means that the record with the key value $o^{nr1}_{t+1,j}$ should be deleted. The cost of this action depends on X_i and is expressed by $CMD_{X_i}(A_t)$. For a further discussion with regard to the function CD and CMD we refer to [Choenni 94b].

We modify T_i such that $T_i = (S_{k,t}, \theta)$. A deletion of an object of class $C_{t+1,j}$ requires only an update of the index on $S_{t+1,w}$ since there is no index on $S_{k,t}$. So, $CMD_{X_i}(A_t) = 0$.

Let us consider the following situation $(S_{k,t}, X_i)$, $X_i \neq \theta$ and $(S_{t+1,w}, \theta)$. Suppose we delete an object of class $C_{t+1,j}$, let say $o^{nr1}_{t+1,j}$, then the index allocated to $S_{k,t}$ should be updated by discarding the record with key value $o^{nr1}_{t+1,j}$. The cost of this action depends on the organization of X_i and is expressed by the function $CMD_{X_i}(A_t)$.

In definition 4.2 (see below) we assign the cost $CMD_{X_i}(A_t)$ to the maintenance cost of the index on A_t and not to maintenance cost of the index on A_{t+1} which actually causes the maintenance.

The maintenance cost of an index record due to insertions can be estimated independent of other indices [Choenni 94a]. This is the case for all index types. The cost involved in maintaining an index X_i due to the insertion of an object in class $C_{l,z}$ is expressed by $CI_{X_i}(C_{l,z})$.

The following definition computes the maintenance cost of an index due to insertions and deletions on a (sub)class in a configuration with degree $m > 1$.

Definition 4.2 Let $P_{1,n} = C_1.A_1.A_2...A_n$, $(n \geq 1)$, be a path with a configuration $IC_m(P_{1,n}) = \{T_1, T_2, ..., T_m\}$, $1 < m \leq n$, $X_i \in \{MX, MIX, NIX, \theta\}$. The maintenance cost ($CM$), due to insertions and deletions on a class $C_{l,z}$, of an index X_i allocated to a subpath corresponding to T_i and having A_{t_i} as ending attribute, is given by:

$$CM_{X_i}(C_{l,z}) = \begin{cases} CD_{X_i}(C_{l,z}) + CI_{X_i}(C_{l,z}) & \\ +K * CMD_{X_i}(A_{t_i}) & \text{if } A_l = A_{t_i} \neq A_n \\ CD_{X_i}(C_{l,z}) + CI_{X_i}(C_{l,z}) & \text{otherwise} \end{cases}$$

in which $K = 1$ if an object is deleted and $K = 0$ if an object is inserted.

4.3 Processing cost of a (sub)path

The processing cost of a (sub)path is defined as the sum of the cost to maintain the indices on the (sub)path and the searching costs of those objects which satisfy to the queries defined on the (sub)path.

The following example illustrates how the part of the processing cost due to queries of a subpath can be computed.

Example 4.3 Let us consider the subpath $S_{Veh,named} = Veh.man.divs.named$ with the load distribution as presented in Table 4. Let us assume that $S_{Veh,named}$ is indexed as NIX. Then the processing cost of $S_{Veh,named}$ due to the queries is defined as $0.6 * CR_{NIX}(Veh) + 0.05 * CR_{NIX}(Bus) + 0.5 * CR_{NIX}(Comp) + 0.2 * CR_{NIX}(Div) + 0.2 * CR_{\theta}(Veh) + 0.3 * CR_{\theta}(Bus) + 0.2 * CR_{\theta}(Truck) + 0.4 * CR_{\theta}(Comp)$. The contribution $0.2 * CR_{\theta}(Veh) + 0.3 * CR_{\theta}(Bus) + 0.2 * CR_{\theta}(Truck) + 0.4 * CR_{\theta}(Comp)$ is due to the workload against the attribute *divs*. Since the NIX organization can not be used in processing queries against other attributes than the ending attribute we are left to a sequential scan to process these queries.

Note, if $S_{Veh,named}$ was indexed as MX or MIX then we were able to process the queries against the attribute *divs* using the indices. □

It should be clear that the processing cost of a (sub)path due to maintenance is the sum of the maintenance costs entailed by each deletion and insertion defined on the classes in the scope of the (sub)path.

Proposition 4.2 determines the processing cost of an index configuration with a degree $m > 1$. The proof can be found in [Choenni 94b]

Proposition 4.2
Let $IC_m(P_{1,n}) = \{T_1, T_2, ..., T_m\}$, $1 < m \leq n$, $X_i \in \{MX, MIX, NIX, \theta\}$ be an index configuration and SP contains all the subpaths corresponding to T_i $i = 1, ..m$. The processing cost of $IC_m(P_{1,n})$ is the sum of the processing cost of each subpath $s \in SP$

Since, we do not need any information about other subpaths to compute the processing cost of a subpath this means that the separability property holds [Whang 81]. This result is used in section 5 to develop an algorithm which is able to select an optimal index configuration for a given workload on a path.

5 An algorithm for the selection of index configurations

In this section we develop an algorithm for the selection of an optimal index configuration for a path given the load distribution on the path. Then we discuss the complexity of the algorithm. Finally we report the result of an experiment.

	MX	MIX	NIX	θ
$C_1.A_1$	<u>9</u>	9	9	18
$C_2.A_2$	10	<u>9</u>	10	20
$C_3.A_3$	<u>7</u>	7	7	16
$C_4.A_4$	8	8	8	<u>5</u>
$C_1.A_1.A_2$	19	<u>16</u>	17	40
$C_2.A_2.A_3$	17	18	<u>16</u>	30
$C_3.A_3.A_4$	<u>15</u>	16	16	41
$C_1.A_1.A_2.A_3$	26	23	<u>12</u>	45
$C_2.A_2.A_3.A_4$	25	<u>19</u>	20	43
$C_1.A_1.A_2.A_3.A_4$	34	32	<u>19</u>	49

Figure 4: Possible subpaths for path $P_{1,4} = C_1.A_1.A_2.A_3.A_4$ with their processing costs using an index organization $X_i \in \{MX, MIX, NIX, \theta\}$.

The algorithm takes as input a path $P_{1,n} = C_1.A_1.A_2...A_n$ with the load distribution on the classes. The output of the algorithm will be an optimal index configuration for the path and an estimate of the cost processing the load with the proposed configuration.

The algorithm consists of 3 procedures, *Cost_Matrix*, *Min_Cost*, and *Sel_Ind_Con* which will be discussed in sequence.

The algorithm starts by executing the procedure *Cost_Matrix*. This procedure computes the processing costs for all possible subpaths with each possible index organization. These costs are represented in a matrix. An element $a_{i,j}$ in the matrix represents the costs in processing the subpath corresponding to T_j with index X_j. A hypothetical matrix is given in Figure 4 for a path $P_{1,4} = C_1.A_1.A_2.A_3.A_4$.

Note, in the case a path has length one and it does not have subclasses the organization for MX, MIX and NIX are almost equivalent. Therefore, the processing costs will be almost same.

Then, the procedure *Min_Cost* determines the minimal costs in each row which indicates the best indexing technique for a subpath. In Figure 4 these costs are underlined.

Finally, the procedure *Sel_Ind_Con* determines an index configuration for the path. The idea of this procedure is based on the consideration of all possible ways to recombine the original path from the subpaths; that is to choose a number of subpaths such that the concatenation of the subpaths will result into the original path (called the recombined path) and each class belongs to exactly one subpath. The processing cost of the recombined path will be the sum of the processing costs of each subpath. A possible way to recombine $P_{1,4}$ is by considering the subpaths $C_1.A_1.A_2$ and $C_3.A_3.A_4$. An index configuration with these subpaths may be achieved by allocating a MIX to $C_1.A_1.A_2$ and a NIX to $C_3.A_3.A_4$. Then, the processing cost of the recombined path $P_{1,4}$ will be 32. However, to avoid an exhaustive enumeration of all possible recombinations we apply the branch and bound technique.

First, we discuss the working of the procedure roughly. Then we discuss how to generate the recombinations.

The procedure *Sel_Ind_Con*, for a path $P_{1,n}$, starts by considering the index configuration $IC_1(P_{1,n})$. It chooses the best indexing technique for this subpath; that is the one with the lowest processing cost (PC). The index configuration $IC_1(P_{1,n}) = \{(P_{1,n}, X_1)\}$ is the one with the lowest processing cost (PC_{min}) until now and will be denoted as IC^{best}. Then, it inspects the configuration containing the subpath $S_{2,n} = C_2.A_2.A_3...A_n$. If the processing cost of $S_{2,n}$ ($PC_{S_{2,n}}$) is greater or equal than PC_{min} then all configurations containing $S_{2,n}$ can be branched. Otherwise we choose the best configuration among them and if this is better than IC^{best} we replace IC^{best} and PC_{min} by the better configuration respectively by the lower processing cost. Then, all configurations containing the subpath $S_{3,n}$ will be inspected in the same way to determine whether IC^{best} can be replaced. This process will be repeated until we reach the configurations containing $S_{n,n}$.

The generation of all the recombinations for path $P_{1,n}$ can be done in the following way. First, we generate all recombinations containing the subpath $S_{1,n}$. It is easy to see that this will result in $(C_1.A_1.A_2...A_n)$. Then we generate the recombination choosing the subpath $S_{2,n}$ as fixed. This results into the recombination $\{\underline{C_1.A_1}, C_2.A_2.A_3...A_{p-1}\}$. The subpath preceding the fixed subpath are underlined which will be used in generating the recombinations containing $S_{3,n}$. From each recombination which includes $S_{2,n}$ two recombinations can be generated including $S_{3,n}$. The first recombination can be achieved by successively discarding the subpath following the underlined subpath, adding attribute A_2 to the underlined subpath and adding the subpath $S_{3,n}$. The second can be achieved by successively discarding the subpath following the underlined subpath, and adding the subpaths $C_2.A_2$ and $S_{3,n}$. Since there is one recombination including $S_{2,n}$ this action will result into the following recombinations containing $S_{3,n}$, $(\underline{C_1.A_1.A_2}, C_3.A_3...A_n)$ and $(C_1.A_1, \underline{C_2.A_2}, C_3.A_3...A_n)$. On basis of the same principle we may generate the recombinations containing $S_{4,n}$ from the recombinations containing $S_{3,n}$.

To generate the recombinations including a subpath $S_{p,n}$ from the recombinations including subpath $S_{p-1,n}$ the following technique can be used in general. For each recombination R containing $S_{p-1,n}$ the following actions should be performed after discarding subpath $S_{p-1,n}$ from R. The recombination R without $S_{p-1,n}$ is called R_{aux}.

1. add $S_{p,n}$ and the subpath achieved by adding attribute A_{p-1} to the preceding subpath of $S_{p-1,n}$ to R_{aux} for the first recombination including $S_{p,n}$.

2. add the new subpath $C_{p-1}.A_{p-1}$ and $S_{p,n}$ to R_{aux}, for the second recombination including $S_{p,n}$.

Note, all recombinations containing a fixed subpath, let say $S_{t,n}$, can be found by computing all possible recombinations for the subpath $S_{1,t-1}$ and adding the subpath $S_{t,n}$ to each recombination of $S_{1,t-1}$.

The processing cost of a recombination is the sum of the minimal processing cost of the subpaths belonging to the recombination. Example 5.1 illustrates the working of procedure *Sel_Ind_Con*.

Example 5.1 Let us apply *Sel_Ind_Con* on the *Cost_Matrix* of Figure 4 for path $P_{1,4}$. The procedure starts by evaluating the configuration $IC_1(P_{1,4})$ and assign it to IC^{best}. From Figure 4 it should be clear that IC^{best} will be initially $\{(C_1.A_1.A_2.A_3.A_4, NIX\}$ and $PC_{min} = 19$.

Then the procedure inspects the configurations containing the subpath $C_2.A_2.A_3.A_4$. Since the minimal costs of $C_2.A_2.A_3.A_4$ is 19 which is equal to PC_{min} all recombinations containing this subpath can be branched.

The procedure continues by inspecting the configurations containing the subpath $C_3.A_3.A_4$

since the minimal processing cost for this subpath (15) is lower than PC_{min}. These configurations are $\{(C_1.A_1.A_2, MIX)(C_3.A_3.A_4, MX)\}$ with processing cost $16 + 15 = 31$ and $\{(C_1.A_1, MX), (C_2.A_2, MIX)(C_3.A_3.A_4, MX)\}$ with processing cost 33. Since the discussed configurations are not better than IC^{best}, IC^{best} and PC_{min} will remain the same.

Finally the configurations containing $C_4.A_4$ will be inspected since the minimal processing cost is 5 which is lower than PC_{min}. First, the configuration $\{(C_1.A_1.A_2.A_3, NIX), (C_4.A_4, \theta)\}$ will be evaluated. Since this configuration leads to processing cost $12 + 5 = 17$, IC^{best} will be replaced by this configuration and PC_{min} will become 17.

Then the configurations $\{(C_1.A_1.A_2, MIX), (C_3.A_3, MX), (C_4.A_4, \theta)\}$ with processing cost 28, $\{(C_1.A_1, MX), (C_2.A_2.A_3, NIX), (C_4.A_4, \theta)\}$ with cost 30 and $\{(C_1.A_1, MX), (C_2.A_2, MIX), (C_3.A_3, MX), (C_4.A_4, \theta)\}$ with cost 30 are evaluated successively. Since these configurations have a higher cost than PC_{min} the proposed configuration by the procedure will be $\{(C_1.A_1.A_2.A_3, NIX)(C_4.A_4, \theta)\}$. This configuration has processing cost 17. □

As regards the complexity of the algorithm we analyze the complexity of each procedure. The complexity of the procedure *Cost_Matrix* is determined by the size of the matrix which should be generated for a path $P_{1,n}$. This depends on the number of subpaths in which a path can be split and the considered index organizations. A path with length n can be split into $\frac{1}{2}n * (n + 1)$ subpaths. The factor $\frac{1}{2}n * (n + 1)$ follows from the fact that there are n subpaths of length 1, $n - 1$ paths of length 2, $n - 2$ paths of length 3 and so on. Since, we considered basically three index organizations and the case of no indexing the size of the matrix will be 4 to $\frac{1}{2}n * (n + 1)$. So, the complexity is $4 * O(\frac{1}{2}n * (n + 1))$.

It should be clear that the complexity of the procedure *Min_Cost* is linear.

The procedure *Sel_Ind_Con* has to evaluate all recombinations for a path $P_{1,n}$ in the *worst* case. The number of recombinations for $P_{1,n}$ is 2^{n-1}. This can be verified easily since we illustrated earlier that for each recombination containing a subpath $S_{p-1,n}$ two recombinations can be generated containing a subpath $S_{p,n}$. It should be noticed that the branch and bound technique is applied in this procedure to avoid the evaluations of all recombinations. Although, this technique does not guarantee that it will reduce the complexity in all cases it has proved to be useful in practice in many fields.

So, theoretically the overall complexity of the algorithm will be $O(2^{n-1})$. Because in practice a path has rarely a length greater than 8 the overall complexity is determined (in most cases) by the expression $4 * O(\frac{1}{2}n * (n + 1))$ which is the size of the matrix.

Note, an exhaustive investigation of all possible configurations taking into account m indexing techniques will lead to a complexity of the order $O(m^n)$ for a path with length n [Choenni 94b]. So, for the specific situation which we consider, 3 indexing techniques and the case of no indexing, the complexity is $O(4^n)$.

Finally, we discuss an experiment presented as Example 5.2.

$n_{l,z}$	= # objects in class $C_{l,z}$
$d_{l,z}$	= # distinct values for attribute A_l of class $C_{l,z}$
$nin_{l,z}$	= average number of values held by a (multi-valued) attribute A_l of an object of class $C_{l,z}$
$rpc_{l,z}$	= # pages to store the objects of class $C_{l,z}$

Table 5: List of used symbols

Example 5.2 Consider the path $P_{Per,named} = Per.owns.man.divs.named$ and the database schema of Figure 1. Before enumerating the database characteristics with regard to the schema of Figure 1 we introduce some symbols in Table 5. The chosen values for the database characteristics are given in Figure 5.

We assume that the average size of an object is 200 bytes. Furthermore, in the case a subpath has length one and the subpath does not have subclasses we organize the NIX and the IIX on this class such that they are equivalent with the SIX organization on the class. In the case a subpath with length one has subclasses the NIX is organized such that it is equivalent with the IIX on the class.

First, we apply the algorithm assuming that the queries in the workload are against the attribute *named* ($LD_{named}(P_{Per,named})$). As second we apply the algorithm assuming that the queries are against *named* as well as against *owns*.

Class	$n_{l,z}$	$d_{l,z}$	$nin_{l,z}$	$rpc_{l,z}$	$LD_{named}(P_{Per,named})$	$LD_{owns}(P_{Per,named})$
Per	200.000	20.000	1	9766	$(0.3, 0.1, 0.1)$	$(0.6, 0.4, 0.0)$
Veh	10.000	5.000	3	489	$(0.3, 0.0, 0.05)$	$(-,-,-)$
Bus	5.000	2.500	2	245	$(0.05, 0.05, 0.1)$	$(-,-,-)$
$Truck$	5.000	2.500	2	245	$(0.0, 0.1, 0.0)$	$(-,-,-)$
$Comp$	1.000	1.000	4	49	$(0.1, 0.1, 0.1)$	$(-,-,-)$
Div	1.000	1.000	1	49	$(0.2, 0.2, 0.1)$	$(-,-,-)$

Figure 5: Database and workload characteristics belonging to the logical schema of Figure 1

The cost matrix for the first case is presented in Figure 6. These costs includes beside the processing cost of the subpath also the costs of retrieving the desired objects from disks. In the case of no indexing we assume that the operations are processed according the forward traversal nested loop technique [Kim 88].

The procedure *Sel_Ind_Con* results into the configuration $\{(Per.owns.man, NIX),$ $(Comp.div.named, MX)\}$ with a processing cost of 202.23. On the first sight the gain seems not to be much. For example, if we had allocated a NIX on the whole path the cost would be 229.04. Furthermore, the differences between the costs using several indexing techniques for a (sub)path seems not to be much also. An explanation for these facts is that relatively many objects had to be retrieved from disks especially for queries which concern the first classes of the path $P_{Per,named}$. So, the cost is mainly determined by this action and not by the maintenance and retrieval costs of the indices.

The cost matrix of the second experiment is represented in Figure 7. The costs include the cost of retrieving the desired objects. Note that the costs of the subpaths (longer than 1) containing the class *Per* increases substantially when a NIX organization is used. This is due to the fact that in these cases the NIX organization can not be used to process the queries against the attribute *owns*. So, in these cases we are left to the sequential scan. Applying the procedure *Sel_Ind_Con* results into the configuration $\{(Per.owns.man.div.named, MIX)\}$ with processing cost 239.66. □

6 Conclusions

The main concepts of object-oriented data models are nested objects and inheritance. To be viable, these models should be supported by an architecture that directly implements the concepts in an efficient way. Several indexing techniques are available for this purpose. Since a database operation leads to the processing of a path, a workload consisting of several operations will lead to several paths. Indexing each path separately may become very inefficient since paths may overlap or are subpaths of each other. Therefore, we construct a single path from all the paths which are related to each other and compute the load on the single path. For this single path we propose an algorithm which is able to split the path in subpaths and allocating the best index (if it exists) on each subpath such that the processing of the subpath can be done with minimal cost in terms of page accesses. For the moment we have considered five indexing techniques and the case of no indexing. As has been shown the five indexing techniques could be reduced to three, multi-index, multi-inherited index and nested inherited index.

The presented algorithm selects the *optimal* index configuration for a path with a *feasible* complexity in practice.

References

[Bertino 89] Bertino, E., Kim, W., Indexing Techniques for Queries on Nested Objects, in IEEE TKD, June 1989, pp. 226-244.

[Bertino 90] Bertino, E., Optimization of Queries using Nested Indices, Proc. EDBT 1990, pp. 44-59.

[Bertino 92a] Bertino, E., On Index Configurations in Object-Oriented Databases, submitted for publication in Int. J. VLDB.

[Bertino 92b] Bertino, E., A Survey of Indexing Techniques for Object-Oriented Databases, to appear in Query processing for Advanced Database applications, Freytag, J., Vossen, G., Maier, D., (eds), Morgan Kaufman.

	MX	MIX	NIX	θ
Per.owns	202.95	202.95	202.95	2929.80
Veh.man	28.39	22.0	22.0	599.65
Comp.div	2.98	2.98	2.98	36.75
Div.named	2.70	2.70	2.70	46.55
Per.owns.man	231.35	224.95	196.55	63232.75
Veh.man.div	31.68	25.12	31.88	33141.25
Comp.div.named	5.68	5.68	5.69	3046.55
Per.owns.man.div	234.31	227.95	212.30	228739.85
Veh.man.div.named	34.06	27.7	31.96	153509.45
Per.owns.man.div.named	237.01	230.66	229.04	897145.55

Figure 6: Cost matrix belonging to the database characteristics of Figure 8 taking the load against *named* into account.

	MX	MIX	NIX	θ
Per.owns	211.95	211.95	211.95	8789.40
Veh.man	28.39	22.0	22.0	599.65
Comp.div	2.98	2.98	2.98	36.75
Div.named	2.70	2.70	2.70	46.55
Per.owns.man	240.35	233.95	6059.35	69092.35
Veh.man.div	31.68	25.12	31.88	33141.25
Comp.div.named	5.68	5.68	5.69	3046.55
Per.owns.man.div	243.31	236.95	6082.28	234599.45
Veh.man.div.named	34.06	27.7	31.96	153509.45
Per.owns.man.div.named	246.01	239.66	6108.60	903005.15

Figure 7: Cost matrix belonging to database characteristics of Figure 8 taking the load against *named* and *owns* into account.

[Bertino 92c] Bertino, E., Foscoli, P., Index Organizations for Object-Oriented Database Systems, to appear in IEEE TKD.

[Bertino 92d] Bertino, E., Guglielmina, C., Optimization of Object-Oriented Queries using Path Indices, Proc. RIDE TQP 92, pp. 140-149.

[Choenni 94a] Choenni, R., Bertino, E., Blanken, H.M., Chang, S.C., On the Selection of Optimal Index Configurations in OO Databases, to appear in Proc. IEEE Int. Conf. on Data Engineering (1994).

[Choenni 94b] Choenni, R., Bertino, E., Blanken, H.M., Chang, S.C., The Selection of Optimal Index Configurations in Object-Oriented Databases, extended version of this paper, available from the authors.

[Kato 92] Kato, K., Masuda, T., Persistent Caching: An Implementation Technique for Complex Objects with Object Identity, in IEEE TSE, Vol 18, No. 7, pp. 631-645 (1992).

[Kemper 90] Kemper, A., Moerkotte, G., Access support in object bases, Proc. ACM-SIGMOD '90, pp. (1990).

[Kim 88] Kim, W., Kim K.C., Woelk, D., Dale, A., Acyclic Query Processing in Object-Oriented Databases, MCC Technical Report ACA-ST-287-88, 21p. (1988). Also appeared in Proc. of ER Conference, Rome, 1988.

[Kim 89] Kim, W., Kim K.C., Dale, A., Indexing Techniques for Object-Oriented Databases, in Object-Oriented Concepts, Databases and Applications, Kim, W., Lochovsky, F., (eds), Addison-Wesley, pp. 371-394.

[Maier 86] Maier, D., Stein, J., Indexing in an Object-Oriented DBMS, in Proc. Int. Workshop Object-Oriented Database Systems, pp. 171-182, (1986).

[Tsangaris 92] Tsangaris, M., Naughton, J., On the Performance of Object Clustering, in Proc. ACM SIGMOD '92, pp. 144-153 (1992).

[Valduriez 87] Valduriez, P., Join Indices, in ACM TODS, Vol. 12, No. 2, pp. 218-246.

[Whang 81] Whang, K., Wiederhold, G., Sagalowicz, D., Separability - An approach to physical database design, in Proc. Int. Conf. VLDB, pp. 487-500 (1981).

The Specification of a Seamless O-O Programming Interface for CAD Tools

M. Sim, W. Gerhardt
Faculty of Technical Informatics and Mathematics
Julianalaan 132, Technical University Delft, The Netherlands
email: <m.sim,gerhardt>@is.twi.tudelft.nl

P. Kist, N. Simon
BitByBit, Information System Development
Kluyverweg 2a, Delft, The Netherlands
Phone: +31 15 682569, Fax: +31 15 682530

Abstract

The programming interface offered by a DBMS should be "seamless" which gives the programmer the illusion that an object is "virtual", i.e. exists in the memory space of an executing tool whenever it is needed. This helps to remove the so-called "impedance mismatch" between the database and programming representations. We provide our view of the term "seamless", the properties of a virtual object and the underlying system. On this basis, we can suggest a specification for the programming interface. The specification puts an emphasis on hierarchical clustering, since our target application domain is CAD.

A conceptual realization and measurements based on a prototype, indicating the feasibility of this approach, are given.

1 Introduction

1.1 Motivation

A bottle-neck in the integration of CAD tools with a DBMS is the so-called "impedance mismatch" [Copeland, 1984] between the representation in the programming language used to implement the tools, and the DDL and DML of a DBMS. This problem is still actual [Atkinson, 1989], [Cattell, 1991]. Cattell notes (page 128) that current virtual systems provide data mapping but lack data hiding. The mapping is achieved by merging the capability of database and programming languages. However, we want a programming interface for CAD that has both mapping and data hiding. Data hiding implies that the programmer need not insert statements related to persistent aspects. To do this, objects must appear virtual to the tool programmer. We use the term **Virtual Object Interface System** (VOIS) [Sim, 1993] to describe an interface that supports virtual objects.

From TOOLS EUROPE '94 (Technology of Object-Oriented Languages and Systems).

1.2 Intentions

We have been active with the "seamless" development for several years, and have created a prototype VOIS. In several publications we describe various implementation aspects [Sim, 1990], [Sim, 1991], [Sim, 1992], [Sim, 1993], [Kist, 1993]. Based on this experience, our intention in this paper is to try and explain what a "seamless" environment is and to provide a specification for a seamless programming interface, that is decoupled from implementation aspects.

1.3 Structure of the paper

We present some related work (1), discuss some requirements of the application domain (2), define the problem of creating a seamless environment (3), explain how a VOIS upholds the seamless environment, the properties of a VOIS and virtual objects (4). We then specify the programming interface (5), present our conceptual realization of the VOIS (6), provide some measurements (7) and draw conclusions in (8).

1.4 Some Related Systems

Various OODBMS's now exist that provide a partial solution. We take Objectivity, Ontos, Alltalk and ODE as examples.

Objectivity provides a set of database facilities [Wade, 1989]. It has a language interface that enables defining object types in C++. It is possible to construct trees, sets and lists. Associations may be unidirectional or bidirectional, and cardinality may be defined. It supports complex composite objects (hierarchically) and provides a browser for browsing through the object heap. The DBMS facilities run in the application's address space and persistent data is loaded on demand. The programming interface is not transparent since special "handle" types are used to define persistent attributes.

Ontos [Ontos, 1991]. In Ontos the programmer also creates C++ class definitions, which are passed to a utility that automatically generates the database schema (in the database). So-called meta classes enable support of several property constraints such as "ordered", "indexed", "required", and "unique". Thus a basis for data integrity checking is present. Aggregate classes can be used as building blocks which are integrated into the object database. Execution of any C++ function can be invoked with an Object SQL query. The interface is complex because the programmer is required to manage the mapping between a C++ object and its database equivalent.

ODE [Agraval, 1989] offers a single integrated data model for both database and general purpose manipulation. We consider its transparency limited, since persistent objects must be defined explicitly.

Alltalk [Kim, 1989] extends Smalltalk-80 by providing persistence to objects without adding a database sub language. In contrast to the previously discussed system, and like the VOIS we propose, it uses a concept of dynamic partitioning. The algorithm prunes the transitive closure of the objects in the process. It provides nice transparency, but in our view lacks clustering functionality, which is important for CAD.

2 The Application Domain

We use the VOIS in a typical CAD environment [Gupta, 1991].

2.1 Architecture Overview

The accepted way to create CAD systems is to define tools in a programming language. A tool communicates with the DBMS through an application programming interface (API). Some of the characteristic requirements are:

- High run-time performance (speed of "C").
- Sharing of design objects among tools.
- Hierarchical clustering of the design objects.
- Control over where the design objects should be stored and in which format.
- Capability to handle very small and very large objects.

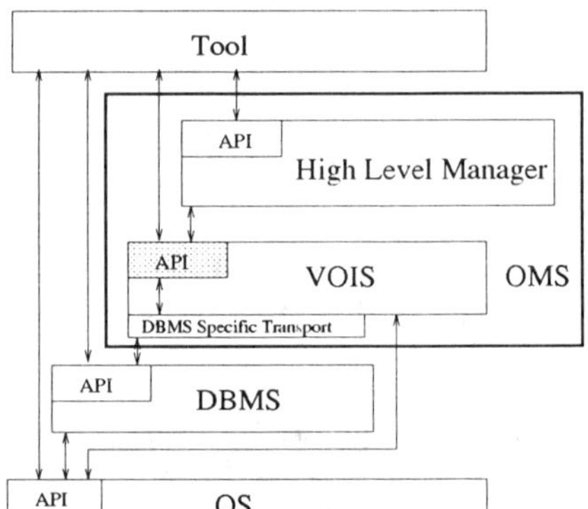

Figure 1: Application domain of a VOIS

Figure 1 shows the strata of a design system environment expressed in major software modules. This environment, excluding the Object Management System (OMS), typifies organizations that extensively use a conventional DBMS, which cannot easily be replaced. In this architecture, the various tools of a design system may interface at different levels.

2.2 OMS Overview

In this architecture, an OMS can minimize the impedance-mismatch. The kernel of an OMS is the VOIS whose task is to support the 'virtual object' properties. **This paper focuses on the specification of the API of the VOIS as depicted in figure 1.** The API interfaces with the Tools, the High Level Manager and with a transporter that communicates with a DBMS of choice. Enhanced management resides in the high level manager and is beyond the scope of this paper. There are several reasons for splitting the OMS in two modules:

- The functionality to support virtual objects can be well defined and implemented as a software module.
- A choice can be made between different high level management modules, depending e.g. on preference of query language.
- A high level manager increases the semantic functionality, however, in some applications, there is no real need for this. The module might unnecessarily increase cost and reduce performance, since the VOIS already provides basic facilities and any addition could be done in the tool(s).

2.3 Clustering for CAD

In figure 2 we illustrate a hierarchical decomposition used to model complex objects. Complex objects are abstracted as clusters that can be nested. The boundary of a cluster is determined by defining a design object to be a **root object** (e.g. cluster A - object a). References between design objects that are used for defining a complex object (bold arrows) are given a special status, because they form the hierarchy. There is a need to define a cluster that represents a database package (Cluster B). Other cluster

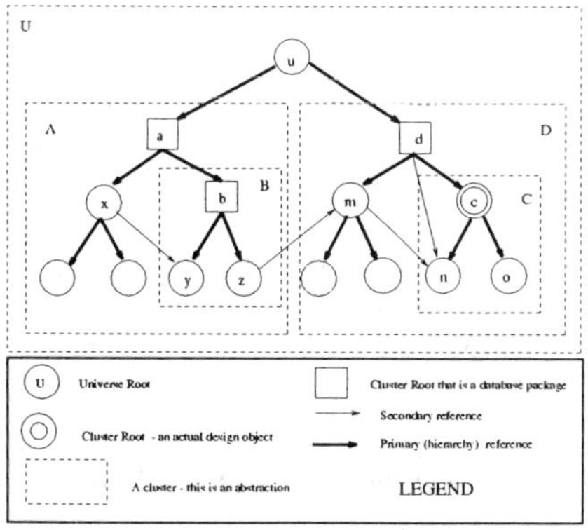

Figure 2: A Clustering Hierarchy

types can be defined to enable data transfer between processes, shared-memory, and to denote aggregate objects. A default cluster (Universe) supplied by the VOIS (universe root) provides the starting point in the cluster hierarchy. The API should provide the means to define such hierarchical structures, without inserting this information explicitly in the code.

3 What is a Seamless Environment and what is the Problem?

3.1 Mapping of design to tool domain

When realizing a certain design system, the functional specifications need to be mapped to tools defined in a programming language. This is called a mapping from the design to the tool domain. Currently, the tool programmer must do this mapping. The mapping involves defining classes (structure and behavior) in the programming language of choice, therefore we consider (the instance of) a class to be the object unit in the tool domain. This mapping problem is outside the scope of this paper.

3.2 The tool domain

The tool domain is a collection of physical sub-domains that may be distinguished by their properties. These sub-domains are at the tool programmer's disposal to implement the functionality of an executing tool with optimal use of the resources. Any object in the tool domain, is represented in the sub-domains by one or more objects each of which requires some memory space to exist. On a standard (UNIX) platform, three important sub-domains are the **process domain**, the **shared domain**, and the **persistent domain** (we consider the persistent domain to be a back-end database).

3.3 Properties of the Tool Sub-domains

We explain the properties of each domain as illustrated in figure 3.

- **Behavior:** Objects are considered to have active behavior if they can communicate with each other through messaging.
- **Lifetime:** The lifetime of an object is finite if it ceases to exist due to the physical property of the domain, rather than an explicit request by the user (e.g volatile memory).
- **Access:** The access to an object is private if it can only be accessed from the domain in which it resides. In the table, the process is considered to have private access. One might argue that inter-process communication enables public access, however, this is limited. Objects cannot freely point to each other. The shared domain enables this, but has some restrictions.
- **Memory:** This is a measure of the amount of memory space available to store objects.

3.4 The Tool Sub-domain Mapping Problem

In systems that don't provide data hiding, the tool programmer is responsible for mapping the tool domain to the sub-domains. The mapping is complex due to the need to move objects between clusters within a sub-domain, and between sub-domains through complicated channels.

Examples
- In the process domain, if an aggregate object is moved to another cluster, the programmer must ensure that the sub-component moves with the aggregate.
- In the persistent domain, the programmer must ensure that a design object will be associated to the right host-machine, database and package.
- In the shared domain, the programmer must ensure that the amount of data shared is minimal.
- The programmer must ensure that an object is loaded from the database when required.

Subdomain / Property	Process	Persistent	Shared
Behavior	**Active**	**Passive**	**Active**
Lifetime	**Finite**	**Infinite**	**Finite**
Access	**Private**	**Public**	**Public (Restricted)**
Memory	**Limited**	**Unlimited**	**Very Limited**

Figure 3: Physical domain properties

3.5 The Tool Sub-domain Mapping Solution

We define a VOIS as a system that automatically performs a correct mapping of design objects between the process, persistent and shared domains, such that the channels are transparent, thereby giving the tool programmer the illusion that there exists one tool domain, which unifies the sub-domains.

The tool programmer can then focus on mapping the design to the tool domain. This concept is depicted in figure 4.

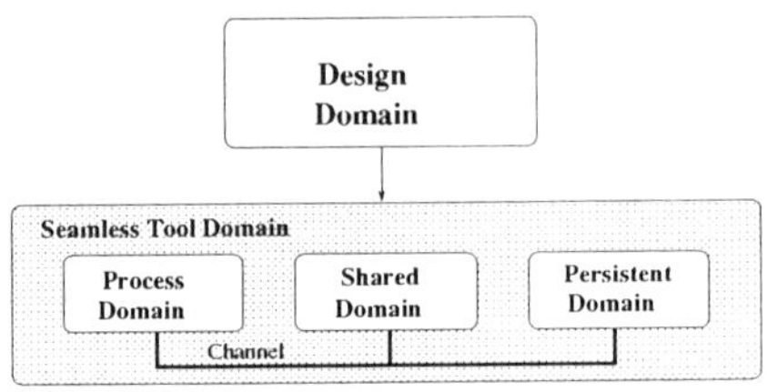

Figure 4: Overview of a seamless environment

4 Properties of a Seamless Environment

When using a VOIS, the tool programmer need only understand the properties of a seamless environment rather than focus on mappings. The properties of a seamless environment can be divided into the properties of the objects and the properties of the interface system.

4.1 Properties of a Virtual Object

1. **durability**: Through configuration information, 'transient' or 'persistent' behavior can be associated to an object.

2. **existence**: When an executing tool manipulates a persistent object, the object will be 'volatile' (demand loading).

3. **mobility**: When a reference to an object changes, it may transparently trigger a 'migration' of the object to another cluster. The mobility property also implies the capability of an object to be transported transparently from one sub-domain to another.

We give a definition of a virtual object expressed in terms of properties: A **virtual object** is an object that is durable, existential, and mobile.

The programmer can assign a different durability to instances of the same class located in different clusters.

Example

Take for example the standard library class 'Collection'. In a tool, an instance of 'Collection' is frequently used to contain transient or persistent objects. In the first case, the 'Collection' instance is transient while in the latter, it is persistent. Through the 'existence' property, the tool programmer need not worry about whether the object is persistent or volatile. The 'mobility' property, reduces the tool programmer's task of relocating instances in the universe to more appropriate clusters. A "misplaced" instance, often a newly created object, will reduce the performance of both tool and DBMS until it is relocated. For example, in the CFI design representation standard [Blinne, 1992], a newly created instance of class 'Port' is modeled to be contained in an instance of class 'Cell'. Another justification for relocating an instance might be that a port 'P' is moved by the tool from cell 'A' to cell 'B'.

4.2 Properties of a VOIS

1. **open tool interface**: The application programmer can use the programming language in a normal way, e.g. she/he is free to define necessary classes, attributes and to use pointers.

2. **open DBMS interface**: The VOIS will correctly interpret the data it receives from a DBMS and will also correctly supply the DBMS with the data it requires.

3. **transparency**: The VOIS hides most virtual functional and temporal aspects from the tool programmer. E.g. an object is loaded on demand and activated in a process, without limitation on the complexity of the referencing to and from the object.

Traditionally, tools utilizing a programming interface must adapt to the internal data structure of the interface. The 'open tool interface' property implies that a VOIS must adapt itself to use the structures as defined by the tool. Likewise, the 'open DBMS interface' property implies that the VOIS must be able to handle the data types defined by the schema of the database and communicate with the DBMS. The transparency in the VOIS is not always total. This is to prevent limitations on flexibility and openness. Examples:

- The tool programmer might wish to explicitly save a cluster at a particular stage.
- The VOIS must be adaptable to a DBMS of choice. It is then possible to create a transparent specialization of the VOIS. For example, a system administrator can define the transport to a particular DBMS, with a required distribution and storage format. The VOIS would then be transparent for the tool programmers.

5 Interface Specification

We give a specification of the API (highlighted in figure 1) of a VOIS to external modules. The specification is composed of three parts: the VOIS configuration, the virtual object and the domain mapping manipulations.

5.1 VOIS Configuration

The 'VOIS configuration' models the relations between clusters, classes and attributes of classes, in the various domains. We first give the definition in BNF notation and follow up with an explanation.

5.1.1 Syntax definition

```
definition list :=        <type definition> |
  <definition list> <type definition>
type definition :=        APPLICATION <name> |
  CLASS <classname> [<relationtype>]
    [ROOT]
    [PARENT <classname> [RELATION <ONE|MANY>]]
    SUPERCLASS <classname>
    <attribute list> |
  TRANSPORT <name> |
  TRANSFORM <name> |
  <setdef>

relationtype      := PRIVATE | REFERENCED |
                     REFERRING | GENERAL
classname         := <name>
attribute list    := <attribute definition> |
  <attribute list> <attribute definition>
attribute definition :=
  ATTRIBUTE <name> [PERSISTENT|TRANSIENT]
    [POINTER [TO (<classname> |
      SET <setname>) [<pointer type>]]
      [RELATION <ZERO|ONE|MANY> TO <ONE|MANY>]]
pointer type      := INTERCLUSTER | INTRACLUSTER
setname           := <name>
setdef            := SET <setname> =
                     <classlist>
classlist         := <classname> |
    <classlist> <classname>
name := [a-zA-Z][a-zA-Z0-9]+
```

5.1.2 Explanation

The syntax is suitable to configure static, i.e. programming language related and dynamic, i.e. VOIS related aspects. The static aspects contain information on the class structure, including its attributes and its inheritance hierarchy. The dynamic aspects contain information on control mechanisms, like clustering, partitioning and transformation of user data.

Static Aspects

- **APPLICATION** identifies the name of the tool this configuration definition applies to.

- **CLASS** is identified by a name.

- **SUPERCLASS** defines the base class (inheritance in object oriented programming).

- **ATTRIBUTE** may be a **POINTER** to a base type (e.g. to an integer), to a virtual class or to a set. The attribute list enumerates the class attributes.

- **SET** describes a set of heterogeneous class-types of which one may be chosen as the target of the pointer.

Dynamic Aspects

- **relation type** specifies the relations of the class relative to its cluster. The examples of relation type given below refer to figure 2.

- **PRIVATE** classes do not point to objects outside their cluster (object o).

- **REFERENCED** implies that the class is pointed to by objects outside its cluster (objects n,c,b,y).

- **REFERRING** classes point to objects outside their cluster but are not referenced (objects u,x,z).

- **GENERAL** class is a combination of REFERRING and REFERENCED (objects a,d,m).

The same relation types can be applied to clusters. Cluster U is PRIVATE, D REFERENCED and A,B are GENERAL. A son cluster is considered to be an object of the parent cluster.

The **relation type** is necessary to perform partitioning of objects into clusters in a transparent and efficient way, e.g. the physical distribution of the persistent data.

- **ROOT** defines the class to be the root object of a cluster.

- **PARENT** identifies the root object of the cluster in which all instances of this class definition reside.

- **RELATION <ONE|MANY>** is used for consistency purposes and may restrict the number of instances of this class in the parent cluster.

- **PERSISTENT—TRANSIENT** behavior can be defined per attribute. The class will become persistent if at least one of its attributes is defined to be persistent.

- **pointer type** applies to pointers to virtual classes.

- **INTRACLUSTER** indicates that the class pointed to resides in the same cluster.

- **INTERCLUSTER** otherwise.

- **RELATION <ZERO|ONE|MANY> TO <ONE|MANY>** specifies the cardinality of the relation and is used for consistency purposes.

- **TRANSPORT** defines the name of a transport method.

- **TRANSFORM** defines the name of a transform method.

The definition of **TRANSPORT** and **TRANSFORM** affects all classes that are defined below these keywords in the configuration definition until another transport or transform method is specified. Transformation and transportation are explained in section 5.3.

5.2 Virtual Object Manipulation

The 'virtual object manipulation' methods enable the tool programmer to control the VOIS and the virtual aspects of the instances. We provide the specification by means of message call examples, using the C++ syntax [Stroustrup, 1987].

Data Type Legend

- **theUniverse** is a virtual object representing the universe cluster (see figure 2).
- **aBoolean** is used to validate correct execution of a message.
- **aVirtual** is an arbitrary (virtual) instance in the universe.
- **aValue** is an arbitrary value of any data type.
- **aName** is a character string that identifies a name-value pair.
- **aRepositoryMode** is one of the following values: INSERT, GET, EXIST, REMOVE.
- **toDestination** is the destination object.

A virtual class is defined through inheritance of a class provided by the VOIS, e.g:
anApplicationClass:public Virtual

The method described in the following sections are generally triggered transparently by the VOIS. However, a tool programmer can use these methods manually, e.g. to enhance performance.

5.2.1 Main Functions

1. aBoolean = theUniverse → Initialize (argumentCount, argumentList)
2. aBoolean = theUniverse → Quit ()
3. aBoolean = aVirtual → Save ()
4. aBoolean = aVirtual → Purge ()

- **Initialize** A tool might desire to control the initialization of the VOIS. The method initializes the interface system and checks the consistency of the configuration data. For example, during prototyping it is useful for the programmer to shut down the virtual system, in which case objects only retain transient behavior.

- **Quit** shuts down the VOIS. This is performed by the VOIS when a tool terminates.

- **Save** performs a (hierarchical) mapping of a (cluster of a) virtual object from the process (or shared) to the persistent domain. This is performed by the VOIS on the Universe root when the tool terminates.

- **Purge** removes an object, without effecting its image in persistent domain. Must be called explicitly.

5.2.2 Ancillary Functions

5. aBoolean = aVirtual → Migrate (toDestination)
6. aBoolean = aVirtual → SetToRoot ()
7. aValue = aVirtual → PrivateRepository (aName, aRepositoryMode, ...)

- **Migrate** enables an (aggregate) object to dynamically switch clusters; its own aggregates will also migrate. This is automatic if there is sufficient configuration information.

- **SetToRoot** enables the programmer to dynamically set the status of an object to be the root of a cluster. The tool programmer might prefer to perform the clustering "manually" rather than supplying the information in the configuration data. The method can also be used to speed up partitioning.

- **PrivateRepository** is an "add-on". Any virtual instance is provided with a local storage repository, that can store, and find keyed values.

(In our implementation, a need arose for such a method, to improve the performance of the VOIS. Because of its usefulness we have opened it to the tool programmer.) Must be called explicitly.

5.3 Domain Mapping Manipulation

This section defines the functions used to map objects across tool sub-domains.

5.3.1 Mapping Concepts

This mapping is accomplished through two basic operations:
- **transformation** is the act of transforming one data format to another
- **transportation** is the act of copying data from one sub-domain (e.g. process) to another (e.g. database).

From the view-point of a particular sub-domain (the source), four activities are possible:
- **implode**; transformation of objects from source to a destination format.
- **explode**; transformation of objects from a destination format to the source format.
- **import**; transportation of objects from a destination to the source.
- **export**; transportation of data from the source to a destination.

These functions must be implemented as methods in a "transfer" class.

5.3.2 Mapping Functions

Data Type Legend

- **anImplodedObj** is a (virtual) object in a destination format.
- **aKey** is a handle to an object in the source sub-domain
- **anIdentifier** is a handle to an object in the destination domain.
- **anImplodedImage** is a collection of imploded objects (originating from a cluster) in their destination format.
- **anImplodedImageSize** is the size of the collection.

The transfer class is sub-classed from *virtual*, the base class of **all** classes that have virtual behavior. It implements the following methods:

8. anImplodedObj = aTransfer → implode (aVirtual)
9. aVirtual = aTransfer → explode (anImplodedObj)
10. aKey = aTransfer → import (anIdentifier, anImplodedImage, anImplodedImageSize)
11. anIdentifier = aTransfer → export (aKey, anImplodedImage, anImplodedImageSize)

- **implode** takes an object and transforms it into a passive form suitable for transportation (e.g. from data structure to a string).
- **explode** will convert objects into an active form, suitable for manipulation (e.g. from a string to a data structure).
- **import** method retrieves, given anIdentifier, the image of a cluster and stores that image at the memory location specified by anImplodedImage. The memory that must contain the image has been reserved by the VOIS. The image size contains the actual size of the memory the VOIS reserved. anIdentifier specifies the external data, suitable to access that data for the first time, e.g. the name of a database, a filename, etc. Reading data from external modules (e.g. DBMS) will usually result in using some sort of generated keys. These keys identify data that is to be manipulated by the external module thus, aKey is the identifier of data used by the external module while anIdentifier is the identifier of the same data used by the VOIS.
- **export** method takes the imploded image and stores it at the location specified by aKey. It returns anIdentifier, completing the aKey-anIdentifier circle so that it can be used again to read the externally stored image.

The transport and transform methods are normally called automatically by the VOIS. The programmer might call the methods in special cases, e.g. to send messages between tools. The system provides a default set of transfer classes. Tool programmers can implement additional transform and transport operations by overriding the default mechanism through subclassing (using the inheritance capability of the chosen language). The configuration data specifies which manager is used.

6 Conceptual Realization

6.1 The Logical Domain

The data traffic between the different subdomains is pipe-lined through an intermediate domain, called the **logical domain**. This domain functions as a buffer that sends or receives transformed objects and is inaccessible to the tool programmer. This makes the channels (figure 4) transparent. The example in figure 5 il-

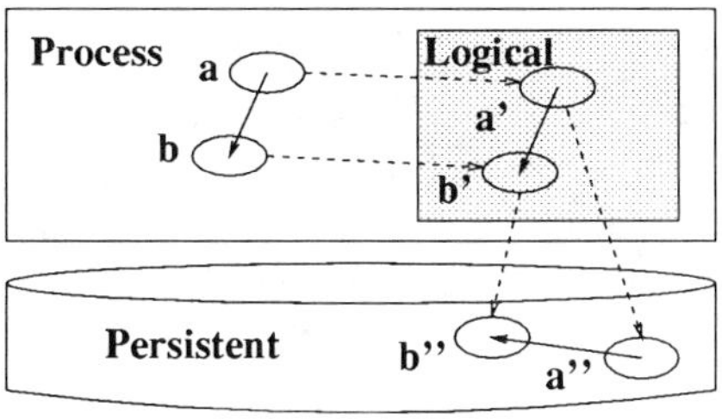

Figure 5: Conceptual realization of domain interaction

lustrates the use of the logical domain. The volatile, persistent objects 'a' and 'b' must be transported from the process to the persistent domain. The objects are transformed and their images are (transparently) stored in the logical domain. The logical domain, upon receive, consequently sends these images to the required destination. This mechanism applies to any **virtual object** regardless of the type of source and destination domain.

6.2 VOIS Managers

The architecture of our VOIS distinguishes the following managers [Sim, 1993]:

- **The object manager** performs key generic operations such as triggering of persistent activities, maintaining the clustering infra-structure and managing the persistent and volatile object addressing. A small set of control functions is available to the tool programmer.

- **The partition manager** assigns objects to the appropriate clusters. The partitioner accesses information stored in a configuration data heap to enhance the partitioning. The partitioning may be controlled by the programmer through a file containing configuration data (section 5.1.1), which specifies the desired relations between object types, and various persistent characteristics.

- **The mobility manager** encapsulates a default transform/transport module for a default DBMS, for shared memory, and for tool-tool communication. The transformation and transportation modules may be extended by the programmer to comply with specific application requirements.

- **The configuration manager** reads configuration files (section 5.1.1), parses the contents and builds internal structures that can be accessed by both the VOIS and the tool programmer. These internal structures are used by all previously listed managers and supply additional information about cluster hierarchies, class structures, etc.

6.3 The Impact of O-O Technology

The data hiding aspects can be realized due to basic characteristics of an object-oriented programming language.

- **Encapsulation** is essential to trigger transparent operations. For example, the data of a cluster of objects is loaded from the database when one of the objects in the cluster is sent a message.

- **Inheritance** enables objects to possess the virtual properties from a base object. For example, migration is handled through inheritance.

- **Overriding/Overloading** (of methods) enables objects to react differently to the same message. In the case of overloading, the constructor of class *Virtual*, for tool programmers, has no parameters, while the VOIS passes a special parameter to this constructor. For the VOIS this will result in a system object.

7 Measurements

Dynamic partitioning - the critical issue.
A vital question in the virtual concept is whether

the run-time overhead caused by automating the partitioning remains small enough to be justifiable. We have performed some simple tests on a prototype system [Sim, 1993], by mapping the process domain to the persistent domain. The tests were performed on a well configured VOIS.

Varying heap, fixed percent non-partitioned.
An important result was that the ratio partitioning time versus a fixed percentage of non-partitioned objects remained linear, for varying quantities of virtual objects (The quantities varied between 100 to 8000 objects resident in a process).

Partition time versus total save time.
Another test involved 50% non-partitioned objects in the process. When the 'Save' method was executed, the time spent on the partitioning was 22%, while the rest was spent on implosion and export.

Varying percent non-partitioned.
Another test measured how the partitioning speed was effected by the percentage of non-partitioned objects. The partitioning time ratio between 17% non-partitioned objects and 85% non-partitioned objects (ratio 1:5) was 1:6, which suggests that worse-case conditions don't cause extreme degradation of the performance.

Factors for effective partitioning.
The key to keeping the partitioning within reasonable limits depends on three factors: A "good" schema for the configuration data, a "good" partitioning algorithm and a "good" definition of the application's configuration information. There are still many open questions with respect to partitioning, e.g. what is the average percent of non-partitioned objects in a process under 'real' design conditions? (Maybe it is considerably less than 50%). Another area open for study is whether the algorithms we have chosen are optimal. This a non trivial problem [Hughes, 1991].

8 Conclusions

8.1 Advantages

- We have shown that it is possible use virtuality to achieve data hiding and mapping thereby reducing the "impedance mismatch".
- The VOIS can be controlled by a small number of interface functions, which do not need to be used often.
- Standardization of an interface would reduce the effort in modifying tool code.
- A standardization effort is simplified due the compactness of the specification.
- The accuracy of the configuration may be changed incrementally, even dynamically (since the environment is configured outside the tool code).
- Incremental configuration conforms to the evolutionary process of building tools from prototype to finalized versions.
- Change of DBMS requires limited changes in the tool code, i.e. in the specific class that regulates transport to that DBMS.
- In the case of design systems that share a common schema, the configuration need only be done once and can be used for many tools (with possibly minor tailoring for specific tools).

8.2 Limitations

In this approach there is no complete transparency (e.g. as in the Smalltalk-80 snapshot); The tool programmer can control which objects (and which attributes) should persist, and how and where they are to be stored, and therefore is aware of persistent aspects.

Our approach has been to keep this information compact and out of the source code. The programmer must include hints (e.g. PRIVATE, REFERRING etc) to achieve effective dynamic partitioning. The current implementation doesn't enable creating classes on the fly, which reduces the flexibility of the system. This however, is a problem inherent in C++ and not in the concept of virtual objects.

We plan to use the VOIS system in several CAD application areas, with large quantities of objects. Only then will it be possible to come to final conclusions regarding the effectiveness of this approach.

8.3 Future Work

- The VOIS specification is not complete. For example, we intend to include the possibility to define dynamic attributes for classes.

- Based on experience, we emphasize the use of the VOIS for CAD applications. However, we believe that it can be put to more general work such as business applications, CASE etc. It is currently being used in the development of a scheduling system for a large organization.

- We are studying the relation between our work and the new object database standard [Cattell, 1993].

References

[Agraval, 1989] Agraval, R. and Gehany, N., "Ode(object database environment):the language and the data model." *ACM Transactions, May, 1989.*

[Atkinson, 1989] Atkinson, M., Bancilhon, F., Dewitt, D., Dittrich, K., Maier, D., Zdonik, S., "The Object-Oriented Database System Manifesto." *Proc. DOOD, December, 1989.*

[Blinne, 1992] Blinne, R. (Editor), "Design Representation Electrical Connectivity Information Model and Programming Interface." *Specification 0.9.6, CAD Framework Initiative, 1992.*

[Cattell, 1991] Cattell, R., "Object-Oriented and Extended Relational Database Systems." *Addison Wesley, Reading MA, 1991.*

[Cattell, 1993] Cattell, R., et al, "The Object Database Standard, ODMG-93." *Morgan Kaufmann Publishers, San Mateo, CA, 1993.*

[Copeland, 1984] Copeland, G. and Maier, D., "Making Smalltalk a Database System." *Proc. Int. Conf on Management of Data, p.p. 316-325, June, 1984.*

[Gupta, 1991] Gupta, R. and Horowitz, E., "Object-Oriented Databases with Applications to CASE, Networks, and VLSI CAD." *Prentic Hall, 1991.*

[Hughes, 1991] Hughes, J., "Object Oriented Databases." *Series in computer science. Prentice Hall Publishing Company, UK, 1991.*

[Kim, 1989] Kim, W. and Lochovski, F.H., "Object Oriented Concepts, Databases and Applications." *Addison Wesley, Reading MA, 1989.*

[Kist, 1993] Kist, P., van Leuken, R. and Sim, M., "Aspects of Realizing the CFI Design Representation Specification in the Nelsis Framework." *Proc. ACM/IEEE European Design Automation Conference, September, 1993.*

[Ontos, 1991] Ontos Inc., "Technical Backgrounder: The ONTOS Product Architecture." *Technical report, Burlington, MA, 1991.*

[Sim, 1990] Sim, M and Dewilde, P., "An Object Oriented Persistent Database Interface for CAD." *Proc. ACM/IEEE European Design Automation Conference, March, 1990.*

[Sim, 1991] Sim, M and Dewilde, P., "Design of a Persistent Programming Environment in an Object Oriented Language Using Clustering and Composite Objects." *Proc. ACM/IEEE European Design Automation Conference, February, 1991.*

[Sim, 1992] Sim, M., Kist, P. and Schot, C., "Data Configuration in an Object Oriented Persistent Programming Environment for CAD." *Proc. ACM/IEEE European Design Automation Conference, March, 1992.*

[Sim, 1993] Sim, M., "Tool and Database Interfacing Based on Virtual Objects." *PhD thesis, Delft University of Technology, Delft, 1993.*

[Stroustrup, 1987] Stroustrup, B., "The C++ Programming Language." *Addison Wesley, Reading MA, 1987.*

[Wade, 1989] Wade, D., "Database Management for Concurrent Engineering." *High Performance Systems, April, 1989.*

Using Object-Orientation in Real-Time Applications : An Experience Report or (1 Application + 5 Approaches = 1 Comparison)

Carlos E. Pereira[#] and Pablo Darscht[+]
Institute of Industrial Automation and Software Engineering (IAS)
University of Stuttgart
email: {pereira, darscht}@irp.uni-stuttgart.de

Abstract: This paper presents some results we have obtained applying object-oriented concepts to the development of real-time applications. It also compares these results with those obtained applying methods based on the functional decomposition. For the sake of restricting the paper's length, two aspects will mainly be focused on: a) The degree of seamlessness achieved by using object-oriented methods along all the development process of a real-time system; b) A comparison among five versions of the software for real-time process control, monitoring and diagnosis of a package routing system, tending to determinate the impact of an object-oriented programming language applied to implement software for real-time systems. Software quality metrics have been used in order to quantify attributes of the resulting software and to allow a better judgement of the strengths and weaknesses of the approaches.

1. Introduction

1.1. Real-Time Systems

The correctness of a real-time system depends both on the logical results of the computation and on the time the results are produced. The extended concept that associates 'real-time' with quickness, considering that the main property of such a system is that it brings a very high performance, is not necessarily true. A system has to satisfy two criteria in order to be considered as *real-time*[Lauber89] [Stankovic88] [Halang92]:

a) timeliness: there are timing constraints to be held by the system and the incapability of the system to meet them will result either in the whole application failure (*Hard* real-time systems) or in the failure of some application tasks (*Soft* real-time systems).

b) simultaneity: the system is embedded in its environment, where many activities occur concurrently.

Until recently, the use of assembly languages and 'programming from scratch'-techniques were a common approach for programming a real-time application. As real-time systems have become larger and more complex, the use of those 'ad-hoc' methods is impractical and new techniques are required. Within this context, the application of software enginnering methods into real time systems development has gaining in importance (see [Ghezzi91]). In fact, the task of building large real-time software systems is very difficult, since it is not only subject to all problems associated with the development of large software systems, but also introduces the additional complexity of handling and satisfying timing constraints [Bihari92].

1.2. Structured approaches

The industry has started to apply structured techniques in the development of real-time systems. Commonly, the methods selected are real-time specialisations of structured analysis that emerged in the past decade (as for example those proposed in [Ward85] and [Hatley88]). They present the same well known shortcomings of traditional structure analysis, as for example: insufficient information hiding, low maintainability and poor reusability. However, it is a great progress in comparison with the absence of a methodology.

From TOOLS EUROPE '94 (Technology of Object-Oriented Languages and Systems).

Supported by the Federal Research Council of Brazil (CNPq); on leave from the Federal University of RGS- Brazil, Electrical Engineering Department

+ Supported by the German Service for Academic Exchange (DAAD); on leave from the National University of Uruguay, Electrical Engineering Institute.

Together with the use of structured techniques, a company of the branch, which aims to set the trends, has introduced[1] other innovations in the developing process of real-time systems, as:

- abandonment of the notion that a real-time system must always be designed 'on bare hardware', which means to substitute cost intensive and non-portable proprietary real-time operation systems by 'off the shelf' ones.
- the restriction of the use of very low level programming languages, like assembly, to critical sections of the code, that usually contain no more than a few lines of code. High level languages are used for the rest of the code.

1.3. A 'new' approach: object-oriented development

Object oriented methods for the development of real-time systems are not so mature as the functional approaches, like the structured analysis[2]. They constitute current subject of research and from the viewpoint of the industry they still lack the required stability to be introduced as a new standard. Although this observation may be correct, we think that this methodology has decisive advantages compared to other (functional oriented) approaches. The experience reported here should reinforce this impression. Among the benefits which can be obtained by applying the object oriented paradigm along all stages of the development process of real-time systems, we should mention:

- modularity: unrelated objects can be completely ignorant of each other, each object represents a self contained piece of the problem which can be examined within the context of the system;
- easy to understand: the abstract software objects can represent entities in the physical world, reflecting the same semantics that are found in the problem domain;
- easy to extend: every change in the real world physical system is easily identifiable, because every physical component that is important in the problem domain has a counterpart on the software side.
- easy to reuse: by means of inheritance and instantiation the reuse of components is motivated.

This list should not induce to believe that the object oriented development methodology is the new 'silver bullet' of Software Engineering: the list contents more a set of objectives than quantitative properties of this approach. Moreover, these properties characterise object-oriented software, not the development process. It indicates that the approach should help a developer to reach the objective of constructing cost-effective applications. However, it is also true that no approach can avoid developers from producing bad software. Finally, there are still many problems to be solved, some of which will also be described along the paper.

This paper focuses on the evaluation of results of case studies we have performed over the past four years, by applying the object oriented development process to real-time systems development. Two major issues will be addressed: the seamlessness in the development of real-time systems using object-oriented methods and a comparison among five versions of the software for a real-time application.[3]

In the next section we present the application selected as case study for this research: a package router system. In section three we compare some aspects of the object-oriented and functional approaches applied during the early phases of the system development (analysis and design) of the package router control software. We come to the conclusion that the 'seamlessness' along all the software life cycle is favoured by the object-oriented approach, but we also mention some points where *semantic gaps* at the development process between consecutive stages still remain. In section four we classify the five versions of the real-time process control software according to the two main properties under consideration: the object-orientation and the real-time capabilities. We compare the different implementations by means of software metrics that give us a clue about the quality of each implementation. Finally, in section five, we present the lessons we have learned from this experience and signal the directions of our future work.

---

[1] A great number of companies still refuse to take this way.

[2] Although the 'roots' of object-orientation are in the late sixties with the development of SIMULA 67, only in the last five years this technique has been gaining a major attention and has been applied to the others phases of the development, such as analysis and design.

[3] A paper describing the previous results of the case-study has been published in [Pereira93a].

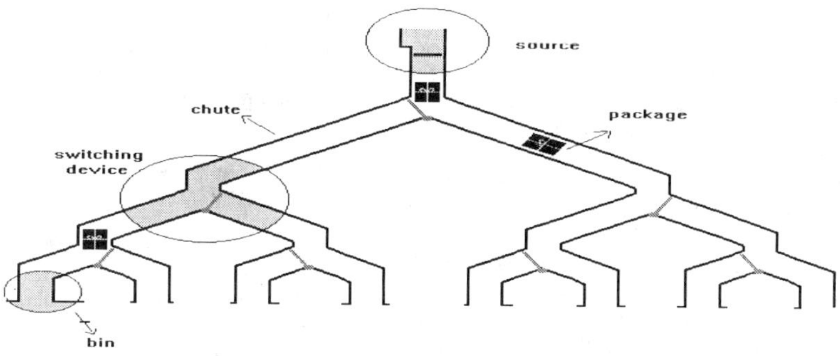

Fig. 1- The Package Router

2. The Package Router.

2.1. The Problem

The case study, whose results will be presented in this paper, consists on the automation of a routing system for distributing packages into destination bins. This system had been used in Germany as a benchmark for real-time development systems, because of the inherent parallelism (more packages are distributed simultaneously) and real-time constraints, while being easy to understand. Similar systems are being installed by German post offices to reduce the time to deliver letters and packages.

At our institute we have a real model of such a system, whose topology is a network consisting of a source and a set of binary switching devices connected by chutes which terminate in bins (see fig.1). Packages move through the network under action of gravity and should be distributed according to their target addresses. A switching device can change its state only when it is empty. Packages may bunch up and, hence, prevent a switch from being set until the entire bunch passes through. The destination of a package is sensed in the source station (i.e. when it first enters the network), where a bar code reader reads the target address. Switches and chutes have no sensors for determining package destination. However, the presence of a package in a chute, switch, or bin are sensed through optic sensors. The problem to be solved by the real-time software is to define a switch controller that maximises the package-'flow', while minimising package misrouting. A monitoring and fault diagnosis system together with a graphical user-interface (that allows a real-time visualisation of the distribution process) complete the automation system.

2.2. Project Scope

This work was carried out within the scope of a research project at our institute, whose overall goal is to investigate the effectiveness of object technology when applied to the development of (real-time) process control and automation systems. The development of the real-time process control software was carried out by undergraduated student teams (1-3 students/team) using CASE tools and programming systems that are commercially available. Participants were industrial automation engineering students in the last terms. The students curriculum comprises lectures related to software engineering and real-time software development. Hence, all the participants were already familiar with concepts like inheritance, classes, tasks, scheduling, and so on. Moreover, all the selected students already had some experience developing software in an industrial environment. The authors have also carefully supervisioned the development of the five versions, trying to avoid discrepancies in the results due to the inherent different skills of team members. In this way, we believe that the results obtained with this case-study can really provide some hints about strengths and weaknesses of each approach[4].

In order to separate the *conceptual solution* of the problem of controlling the package router from its *implementation*, these two tasks were commended to different student teams. In a first stage, two documents containing the software requirements specification and a preliminary

[4] Of course, it would even be better to have five teams with experts in each approach, all of them with several years of experience in developing software in industrial environments. In order to guarantee unbiased results, participants' QI should be almost identical, too. However, this ideal configuration to a comparison is unfortunately far away of being practicable.

software design were produced. The first one, following the Object Modelling Technique (Rumbaugh et al, General Electric, [Rumbaugh91]), has later been used as a basis for the object-oriented programming. The second one, an EPOS-R and EPOS-S[5] description, as the starting point for the process-oriented implementation. Before being used as a base for the different implementations, these design documents had carefully been checked, in order to ensure their completeness and correctness. Such an aspect is very important, since we wanted to compare different possibilities to implement *the same* design solution. Each of the versions of the control software corresponds to a different approach to real-time software implementation, varying from high-level real-time programming languages (based on concurrent processes) to object-oriented languages under real-time operating systems. One should mention at this point that we also tried to include existing real-time object oriented languages, such as RTC++ [Ishikawa90] and real-time Talk [Brorrsson92] in our comparison. However, no commercial version of such environments was available at the time of our case study (we also had no succes trying to get a runable beta-version of these environments for our comparison). The same occurred concerning ADA-9x, whose compilers were under implementation.

2.3. Project Status

Five versions of the software for the automation of the package router problem were implemented. All versions fulfil the functional and timing requirements and are able to distribute packages in the model. On average, it took 6 months[6] for each team to deliver a executable program.

3. From Requirements to Implementation

It is well known that, because of its iterative nature, the object-oriented development process can't be described as a linear succession of phases. Nevertheless, for the sake of clarity, in this section we describe our experiences leading to a complete design of the software for the package router using classic milestones to distinguish the different stages of the development process.

3.1. The beginning of the development process

3.1.1. Modelling the current system

An important characteristic of process control and automation software, that distinguishes it from other kinds of software, is its tight coupling with the physical process under control, i.e., it must integrate to a more complex structure, which includes the physical devices it controls. Therefore, software developers must fully understand the process and devices under control, and to achieve this, they have to build a model of the existing reality. This analysis phase must take place independent of the development methodology. Subsequently, by comparing the current system expressed by the model with the desired system described by the custommers' requirements, the functionality to be added by the software is determined.

We have confirmed that the quality of the obtained solution strongly depends on the ability to *integrate* the model of the current system in the software under development. Moreover, the experience obtained by applying different approaches to the development of the package router control software shows that existing object-oriented methodologies help to reach a high degree of integration. In effect, they investigate the requirements to find *objects* and use them to build a model of the system. In the case of automation systems like the package router, some objects are very easy to find[7]: chutes, packages, switching devices, bins, and the like. As we will show later, these objects constitute the skeleton of the software to be built.

On the other hand, the functional approach must tackle a big *semantic gap*, because, while stating the requirements and modelling the current system, it describes what the system shall perform as seen from an external point of view. This is later reformulated into how-terms to

[5] EPOS is a fully integrated CASE-Tool developed at our institute and since 1980 commercially available by the firm GPP in Germany. It has been installed for a growing number of users in industry, governmental agencies, research institutes and universities. EPOS was conceived for the development of hardware/software projects. EPOS-R is a specification language for requirements definition and EPOS-S a specification language for describing system design (see also [Lauber87]).

[6] The starting point was the preliminary design mentioned in the previous paragraph.

[7] It is not meant that *all* the objects are easy to find. But due to the tangible nature of the technical plant under control in several real-time applications, such as the package router, there is a set of 'things' to be described. On the other hand, other objects are to be added during the development.

enable the functional breakdown inherent to these methodologies[8][Jacobson92].

3.1.2. Describing behaviour

We have found that in this kind of applications, often called *reactive systems* to remark the high degree of interdependence with the environment, the description of the behaviour of each object and its interrelations plays a very important role. The OMT's *dynamic model*, as presented in [Rumbaugh91], is in some aspects too vague to adequately describe complex behaviours, in particular timing constraints, which are a substantial aspect while considering real-time systems. In the case of the package router this part of the behaviour was described in declarative form, using an object-oriented framework for the specification and analysis of timing requirements developed at our institute[Pereira93b,c]. This framework intends to enhance existing object-oriented analysis methods concerned to a better support in generating a real-time system specification that is easy to understand while also being formal enough to allow a checking of the descriptions correctness, a very important point during the requirements stage [Kemmerer93].

3.2. The transition to design

For the purposes of this paper, we consider the design as the stage of the development process in which the developer delineates the methods to be used by the software to achieve its objectives. We are aware that this definition does not correspond to those given in the 'object-oriented literature', and in fact it is difficult to find two authors that give the same definition of design. As we have observed, a high degree of seamlessness in the transition analysis →design motivated by the object-oriented approach exists. This is probably the cause for this multitude of definitions.

In the case of developers applying an object-oriented approach, the starting point of the design is the model of the current reality based on objects that correspond to entities of the real world. These initial objects usually correspond to 'dummy' entities, such as valves, tanks, chutes, etc. They are usually passive objects, which don't know how to behave themselves and how to co-operate with the other objects in order to satisfy the requirements. The developer carries out the design process by incorporating the missing skills to these dummy objects, giving them, in some sense, intelligence and autonomy. Nevertheless, as we have observed, sometimes more abstract objects, that do not have a physical nature, are needed (for instance, a control object to coordinate the operation of other objects). Despite of that, the physical structure of the real-time system to be controlled is an excellent starting point to build an object class network. In the case of the package router, as it can be observed in figure 2 -a static view of the model of the *desired system*-, practically all classes correspond to a physical entity. Another common characteristic of technical systems can be recognized in the figure 1: several entities appear 'replicated' in a system. For instance, the package router system has seven switch devices, each one being identical in behavior and structure. The use of instantiation (class-instance relationship) is very helpful in order to obtain shorter descriptions. Similarly, the generalization/specialization-concepts present in the object-oriented paradigm also contributes to the production of a more compact specification, since commonalities among classes can be inherited. This enhances not only the understandability of the model, but also improves its maintainability. As the desired behaviour is added to the initial model, it ceases to represent the *current system* and gradually becomes a model of the *desired system,* and this suits the idea of *seamlessness* of the method very nice.

On the other hand, we have observed that the use of object-oriented notations don't conduce inexorably to an object oriented development: inexperienced developers tend to use many independent 'functional' objects to incorporate the required behaviour to the system, leading to results that are even more difficult to understand (and to modify, to maintain, etc.) than well engineered function oriented approaches, because they lack the modularity of the latters. We attribute this to a misunderstanding of the object oriented paradigm, that ends in a meagre functional design expressed in object-oriented terms.

3.3. At the transition between design and implementation

As stated before, we have found that the object-orientation contributes to achieve a smooth transition between the requirements and the conceptual solution. This is also true for the transition between design and implementation, although some restrictions can be found in this case. The first observation is that typical

[8]The consideration of the actions, which the desired system must accomplish in order to satisfy the requirements, is obligatory -also for object-oriented approaches-, since we are considering only procedural methodologies. The differences between both approaches reside in the moment and in the method used to do this.

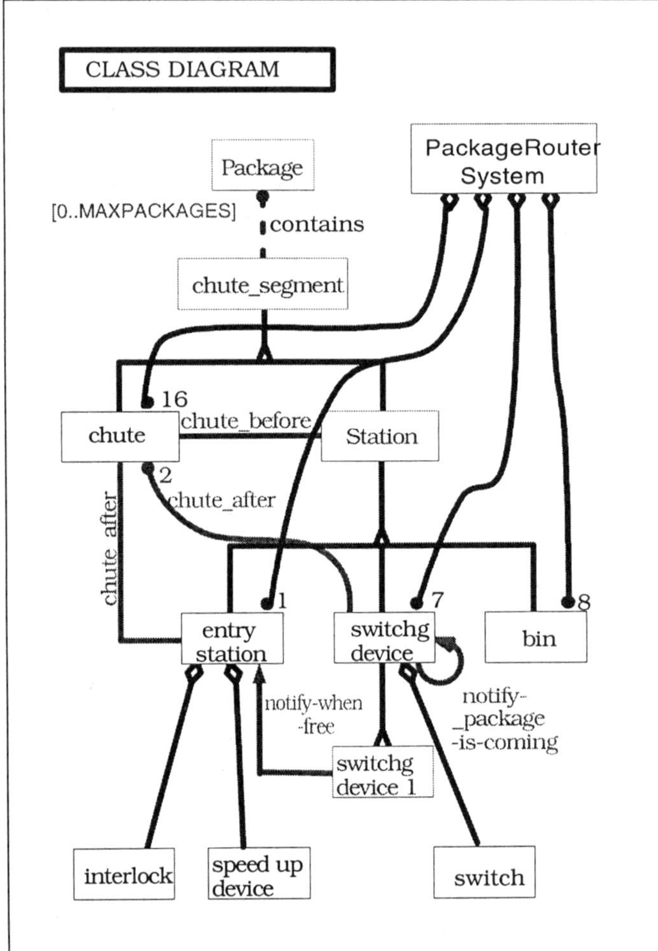

Fig. 2- The object model of the package router (Notation: OMT).

characteristics of object-oriented programming languages collide with the requirement of timeliness that real-time systems have to fulfil. In particular, issues like dynamic linking and garbage collection are in general irreconcilable with the time response determinism demanded by real-time applications. As a result, 'pure' object-oriented languages are pratically out of consideration for real-time applications, and the developers are forced to use hybrid ones.

The following reflections refer to the experiences gained while translating the design of the package router control software in C++. This language possesses some properties that map directly to concepts used during earlier stages of the development, such as classes, inheritance, virtual functions, etc. This reinforces the smoothness of the transition design→ implementation and the traceability of the development. On the other hand, the fact that C++ is a *single threaded* language obliges one to adapt the previous conceptual solution in order to be implemented with this limitation. For instance, C++ objects running under DOS, on the contrary to those used during the analysis and design, must be passive and the communication among them resembles much more the subroutine call mechanism[9] than the idealised message passing used before. The approaches adopted by the current C++ implementations are described in paragraph 4.4.2, and in the last section of this paper we outline our current attempt to give a better solution to this problem by extending the programming language by *active* object classes.

[9] Due to object-oriented concepts like late-binding or polymorphism, the 'jump to subroutine' is more elaborated than in the trivial case.

4. Comparing five implementations of the control software

4.1. Tools and Methods used in the comparison

The choice of a suitable pair 'programming language - operating system' plays a very important role in the implementation of real-time software. On one hand, the use of a programming language that takes into account the time dimension of an application leads to the production of more compact, reliable and maintainable systems. On the other hand, a efficient operating system helps to ensure that the timing constraints will always be met. Besides, it allows to achieve a good degree of portability, decisive if it is intended to remain competitive in spite of the rapid evolution of the hardware . By additionally considering whether the programming language used is object-oriented or not we get the following classification schema that leads to the five different approaches used in our case studies.

In order to visualise the two principal dimensions that differentiate the pairs shown in table 1, we use the neologisms 'real-timeness' and 'object-orientedness'. The first of them refers to the pair *'programming language - operating system'*, and indicates the combination of the characteristics of a real time operating system and the existence at the language level of real-time constructs, such as synchronisation primitives. The second should give an idea of the support provided by the language to object-oriented concepts. We expressly stress that both 'magnitudes' shown in figure 3 have a qualitative nature, and the only intention of the picture is to remark the two main properties under consideration in this research.

programming real-time?	language OO ?	runtime-system real-time?	Programming System	Summary
yes	no	yes	PEARL (Werum GmbH Germany)	high-level real-time programming language standardised in Germany (DIN66253) with tasks (concurrent process), real-time constructs, scheduling of task activation's by the occurrence of timing and other events
yes	+/-	yes	ADA (Meridian)	high-level real-time programming language, tasks, abstract data types (packages), object-based
no	no	yes	C under the real-time operating system QNX (WATCOM-C compiler and Quantum Systems)	conventional C programming language under a real-time UNIX-like operating system (POSIX). The real-time features of QNX (such as timers, interprocess communications and process scheduling) are made available in C through a run-time library.
no	yes	no	C++ under DOS (Borland)	object-oriented, no real-time features; user-friendly debugger and programming environment
no	yes	yes	C++ under QNX (INTEK-C++)	object-oriented, real-time , message-passing (synchronous and asynchronous)

Table 1- The five programming environments used in the comparison

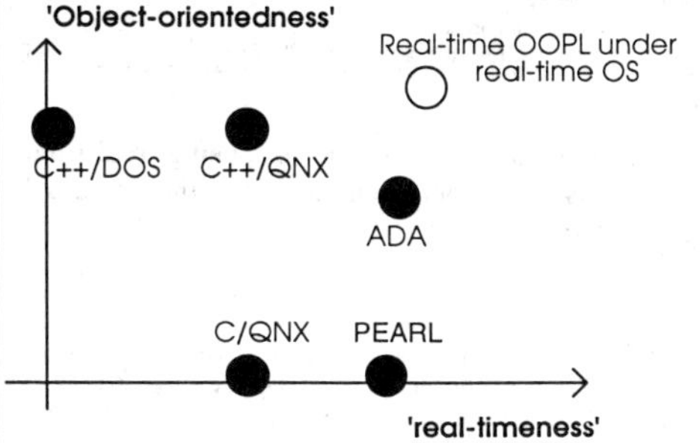

Fig. 3- Properties of the pair programming language - operating system.

The comparison of the final versions of the software for real-time process control has been conducted using complexity metrics. They will be represented in a three-dimensional way, using as independent 'variables' those shown in the figure 3, in order to obtain a good idea of the influence of these properties on the measurement achieved.

4.2. Factors influencing the size

The figure 4 depicts the relative size of the source code of the different implementations. This 'relative' size was measured as the total amount of lines of code excluding comments and blanks. The first observation is that it decreases with the 'object-orientedness': the validity of this conclusion is specially clear, considering that this property is the only difference between the pairs C/QNX and C++/QNX. We interpret this result as the consequence of the use of powerful abstraction concepts such as classes and inheritance (the instantiation permits that after defining a class, several instances can be generated with a simple declaration, independent of the complexity of the behaviour of the class). The comparison of the implementation with ADA (an object-based programming language) and PEARL (with abstraction capabilities comparable to PASCAL) also confirms the incidence of abstraction in reducing the size of the code.

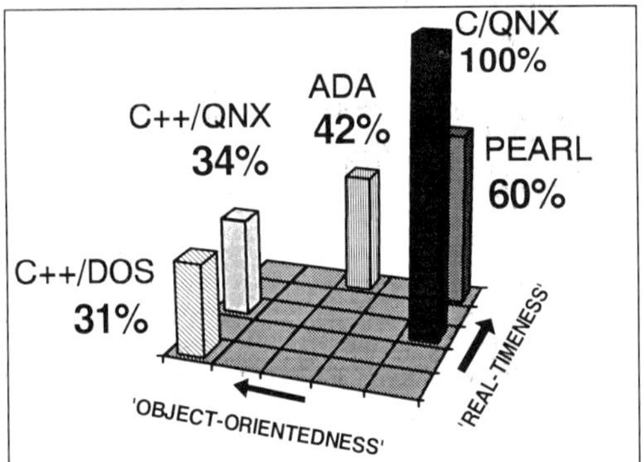

Fig. 4 - Comparison of the size of the resulting source code.

As can be observed, the size of the resulting real-time software in PEARL was considerably smaller than that obtained with C/QNX. It confirmed our expectations that the use of a 'real' real-time programming language facilitates the implementation of a real-time application[10]. This becomes evident if we consider for example the amount of code required to program a cyclic activation of a task: figure 5 shows comparatively the implementation of a cyclic monitoring activity both in PEARL (where just 1 line of code is needed) and in C/QNX (where more than 20 lines of code are needed). With regard to the size, the combination of the object-orientation with real-time constructs seems promissory.

4.3. Cyclomatic complexity

In order to obtain high quality software it is very important to keep its complexity low[11]. One metric usually applied to measure complexity is the so called cyclomatic complexity as defined by McCabe [McCabe76], which counts the number and the nesting of control flow decisions (IF, CASE, FOR, WHILE statements). Some authors, such as Jacobson [Jacobson92], even state that this factor determines the lifetime of the system. Before presenting the results obtained, it is interesting to consider the suitability of the index used: one tends to think that the number of decisions in the control flow of the program is a very partial view of complexity. Returning again to the piece of code shown in figure 5, the complexity index are 0 and 1 for the PEARL and C/QNX versions respectively, while every 'impartial observer' would probably affirm that the difference in complexity is much greater.

Nevertheless, by comparing the results achieved for C/QNX and PEARL, as shown in figure 6, we conclude that the biggest reduction of the complexity is achieved by using real-time constructs, in concordance with the 'feeling' gained from figure 5.

PEARL:	C or C++/QNX

MainTask
ALL 0.01 SEC ACTIVATE MonitorChute
 	
Task MonitorChute
- Code
	Monitor Class
	
	task_id=qnx_name_attach(0,'Name)
	// register the calling task under a name
	proxy=qnx_proxy_attach(Parameter) // creation of a proxy process
	timerid=mktimer(proxy, Parameter) // creation of an interval timer
	TimerStruct.Par1=x; TimerStruct.Par2=y // set the timer parameters
	reltimer(timerid, &TimerStruktur)
	while(true) { receive(proxy,Parameter)
	Code;}; // wait for the proxy to run the code

Fig. 5 - Cyclic activation of a task using PEARL and C

[10] The comparison of the two C++ versions cannot be considered a counterexample: by 'paying' with a very small increase of the code size the advantages of the use of a real-time operating system are gained.

[11] The complexity inherent to the system cannot be changed, but it can be managed. On the other hand, the software aggregates complexity to the entire system. This later type is referred here.

As expected, there is a great correlation between size and cyclomatic complexity; still, the impact of the real-time constructs is even greater here. When comparing ADA and PEARL, we attribute the better metrics of the former to the presence of inter-task communication facilities, which at the same time signals a weakness of PEARL.

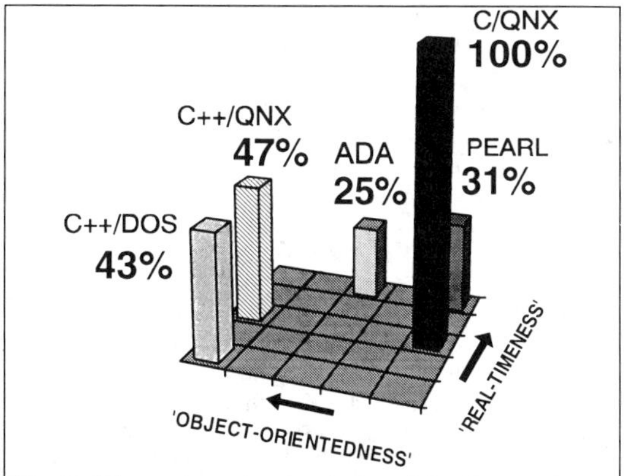

Fig. 6 - The cyclomatic complexity of the five versions.

4.4. Parallelism and Data flow

We will analyse these two metrics together, because both are in direct relation to the communication model supported by the language (and the operating system). The data flow metric depicts the number of global variables and the parallelism is determined by the number of concurrent threads of control.

4.4.1. Why global variables?

We have not only considered the data structures that are known for all the modules of the program as 'global variables', but also the functions declared as *friend* in C++, because they are also a violation of the information hiding principle. As the developers of the C++/DOS version of the software made extensive use of these kind of functions (contrary to the implementers of the C++/QNX version), the data flow metric achieved a considerable high value. This 'deviation' would not have been permitted by Smalltalk[Goldber83] or Eiffel[Meyer88], object-oriented languages with stronger encapsulation concepts.

With respect to the other versions, the global variables were used mainly to implement inter-task communication, and the developer of the ADA version could completely avoid them. In the case of the two implementations based on QNX, the number of global variables corresponds approximately with the number of tasks, because they operate as buffers in the inter-task communication. Due to the support given by the operating system to this interaction, the number of global variables could be maintained manageable, in spite of the great number of tasks employed. Exactly the opposite situation occurred with the PEARL version: the inter task communication was so complex to implement, that the developers chose to use fewer tasks in order to keep the number of global variables under control.

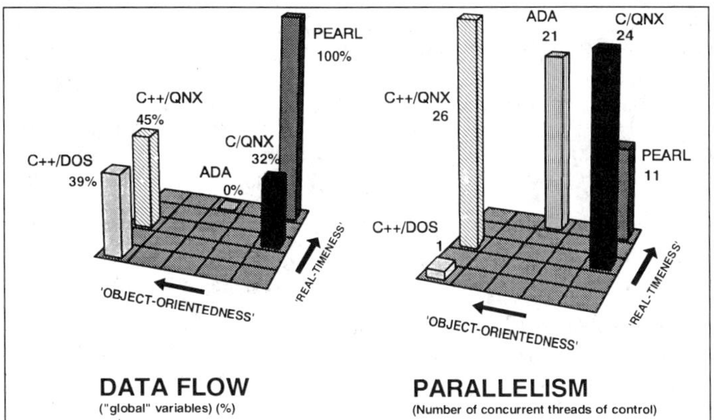

Fig. 7 - Data flow and parallelism

4.4.2. Communication models

The message passing communication model of the object-oriented language enforced the use of concurrent processes (26 tasks, where there was 1 task for each active object, like for example the switch devices, see figures 1 and 2), while reducing the amount of global variables (the object-orientation leads to a better information-hiding).

Almost all programming systems used in the comparison allow the reflection of the real world parallelism in the application program through tasking mechanisms, although under different points of view. While in the process-oriented implementations a task normally represents an action, in the object-oriented versions the natural unit of parallelism is an object.

It is difficult to judge which approach is the best one. One could even consider the possibility to combine both approaches in order to obtain objects where the degree of internal concurrence could be dynamically configured. It would allow the definition of objects with full parallelism in their operations (where the synchronisation of the access to the objects attributes must be carefully taken into account) as well as objects with no internal concurrence (see for instance [Bihari92]).

However, as stated before, C++ is a single threaded language. To overcome this problem and implement concurrent objects, implementers have allocated each 'active object' to a QNX[12] task, implementing the intercommunication between objects as messages between tasks. This allowed them to circumvent the restriction imposed by the programming language, at the cost of degrading the quality metrics obtained for this version (see for example the data flow measurement in figure 7).

5. Lessons learned and future work

The real-time software development differs considerably from the software development process of information systems, and therefore one has problems when trying to adapt existing methods that were conceived for information systems development to the real-time systems field. Even for the development of middle-size real-time applications the complexity of the software management is not to be underestimated, mainly if aspects like readability, reliability, maintainability are intended.

[12]Of course the version using C++/DOS cannot simulate 'active objects'

The object-orientation is a promising approach to tackle these problems concerning the development of complex real-time systems. It induces to build the solution starting from an object-oriented model of the existing system (in the case of process control and automation, the technical plant). Although this initial model is enriched during the further phases (design and coding), the original structure is preserved along the development cycle until implementation. Since the abstract objects within the computer represent and behave like the corresponding physical objects in the real world (and in the model of the real world), the automation software has the semantics that are found in the problem domain. Because of this, the object-oriented paradigm brings the bests results when it is applied during the *whole* development process, since the use of a uniform 'way of thinking' derives in smooth transitions between the different phases of it.

The academic nature of this case study has determined its environment and its objectives. Nevertheless, the following promissory conclusions are particularly interesting for the industry while considering the introduction of object-oriented technologies:

❑ The transition between the different steps of the object-oriented software development process is smooth. Therefore, the communication between analysts, designers and programmers is easier, and the traceability of the decisions taken along the different development steps is very high.

❑ The object-oriented paradigm is more than a set of new notations or a new programming language. In order to be able to exploit its advantages, the developer must learn to 'think object-oriented', and in the first place, he must know the concepts behind the new notations and languages.

❑ For new developers (as in the case of our students) the object-oriented technologies are not much more difficult to master than the function-oriented ones (neither are they easier than those).

❑ The object-oriented programming language chosen must support the concepts used during the earlier steps of the development process. Simultaneously, it order to be suitable for real-time applications, the language should provide high-level constructs for dealing with time.

From a strictly technical point of view, the major lesson learned from our case studies is that existing object-oriented approaches are still not THE solution for the development of real-time applications, mainly because they still lack a mechanism to handle timing semantics (both specification and implementation) and the deficiencies of commercially available programming languages to map to the abstract concepts used during analysis and design.

Solutions for these problems are subject of research at our institute. As stated before, a declarative language to describe timing constraints, including time-outs, deadlines, simultaneity, order of events, etc., has been defined and a prototype of a framework for describing temporal relations and performing temporal reasoning is currently under implementation. By adding these real-time features to object-oriented concepts a very powerful mechanism to describe and design real-time applications can be achieved.

Aditionally, another current topic of research deals with improvements to existing real-time programming environments, such as those for the development of programs in C and C++, whose target code should run under real-time UNIX operating systems (from now on RT-UNIX). With the attempt to standardize the user level interface of the operating system through the POSIX 'Portable Operating System Interface for Computing Environments', the number of such environments has abounded in the last years. Different ways of augmenting the capabilities of such systems with real-time constructs similar to those available in PEARL (see figure 5 for an example) have been implemented. One of them consisted in the implementation of a PEARL-based real-time library for RT-UNIX-based environments in C [Belschner94]. Another approach currently under development consists in an attempt to combine the object-orientedness of C++ with the realtimeliness of RT-UNIX operating systems. The main idea is to map the 'logically distributed' model of an object-oriented language, like C++, to the physically-distributed model of a real-time process-oriented operating system. Contrary to existing concurrent object-oriented programming languages, such as PANDA[Assenmacher93], POOL[America92], ConcurrentSmallTalk [Yokote87], ACT++ [Kafura93], etc. which have been developed for distributed systems, our approach focuses on real-time aspects of an application. It also differs from others real-time object-oriented programming languages, such as DROL [Tokoro92], RTC++ [Ishikawa90], FLEX[Lin91], since the number of added primitives is kept very low (we don't intend to define a new language but rather to achieve a powerful real-time programming environment). We have adopted an approach similar to that of RTO++[Nigro93], where the concept of active classes inheriting the properties of a pre-defined super-class has been introduced. However, since our 'root' active class makes use of several real-time features of RT-UNIX, such as the mapping of C++ inter-object communication to real-time interprocess-communication, the timeliness necessary for a real-time software can be better ensured (RTO++ has been implemented under DOS, definetely a non real-time operating system). In our first version, each instance of an active class has its own thread of control. It communicates with other classes either synchronously or asynchronously, where deadlines for the communication as well as operations for handling time-outs can be specified. At the time this paper was written, a pre-processor that translates the extended C++ code was under beta-testing.

We are also just starting a project to investigate the automatic code generation from a specification delivered with the framework proposed. Due to the seamlessness of the object-oriented paradigm, such an automatic translation seems to be very interesting, mainly to obtain a rapid prototype of specifications.

REFERENCES

[America92] America, P. :*Design Issues for Parallel Object Oriented Languages* In: Heeg,G. et all - TOOLS 7 Technology of Object-Oriented Languages and Systems, Tutorials Notes, Dortmund, Germany, Prentice-Hall 1992.

[Assenmacher93] Assenmacher, H.; Breitbach, T.; Buhler, P.; Hübsch, V.; Schwarz, R.: *"PANDA - Supporting Distributed Programming in C++"*.in: Proceedings of ECOOP'93, July 1993. Ed. by O. Nierstrasz, (LNCS 707), Springer-Verlag, Berlin

[Belschner94] Belschner, R., Pereira, C. and Schlatter, P.: *Mapping PEARL's High-Level Real Time Constructs to a C Run-Time Library under a Real Time UNIX.* (submitted for publication)

[Bihari92] Bihari, T. and Gopinath, P.: *Object-Oriented Real-Time Systems: Concepts and Examples* IEEE Computer, December 1992, pp. 25-32.

[Brorrsson92] Brorrsson, E. et al.: *RealtimeTalk an Object-Oriented Language for Hard Real-Time Systems.* IFAC International Workshop on Real-Time Programming. Brugge-Belgium. pp. 81-86. 1992

[Ghezzi91] Ghezzi, C.; Jazayeri, M.; Mandrioli, D. *"Fundamentals of Software Engineering".* Englewood Cliffs: Prentice-Hall, 1991

[Goldberg83] Goldberg, A. and Robson, D.: *"Smalltalk-80: The language and its implementation".* Reading, MA: Addison-Wesley, 1983

[Halang92] Halang, W.: *Real-Time Systems: Another Perspective.* The Journal of Systems and Software, April 1992, pp. 101-108.

[Hatley88] Hatley, D. and Phirbhai, I.: *Strategies for Real-Time System Specification.*New York : Dorset House 1988.

[Ishikawa90] Ishikawa, Y. et al: *Object-Oriented Real-Time Language Design: Constructs for Timing Constraints.* OOPSLA/ECOOP'90 pp. 289-298. 1990

[Jacobson92] Jacobson,I., Christerson,M., Jonnsson und Övergaard,G.: *Object-Oriented Software Engineering - A Use Case Driven Approach.* ACM Press, Addison Wesley, Reading, MA, 1992.

[Kafura93] Kafura, D., Mukherji,M. and Lavender, G.: *ACT++: A class library for concurrent programming in C++ using actors.* Journal of Object-Oriented Programming. October 1993, pp. 47-55.

[Kemmerer93] Kemmerer, R. and Ghezzi, C.: *Guest Editors' Introduction: Specification and Analysis of Real-Time Systems.* IEEE Transactions on Software Engineering. Vol.18, No 9, pp. 766-767, September 1992.

[Lauber87] Lauber, R. and Lempp, P.: *"EPOS Overview".* Institute for Control Engineering and Industrial Automation (University of Stuttgart) and GPP Gesellschaft fuer Prozessrechner-programmierung mbH, Germany, Oct. 1987

[Lauber89] Lauber, R.: *Prozeßautomatisierung - Band 1.* Berlin, Heidelberg, New York: Springer-Verlag 1989. (in German)

[Lin91] Lin, K.; Liu, J.; Kenny, K.; Natarajan, S.: *"FLEX: A Language for Programming Flexible Real-Time Systems".*in: Foundations of Real-Time Computing, Formal Specifications and Methods, ed. by A. Tilberg and G. Koob, Kluwer Academic Publishers, Boston, 1991

[McCabe76] McCabe,T.: *"A Complexity Measure."* IEEE Transactions on Software Engineering, Vol. 2, No. 4, Dec. 1976.

[Meyer88] Meyer, B.: *"Object-oriented Software Construction."* 1988, Prentice Hall International (UK) Ltd, Hertfordshire

[Nigro93] Nigro, L.; Tisato, F.: *"RTO++: a framework for building hard real-time systems".*Journal of Object-Oriented Programming, Vol. 6, No. 2, pp. 35 - 47, May 1993

[Pereira93a] Pereira, C.E.: *Putting OO to work: Results from Applying the Object-Oriented Paradigm during the Development of Real-Time Applications.* First IEEE Workshop on Real-Time Applications, pp. 166-170. New York, NY, May 13-14, 1993.

[Pereira93b] Pereira, C.: *'A Framework for Describing Timing Requirements of Real-Time Systems at an Object-Oriented Requirements Engineering Phase'.*Technical Report, Institute for Control Engineering and Industrial Automation, University of Stuttgart, September 1993

[Pereira93c] Pereira, C.: *'On Describing Timing Requirements within a Real-Time Object-Oriented Requirements Engineering Phase'.* Workshop #4: Object-Oriented Real-Time Systems Analysis and Design Issues, OOPSLA '93.

[Rumbaugh91] Rumbaugh, J. et all: *Object-Oriented Modelling and Design* .Englewood Cliffs, NJ, Prentice-Hall 1991.

[Stankovic88] Stankovic,J.: *Misconceptions About Real-Time Computing: A Serious Problem for Next-Generation Systems.* Computer, October 1988, pp. 10-19.

[Tokoro92] Tokoro, M.; Takashio, K.: *"DROL: An Object-Oriented Programming Language for Distributed Real-Time Systems".* Proceedings of OOPSLA'92 , pp. 276-294

[Ward85] Ward, Paul and Mellor, S.J.: *Structured Development for Real-Time Systems.* New York : Yourdon, 1985 (3 Volumes).

[Yokote87] Yokote, Y. and Tokoro,M.: Yokote, Y. and Tokoro, M.: *Experience and Evolution of ConcurrentSmalltalk* In: OOPSLA'87 Proceedings October 4-8, 1987. pp.406 - 415.

METHODOLOGY (PART 1)

Limits of Seamlessness in Object Oriented Software Development

Dorothea Beringer
GfAI, Gruppe für Angewandte Informatik AG
CH - 3037 Herrenschwanden
and
Swiss Federal Institute of Technology
Software Engineering Laboratory
EPFL-DI-LGL
CH - 1015 Lausanne
dorothea.beringer@di.epfl.ch

Abstract

Seamlessness is a promise often used to promote object orientation, and the use of object orientation in the different domains and in the different stages of the software development process has brought great improvements in seamlessness.

Where can we find seamlessness? And are there different kinds of seamlessness? In this paper we look at seamlessness starting with the different models found in large software developments. To give a common base for the discussion a model architecture is presented and different aspects of seamlessness are defined. We then show on a general level, where object orientation has already brought some seamlessness, where it will hopefully bring a higher degree of seamlessness in the future and where it cannot bring seamlessness due to restrictions inherent to the model architecture. The emphasis of the discussion is not to present a complete theoretical treatment but rather to help software developers to judge the many claims about seamlessness.

From TOOLS EUROPE '94 (Technology of Object-Oriented Languages and Systems).

1 Introduction

In software development the most evident seams are found between analysis and design and between design and implementation. Such seams have been blamed for many delays and failures in software development when structured methods like Structured Analysis and Structured Design were used, but could never be bridged in a convincing way. Another seam is found between database models and application models. In applications where procedural languages are used together with relational databases, this last seam is very evident. The developer has to master two different paradigms and uses special tools like embedded SQL to bridge the gap. There are still other seams that are not so evident, e.g. between the external view of a user interface and its internal design, or between the conceptual data models and the logical database design.

With the penetration of object orientation into design and analysis as well as databases, the promise of seamlessness is often emphasized: using the object model in all of these areas would allow to have the same syntax and the same semantics in all models, thus avoiding any seams between the models or at least making the transition from one model into another very smooth.

Discussions about seamlessness often end in misunderstandings due to different presumptions about the development process. Therefore, before the degree and the places of seamlessness are discussed, we need to define our view of the development process. We do this by describing a model architecture. This will be the basis for the actual goal of the paper: to show on a general level where object orientation has already brought some seamlessness, where it will hopefully bring a higher degree of seamlessness in the future and where it cannot bring seamlessness, due to restrictions inherent to the model architecture. Chapter 2 presents the model architecture, in chapter 3 we define several aspects of seamlessness, chapter 4 then investigates seamlessness according to the criteria of chapter 2 and 3. Finally, some often heard misconceptions about seamlessness are briefly mentioned in chapter 5.

This paper is written from a developers point of view. Its purpose is to shed light onto some practical aspects encountered in rather large development projects, but it does neither aim at resolving the open questions nor at discussing in depth all aspects of the field.

2 The model architecture

The reason for presenting the frame of a model architecture here is that our discussion of seamlessness will be based on it.[1] The model architecture defines the most important models of a software system that are produced during its development. For each model it describes the purpose of the model, its syntax and its semantics. As part of the metamodel of the development process it only defines the most important results of the process. The model architecture shows the static side of the methods used (the models that are developed), but it does not show the process side of the methods (how the models are developed).

A single model architecture may serve as a base for several life cycle models. It only fixes which models are to be developed and what their static relationships are, but it does not make any constraints on the order in which the models are developed or on the development process itself. A model architecture thus enables sequential and iterative approaches. Prototyping is no contradiction to having a model architecture. Prototyping is an aid in the process to attain certain models (e.g. experimental prototyping for the models of the system architecture) and a prototype can even be part of a certain model (e.g. part of the user interface specification can be modelled by a prototype). Figure 1 shows the different abstraction levels of the model architecture that is the base for this paper.

Different methods with different kinds of models can be fitted into this frame. Many of the current OO-methods do not provide a complete model architecture that fills the whole frame presented here. Most of them cover the models of the detailed design and to some extent the system analysis. Other parts like the external specification of large user interfaces or the domain analysis are still very immature. Depending on the method used, each level can contain more than one model. As an example, the analysis model of OMT is made up of the object model, the dynamic model and the functional model [Rumbaugh 91].

In the following description of the different levels of the frame of a model architecture we concentrate on the purpose of the models. But we do not describe any possible syntax or semantics of them, which would then make up a concrete definition of a model architecture.

Models of the Domain and Problem Analysis:[2]

These models describe the universe of discourse on a very coarse level of granularity. The universe of discourse may contain one or more existent or planned computer systems but is in any case larger than the one defined by the system boundaries in system analysis.

The purpose of the domain analysis model is the following:

- To identify concepts and models which span multiple applications in a given domain.
- To describe the universe of discourse in the language and in the way of thinking of the

1. There are some more reasons to emphasize the model architecture and to define it explicitly, namely:
   - The model architecture defines the static view of methods in a very condensed way.
   - The same model architecture may be valid throughout projects with different life cycle models, whereas the process has to be adapted.
   - The model architecture also serves as the basis for quality assurance, project control and metrics.
   - Those models that are to be maintained throughout the lifespan of a system can be defined easily based on the model architecture.

2. D'Souza has proposed a similar frame of a model architecture in [D'Souza 93].

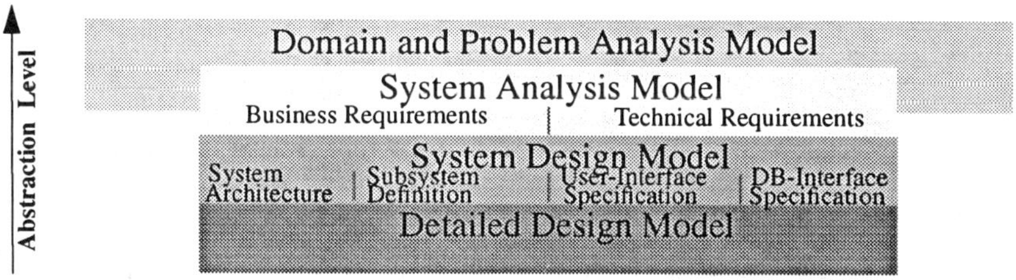

Figure 1

domain experts and users.

The purpose of the problem analysis model is:

- To describe one real-world problem in its environment.
- To model the problem in the language and in the way of thinking of the domain experts and users.

Models of the System Analysis:

The system analysis (also called conceptual modelling or functional requirements) focuses only on the part of a problem that will be implemented in a software system and differs from the problem analysis model mainly in the level of granularity and in the exact definition of the system boundaries. Before we can describe the outside view of the system, we need to know the exact system boundaries on a conceptual level. This must not to be mixed up with the user-interface specification, which is based on the specific technical constraints, goes into much more details, and is a model of the system design and not of the system analysis. The purpose of the system analysis model is:

- The system is modelled in the world of the user, in the way he is used to think. This may include business rules or business transactions that affect many different objects as well as objects that do not take any actions in the real world.
- The system is viewed and described from the outside. The overall features of the system must be determined. The main focus is on the external events acting on the system as a whole, together with their input and output characteristics.
- In order to support the definition of the business requirements (external view) it may be helpful to model the internal view on a very high level for structuring purposes. But the main focus lies on modelling what the business is (external view), not how it is solved by a certain system (internal view).

Examples of the semantics and syntax of system analysis models as defined above may be found in the requirements analysis of OOSE [Jacobson 92], the analysis model of Fusion [Fusion 93], or in Modern Structured Analysis [Yourdon 89].

Requirements concerning the technical constraints (also called non-functional requirements) also belong to the system analysis, but are not discussed here.

Models of the System Design:

While in the system analysis the business itself is modeled, the system design (also called system specification) defines the architectural requirements of one specific solution. The importance of the system design model depends on the complexity of the solution. For more complex systems the system design includes:

- Specification of the user interface: the purpose is to define exactly the "look and feel" of the interface from the users point of view. This is again an external view on the system as it does not describe how the user interface is designed internally.
- Specification of interfaces to other computer systems.
- Model of the system architecture and of the subsystems: the goal is the exact definition of the interfaces and responsibilities of the subsystems, which will then be designed independently.

The system design model thus shows how the requirements of the user are met by a certain software architecture. It is a technical model, using the language of the developer. Though some OO-methods stress the importance of the system design model (e.g. [Rumbaugh 91] and [Shlaer 93]), they do not provide modelling techniques for all parts of it.

Models of the Detailed Design:

Within the detailed design there are two kinds of models: the design model that is basically independent of a certain programming language and concentrates on the interface definition of the classes, and the implementation model that reflects the implementation and may be represented directly in the source code. The purpose is to define an object model that achieves as best as possible quality criteria like reusability, extendability, correctness and so on. The detailed design reflects the inside view of the system and incorporates all the details that are necessary to get a complete object model.

Not in every project models are needed at each level. There are many projects that start right away with the system analysis, the system design or even the detailed design. In these cases either the problem to be solved is very simple (the problem is implicitly defined in the minds of those, who solve it), or certain models are already defined in some other specifications, e.g. a hardware specification, a comprehensive and consistent problem statement or a company wide domain analysis.

Because the object oriented paradigm was first used in programming languages, there are many OO-methods that primarily address the detailed design. This, however, must not mislead us to forget the importance and purpose of the higher levels of abstraction.

3 Different kinds of seamlessness

For the further discussion it is useful to distinguish between different kinds of seamlessness, namely:

Seamlessness in the syntax

We speak of seamlessness in the syntax in different models or languages if they have the same set of symbols and if the rules how the symbols are put together to form a model or a program are equal. Of course, this does not mean that in every model every symbol must be used.

Seamlessness in the semantics

We speak about seamlessness in the semantics if the meaning and interpretation of the symbols is the same in the different models or languages. In the following examples we have seamlessness in the syntax, but no seamlessness in the semantics.

Example 1: The association symbol used in the analysis model may be the same as the one used in the design model. But the meaning of the symbol is different: in the analysis model it denotes a relationship that may be in both ways and may be a many-to-many relationship. In the design the symbol denotes a pointer, which is a one-way relationship and only points to one object.

Example 2: Depending on the context the symbol "class" may denote a type or a collection.

Seamlessness regarding the purpose of models

Every model has a certain purpose that determines its content and reflects a certain view of the system and a certain way of thinking. There are differences between modelling the business and modelling the software structure and there are differences between the outside view of a system, subsystem or object and its internal view. Two models are seamless in regard to their purpose, if they have the same purpose and reflect the same view of the system.

Seamlessness regarding the relation of two models

Even if two models differ in syntax, semantics and purpose, there may still be a weaker form of seamlessness: the seamlessness in the relation of two models. We say that two models are seamlessly related to each other if notions which were introduced in one model are represented in the other model in a very simple and straightforward manner [Jacobson 92]. This means that the relation between the components of different models and the transition from one model to another is well defined. Almost every model architecture claims this kind of seamlessness to a certain degree. But there are big differences in how smooth, precise and complete the transitions and relationships are defined.

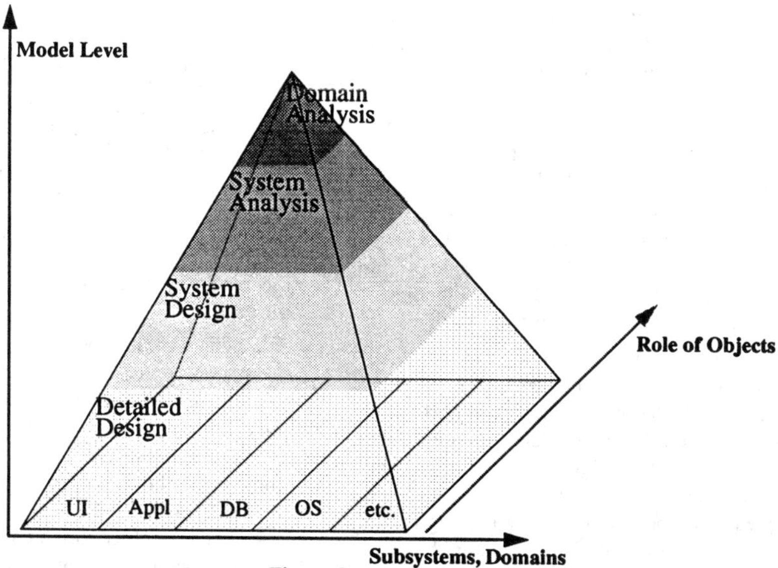

Figure 2

4 The three dimensions of seamlessness in the object oriented development

The above discussion of model architecture and seamlessness is independent of the paradigm used. It can be applied both for structured and object oriented methods and languages. In this paragraph we will now see what we can conclude for the object oriented software development. For this purpose, the different models are presented in a three-dimensional pyramid in figure 2. The first dimension is given by the different levels of the model architecture as described in chapter 2. The second dimension divides the object model into different subsystems or domains. Common subsystems are the user interface domain (UI), one or several application domains (Appl), a data base domain (DB) and the operating system domain (OS). The third dimension distinguishes the objects according to the role they have in the object model.

4.1 The different model levels

Because the different model levels have a different purpose by definition, there is clearly no seamlessness in purpose. What about the seamlessness in the semantics and syntax of these models as far as object oriented software development is concerned? This question is difficult to answer, because there is still no common agreement about the characteristics of object oriented analysis and design models, and because the characteristics used to determine if a programming language is object oriented or not do not apply directly on higher level models.

If we look at the system analysis models as proposed in [Fusion 93] and [Jacobson 92] it becomes clear, that they differ as well in semantics as in syntax from the models of the detailed design. They incorporate some, but not all of the semantics found in lower level models, and they add some more semantics to achieve purposes that are specific to their abstraction levels.

Even if object orientation cannot bring seamlessness regarding the purpose of the models, and has not yet brought the desired seamlessness in semantics and syntax into the first dimension of the model architecture, it has brought seamlessness into the relation between the models:

- As all the models are based on the object oriented paradigm, some characteristics, e.g. identifiable objects, classification, messaging and encapsulation are found in most models at the different levels. This is a great advantage compared to those methods that use completely different modeling paradigms for analysis and design (like Structured Analysis and Structured Design), and where neither the relation between the different syntax and semantics is obvious nor any methods that really support a clean transition are available.

- The way in which the elements of one model are related to the elements of another model can be well defined (see e.g. [Fusion 93], [Jacobson 93] and [OMT 91]), though no automatic transformation can be provided.

In the first dimension the seamlessness concerning the relationship is the most important one and here object orientation has brought a great breakthrough. Developers need different models to express different views. But the relations between these views must be clear and together these models should give a complete description of the system through different levels of abstraction. The goal for the future should be to improve the methods in supporting this kind of seamlessness, and not to enforce seamlessness in syntax and semantics to a degree where the different purposes of the model levels get lost.

4.2 The different domains

Though the different object oriented programming languages (OPLs) all incorporate the characteristics of object oriented languages, they differ in the details of the underlying object model (e.g. multiple inheritance in C++, class variables and methods in Smalltalk, pre- and postconditions in Eiffel) and in their syntax. Of course there are interfaces to bridge the seam between subsystems designed and implemented in different languages, but the seam remains.

Another source of seam in syntax and semantics are different libraries and different frameworks for the different subsystems. If we use different libraries for the user interface, for the application domains and for the database subsystem, these libraries do not necessarily match in the common parts. Certain user interface management systems (UIMS) and object oriented database management systems (ODBMS) even force the developer to use their underlying object model and their library for all communication. Therefore a mismatch cannot be avoided. The only help here is a very careful system

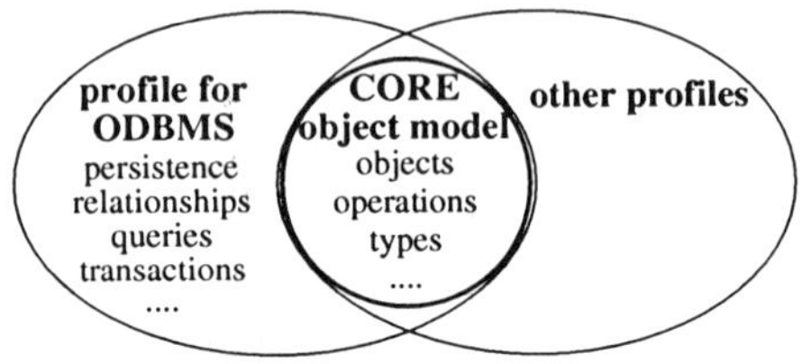

Figure 3

design and a wise choice of the tools and libraries to be used.

The big breakthrough object orientation has brought into the second dimension concerns the seamlessness between applications and database management systems (DBMS). One big concern in classical software development is the seam between the procedural languages and the relational calculus of the DBMS. By using object oriented languages together with object oriented database systems it is hoped to avoid this seam. As far as the underlying paradigm is concerned, the seam has indeed been closed and there is no more change of paradigm between relational and procedural models. But the seamlessness between the applications and the ODBMS is not yet perfect. Up to now the meta models underlying the different ODBMS differed from each other and they differed also from the meta model underlying the OPLs. Some of the latter differences are due to the fact that ODBMS fulfil requirements that are not found in most OPLs, e.g.:

- Each object in the database needs some kind of handle that is persistent over time and can be retrieved when the application is started again.
- The objects in the database may be used concurrently by several applications.
- Most OPLs do not differentiate between the type definition of an object and the collections of objects, a distinction necessary in data bases.

To overcome these differences in the object models and to allow the programmer to experience as much seamlessness as possible across different ODBMS and with certain programming languages, the Object Database Management Group (ODMG) has defined the Object DBMS Standard, which contains a common object model. The members of the ODMG will sell ODBMS that are based on this model [ODMG 93]. The Object DBMS Standard includes the core components of the OMG Object Model and will be proposed to become an accepted profile in the OMG architecture as illustrated in figure 3.

4.3 The role of objects

Within each model we find objects with different roles. Some objects provide low level services, e.g. mathematical functions or collection classes, others reflect the essence of a subsystem. Some objects act as servers, just being there to help other objects fulfil their responsibilities, while others have the role of interfaces between some groups of objects or are controllers that incorporate control mechanisms. In the design of a model it is often helpful to distinguish between the different roles of objects. Some methods even use different syntax for objects with different roles (e.g. entity objects, control objects and interface objects in the analysis and design models in [Jacobson 92]).

There are several schemes that may be used to distinguish between the roles of an object, e.g.:

- Classification according to the behavior and the responsibility of an object within a group of objects (see also [Wirfs 93]):
  - Server objects: objects that do not use other objects but only provide services.
  - Controller objects: objects whose main responsibility is controlling some higher level aspects.
  - Coordinator objects: objects that help to reduce the coupling.
  - Interface objects: objects that are used as an entrance point for accessing a group of objects from the outside.
- Classification according to the essence of an object for the system:
  - Essential objects: these objects reflect the essence of a certain subsystem.
  - Architectural objects: these objects complete the object model of a subsystem to get a higher level design.
  - Low-level objects: objects typically found in libraries, e.g. building blocks for lists, mathematical functions and collection classes.

Though the role of the objects may differ, they have the same syntax and the same semantics in the design. The quality metrics are the same for all different objects as far as their role is concerned. Therefore, if object oriented techniques are used, there is a high level of seamlessness in syntax and semantics in the third dimension of our system pyramid.

5 Misconceptions about seamlessness

5.1 Mismatch between abstraction levels and roles of objects

For the classifications of the roles of objects according to their essence for the system, there are also other terms in use, namely: analysis objects, design objects and implementation objects. Analysis objects in the design and implementation models are those objects that are derived from some objects already present in the analysis model. They represent the key concepts of the problem domain. Essential objects from other subsystems (e.g. objects for the user interface) and architectural objects are called design objects. The implementation objects are those objects that do not have any predecessors in higher level models (see also [Meyer 93]). Figure 4 shows this classification for the implementation model.

The misconception comes in when this classification is used as an argument for the seamlessness in syntax, semantics and purpose of the analysis, design and implementation model. If we call the part of the implementation model that is made up of analysis objects the analysis model, that analysis model corresponds no longer to the analysis model defined in our model architecture. It is just a first cut of the implementation model. In this case there is only one level of abstraction, and only one model being developed during the whole development process, namely the implementation model[3]. As a consequence the models of analysis, system design and detailed design do not address different purposes, different views (external and internal views) and different experts (domain, user and programming experts), but denote only what kind of objects are added to the model.

3.This view is promoted by those CASE-Tools that either advocate code generation out of analysis models or allow only one abstraction level of the model architecture.

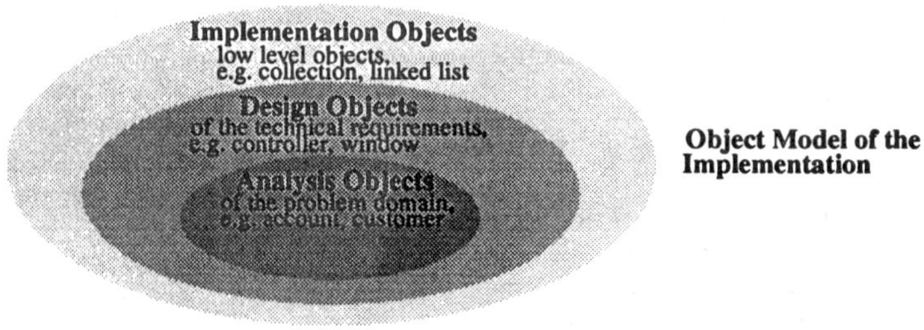

Figure 4

Thus if we do not distinguish clearly between the abstraction levels of models and the role of objects, we are likely to run into some of the following problems:

- We degrade analysis to be the first draft of design. This means that we just start with design and use the quality criteria and semantics of the detailed design already in the first steps of analysis.
- The focus in the analysis model is on describing the real world according to the purposes and criteria of the analysis model. When the resulting objects are just carried over into the design, this can result in a bad design, because the different purpose and semantics of the analysis and design models also imply different quality criteria.
- The essential objects of the domains other than the problem domain are often handled as less important add-ons, thus neglecting a careful system design.

As far as seamlessness is concerned, considering the analysis model as being just a part of the implementation model results in a very high degree of seamlessness, but it is a seamlessness in the third dimension (the role of objects) of our system pyramid and not in the first one (the abstraction level of models).

5.2 Object models based on an extended entity relationship model

One popular way of developing an object model is the data driven approach. In a first step, some kind of extended entity relationship model (ERM) is developed. In a second step, operations and messages are added. Though the model gets refined and completed by further classes, the entities and relationships discovered and modelled in the first step remain more or less the same during analysis, design and implementation. The entities modelled by the criteria of data modelling are then the objects that should satisfy encapsulation, high cohesion, low coupling and a good subsystem structure. There seems to be a high degree of seamlessness, but this seamlessness is primarily one in the syntax. The syntax of an ERM is a subset of the syntax of the object model of the analysis and the design. But what about the semantics of the models?

- ERMs have a flat structure. The unit of encapsulation is a very small one: entities. These entities can be put into aggregations, but the aggregations are always viewed as a loose collection of entities and their inside is known to the rest of the model.
- Normalization is a very important notion in ER-modelling. But normalization makes it necessary to handle structured or polyvalent attributes as separate entities (e.g. in [Coad 91]). In an object model, however, objects may have a complex structure.
- ERMs do not support information hiding. Every entity and everything inside an entity is visible to any other entity in the model. The interface to the entity is defined by its internal structure. Visibility criteria do not play any role in the modelling of an ERM. In an object model, however, there is a clear distinction between the interface and the internals of a class and it should also be clearly stated, to which other classes a class is visible.
- Attributes and operations are distinguished from the beginning of the modelling process.

But analysis should only answer the question which features and responsibilities a certain class or group of classes has, and not if they are provided as data or as operations. This design and implementation decisions should remain the responsibility of the detailed design, and not be decided upon in the first steps of analysis.

- The quality of an object model can be measured by the degree of cohesion inside the classes and the coupling between the classes. In order to achieve good quality the interface of a class, i.e. its operations, must be determined according to these criteria. If classes are determined only based on the static data that resides in them and all other features are added later on, either the model has to be thoroughly redone (i.e. transformed into a totally new model), thus sacrificing the claimed seamlessness, or the object model will be of a bad quality.[4]
- Large systems are divided in subsystems according to the criteria of high cohesion and low coupling. An ERM itself does not support the notion of subsystems. If they are introduced later on, either the subsystems cannot satisfy the mentioned criteria, or the model must be thoroughly revised, thus sacrificing the seamless extension of an ERM into an object model.

So there is seamlessness in the syntax, but not in the semantics between an ERM and an object model, and there is certainly no seamlessness in purpose between an ERM of the analysis and an object model of the design.

If we nevertheless want to use the ERM in the analysis, there are two possibilities: First, we may enforce a seamless extension of the ERM into the object model by just adding to the data model of the analysis operations and further classes as necessary for the design and the implementation. Then the resulting object model will have a high degree of coupling between the classes, and size, complexity and visibility of the classes are not minimized.

The second possibility is to sacrifice seamlessness in order to get a really good design. The data driven approach is used in analysis (with or without defining operations for the classes). The object model of the design uses the analysis model only as a source of well defined information but is made according to the quality criteria of the design, thus introducing a clear seam between the two models (though they may have the same syntax):

- ERMs are a good modelling technique to investigate the data especially in information engineering and to model part of the system requirements. We can use ERMs as part of the problem analysis in order to describe the data-side of the requirements and with the goal of modelling the problem from a user's perspective.
- After the analysis and after having decided upon the overall system architecture, we can use the ERM as an input to the object models of the application domains. However the object model must be built according to the criteria of good object design and does not necessarily resemble the original ERM from analysis. The developer then makes the design with the goal to get easily maintainable, extendable and reusable classes.

5.3 "The use of OPLs has made all higher level models superfluous"

In the times of assembler programming the gap between the description of an algorithm in structured English and its code was quite large. When the first third generation languages appeared, this gap nearly vanished, because these languages were just as expressive as structured English. Still the overall program structure, especially the interfaces to the different modules, had to be described separately. With more advanced programming languages like Modula2, Ada or Eiffel, even this could be done just as nicely in the programming language. As a matter of fact, there are many well documented systems around that are structured and documented directly in the source code, using the features of the programming languages (and comments, of course). Having now object orientation, and thus languages

4. A comparison of the quality of an object model developed according to the data driven approach and the quality of one developed according to other approaches may be found in [Sharble 93]

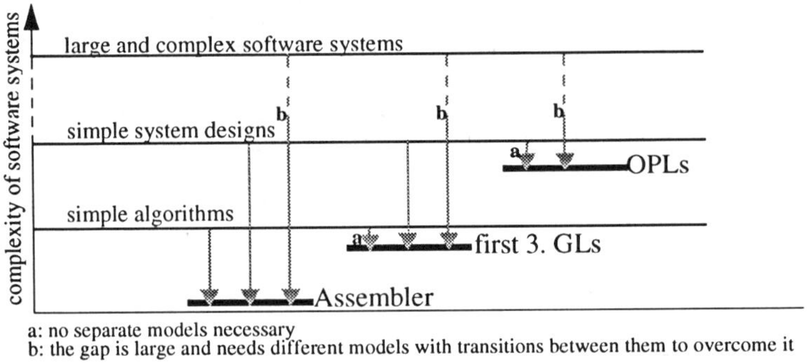

Figure 5

that allow to implement directly all features of an object oriented system, are there still any higher level models necessary? If we look at certain systems that were implemented some years ago and that needed several transitions from the problem statement down to the assembler coding, we are tempted to say no, because their problem definitions are simple enough to be described directly in modern OO-languages, obtaining total seamlessness by having only one model. We get the same picture if we look into books on object oriented programming where many examples with a textual problem statement can be directly implemented in a high level OO-language.

Nevertheless there are two reasons, why still several model levels are necessary and why the problem definition and the system design in general cannot be directly included into the source code:

- Complexity of the problems to be solved: As the programming languages evolved the systems to be built also became more complex. The system architecture and the user interactions are much more complex today. The systems are larger, different software systems need to be connected and the use of off-the-shelf components like DMBS, UIMS and networking software became much more important. For complex systems it is not possible to model all the different views in one model. The danger to get lost in a complex project is too high.
- Abstraction levels, ways of thinking: Even if we have very mighty programming languages (even mightier ones than todays OPLs), there will still be the difference in the purpose between designing a system by system experts and analyzing the problem domain by domain experts. There must be a transition from the analysis model to the design model, because they represent different ways of thinking, are approved by different kinds of people and are created according to different quality criteria. As long as we want to reflect the business world as directly as possible, we need object models that are able to reflect the way of thinking of the business world. Thus a transition form the object model of the business to the object model of the implementation is unavoidable (see also [Palmer 93]).

6 Conclusions

In this paper we have discussed object oriented software development with respect to seamlessness. In order to lay a common foundation, we have first defined a model architecture consisting of different abstraction levels, and a classification of seamlessness according to the seam in the syntax, the semantics, the purpose, and the seam in the relationship. In a second step we have examined seamlessness with respect to three dimensions, namely the different abstraction levels, the different subsystems or domains found in a system, and the different roles of objects in a model.

As far as the different roles of objects in a model are concerned, seamlessness in syntax and semantics is already available today.

For the different domains, object orientation can bring seamlessness in syntax and semantics at least to a certain degree, too. However, due to differences in syntax and semantics of different OPLs, ODBMS, UIMS and libraries, the maximum degree of seamlessness has not yet been reached. As soon as a standard object model will be generally acknowledged and incorporated, the situation will be much better. Corresponding efforts of the OMG concerning a core object model and of the ODMG concerning database systems are on the way.

Another advantage of the object oriented software development is the seamlessness in the relationship between the models of different abstraction levels (the first dimension in the system pyramid). The fact that all models are based on the same object oriented paradigm makes well defined transitions from one abstraction level to another possible. But because purpose and content of the different abstraction levels are different by definition, there will always remain a seam in purpose between them. The question to what extent seamlessness in semantics between different abstraction levels can be reached remains open because todays methods do not yet cover all areas of the model architecture, and because new methods are still emerging.

7 References

[Booch 91] Object Oriented Design, G. Booch, Benjamin/Cummings, 1991

[Coad 91] Object-Oriented Analysis, P. Coad and E. Yourdon, Prentice-Hall, 1991

[D'Souza 93] Comparing OO Analysis and Design Methods, D. D'Souza, Proceedings of the OOP93 in Muenchen

[Fusion 93] Object-Oriented Development: The Fusion Method, D. Coleman et al., HP Laboratories, 1993

[Jacobson 92] Object-Oriented Software Engineering, I. Jacobson, Addison Wesley, 1992

[Meyer 93] Design by Contract, B. Meyer and J. M. Nerson, Proceedings of the Summer School of EDBT in Leysin, 1993

[ODMG 93] The Object DBMS Standard, Th. Atwood, Object Magazine, Sept.-Oct. 1993; The ODMG Object Model, M. Loomis, JOOP June 1993

[OMG 92] The OMG Object Model, Object Management Architecture Guide V2, OMG, 1992

[Palmer 93] Seamlessness or shamelessness?, J. Palmer, Object Magazine, Sept.-Oct. 1993

[Rumbaugh 91]Object Oriented Modelling and Design, J. Rumbaugh et al., Prentice-Hall, 1991

[Sharble 93] The Object-Oriented Brewery: A Comparison of Two Object-Oriented Development Methods, R. Sharble and S. Cohen, ACM Software Engineering Notes, April 1993

[Shlaer 93] A Deeper Look at the Transition from Analysis to Design, S. Shlaer and S. Mellor, JOOP 5(9), 1993

[Wirfs 90] Designing Object-Oriented Software, R. Wirfs-Brock et al., Prentice-Hall, 1990

[Wirfs 93] R. Wirfs-Brock, talk given at the CHOOSE-Forum (Zuerich, Switzerland, 1993)

[Yourdon 89] Modern Structured Analysis, E. Yourdon, Prentice-Hall, 1989

A Development Framework for Object-Oriented Specification and Refinement

Graeme Smith

CRIN-CNRS and INRIA Lorraine
Nancy, France

Abstract

This paper presents a language-independent framework for developing formal specifications in an intuitively object-oriented style. Within the framework, object-oriented concepts and design strategies are captured by the application of development operators. The operators, by effectively hiding the technical details of how object-oriented concepts are captured in a given specification language, allow the specifier to develop specifications in an intuitively object-oriented fashion. They also present a flexible approach to object-oriented specification as libraries of operators can be defined allowing many different definitions of object-oriented features to be available. This enables a close mapping to be achieved between the specification and the implementation in the chosen object-oriented programming language. The framework also records the history of operator application enabling "classes" and "modules" to be identified in the resulting specifications and, hence, the possibility of modular verification and refinement.

1 Introduction

Formal methods of specification, verification and refinement[1] have long been advocated as a means of reducing design errors and increasing confidence in developed software systems. Recently, several approaches have been proposed for combining object-oriented concepts with formal methods. Most of these have involved the extension of existing specification languages or techniques with object-oriented concepts[Alencar 91, Clerici 88, Duke 91, Engelfriet 91], while others have simply suggested conventions for using existing specification languages in an object-oriented style[Cusack 90, Hall 90, Whysall 91].

To the object-oriented programming community, these approaches have the potential for offering a means of formal software development where the same design concepts and system structuring can be used from specification through to implementation. Also, they can improve the efficiency and confidence in software reuse by providing precise documentation of existing software components. However, they are still generally regarded as being too difficult or too impractical to use.

The approaches based on extending an existing language require that the semantics of the language be extended or completely modified to incorporate the object-oriented features. Therefore, they cannot directly use existing methods of verification and refinement and support tools already developed for the language. Moreover, the resulting language and, in particular, its semantics can be quite complex making the development of new methods and tools difficult. A further problem with these approaches is that, in order to reasonably limit the size of the language, the language designer must decide on specific definitions of particular object-oriented features when, in fact, a range of possible definitions may exist. If a precise mapping between features in the specification and implementation is desirable, such decisions may limit the object-oriented programming languages with which the approach can be effectively used.

The approaches based on using conventions, on the other hand, don't complicate the specification language and its semantics and are also more flexible since it is always possible to define further

[1] Refinement is the process of transforming a specification into, or towards, code.

From TOOLS EUROPE '94 (Technology of Object-Oriented Languages and Systems).

conventions to capture alternative definitions of particular object-oriented features. However, often the conventions are difficult to use and don't allow the specifier to develop specifications in an intuitively object-oriented fashion.

A further problem with nearly all of the approaches is that classes are the only structuring form[2]. Consequently, modular refinement of object-oriented specifications has been concerned only with the refinement of individual classes[Utting 91, Whysall 91]. This is, however, too restrictive. Often an invariant best expressed in terms of one class at a high-level of abstraction is better expressed in terms of one or more other classes at implementation. This notion is central to development methodologies based on responsibility-driven design[Dubois 93, Feather 87]. Therefore, a practical notion of refinement needs to be concerned, not only with classes, but also with *modules* which group related classes.

This paper presents an approach which overcomes the problems described above. It is language-independent and so can be used with existing specification languages and, hence, already developed methods of verification and refinement. Object-oriented concepts are modelled by the application of *development operators*, i.e. operators which enable the incremental construction and modification of specifications. Such operators are defined within a specification development framework in which the specification itself is a component. They enable the specifier to develop specifications in a more intuitively object-oriented fashion by separating the use of object-oriented concepts from the technical details of how they are captured. The approach also offers flexibility since it is possible to define a library of operators capturing alternative definitions of particular object-oriented features.

By also recording the history of operator application in the framework, "classes" and "modules" can be identified in the resulting specification and modular verification and refinement can be carried out. The history, by providing information concerning the design decisions taken during the specification's development, represents a deeper understanding of the specified system than the specification alone. This information may also be useful for adapting and modifying the specification as the system evolves.

The proposed approach is intended to form the basis of an interactive specification development tool. It is based on work done on the SACSO system[Finance 90] and continued in the ESPRIT project ICARUS concerned with the incremental construction of specifications[Souquières 93]. The latter proposes a language-independent framework in which the development of a specification is formalised in terms of a *product*, denoting the specification, and a *workplan*, denoting the history of goals to be achieved and the corresponding application of development operators. Section 2 describes this development framework and Section 3 illustrates how it can be used for developing specifications in an object-oriented fashion. Section 4 presents a simple case study and Section 5, referring to this case study, describes how the framework can be used to enable modular refinement.

[2]The approach of [Alencar 91] also supports notions of modules, theories and views[Goguen 87].

2 Development Framework

This section describes the proposed development framework. The development of a specification can be viewed as a sequence of steps where each step corresponds to the application of a development operator to the development state. The development state consists of a workplan, denoting the history of goals and development decisions, and a product, denoting the specification. Links associate sections of the workplan and product.

2.1 Workplan

The workplan consists of a collection of *tasks* describing goals to be achieved in order to produce the required specification. A task is *reduced* by the application of a development operator. A reduction consists of decomposing the task into several subtasks. These subtasks together achieve the same goal as denoted by the original task. For example, during the development of a specification, a task of the form Specify Queue may be reduced by a development operator to the subtasks Specify Queue State and Specify Queue Operations. This is represented graphically as in Figure 1.

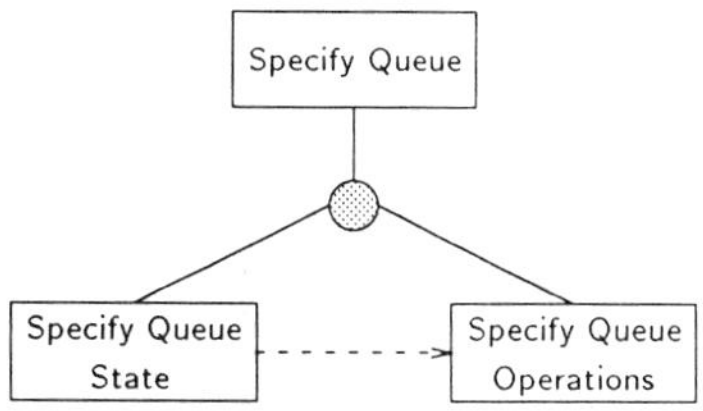

Figure 1: Reduction of the task Specify Queue.

In general, there may be several possible reductions for any given task. A task may, therefore, be reduced by a number of different development operators.

Often it is desirable to decompose a task into its subtasks progressively, i.e. to apply an operator which produces only one, or a limited number, of the required subtasks at a time. For example, the task Specify Queue Operations could be reduced to a single subtask Specify Join Operation and then later, after the specification of the Join operation is completed, a subtask Specify Leave Operation could be added. To enable this, a reduction can be either *partial* (represented by a non-shaded circle) or *complete* (represented by a shaded circle as in Figure 1). A partial reduction is one which allows the list of its subtasks to be extended.

Subtasks of a given task may also be related by a *precedence relation* indicating that certain of them must be reduced before others. A precedence relation is a strict partial order on tasks and may be either *strong* (represented graphically by a full arrow between the tasks) or *weak* (represented graphically by a dashed arrow between the tasks as in Figure 1). A strong-precedence relation between tasks T1 and T2 indicates that T2 cannot be reduced until T1's reduction is completed. A weak-precedence relation between T1 and T2, on the other hand, indicates that T2 cannot be reduced until the reduction of T1 has made "sufficient progress". This notion is informal and can only be decided by the specifier. The weak-precedence relation, therefore, acts as a hint to the specifier as to which subtask to reduce first.

2.2 Product and Workplan-Product Links

The product consists of both formal and informal text. The role of the informal text is to aid the understanding of the formal text. During the development of a specification, an incomplete part of the product is represented by a *placeholder* which is linked to a single non-reduced task in the workplan. It is replaced by formal or informal text by the application of development operators to the task and its subsequent subtasks. When this occurs, the links between the workplan and product are maintained so that each completed part of the product is linked to the tasks in the workplan which produced it. In the context of object-oriented specification, these links enable the identification of parts of the product with object-oriented structures such as classes and modules. As the specification language may not support such structures, they are not necessarily evident in the product alone.

2.3 Development Operators

Development operators work simultaneously on the workplan and product to reduce tasks and construct or modify the product text. They obtain parameters interactively from the specifier and also from the existing workplan and product. Since they manipulate product text, development operators are necessarily language-dependent. An operator typically adds to the product a parameterised text which, together with the structuring implied by the workplan, captures the desired object-oriented concept.

For simplicity, the operators in the next sections will be presented without reference to a particular specification language. For interested readers, a set of operators for constructing object-oriented specifications in the formal specification language Z can be found in [Smith 94].

3 Operators for Object-Oriented Specification

This section presents several operators for the framework described in Section 2. The operators enable a particular approach to object-oriented development to be followed. Alternative approaches could also be made available by extending the set of operators. In particular, operators based on existing object-oriented design methods (e.g. [Booch 91, Rumbaugh 91]) could be developed.

In general, the operators fall into three categories: those that correspond to applying a particular design strategy, those that correspond to the identification of particular components, e.g. classes or operations, to be specified and those that correspond to the task of specification itself.

3.1 Applying design strategies

The first group of operators are used to apply a particular design strategy. They are used in the preliminary stages of the specification of a particular component in the product. Generally, such operators produce complete reductions and precedence relations between their subtasks. They replace a single placeholder in the product with a text interspersed with two or more new placeholders. The text is derived entirely from the existing product and workplan. For example, to specify a previously identified class one of the three following strategies could be chosen.

- The class could be defined explicitly in terms of its state and operations possibly instantiating existing classes.
- It could be defined as a subclass of one or more existing classes.
- It could be defined by first defining one or more other classes which it inherits or instantiates.

Let the operators which apply these strategies be called Specify Class, Specify Subclass and Specify Module respectively. A workplan reduction corresponding to Specify Class was shown in Figure 1. A more general representation of this reduction is shown in Figure 2 where CLASS is a parameter, representing the class name. When a parameter is used in the name of a task it is automatically passed to any operator used to reduce that task.

The reduction associated with Specify Subclass is shown in Figure 3. The subtask Identify CLASS Inherited Classes would typically be linked to several placeholders in the product. These placeholders would be replaced by text parameterised with information derived from the existing product, i.e. information associated with the inherited classes. The subtasks Specify CLASS State and Specify CLASS Operations correspond to specifying additional state information and operations, respectively, in the subclass.

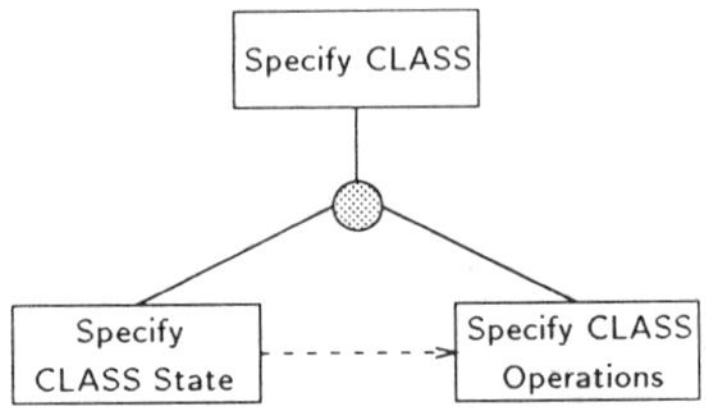

Figure 2: The operator Specify Class.

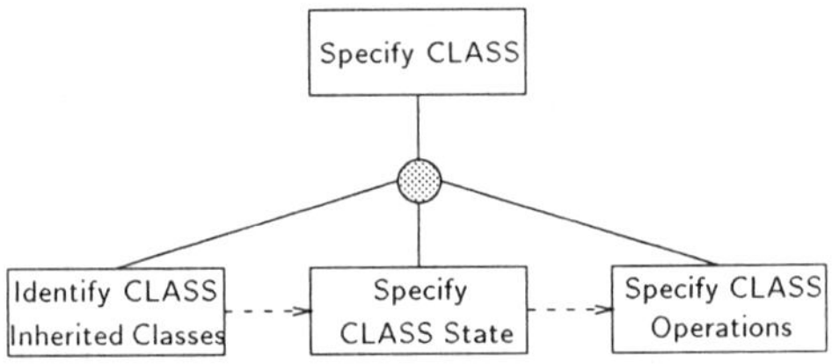

Figure 3: The operator Specify Subclass.

The reduction associated with Specify Module is shown in Figure 4. The first subtask involves the specification of the classes required in order to specify the desired class. The second subtask involves the specification of the desired class using the classes defined in the first subtask.

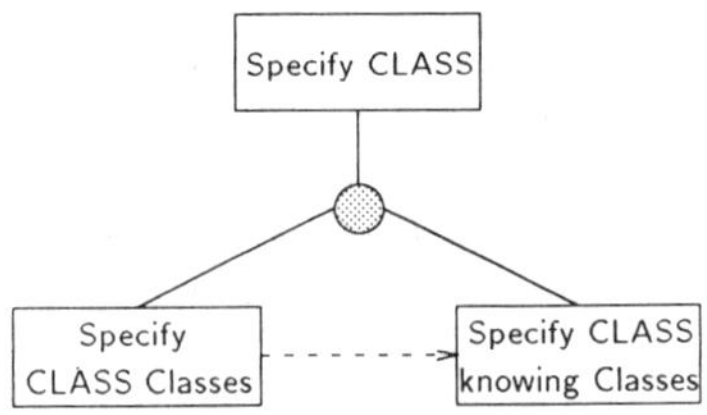

Figure 4: The operator Specify Module.

Other operators in this group are the operators for specifying the state information of classes and for specifying previously identified operations. Let these operators be called Specify State and Specify Operation respectively. Their reductions are shown in Figure 5.

3.2 Identifying components of the specification

The second group of operators are used to identify similar components in a specification when an arbitrary number of such components may ex-

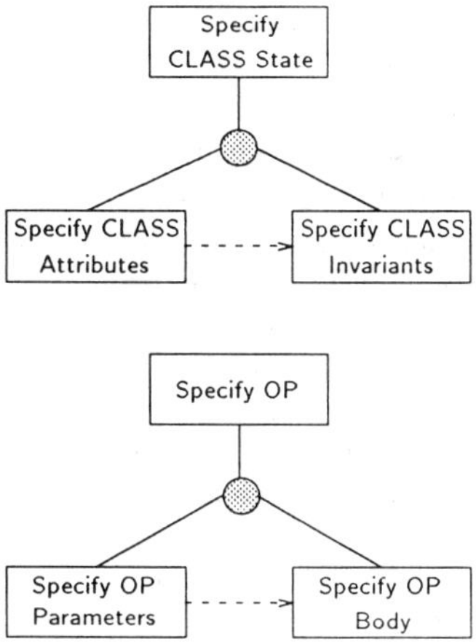

Figure 5: The operators **Specify State** and **Specify Operation**.

ist. They are used in the intermediate stages of the specification of a particular component of the product. Generally, such operators produce partial reductions (so that more components can be identified at a later time) and no precedence relations between their subtasks. For example, the task **Specify CLASS Operations**, produced by the operators **Specify Class** and **Specify Subclass**, could be reduced by an operator **Identify Operations** which requires the specifier to interactively provide the names of the operations and produces subtasks corresponding to the specification of each. The reduction associated with this operator is shown in Figure 6; OP_1, OP_2, etc are the parameters provided by the specifier.

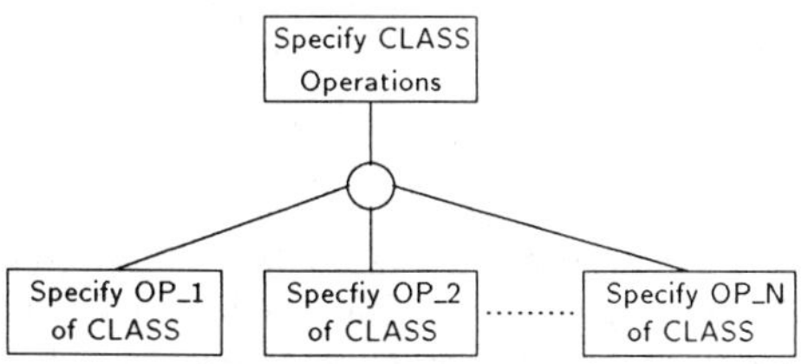

Figure 6: The **Identify Operations** operator.

Similarly, the subtask **Specify CLASS Classes**, produced by the operator **Specify Module**, could be reduced by an operator **Identify Classes**. The reduction is shown in Figure 7.

A similar operator could be used to reduce the

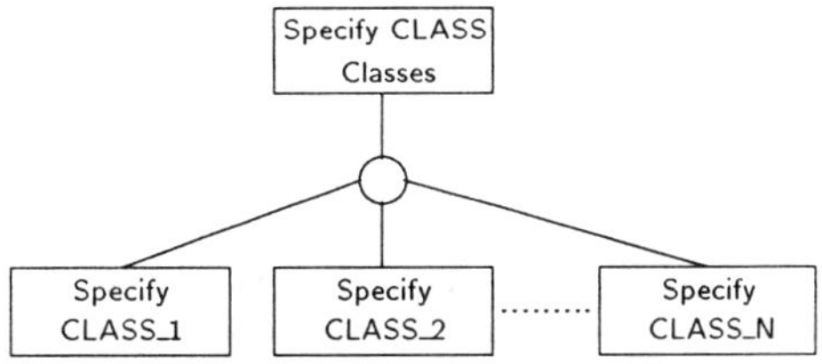

Figure 7: The **Identify Classes** operator.

task **Identify CLASS Inherited Classes** produced by the operator **Specify Subclass**. In this case, however, the subtasks would depend on the type of inheritance being modelled. For example, if inherited operations were allowed to be redefined then the subtasks could be of the form **Redefine CLASS_N Operations in CLASS**. On the other hand, if no modifications were allowed to be made to the inherited classes then no subtasks would be required.

3.3 Specifying components of the specification

The final set of operators are used to complete the specification of a component of the product. Generally, they have no subtasks and produce a partial reduction. These operators would be used to reduce the subtasks of the **Specify State** and **Specify Operation** operators. They are the most language dependent of the operators as they require the specifier to interactively input either specification text or text from which the required specification text can be derived. For example, the subtask **Specify CLASS Attributes**, produced by the operator **Specify State**, would be reduced by an operator which would require the names of attributes and their types to be interactively input by the specifier. In the case of a state-based specification language, i.e. a specification language which includes an explicit notion of state, such information could be placed directly into the product. For example, for the specification language Z[Spivey 89], the operator, given the parameters corresponding to an attribute A of type T, would produce the following product transformation (placeholders are represented by '...').

```
┌ CLASS ────────                 ┌ CLASS ────────
│ ...                            │ A : T
├──────                 ⟹        │ ...
│ ...                            ├──────
└──────────────                  │ ...
                                 └──────────────
```

In the case of a specification language which doesn't support an explicit notion of state, the operator could be considerably more complex. For example, for the algebraic specification language Glider[FUN (Namur) 90], the operator, given the parameters corresponding to an attribute A of type T, may produce a product transformation as follows.

```
Type cluster  CLASS              Type cluster  CLASS
 ...                              ...
 ...                     ⟹        operation  Access_A
end  CLASS                         arity  CLASS — T
                                    ...
                                   end  Access_A
                                  ...
                                 end  CLASS
```

Since Glider, being algebraic, has no notion of state, the attribute A is simulated by an operation *Access_A* which returns the value of A when it is called. The equations defining this operation would be derived automatically from the definition of the class operations. The full definition of a development operator which uses such an approach to enable an attribute to be added to an already defined class can be found in [Souquières 93].

Such operators illustrate the kind of technical details needed to capture object-oriented concepts in most existing specification languages. The proposed framework effectively hides these details from the specifier during the development of a specification. For the operator above, the specifier need only provide the name of the attribute and its type.

4 Case Study: A simple communications network

In this section, a case study is used to illustrate how the framework and the operators presented in the preceding sections can be used to aid the development of a specification in an object-oriented style. The case study is of a simple communications network. The network is composed of a number of interacting nodes. A node receives messages from the network, processes them and then sends them on. Each node has an input queue of received messages which have not yet been processed and an output queue of processed messages which have not yet been sent.

The workplan of the specification development is shown in Figure 8. (The parts of the development corresponding to the specification of states and operations are elided.) The first step corresponds to choosing the design strategy for the development of the class **Network**. Since the network is composed of a collection of node objects, it is necessary to first define the node class and, hence, the operator **Specify Module** is chosen. The subtask **Specify Network Classes** produced by the application of this operator is then reduced by application of the operator **Identify Classes** and the identification, by the specifier, of the single class **Node**.

The next step involves the specification of the class **Node**. Since a node is composed of queue objects, the task **Specify Node** is reduced by another application of the **Specify Module** operator. This is followed by the reduction of the subtask **Specify Node Classes** with the operator **Identify Classes** and the identification of the single class **Queue**.

The next step involves the reduction of the task **Specify Queue**. This class can be specified directly in terms of its state and operations and, hence, the operator **Specify Class** is chosen. The step is followed by the reduction of its subtasks. For example, for the specification language Z, the application of the operator **Specify Class** would produce the following product transformation.

```
                        ┌ Queue ────────
 ...           ⟹        │ ...
                        └──────────────
                         ...
```

The two new place holders would be linked to the subtasks **Specify Queue State** and **Specify Queue Operations**. **Specify Queue State** would be reduced by the operator **Specify State** followed by an operator corresponding to the declaration of an attribute *msgs* representing the sequence of messages in the queue. (No invariants are specified on the queue at this level of abstraction.) The product transformation is shown below (where *Msg* denotes the set of all possible messages and seq *Msg* the set of all possible sequences of such messages).

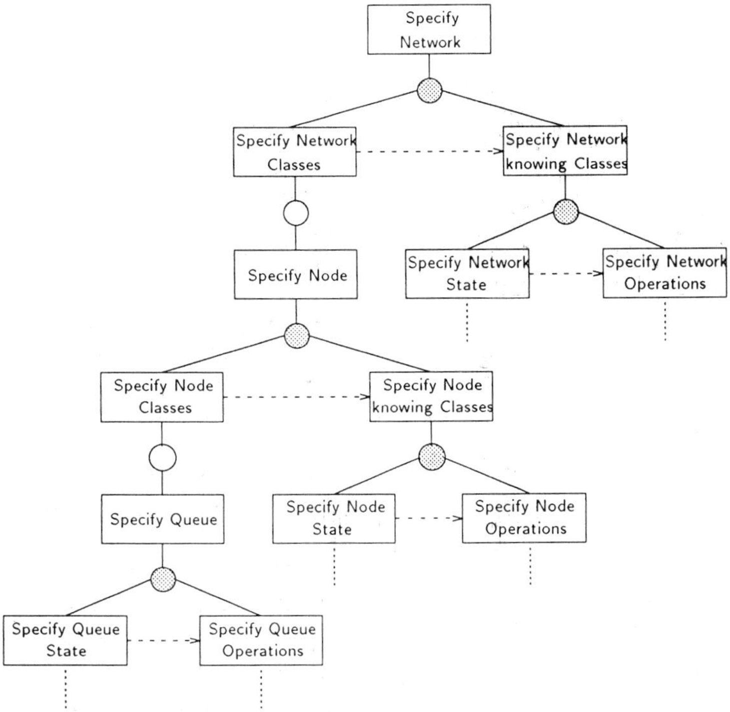

Figure 8: Workplan of **Network** specification.

Queue
...

...

$\Longrightarrow$

Queue
msgs : seq *Msg*

...

The specification of the queue class is completed by identifying and specifying the possible operations[3]. Application of the **Identify Operations** operator produces the following product transformation (where *Join* and *Leave* are the operation names provided as parameters by the specifier).

Queue
msgs : seq *Msg*

...

$\Longrightarrow$

Queue
msgs : seq *Msg*

Queue_Join
Δ*Queue*
...

Queue_Leave
Δ*Queue*
...

[3]The operator Specify Class does not allow the initial state of objects of a class to be defined. If this were necessary an alternative operator could be defined and used.

This operator demonstrates how the object-oriented development of specifications can be made more intuitive. Since Z has no notion of classes or encapsulation, name clashes occur unless all operations in a specification are given distinct names. Furthermore, it is necessary to declare explicitly which part of the specification state an operation may change. The specifier, however, may ignore these concerns as they are handled by the operator. The operations produced have the names *Queue_Join* and *Queue_Leave*, i.e. the specified names prefixed with the class name *Queue*. This enables the specifier to use the same names for operations in other classes without name clashes occurring. Also, the declaration Δ*Queue*, stating that the operations change the state associated with the queue class, is included automatically in each operation.

The operations are completed by application of the operator **Specify Operation**, to each of them. This is followed by appropriate operators, similar to that used to declare an attribute, to define their parameters and bodies (the predicates of the operation bodies would be input directly by the specifier). The complete product is shown below.

Queue

$msgs : \text{seq}\ Msg$

Queue_Join

$\Delta Queue$
$in? : Msg$

$msgs' = msgs \frown \langle in? \rangle$

Queue_Leave

$\Delta Queue$
$out! : Msg$

$msgs = \langle out! \rangle \frown msgs'$

The specification development is completed by the reductions of the tasks Specify Node and Specify Network in a similar fashion.

5 Object-Oriented Refinement

In this section, the case study is used to illustrate how the framework can aid the modular refinement of object-oriented specifications. By examining the workplan, parts of the product corresponding to classes and modules can be identified. These parts represent sub-specifications which can be refined in isolation. By adding appropriate tasks to the workplan, such refinements can also be carried out by the application of development operators.

5.1 Refining classes

Classes are identified as those parts of the product linked to the tasks following, and the task immediately preceding, any reduction produced by the operators Specify Class or Specify Subclass. In the specification of the communications network three classes can be identified. These classes are associated with the subtrees beginning with the tasks Specify Queue, Specify Node knowing Classes and Specify Network knowing Classes.

Assuming the operators which create and use classes have been defined, or used by the specifier, in a way which respects the notion of class encapsulation, the classes within a product can be refined in isolation thus simplifying the overall refinement process. To simplify the identification of classes and aid the process of refinement, subtasks corresponding to the refinement of classes could be introduced. For example, the operator Specify Class could be modified to produce the workplan reduction shown in Figure 9.

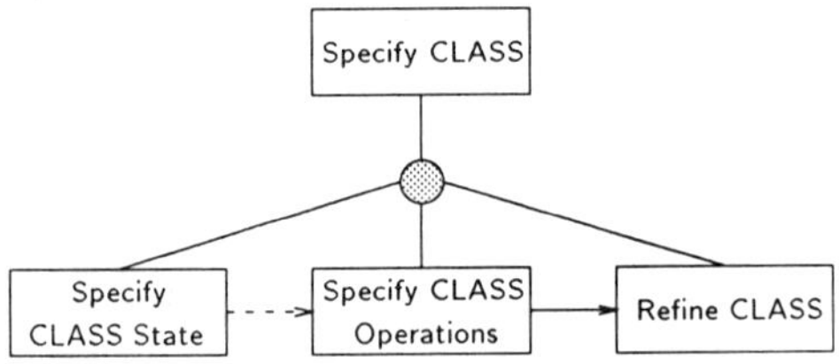

Figure 9: The operator Specify Class.

The operator Specify Subclass could be modified similarly. The reduction of the task Refine CLASS and its subsequent subtasks would require a set of development operators reflecting the refinement methods suitable for the specification language being used. Like the operators for specification, such operators could be grouped into three categories: those that apply a particular refinement strategy, those that identify components of the product to be refined and those that correspond to the task of refinement itself. As well as producing the refined version of the specification, these final operators would introduce subtasks corresponding to the necessary refinement proof obligations.

5.2 Refining modules

Like classes, modules can be identified by examining the workplan. They correspond to those parts of the product linked to the tasks following, and the task immediately preceding, any reduction produced by the operator Specify Module. In the specification of the communications network, two modules can be identified. These modules are associated with the subtrees beginning with the tasks Specify Network and Specify Node. The latter module is, in fact, a component of the former.

To enable refinement of modules in isolation, classes first identified within a module must not be used outside the module. For example, in the communications network case study, an object of the class Queue cannot be instantiated within the class Network. If this were required, the class

Queue should have been identified in a reduction of the task Specify Network Classes. This notion of module encapsulation could be enforced automatically by building it into the definition of the relevant development operators or, alternatively, left as the responsibility of the specifier.

Allowing modules to be refined, in addition to classes, results in a more flexible and practical notion of refinement. For example, assume that within the communications networks there were many possible paths which a message could take to get to its destination. To avoid congestion at a particular node, an invariant could be introduced in the class Node which states that a message will not be accepted unless the number of messages already at the node, either waiting to be processed or sent, is less than some constant n. This may be realised in an implementation by an invariant in the class Queue which restricts the length of a queue to be $n/2$. The necessary refinement could be achieved by refining the module which contains the classes Node and Queue. It could not be achieved, however, by refining the classes Node and Queue separately.

As with classes, subtasks can be added to simplify the identification of modules and aid in their refinement. The operators concerned with the actual task of refinement would be identical to those for class refinement, i.e. they would simply apply refinement techniques suitable for the specification language being used. The operators for applying particular refinement strategies, however, would apply strategies relevant to groups of classes. One such strategy is that of distributing an invariant between classes as described above. Other strategies would include the addition and deletion of classes to restructure modules and the introduction of aliasing, i.e. sharing objects between classes, when refining from a specification language where objects values are present within classes to an implementation language where only pointers or object identities are present. Each of these strategies is seen to be vital in the refinement of object-oriented specifications.

6 Conclusion

This paper has presented a language-independent framework for the development and refinement of object-oriented specifications. The framework is based on that proposed in the ESPRIT project ICARUS concerned with the incremental construction of specifications. Development operators are used to simultaneously construct or modify a workplan, denoting the history of goals to be achieved and corresponding application of operators to these goals, and a product, denoting the specification. The utilisation of such operators enables complex specification techniques to be captured in terms of parameterised texts.

The operators, by effectively hiding the technical details of how object-oriented concepts are captured in a given language, allow the specifier to develop specifications in an intuitively object-oriented fashion. They also present a flexible approach to object-oriented specification as libraries of operators can be defined allowing many different definitions of object-oriented features to be available. This enables a close mapping to be achieved between the specification and the implementation in the chosen object-oriented programming language.

The workplan enables classes and modules to be identified in the resulting product and thus enables the possibility of modular refinement. The use of modules results in a more practical and flexible notion of refinement than can be obtained with class refinement alone. The identification of classes and modules could also enable modular verification to be carried out. If operators were designed, or used by the specifier, in such a way as to respect class encapsulation and preserve properties through inheritance, properties verified for classes which are inherited or instantiated within a given class could be used in the verification of properties of that class.

The practicality of the proposed approach is dependent on an environment which manages the workplan and product and the links between them. Such an environment is under development within the ESPRIT project ICARUS. A prototype of the environment is already implemented and allows simple operators to be chosen via a menu which is dynamically defined according to the current task type. A more flexible notion of operator and an interface to facilitate the implementation of such operators is presently being developed.

Finally, an important area of current work is the application of the framework to particular specification languages. A set of object-oriented development operators have been designed for the state-based specification language Z. These include operators for declaring and applying operations to objects either individually or in aggregates of arbitrary size. Operators for simulating state-based inheritance in the algebraic specification language Glider have also been developed.

Acknowledgements

The author is supported by a post-doctoral fellowship granted by the Direction de la Recherche et des Etudes Doctorales (D.R.E.D) and financed by the Ministère des Affaires Etrangères, France. Thanks to Guido Bosch, Jean-Pierre Jacquot, Nicole Lévy and Jeanine Souquières with whom this work was carried out.

References

[Alencar 91] A. Alencar and J. Goguen. OOZE: An object oriented Z environment. In P. America, editor, *Proceedings European Conference on Object-Oriented Programming (ECOOP'91)*, volume 512 of *Lecture Notes in Computer Science*, pages 180–199. Springer-Verlag, 1991.

[Booch 91] G. Booch. *Object-Oriented Design with Applications*. The Benjamin/Cummings Publishing Company Inc., 1991.

[Clerici 88] S. Clerici and F. Orejas. GSBL: An algebraic specification language based on inheritance. In S. Gjessing and K. Nygaard, editors, *Proceedings European Conference on Object-Oriented Programming (ECOOP'88)*, volume 322 of *Lecture Notes in Computer Science*, pages 78–92. Springer-Verlag, 1988.

[Cusack 90] E. Cusack, S. Rudkin, and C. Smith. An object oriented interpretation of LOTOS. In S. Vuong, editor, *Formal Description Techniques, II (FORTE'89)*, pages 211–226. North-Holland, 1990.

[Dubois 93] E. Dubois, P. Du Bois, and M. Petit. O-O requirements analysis: an agent perspective. In O. M. Nierstrasz, editor, *Proceedings European Conference on Object-Oriented Programming (ECOOP'93)*, volume 707 of *Lecture Notes in Computer Science*, pages 458–481. Springer-Verlag, 1993.

[Duke 91] R. Duke, P. King, G. Rose, and G. Smith. The Object-Z specification language. In T. Korson, V. Vaishnavi, and B. Meyer, editors, *Technology of Object-Oriented Languages and Systems: TOOLS 5*, pages 465–483. Prentice-Hall International, 1991.

[Engelfriet 91] J. Engelfriet, G. Leih, and G. Rozenberg. Net based descriptions of parallel object-based systems or POTS and POPS. In J. W. de Bakker, W. P. de Roever, and G. Rozenberg, editors, *Foundations of Object-Oriented Languages*, volume 489 of *Lecture Notes in Computer Science*, pages 229–273. Springer-Verlag, 1991.

[Feather 87] M. Feather. Language support for the specification and development of composite systems. *ACM Transactions on Programming Languages and Systems*, 9(2):198–234, April 1987.

[Finance 90] J.P. Finance, N. Lévy, J. Souquières, and A. Valdenaire. SACSO: un environnement d'aide à la spécification. *T.S.I.*, 9(3):245–261, 1990.

[FUN (Namur) 90]
FUN (Namur), CRIN (Nancy), and PRLB (Brussels). Presentation of Glider. Technical Report Specfunc-016-R, ICARUS, 1990.

[Goguen 87] J. Goguen and J. Meseguer. Unifying functional, object-oriented, and relational programming with logical semantics. In B. Shriver and P. Wegner, editors, *Research Directions in Object-Oriented Programming*, pages 417–477. MIT Press, 1987.

[Hall 90] A. Hall. Using Z as a specification calculus for object-oriented systems. In D. Bjørner, C.A.R. Hoare, and H. Langmaack, editors, *VDM'90: VDM and Z!*, volume 428 of *Lecture Notes in Computer Science*, pages 290–318. Springer-Verlag, 1990.

[Rumbaugh 91] J. Rumbaugh, M. Blaha, W. Premerlani, F. Eddy and W. Lorensen. *Object-*

Oriented Modeling and Design. Prentice-Hall International, 1991.

[Smith 94] G. Smith. An object-oriented development framework for Z. To appear in *8th Z User Meeting (ZUM'94)*, Cambridge, June 1994.

[Souquières 93] J. Souquières and N. Lévy. Description of specification developments. In *Proceedings IEEE International Symposium on Requirements Engineering*, San Diego, January 1993.

[Spivey 89] J.M. Spivey. *The Z Notation: A Reference Manual*. Series in Computer Science. Prentice-Hall International, 1989.

[Utting 91] M. Utting and K. Robinson. Towards an object-oriented refinement calculus. In *Proceedings 14th Australian Computer Science Conference (ACSC-14)*, February 1991.

[Whysall 91] P. Whysall and J. McDermid. Object oriented specification and refinement. In J. Morris and R. Shaw, editors, *4th Refinement Workshop*, pages 150–184. Springer-Verlag, 1991.

Constraints in Object-Oriented Analysis and Design

Stefan Van Baelen*, Johan Lewi and Eric Steegmans

Katholieke Universiteit Leuven, Department of Computer Science
Celestijnenlaan 200A, B-3001 Leuven (Heverlee) - BELGIUM
Tel: +32 16-20.10.15 x 3596 - Fax: +32 16-20.53.08
E-mail: Stefan.VanBaelen@cs.kuleuven.ac.be

* Research Assistant of the Belgian National Fund for Scientific Research

ABSTRACT : Many object-oriented analysis methods provide support for the specification of constraints to reflect rules of the problem domain in the analysis model. Constraints describe properties that must be true at each moment in time for the entire system, without determining how they are to be preserved. The specification of constraints is mostly done by using informal text, operational restrictions or integrating constraints in existing model concepts. Two new specification formalisms to specify constraints are presented in this text. The first formalism treats constraints as a distinct concept of the model, specifying constraints in a formal way by using first-order logic assertions. The second formalism incorporates existential dependency constraints in the model structure in order to highlight the logical problem domain structure in the analysis model structure.

In addition, a design transformation approach is presented to implement the introduced analysis formalisms. During this transformation, the way constraints are handled in the actual software is being determined. On the one hand, a four-level transformation approach is presented to realize constraints by means of invariants, ensured assertions and require clauses. On the other hand, design issues concerning transformation and optimization of analysis model structures to classical implementation structures are presented.

From TOOLS EUROPE '94 (Technology of Object-Oriented Languages and Systems).

Key Words : Object-Oriented Analysis & Design, Constraints, Object Model Structure, Invariants, Require Clauses, Model Optimization.

1. Introduction

Many object-oriented analysis methods provide support for the specification of constraints to reflect rules of the problem domain in the analysis model. Constraints play an important role in the problem domain and are generally of utmost importance, whether they express rules and regulations, policies, logical rules and physic or human-defined laws. Therefore, they should be reflected directly in the object-oriented analysis model build of the problem domain. Constraints are a means to express general properties for the system, without specifying how they are being realized. They must hold during the entire life time of all objects of a class, restricting object structure and behavior [Odell 93a]. On the one hand, the number of possible valid instances of the specified model is diminished because the information present in the system must obey the constraint rules. On the other hand, certain events and actions causing unallowed model transitions are forbidden. By means of constraints, intrinsic properties of the system to be modeled can be described in a very elegant way. Indeed, in formulating constraints at the analysis level, only the aspect of '*which properties must be satisfied by objects*' is covered, thereby abstracting from how and when these properties must be controlled and how the system must react. These aspects are deferred to the design phase of the software life cycle.

The importance of constraints in a certain analysis method is mostly reflected in the provided specification notation. The formalisms in which these constraints can be specified in the model differ from method to method. In the first part of the text the classical ways of specifying constraints and its shortcomings are presented. Hereafter, two new specification formalisms for constraints are presented. A more detailed comparison of constraint specification formalisms can be found in [Van Baelen et al. 93]. The second part of the text presents a design transformation approach for the introduced constraint specification formalisms.

2. Constraints in Object-Oriented Analysis

2.1 Constraints as Informal Text

Most object-oriented analysis methods, such as [Shlaer & Mellor 88, 92], [Wirfs-Brock et al. 90], [Coad & Yourdon 91], [Rumbaugh et al. 91], [Embley et al. 92] [Jacobson 92] and [Booch 94], have only informal support for specifying general constraints on the model structure. Although they provide some specific restricted forms of formal constraint notation, they generally neglect the importance of constraints to a certain extent. General properties of the external world cannot be expressed explicitly but only in plain English [Odell 93b], mostly just as an additional part of the OOA documentation set.

Although constraint have an important role in the external world, they never get the same impact on the developed software model. Although the analysis process must keep its creativity, its outcomes must be formal. Indeed, if the design phase must start with an informal analysis description, errors will almost certainly be inevitable. An informal specification is exposed to human interpretation, often not corresponding with the intention of whoever formulated it. If a formal analysis description with clear, well-defined semantics is produced, the following phases of the software life cycle have a solid base to go on with the development of the software system. In addition, formal verification techniques can be used to verify the obtained analysis model before going into design. This will prevent logical development errors from the analysis phase on. Constraints are important items of an object-oriented analysis model, just like classes, attributes, relations, and events and actions. Therefore, next to a formal description of the effect of events and actions, a formal definition of constraints instead of an informal textual definition is advisable.

We will illustrate the specification of constraints with a simple example which we will use throughout the text. Consider a banking system in which banks grant car loans to their clients. A person can only get a car loan if (s)he is client at the bank ((s)he owns an account) and if (s)he has reached the legally defined adult age. A possible model for such system is presented in Fig. 1.

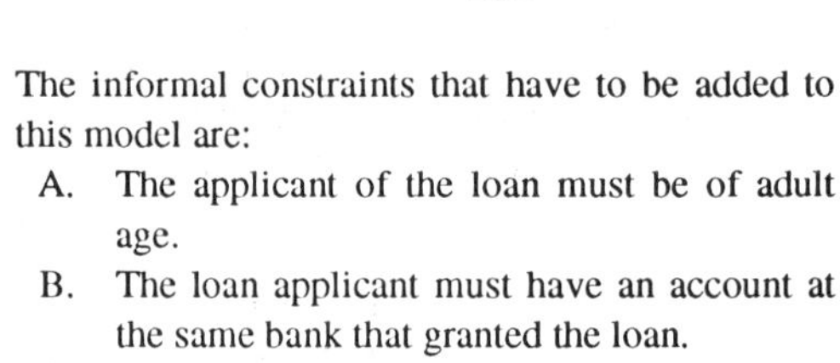

Fig. 1

The informal constraints that have to be added to this model are:

A. The applicant of the loan must be of adult age.

B. The loan applicant must have an account at the same bank that granted the loan.

C. A minor cannot go below zero, an adult can go 1000 $ below zero.

2.2 Constraints as Operational Restrictions

One possibility to obtain a more formal description of constraints is by controlling the execution of actions. This is supported by almost all current object-oriented analysis methods. By means of state transition diagrams, control flow diagrams or pre- and postconditions on actions, violations of the real world properties can be avoided. Such approach causes several problems.

A first problem is the gap that is introduced between the problem space and the obtained analysis model. Instead of describing what rules apply in the real world, this kind of constraint specification describes how they are realized. This must certainly be specified during the development, but at the design level rather than at the analysis level. The analysis phase must be centered around the reflection of the external world into the developed analysis model, and this in a natural instead of an artificial way.

Another problem concerns future revisions and modifications. When a constraint is specified as an independent item, it will remain present as such in revised and modified systems. However, when the constraint is realized in an operational way, it would be hard to satisfy the constraint again when new additions or changes to the model are made. The revisor must perform a sort of reverse engineering by extracting the constraint from its realization to keep the system consistent. It introduces the same problems as the realization of class invariants by means of pre- and postconditions in Eiffel [Meyer 88].

To realize the previous described constraints by controlling the execution of actions, every constructor and mutator of classes *ACCOUNT*, *BANK*, *LOAN* and *PERSON* are influenced. Indeed, these classes can contain a mutator that causes a violation of a specified constraint, because every class has the possibility to change the instances of the relations in which it takes part.

For instance, constraint A can be expressed by means of a precondition on the creation of *LOAN* objects:

```
class LOAN is
  constructor
    create ( p : PERSON, ...)
      require : p.is adult¹
  ...
end LOAN
```

However, if a new action is added to change the loan applicant, it also has to be controlled. When the constraint was formulated directly this would not be the case, because the constraint remains logically the same. Future additions of actions do mostly not give rise to revisions of constraints, but only of their realization.

In the same way, constraint B can be realized by controlling the creation of loans and destruction of accounts, and constraint C by controlling the creation of accounts and withdrawals on accounts. Addition of new actions, such as changing the loan applicant and account owner influences constraint B, whereas changing the account owner and introducing a bank transfer, an automatic savings instruction or a payment domicile influences constraint C. After each addition, one is obliged to review the entire state diagram or all preconditions of the control mechanism to keep its correctness. Therefore, it is very hard to keep consistency during the software life cycle which contains many revisions, modifications and adaptations. The analysis description should be declarative, describing what must be valid in the system, instead of operational, describing how the system will keep its consistency.

1. Actually, we can check if a person is adult by 'p.age ≥ DURATION'adult age' or '**now** - p.Date of Birth ≥ DURATION'adult age'. In these expressions, '**now**' stands for the current time and adult age is a predefined value of the domain *DURATION*, an abstract data type to indicate a period in time. Because to be adult is a semantic real world property of a person, we will define it as a query *is adult* for the class *PERSON*. As such, it can be seen as a derived property from the date of birth.

2.3 Constraints Integrated in Existing Model Concepts

Current object-oriented analysis methods that try to incorporate certain kind of constraints in the analysis model in a more formal and explicit way, integrate them with other concepts of the method, mostly restricted to one model item of one concept (e.g., in one attribute definition)[2]. Constraints about relations and attributes are integrated in the definition of the relation and attribute, whereas general constraints about objects of a class are specified as part of the class description. This can be very useful and adequate for certain kind of constraints, such as connectivity (also called cardinality or multiplicity) constraints for relations, multiplicity constraints for attributes (one or many possible attribute values for an object), and mutability constraints for both. Obviously, such constraints are a basic part of the relation and attribute definition. These constraints can be integrated easily because they only bear upon a single item of a concept of the analysis method. Other constraint however are integrated with one model item of a concept although they can spread out over a larger part of the model.

However, if a constraint can spread out over a large part of the model, existing of several items of one of more concepts, it is not possible to integrate constraints with a particular item in a decent manner. Constraints over several relations cannot be placed with one particular relation definition. Some methods place constraints between attributes of the relation participants in the relation definition (e.g., as [Rumbaugh et al. 91] and [Odell 93b, 93c], however not in a formal way). But, for instance, rules between attributes of objects connected by several successive relations, or join and anti-join constraints in a relation ring (if an object *a* of class A is connected through successive relations with *a'*, also of class A, then a = a', respectively a ≠ a') cannot be adjudged to a particular dedicated relation or class. When such constraints are placed in a single class or with a single relation, arbitrariness will have a huge impact on the model. Indeed, the constraint is only visible in the dedicated element and not in the other involved elements. Useful information for classes is hidden in the definition of other classes, relations or attributes. Bad placement of constraints in the model will also lead to the diminishing of reuse. It will be very hard to get a proper insight in the existing structure, which will encourage the analyst to start all over again.

It is difficult to allocate the previous described constraints of our example to the best fitted model items present. Constraint A can be placed with the classes *PERSON* or *LOAN*, but also with the relation *Applicant* or with the attribute *Date of Birth*. Constraint B is an example of a sort of join constraint in a relation ring, where four classes and four relations are involved. Constraint C can be placed with the classes *PERSON* or *ACCOUNT*, with the relation *Owner* or with the attributes *Balance* or *Date of Birth*. The choice between these alternatives will always remain rather arbitrary. No matter which criteria we choose to select an element to place the constraint, it will always introduce arbitrariness and asymmetry in the model.

2.4 Constraints as a Separate Concept

To obtain a formal, declarative and separate constraint specification in object-oriented analysis models, a notation formalism for constraints is developed as part of the ER@S project[3] [Van Baelen et al. 92, Lewi et al. 93]. This approach treats constraints as a distinct concept of the

2. There is a slight difference between a concept (attributes, relations) and a model item of a concept (1 attribute, 1 relation). Constraint can spread out over several concepts, such as constraint A that includes both an attribute and a relation, or over several model items of one concept, such as constraint B that only deals with relations between classes.

3. ER@S is an object-oriented development method that supports the full software life cycle, from analysis through design and implementation to the maintenance and running (evolution) phase. A full description of the ER@S method falls beyond the scope of this paper.

analysis model, next to classes, relations, attributes and so on. Each constraint definition contains the actual specification of the constraint itself in first-order logic, a name as a mnemonic for it, and a description of the model part that is involved.

The actual specification of the constraint is a first-order logic assertion that specifies a condition that must be true at all times. This expression is formulated viewing from one class and as such specified for all object of that class. In the logic assertion, navigational expressions may be used to reach other objects or attribute values. These navigational expressions results generally into a bag of objects, although a singleton set is obtained when the relation has a 1-connectivity at the related side. As such, the expression 'a.Relation Name' stands for the objects to which the object *a* is related by the relation 'Relation Name'. The expression 'a.Attribute Name' stands for the value or values of attribute 'Attribute Name' that is associated with the object *a*. Finally, applying the expression on a bag of objects results in the (bag) union of their result on each object.

The affected model part is automatically derived from the actual specification of the constraint by examining the items used in the specifications, and is especially useful for design purposes (see further). It indicates all model items that are affected by the constraint. The specification of the involved classes can include the constraint name to highlight the restriction on their instances. However, the constraint definition will be a separate information item of the model, not integrated in a particular model element. Otherwise, the problems specified earlier would appear again. The specification of the previous introduced constraints, using the same names as given earlier, are presented in Fig. 2.

```
constraint A
--   for LOAN with relation Applicant
--        to PERSON with attribute Date of Birth is
for each l in LOAN :
   l.Applicant.is adult
end A
```

```
constraint B
--   for LOAN with relations
--        ( Applicant to PERSON with relation Owner,
--          Grantor to BANK with relation Provider ) is
for each l in LOAN :
   l.Applicant.Owner intersection
     l.Grantor.Provider ≠ empty set
end B
```

```
constraint C
--   for ACCOUNT with attribute Balance
--        with relation Owner to PERSON
--             with attribute Date of Birth is
for each a in ACCOUNT :
   if a.Owner.is adult
       then a.Balance ≥ -1000 $
       else a.Balance ≥ 0 $
end C
```

Fig. 2

The only arbitrariness in this specification arises from the fact that the constraint is described starting from one of the involved classes. For instance, constraint A could also be specified as

```
for each p in PERSON :
   if p.Applicant ≠ empty set
       then p.is adult
```

However, this affects only the specification of the constraint itself, not the place of the constraint in the analysis model. The constraint is a distinct part of the model, independent of any item.

The notation of constraints as a formal, declarative and separate concept leads to a consistent, unambiguous and symmetrical constraint specification and placement for all constraint types. But certain important structure dependencies are hidden in these constraint specifications, instead of being part of the basic model structure. Indeed, classes that are actually materializations of relations, such as *ACCOUNT* (between *PERSON* and *BANK*) and *LOAN* (between *PERSON*, *BANK* and *CAR*), always imply an additional constraint on the presence of an object of the participant classes. It can be expressed by means of the above notation or by integrating existential dependency in the definition of a relation. Another existential dependency in the model is the one of constraint B, expressing that a loan is dependent on an account of the loan applicant. Such constraints are like glue, holding the model instances consistent with respect to the problem space This approach is not favorable, neither from the viewpoint of the model developer nor from that of the model reviewer and re-user. This is because the logical structure dependencies are only specified by means of additional constraints, not by the model structure elements themselves. The modeler has to make an explicit transition from the logical structure of the problem space to the model equivalent, a combination of structure and explicit constraints. Instead of highlighting the basic structure of the model, one of the important things of an analysis description, this structure is neglected and shifted to the specified constraints. Therefore, a good model should capture many constraints through its structure.

2.5 Constraints Implied by the Model Structure

To diminish the gap between the problem domain and the analysis model, we developed a hierarchical relation structure to enrich the expressive power of the model, reflecting the logical structure dependencies directly into the model structure. A hierarchical relation structure will treat relations as classes themselves.[4] As such, the choice to model a certain relational thing, e.g., accounts, as a relation or a class will disappear. It will be modeled as both class and relation at the same time. Such class will be called a refined class (or a class refined by a relation), because the relation refines the objects of the class as relationships between objects of other classes. This approach captures implicitly the structure existential dependency constraints. By defining the class *ACCOUNT* as a class refined by a relation between *PERSON* and *BANK*, it is stated that account objects also represent a relationship between a person and a bank. Therefore, such objects cannot exist without being related to a person and a bank.[5]

Because refined classes can be used as participants themselves, a relation hierarchy is created expressing existential dependency constraints between the objects. Because the existential dependency is transitive, an object of the class that is refined by another refined class is also existential dependent on objects of the deeper participants. As such using class *ACCOUNT* as participant of *LOAN*, each loan object is not only existential dependent on an account object, but also on a person and a bank object. This is exactly what we wanted to specify earlier with constraint B. The final model is presented in Fig. 3. The circle for *LOAN* represents the relation (between *ACCOUNT* and *CAR*) that is encapsulated in the class *LOAN*. The double circle for *ACCOUNT* indicates that duplicates are allowed for the encapsulated relation. So a person can have more than one account at the same bank. Duplicates are indeed possible when relationships are considered as objects. Indeed, the object identity will always present, even if two objects have the same participants.

4. [Rumbaugh et al. 91], [Embley et al. 92] and [Shlaer & Mellor 88] also provides the possibility to model a relation as a class. But it is not really a class of objects with their own identity, but merely a class of associations of two objects, which identities are defined as a combination of the identities of the objects part of the association. Duplicates, for instance, are not possible. Furthermore, one has to make a choice at the analysis level whether a problem space relation is going to be modeled as a straight relation, a relation as a class (actually an exceptional case, not often used), or just a class with two additional relations for the two participants. In this approach, every relation is automatically encapsulated in a class. It is only in the design phase that one has to decide if a relation will be implemented by means of a class or an ordinary association.

5. Existential dependencies among objects may seem sometimes too restrictive for the ultimate system. A great deal of run-time flexibility, for instance in populating the model with instances, would be lost. However, object-oriented analysis is basically concerned with building an abstraction of the external world. Therefore, focusing on the external world in its *normal* appearance should have priority over the run-time issues during analysis.

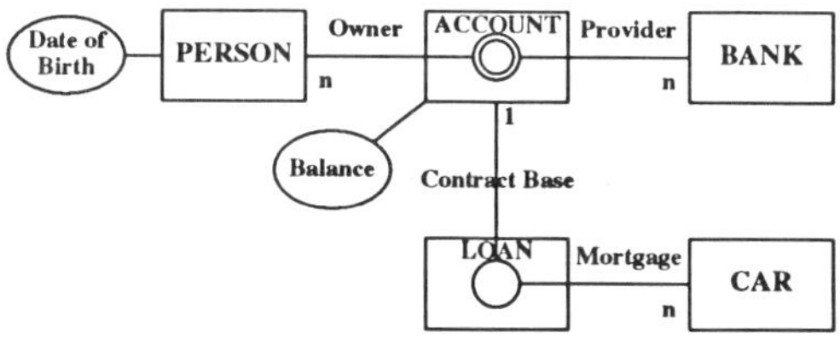

Fig. 3

When a class is existential dependent of more than two other classes, a binary equivalent in conformity with the problem domain is used as a representation, as illustrated by the the *LOAN* class of our example. When a class is existential dependent of only one other class, this can be expressed as in Fig. 4. In this case, the class is refined by a unary relation of the participant class. It is also possible to define a duplicate connectivity for a unary relation to indicate whether several refined objects can be containing the same participant object.

Fig. 4

Notice that we can now avoid arbitrariness in the constraint specifications. The description of the constraint will be formulated from the highest classes in the relation hierarchy. As such, there is only one way to formulate a constraint. The remaining constraints are presented in Fig. 5.

constraint A
-- **for** LOAN **refined with** ACCOUNT
-- **refined with** PERSON
-- **with attribute** Date of Birth **is**
for each l **in** LOAN :
l↓Contract Base↓Owner.is adult
end A

constraint C
-- **for** ACCOUNT **with attribute** Balance
-- **refined with** PERSON
-- **with attribute** Date of Birth **is**
for each a **in** ACCOUNT :
if a↓Owner.is adult
then a.Balance ≥ -1000 $
else a.Balance ≥ 0 $
end C

Fig. 5

The query 'a↓Role Name' (e.g., l↓Contract Base) in the constraint specification stands for the object of the Role Name class that is a basic part of the relationship object *a*. The inverse query 'b↑CLASS NAME' stands for the set of objects of the CLASS NAME class in which *b* participates. If a ≈ (b,c)[6] then a↓Role B = b, a↓Role C = c, a ∈ b↑A and a ∈ c↑A. This notation supports the view of zooming into the elements that are part of an object (projection ↓), and zooming out to the items that contains the object (election ↑).

One can try to go even further and capture the remaining constraint also in the model structure by providing additional constructs. However, a trade-off is necessary between model complexity and model simplicity and understandability. The step from a flat relation structure to a hierarchical relation structure has shown its use in practice. It provides a solid base for mapping the problem space into an analysis model. Whether or not more constraints have to be supported explicitly in the model structure, is not clear yet. But we are experiment with new structure mechanisms to capture more constraints into the model structure.

3. Realization of Constraints during Object-Oriented Design

The analysis of a software system must be focused on the problem domain. The final outcomes of the analysis phase contains, amongst others, a complete description of the entire system on a high level of abstraction. Aspects of the solution domain are not incorporated in the analysis model. Therefore, constraints are introduced as a high level specification mechanism

6. a is not really equal to (b,c), but it contains (b,c). In addition, it has its own object identity, which allows also that another object of class A, say a' ≈ (b,c).

for rules and regulations of the problem domain, without yet deciding how and when they are going to be checked and realized. The design phase is the right place and time to take decisions regarding to the realization of the specified constraints.

The development of a software system comprises a wide variety of aspects. A possible way to control this amount of information in a decent manner consists of dividing the design into different partitions, each focussed on a certain design aspect. Combining such partitions may result in the whole model in all its details, or in a partial view on certain aspects of the system. As such, each design aspect can be described independently, without order restrictions. If one wants to ignore certain issues at a certain moment in time, one can just skip a design partition. If the introduction of new technology requires an additional design partition, or give rise to a possible deletion of a partition, the design method can easily be adapted. Such partition-based design can contain one partition centered around the realization of constraints. This section will present some design issues regarding constraints.

Constraints can be stretched out over one or more classes. They reduce the number of possible instances of the model, and the number of possible events and actions that can occur at a certain time. At each moment in time, the information present in the system must always obey the constraint rules. To realize these constraints at the design level, a trade-off has to be made between efficiency and consistency. The design approach presented here is aimed at classical object-oriented languages, such as Smalltalk, C++ and Eiffel. Further research about design issues that arise when constraint-based languages are used as a target language is planned in the near future.

3.1 Design Issues for Separate Constraints

Constraints specified as a separate concept, as described in a previous section, still have to be realized in the lower levels of the system development life cycle. At the design phase, several topics arise during the constraint realization. The main issues are concerned with the place and time the system must be checked for possible constraint violations, and the actions that must be performed when a violation is going to occur or has occurred. Two distinct approaches can be applied :

- One approach consists of preventing the occurrence of a constraint violation. First of all, the set of actions that can be the source of a constraint violations are derived. For each action, a precondition can be determined that must be fulfilled before the action can be executed. These preconditions will prevent the system of going into a wrong state. The execution of certain actions cannot be tolerated for certain system states. This approach causes a loss of efficiency due to a high number of tests, but keeps the system in a highly consistent state at each moment in time.
- Another approach consists of detecting fault system states, whereupon the system itself will perform either a sort of rollback to an older valid state, or the invocation of an error recovery procedure that tries to fix the system. This results in an important gain of efficiency, but leaves the system in an inconsistent state during a certain time.

The choice between these two approaches is often situation specific. A trade-off has to be made between efficiency and consistency, depending on which criteria are of utmost importance for the required system. The rest of this section presents an approach for preventing constraint violations.

A first way to prevent constraint violations - a rather simple, but very time consuming and unrealistic way - is to check each constraint at initialization time of the system and then for every single action invokement in the entire system. However, not every object will be changed by every action and therefore not every constraint can be violated. Because actions have only local effect on the state of the entire system, most of the constraints will still be valid after the execution of an action if they were valid before the action. This will depend on the invoked action, the involved objects and the classes to which the objects belong.

A more tunable constraint realization approach by preventing constraint violations is developed as part of the ER(X)S project. The decisions that have to be made are ordered in several successive levels for a separation of concern. We will locate where and when each constraint can be violated. This will determine the exact moments, objects and actions to check a certain constraint. It is done in four steps:

- Firstly, the classes that are involved in each constraint are determined. Only actions involving objects of these classes can cause a violation of the constraint. Actions involving only objects of other classes cannot be of any influence on the validity of the constraint.
- Then, the set of objects of the involved classes that have to be verified when an action on an object of the class is invoked, will be determined. Mostly, it will not be necessary to check each object of the class when an action is executed on a certain object of that class; checking the involved object will be sufficient.
- Thirdly, the actions that can cause a constraint violation must be determined. Actions concerning certain characteristics of an object will mostly not violate constraints about other characteristics.
- Finally, the require conditions that have to be tested before each action can be invoked safely, are derived. Mostly, these require conditions can be made simple and efficient, compared to the actual constraint expression.

Actions can be divided in two types. Local actions are actions on an object that only have a local effect. This means that such action cause only a state transition of the object involved in the action[7]. Global actions are actions on an object that have a global effect. Such action cause a state transition of the object involved in the action and of other objects in the model. Global actions can be seen as a compound of several local actions. This is often modeled as such in order to keep proper encapsulation of the effect of an action on the whole model. If the separation between local and global actions is not made, one can introduce additional local actions to rebuild all global actions out of the defined local actions. In the presented steps, we will only concentrate on the local actions. Hereafter, we will discuss some issues concerning global actions.

3.1.1 Determination of the Involved Classes

As stated above, not every action on an object of a class give rise to a violation of all constraints. Therefore, we will determine for each constraint the classes where it can be violated. This means that a local action on an object of that class can violate the constraint. In this way, one is certain that the constraint doesn't have to be checked when an action of a not involved class is invoked. The analysis constraints are transformed into design class invariants, expressing a property for each object of that class. Each class invariant must and will always be preserved. The transformation of a constraint consists of first deriving the involved classes, and hereafter reformulating the constraint as a class invariant for the objects of those classes. Unlike constraints, that covers the whole model, class invariants only impact the class for which they are defined.

7. When part of a state is shared between two objects, e.g., a relationship between object *a* and *b*, an action changing this shared state part is also considered a local action. So a local action on an object may change only its own state or the state parts shared with other objects. This means that if an action on object *a* changes its relationship participation from *b* to *c*, it is still considered as a local action, although the state of the objects *b* and *c* change also indirectly.

A constraint spreads out over a number of classes, relations and attributes. In general, the class directly involved in the constraint, together with the classes part of an involving relation form the total set of involved classes. Indeed, local actions of a class can only change the attributes and the own relationships of the objects of that class. Just because the shared state of objects of class can be changed via the verge classes on the other side of the relations, we have also to consider these verge classes.

Because additional rules regarding the change of relationships apply in ER_{OO}S, we can give a more precise description of the set of involving classes. In ER_{OO}S, only a refined object may change its participating objects. It is not possible for an object to change its refined object in which it participates. This must be done via the refined object directly. This means that an account object may change its participant bank object and person object, but the bank object and the person object may not change the account object in which they participate directly. Also, the person related to the bank via the *ACCOUNT* relation can not be changed by the bank object itself. This must also be done via the account object.

As an illustration, we will use the constraint A, presented in Fig. 5. It expresses the fact that the loan applicant must be of adult age. The classes involved in this constraint are *LOAN*, *ACCOUNT* and *PERSON*. A loan object may change its participant account object, the account object may change its participating person object and the person object may change its attribute value *Date of Birth*. Constraint A cannot be violated after an object action of the classes *BANK* or *CAR*. These classes corresponds exactly with the classes of the affected model part of the constraint, which can be derived from the constraint specification. In addition, the bottom classes of this model part hierarchy without any involving attributes can be excluded from the set of involved classes. Indeed, their attributes are not involved in the constraint, and the involved relation in which they participate cannot be changed via them, but only via the refined class.

If we have determined the involved classes, we can reformulate the constraint as a class invariant for the involved classes. Because the original constraint was formulated starting from *LOAN*, we only have to reformulate it for the classes *ACCOUNT* and *PERSON*. The resulting class invariants are given in Fig. 6.

```
class LOAN is
  class invariants
  A : for each l in LOAN :
    l↓Contract Base↓Owner.is adult
  ...
end LOAN

class ACCOUNT is
  class invariants
  A : for each a in ACCOUNT :
    if a↑LOAN ≠ empty set
      then a↓Owner.is adult
  ...
end ACCOUNT

class PERSON is
  class invariants
  A : for each p in PERSON :
    if p↑ACCOUNT↑LOAN ≠ empty set
      then p.is adult
  ...
end PERSON
```

Fig. 6

3.1.2 Determination of the Involved Objects

In the previous section, we have determined the classes where a certain constraint can be violated. As a result, we can be certain that the constraint doesn't have to be checked when an action of a not involved class is invoked. Class invariants have been formulated for each constraint to determine the set of properties that each object of a class must satisfy. The defined class invariants can be checked for all object of the class, each time an action on any object of the class is executed. However, a local action can only change the state of the object involved in the action, not the state of other objects of the class. Therefore, each time a local action is invoked, only the object on which it was applied must be checked whether it still fulfill its class invariants. E.g., when a mutator to change the account owner is invoked on a certain account, only this account has to be checked whether it still fulfills all class invariants. All other accounts are not changed and thus they keep fulfilling the class invariants.

3.1.3 Determination of the Involved Actions

After the determination of the involved classes and the objects to check when a local action is invoked, we determine the set of actions that can violate a class invariant. Suppose we have a number of mutators for a certain object, but only one to change the value of a particular attribute. Then it is only necessary to check a class invariant depending on the possible values of the attribute, after the construction of the object and after each invocation of that particular mutator. In this way, the exact actions of a class that can cause a violation of a class invariant are determined so that checks must only be performed when it is certain that a violation can occur. To determine the actions where a certain class invariant for a class must be checked, we can use the following rules in ER(O)S:

- Queries on the system cannot violate any class invariant. Queries only interrogate the system, they don't update the system state.
- Constructors, which are local actions that construct a new object, can only violate the class invariant of which their class is the top class of the corresponding constraint. If the class of the constructor is an intermediate class of the constraint model tree, the created object is not part of any object of a higher level, again because this must be done via an object on a higher level. So when a new account object is created, it cannot be part of any loan object yet. Therefore, the class invariant is not affected by the creation.
- Mutators of attribute values can only violate those class invariants that explicitly use the attribute. Other attributes than the ones used are of no importance for the class invariant.
- Mutators of relation participants can only violate those class invariants that explicitly use the participant class. Other participants than the ones used are of no importance for the class invariant.
- Destructors cannot violate any class invariant. A destructor only destroys an object, so the truth value of the class invariant cannot be changed. However, some implicit dependency constraints can be violated. These constraints are not formulated as a separate constraint but implied by the model structure. They must be dealt with when the model structure is been transformed.

The set of action for which the class invariant must be checked can sometimes be reduced even more based on a detailed semantic study. In the case of the banking problem, the class invariant stating that the balance of an account may not go below zero needn't be checked after a deposit but only after a withdrawal, although a deposit changes the balance of an object too. For the example of constraint A, formulated in Fig. 5, the actions that have to be checked are:

- When constructing a loan object
- when mutating the *Contract Base* of a loan object
- when mutating the *Owner* of an account object
- when mutating the *Date of Birth* of a person

For each action that can cause a violation of the constraint, an assertion is formulated that have to be assured over the invocation of the action. This ensured assertion formulate an expression that must stay valid after the action is executed. If this is not the case, the action may not be executed. The ensured assertions for the construction of a loan object, the mutator of the person participant of an account object and the mutator of the *Date of Birth* of a person, ensuring constraint A are presented in Fig. 7 (formulated separately, although they can also be integrated in the formulation of the actions themselves).

ensured assertion
imposing constraint A
for constructor construct loan **of class** LOAN **is**
self↓Contract Base↓Owner.is adult
end ensured assertion
(analogous for mutator change contract base)

ensured assertion
imposing constraint A
for mutator change owner **of class** ACCOUNT **is**
if self↑LOAN ≠ **empty set**
then self↓Owner.is adult
end ensured assertion

ensured assertion
imposing constraint A
for mutator change date of birth **of class** PERSON **is**
if self↑ACCOUNT↑LOAN ≠ **empty set**
then self.is adult
end ensured assertion

Fig. 7

How these ensured assertions have to be checked is still not yet defined at this point in the transformation. This can be done by preventing violations by means of requirements, by correcting violations by means of a rollback mechanism or by creating alternatives by means of assertion additions of the effect clauses (a sort of exception handling mechanism). It can be deferred to the implementation phase or been integrated in a fourth transformation step. The fourth step presented next will prevent violations by means of the introduction of require clauses in order to prevent the execution of an action that will cause a constraint violation.

3.1.4 Determination of the Require Clauses

Until now, we have determined for each constraint the set of actions, invokable on objects of the involved classes, that can cause its violation. For these actions, an ensured assertion is formulated to be preserved over the execution of the action. In this way, the checks for realizing constraints are determined exactly. This level consists of a transformation from an ensured assertion into a requirement clause that can be tested before an action is invoked. The require clause will fail only if the action causes a constraint violation.

The require clauses are based on (1) the current state of the object on which the action occurs, (2) the parameters that are supplied with the action and (3) the effect that the action will realize. For each ensured assertion, a require clause is formulated that prevents forbidden action invocations. These require clauses formulate an expression that must be valid before the action is executed. The require clauses deducted from the ensured assertions of Fig. 7 are presented in Fig. 8 (also formulated separately, but they can also be integrated with the actions).

require clause
imposing constraint C
for constructor construct loan (account, car)
of class LOAN **is**
account↓Owner.is adult
end require clause

require clause
imposing constraint C
for mutator change contract base (new account)
of class LOAN **is**
new account↓Owner.is adult
end require clause

require clause
imposing constraint C
for mutator change owner (new person)
of class ACCOUNT **is**
if self↑LOAN ≠ **empty set**
thennew person.is adult
end require clause

require clause
imposing constraint C
for mutator change Date of Birth (new date of birth)
of class PERSON **is**
if self↑ACCOUNT↑LOAN ≠ **empty set**
then now - new date of birth
≥ DURATION'adult age
end require clause

Fig. 8

By defining these four steps for the constraint transformation (determination of the involved classes, objects, actions and formulation of require clauses), we can exactly define the moments on which constraints have to be checked and the objects on which they have to be applied. As such, a detailed constraint realization protocol can be implemented, that will preserve all constraints formulated at the analysis level at all times. This process can be performed semi-automatically, and can still be mapped to any classical object-oriented language[8].

3.1.5 Global actions and Constraint Realization

In the presented four constraint transformation steps, we have only considered local actions. For dealing with global actions, it is mostly sufficient if the constraints hold after the execution of the whole global action, and not during intermediate states of it. If we use the previous scheme, we imply that the constraint cannot be violated over each local action, part of the division of the global action. This will of course realize the constraints, but it is too strong.

However, we can merge the ensured assertions of all local actions part of a global action without becoming too restrictive. Indeed, if a certain property *can* be violated by a local action, this is also possible by a global action containing this local action. It is possible that certain ensured assertions become trivial due to the fact that the other local actions, part of the same global action, imply the stated assertion. E.g., when a deposit and a withdrawal are combined in such a way that the deposited amount is higher than the withdrawn amount, the constraint for imposing a positive balance doesn't have to be checked at all. Also, when two participants that must be the same, are being changed together to the same new object, it is not necessary to check the equality, although this has to be done when only one participant is changed. Determining which ensured assertions have become superfluous and which ones have to be tested explicitly, can be deduced from the combination of the local actions part of the global action.

The merging of the ensured assertions is possible because they only state a property that has to be preserved over two moments in time. At the previous moment, the constraints are certainly guaranteed. At the future moment, after execution of the total action, they have to be valid again. When we divide global action in several local actions, we must move our control mechanism over the total period of the global action, not over a single local action. A require clause, however, is based on the current state of the object on which the action occurs, the parameters that are supplied for the action and the effect that the action will realize. This is highly dependent of the actions that are being executed before and after it.

Therefore, we have to deduce the exact require clause for a global action from (1) the set of ensured assertions of its local actions, (2) the effect of the global actions, as a concatenation of the effects of its local actions, (3) the current state of the system and (4) the parameters supplied for the global action. E.g., the require condition for a combination of a deposit and a withdrawal that must keep the balance positive, will be that the difference between the withdrawn amount and the deposited amount may not exceed the actual balance of the account.

3.2 Design Issues for Implied Constraints

A hierarchical structuring of relations may result in more classes and a more complicated structure to implement. Therefore it is advisable to transform the hierarchical relation structure to a simpler structure such as a classical flat one. It is rather straightforward to transform the developed hierarchical model into a bipartite, flat model, consisting of classes on the one hand and flat relations on the other. Flat relations are preferred at the design level for reasons of simplicity and

8. We have already implemented these require clauses in Smalltalk, Eiffel and C++.

implementation ease. There is no identity or functionality associated with a flat relation. A flat relation corresponds with the relation concept of entity-relationship modeling and many object-oriented methods.

A refined class can be transformed in two ways. On the one hand, it can remain a class, having a flat relation to each of its participants. These flat relations express the same information as the corresponding hierarchical relation. However, implicit existential dependency constraints need to be stated explicitly. On the other hand, a refined class can be transformed into an ordinary relation, so that the relational objects become plain relationships. In this case, the functionality of the optimized class (its attributes, participations, actions etc.) must be shifted to neighboring classes, and its object life cycle may be simulated by additional attributes. This transformation is presented in Fig. 9. The design level is the right place to decide which classes have to be optimized and which ones have to be kept as a class. The main concern here is to find a good balance between the data amount and the procedural amount of the design.

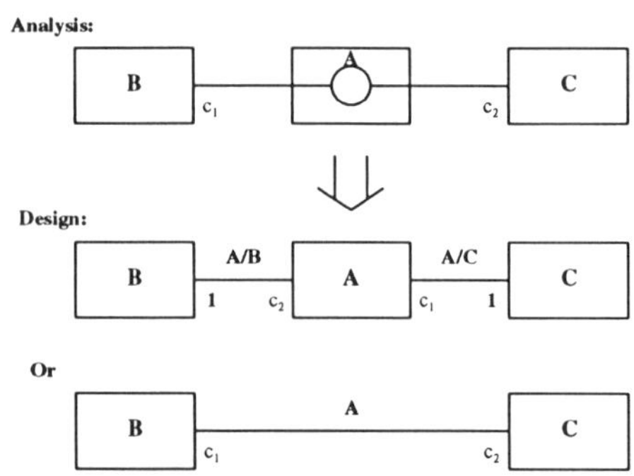

Fig. 9

4. Conclusion

The classical techniques for the specification of constraints are not well fitted to describe general constraints of the problem domain:

- Specifying constraints as informal text is too informal as an outcome of the analysis phase. This will introduce human interpretation errors during later stages of the development.
- Specifying constraints explicitly as operational restrictions is of too low level during analysis. It causes a gap between the problem space and the analysis model. Instead of describing what rules apply in the real world, the analysis model describes how they are realized. This creates consistency problems when future revisions and modifications are made.
- Certain constraints, such as connectivity and mutability constraints, can easily be integrated in one existing model concept. When constraints spread out over a larger part of the model, they cannot properly be integrated in one dedicated model item.

Two new specification formalisms are presented to specify constraints at the analysis level:

- On the one hand, general constraints are specified in a formal, declarative and separate way as independent items of a distinct model concept. Each constraint definition contains the actual specification of the constraint itself in first-order logic, a name as a mnemonic for it, and a description of the model part that is involved. However, existential dependency constraints are hidden in the constraint specifications instead of being supported by the model structure.
- On the other hand, a hierarchical relation structure is used to enrich the expressive power of the model by capturing existential dependency constraints implicitly by the model structure. This structure encapsulates every relation into a class, so that the choice to model a certain relational thing as a relation or a class will disappear. A hierarchical relation structure highlights the logical structure of the model to its right extent.

To realize the specified general constraints at the design level by preventing constraint violations, a four-level transformation approach is developed: determination of (1) the classes involved in a constraint, (2) the objects that have to be checked, (3) the actions that can cause a violations and (4) the require conditions that have to be tested before each action can be invoked safely. This will determine the exact moments, objects and actions to check a certain constraint.

The hierarchical relation structure can be transformed to a flat relation structure during design, finding a good balance between the data and procedural part of the design. A refined class can be kept as a class during design, having a flat relation to each of its participants, or can be optimized to an ordinary relation, with a shift of its functionality to its participants.

References

[Booch 94] Booch, G., *Object-Oriented Analysis and Design with Applications, Second Edition*, Benjamin/Cummings, Redwood City, California, 1994.

[Coad & Yourdon 91] Coad, P., and Yourdon, E., *Object-Oriented Analysis Second Edition*, Yourdon Press, Englewood Cliffs (New Jersey), 1991.

[Embley et al. 92] Embley, D.W., Kurtz, B.D., and Woodfield, S.N., *Object-Oriented Systems Analysis*, Yourdon Press, Englewood Cliffs (New Jersey), 1992.

[Jacobson et al. 92] Jacobson, I., Christerson, M., Jonsson, P., and Overgaard, G., *Object-Oriented Software Engineering: A Use Case Driven Approach*, ACM Press, Reading, Massachusetts, 1992.

[Lewi et al. 93] Lewi, J., Steegmans, E., Dockx, J., Swennen, B., Van Baelen, S., and Van Riel, H., *Object-Oriented Software Development with EROOS: The Analysis Phase*, Department of Computer Science, K.U.Leuven, CW Report 169, 1993.

[Meyer 88] Meyer, B., *Object-Oriented Software Construction*, Prentice Hall, New York, 1988.

[Odell 93a] Odell, James J., Specifying requirements using rules, *Journal of Object-Oriented Programming*, Vol. 6, No. 2, May 1993, pp. 20-24.

[Odell 93b] Odell, James J., Using business rules with diagrams, *Journal of Object-Oriented Programming*, Vol. 6, No. 4, July-August 1993, pp. 10-16.

[Odell 93c] Odell, James J., Specifying structural constraints, *Journal of Object-Oriented Programming*, Vol. 6, No. 6, October 1993, pp. 12-16.

[Rumbaugh et al. 91] Rumbaugh, J., Blaha, M., Premerlani, W., Eddy, F., and Lorenson, W., *Object-Oriented Modeling and Design*, Prentice Hall, Englewood Cliffs (New Jersey), 1991.

[Shlaer & Mellor 88] Shlaer, S., and Mellor, S. J., *Object-Oriented Systems Analysis : Modeling the World in Data*, Yourdon Press, Englewood Cliffs (New Jersey), 1988.

[Shlaer & Mellor 92] Shlaer, S., and Mellor, S. J., *Object Lifecycles : Modeling the World in States*, Yourdon Press, Englewood Cliffs (New Jersey), 1988.

[Van Baelen et al. 92] Van Baelen, S, Lewi, J., Steegmans, E., and Van Riel, H., EROOS : An Entity-Relationship based Object-Oriented Specification Method, *Technology of Object-Oriented Languages and Systems TOOLS 7*, Heeg, G., Magnusson, B., and Meyer, B. (ed.), Prentice Hall, Hertsfordshire, UK, pp. 103-117.

[Van Baelen et al. 93] Van Baelen, S, Lewi, J., Steegmans, E., and Swennen, B., Constraints in Object-Oriented Analysis, Object Technologies for Advanced Software, Nishio, S., and Yonezawa, A. (ed.), *Lecture Notes in Computer Science 742*, Springer-Verlag, Berlin, Germany, pp. 393-407.

[Wirfs-Brock et al. 90] Wirfs-Brock, R., Wilkerson, B., and Wiener, L., *Designing Object-Oriented Software*, Prentice Hall, Englewood Cliffs (New Jersey), 1990.

BUSINESS AND FINANCIAL APPLICATIONS

Beyond the Use Case: Combining task analysis and scripts in object-oriented requirements capture and business process re-engineering

Ian Graham

Swiss Bank Corporation
1 High Timber Street, London EC4V 3SB, England
email: grahami@gb.swissbank.com

Abstract

Most methods of object-oriented analysis are weak in the area of requirements capture, usually assume that a written requirements document already exists. The danger here is that such documents often contain implicit functional decomposition assumptions that interfere badly with the task of generating a truly object-oriented specification. An exception is the Objectory method [Jacobson 92] whose "use case" offers developers a chance of beginning in an object-oriented fashion rather than grafting object-oriented ideas onto a functional specification of the traditional kind.

This paper is based on some observations about use cases and their connexions with related ideas in computer science and on our practical struggle to build object-oriented systems within an environment that must build on the conventional skills of existing developers as well as the most advanced object-oriented techniques and tools.

The two observations to be made about use cases concern their similarity to the task descriptions of hierarchical task analysis as used commonly by HCI designers and to the stereotypical scripts used in AI. The former emphasize the relation of tasks to goals and the decomposition of those tasks to primitive units. The latter place the stress on tasks as prototypes for business processes. This enables us to view the task model as a bona fide object model and to view tasks as plans for work-flow execution. The latter emphasizes the character of object-oriented methods as techniques for modelling and simulation, rather than procedural descriptions of businesses.

The remainder of this paper is a concise description of our overall approach. We take as read the use of some particular notation for object modelling per se. *We use the SOMA approach of [Graham 94] but are equally happy with the use of other sufficiently rich analysis notations such as those of [Booch 93], [Desfray 92], [Jacobson 92], [Nerson 92] or [Rumbaugh 91]. The advantage of SOMA is its support for rules, which enables analysts to capture business knowledge in a direct manner and not to lose information by applying unnecessarily formal semantics too early in the life cycle.*

From TOOLS EUROPE '94 (Technology of Object-Oriented Languages and Systems).

1 Introduction

Many object-oriented analysis and all object-oriented design methods assume that a written requirements specification is available and that business priorities and feasibility are issues that have already been hammered out. This is a major assumption and, if true, it is likely that the requirements capture work has proceeded using functional decomposition techniques that will present fundamental, latent incompatibilities to an object-oriented approach to analysis. In order to obtain the full benefits from the object-oriented metaphor it were better that it was applied from the outset. The approach described in this paper was arrived at during practical attempts to produce properly object-oriented requirements statements using developers with conventional systems development backgrounds. The main results are that the approach works and that users and developers understand it.

To obtain requirements one may either guess at them (not recommended), conduct interviews or run workshops. Currently, workshop based approaches to rapid development are popular and have proved effective. This approach is commonly called Rapid Application Development (RAD) because it is usually associated with rapid, incremental delivery of software components. Most existing approaches to rapid application development are based on functional decomposition and relational entity modelling techniques that are fundamentally incompatible with the object-oriented metaphor. In fact the almost instinctive reaction of traditionally trained developers is to decompose and an outlet needs to be found for this urge. In the approach adopted here we satisfy this craving for decomposition by encouraging it in the task domain in the hope that it can be avoided during object modelling *per se*.

Before requirements capture can begin, analysts must have a clear understanding of object modelling and the principles behind object-oriented software engineering. This is because if such an understanding is not present, the whole elicitation process may be structured in such a way as to ensure that the model produced is not object-oriented; if you don't know what you seek you will not find it. The danger is that questions will be asked based on an incremental functional decomposition that is formulated in the analyst's mind as discovery proceeds and based on the existing functional practices of the business rather the on essential business processes and goals. Users can be easily led along such a path even when they start with their own, business-oriented, mental object model - as they often do. The analysts may construe things after their own, functional fashion instead of going to the roots of the user's conception of the world. Of course, object-oriented analysts also construe the world in the own, biased manner, but it is assumed that an object-oriented description is required and, I would argue that such an object-oriented model will map more closely onto the conceptual structures of a user than ones based on functional specialization. This view is supported by modern management theory and practice, where it is found that models of business processes based on communicating actors are both more stable and more flexible than those based on functional views of organizations.

Before we can capture knowledge we need some form of representation. An object-oriented approach dictates that the representation should be in the form of objects, so we shall assume that the SOMA representation as described in [Graham 94] is adopted though any notation such as that of [Rumbaugh 1991] - with suitable extensions - can be used. The extensions required principally concern the way associations and rules are represented and the various annotations that should be made to attributes and operations. In SOMA objects (which are either classes or instances) encapsulate rulesets as well as attributes and methods. Rulesets are inheritable and describe those aspects of objects that are not conveniently dealt with as attribute constraints or method assertions. They generally have a second order quality or express some kind of quantification and are expressed non-procedurally as in an expert systems language. At the requirements capture stage they serve as a repository for requirements that are not easily slotted into the more usual object model without further analysis or the taking of some design decision. There is not space to discuss this topic in this paper and the reader is referred to [Graham 94, 94a] for the details.

Developers trained and steeped in traditional methods have two ingrained reactions to a problem; if it can be represented as a static entity they want to normalize and if it can be regarded as a function they want to decompose it. It has been found that a workshop that ends with a very good object model can easily lead to the production of documentation in the form of normalized entity models and hierarchical, functional decompositions. This can be discouraged by education but it is hard to prevent completely. One, rather devious, technique is to allow developers to decompose but to do so within the task domain rather than the object domain. This gives them a suitable feeling of closure without violating the principles of object-orientation. That is not to say that they need not understand the object-oriented approach thoroughly, only that their natural, functional reflex is inhibited.

This approach leads to a novel view of the whole requirements capture process as an iterative waterfall cascading from task analysis through to object modelling down to detailed design and implementation modelling. As with all waterfalls, there can be elements of the task object model that are not discovered until the analysis and implementation models are built. Incidentally, I begin to feel that we should ban the word "functional" from the development vocabulary as it is so overlaid with meaning, nuance and emotion.

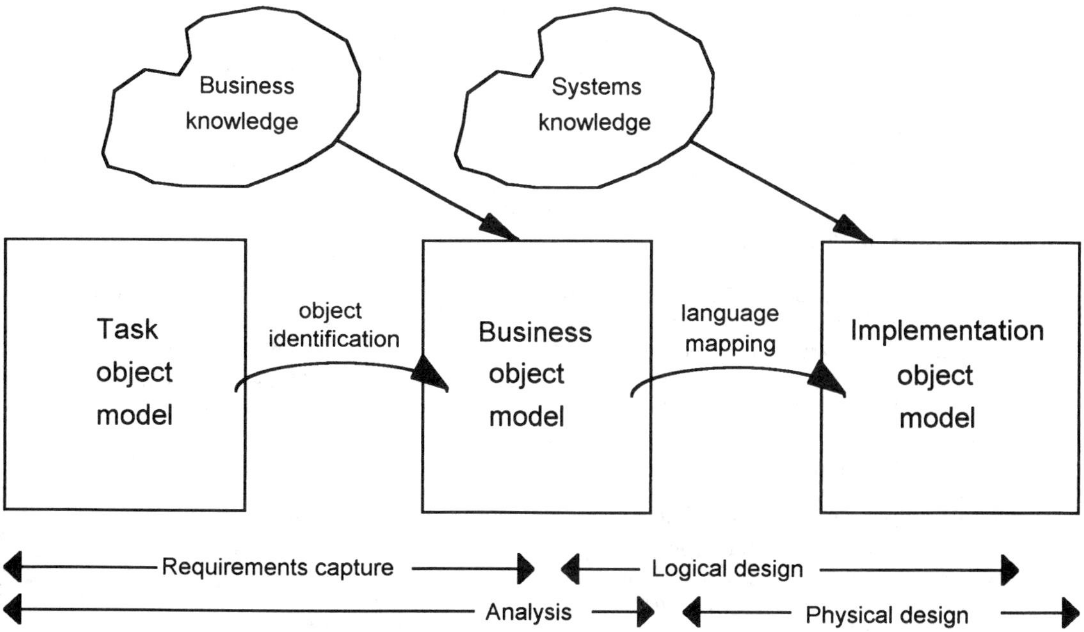

Figure 1 - Stages of object-oriented development

The TOM elicits business processes, goals and tasks and *not* functions. This new view of development can be illustrated diagrammatically as shown in Figure 1.

The TOM delivers an object model in the full sense but its objects represent users' tasks not domain and application objects. As we shall see, a textual analysis of the task model helps us discover these analysis objects though business and modelling expertise is required to complete the model. Lastly, the business object model is modified to a model that can be expressed in the semantics of some particular language. In the case that this language is C++ we can use the Booch's 1993 method to formalize this step. Booch'93 can, for example, represent pre-conditions but cannot represent rules. Thus part of the conversion is the mapping of rules to assertions. Ambiguities in the Business Object Model (BOM) with respect to the language syntax must now be eliminated and any loss of expressiveness noted to ensure traceability. A further step could be to create a suite of mappings to different object-oriented design notations, following Desfray's [94] idea of hypergenericity or equivalently Shlaer and Mellor's [92] recursive design.

There is no reason why this model should not be applied to business and enterprise modelling as well as systems modelling. There are really no changes. The language referred to need not be a programming language but a set of business imperatives. Anything with precisely defined semantics will do.

Our approach to object modelling uses deliberately imprecise, though rigorous, semantics. This may be justified by the observation that precise semantics entail commitment to a particular logic and that it is known that all logics have a restricted expressive power. What can be expressed in non-monotonic logic or fuzzy logic may be impossible or difficult to express in first order predicate calculus for example. Human reasoning is inherently imprecise and the more detailed the understanding the fuzzier it usually gets. Our object model must capture the detail of even the vaguest requirements although later the imprecision must be removed to implement on a machine. Some requirements are even too vague for this approach and may only be discovered after a prototype has been presented for critique.

Message name	Trigger event	Source	Target	Information sent/received	Expected result	Goal

Figure 2 - Message table

2 Context modelling

The construction of a task object model begins with the construction of a model of the business context. We will assume, unless otherwise stated, that the analysis is being carried out during a RAD workshop. The most common context modelling technique is to use a level-0 DFD. A slight extension of this approach carries over to object-oriented projects provided that there are some changes in interpretation. Facilitators and analysts must understand that it is objects with responsibilities that are being sought and not functions. Data flows should be regarded strictly as message flows between the system object and the external objects, which may be actors (that is users playing a particular rôle), external systems or anything else that interacts with the system. It is important that message flows are related to events at this stage. The format should be as shown in Figure 2. There is one message row for every interaction on the context diagram. Such a context diagram is illustrated in Figure 3.

Every message is regarded as a closed loop and the most important ones usually originate outside the context. The expected result may be void, as with the broadcast messages from a data feed. Diagrams need not show every such relationship between clients and servers as long as this table is complete. That is, where there is more than one message flow between the same source and target then only one arrow need be drawn. A distinction between temporal and external events is often useful and this is indicated by the nature of the trigger event; "every Friday", "customer action", "when the index records an uptick", etc. The characteristic feature of the message is its goal; why the message is being sent and what the sender hopes to achieve.

As an example, consider a counterparty who phones an equity trader to make a sale of equities. We might then record the message as "external sale request" between counterparty and trader and specify that counterparty identity, instrument, limit price and quantity are passed as parameters. The result is a trade confirmation and an instruction to Settlements. The trigger is random action by counterparty. Note further that these messages can be classified. External sale requests could be for equities, bonds, foreign exchange and so on.

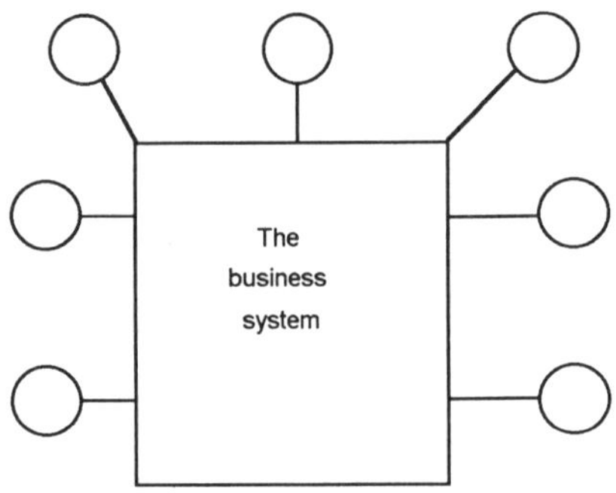

Figure 3 - Context model, stage 1: Find connexions with external entities and systems

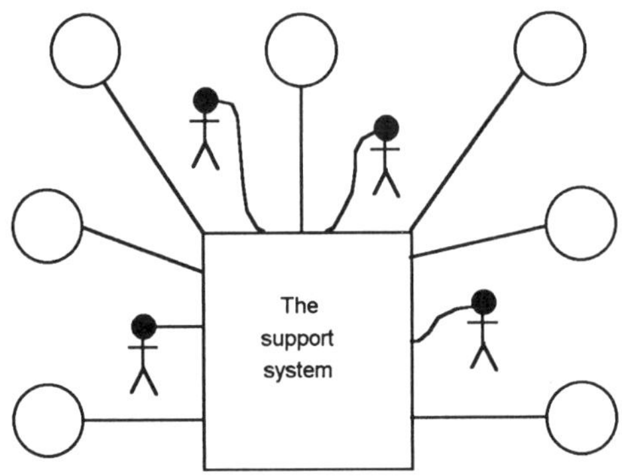

*Figure 4 - Context model, stage 2: Identify **actors**: users adopting a rôle*

There are three stages. As indicated by Figures 3 and 4, the first two are to identify significant external entities and communication with the business system including manual operations and then shrink the context so that human users are seen as communicating with a support system or computer system. Once the external environment has been discovered the next step is to identify the actors. **Actors** are *users adopting a rôle to interact with the system for some purpose*. These actors now communicate with the system as external entities. What sort of people or systems will make use of any proposed system and how will they expect it to behave? What responsibilities does the system have towards its users? The third stage is to complete the message flow tables.

During these stages it is important to find out about the likely skills of the proposed users and describe the skill profiles of the actors. Later these skills can be related to those required to carry out the lowest level tasks in component task scripts.

The most important messages are usually those sent by the actors to the system. For example, a trader may ask "what is my position?". Note that the message source is the trader even though the data flow substantially from the system to the trader. Every such message has a goal and this must be discovered because it then becomes possible to ask what tasks must be performed by the system to assist the user in accomplishing this goal. The elicitation of goal completes a description of the system's scope. Now a more detailed task analysis begins to build a requirements model.

3 Task-scripts, subscripts, component scripts and side-scripts

Jacobson's [92] use cases offer a clue as to how one can proceed from here. However, the phrase "use case" often leads to confusing sentences; being - I guess - a literal translation from the Swedish. Further, it appears as if use cases are new, whereas there are several related ideas within computer science already. First, there is a connexion with the process bubbles of a DFD. Second, the use case descriptions resemble the stereotypical scripts of [Schank 77]. Last, use cases resemble the tasks of hierarchical task analysis which is widely, if not universally, used in HCI design. We will use the term **task-script** to emphasize these honourable forebears. In doing so we can draw on the riches of both script theory, which has direct implications for object modelling of stereotypical behaviour or business processes, and of HCI, where it is known that tasks can be recursively decomposed and that objects are usually found during this process. We retain the idea from Jacobson that the task-scripts will be used as the basis for test scripts later on. The most remarkable observation that can be made about this synthesis of ideas is that task scripts can be regarded as objects that may participate in classification, composition and usage structures, albeit in a different domain. Further, every task script is related to a goal that its execution facilitates. Task scripts, like use cases, are prototypical.

Task scripts are primarily used to discover business objects and retained for testing purposes. The components of a script are arrived at by using task analysis and are called **component scripts**. This is where the hierarchical decomposition takes place down to the level of atomic tasks that refer directly to objects and their operations. Classifying scripts into more specialized versions gives rise to **sub-scripts**. When exceptions require the flow of control to be redirected to a script dealing with a special case, the latter is dealt with by a **side-script**. It is important to emphasize that task scripts deal with business processes and not business functions to avoid the danger of capturing the requirements in the form of narrow functional specializations which are often present in the existing organization.

For each incoming message flow in the context model, it should be established what the rôle player or external agent would normally expect to happen in the form of a stated goal and a script beginning with an event.

We have looked at the external interactions now let us look at the interactions internal to the business area and posit a "system" within it. The diagram in Figure 5 shows a fragment of the task-script diagram for a general trading system. Exploring the "confirm deal" script reveals that there may be a "check position" component-script and that various objects are required to implement the script. This component-script does not record an exception. The script might read:

"To confirm a deal the trader enters the *counterparty* and *security* details and checks the limits on his *position*. If the limits are OK the deal is struck and confirmed" Here there are at least three objects (in italics).

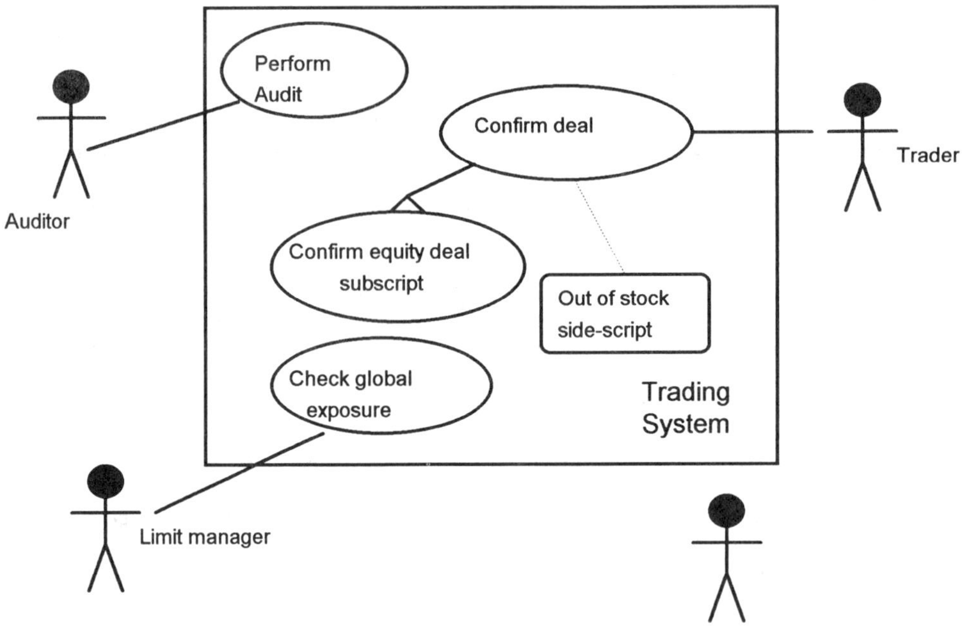

Figure 5 - Context model for a trading system with task-scripts added

An exception or side-script is far more useful. For example, the "settle trade" script might read "on receipt of ticket, match trade and record data". When the match fails, a side-script such as "alert exception manager and print letter" must be added.

It should be apparent that task scripts are being modelled as objects and given classification, composition and usage structures corresponding to sub-, component and side-scripts respectively. These three structures correspond to the views taken in use case analysis, task analysis and script theory respectively. It is necessary to realize that these objects are not objects in the problem domain but in the domain of task modelling; they are nevertheless objects though they do not usually have significant operations.

Tasks are carried out in order to achieve goals. Goals are desirable states to be achieved. Preliminary scoping elicits goals. Analysis discovers the tasks behind them.

The end product is a set of high level objects and their responsibilities together with a message list as above. We may also have elicited some composition and classification structures and these should be recorded. Techniques for extracting these objects from the task-scripts are discussed briefly below. Any objects mentioned in discussion should be recorded uncritically for later analysis.

A notation similar to the class cards used for object modelling is recommended for recording the task. Thus, a task is represented as shown in Figure 6.

High level objects are sometimes aggregates of lower level objects and may represent departments or service providers and the like. Such an object is called a layer. A typical layer will be a department, organization, existing system or (rarely) a conceptual structure. Organization into layers can proceed bottom-up by assembling objects which have been discovered to participate in composition structure or merely identified directly. Doing the latter imposes a top-down decomposition to make the problem more tractable but corresponds well to the notions of subsystem, subject or layer found in various object-oriented analysis approaches. Each layer will receive messages and encapsulate its structure. A matrix of events and objects affected

Task Name	
Supertasks (AKO)	
Component tasks	
Task body	
Associated tasks	
Exceptions	Side-scripts
Rulesets	

Figure 6 - A task card

should be produced and risk identification attempted at this stage if time permits.

At first sight the similarity of task scripts is use cases is more apparent than the differences that exist. Therefore it is worth clarifying that the stereotypical nature of scripts is what makes then into classes in the TOM. They represent tasks that are *understood* and which may describe processing deep inside the system rather than merely the tasks at the interface. Anecdotal evidence from one user of Objectory user suggests that use cases are better at modelling the interface than system internals. We have not found this with task scripts[1]. Tying the tasks to a goal is an important addition too and the wholesale import of techniques from task analysis is more convenient that re-inventing them.

[1]This was reported during a Birds of a Feather session at Object Expo Europe in 1993.

4 Identifying objects

Once the task object model has been built we have a textual source that can be mined for objects, attributes, operations, structures and rules. However, it is always possible to pre-empt this process by skilful questioning during a workshop or even a one-to-one interview. The techniques involved are also useful for the analyses of the protocols contained in task scripts and so we will present them first.

Several of the methods which have been developed by knowledge engineers trying to elicit knowledge from human beings with the aim of building expert systems can be used to obtain concepts in any domain. These concepts often map onto objects. This is not the place for an exegesis on methods of knowledge acquisition, but we should mention the usefulness of methods based on Kelly grids (or repertory grids) [Kelly 55], protocol analysis, task analysis and interviewing theory. Protocol analysis [Ericsson 1984] is in some ways similar to the procedure of analyzing parts of speech, and task analysis can reveal both objects and their operations. Task analysis is often used in user interface design [Daniels 86, Johnson 92]. The details of these techniques can be found in any decent book on knowledge acquisition; e.g. [Hart 89], [Graham 88]. We normally proceed as follows:

1. Textual and protocol analysis are used to extract candidate classes, attributes, rules and operations from the decomposed task scripts. An additional step attaches the attributes, operations and rules to the objects.
2. Repertory grids, card sorts, laddering, etc. are used to discover associations and classification and composition structures. The original objects are critiqued on the basis of this new knowledge. A mnemonic for the use of repertory grid techniques may be stated as follows:
   - Ask for the opposite of everything and discard logical opposites.
   - Ask for the general names for groups of two or more objects.
   - For every triad of objects ask for a property that two have and the other does not. Do this for each pair in the triad
3. Class cards are prepared for each class identified.

Object templates, which are similar to our class cards, have been used in knowledge acquisition for expert systems. The knowledge engineering approach emphasizes that classes should correspond to concepts held by users and experts. High level classes represent abstractions that may be reusable across several similar domains.

A few common sense guidelines for object identification would be worth including at this point if space permitted. Analysts should avoid objects arising solely from normalization or the removal of many-to-many relationships. The rule is: if it's not a real-world entity then it's not an object. For example, the many-to-many relationship between ORDERS and INVOICES may be removed by introducing a new class ORDER-LINE. This is fine, the lines are real things; they get printed on the invoice. On the contrary there seems to be no such natural object that would remove the many-to-many relationship between cars and the colours they may be painted or products and the regulations that apply to them.

It is beneficial to make a preliminary list of objects and operations based on their text prior to RAD workshops. This is used to kick start object identification and there is a well tried and fairly mechanical means for doing this known as Abbott Textual Analysis [Abbott 83]. Roughly speaking, nouns are candidate objects and verbs are candidate operations. Obviously, this technique only suggests business objects and knowledge of the business and of object-oriented principles is required to complete the transformation. In workshops it is the users who perform the text analysis - and they enjoy it. They then work with the analysts to build the BOM.

5 Building the object model

The objects identified so far may now be assembled into an object model and data semantics added. This model may show up incompletenesses but analysts are to be warned to resist the temptation to normalize unnecessarily. Many to many relationships may be tolerated. First normal form is quite irrelevant in object-oriented analysis. The golden rule is: "If it isn't a real world thing or concept then it's not an object". This rule must not, however, be interpreted as saying that domain specific abstractions are not permitted. What is in the "real world" depends on the purpose of the development.

Following the identification of an object-type such as "securities" we must now ask: "are all securities handled in the same way?", which will help us to discover the classification structure of securities. Similarly, given three objects of a type we should ask, for instance, if the users can think of a property that equities and warrants share but that bonds do not. Maybe the answer is that bonds are always "listed" on the stock exchange. This helps to discover both subclasses and attributes and can be repeated for all object triplets. It is also often useful to ask for the opposites of concepts as they are not always logical opposites. For example, the opposite of an equity may be considered to be a bond. This is a useful questioning technique for discover more specific object-types or even attributes. A useful technique for discovering generalizations is to ask, say: "Is there a concept that covers the situation where a counterparty doesn't have the funds to settle and the one where settlement fails due to a non-existent counterparty?". The answer may produce an object called something like "settlement failure" at a higher level of generality. What we are doing here is applying one of the object elicitation techniques of SOMA; the method of repertory grids. These methods are described in more detail in [Graham 94, 94a].

In a trading domain, for example, we may well end up with a structure of the sort shown in the fern diagram in Figure 7.

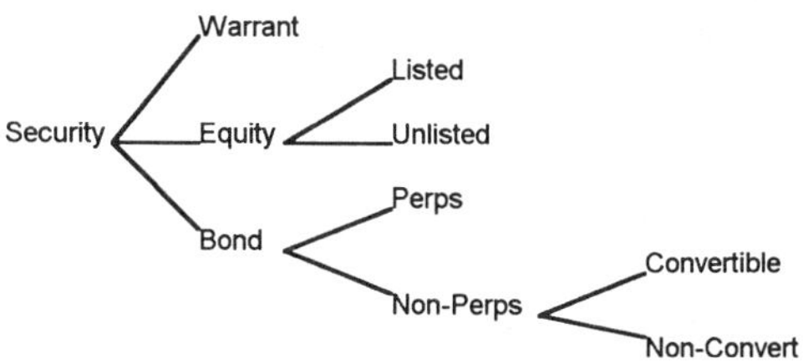

Figure 7 - A fern diagram for the class Security

Note that Coupon is an attribute of Bond but not of Perps. Any instance of Perps will inherit the Coupon attribute and the "gross yield to redemption" operation.

It is important to avoid mixing classification structures like this with composition hierarchies. For example, a warrant could be viewed as a composite instrument consisting of an equity and an option. This is **not** the same as equity inheriting from warrant. Beginners often suffer from this confusion and even experts slip up occasionally.

Producing a sound reusable structure is hard. It should not be expected that a workshop will produce a perfect version first time. Subsequent analysis is usually necessary to refine the structures.

Now we have some objects (nouns) we must identify their responsibilities (i.e. the services they provide to other components or actors or the operations they can perform. To do this we may examine the verbs present in the scripts. These operations must then be attached to a suitable object-type. The guiding principle is encapsulation; objects should contain and hide their data behind their operations. For example, a share register hides registrations behind an interface which permits it to send certificates to new registrants, pay dividends and so on. In RAD workshops the functions will be tied to these and further objects.

Key questions that should be asked are:

- Who is involved in an interaction to carry out the responsibility?
- What exceptions may occur? (E.g. credit limit exceeded)
- What services must be provided to execute the interaction?
- Which objects may provide such services?
- Which data does a service need to access? (These should be encapsulated by the object to which the operation is tied if possible)

The task-scripts that were identified at the context modelling stage should be further refined and checked for completeness. Have all potential actors and uses been identified? Have all exceptions been covered sufficiently?

Task scripts may be decomposed into component scripts. The level of detail to which this is done depends on the purpose. If the user interface is being designed then quite a low level is appropriate. For business requirements this is less likely. In either case the component scripts will offer a further source of nouns and verbs. The rule is that task scripts should be decomposed to the level where further decomposition fails to reveal relevant objects.

Entities should be classified into **interface objects** (if any) and system objects. System objects should be further divided into **application objects** and **domain objects**. Domain objects are persistent and likely to be fairly stable in structure throughout the lifetime of the application, though their instances may change rapidly. Typical examples might include Share-Register, Client-Database, Parts-Inventory, etc. Application objects are more volatile. They contain the operations that are not firmly tied to long-term stored data. Making this separation helps with the maintainability of the system in future and corresponds to the traditional notion of data independence. For those familiar with Sybase and roughly speaking, a Sybase server table with stored procedures will correspond to a domain object. The client would store the operations of application objects.

Each operation can now be provided with a process description exactly in the manner of conventional top-down methods, but these **must** be attached to an object. This also provides a further check that no operation has been missed.

Rules and constraints that connect attributes and operations to each other and specify things like conflict resolution strategy are also written down.

Existing systems are best regarded as entire objects that can send or be sent messages. During implementation this may require the construction of an **object wrapper** (see [Graham 92]) around each such system or the use of an object request broker.

For a system where declarative rules are important, such as mortgage lending or trade matching in a settlement system, this step is highly significant for two main reasons. First, recording the rules to which an object must conform directly as rules matches the way users think about the problem and is far easier to use as a communication tool. The alternative would be to record these rules as pre-processing steps within procedures which is much harder to understand and, worse, makes implicit assumptions about the style of implementation. Secondly, where there is a corpus of declarative knowledge expressed as rules, it may be advantageous to implement these rules directly in a knowledge based system component of the final system - with considerable benefits in terms of both rapidity of development and maintenance as regulations, say, change in future. Objects with many rules can be implemented directly as the rule-sets of an expert systems development tool.

It is recommended that a simple IF/THEN syntax is used to record rules as described by [Graham 94,94a). The ordering of a set of rules is not significant. If it is, in the real world that is, then an operation should be defined instead.

If an expert systems implementation is not desired then the rules can be converted to assertions and then operations mechanically at design time.

6 Creating class cards and walking through the system

A CRC approach is most beneficial at this stage and the next step is to conduct a brainstorming session. Class names are written on large cards. For each entity, add its responsibilities. These come from the preliminary task model and from

Class Name	Abstract/Concrete
Superclasses	Domain/Application/Interface
Parts	
Attributes and relationships	
Operations	Servers
Rules	

Figure 8 - A class card

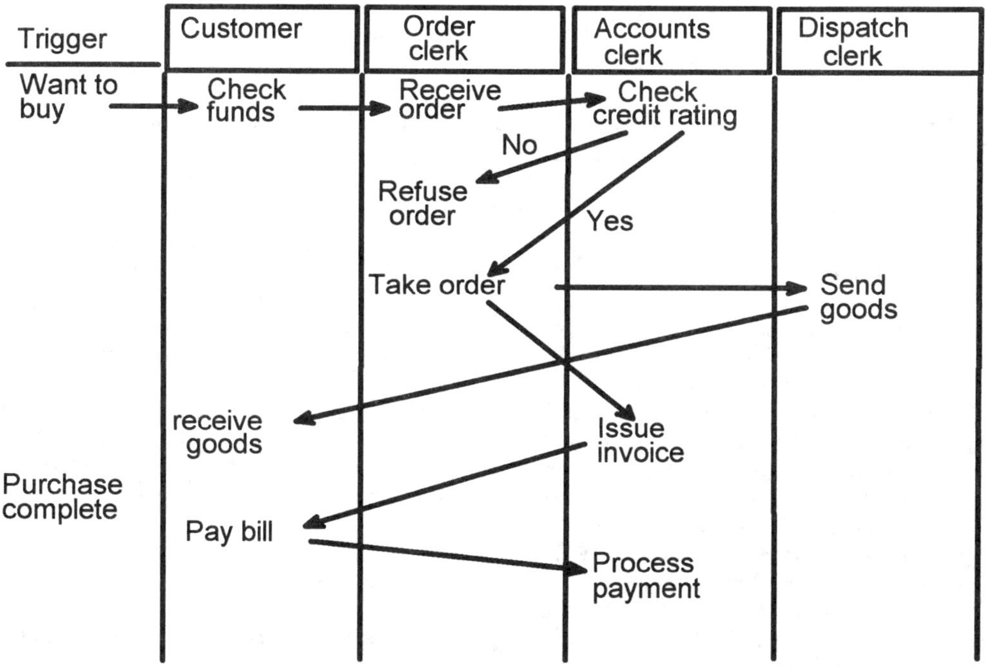

Figure 9 - Incomplete event trace for a mail order goal

brainstorming. Next it must be established which other entities collaborate with each object to carry out each operation identified. During this process an attempt is made to organize the cards into classification and aggregation structures.

At this point rôle play may be carried out. Each participant takes one or more cards and acts its part. The facilitator issues events based on the task-scripts and the messages are passed round verbally noting changes of state on the back of the cards. In this way the responsibilities and collaborations are "debugged" and issues exposed.

Finally any constraints and rules that the objects are subject to should be recorded on the cards. The format for a SOMA class card is shown in Figure 8.

Attributes have a type which is an object-type or a primitive; e.g. DoB(Date). Attributes that represent relationships have multiplicity and modality constraints; e.g. WorksIn(Dept,0,1). It is important to note that relationships are to be regarded as one-way pointers **out** of the object and not as two-way links between objects. If a two-way link is required then an object representing the relationship must be defined, especially if the relationship has attributes itself.

The output from this stage is the completed cards and a series of event traces. A useful notation for recording event traces has its origins in the document flow diagrams of early systems analysis. [Lorenz 93] proposes a similar notation. The objects and actors are written across the top of a large page and the triggering event is noted to the left. Figure 9 shows a very simple, and incomplete example concerned with mail order. Descent of the columns underneath the objects represents the passage of time. The arrows indicate the flow of messages and are annotated with decisions temporal constraints and so on.

Object-types should be divided into those with complex, significant states and others. Where the states are complex a state transition model can be used to discover further operations. The notation for state models is that of [Harel 87] as presented by [Rumbaugh 91].

	Objective 1	Objective 2	Objective 3	Total
Object 1	76	30	80	186
Object 2	88	30	50	168
Object 3	15	40	5	60
Total	179	100	135	

Figure 10 - Object/Objectives matrix

7 Object-oriented RAD workshops and subsequent development

After establishing the basic mission of a project, the first task is to set the primary business objectives. It is beneficial if participants are encouraged to suggest how the attainment of each objective could be measured. It is often hard to find such measures for objectives but a formal step which asks people to think about the question helps considerably. [Rubin 92] makes a similar point.

Next we ask participants to try to prioritize the objectives. This involves placing a rough forecast of the benefit expected to be derived from achieving each objective. It tends to reveal grouping among objectives; when one objective cannot realize its benefits without another being also achieved say. The most important benefit of this prioritization is that, in later project phases, it enables project managers to place emphasis on the critical modules. This is especially important where prototyping or rapid development is contemplated. The priorities should be traced through to modules therefore wherever possible. Once objects, and especially high level 'layers', have been discovered these should be scored against the objectives. This will typically happen after context modelling, task script analysis and walkthroughs have been completed as described below. The objects/layers with the highest scores have *ceteris paribus* the highest development priority. Total scores for the objectives will confirm or deny the original business priorities or may be used to apply weighting to the horizontal scores, or used directly as illustrated in Figure 10. In the diagram Object 1 clearly has a high priority while Objectives 1 and 3 can be mostly satisfied by delivering Objects 1 and 2.

Facilitators must zealously crush attempts to describe a systems solution during requirements capture - it is what has to be done that is required not how it is to be done.

Normally, RAD workshops and interviews are a precursor to rapid development. The deliverables from requirements capture should form input to a planning process which will set up a project lasting about three months elapsed time during which a small team will prototype the objects representing the objective with the highest priority. Evaluation of the prototype should be based on the views of an independent evaluation team and upon the task-scripts developed in the context model.

8 Conclusions

The method has been a success on projects in enabling traditionally trained developers to avoid the worst excesses of functional decomposition and "structured" analysis. It has also been popular with the user population, who are frequently involved in rapid application development (RAD) workshops, because of our insistence on building models in terms of familiar business objects and avoiding jargon and unnatural constructs.

In our environment, which uses object-oriented languages such as C++ and advanced tools such as NeXTstep extensively, we faced the need to capture and analyze requirements in an object-oriented fashion. We wanted seamlessness between development phases and activities and we wanted to apply the benefits of reuse at the level of specification as well as at the code level. Early experiences have been encouraging. RAD is widely accepted. Early attempts at object-oriented analysis produced specifications that were still too "functional". Gradually, as we begin to apply the methods outlined in this paper, we are producing specifications in terms of object descriptions. The task oriented approach forces, or at least encourages, analysts to converge on object-oriented models and there is now a defined, step-by-step approach to doing this that can be taught. We have found that this approach is largely independent of the notation used for object-oriented analysis, though the expressive power conferred by the use of rules - not discussed in this paper - is still a benefit of SOMA. My chief conclusions therefore, based on this experience, are that:

1. it works;
2. both users and developers understand the approach; and
3. the approach can be added to most existing OOA/D methods without disrupting them.

A remarkable finding is that business process re-engineering can use exactly the same approach as system development merely by changing the scope of the TOM to include the business network and changing the granularity of the model.

A tool to support the approach is currently under development with release planned for late 1994.

9 Acknowledgements

I would like to thank the referees for their helpful comments.

10 References

[Abbott 83] Abbott, R.J., Program Design by Informal English Descriptions, *Communications of the ACM* **26**(11), 882-8941983

[Booch 93] Booch, G., *Object Oriented Design with Applications*, 2nd Edition, Benjamin/Cummings, 1993

[Daniels86] Daniels, P.J., The user modelling function of an intelligent interface for document retrieval systems, in: Brookes, B.C. (Ed.) (1986) *IRFIS 6: Intelligent Information Systems for the Information Society*, Amsterdam: North Holland, 162-176

[Desfray 92] Desfray, P., *Ingénerie des objets: Approche classe-relation application à C++*. Paris: Editions Masson., 1992

[Ericsson 84] Ericsson, K.A. and Simon, H.A., *Protocol Analysis: Verbal Reports as Data*, Bradford Books, 1984

[Graham 88] Graham, I.M. and Jones, P.L.K., *Expert Systems: Knowledge, Uncertainty and Decision*, Chapman & Hall, 1988

[Graham 92] Graham, I.M., Interoperation: Combining object-oriented applications with conventional IT, *Object Magazine* **2**(4), 36-37

[Graham 93] Graham, I.M., Migration using SOMA: A Semantically Rich Method of Object-Oriented Analysis, *Journal of Object-Oriented Programming* **5**(9), Feb. 1993

[Graham 94] Graham, I.M., *Object-Oriented Methods, 2nd Edition*, Addison-Wesley

[Graham 94a] Graham, I.M., *Migrating to Object Technology*, Addison-Wesley (to appear)

[Harel 87] Harel, D., "Statecharts: A Visual Formalism for Complex Systems", in *Science of Computer Programming 8* 231-274, North Holland, 1987

[Hart 89] Hart, A. *Knowledge Acquisition for Expert Systems* (2nd edition), London: Kogan Page, 1989

[Jacobson 92] Jacobson, I., Christerson, M. Jonsson, P. and Overgaard, G., *Object-Oriented Software Engineering*, Addison-Wesley, 1992

[Johnson 92] Johnson, P., *Human Computer Interaction: Psychology, Task Analysis and software engineering*, London: McGraw-Hill, 1992

[Kelly 55] Kelly, G.A., *The Psychology of Personal Constructs*, New York: W.W. Norton, 1955

[Lorenz 93] Lorenz, M. (1993) *Object-Oriented Software Development: A Practical Guide*, Englewood Cliffs NJ: Prentice Hall

[Nerson 92] Nerson, J., Applying Object-Oriented Analysis and Design, *Comms. ACM* **35**(9), 63-74

[Rubin 92] Rubin, K. and Goldberg, A., Object Behaviour Analysis, *Comms. of the ACM*, Sept 1992, 49-51

[Rumbaugh 91] Rumbaugh, J., Blaha, M., Premerlani, W. *et al.*, *Object-Oriented Modelling and Design*, Englewood Cliffs NJ: Prentice Hall, 1991

[Schank 77] Schank, R.C. and Abelson, R.P., *Scripts, Plans, Goals and Understanding*, Lawrence Erlbaum Associates, 1977

[Shlaer 92] Shlaer, S. and Mellor, S.J., *Object-Lifecycles: Modelling the World in States*, Yourdon Press, 1992

Experiencing full object oriented lifecycle in a complex financial domain

Stefano Sappino, Tecsiel S.p.A. (1)
(E-mail Sappino@tecpi.tecsiel.it)
Brunella Vaglieco, Elasis S.c.p.A. (2)
Ernesto Bauchiero, I.T.S. G.E.I.E. (3)
Valeria Gioia, Tecsiel S.p.A. (1)
Domenico Macrini, Elasis S.c.p.A. (2)
Giuseppe Capretto, Elasis S.c.p.A. (2)

(1) Via del Ponte di Piscina Cupa, 43 00128 Roma Italy tel 39-6-505091 fax 39-6505088
(2) Viale Impero s.n. 80038 Pomigliano d'Arco Italy tel. 39-81-8036421 fax 39-81-8036472
(3) Via Issiglio 63/A Torino Italy tel. 39-11-6853019 fax 39-11-6853583

ABSTRACT

Object oriented technology is often regarded as immature to be applied to traditionally mainframe-based systems where structured analysis techniques still dominate. The work flow process based on managerial strategies applied to bookkeeping and finance is one of these sectors.

This article shows the experience acquired applying a totally object oriented approach to the analysis and the development of a system used by financial management. The system must manage the active life (4 years forecast) of a important international agreement between the Fiat Auto car manufacturer and the Republic of Algeria.

The complexity of the domain and the strong mission critical integrity constraints–represented a significant test against which evaluate the promises of object-oriented technology.

INTRODUCTION

Object-oriented technology is by now largely used in many contexts such as research and implementation of systems with advanced user interface and high-complexity software in CAD/CAM, CASE and simulations fields; however, a heavy–pressure in the software development comes from the company's work flow automation, with special attention to bookkeeping and finance.

From TOOLS EUROPE '94 (Technology of Object-Oriented Languages and Systems).

Currently the above mentioned contexts are only marginally influenced by the new methodologies and techniques of the object-oriented approach.

In this paper we describe the work made under a cooperation between Elasis, I.T.S. and Tecsiel in realizing a generalized software system for international agreements' management; the specific instance is represented by the agreement between Republic of Algeria and Fiat Auto S.p.A. aimed at building up a brand new car factory in Algeria.

Elasis is the Fiat research and development company located in South Italy. In the software field, Elasis is interested in testing new technologies within the software production process to provide Fiat Auto with a competent know-how.

I.T.S. is the Fiat Group company which supplies Information Technology services.

Tecsiel is the research and development company of the Finsiel Group, the second computer science Group in Europe, as far as the billing is concerned. Tecsiel's major interest fields are software engineering, open systems, object oriented technology and ISO/OSI networking.

This paper is organized in three sections. In the first one, we give an overview of the context in which the project evolved, trying to point out the specific challenges of the domain; in the second one, the aspects belonging to the actual project development are reported, paying special attention to software metrics; finally, a discussion concerning emerged problems of general interest is reported.

CONTEXT OVERVIEW

Financial management of an international agreement requires a strict observance of the following constraints:

- movement of capitals is subject to formal, strict rules;
- as a bridge between different legal and financial environments, it must match and satisfy a set of requirements represented by the intersection of the involved systems;
- its reliability is critical to properly acquire all the economical opportunities;
- it must be able to promptly react to a wide spectrum of external events;
- its internal coherency must be maintained even in its most complex and intricate aspects;
- its expected life-cycle covers many years in which several thousand of entities must be processed;
- it must interact with older "legacy" systems aimed at managing company's financial assessments.

Business procedures devoted to handle the flow of an international agreement are rather complex because of the number of involved Subjects (States, Independent Companies, Departments in a company), their world-wide dislocation and the external constraint established by Italian and Algerian laws and the international trade rules.

Fiat Auto aimed at developing a software management system flexible enough to quickly adhere to the ever-changing requirements coming from the internal departments, in charge to decide internal procedure. In addition, the system had to be general enough to represent a support basis to the forecoming international agreements.

The specific project goal was to design and implement a system controlling the contract work flow from the Fiat Auto point of view.

The automation and optimization of the most complex intricacies in the business work flow represents a constraint to be accomplished within a short-term plan dealing with a high degree of uncertainty in the final specifications.

Previously, a mainframe based "classical" application was a partial IT support to the management of this kind of contracts. However, such an application was not able to timely absorb the amount of not completely foreseeable needs of an international agreement.

I.T.S., knowing the uncertainty of the final requirements, and forecasting a long period of time in which they could keep evolving and emerging, decided that a new approach would be of interest. The object-oriented technology was, considering its claims, the natural choice.

Elasis had previously developed an object-oriented experimental prototype to automate an existing international agreement. This prototype was shown to the Fiat management. and demonstrated itself as an useful support to the actual project start-up.

Tecsiel has been an active company in the object-oriented technology field for a long time. Thanks to this ability, it was involved as a consultant to drive analysis from a methodologically correct point of view and to participate in software implementation.

The project work group was made up of 3 C++ programmers (with different level of experience) and 2 project managers, whose one mostly devoted to emphasize the correctness of the OO approach.

TARGET HARDWARE/SOFTWARE

The target environment has been a PC platform with MS-Windows 3.1 and ORACLE RDBMS.

The RDBMS technology has been in line with the company software policy; the new system was going to be integrated in an environment where PCs have been in use for office automation with access to business software through mainframe terminals .

Development environment was made up of the Glockenspiel C++ precompiler, Glockenspiel's CommonView 3.0 (a GUI class library) and the

CommonBase 1.2 class library to encapsulate the RDBMS. The C compiler was MS C 6.0, running under OS/2 1.3.

PROJECT DEVELOPMENT

ANALYSIS

At the project start-up a draft analysis document was available. This document was the result of some interviews to the final user who has been the owner of "the way we do it" knowledge in the field of the international agreement's everyday management.

The document did not adhere to any formal OO methodology but was structured in an OO-like style.

In order to formalize the analysis, the Coad-Yourdon notation was chosen together with the support of the CASE tool Object Maker, from Mark V systems. Object Maker was planned to be used as a code generator, class browser and documentation tool. A reverse engineering tool was scheduled from Mark V to be released in a short time.

The analysis phase exclusively focused on domain understanding; this approach allowed a depth knowledge of the domain internals without "side effects" caused by the adoption of an implementation-driven point of view .

The normalization of the available specification brought to an object model containing:

- classes/objects;
- a draft subject division hypothesis;
- instance and part-of connections;
- high level message connections;
- and, for each class/object, the most relevant attributes and methods.

A specific abstraction pass was performed in order to obtain abstract classes from which derive by inheritance.

To achieve the maximum from the interaction with the end user, only terms taken from the user's vocabulary was used to describe analysis class/objects.

One important result of this activity of normalization was the identification of several ambiguities, inconsistencies or "holes" in the domain understanding, as it had been perceived from the end user. One of the most challenging activities for the work group in the whole project was "querying for specification", often providing hints and solutions to establish a formal procedure.

The analysis phase was repeated several times; at the end (when the work group agreed on the fact that no further specification could have been obtained from the end user, as far as the user himself was conscious), a formal model, constituted by 7 subjects was produced. Tracking the model's history, subjects grew up from 5 to 7; the class/object number changed about 15%, mainly due to substantial changements of requirements.

It should be pointed out that the analysis phase stopped at a rather high level with respect to class/objects and attributes/methods specification, while a well detailed description of class/objects relationships was obtained.

As a side effect of the analysis, for each subject in the analysis model, a class playing a central role was identified. Those classes acted as coordinators of the activities performed by the other classes of the subject. Moreover, these classes provided primary services to other subjects.

DESIGN

The aim of the design phase was to add to the analysis model all the class/objects needed to reach a computer-based solution. Even this phase was performed several times.

Because of an explicit, strategic assumption the design of GUI objects was not included in this phase. GUI objects were to be considered as highly volatile during the end user validation steps; furthermore, GUI objects were viewed as easily obtainable from the GUI class library and the design object model. Besides, the previously developed prototype code heavily connected GUIs aspects and RDBMS aspects. The capability and the achieved results in reusing such a code was one of the project goals.

The final version of the design model contains 86 class/objects and 7 subjects, ranging from 24 to 3 class per subject. In this model 19 class/objects identified as "not to be implemented" were included.

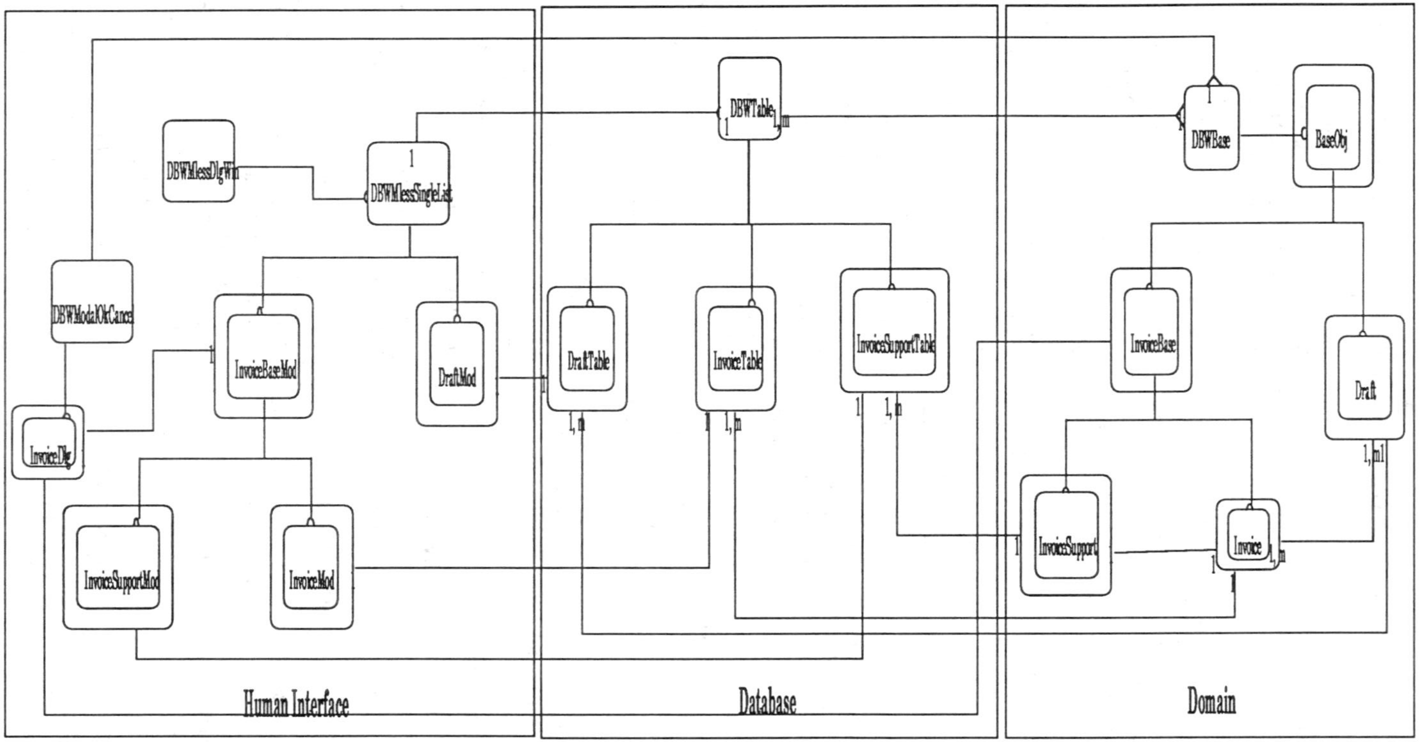

Figure 1: a section of the Object Model, showing human interface, database and domain subjects related to invoice and draft domain objects (a draft is a colletion of invoices)

Anyway, an in-depth discussion concerning the interaction philosophy to be adopted was executed.

IMPLEMENTATION

Implementation phases were conducted in parallel with analysis and design cycles.

From a technical point of view, every subject was resolved in a separate DLL (dynamic link library) and every class was implemented in a distinct source file, preserving in such a way a significant continuity of representation from the analysis object model through the object code.

A significant effort was spent in optimizing the class library previously developed to implement the prototype; this library, not specifically designed for reuse, actually generated more problems than it helped to solve; it is conceivable that a new one would have been a better choice in terms of flexibility and design correctness. Anyway, from the cost management point of view, the availability of such a library reduced significantly the development elapsed time.

The development environment proved to be reliable enough; long compilation time and lack of an efficient class browser badly affected productivity.

Both user interface efficiency and functional validation were provided through a set of intermediate releases. For each release, interesting feedback in terms of both usability and better specification emerged. Comparison and integration of user and analyst point of views and knowledge were the foundation to build up an efficient product exploiting the available technology power.

METRICS

Three cycles of a spiral software life cycle were performed. The break-point for each cycle was determined by the availability of new user requirements.

The following table shows development effort details. All man-months data reported in this section are the actual time spent on the activity.

Activity	*man-month*	*involved resources*
PHASE 1		
Analisys	4	3
Design	1.5	3
Data Base Design	0.5	1
UI Design	2	2
Prototype re-engineering	4	2
Totals	12	
PHASE 2		
Analisys	1.5	2
Design	1	1
Data Base Design	0.5	1
Develoment and test	18	3
Totals	21	
PHASE 3		
Analisys	1	1
Design	1.5	2
Data Base Design	1	2
Development and test	18	2
Totals	21.5	
Total effort	54.5	

Table 1: project's schedule details

Total elapsed: 1.5 years.

An additional resource who joined the work group at the end of the first phase was non effective because of the time involved in mastering fundamentals in OO design and programming.

The following table shows in detail the overall metrics of the project.

	Totals
Processed files	805
Total line #	76536
Locs #	52092
Total comments #	3893
Total methods #	4357
Total attributes #	1635
Class #	413
Methods/Class	10.55
Attributes/Class	3.96
Locs/Methods	11.96
Locs/Comments	13.38

Table 2: project's metrics

By comparison, we are reporting herewith the available metrics of the mainframe-based existing system in FIAT for general bookkeeping management. This is the system that should have been extended if this project had not been proposed.

Activity	man/month
Analisys	33
Design	67
Development and test	350
Total	450

Table 3 : a "comparable" mainframe-based project

Total elapsed: 4 years.

50 man-months were spent to connect this system to other company information systems.

Extreme caution must be used in evaluating these data: the involved system are different by hardware, technology, number of allowed users, development date and supported functionality; mainframe actual system supports less general functionalities, but it is more detailed in what it is concerned.

OBTAINED GOALS AND PROBLEMS ENCOUNTERED

GLOBAL CONSIDERATIONS

The main goal, i.e. the implementation of a complete management system for a complex financial domain was completely reached. All the intricacies of the analysis context was formalized and implemented even dealing with a high degree of specification uncertainty and volatility.

The produced code demonstrated a few bugs, even in its early development phases, and an overall good robustness and usability.

The end users have accepted the system with satisfaction as it resulted to be compliant with their effective needs, and because it was coming off from their active participation in all phases of the project.

Such a good quality level of interaction between analyst and final user is usually difficult to be achieved with traditional analysis and development methods without specific user training in analysis and design notation and structure.

Original project schedule was negatively affected by an over-evaluation of the effectiveness of the domain comprehension obtained with the pre-analysis phase; furthermore, specification volatility was even greater than what had been supposed. However, this problem was in the scope of project goals, and a global evaluation of the elapsed time shows a significant advantage for this system if compared with implementations of traditional systems.

ANALYSIS

The analysis object model proved itself as an extremely useful tool to capture the space domain complexity in a compact and understandable way. This model was used as a discussion base even with the end user, as it allows a punctual and effective procedure when pointing out difficult questions or specification problems.

The model proved itself to be rather stable during project life cycle; the extended requirements modifications had localized impact on the model.

Coad-Yourdon notation showed some lack of usability to represent message connections as the model complexity grew up; moreover, there is no way to specify which method sends a message; this constitutes a limit to the capability of tracking with precision system behaviour.

On the other hand notation turned out to be clear, understandable and effective.

The OO point of view allowed the user to flawlessly join the analysis team every time it was needed; no "different languages difficulties" troubled the team.

DESIGN

The design object model was realized in a short time and demonstrated a good stability. Most of the work in producing the design model consisted in re-mapping instance and part-of relationships into implementation classes such as lists and containers.

A third normal form description of RDBMS logical and physical design was a straightforward translation of the design object model; links between the RDBMS and the domain object was provided by the prototype-developed class library.

As a subproduct of this activity, a simple but useful, abstract and reusable class library to ensure RDBMS integrity on objects deletion was implemented.

A not entirely satisfying aspect in the design phase was represented by the impossibility to completely track the GUI design phase. Three main causes can be identified:

- CASE tool inability to cover the entire software life cycle (lack of reverse engineering and code generation);

- the need of reusing previously written code not completely engineered turned out into a heavy process of continuous changes;

- frequent GUI classes fine-tuning on the basis of the user feedback.

As a consequence of such a situation (and by time pressure) a proliferation of GUI-specific classes came out; *a posteriori*, while a detailed GUI classes model would have resulted as time-consuming and scarcely useful, a mid-level of formal specification (focused on the production of abstract and truly reusable GUI classes) could have been reached, avoiding the great part of implementation dissipating effects.

CASE TOOLS

Our opinion about the experience we had with CASE reflects some of the contradictions the CASE products are dealing with: while the use of an automated instrument leveraged us from many low-level activities, providing us a precious, solid and understandable common base of discussion, our attempt in using it as an everyday working tool came out in frustrating disillusions.

The CASE tool Object Maker in its release 2.04 under Windows 3.1 environment is somewhat slow and it is impossible to use it as a class browser and documentation tool, even if this can be done in small projects.

A serious lack was represented by the Mark V fault in releasing the long-awaited C++ reverse engineering module. The team did not have a productive way to efficiently analyze and integrate commercial and built in-house class libraries. Another problem with the Object Maker's Coad-Yourdon notation support was represented by bugs in breaking down complex model in simpler ones.

Object Maker was anyway invaluable in creating the models we used through the entire project; a global evaluation of its use is positive.

OO AND THE HUMAN FACTOR

The OO technology knowledge obtained by people involved in the project can be considered good.

Those components of the team who came from a coding-only OO background, experienced some difficult to move to a more abstract point of view in the analysis and design phases. Such a factor should be taken into account: the knowledge of an OO language does not imply an automatic capability to produce a good OO software design. A formal, company-driven approach to OO analysis and design seems to be preferable to the bottom-up growth.

According to the user, for the first time he was given the possibility to directly drive specification and validation phases; the release of 5 intermediate prototypes helped very much in identifying incomplete or obscure requirements.

As a consequence of the in-depth domain knowledge acquired, the work group has been able to identify and solve problems affecting the coordination between the various actors playing a role in the international agreement management. The formal results of such activities constitutes a de facto reference manual of the operations inside the entities involved.

SUMMARY

The implementation of an object-oriented financial, complex management system for a major car manufacturer group has been a success. Its integration with a context equipped with mainframe-base "legacy" systems has been obtained with little technical effort.

The spiral software life cycle demonstrated itself as a good model for the actual project management; the object-oriented methodology turned out to be a good way to model even the most complex aspects of financial domains.

User control over project results was simplified by the ability to effectively communicate in common and meaningful (from both sides' points of view) terms.

Project effort was considerably lower than the one spent for previously developed projects with a traditional approach in the same domain, while maintaining a higher level of user satisfaction.

OO analysis and design model demonstrated a high degree of stability and flexibility against time and requirements changes. According to involved development companies, structured analysis techniques used in similar context showed a much lower degree of understandability, maintainability over time and flexibility.

Development and CASE tools used in the project were found adequate and satisfactory enough to support a real cost-effective, efficient and complete object oriented software life cycle.

REFERENCES

[Blaha88] Blaha M., Premerlani W., Rumbaugh J.
Relation database design using an Object-Oriented methodology
Comm. of the ACM, apr 1988

[Booch91] Booch, G.
Object-Oriented design
Benjamin/Cummings, 1991

[Burnstine 90] Burnstine R., Rin A.
Object-oriented technology and its relationship to commercial application development and case
Software engineering strategies, jul 1990

[Coad 92] Coad P.
Object oriented pattern
Comm. of the ACM, oct 1992

[Coad 91a] Coad P., Yourdon E.
Object-oriented analysis
Prentice Hall, 1991

[Coad 91b] Coad P., Yourdon E.
Object-oriented design
Prentice Hall, 1991

[de Champeux91] de Champeux D., Faure P.
A comparative study of object-oriented analysis methods
JOOP, march/april 1991

[Henderson-Sellers90] Henderson-Sellers B., Edwards j.
The object-oriented systems life cycle
Comm. of the ACM, sep 1990

[Jacobson 93] Jacobson I.
Is object technology software's industrial platform?
IEEE Software, jan 1993

[Kilian 91] Kilian M.
Bridging the gap between O-O and E-R
Entity relationship approach 1991 conference proceedings

[Meyer 88] Meyer B.
Object-oriented software construction
Prentice hall, 1988

[Meyer 91] Meyer B.
Object-oriented software development
ESEC 1991 Tutorial

[Pittman 93] Pittman M.
Lessons learned in managing object-oriented development
IEEE Software, jan 1993

[Wirfs-Brock90] Wirfs-Brock R., Johnson R.
Surveying current research in Object-Oriented design
Comm. of ACM, sep 1990

[Wybolt 90] Wybolt N.
Experiences with C++ and object-oriented software development
ACM SIGSOFT apr 1990

REUSE AND METRICS

Supporting Object-Oriented Design with Metrics[!!]

M. Campanai[!] P. Nesi*

*Department of Systems and Informatics, Faculty of Engineering, University of Florence
Via S. Marta 3, 50139 Firenze, Italy, nesi@ingfi1.ing.unifi.it

[!] CESVIT, Center for Software Quality, CQ_ware, Fortezza da Basso, Palazzina Lorenese, Viale Strozzi, Firenze

[!!] This work was partially supported by the Italian Research Council, CNR (Consiglio Nazionale delle Ricerche).

Abstract

A framework for the estimation of object-oriented system specifications by using a set of metrics covering technical, cognitive and process-oriented views is presented. The parameters defined in this paper allow the evaluation of a prevision model to quantify expected efforts as a function of the life-cycle stages. The use of metrics for the estimation of reusability, modularity, maintainability and testability is analyzed. Metrics are integrated in a CASE tool named TOOMS which has been defined by our research group for the specification of reactive systems. TOOMS is based on TROL, a dual object-oriented language with both descriptive and operational capabilities. TOOMS allows to describe the system at different levels of structural abstractions, and at different levels of specification detail. The metrics proposed are able to produce estimation at each level of system specification, thus allowing the incremental specification/metrication.

1 Introduction

There is an over-abundance of metrics in the literature. Complexity and size are often defined on the basis of available metrics; many attempts to metrics validation have been presented, but unfortunately for each positive validation there is a negative one. Some empirical studies with metrics and measurement frameworks for object-oriented systems have been presented in [Laranjeira90], [HendersonSellers93], [Yap93], [Meyer90], [Coulunge93], in which general concepts for the estimation of size, complexity and reuse level, have been proposed. Furthermore, an analysis of the impact of the *"reuse, as the most enticing promise"*, in the object-oriented development has been carried out in [HendersonSellers93]. However, it should be noted that in the measurement of object-oriented systems, a general poor design and a lack of adherence to proper measurement principles are still present. This lack is also due to the different definitions of what the object-oriented paradigm is. Moreover, several formal definitions of correct measurement principles have been presented in [Fenton91], and [AMI92], but they are still oriented to the structured approach.

At each stage of software life-cycle, metrics should be used to quantify (i) the expected effort and the system size (e.g., *process-oriented view*), (ii) the quality of the system and conformance to requirements (e.g., *technical view*), and (iii) the understandability of system components and library (e.g., *cognitive view*). All these measurements should be estimated even if the system under development is not yet completely specified. In object-oriented system development, more effort is required in the design phase, and considerably less in program maintenance. For these reasons, the metrication of system specifications assumes a high relevance from the early stages of system design.

It should be noted that, the attention shift from *software code to design metrics* and from *structural complexity to logical correctness* rendered many well-known software metrics unusable since they are too much focused on code details. The growing attention on the process of software development has created the need to get process-oriented information and to integrate metric into the software development process. Furthermore, owing to presence of many differences among projects in the same company, it is important to create an integrated environment for developing project-oriented tailored measures.

In this paper, a shift on prospective is presented (a) in the definition of metrics, (b) in the integration of metrics in the development process at

From TOOLS EUROPE '94 (Technology of Object-Oriented Languages and Systems).

method level, by providing an integrated framework for measurements. In fact, the metrics proposed have been integrated in TOOMS, a CASE tool for the visual and textual specification of real-time systems which has been implemented by our research group [Bucci93]. TOOMS is based on an object-oriented formal language and model named TROL [Nesi93], [Bucci94]. TROL allows the designer to specify all system specification details and to describe the structural, functional and behavioral aspects. TROL adopts a dual model which is able to integrate operational and descriptive formalisms; furthermore, its features and similar to other object-oriented specification languages and methods – e.g., TRIO++ [Mandrioli93b], ObjectCharts [Coleman92], Object-Oriented version of SDL (OSDL) [Braek93], ObjectTime [ObjecTime93]. The set of metrics proposed in this paper can be also applied to these formalisms. These high-level metrics are independent of the programming language; thus, can be applied to other specification object-oriented processes. The measurement framework was integrated in TOOMS in order to evaluate the evolution of some characteristics of the systems under specification. In TOOMS, quantitative parameters and related metrics have been defined for evaluating the static and dynamic aspects of the system under specification with a great attention to the specification reusability and testability.

In Sect.2, the TOOMS/TROL model and notation are presented. In Sect.3, the metrics defined (integrated in TOOMS) are presented. The mapping of general concepts with respect to the metrics proposed is reported in subsection 3.4. Conclusions are drawn in Sect.4.

2 TROL Model and Notation

TOOMS/TROL adopts a dual model presenting both descriptive and operational aspects. Differently from other dual models and languages, TROL is mainly based on reusing both the static and dynamic aspects of specifications. TROL has the capabilities for specifying system behavior, structure and functionality, and allows the verification and validation of composition/decomposition mechanisms. This feature is strongly useful when a component under reuse is verified and validated in order to check if it satisfies the initial requirements. Moreover, TROL supports the incremental specification of system description.

In TOOMS/TROL, an object is a software entity which makes state transitions over time. The state of an object is persistently encapsulated in the object itself and hidden to the outside world. An object is an instance of a class. Classes are defined by means of

```
Class Sample1
   Provided_services: // i.e., inputs
      IA [3.2,4.5]: IA_Type;
      IB : IB_Type;
      IC : IC_Type;
   Required_services: // i.e., outputs
      OA : OA_Type;
      OB : OB_Type;
   Clauses:
      CLA1 : New(IA) → Ready(OB) - - [2.1,4.5];
end;
```

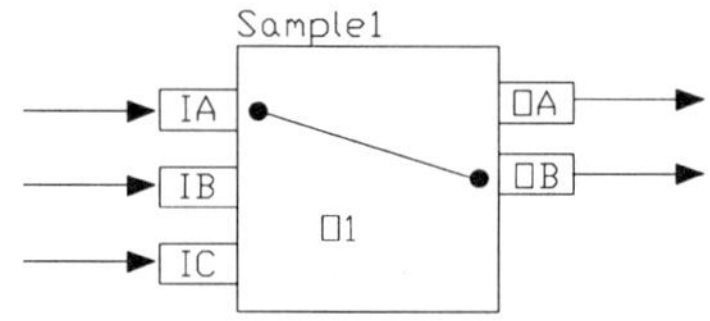

Figure 1: External class description of class Sample1, and visual representation of Object O1 of class Sample1.

their external and internal class descriptions, which correspond to public and private class members according to the object-oriented paradigm. An object is seen from the outer objects only through its public features. The following subsections summarize the main features of the TROL language, and a complete description is reported in [Nesi93].

2.1 External class description

The external class description (see Fig.1) reports the public features of the class. These are **Provided_services**, **Required_services**, and **Clauses**. Provided and required services can be regarded as input and output ports (gates), respectively [Coleman92]. This model is called IO-based, as opposite to the method-based model of many object-oriented models and languages – e.g., [WBrock89], [Walker92]. The external class description presents the services it *provides*, but also the services it *requires* (see Fig.1).

In the early steps of reactive system specification, some temporal requirements on system behavior are usually imposed. Time analysis is needed to ensure the system predictability with respect to real conditions. In the TROL external class description, time is modeled by means of the four types of temporal constraints as proposed by Dasarathy [Dasarathy85]. These constraints are associated with services and clauses. The first two types of temporal constraints are associated with services, such as service IA in Fig.1, which describes the minimum and the maximum rate of that service in time units. In particular, bounds for the rate of an input signal are associated with the corresponding provided service, and bounds

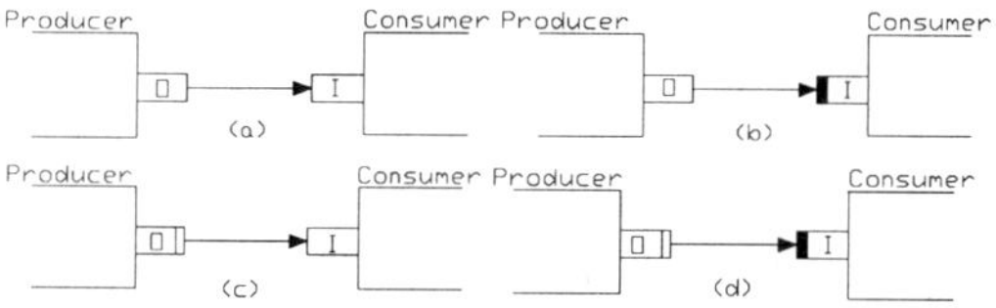

Figure 2: Possible combinations between provided and required services define the communication mechanisms between objects: (a) synchronous communication where both sender and receiver are blocked; (b) asynchronous communication with a non-blocked sender and a blocked receiver (when the buffer is empty); (c) asynchronous non-blocked communication corresponding to the request of the latest information value from the sending object (overwriting mechanism); (d) asynchronous non-blocked communication, where a message is stored in the buffer only if it is changed with respect to the last value.

for the rate of an output signal with the required service. The other two types of temporal constraints are associated with **Clauses**. Since the services are only a static class description, in the TROL model, clauses which describe the external class behavior have also been included in the external class description. In the visual representation of TOOMS clauses are represented by lines drawn inside the box (ending with dots). Clauses represent a dependence between the services corresponding to the connected IOs, and are structured as:

$$< \text{action-condition} > \rightarrow < \text{consequent-condition} > - - [T_m, T_M];$$

which means: if the <action-condition> is true at time t then the <consequent-condition> will be true at an instant of the time interval $(t+T_m) \div (t+T_M)$. Referring to Fig.1, clause CLA1 specifies that when a new message arrives on IA, object O1 will make ready a request on OB in the specified time interval. Temporal constraints associated with clauses describe the bounds for the time of reaction [Dasarathy85]. Since a clause describes the external class behavior, conditions must be expressed only in terms of public references. Only simple clauses – i.e., clauses in the definite form [Maier88] – are allowed. However, the clauses represent a non-exhaustive description of class behavior; these are very useful during the composition/decomposition process of a class and for the definition of the abstract behavior in the early phases of system specification.

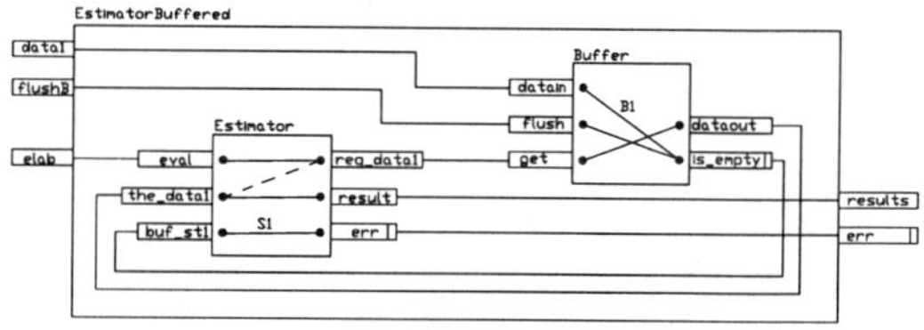

Figure 3: The class EstimatorBuffered composed of S1 and B1 sub-objects (i.e., its attributes).

2.2 Object communications

When two objects are connected together through their services (required-to-provided) a channel of communication is established. The connection is allowed only between services belonging to the same type – e.g., Boolean with Boolean. At run time, the TROL environment consists in a number of concurrent communicating objects. The default communication model is synchronous on unidirectional channels (represented in Fig.2b), as in the timed CSP model [Hoare85] proposed by Shaw in [Shaw92]. Client/server communications are supported through *message passing*; messages are considered as tokens irrespective of their content, i.e., data, (control) commands or both.

In TROL, there are two kinds of provided services: normal and buffered[1] (**buffered**), and two kinds of required services: normal and always available[2] (**available**). The default value is normal for both kinds of services, and the above keywords in bold are reported in the textual description to specify the other types of service, when needed. Through the connection of these types of services four types of communication mechanisms are defined (see Fig.2).

2.3 Internal class description

The internal class description corresponds to the class implementation. In the TROL model, classes are divided into *non-basic object classes* and *basic object classes*.

A **non-basic object class** is implemented in terms of a set of communicating sub-objects, which in turn belong to their classes. This leads to a hierarchical organization of software structure. The definition of a non-basic object class corresponds to the relationship of aggregation of the object-oriented

[1] implemented by means of a buffer with an infinite dimension.

[2] when the associated information is always there, that is, when the service has its information always ready for the receiver. Available services can be used to present outside the object state.

```
Class EstimatorBuffered specializing non_basic_object_class
  Provided_services:
    data1 : DataType;
    flushB : Signal;
    elab : Signal;
  Required_services:
    results : Real;
    err available : EstimatorErrType;
  Clauses:
    ESTIMATION: New(elab) ∧ err==OK → Ready(results);
    FLUSH : New (flushB) → err==EMPTY;
    DATA : New (data1) ∧ err==EMPTY → err==OK;
  /*** private parts ***/
  Attributes:
    B1 : Buffer;
    S1 : Estimator;
  Connections:
    data1 - - B1.datain;      elab - - S1.eval;
    S1.result - - results;     S1.err - - err;
    S1.req_data1 - - B1.get;     B1.dataout - - S1.the_data1;
    B1.is_empty - - S1.buf_st1;     flushB - - B1.flush;
end;
```

Figure 4: Description of the class EstimatorBuffered with the external description of class Estimator, where EstimatorErrType is defined as an enumeration: **enum** EstimatorErrType {EMPTY,OK};. The description of class Buffer will be provided later.

paradigm. Fig.3 is the visual representation of a class – i.e., EstimatorBuffered – composed of two sub-objects, S1 and B1, belonging respectively to classes Estimator and Buffer. Objects which are part of a given class are drawn inside the box corresponding to the class itself. In Fig.4 (descriptive counterpart of Fig.3), the definition of class EstimatorBuffered includes the declaration of two **Attributes**, B1 and S1. The public part includes provided services, required services and clauses, while private parts are connections among sub-objects, and class attributes. Temporal constraints in the class description allow the verification of object composability also with respect to the behavior with temporal requirements. Rates of service and clauses with temporal constraints are propagated from a level of structural hierarchy to the lower following class *Connections* [Bucci93]. The formal definition of temporal constraints in the class description simplifies the propagation and the top-down verification.

Basic object classes are those that cannot be regarded as a composite object; these can be implemented by using: (i) an extended state machine formalism called "eXtended State Machine" (XSM) model, or (ii) a set of pure data transformations of input into output data (without any notion of state variables) called "eXtended Combinatorial Machines" (XCMs). Therefore, a TROL environment presents, at the lowest level of hierarchy, a lattice of communicating basic objects which are implemented either as XSMs or XCMs. Objects implemented as state diagrams have also been proposed by [Shlaer91], [Rumbaugh91], [Coleman92], [ObjecTime93]. On the contrary, the XSM model of TROL is quite different since it has been defined to be integrated with the description in terms of clauses. The computational model adopted for describing basic objects as state machines (XSM) in TROL has been derived by the model proposed in [Shaw92]. In Fig.5, the implementation of class Buffer as an XSM is presented. In this figure, the arrow which starts from a short line on the background of the state machine marks the initial state. The XSM model supports the definition of typed auxiliary variables (e.g., Buff[∞] in Fig.5). From the object-oriented point of view, these variables are class **Attributes**. In the XSM model, outputs depend on machine state, inputs and auxiliary variables, while the conditions for state transition depend on inputs (provided services) and on auxiliary variables. A set of statements is associated with each state, and statements can be either assignments, or procedure calls.

In TROL, time is considered as continuous, thus avoiding the problem related to the tick size [Shaw92]. Time is added by using again the temporal constraint concept which is represented by $[D_{min}, D_{max}]$ where D_{min} and D_{max} are time **Duration** with: $0 \leq D_{min} \leq D_{max}$. In an XSM, temporal constraints can be applied to different predicates, such as the conditions associated with state transitions, requests of provided services, sending of required services, numerical expressions, and procedure calls. However, the temporal constraints assume different meanings in different places [Bucci94]. In Fig.5, the complete description of class Buffer is reported. In this figure the class implementation (Attributes, States, Paths) has been reported. Since the class Buffer is defined as an XSM, the field **Connections** is missing.

It should be noted that, in the XSM model, a basic object may present a state diagram with a central state – e.g., state named CENTRAL in Fig.5. A number of transitions start from such a state, and each transition identifies a typical branch or aggregate of states called class *path*. For example, the class Buffer in Fig.5 presents three **Paths** (INIT, PUT, GET). In TROL, each class implemented as an XSM is an active object which in turn is implemented with one thread of execution for each path (the concept of path in TROL is equivalent to that of process in SDL). In this way an object can satisfy concurrent request of services, if they belong to different paths. These threads (i.e., paths) are signal sensitive meaning that they are waiting for a signal to change state; hence, their execution is causal (i.e., event-driven).

```
Class Buffer specializing XSM
  Provided_services:
    datain : DataType ;
    get : Signal ;
    flush : Signal ;
  Required_services:
    dataout : DataType ;
    is_empty available : Boolean;
  Clauses:
    GET : New (get ) ∧¬ is_empty → Ready (dataout );
    FLUSH : New (flush) → is_empty;
    DATAIN : New (datain) ∧ is_empty → ¬ is_empty;

  /*** private parts ***/

  Attributes:
    in : Integer ;
    out : Integer ;
    is_empty : Boolean ;
    Buff : DataType [∞ ];
  States:
    START: { in=0; is_empty=TRUE; out=0; }
    CENTRAL: { }
    WRITEIN: { in=in+1; Buff[in]=datain; is_empty=FALSE; }
    WRITEOUT: { dataout=Buff[out] - - [0,10.3]; out=out+1; }
    ISEMPTY: { is_empty=TRUE; }
  Paths:
    INIT: { START: → CENTRAL;
        CENTRAL: New(flush) → START; }
    PUT: { CENTRAL: New(datain) → WRITEIN;
        WRITEIN: →CENTRAL; }
    GET: { CENTRAL: New(get) ∧¬ is_empty → WRITEOUT;
        WRITEOUT: in != out → CENTRAL;
        WRITEOUT: in==out → ISEMPTY;
        ISEMPTY: → CENTRAL;
        WRITEOUT: Fail(TIMEFAIL) → CENTRAL; }
end;
```

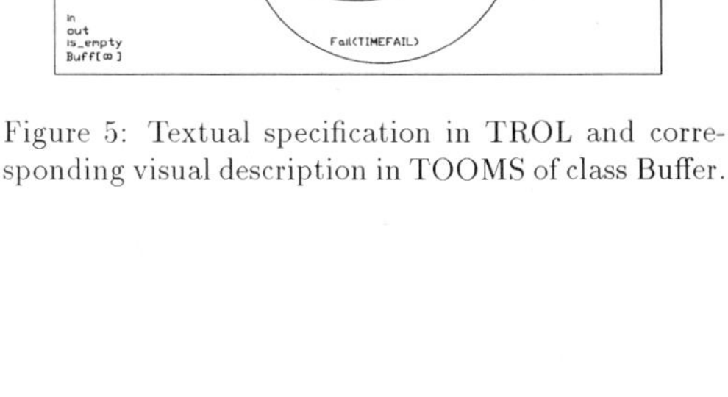

Figure 5: Textual specification in TROL and corresponding visual description in TOOMS of class Buffer.

A particular case of basic object class is that which does not present any form of state variable. These classes are called "eXtended Combinatorial Machines", XCMs, and are implemented as state machine with a single state, where the auxiliary variables do not maintain their values from an execution to the next.

2.4 Class specialization

In TROL, the specialized non-basic object classes inherit attributes, provided and required services, connections, and clauses from their super-class. In particular, class services and attributes can be added or specialized from those of the super-class; connections can be deleted or added; new clauses can be added, while inherited clauses can be overwritten by homonymous clauses.

For classes implemented in terms of XSM, the specialization mechanism consists in adding or specializing services and/or attributes (auxiliary variables). In addition, the state diagram can also be changed, since its modification corresponds to the modification of the class behavior. In particular, class states and paths can be added and/or modified. This means that states and paths of the superclass must be present in the sub-class; for this reason, in the formal description of a sub-class some states can be missing, since they can be inherited from the superclass.

2.5 The TOOMS Tool

The structure of the TOOMS tool is comprised of: a set of visual editors, an Object Database, and a set of utilities (see Fig.6). In TOOMS, the user interacts with the visual editors describing the system under specification by means of few graphical symbols. The syntax and semantics of each software specification details in TOOMS are constrained to be in accordance with the TROL model and language [Nesi93]. Each specification detail defined by means of the visual editors is translated in the TROL formal language. In particular, the Block Editor is adopted to specify non-basic object classes, the Machine Editor to specify XCMs and XSMs (see Fig.7), the Function Editor to implement functions and procedures, and the Type Editor to define new types [Bucci93]. Moreover, in the TOOMS tool, a set of utilities, to provide metrication, verification, validation, and simulation is directly integrated in the visual editors. A code generator, which transforms the system specification from TROL language into a C++ code, is also available. The automatic generation of reports describing the system under specification and the results of verification, validation and simulation is provided.

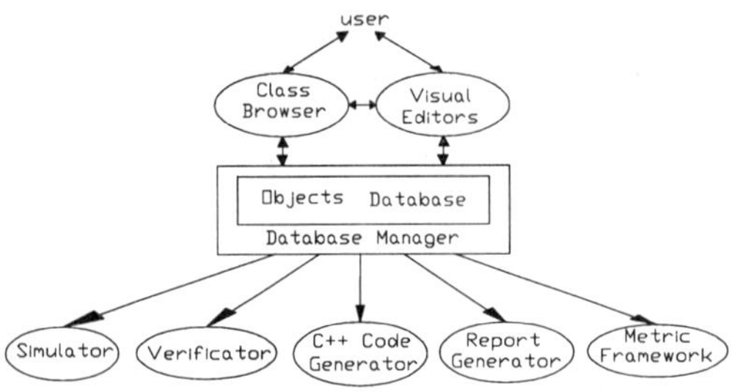

Figure 6: TOOMS, system overview.

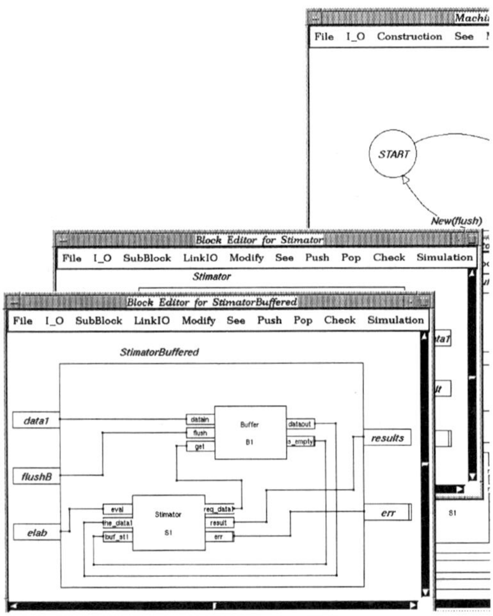

Figure 7: Block and Machine Editors of TOOMS tool.

Each type of software entity specified by means of the visual editors is collected for its future reuse into the Object Database. In TOOMS, complete applications are considered classes as well. This allows to build more complex applications starting by simple ones and by their components, and to shorten the development time of a system prototype. The information available into the database can be inspected by means of the Class Browser that is an interactive program which allows the database navigation and queries. More details about the structure of TOOMS tool can be found in [Bucci93], and details about TROL language in [Nesi93], [Bucci94].

3 TOOMS Quality Model

Many efforts have been made in order to define appropriate frameworks for software quality evaluation, in the literature. Metrics for code evaluation have usually extended to be used during the analysis and design phases; for providing software developers and managers with appropriate instruments for establishing software quality, since the early stages of system development.

In this section, the quality model for object-oriented design is presented. The model proposed has been defined in order to give at the TOOMS/TROL users a reasonable help for evaluating their work. On the other hand, the concepts proposed are general enough to be used with other object-oriented approaches with minor changes – e.g., with [Mandrioli93b], [Coleman92], [ObjecTime93], [Braek93].

Many classifications of metrics have been presented in the literature – e.g., [HendersonSellers91]. Our approach is based on three different views of the design: a *technical*, a *cognitive*, and a *process oriented* view. The technical view refers to the software engineering aspects of system specification (size, complexity, testability, etc.); the cognitive view takes into account the external understandability of system components (i.e., classes); the process-oriented view refers to system aspects that are influenced or can influence the process of system development. These three views are evaluated in a common measurement framework in which each view can influence the others. Each view can be used in different phases of system evolution: *cognitive metrics* during the development and/or in the system maintenance, the *technical* view for the evaluation/certification of some specific characteristics of the system; the *process-oriented* view for the impact of technology on the whole development process.

In the TOOMS tool [Bucci93], some features for

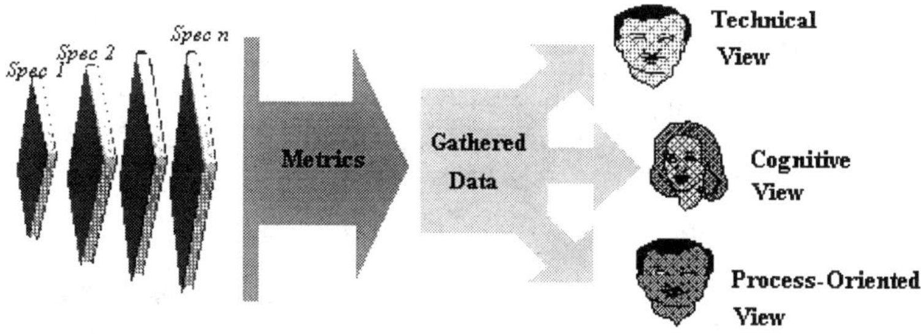

Figure 8: A continuous approach to quality improvement through metrics.

the specification and metrication of reactive systems have been added in order to create an integrated environment. The aim of the integration is to cover the entire life-cycle of the system under specification by using a unique tool.

3.1 Technical Metrics

In this section, metrics to evaluate the class complexity in a TROL like environment will be given.

The following symbols will be used: NRS number of required services, NPS number of provided service, NA number of class attributes, NC number of class clauses, and NP number of class paths (see Sect.2.3). The above numbers are comprehensive of the features inherited from the superclasses of the class under consideration according to the object-oriented paradigm. In the case of a method-based approach the number of paths corresponds approximatively to the number of class methods or class processes. The list of symbols is reported as a glossary in App.A to facilitate the readability of the paper.

3.1.1 Class Complexity, CC

The Class Complexity (CC) is the weighted sum of Internal and External Class Complexity (ICC and ECC):

$$CC = w_{ICC}\ ICC + w_{ECC}\ ECC$$

where w_{ICC}, and w_{ECC} are tailorable weights. Note that, since ICC and ECC take into account the complexity of the class considering all its superclasses, then CC is also comprehensive of such complexities.

3.1.2 Internal Class Complexity, ICC

The Internal Class Complexity (ICC) takes into account the Class Path Complexity (CPC) and the Class Attribute Complexity (CAC) according to the TROL model. In addition, ICC describes also how the *Paths* of a given class are internally coupled in using class attributes by means of term $CCPC$, (Class Coupling Path Complexity). The ICC is also influenced by the intrinsic concurrency of the class (Class Internal Task Complexity, $CITC$) – e.g., a class comprised of only one **Path** is obviously less complex than the same class implemented with two **Paths** (i.e., which correspond to two processes). The object-oriented design usually consists in a process of class decomposition and/or object composition for defining new classes. At this level, the Class Path Complexity has no sense since the paths are not yet implemented. On the contrary, in the phase of design, it is very important to evaluate the class complexity on the basis of how the class attributes (which in turn are instances of some class) exchange information. This fact is measured with the Class Internal Communication Complexity, $CICC$.

Therefore, the internal class complexity has been defined as:

$$ICC = w_{CAC}\ CAC + w_{CPC}\ CPC + \\ w_{CCPC}\ CCPC + w_{CITC}\ CITC + w_{CICC}\ CICC$$

where w_{CAC}, w_{CPC}, w_{CICC}, w_{CCPC} and w_{CITC} are application-dependent weights.

In the following, details about the above coefficients are given.

Class Attribute Complexity, CAC

The complexity of each attribute (Attribute Complexity, AC) is equal to the class complexity of the attribute itself, thus $AC = CC$. Hence the class attribute complexity, CAC, is obtained by considering all the class attributes:

$$CAC = \sum_{i}^{NA} AC_i$$

In many object-oriented languages, such as in C++, there is a set of predefined basic types which are not implemented as classes. For these basic types the class complexity CC must be predefined. In TROL, a suitable class has been defined for each basic type [Bucci93].

Class Path Complexity, CPC

The Class Path Complexity is estimated by using the expression:

$$CPC = \sum_{j}^{NP} PTC_j$$

where PTC is the Path Complexity defined as:

$$PTC_j = w_{PMC}\ PMC_j + w_{PEC}\ PEC_j + w_{PIC}\ PIC_j$$

where: PMC_j is the sum of McCabe-like complexities of the statements which are present in the class path j [McCabe76], [HendersonSellers92]; PEC is the path external complexity which estimates the cost of the external procedure calls:

$$PEC_j = \sum_{i}^{AllCallsIn(j)} CallComplexity(i,j)$$

where the $CallComplexity(i,j)$ is evaluated by considering the complexity of the procedure parameters (the term 'call' means only the use of a function from the library or of a function defined with the Function Editor); PIC is the path internal complexity which estimates the cost of the access to class attributes. The PIC for path j holds:

$$PIC_j = \sum_{i}^{NA} AC_i\ USE(i,j)$$

where $USE(i,j)$ assumes the value: 0 if the attribute i is not used by path j, 1 if it is only read, and 2 if it is read and/or written; and AC is the already defined Attribute Complexity.

In TROL, the concept of Path is present only for basic objects; therefore, for non-basic objects $NP = 0$ and thus the CPC is equal to zero. The weights w_{PMC}, w_{PEC}, and w_{PIC} mainly depend on the application field under analysis. For example, in the case of real-time system specification in TROL, they are usually assumed to be 1, 1, and 2, respectively. In this way, a higher weight of the costs of attribute sharing among internal processes (i.e., paths) of an object is given.

Class Coupling Path Complexity, $CCPC$

This factor gives a measure of how the class paths act on class attributes. In fact, as in method-based object-oriented languages, several class methods can work on the same attributes; thus, in TROL, several paths can work on the same attributes. For this reason the complexity of path coupling in working on attributes can be estimated by using:

$$CCPC = \sum_{i}^{NA} \sum_{j}^{NP} AC_i\ PRS(i,j)$$

where $PRS(i,j)$ is the number of the presences of attribute i in path j; AC is the already defined attribute complexity. Note that $CCPC$ is higher when a same attribute is frequently used in more than one path. Since in TROL (as in OSDL) the concept of Path (i.e., process in OSDL) is present only for basic objects (basic block in OSDL), for non-basic objects $NP = 0$ and, thus, $CCPC$ is equal to zero.

Class Internal Task Complexity, $CITC$

As to concurrency, the class internal complexity mainly depends on the number of tasks which are present inside the class itself. For this reason the $CITC$ has been considered equal to the number of internal processes of the class. In TROL, this measure is very simple: if the class is a basic object class, the number of internal process of a class is equal to the number of paths – i.e., $CITC = NP$. On the contrary, at level of non-basic object classes, when the system under specification is only partially defined, the number of class paths is not yet defined since the low-level classes are not yet defined at all. In this case, it is supposed that the number of tasks is at least equal to the number of class sub-objects (i.e., attributes), thus $CITC = NA$.

Class Internal Comm. Complexity, $CICC$

In the TROL model, the measure of Class Internal Communication Complexity has a sense only for non-basic object classes, while for basic object classes it is equal to zero, $CICC = 0$. This is a complementary

measure with respect to the Class Path Complexity (CPC) previously presented.
The structure of non-basic object classes is defined in terms of communicating sub-objects:

$$CICC = \sum_{i}^{NCON} MSGC_i \; CTYPE(i)$$

where: $NCON$ is the number of connections among the sub-objects of the class (see Sect.2.3); $MSGC_i$ is the message complexity that depends on the complexity of the message class; $CTYPE(i)$ is a coefficient which takes into account the kind of communication between objects. In TROL, four types of communication mechanisms are obtained for the combination of the different service types (see Fig.2); hence, $CTYPE$ is equal to 4 for normal-to-normal, 3 for normal-to-buffered, 2 for available-to-buffered, and 1 for available-to-normal communications. The complexity of message, $MSGC$, depends on the complexity of the class which has been used to define the message structure, since in the object-oriented approach, as in TROL, messages are also class instances. For this reason, $MSGC$ is equal to the CC of the message. With this assumption the costs for manipulating the message itself are also included in that measure.

It should be noted that a value for $CICC$ can be obtained since the early stages of system specification. Therefore, it can be very useful as a basis for defining a process-oriented metric.

3.1.3 External Class Complexity, ECC

The External Class Complexity (ECC) takes into account the complexity of provided and required services (Provided Service Interface Complexity, $PSIC$, and Required Service Interface Complexity, $RSIC$, respectively) of the class, considering also their interdependencies by means of the measure of Service Complexity, SC. The SC term measures also how much the class is able to produce autonomous requests to the outer objects:

$$ECC = w_{PSIC} PSIC + w_{RSIC} RSIC + w_{SC} SC$$

In the following, the terms $PSIC$, $RSIC$ and SC are discussed separately. The values of weights w_{PSIC}, w_{RSIC} and w_{SC} depend on the application field under analysis. For example, in the case of real-time system specification in TROL, they are usually assumed to be 1, 1, and 1.5, respectively. This choice is due to the fact that in real-time systems the dependency among objects through services is an index of the event propagation inside the system. Therefore, SC must have a bigger influence on ECC with respect to the others.

Provided Service Interface Complexity, $PSIC$

The complexity of the provided interface of a class is estimated with:

$$PSIC = \sum_{i}^{NPS} MSGC_i \; PMEC_i \; PTCPS_i$$

where NPS is the number of provided services; $MSGC$ is the already defined message complexity (equal to the CC of the message); $PMEC$ is a weight which takes into account the type of communication mechanism of provided services (equal to 1 if the provided service is **buffered** or 2 if it is normal); $PTCPS_i$ marks the presence of temporal constraint for the provided service i (it is equal to 2 if the temporal constraint specifying the service rate has been defined, otherwise a value equal to 1 is assigned).

Required Service Interface Complexity, $RSIC$

Differently from the method-based object-oriented models in which the requests of services are hidden inside the methods body, in the case of IO-based model, such as in the TROL language or OSDL, etc., the complexity of the required interface of the class can be simply estimated by means of:

$$RSIC = \sum_{i}^{NRS} MSGC_i \; RMEC_i \; PTCRS_i$$

where NRS is the number of required services; $MSGC$ is the already defined message complexity; $RMEC$ takes into account the type of communication mechanism of required services (equal to 1, if the required service is **available**, or 2 if it is normal); $PTCRS_i$ marks the presence of the temporal constraint for the required service i (it is equal to 2 if the temporal constraint specifying the service rate has been defined, otherwise a value equal to 1 is assigned).

Service Complexity, SC

The complexity of class services, SC, measures how much the provided services of a class are related to the required services of the same class. This measure represents how the required services (i.e., outputs) of the class depend on the provided ones. It is a measure of class behavior complexity. In general, for a class, two kinds of required services can be present, that is, autonomous and non-autonomous. The former are those which are generated directly from the class without any external request. The latter are those which are indirectly due to requests of other system objects, such requests reach the object by means of provided services. For these reasons, the Service Complexity is defined as:

$$SC = NAR + NASC$$

where NAR is the Number of Autonomous Requests. This is equal to the number of required services which are generated by paths independently of the provided services of the class. On the contrary, the Number of Non-Autonomous Requests of a class, $NNAR$, is equal to $(NRS - NAR)$. Hence, the complexity of non-autonomous services of a class, $NASC$ is estimated by:

$$NASC = \sum_{i}^{NNAR} NPS(Path(i))$$

where $NPS(Path(i))$ is the number of provided services which are present in the $Path(i)$, and function $Path(i)$ identifies the path which generates the non-autonomous request i.

In TROL, this measure can be directly derived from the definition of class clauses from the early phases of software life-cycle.

3.2 Cognitive Metrics

In the object-oriented approach, cognitive metrics should give a measure of how easy it is, for the user, to understand the nature of a class by observing its external description. To this end, a significative cognitive measure is given by the Complexity Ratio, CR. Moreover, the estimation of system and sub-system verifiability is another important cognitive metric, this factor is measured by the Verifiability Index, VI.

3.2.1 Complexity Ratio, CR

The Complexity Ratio is a measure of how much the nature of a given class can be understood through its external description:

$$CR = \frac{ECD}{ICC}$$

where ECD is a measure of the External Class Description, and ICC is the Internal Class Complexity. A high CR means that the class external description is very detailed with respect to its internal complexity. Note that, in TROL, the external class description is comprehensive of provided and required services describing the class static interface, augmented by clauses describing the class behavior. We have been chosen to define ECD instead of using the already defined ECC since the latter does not represent only the external class complexity as can be observed by the analyst. In fact, ECC has been defined also considering the SC which in turn is based on the knowledge of dependencies between required services and the class paths.

The ECD gives a measure of the external class description as can be observed by the analyst in the phase of class reuse. In the method-based model the External Class Description consists in the method description plus preconditions and post-conditions, if these are available at the external class level. In other languages, assertions or clauses for describing the internal class behavior at the external level can be present. In the last case, the External Class Description is more complete such as in TROL.

ECD is defined as the weighted sum of Class Static Description, CSD, and Class Dynamic Description, CDD. The static description covers the structural aspect while the dynamic description the behavioral aspect:

$$ECD = w_{CSD}\ CSD + w_{CDD}\ CDD$$

where w_{CSD} and w_{CDD} are application-dependent weights – for example in specifying real-time systems the values 1 and 2, respectively, have been usually assumed to give more importance to the description of system behavior.

CSD is obtained by means of the $PSIC$ and $RSIC$ already defined in Sect.3.1.3:

$$CSD = w_{PSIC}\ PSIC + w_{RSIC}\ RSIC$$

CDD describes how many details regarding the class behavior are reported in the class external description with respect to what should be given to fully describe the class behavior. For the TROL model, this measure holds:

$$CDD = \frac{NSPSR}{NPS} + \frac{NSRSR}{NRS} + CCC$$

where $NSPSR$ is the number of specified **Provided_service** rates; $NSRSR$ the number of specified **Required_service** rates; CCC class clause complexity defined as:

$$CCC = \sum_{i}^{NC} CLC_i$$

where CLC is the CLause Complexity estimated with:

$$CLC_i = NPS_i + NRS_i + NOP_i + PTCC_i$$

while NOP_i is the number of Boolean and comparative operations in the clause i; NPS_i is the number of provided services in the clause i; NRS_i is the number of required services in the clause i; $PTCC_i$ marks the presence of temporal constraint for the clause i (it is equal to 1 if the temporal constraint has been defined, otherwise is assigned a value equal to 0).

3.2.2 Verifiability Index, VI

In TROL, class and system verifiability is guaranteed by means of the definitions of provided services, required services, and clauses with their respective temporal constraints. Basic objects such as XSMs and XCMs are implemented according to the clauses defined in their external class interface. Therefore, the external class description given in terms of clauses verifies the class implementation expressed by means of a set of communicating sub-objects (i.e., non-basic object class) or as a basic object class (i.e., XSMs, XCMs). To this end, the verifiability index for a given class is defined by the ratio between the ECD expressing the complexity of the external class interface and CC the complexity of the class itself:

$$VI = \frac{ECD}{CC}$$

This index gives a measure of how the class can be verified with respect to its complexity. For example, if a given class reports to the external level (by means of provided services, required services and clauses) a lot of details with respect to its total complexity, then it is more verifiable than a class that, having the same total complexity, is less described at the external level. Therefore, VI can be regarded as measure of class verifiability.

3.3 Process-Oriented Metrics

When Managers and Software Quality Assurancers plan budgetary and personnel resources for a new project, they feel more comfortable to use estimation models than just to rely on rules of thumb or entirely subjective judgments. For this reason, they need objective information from the projects under development. At the process level, the metrics which can be useful to control the development are: productivity, expected size and cost [HendersonSellers93c].

Technical metrics can be adopted to manage a software project. The estimation of expected size metrics can help managers to predict the system evolution. According to the TOOMS/TROL model, the measurement approach must be incremental too. Since the early stages of software life-cycle, technical measures estimate system size and complexity. A subjective continuous growth of size and complexity means that developers are extending specifications with their usual productivity rate.

It should be noted that, the trend of reuse level in the project can also be a good measure of the development process behavior. In the following, coefficients to estimate productivity, reuse level, expected size and cost, of the system, are reported.

Another very important factor is the evaluation of need of testing during the development process. Although the phases of system testing should be defined in advance, it is also important to detect when a class or a sub-system under development has grown too much without being tested. These conditions can be easily detected by using the last metric of this section (i.e., TI).

3.3.1 Productivity Index, PI

At each time instant of system development, a good measure of the productivity can be given by the Productivity Index, PI, which is defined as:

$$PI = \frac{\sum_i^{NewCls.} CC_i + \sum_i^{NewSpec.Cls.} INCCC_i}{\sum_i^{NCL} CC_i}$$

where: $NewCls.$ are the classes which have been added with respect to the last check point of PI estimation; $NewSpec.Cls.$ are the classes which have been specialized with respect to the last PI estimation; NCL is the number of classes which are globally present in the system under development; and $INCCC$ is the increment of class complexity (in this case it is estimated only for the new specialized classes):

$$INCCC_i = CC_i - \sum_j^{SuperClassesOf(i)} CC_j$$

where $SuperClassesOf(i)$ are only the direct superclasses of class i.

Note that PI represents a measure of how much software has been produced by the designer with respect to the last version. This measure is obtained in terms of system complexity. The definition of PI measure is due to the fact that the metrics usually adopted are not a significative measure. These are based on the number of new and specialized classes divided by total number of system classes. In fact, as can be noted by observing a typical object-oriented project, it is often necessary to create many simple- and low-complex classes – i.e., with few attributes and simple paths (methods).

Since this measure is obtained with respect to the last value, the sequence of PI in time should be estimated by using a constant time interval. A normalized version is obtained by dividing PI for the time interval expressed in work-time – i.e., $NPI = PI/WT$.

3.3.2 Reuse Index of the system, RI

At each time instant of system development, a good measure of the reuse level in the system is given by the Reuse Index, RI, which is defined as:

$$RI = \frac{\sum_i^{AllSpec.Cls.} INCCC_i}{\sum_i^{NCL} CC_i}$$

where $INCCC_i$ is, in this case, the increment of class complexity for the specialized class i; $AllSpec.Cls.$ are the classes which have been specialized with respect to the initial condition of class library.

3.3.3 Expected System Size, ESS

The Expected System Size, ESS, is a prediction of system size at the next estimation of ESS. The estimation of this value is obtained on the basis of the company experiences (based on historical data) and it considers the increment in both class size and class number:

$$ESS = (NCL + ENCL)\ AVGCC\ SizeEvolution$$

where $AVGCC = \frac{1}{NCL}\sum_i^{NCL} CC_i$ is the averaged value of class complexity CC of the system; NCL is the number of system classes at the time of measuring; $ENCL$ is the expected number of new classes which will be implemented until the next check point. The $SizeEvolution$ and the $ENCL$ are time-dependent coefficients which are defined by the company on the bases of its experiences in developing software systems.

3.3.4 Expected System Cost, $ESCost$

The Expected System Cost, $ESCost$, can be regarded as the sum of costs which are due to the reuse of old classes, $ESCost(reuse)$, plus the cost of development of new ones, $ESCost(development)$, plus the cost of specialization of already implemented classes, $ESCost(specialization)$:

$$ESCost = ESCost(development) + ESCost(reuse) + ESCost(specialization)$$

The cost related to the development of new classes assumes the form:

$$ESCost(development) = CMA(development)\ NewCls. \sum_i^{NewCls.} CC_i$$

where $CMA(development)$ is a company-dependent coefficient. This is estimated considering the averaged costs observed from a congruent category of already developed applications. The cost of reuse and specialization holds:

$$ESCost(reuse) = \sum_i^{ReusedCls.} CC_i\ CR_i$$

$$ESCost(specialization) = CMA(specialization)\ NewSpec.Cls. \sum_i^{NewSpec.Cls.} INCCC_i$$

where $CMA(specialization)$ is a company-dependent coefficient estimated in the same manner as the already defined $CMA()$ coefficient.

It should be noted that, for the estimation of the general cost, we have used both technical and cognitive metrics defined in the previous sections. This is possible since most of those measures lead to a value even if the system is only partially specified. This characteristic is congruent with TOOMS/TROL, TRIO, OSDL, capabilities.

3.3.5 Test Index, TI

At each instant of the developing process, it is very useful to identify the classes (i.e., sub-systems) for which the test is needed. With this metric it is assumed that the test of a class is needed when its complexity has grown too much with respect to the last testing section. In TROL, the testing can correspond to (i) the verification of high-level class behavior by means of clauses execution, (ii) the validation of system composition/decomposition and (iii) the validation of an XSM in terms of clauses [Nesi93]. Analogous mechanisms are present in similar languages.

Therefore, the Test Index for a given class i is estimated as a relative change of class complexity:

$$TI_i = \frac{CC_i(ActualVersion) - CC_i(LastTestedVersion)}{CC_i(LastTestedVersion)}$$

As a conclusion, classes which have a TI bigger than a threshold must be tested before to going on in the development process. The threshold is defined on the basis of company experience in the specific field of measured application. This measure can be extended to the entire system by evaluating the TI of the class which represents the system itself.

3.4 Metric Framework

The classification scheme reported in Table 1 explains some aspects of the measurement model integrated in TOOMS. The Table shows the mapping of general metrics to the TOOMS metrics. As it was pointed out by many authors, metrics must fit the

General Concepts	Measurements
Class-Level	
Interface Metrics	ECC, $PSIC$, $RSIC$, SC
Method Metrics	$CCPC$, CPC
Class Features	ECC, $CITC$, CAC, CPC
CLASS complexity	CC, ECC, ICC, VI
Timed complexity	$PSIC$, $RSIC$, CCC
Logic complexity	$CCPC$, CPC, $CITC$
Input/Output	NRS, NPS, PEC
Communication	$CICC$, $RSIC$, PEC, $PSIC$
Reuse-Level	
Inheritance	RI
Class Features	ECC, CR
System/Subsystem	ECC, $CICC$
Cognitive Metrics	CR, VI
Test-Level	
Complexity Metrics	CR
Timed complexity	CCC, $PSIC$, $RSIC$
Logic complexity	ECD, $CCPC$, $CITC$
Test coverage	VI, TI
Process-Oriented Level	
Productivity	PI
Reusing	RI
Size estimation	ESS
Cost estimation	$ESCost$

Table 1: Mapping of general concepts to TOOMS metrics (see App.A for the glossary of the metrics proposed).

main needs of developers and managers; data collection and data gathering have to be an automatic support for the development process. Note that the approach proposed is similar to the GQM approach of [Basili84], defining a set of metrics capable to express meaningful indicators and some conformance to the ISO 9126 standard.

Technical metrics are independent, while a correlation exists among the different views. In fact, some metrics assume different meanings according to the adopted view. Thus, different views use the same metrics in different contexts. Moreover, in our experience, developers do not need to get an absolute value, but they need to understand the values trend in order to identify discontinuity and changes from the usual trend. As a consequence, the metrics proposed can be suitable adopted.

It should be noted that the classification is related to a real need for gathering different kinds of metrics and for correlating metrics to produce a readable and understandable data output.

4 Conclusions

A set of metrics for object-oriented development and its integration in the CASE tool, TOOMS, has been presented. The proposed metrics have been defined for a formal object-oriented model and language, mainly focused to the specification of reactive systems (i.e., TROL). These metrics cover all aspects of system specification helping the TOOMS users to produce well stated applications. Metrics are only a support to improve the quality of the specification, which is guaranteed to be formally correct by means of the TOOMS facilities for system validation. Moreover, metrics are useful for estimating and validating of the product quality.

Most of the metrics defined are new, but they are equivalent in general terms to others which have been proposed in the literature. The metrics proposed have been defined to ensure their applicability in all phases of software life-cycle; in fact, most of them can estimate congruent values even if the system is only partially specified according to the capability of many new languages, such as OSDL, TRIO+, TROL.

The TOOMS tool with metrics has been used on several case studies showing the advantages of our model. The use of the metrication framework has demonstrated its general validity for quality evaluation of object-oriented specifications.

Acknowledgments

The authors would like to thank Prof. G. Bucci for his valuable suggestions, the collaborators from CQ_ware: M. Traversi, and O. Morales for their discussions on Software Quality, and the anonymous reviewers for their comments.

A Glossary

AC	Attribute Complexity, CC of attribute;
$AVGCC$	Averaged value of class complexity (CC);
CAC	Class Attribute Complexity;
CC	Class Complexity;
CCC	Class Clause Complexity;
$CCPC$	Class Coupling Path Complexity;
CDD	Class Dynamic Description;
$CICC$	Class Internal Communication Complexity;
$CITC$	Class Internal Task Complexity;
CLC	CLause Complexity;
CMA	A company-dependent coefficient;
CPC	Class Path Complexity;
CR	Complexity Ratio;
CSD	Class Static Description;
$CTYPE(i)$	Communication type of the connection i;
ECC	External Class Complexity;
ECD	Measure of the External Class Description;
$ENCL$	Expected number of new classes;
$ESCost$	Expected System Cost;
ESS	Expected System Size;
ICC	Internal Class Complexity;
$INCCC$	Increment of class complexity;
$MSGC$	Message complexity;
NA	Num. of class **Attributes**;
NAR	Num. of auton. requests in the class;
$NASC$	Complex. of non-auton. serv. of a class;
NC	Num. of **Clauses** in the class;
NCL	Num. of system classes;
$NCON$	Num. of **Connections** in the class;
$NNAR$	Num. of non-auton. req. serv. in the class;
NOP	Num. of Boolean and compar. operations;
NP	Num. of class **Paths**;
NPS	Num. of Prov. serv.;
$NPS(j)$	Num. of Prov. serv. in the **Path** j;
NRS	Num. of Req. serv.;
$NSPSR$	Num. of specified prov. serv. rates;
$NSRSR$	Num. of specified req. serv. rates;
$Path(i)$	Path generating the required service i;
PEC	**Path** external complexity;
PI	Productivity Index;
PIC	**Path** internal complexity;
PMC	McCabe complex. of statements in a **Path**;
$PMEC$	Weight of commun. mec. of Prov. serv.;
$PRS(i,j)$	Num. of presences of attrib. i in path j;
$PSIC$	Prov. Serv. Interface Complexity;
PTC	Complexity of a single **Path**;
$PTCC$	Presence of temp. const. for the **Clause**;
$PTCPS$	Presence of temp. const. for the prov. serv.;
$PTCRS$	Presence of temp. const. for the req. serv.;
RI	Reuse Index of a system;
$RSIC$	Required Service Interface Complexity;
$RMEC$	Weight of comm. mec. of Req. serv.;
SC	Service Complexity of a class;
TI	Test Index of a class;
VI	Verifiability Index of a class;

References

[AMI92] "AMI Handbook", tech. rep., AMI consortium, ESPRIT 5494, January 1992.

[Basili84] V. Basili and D. M. Weiss, "A Methodology for Collecting Valid Software Engineering Data", *IEEE Trans. on Software Engineering*, Vol. 10, No. 6, 1984.

[Braek93] R. Braek and O. Haugen, *Engineering Real Time Systems: An object-oriented methodology using SDL*. New York, London: Prentice hall, 1993.

[Bucci93] G. Bucci, M. Campanai, P. Nesi, and M. Traversi, "An Object-Oriented CASE Tool for Reactive System Specification", in *Proc. of 6th Int. Conf. on Software Engineering and Its Applications*, (Le CNIT, Paris la Defense, France), 15-19 Nov. 1993.

[Bucci94] G. Bucci, M. Campanai, P. Nesi, and M. Traversi, "An Object-Oriented Dual Language for Specifying Reactive Systems", in *Proc. of IEEE Int. Conf. on Requirements Engineering, ICRE'94*, (Colorado Spring, Colorado, USA), 18-22 April 1994.

[Coleman92] D. Coleman, F. Hayes, and S. Bear, "Introducing Objectcharts or How to Use Statecharts in Object-Oriented Design", *IEEE Trans. on Software Engineering*, Vol. 18, pp. 9–18, Jan. 1992.

[Coulunge93] B. Coulunge and A. Roan, "Object-Oriented Techniques at work: Facts and Statistics", in *Proc. of TOOLS Europe 93*, (Versailles, France), pp. 89–95, 8-11 March 1993.

[Dasarathy85] B. Dasarathy, "Timing Constraints of Real-Time Systems: Constructs for Expressing Them, Methods of Validating Them", *IEEE Trans. on Software Engineering*, Vol. 11, pp. 80–86, Jan. 1985.

[Fenton91] N. E. Fenton, *Software Metrics: a Rigorous Approach*. London: Chapman and Hall, 1991.

[HendersonSellers91] B. Henderson-Sellers, "Some Metrics for Object-Oriented Software Engineering", in *Proc. of TOOLS 6 Pacific 1991*, pp. 131–139, TOOLS USA, 1991.

[HendersonSellers92] B. Henderson-Sellers, "Modularization and McCabe's Cyclomatic Complexity", *Communications of the ACM*, Vol. 35, pp. 17–19, Dec. 1992.

[HendersonSellers93] B. Henderson-Sellers, "The Economics of reusing Library Classes", *Journal of Object Oriented Programming*, July-August 1993.

[HendersonSellers93c] B. Henderson-Sellers, D. Tegarden, and D. Monarchi, "Object-Oriented Metrics", in *Proc. of 7th European Conf. on Object-Oriented Programming, ECOOP'93, Tutorial notes*, (Kaiserslautern, Germany), July 1993.

[Hoare85] C. A. R. Hoare, *Communicating Sequential Processes*. NY, USA: Prentice Hall International, 1985.

[Laranjeira90] L. A. Laranjeira, "Software size estimation of object-oriented systems", *IEEE Trans. on Software Engineering*, Vol. 16, No. 5, pp. 510–522, 1990.

[Maier88] D. Maier and D. S. Warren, *Computing with Logic*. Menlo Park, CA, USA: The Benjamin/Cummings, Inc., 1988.

[Mandrioli93b] D. Mandrioli, "The Object-Oriented Specification of Real-Time Systems", in *Tutorial at TOOLS Europe '93*, (Versailles, France), 8-11 March 1993.

[McCabe76] T. J. McCabe, "A Complexity Measure", *IEEE Trans. on Software Engineering*, Vol. 2, No. 4, pp. 308–320, 1976.

[Meyer90] B. Meyer, "Lessons learned from the design of the Eiffel libraries", *Communications of the ACM*, Vol. 33, No. 9, 1990.

[Nesi93] P. Nesi, "An Object-Oriented Language and Compiler for Reactive Systems", tech. rep., RT 3/93 Dip. di Sistemi e Informatica Facolta di Ingegneria, Universita di Firenze, Florence, Italy, 1993.

[ObjecTime93] NorthernTelecom, "ObjecTime: Object-Oriented CASE for Real-Time Systems", tech. rep., Bell-Northern Telecom, 1993.

[Rumbaugh91] J. Rumbaugh, M. Blaha, W. Premerlani, F. Eddy, and W. Lorensen, *Object-Oriented Modeling and Design.* New Jersey: Prentice Hall International, Englewood Cliffs, 1991.

[Shaw92] A. C. Shaw, "Communicating Real-Time State Machines", *IEEE Trans. on Software Engineering*, Vol. 18, pp. 805–816, Sept. 1992.

[Shlaer91] S. Shlaer and S. J. Mellor, *Object Life Cycles: Modeling the World in States.* New Jersey, USA: Prentice Hall, Englewood Cliffs, 1991.

[Walker92] I. J. Walker, "Requirements of an Object-Oriented Design Method", *Software Engineering Journal*, pp. 102–113, March 1992.

[WBrock89] R. Wirsf-Brock and B. Wilkerson, "Object-Oriented Design: a responsibility-driven approach", in *Proc. OOPSLA'89*, (New Orleans, Louisiana), pp. 71–75, SIGPLAN NOT, ACM Press, Oct. 1989.

[Yap93] L.-M. Yap and B. Henderson-Sellers, "Consistency considerations of object-oriented class libraries", tech. rep., University of New South Wales, Information Technology Research Centre, n.93/3, Sydney, Australia, June 1993.

Reuse Inhibitors with, and Requirements for Collection Class Libraries

Hans Albrecht Schmid
FB Informatik
FH Konstanz

Abstract

This paper addresses the problem why collection class libraries are hard to reuse in real life production applications. It seems that the current first generation of class libraries is not mature enough.

A mini case study identifies different kinds of problems that may make reuse difficult or inhibit it. It uses state of the art C++ collection class libraries as examples. The problems identified include: impossible composition of collection components with given element types, performance problems, missing functionality, missing collection components, difficult exchange of representations, and no ease of learning and use due to missing uniformity.

General requirements for collection class libraries are derived, explained and presented. They include: genericity of element composition and of representations and implementations, functional completeness and collection completeness, abstraction from the representation and implementation, and uniformity.

1. Introduction

Though a large number of C++ class libraries are commercially offered, and many of them available with a compiler, it seems that reuse is practised less frequently in production environments than supposed, with the exception of user interface libraries.

From TOOLS EUROPE '94 (Technology of Object-Oriented Languages and Systems).

Our experience is that even when the psychological reuse problems like egoless programmer and NIH-syndrom (not invented here) are overcome, and even when both developer and management attitude are very positive towards reuse, it is in practical applications and production projects (compare [Lenz87]) often difficult, or even impossible, to reuse components from class libraries.

Current class libraries, which form the first generation of class libraries for production languages (excluding Lisp/CLOS, and Smalltalk as interpretive languages), do not seem to be mature enough to lend themselves easily for reuse (with the exception of user interfaces).

This general claim will be substantiated in this paper with the example of collection class libraries, and of abstract data types or high level objects that originate from the analysis of an application (without a consideration of data structures). Stroustrup calls them "abstract types", in contrast to concrete types, which are just an operational manifestation of a concrete data structure [Stroustrup92].

Using a very small, but realistic example, different cases will be shown in which collections from class libraries cannot easily be reused. The examples are drawn from currently available libraries, in particular from the Booch library [Rational93], since it is well known, and its original Ada library is scientifically very well documented [Booch87]. Some hard reasons will be identified that prevent reuse, and other, less hard, reasons impeding it.

From this analysis, requirements for collection class libraries will be derived that enable the reuse of collections and make it more easy. Many of these requirements are based on ideas expressed in [Uhl90]. A large part of these requirements can easily be generalized from collection libraries to general reusable class libraries.

2. Mini Case Study

2.1 Description

Throughout most of the paper, we will use the following example: A word count application counts the frequency of words in a text. The user can access the word-frequencies, sorted according to their frequency, in a word-frequency collection.

The reuse potential is very great: the user interface, and the objects: word, text, and word-frequency collection, are reuse candidates. In the following, we shall consider the word-frequency collection and see, how we can reuse components from collection libraries to implement it.

2.2 Determine the Reusable Component

The word-frequency collection, containing words and their asociated frequencies, is a container or collection object (in the object oriented terminology) or an abstract data type (in the more conventional programming languages terminology).

There are two phases of the application, counting the word frequencies, and outputting them, in which it is used differently. In the first phase, the word-frequency pairs are selected according to the value of the word, in the second, according to the frequency value. For this reason, we are going to use two different collection components in the two phases, and transfer the word-frequencies from one into the other one.

To determine which kind of collection is required, we look for the application operations that are applied to the word-frequency collection, and, complementary, to the structures that exist among the elements of the application:

- In the first application phase, the main operation is to add a word-frequency, which means: if the word is not yet in the collection, store it with a frequency count of one, otherwise increase the frequency count by one. The structure is a mapping from words to frequencies; no other structure is defined among the word-frequency pairs. Thus, we select a map collection component (called also directory or dictionary), with the word as a key, and the frequency as a value.
  In the second application phase, the main operation is to get the words in a sequence sorted according to their frequency. A "greater" relation is defined as an order relation among the frequency counts. This proposes to use a sorted collection ordered on frequency counts.

In the sequence, we will consider mainly the first application phase, and see with which obstacles one may be faced when one is going to implement the word-frequency collection by a map from a class library.

3. Composability with Elements

Collection classes contain elements that are all of the same type (as e.g. a stack of floats or a stack of windows), which may also be a polymorphic type. A collection component from a library must provide mechanisms to create different collection classes for different user-supplied element types. This is a special kind of horizontal composition [Goguen87]. It would be desirable that a collection component could be composed with all possible kinds of user-supplied element types, be it language defined types or user defined types (e.g. classes, structures, or unions in C++).

3.1 Composability Restrictions

However, normally there are restrictions regarding the range of element types that a user may supply, or special requirements are set up for user-supplied types (e.g. that they might have to provide methods with certain names). The more restrictions and requirements, the more difficult reuse becomes. In production applications, they may even become a serious reuse inhibitor.

In non-production applications as e.g. university projects, it may be often possible to modify the type of a user-supplied element to make it fit to the collection component requirements and restrictions.

However, this is usually not possible in a production project, because different components like a collection and its element may be designed quite independently, possibly by different teams.

Typically, the element component will be developed in, or be available from the project, and is designed to meet the project requirements. If a reuasable component from a class library cannot be composed with a given element component, it will often not be possible to modify the element component. Consequently, reuse is impossible.

3.2 Case Study: Missing Element Support

Suppose that the word, a component originating from the project, is represented by a string (i.e a Null-terminated character array) according to C conventions. The map, to be reused from a class library, has two element types, a key and a value. It is to be composed with the word type, as a key, and an integer type, as a value, to form the word-frequency collection.

Let us consider, as an example, the Map from the Booch library [Rational93] for reuse. It is provided as a class template

```
template < class Item, class Value,
                    unsigned int Buckets>
class Map { ... };
```

such that it may be tailored and adapted to different, user-supplied key (called Item) and value types. Both the Item type and the Value type "may be a primitive type or a user defined class" [Rational93]. This provides quite a degree of genericity, but does not include the type of the word component from our example application, which is the informal string type, and formally of type char*.

Though, technically, the type "char*" may be substituted for the template type T:

```
typedef Map< char*, int, ...> WordFrequencyMap;
```

the WordFrequencyMap will not work as intended since it performs the operator= and operator== on the pointers, and not on the character arrays. This means it will insert just pointers, but not C strings as a key into the map. As a result, all key pointers in the WordFrequencyMap may point to the same character string, or, even worse, to an empty buffer, depending on implementation details of the user program. Another problem is that comparing words for equality will not work correctly: equal words at different storage locations are considered as different.

As a consequence, reuse of the Map component from this library is, acccording to the description cited above, not directly possible, but would require modifying the word component. If such a modification is precluded as in a production project, reuse is inhibited.

A class library designer will use primarily programming language constructs as e.g. generic packages in Ada or templates in C++ to support the desired element types. If the language constructs do not suffice, additional mechanisms are required.

The C++ template language construct [Stroustrup92] has made provisions for the case that some particular data types need as template types a specialized treatment. It allows the developer of a class to complement the class definition:

```
template< class T>
class X {
  void ExampleFunction( T aT);
};

template< class T>
void X<T>::ExampleFunction( T aT)
{ /* treat any regular template type */ };
```

by specialized definitions (i.e. implementations) for particular template argument types, as for the type char*:

```
void X<char*> ::ExampleFunction( char* aT)
{ /* treat template arguments of type char* */ };
```

For a class library designer, this language feature would be a solution for the described and some other similar problems. However, it seems that it cannot be applied to template classes with several template types. A study of [Stroustrup92] does not reveal any restrictions; but our experience is that, at least, current compilers with template support [Borland92], [Zortech93] do not support specialized member function definitions for template classes with more than one template argument.

3.3 Common Base Class Problem

A different kind of problem may be found in class libraries that are designed in a Smalltalk-like style. They require that the element type of a collection class is derived from a library supplied base class named "Object" or similarly.

For example, consider the Glockenspiel container library, or the Borland class library. Since the Borland V.3 library, called BIDS, which supports templates, does not contain a map, the older V.2 class library that contains a "directory" class is to be used. Both libraries require that the key and the value component of a map have to be derived from the class Object.

Such a requirement makes sense in a seamless application development framework (see, e.g., [Gamma90]), where a complete application is developed using classes from the framework. In production applications, where this is not the case, the requirement is very restrictive. Obviously, in our example application, it would prevent us from reusing the directory class, or we had to change the design of other project components like the word component.

3.4 Element Genericity Requirement

We conclude that, generally, the genericity of a collection component may be missing regarding its composition with differing element components. The missing genericity is a K.O.-criterion that may prevent reuse. To cope with this serious reuse inhibitor, the following requirement must be met by collection components:

Element genericity requirement:
A collection library should provide sufficient genericity with regard to the kind of element type, such that all fairly common classes of element types (both formally and informally C++ language defined types and user defined types with/without constructors/destructors) can be composed with the collection components.

This requirement is easily generalized to all kinds of class libraries in form of a composability genericity requirement, which requires that library components provide sufficient genericity regarding their composability with user supplied components.

4. Representation and Implementation Variants

The second reuse K.O.-criterion in production applications is the performance of the reuse solution. A reuse solution should offer about the same time and/or space performance as a solution implemented particularly for an application. If reuse does not provide the same performance, an application developer has to make a decision if the loss of performance is acceptable, or if it is outweighted by other advantages as e.g. the gain in development effort or an earlier time to market. Time performance drawbacks of some percent up to some ten percent seem to be acceptable for many production applications.

4.1 Case Study: Missing Representations

Suppose that the word frequency map is being implemented by reusing either the CMapStringToOb from the Microsoft Foundation library [Microsoft92], or the unbounded form of the Map from the Booch library [Rational93].

Performance prototyping of the word-count application yields the expected time performance, but lets us discover a substantial space performance problem. The problem is that only about 30 000 word-frequency pairs do fit into 1 MByte of memory, which is, given that a word with an supposed average length of 7 characters and a count of 4 Bytes totals 11 Bytes on an average, around a third of the value that would be reached when no space is wasted. An analysis shows two reasons for the space overhead.

The first one, being due to the word representation (by pointers to a variable length array in the heap, yielding an overhead of 4 Bytes for the pointer and of 2-4 Bytes for the storage administration length count, depending on the C++ compiler), is not of relevance to the subject of this section, but to that of section 3. Its reduction would require a redesign of the word representation, and a change of the syntactical form of a word into a class. The element genericity would allow us to adapt the map component to this change.

The second reason for the space overhead is due to the map representation. The map representations from both libraries use a hash chaining scheme, which stores a pointer to a chained list of key-matching elements in a hash table entry. For each hash table element, there is an overhead of 1 or 2 Bits for administration information, and of 4 Bytes for the list pointer. For each list element, there is an additional overhead of 4 Bytes for the pointer to the next list element and of 2-4 Bytes for the heap storage administration. The total map space overhead amounts to 4-5 Bytes per table entry and 6-8 Bytes per element.

It should be easy to reduce the space overhead by selecting a different map representation: The hash table overflow list overhead of 6-8 Bytes per element may be reduced to practically zero

- either by using for the overflow lists of the hash table a tabular representation with chained element arrays,
- or by using an open hashing representation. This is only possible when there is a good estimate for the maximal number of elements.

As a consequence, we require a map component with a given representation from a class library, either with a hash chaining, tabular overflow list representation, or with an open hashing representation, in order to reach the same space performance as an application specific solution. It needs to have the same interface as the previously used map, in order to not cause application program modifications (compare section 7).

No map component with either of both representations is available in the Microsoft Foundation library [Microsoft92]. This might be a serious reuse inhibitor. When we want to reuse the available map component, we have to accept a space performance overhead of 6-8 Bytes per element. If we cannot accept this, in some cases quite considerable, space overhead, the only other choice is not to reuse a map from the library and to develop one on our own.

The Booch library also does not offer an unbounded map with an hash chaining, tabular overflow list representation, but it offers one with a open hashing representation (named bounded form), which could be used.

4.2 Which Representations to Provide?

It might seem that the class library designers made just a bad choice in selecting the hash chaining representation. However, this is not the case. If they had selected the open addressing representation, this would fit well to our example application characteristics, but might not fit to other application characteristics (e.g. where the number of hash table elements is not known and cannot be estimated in advance). For again other application characteristics (e.g., where the number of elements is very dynamic, or where the elements are to be visited in key order) no hash, but a sorted tree representation would be required.

The problem is that, for a collection class or an abstract data type, there is no single representation that is the best one and suitable for all application characteristics. If a reusable component provides only one representation, this will fit well to the characteristics of some applications, but not to those of other ones. A large amount of genericity, as we have seen in section 3 with regard to element types, is required with regard to the representation to make a reusable component fit to many different application characteristics.

4.3 Representation/Implementation Genericity Requirement

This is expressed in form of the "representation/ implementation genericity requirement":
A reusable library should offer all major representation and implementation choices for each of its components, which a developer might, reasonably, use for an application case when he or she implements the component self.

A very comprehensive form of representation/ implementation genericity is described in [Uhl90] for an Ada abstract data type library. It is applied in [Schmid93] to an extremely generic collection class library, where the C++ template construct is used to provide implementation hierarchies, where the hierarchically lower used class may be selected from the user as a template parameter from a range of offered classes. An open point here is that only a selection of different representations, but not of different algorithms is possible in this way.

Apart from these libraries, the referenced libraries provide either none or an insufficient number of representation/implementation alternatives. Only the Borland V.3 BIDS library goes a small step towards representation genericity. It defines so-called collection template classes: Bag, Set, Array, SortedArray, Stack, Queue, and Deque, and so-called representation classes: Vector, SLList, DLList. The idea is that collection template classes may use diferent representation classes for their representation. However, there is a restricted representation choice only for the Stack, Queue, and Deque, which can be represented either by the Vector or by the SLList, respectively the DLList.

5. Functional Completeness

The requirement for functional completeness of the services, which a reusable class should provide, is generally accepted (compare [Johnson88], [Booch87, p.35]), but interpreted in different ways. Sometimes, it is considered as providing a minimal set of simple orthogonal services, from which every other service can be composed, same as one proceeds in an operational specification language. We will show that following this definition of functional completeness, as it seems to be done in some class libraries, reuse may be prevented in many cases.

5.1 Case Study: Missing Services

So far, we have not considered the services that are provided from a collection class map. Our interest is to see how these services can be used to implement the application operation of adding a word frequency to the word frequency map.

All maps from different class libraries offer - somewhat different - services "insert a pair", "find a pair with given key", "remove a pair", and "get value of a pair". Thus, they provide a minimal functional completeness with regard to the operation add a word-frequency, which is implemented as follows:

```
if (! aWordFrequencyMap.FindPair( key) )
//if the word is not yet in the collection
//store it with a frequency count of one
  aWordFrequencyMap.InsertPair( key, 1)
else
// otherwise increment the frequency count by one
  aWordFrequencyMap.GetValue( n)
                                  //of found pair
  aWordFrequencyMap.RemovePair( key)
  aWordFrequencyMap.InsertPair( key, n+1)
```

The problem is that this implementation yields a very bad time performance. In case of the key being not yet in the collection, the data structure is searched twice to find the entry corresponding to the given key (with FindPair, and with InsertPair). In case the key is in the collection, it is even searched three times (with FindPair, RemovePair, and InsertPair).

If one would develop an own map, instead, one would search the data structure once, and keep either the entry of the found pair, or the position where the pair is to be inserted, if not found. This would require one search, which is a half or third of the searches, and of the execution time, of the reuse solution.

Since the operation "add a word frequency" is central for the overall application time performance, increasing it by between 100% and 200%, would, clearly, not be acceptable. As a consequence for a production application, reuse would be excluded. However, the operation cannot be implemented more efficiently with the minimal functional complete set of operations. Due to the object encapsulation, it cannot - and should not - be implemented directly. This is not an argument against encapsulation and also not against reuse, as one may hear sometimes, but that a larger set of operations is required.

An additional service "modify value" that modifies the value component of a found pair (which is referred to by an internal or external cursor that is set by FindPair), can be used to replace the last two service calls, RemovePair and InsertPair. Some maps from class libraries (e.g., the Booch Ada Map [Booch87], and the dictionary and association class from [Borland92]) do not provide such a service .As a consequence, reuse of these maps could not be justified to implement our example application.

With a modify service, only one search is required, if the key is in the collection. However, still two searches are required, if the key is not in the collection. This yields a time performance overhead between a few and hundred percent, depending on the ratio of calls where the key is in the collection, and where it is not. Compared to the first implementation, this is a great improvement, but the overhead might still not be acceptable and prevent reuse.

To overcome this problem, a single service must be provided that either finds the pair with given key and sets or returns a cursor to it, or that inserts a pair with given key and value, indicating by a boolean parameter the case selected. This service, called "FindOrInsert" in [Uhl90], does only one search. Using this service, we reach the same time performance (expressed in the number of searches) as own development would yield. Some collection class libraries provide this or a similar service for maps [Microsoft92], [Zortech93].

5.2 Functional Completeness Requirement

Generally speaking, the functional completeness requirement is:
A functional complete set of services is to be provided from any component. It should contain not only a minimal set of simple services, but also composed services, which

1. provide an essentially better performance than the respective combination of simple services (compare with Booch's notion of primitive operation [Booch87, p.35])
2. are used frequently from users, and cannot be realized by a direct combination of simple services without writing an additional amount of code. Then it is more economical to invest once into providing the service than having every user do it.

An example for the second item is providing the last and previous service also with singly linked lists, or a direct access to the n-th element of a sequence (list or array/table).

6. Collection Completeness

Different class libraries contain different kinds of collection components. Apart from smaller differences, major components seem to be missing in libraries as shown in the following.

6.1 Case Study: Missing Components

For the second application phase, a sorted collection is required, which has the word-frequency elements ordered according to the frequency values, such that the most frequent or infrequent words may be accessed. A collection class "sorted collection" (called also sort or sorted sequence) orders key-value-elements according to their key, which is the frequency in the example, or according to the whole element. In the latter case, a record with the frequency as a first component and, consequently, as the primary sorting criterion is to be supplied as an element.

Note that a sorted collection is abstractely defined. It may be represented in different ways, a table or array representation, and a sorted binary tree or a Btree representation being the most important ones. The tradeoff is a slower insertion time with tabular representations against space for the tree pointers with tree representations. A SortedArray, as it is provided in the Borland BIDS library [Borland92], is a specialization of a sorted collection.

No sorted collection class can be found, for example, in the Booch [Rational93] and the Microsoft [Microsoft92] class library. Using other collection components like a unsorted Tree from the Booch library, or an Array from the MicroSoft library, would require implementing all sorting algorithms with the very basic tree services, respectively array services. Consequently, only very small savings would be the benefit from reusing these components.

The problem is that, if important collection concepts are missing in a collection class library, they need to be developed by the user. The reuse potential is not exhausted.

6.2 Collection Completeness Requirement

To judge which collection components should be provided we consider the Ada systematic catalogue of abstract data types [Uhl90], the Smalltalk class hierarchy and the referenced libraries. Our conclusions are expressed in the collection completeness requirement:
A collection class library should contain as basic components (names separated by a "/" are used as aliases):

- linked list/sequence,
- tabular list/tabular sequence/array,
- tree and binary tree,
- sorted collection,
- set,
- map/dictionary,
- bag.

From these, other components are derived by restricting, combining and renaming services of the basic components:

- stack, queue, deque, priority queue, circular queue.

7. Abstraction from the Representation/ Implementation

During the application development process, one acquires more knowledge and experience, possibly by prototyping, about the application and its characteristics, and about performance issues that are too difficult to calculate beforehand. As a consequence, one might have to exchange the previously selected representation with another, more suitable one. The same may happen during the life time of an application where the application characteristics may change. For example, the number of elements in a collection may increase, or new functions may be added to an application that change the relative frequencies with which different services of a collection are called.

7.1 Exchanging Representations

Suppose, for example, that an application reuses a doubly-linked representation of a list from a class library as e.g. [Rational93], [Zortech93]. Among other services, it uses the previous service that yields acces to the preceeding element.

However, it might be found out during development, or, alternatively, during the application life time due to an increasing number of list elements, that the space overhead of the double links cannot be tolerated. The time overhead for an inefficient previous service may be accepted since it is called very infrequently. That means the double linked representation is to be exchanged against a single linked one. This exchange causes larger program modifications since the single linked list representation from these libraries does not offer a previous service.
This example demonstrates an frequent case, since in real life projects, one is faced with unanticipated and/or changing application characteristics. Therefore, it is neccessary that one representation of a collection component may be exchanged against another one without much effort. The exchange should not cause any program modifications, except for the one place in the program, where the representation is selected.

7.2 Representation Abstraction Requirement

An easy exchange of representations is only possible if the interface of all different representations is exactly identical, regarding both the amount of services provided, and their detailed syntax and semantics.

This is formulated as the "representation abstraction requirement":
The interface of a component should be an abstraction (called also protocol) that is strictly separated from the representation and implementation of classes. This means that all representations and implementations should have one and the same abstraction, i.e. one identical interface.

Theoretically, when we think in abstract data types, this requirement is self-evident, since a type is defined by its applicable operations. Thus, types are different when their operations differ. But in pratice it is often violated, as shown for single and double linked lists. Though Booch builds on the notion of an abstract data type, and differentiates it from that of a form, which provides a representation/implementation, this separation is not strictly followed as shown above, and abstract data types provide a differing set of operations for different forms [Booch87], [Rational93].

Please note that the implications of representation abstraction can be far reaching and influence heavily the component interface. For example, if a list is considered as a sequence of nodes [Booch87], [Rational93], no previous service can be provided with a single link representation.

There are also more subtle violations as e.g. in the library [Microsoft92]: With an Array of objects, the RemoveAt or RemoveAll services will remove the objects only from the array, but the user has to delete them himself or herself. Whereas with an Array of strings, the deletion is done by the respective Remove service itself. Working with or exchanging these different kinds of elements may lead to subtle errors that are very difficult to find.

In [Uhl90], it is shown that all component representations may offer exactly an identical set of services, though the service time and/or space performance may be different.

7.3 Separation of Design and Implementation Issues

Meeting the representation abstraction requirement gives not only the benefit of easy representation changes, but also allows to separate two different issues, namely the selection of the abstraction (i.e the interface) and the selection of the representation/implementation into two different time points during the development process.

The interface, i.e. the functionality, is important during the design phase: a collection, or another reusable class, is to be selected according to its functionality. There is no need to consider the representations if the representation/ implementation genericity requirement is fulfilled, that means if one is sure that all important representations are offered for an abstract type.

During the implementation phase, the performance becomes important: one has to select the suitable representation for a previously determined class.

In addition, the selection of a collection during the design phase is made easy, because the number of different abstractions is relatively small, compared to the number of different representations/ implementations that may amount in the order of thousands per abstraction. When the abstraction is determined, it becomes more easy to select the representation/implementation than to select both at a time.

8. Uniformity among Collection Components

Suppose that we have used, the first time, a collection component, e.g. the map, from a library, and are going to use another collection component from the same library. The second use should be much easier than the first time use. This is true under the presupposition that there is a uniformity of design among all components of a library.

One aspect of uniformity is the underlying semantics of all services. It should be the same, e.g. either a copy or a reference semantics, whereas e.g. in the Booch library [Booch87], [Rational93] both semantics are used.

Another aspect is that same or similar services should have the same or similar syntax and semantics. For example, if one inserts a key-value pair into a map with

```
void Insert(   const KeyType& k,
               const ValueType& V)
```

one would suppose that one inserts an element into a Set similarly with

```
void Insert( const ElementType& E).
```

However, many class libraries will disappoint this expectation to a smaller or greater degree. For example, the Booch library inserts a key-value pair into the Map with

```
... Bind( const Item&, const Value&)
```

whereas an element is inserted into a Set with

```
... Add( const Elem&),
```

and into a List with

```
... Insert( const Elem&).
```

Most of the collection classes have different insert- and remove-services.

Though there may be reasons for this approach, it does not seem to help a user in "learning" a library, but makes it more difficult. The more similarities there are among different classes, the easier it is for a user to learn and remember the classes. The latter is of great importance when he or she is only a casual user.

From this considerations, the "uniformity requirement" follows:
The same or a similar set of services (both from a syntactic and a semantic point of view) should be provided for all collection components, where applicable, or to a large subset of them.

9. Conclusions

It has been shown that there are a number of characteristics which may make, in certain situations, the reuse of the current, first generation C++ class libraries difficult or even sometimes impossible.

Six requirements to class libraries have been derived. A central requirement is that for genericity of a collection component, both with regard to the type of the collection elements, and to the representation and implementation variants of a collection. Nearly of the same importance is the requirement for functional completeness of a component. When these requirements are met, then it is made sure that, in most application cases, a component can be used and provides the necessary performance.

The requirement for component completeness ensures that all necessary components are provided. Whereas the requirements for representation abstraction and component uniformity provide for an easy finding and handling of components.

10. Acknowledgements

Thanks are due to J. Uhl. A number of the ideas expressed in this paper are based on common work.

11. References

Turbo C++ Programmierhandbuch V.3.0; Borland GmbH, Starnberg, 1992

G.Booch: Software Components with Ada; Benjamin Cummmings, Menlo Park, 1987

E.Gamma, A.Weinand: ET++ - A Portable C++ Class Library for a UNIX Envvironment; Tutorial OOPSLA/ECOOP'90, ACM Press

J.A.Goguen: Reusing and Interconnecting Software Components; IEEE Computer, February 1986, 16-28

R.E.Johnson, B.Foote: Designing Reusable Classes; Journal of Objectoriented Programming Vol.1/ No.2, June 88, 22-35

M.Lenz, H.A.Schmid, P.Wolf: Software Reuse through Building Blocks; IEEE Software, July 1987, 34 - 42

Microsoft C++ Class Libraries User Guide V.7.0; Microsoft C++ Class Libraries Reference V.7.0; Microsoft Corporation, 1992

C++ Booch Components; Rational, Santa Clara, CA, 1993

H.A.Schmid: An extremely generic C++ collection library; prepared for publication

B. Stroustrup: Die C++ Programmiersprache; Addison-Wesley, Bonn, 1992

J.Uhl, H.A.Schmid: A Systematic Catalogue of Reusable Abstract Data Types; Lecture Notes in Computer Science 460, Springer, Berlin, 1990

Zortech C++ Tools Reference V.3.1; Symantec Corporation, Cupertino, CA, 1993

THEORY

On the Construction of Extensible Systems

Jawahar Malhotra*

Computer Science Department, Aarhus University
Ny Munkegade 116, DK-8000 Aarhus C. Denmark
e-mail: jmalhotra@daimi.aau.dk
tel: (+45) 8942 3271
fax: (+45) 8942 3255

Abstract

Extensible systems are systems which can be extended, by adding new code, without requiring any modification to the original system's source code, without recompilation of the original system, and possibly, without even having access to the original source code. An approach which enables the construction of highly extensible systems is described. It is based on a metaphor: construct the system so it resembles a piece of computer hardware, in that it has a mother-board with slots, and extension boards that plug into these slots. Language mechanisms, that support the construction of systems in this manner, are described. Concrete examples of this approach are presented. The realization of these mechanisms in the programming language Beta, an object-oriented language, are shown. The approach is general enough to be adaptable to other languages. Three alternative techniques for processing extensions are discussed. An attempt is made to classify all changes that can possibly be made to an object-oriented system. This is used to determine which types of changes can be supported, by installing extensions in a possibly redesigned system, rather than by modifying the source code and recompiling.

*Research supported by the Danish Research Programme for Informatics, grant number 5.26.18.19

From TOOLS EUROPE '94 (Technology of Object-Oriented Languages and Systems).

1 Introduction

This report describes work in the context of the DeVise project at Aarhus University. The overall goal of the DeVise project is to create concepts and tools for experimental system development. A subgoal is to explore the area of user-tailorable systems. To support tailorable systems, one needs the concept of system extensibility, especially of the dynamic kind. Hence, the area of extensible systems been explored in order to gain some insight into what support a programming language should provide to allow extensible systems to be written.

An extensible system tends to have wider applicability than a rigid one. This is because more people can adapt it to their use situation. It also tends to have a longer lifetime as it can grow with the user's needs. Furthermore, it acts as a catalyst for new ideas: advanced users can easily experiment with various extensions, leading to some very creative uses of the system not conceived of at development time. GNU Emacs (Stallman, 1984) is a good example of this.

By an extensible system, is meant one that is executable, yet has the potential of accepting new code; code which may either replace or enhance existing parts. Furthermore, in order to make the extension, there should be no need for the source code of the original system (only symbol-table information is required), nor, preferably, should there be any need for the entire development environment. Needless to say, the source code of the original system must not be modified or require recompilation. In the terminology of (Nørmark, 1992) who introduces the notion of an *open point* as a behavioral parameter of a program, an extensible system is a system with open points.

When one tries to develop a system under such constraints a number of interesting issues arise.

- **Structuring the System to be Extensible.** A system comprises of a number of components.[1] What should these components be, and how should they be organized, so that significant changes in the behavior of the system can be effected by replacing these components by newer versions? If the components are too fine-grained, simple changes of behavior will involve many components, thus making the extension process laborious and error-prone. If they are not comprehensible in their own right, they will be difficult to extend. A good component-level architecture will also make it easier for the person tailoring the system to gain an overall understanding of the system and to identify which components need to be replaced in order to install a certain extension.

- **Writing Open Components.** There is a need to write components in a way such that they may be specializable later without changing their original source code. This is essential if the system is to be extensible without modification of the original sources. Callbacks or hooks are an example of a mechanism for writing functions/procedures which may be extended without modification of the original sources.

- **Ensuring a small Semantic Gap.** End-users typically know what functionality they would like to change or add. It is not very easy for them to find what they need to specialize or to find exactly where they should add it. Hence, there is a need to write the system components in a way such that they correspond, more or less, to the functionality of the system. This will reduce the semantic gap, thus facilitating the location of code. Tool support can also aid this process. So, it is imperative that all the bits and pieces that go together to implement some feature of the system be packaged together, as much as possible, within a component.

- **Installing Extensions.** Once an extension has been written (i.e. an original component has been located, comprehended, and specialized), it is still necessary to make the compiled application use the specialized version instead of the original version. In a language with dynamic scoping (e.g. Smalltalk (Goldberg & Robson, 1983)), the replacement could be done by giving the extension the same name as the original. But, in a language with static scoping, this would not work. There is a need for some additional mechanism to support this; e.g. use variables: if the original component was referred to through a variable, then assigning the new extension to that variable would have the desired effect.

[1]By components is meant the parts (functions, procedures, classes, modules,...) of the application.

It is interesting to examine the types of language mechanisms necessary to handle these issues.

Using an example of a spreadsheet system, and the programming language Beta, techniques and language mechanisms which help write such extensible applications are illustrated. Beta is a strongly-typed, statically-scoped, block-structured, object-oriented language in the spirit of Simula (Dahl *et al.*, 1968).

The hardware metaphor which suggests that a system be structured so it resembles a piece of computer hardware, in that it is has a mother-board with slots and extension boards that plug into these slots, is introduced. This simple metaphor proves surprisingly useful in guiding the overall architecture of the extensible system. Various language mechanisms that support this approach are identified; their realizations in Beta are illustrated and discussed. The author feels that Beta has a number of interesting features that make it particularly elegant for writing extensible systems.

In addition to exploring the construction of extensible systems, this report also explores the extension process; i.e. handling extensions. Extensions must be processed, i.e. compiled, or interpreted, before they can be installed into the extensible system. Three alternatives for processing extensions are explored.

In order to gain an understanding of the power of this approach, an attempt is made to classify all changes that can possibly be made to an object-oriented system. This is used to determine which types of changes can be supported, by installing extensions in a possibly redesigned system, rather than by modifying the source code and recompiling.

Section 2 describes, as an example, an extensible spreadsheet system which is characteristic of the types of extensible systems this work tries to support.

Section 3 presents guidelines for constructing extensible systems and then illustrates how the spreadsheet system can be constructed in accordance with these guidelines, using Beta as the programming language. Section 4 covers the alternatives available when it comes to processing extensions. Section 5 examines the types of changes one can make to an application and shows if they can be supported by the extensibility mechanisms presented earlier.

2 The spreadsheet example

As an example, consider an extensible spreadsheet system which allows users to specialize existing cell-types and define new types of cells; e.g. cells, which are designed to contain free-format text, can be specialized to support formatted text, or, a new type of cell which contains video can be defined. These changes or additions should be definable by the user and incorporable into the application executable without recompilation of the original sources.

This incorporation could happen dynamically, during the execution of the spreadsheet system; the spreadsheet system could load the new extension. It could also happen statically; the extension could be patched into the original executable yielding a new extended executable.

It is important to keep in mind that it is the end-user[2] of the spreadsheet system who, without having access to the source code of the system, and preferably without having the original development environment, will write these extensions.

3 Building the extensible spreadsheet in Beta

The problem then, is to write such an extensible spreadsheet application and to identify what special language mechanisms were used to accomplish this task.

Computer hardware is designed to be highly extensible. This is primarily because it is not very easy and economical to produce completely new hardware each time an extension has to be made. What aspects of hardware make it so extensible? It is primarily the overall architecture which comprises of a mother board with slots. Much of the extensible functionality resides on extension boards which are plugged into these slots. Users can typically handle the following tasks themselves:

- add a new board in an empty slot
- specialize an existing board (e.g. add new memory SIMMs)
- replace an existing board by a newer version

If software could be constructed in this manner, similar benefits could be availed of. One way to look at it is as follows: the mother board of a program is the main program and the slots are open points (e.g. callbacks in many languages). The extension boards are the various software components (classes, procedures, functions, types, ...) which fill the open points. This structure (of mother board, slots and components) can be replicated within each software component.

Extending a software system can then be viewed as a process very similar to extending a piece of computer hardware. With software, in addition, to just swapping boards, it would also be possible to allow users to construct new boards (generally by modifying existing ones). It may also be possible to support modifications of the mother board.

The development of the spreadsheet application in Beta follows this theme: it is constructed in the manner prescribed above. The construction is presented in stages — primarily to illustrate all the features without too much complexity. In the first attempt, is presented a version which doesn't allow dynamic extensibility. It serves to introduce the general framework of the application and acts as a reference with which to compare the dynamically extensible version. The second attempt presents a version which can be dynamically extended.

Appendix A presents a brief introduction to Beta.[3] It is recommended that the reader glance briefly at it.

3.1 The first attempt

Here is an abstract presentation of a spreadsheet system. Only details relevant to this discussion are presented. `SpreadSheetSystem` is declared as a Beta

[2] who, probably, should be a programmer, better known as a super-user.

[3] For a detailed description of Beta see (Kristensen *et al.*, 1987; Madsen *et al.*, 1993).

pattern; nested within it are declarations of `Cell`, `TextCell` and `PictureCell`; the latter two are sub-patterns of the first. A few variables, `Row` etc., are declared. Finally, there is the do-part which is the body of `SpreadSheetSystem`; it gets executed when `SpreadSheetSystem` is executed; it creates instances of `TextCell` and `PictureCell`.

Listing 1.

```
SpreadSheetSystem:
(#
  (* Cell pattern *)
  Cell:
  (#
    loc: @Position;
    (* ':<' means virtual declaration *)
    draw:< (# ...INNER... #);
    edit:< (# ...INNER... #);
    update:< (# ...INNER... #)
  #)
  (* TextCell specialization *)
  TextCell:< Cell
  (#
    value: @Text;
    (* '::<' means further *
     * binding of virtual  *)
    draw::< (# do ...textOutput value;
                       INNER... #);
    edit::< (# do ...invoke text editor;
                       INNER... #);
    update::< (# do ...recalc value;
                       draw; INNER... #)
  #);
  (* PictureCell specialization *)
  PictureCell:< Cell
  (#
    value: @Bitmap;
    draw::< (# do ...bitmapOutput value;
                     INNER... #);
    edit::< (# do ...invoke bitmap editor;
                      INNER... #);
    update::< (# do ...recalc value;
                       draw; INNER ... #)
  #);
  (* array of refs to Cell objects *)
  Row: [100]^Cell;
  (* array of refs to Row objects *)
  Sheet: [100]^Row;
  (* ref to a Row object *)
  aRow: ^Row;
do
   ...
   (* Get REF to row 10 *)
   Sheet[10][] -> aRow[];
   (* create a text cell at
    * position (10,10) *)
   new(TextCell) -> aRow[10][];
   (* invoke edit new cell *)
   aRow[10].edit;

   (* create a picture cell at
    * position (10,11) *)
   new(PictureCell) -> aRow[11][];
   aRow[11].edit;
   aRow[10].update;
   ...
#)
```

To run this spreadsheet system, one must create an instance of `SpreadSheetSystem` and execute it in some runtime environment.

Listing 2.

```
main:
(#
  SpreadSheetSystem : (# ... #);
  aSpreadSheet : ^SpreadSheetSystem;
do
  ...
  new(SpreadSheetSystem) -> aSpreadSheet[];
  aSpreadSheet; (* execute it *)
  ...
#)
```

If this were a real implementation of a spreadsheet system, rather than just an illustrative one, the do-part of the `SpreadSheetSystem` would invoke some user-interface loop which would present some standard spreadsheet-like interface. Statements such as `new(TextCell)` etc., shown being executed directly in the do-part, would typically be executed indirectly through this user-interface. As the user-interface aspect is not relevant to this discussion, it has been omitted for the sake of simplicity.

When `main` executes `SpreadSheetSystem`, by creating an instance of it and executing that instance, control is in the do-part of the spreadsheet pattern. The `new(TextCell)` creates an instance of the `TextCell` pattern and stores a reference to it in position `(10,10)` of the sheet. When the method `draw`, for example, is invoked on this instance of `TextCell`, execution begins in the `draw` method declared in `Cell`; when it hits the `INNER` construct it enters the `draw` method declared in `TextCell`. Upon completion of this, control returns to the `draw` method in `Cell` at the statement following the `INNER`. The same applies for the other virtual methods in `TextCell` and `PictureCell`.

In this implementation of the spreadsheet system, the following language mechanisms are utilized to implement the system so it is extensible:

- **Block Structure.** Block structure allows one to construct a software system as one would construct a hardware device i.e. as a number of sub-units (boards or components) which are part of a larger unit and so on. As in a piece of hardware, there are component boards, in a software system there are blocks. Nesting of blocks, as in Beta and Simula, allows one to model the building blocks of a system at a coarser level than just ordinary unnested classes. It also serves to package together related functionality. For example, the `SpreadSheetSystem` pattern models a spreadsheet building block and the `TextCell` pattern models a text-cell building block.

  Once a system is structured in the form of such building blocks, making extensions is conceptually easier: replace the appropriate building block by an extended version. This is similar to what happens in the hardware world: a computer's networking capabilities are extended by replacing its existing ethernet board with a newly released version.

- **Virtual Patterns.** A virtual pattern allows one to model a component that is open i.e. has some deferred functionality, yet, possibly has some default behavior. They are essential if one has to write components which must be extensible without any changes to their original definition.

  In Beta, patterns unify types, classes, procedures, and functions. As a result, the concept of virtual pattern in Beta, spans all of these related concepts of virtual types, virtual classes etc. Sandvad and Nørgaard, in their report (Nørgaard & Sandvad, 1990), show how virtual patterns can be used to defer actions, values, and substance i.e. declare components in which these aspects may be specified later or their existing definitions specialized, all without modification to their original definitions.

  In the example, `Cell` is written with virtual procedures (deferred action): `draw`, `edit`, and `update`. In addition, `SpreadSheetSystem` is written with virtual classes (deferred substance): `TextCell` and `PictureCell`.

- **Further binding of virtuals in all specializations.** In Beta, unlike Simula and most other object-oriented languages, a further binding of a virtual *does not* override the original definition or previous bindings. For example, in `SpreadSheetSystem` in the declaration of `TextCell`, the further binding of `draw` doesn't override the original declaration of `draw` in `Cell`; it extends it. In a further specialization of `TextCell`, a further binding of `draw` would not override the original declaration in `Cell`, nor would it override the binding in `TextCell`; it would extend them.

  This allows for multiple levels of refinement and is particularly useful as it allows an extension made to an extended component to behave as expected. With overriding, an extension made to an already extended component would end up losing its previous extensions unless it was explicitly programmed to utilize them, thus putting an additional responsibility on the shoulders of the extension programmer. Put simply, with the Beta model for further bindings, by making an extension it isn't possible to easily break what already works.

- **The INNER construct.** This allows one to specify precisely when, in an extensible action component, control should be transferred to the specialization. It models the fact that the extensible component decides when the extension should be invoked; not the other way around. Extensions don't need to be concerned with specifying when they should be invoked.

- **Nested Specialization.** In other words, the ability to build a new component from an existing one by specializing some nested component. For example, one could specialize the `TextCell` component by creating a new spreadsheet system as a specialization of the old:

  Listing 3.

```
(* create a new system which is  *
 * identical to the old, except: *)
NewSpreadSheetSystem: SpreadSheetSystem
(#
  (* text cells differ slightly *)
  TextCell::<
  (#
    (* in their edit command *)
```

```
        edit::< (# do ...issue warning;
                  INNER #);
     #)
   #)
```

A new spreadsheet system has been constructed, reusing the old, and specializing `TextCell` to issue a warning whenever edited. This is equivalent to constructing a new piece of hardware by copying most of the old and replacing some of the old parts by new extended versions. This is an elegant, powerful, and conceptually clear way to specify an extension to a system.

3.1.1 Building a new executable

In order to build an executable for the `NewSpreadSheetSystem` shown above, it is necessary to write a new `main` (similar to the one for `SpreadSheetSystem`) and to compile and link it into a new executable. For this process, only the object code for the original `SpreadSheetSystem` and the necessary symbol-table information is necessary. No modifications to, or recompilations of, the original source code are necessary.

Another approach that uses Beta's pattern variables (see Appendix A.1), the interpreter (see (Malhotra, 1993)), and doesn't require the rewriting, or recompilation, of `main`, can be written as:

Listing 4.

```
main:
(#
    (* same as original *)
    SpreadSheetSystem: (# ... #);
    (* pattern variable *)
    theSSSystem: ##SpreadSheetSystem;
  do
    (* load extended version *)
    (extensionFile) -> interpret
       -> theSSSystem##;
    if theSSSystem## = NONE then
       (* extended version not found *)
       (* install default version *)
       SpreadSheetSystem## -> theSSSystem##;
    (* execute installed version *)
    theSSSystem;
#)
```

The original `main` has been rewritten to be extensible. An executable obtained by compiling this main behaves as follows: upon startup, it attempts to load an extension from a designated extension file. If found, the extended version of the spreadsheet system is loaded and executed, else the original default version is executed. To extend the system, one simply needs to put the source code for an extension such as `NewSpreadSheetSystem` in the designated extension file and restart the executable. No compilation or linking is required.

The extension is loaded via the interpreter. The return value of the interpreter is a value denoting a pattern. It is like a function-closure; it is called a structure value in Beta terminology. Structure values are stored in pattern variables. In the code above, `theSSSystem` is a pattern variable. These concepts of pattern variables and structure values are discussed in Appendix A.1.

The problems of processing extensions are covered in more detail in Section 4.

3.1.2 Problems with the first attempt

It is possible to construct a new spreadsheet system using the old. It isn't possible to modify the old system in place. To get the effect of an extension, the new system must be started instead of the old. It isn't possible to make extensions dynamically i.e. during the execution of the old system, as it is necessary to abort the execution of the old system and execute the new system.

As a result of this, it is impossible to write a spreadsheet system which has a command, which allows its user to specify the code for a new cell type and, upon completion, allows the system to resume execution with the new cell type defined.

3.2 The second attempt

To make the spreadsheet dynamically extensible, we must define it as follows. Lines marked with a vertical bar are changed/added with respect to the first attempt.

Listing 5.

```
DynExSpreadSheetSystem:
(#
  Cell:
  (#
    loc: @Position;
    draw:< (# ... #);
    edit:< (# ... #);
```

```
    update:< (# ... #)
  #)

| TextCellDefault: Cell
  (#
    >>Identical to TextCell
      in SpreadSheetSystem<<
  #)

| PictureCellDefault: Cell
  (#
    >>Identical to PictureCell
      in SpreadSheetSystem<<
  #)

  (* pattern variables *)
| TextCell: ##TextCellDefault;
| PictureCell: ##PictureCellDefault;
| xxxCell: ##Cell;

  Row: [100]^Cell;
  Sheet: [100]^Row;
  aRow: ^Row;
do
    ...
    (* store defaults *)
|   TextCellDefault## -> TextCell##;
|   PictureCellDefault## -> PictureCell##;
    ...

    (* create via pattern variables *)
    (* a new TextCell *)
    new(TextCell) -> aRow[10][];
    ...

    (* a new PictureCell *)
    new(PictureCell) -> aRow[11][];
    ...

    (* a new xxxCell *)
|   new(xxxCell) -> aRow[12][];
    ...
#);
```

`TextCell` and `PictureCell` have been renamed to `TextCellDefault` and `PictureCellDefault`. Pattern variables, with names `TextCell` and `PictureCell`, and types `TextCellDefault` and `PictureCellDefault` respectively, have been declared. The default patterns for text and picture cells (i.e. `TextCellDefault` and `PictureCellDefault`) have been stored in the corresponding pattern variables. With the exception of the use of the pattern variable `xxxCell`, this version of the spreadsheet (`DynExSpreadSheetSystem`) will behave identical to the previous version (`SpreadSheetSystem`).

`DynExSpreadSheetSystem`, however, leaves open the possibility of change in the definition of its text and picture cells, as well as the introduction of a new cell type, all without any modification, or recompilation of its source code. If the following statement were compiled into the above application, executing it would change the pattern denoted by the pattern variable `TextCell` to a dynamically-loaded extension (which must be sub-pattern of `TextCellDefault`).

Listing 6.

```
(TextCell Extension Source Code)
    -> interpret -> TextCell##
```

Here, `TextCell Extension Source Code` is the source code of this extension, presumably obtained from the user. Execution can resume after this statement; there is no need to restart the entire spreadsheet system. All uses of `TextCell` will see the new extended version once this statement has been executed. An example of a text cell extension could be the following:

Listing 7.

```
TextCellExtension: TextCellDefault
(#
  edit::< (# do ...issue warning; INNER; #)
#)
```

If in an execution of `DynExSpreadSheetSystem`, the above extension were loaded, all subsequently created text cells would issue a warning every time they were edited.

Using pattern variables and the interpreter in this manner, it is possible to write systems which allow parts to be dynamically replaced by specialized parts, all without any modifications, or recompilations of the original source code. It isn't even necessary to restart the application.

This example also defines the pattern variable `xxxCell`. This is defined in order to allow the introduction of new types of cells, as opposed to changing the behavior of existing types of cells. If the following statement were compiled into `DynExSpreadSheetSystem`, executing it would store a new dynamically loaded pattern (which must be a sub-pattern of `Cell`) in `xxxCell`.

Listing 8.

```
(NewCell Source Code) -> interpret
    -> xxxCell##;
```

Once again, `NewCell Source Code` is the source code of the new cell type, obtained from the user, and could contain, for example, the following:

Listing 9.

```
VideoCell: Cell
(#
  value: @Video;
  draw::< (# ...playVideo value;
               INNER ... #);
  edit::< (# ...invoke video editor;
               INNER ... #)
  update::< (# ...recalc value; draw;
                 INNER ... #)
#);
```

`DynExSpreadSheetSystem` could load such a definition, enabling it to support video cells, a feature that was not conceived of at development time.

Pattern variables truly allow one to model the concept of slots in hardware. Given a system, we can replace what is contained in a pattern variable or add something into an empty pattern variable, all without building a new system. This is exactly how it is in the hardware world.

Virtual patterns don't accomplish this. A virtual pattern also denotes a kind of slot, but a slot with something already built into it; that pre-built part cannot be removed or replaced. To put something new into this slot, one must replicate the entire machine; the new component then becomes a pre-built part of the same slot in the replicated machine. This is effective in software as this replication process is relatively easy and cheap.

3.3 Comparison with other languages

It is interesting to see how extensions can be defined in procedural languages such as Pascal (Jensen *et al.*, 1985) and C (Kernighan & Ritchie, 1988). In these languages, everything is modeled as types and procedures (or functions). For example, one may model a Cell by declaring a record type, a create function which returns newly allocated space for a Cell record, and functions/procedures which model the operations that can be performed on Cells. We can define an extension of a Cell (e.g. to a VideoCell) by defining a new record type called VideoCell which must include all the fields of a Cell along with any additional fields.

In other words, it isn't possible to construct software in the "hardware style" advocated earlier. It is possible to view procedures/functions as the component boards and procedure/function variables as slots; this is not very useful for extensibility purposes as the granularity of the components is very fine. Furthermore, other features useful in the construction of extensible systems, e.g. reuse, small semantic gap, etc. are not easily realizable in these imperative languages.

Other OO languages, such as Smalltalk (Goldberg & Robson, 1983), C++ (Ellis & Stroustrup, 1990), and CLOS (Keene, 1989), support reuse, easy definition of extensions, small semantic gap, etc. Smalltalk, and CLOS, due to their dynamic nature are very suitable for writing, processing, and installing dynamic extensions. With CLOS, in addition, it is also possible to use the Meta Object Protocol (Kiczales *et al.*, 1991), a very powerful means to extend and tailor a system.

All of these languages, however, lack some of the features identified as very useful for constructing extensible systems. These include block structure, virtual patterns (as opposed to just virtual methods), further bindings, the inner construct, and pattern variables.

3.4 Summary

An approach for constructing statically and dynamically extensible systems has been presented. The approach is based on constructing software in a manner analogous to hardware in order to attain high degrees of extensibility. The primary language mechanisms that make this type of construction possible are identified, related to the hardware metaphor, and discussed.

Using this approach, and the language Beta, extensible systems can be elegantly constructed. Furthermore, the construction of extensions is also very simple and elegant.

4 Processing Extensions

Given the executable for an extensible system (along with some signature information) and the source code for an extension, it must be possible to process (compile or interpret) the extension in the context of the extensible system. The goal is to arrive at a new executable which includes the extension.

If the extension is to be processed statically (Section 3.1), then a compiler, which can handle separately-compiled parts, and a linker are all that is needed. The extension can be compiled as a separate module using the signature information about the object code that is part of the executable; it can then be linked with the original executable to produce the new executable.

Processing the extension dynamically is a little more difficult. It should be possible for an executing application to load the extension into itself and continue execution. A number of alternatives are possible; here are a few:

1. Ordinary (non-incremental) compiler with a dynamic linker and loader.
2. Incremental Compilation and Execution environment.
3. An interpreter compiled into the extensible application.

4.1 Ordinary compiler with a dynamic linker and loader

When the application needs to load an extension it invokes the compiler, providing it the source code of the extension. The compiler may or may not be embedded within the application. If it isn't, then it can be invoked via the appropriate inter-process-communication routines. The compiler must be capable of handling separately compiled units; it is the responsibility of the application to package the extension as a separately-compilable unit. Once the compilation is complete, the application invokes a dynamic linker and loader to load the resulting object code into the current execution. The loader provides the application with a reference to the extension. This is used to incorporate the extension into the application's execution.

This approach was adopted by (Agesen & Frølund, 1989) in their attempts to introduce extensibility into Beta applications. In their implementation, an extension is packaged as a separately-compilable module upon which a compile process is started. The compiled code is then linked and loaded into the – possibly executing – system.

4.2 Incremental Compilation and Execution environment

Given a set of modifications to an application's source code, and its executable, an incremental compiler is capable of producing a new executable with as little recompilation as necessary. Furthermore, some environments (such as the The Mjølner Orm system (Magnusson, 1993)) are even capable of resuming the original execution after such a recompilation.

In a system like the Mjølner Orm System, the extensible application would have to be executed within the provided execution environment. An extension could be installed by using the environment to suspend execution, incrementally compile the extension and produce a new executable, and continue execution. Note that in this scenario it is the environment and not the application that is responsible for installing the extensions.

This is clearly a useful approach; it is also much more general, as arbitrary changes to the original application can be supported. The types of extensions presented in this report don't require any changes to the source code of the original application; they don't require the generality of incremental compilation. Hence, if one is only interested in these types of extensions, incremental compilation is a bit of an overkill.

4.3 Interpreter compiled into the extensible application

The interpreter is embedded within the application. When the application needs to load an extension it invokes this interpreter, providing the source code of the extension as an argument. The interpreter processes this source code, creates appropriate runtime objects in the current execution's image, and returns a reference to this interpreted entity. The application then refers to the extension via this reference.

If the extension refers to a symbol already defined in the system being extended, the interpreter should be able to resolve this to the appropriate compiled part of the system. It should not require the referred part to also be interpreted.

Should the extension refer to a symbol in a library not already part of the system being extended, the interpreter should be able to incrementally load and link the necessary libraries into the extensible system before resolving the name to the appropriate compiled part.

It is also possible to design the interpreter to exist as a separate entity i.e. not embedded within the application. The application could then interact with it as it does with the compiler and dynamic linker/loader.

4.3.1 The Beta interpreter

An embeddable interpreter for Beta has been built and is described in (Malhotra, 1993). It is written almost entirely in Beta, has an object-oriented design, and interprets Beta Abstract Syntax Trees directly. Compiled code may invoke interpreted code and vice-versa. The interpreter is packaged as a library with an Application Programmer's Interface (API) which includes the following:

AddDecl: `(context * declText) -> ()`
MakeDeclExecutable:

```
        (context * originObject * declText)
              -> executablePattern
```

These are functions which a Beta program can use to load extensions via the interpreter. The function `MakeDeclExecutable` returns a reference to the interpreted pattern; a reference which can be executed. To build a Beta application which uses the interpreter, one simply includes a file defining the interface to the interpreter, and uses the above functions. When the Beta system links the application, the interpreter is embedded within it.

5 Extensions as viewed from the Inheritance Hierarchy

It is useful to classify the different types of changes one can make to an application. One can then determine if it is possible to program the application so that these classes of changes can be accommodated without modification to the original sources i.e. by simply loading extensions into the application. In other words, it helps answer the question: what kind of changes, to the application, can be made by simply loading new extensions?

For an object-oriented application, one possible way to classify changes is to view them as different types of modifications of the application's inheritance hierarchy. The following list contains such a classification of changes along with suggestions for how they could be accommodated in Beta.

1. Modification of a leaf node i.e. a pattern not used as a super-pattern. If the modified leaf node *cannot* be expressed as a sub-pattern of the original, then it becomes necessary to replace the original by the modified at the source-code level and recompile.

   If the modified leaf node *can* be expressed as a sub-pattern of the original, then this can be supported. The modified leaf node can be loaded as an extension and all points in the executable that referred to the original can be made to point to the new e.g. by using a pattern variable. For example, if one wanted to handle modifications of a pattern `P`, which was not used as a super-pattern, by loading extensions, one could declare a pattern variable `PV` of type `P` and replace all uses of `P` with `PV`. Then, modified versions of `P` could be loaded and, provided they were sub-patterns of `P`, could be assigned to `PV`. The resulting application would behave as if it had been compiled with the modified `P` instead of the original.

2. Modification of a non-leaf node i.e. a pattern used as a super-pattern. Once again, if the modified version *cannot* be expressed as a sub-pattern of the original, then the change has to be made at the source-code level and the application recompiled.

   If it *can* be expressed as a sub-pattern, it is possible to load it as an extension and, with one exception, update all references to the original by the new version. The exception: patterns for which the original was a super-pattern cannot be updated to have the new version as a super-pattern. This is because, in Beta, super-patterns cannot be dynamically changed. This is a limitation with the implementation of Beta.

   It seems logical to use pattern variables to solve this problem in the following way:

   Listing 10.

   ```
   WindowP : Component(# #)
   Window : ##WindowP;
   ```

```
(* pattern variables
   as super-patterns *)
Dialog : Window (# ... #);
TextEditor : Window (# ... #);
```

With this setup, one can dynamically change the super-pattern of `Dialog` and `TextEditor` to a specialization of `WindowP` by assigning to the pattern variable `Window`. A modification of `WindowP` could be loaded as an extension and stored in `Window`; as a result all uses of the pattern variable `Window` would get the updated version. The problem is that the current implementation of Beta doesn't allow pattern variables to be used as super-patterns. It is possible to implement this feature; it would add overhead which would be experienced even when it was not used, a good reason to disallow it.

3. Addition of a leaf node. This amounts to loading a new pattern, which could be a sub-pattern of some existing pattern, and executing it. This can be handled easily.

4. Addition of a non-leaf node. This amounts to loading a new pattern, which is a sub-pattern of some existing pattern, and making it the super-pattern of some existing pattern. If it were possible to dynamically change super-patterns, this type of change could be accommodated.

5. Other modifications of tree structure e.g. change the super-pattern of a pattern. These cannot be supported without making source changes and recompiling. Once again, dynamically changeable super-patterns would solve this problem.

6 Related Work

(Nørgaard & Sandvad, 1990) present a detailed discussion of reusability and extensibility in the Beta system. Their work has also been a source of inspiration for this work. Their focus is "extensibility of software components with the point of view of reusability." In other words, if one has a library with a class defining a general purpose window, how can one reuse (in another application) the class while extending and customizing it to one's needs. Although we also need such capabilities, we are also interested in how these extensions can be made in a "ready to run" or running application. This work has built upon their work, especially in the area of using virtual patterns to defer specification of action, substance, and values.

Another inspiration for this work has been the report (Nørmark, 1992) which explores the concept of an *open point*. An open point is defined as a behavioral parameter of a program. With respect to Beta, Nørmark doesn't talk about pattern variables and also states that "...open points simulated via virtual patterns are closed too early relative to the execution of the program." This report shows that with the availability of pattern variables and the Beta interpreter, this is no longer true. Nørmark also discusses the issue of documenting open points.

Meyer, in his book (Meyer, 1988), addresses extendibility as an external quality factor of a software system. He describes extendibility as "the ease with which software products may be adapted to changes of specifications." He identifies the concepts of polymorphism and dynamic binding as concepts that support extendibility. The two principles proposed by him as essential for improving extendibility, *design simplicity* and *decentralization*, are fully supported by the views presented in this report.

The seminal system and paper on extensible systems is (Stallman, 1984). Stallman presents a list of language requirements for the purpose of writing extensible systems. Among these, he lists dynamic scoping and no typing as essential. This work shows that this is not entirely true; it demonstrates that extensible systems can be written in a static-scoped language with static type-checking.

Notkin and Griswold (Notkin & Griswold, 1987) describe an extension interpreter which relies on call arbitration, dynamic linking, and multi-language extensions. The extension interpreter is able to load an application's object code, given its interface specification. It is also able to interpret one or more extensions, written in any extension programming language. The extension(s) may use the procedures of one or more loaded applications, thus extending each of them and creating a single extended application.

In (Ossher & Harrison, 1992), the authors show how the inheritance hierarchy of an application can be extended by merging it with another, possibly sparse, extension hierarchy. An interesting discussion of extensible visual formalisms, including extensible spreadsheets, is presented in (Johnson *et al.*, 1993; Zarmer & Chew, 1992).

On the comprehension of systems, in order to tailor them, Mørch (Mørch, 1993) argues that the rationale for the system design should be coupled with the system and provided to the person tailoring the system. Ossher (Ossher, 1987) also discusses a mechanism for specifying the structure of large systems; this could be prove very useful for gaining an understanding of the system before attempting to tailor it.

Reflective techniques are also very useful for writing extensible systems. The more an implementation is reflected, the more information there is available at runtime, thus making it easier to process and install extensions efficiently. The book (Kiczales *et al.*, 1991) presents an excellent and detailed discussion of the use of reflective techniques for making extensions in CLOS. There is also some work on reflection and C++ (Chiba & Masuda, 1993); here a version of C++ called OpenC++ is presented. In OpenC++ classes, and selected methods within them, may be declared reflective. Reflective classes have metaobjects which can be used to extend or change the semantics of method calls.

The idea of pattern variables was originally introduced in (Agesen & Frølund, 1989). In their report, Agesen and Frølund present a mechanism for building extensible systems using dynamic linking and loading. We have built upon their ideas in coming up with a general extensibility mechanism for Beta.

In practical use today are applications on the Apple Macintosh which utilize the concept of "add-on." So, an application extends itself dynamically by loading an add-on which blends in with the original application. The add-on shares the original system's runtime environment. As an example, spelling checkers are generally add-ons which are loaded by word processors when needed. The word-processor and the spell add-on communicate using some event mechanism. The Macintosh add-on concept can be elegantly modeled using the mechanism we provide.

Listing 11.

```
WordProcessor:
(#  SpellCheck : ##AddOn;
 do ...loadAddOn -> SpellCheck;
    ...SpellCheck...
#)
```

Here `AddOn` is a predefined pattern which describes the interface common to all AddOns; `loadAddOn` loads a precompiled version of `SpellCheck`; we could also have used the interpreter instead. Then, a spelling checker can be defined and loaded dynamically into the word processor.

(Pedersen *et al.*, 1987) presents a discussion of the Beta shadow language. Their focus is primarily in designing techniques to monitor and debug programs. In a sense, they want to support the age-old debugging technique of putting print statements into programs without actually modifying the source code of the program or recompiling the program. This is equivalent to extending the original application without changing its source code or recompiling it, something very similar to what has been described in this report. They propose a runtime representation amenable to extensibility e.g. consult a jump table after each statement. Although interesting, such an approach would exact a high efficiency overhead. (Bendix & Østerbye, 1986) also presents techniques useful for monitoring and debugging of, primarily concurrent, Beta programs.

(Trigg *et al.*, 1987) describe the concept of system adaptability. According to them, a system can be adaptable in four ways: it can be (1) flexible (2) parameterized (3) integratable (4) tailorable. Our focus has been primarily in finding techniques to support (3) and (4). Although we don't say much about these concepts in this paper, we agree that these are useful concepts in the world of the application builders and users. We feel that the choice of how the application should be adaptable and what tailorability language should be presented to the end-user is left entirely up to the application designers and builders.

7 Conclusions

This report has identified techniques and language mechanisms useful for constructing extensible systems. The usefulness of these mechanisms is premised upon the belief that computer hardware is highly extensible in its construction and hence, software that can be constructed in a similar manner will also be highly extensible. This simple metaphor has proven surprisingly useful in guiding the overall architecture of the extensible system.

This approach to writing extensible systems relies heavily on the power of object-oriented programming in creating highly reusable, generic, polymorphic, and encapsulated components. In particular, it is the polymorphic nature of the extensible application's code (its pattern variables) that allows one to replace a pattern by its sub-pattern, in the executable, without requiring a recompilation of the code that uses the pattern.

The usefulness of these mechanisms has been backed by examples written in Beta. Elegant techniques for writing extensible systems and for extending them have been demonstrated. In addition to the illustrative examples presented here, these concepts have been tested in much larger practical examples. In all cases, they have worked as expected. The approach and mechanisms are not limited to Beta; they can be adapted to other languages.

For processing extensions, the interpreter approach has been very successful. The interpreter has also proven useful for a number of additional applications, like an incremental execution environment, and a source level debugger. The overheads of embedding the interpreter into an application have not been much; for most reasonable sized applications, it has not even doubled the size of the executable.

Extensibility is generally introduced at the expense of efficiency. It may be acceptable for the extensions to be less efficient than pre-built parts. It is, however, less desirable to sacrifice the efficiency of pre-built parts in order to allow them to be extensible. A system which doesn't use the extensibility features shouldn't have to pay for them, while one that does use them should still run acceptably efficiently.

In the presented approach, open points are introduced by using pattern variables. These introduce a level of indirection and, hence, some overhead which is experienced even when pre-built parts are used. A solution would be a scheme which doesn't require all uses of a pattern to be via a pattern variable, yet allows the pattern to be dynamically replaced. This could be done if one could know all the use points, in the executable, of the pattern. One could then patch these to correspond to the new pattern.

8 Future Work

Object-oriented modeling techniques are geared for producing highly reusable components. These components are designed to be reusable as library components — they can be reused when constructing a new application, or another part of the same application. This is very useful in designing components for extensible systems; here also, components are reused, albeit in a different manner. One can view the process of extending a system as identifying a component, reusing it to make a new specialized version, and replacing the original with the new version. It is, however, possible that certain bits of functionality of the extensible application, that would normally *not* be modeled by the standard techniques, need to be modeled when designing an extensible system. For example, in a spreadsheet system, using standard techniques, one may blend the constraint solver into the functionality of the cells. But this would not be so desirable if one wanted to make this constraint solver extensible. We plan to study how the standard techniques need to be modified to produce models for extensible systems.

Tailorability issues come heavily into play while mapping this object-oriented model into an implementation. It is how the various modeled components are put together into a working application that determines how easily one will be able to replace them with specialized versions. We plan to explore techniques for mapping object-oriented models into implementations that are tailorable.

As an end-user of an application, one is not so aware of the internal program structure of the application. One deals with concepts in the application domain and not in the programming domain e.g. it is easier to phrase a statement like "when I select that window" rather than "when that window object receives a mouseDown message followed by a mouseReleased message." Object-oriented programming has reduced this gap between application-world concepts and programming-world concepts by allowing real world objects to be modeled by program objects. There still remains, however, quite a gap between these two worlds. We would like to build tools which allow users to identify extension points in terms of the functionality-view of the application rather than the source-code view of the application. We are also interested in developing techniques and tools which enable the user to comprehend the system being tailored.

The concepts presented in this report are being tested currently in the context of a large application: the DeVise Hypermedia System. This application has already been built in Beta and doesn't have any explicit support for being extensible. It is now being made extensible using the approach presented here.

It is hoped that this experiment, in addition to yielding a highly extensible hypermedia system, will also lead to some design guidelines for extensible systems and some ideas for languages and environments for writing extensions.

The relation between reflective techniques and extensibility is also an item of future work. It is clear that much can be gained, in terms of extensibility, by reflecting the implementation of a system. The interesting issues will be to determine how this can be done efficiently.

Acknowledgements

This work has benefited from the contributions of Prof. Ole Lehrmann Madsen, Görel Hedin, Kaj Grønbæk, Randall Trigg, Anders Mørch, Jørgen Lindskov Knudsen, Elmer Sandvad, Jørgen Nørgaard, as well as many members of the DeVise project and the employees of Mjølner Informatics.

A A brief Beta primer

This very brief primer provides a very superficial introduction to Beta. Concepts used in the main text, but not presented here, are generally presented where they are used. For more detailed treatment, please consult the Beta book (Madsen *et al.*, 1993).

A Beta program execution is a collection of objects.[4] An object is statically or dynamically created as an instance of a so-called *pattern*. The pattern is an abstraction mechanism that unifies type, function, procedure, and class.

Due to the pattern concept, the size of the language is relatively small. At the same time, however, it implies that type, function, procedure, and class definitions have the same syntax; a feature that might confuse inexperienced users.

A pattern `PP` is written as:

Listing 12.

```
PP:  P
(#  (* attribute-part *)
    Decl1; Decl2; ...; Decln
    (* enter-part *)
 enter Inputs
    (* do-part *)
 do Imperatives
    (* exit-part *)
 exit Outputs
#)
```

where `P` is the super-pattern. The declarations `Decli` can be of the form:

1. `A: @Q` where `Q` is a pattern. This means that an instance of `Q` is part of every instance of `PP`.
2. `A: ^Q`. This means that a reference to an instance of `Q` is part of every instance of `PP`.
3. `QQ: Q (# ... #)`. This is a declaration of a new pattern `QQ` nested within pattern `PP`. It has the same structure as the declaration of `PP`.

The enter-part, `Inputs`, describes the input parameters (formal parameters), `Imperatives` describes the actions to be performed (body), and `Outputs` describes the output parameters (return value). The Beta syntax unifies assignments and procedure calls; the symbol `->` denotes both of these operations. For this paper, one should understand `E1 -> E2` as `E2 := E1` if `E2` is an l-value; otherwise, it means `E2(E1)`.

`PP` inherits all the attributes of its super-pattern `P`. The enter-part, do-part, and exit-part of `PP` are derived by combining `P`'s parts with the corresponding parts specified in `PP`.

A pattern may be used as a type or a procedure. As an example of its use as a type consider:

Listing 13.

```
Cell:
(# Position : (# x : @integer;
                 y : @integer; #);
  loc : @Position;
#)
```

Here `Position` is used as a type. As an example of a pattern's use as a procedure consider:

Listing 14.

```
SpreadSheet :
(# Cell: (# ... #)
   CreateCell:
   (# (* local variables *)
      x : @integer;
      y : @integer;
```

[4] Some ideas for this brief introduction borrowed from (Nørgaard & Sandvad, 1990).

```
        newCell : ^Cell;
      enter (x,y)
      do new(Cell) -> newCell[];
         x -> newCell.x; y -> newCell.y;
      exit (newCell[])
    #)
    aCell : ^Cell;
  do ... (10,10) -> CreateCell -> aCell[];...
#)
```

Here `CreateCell` is defined and used as a procedure. In the definition, the construct `new(Cell)` means "create a new instance of pattern `Cell` and return a reference to it." Executing a pattern (e.g. `(10,10) -> CreateCell`) implies creating an instance of it, transferring the input parameters into this instance, executing its do-part imperatives, and returning the output parameters from the instance. We interchangeably use the terms *procedure* or *pattern* for a pattern defined as a procedure; the same applies for patterns defined as functions.

A special variant of a pattern is called a *virtual pattern.* A virtual pattern allows one to defer the specification of some of its details until later. It is declared and specialized as follows:

Listing 15.

```
P : (# V :< (# ... #) ... V ... #)
Q : P (# V ::< (# ... #) ... #)
```

In `P`, `V` is declared as a virtual; there is also a reference to `V` within the body of `P`. In `Q`, the inherited virtual `V` is further bound. Hence, in an instance of `P`, the `V`-reference refers to the `V` declared in `P`, while in an instance of `Q`, the same `V`-reference (inherited from `P`) refers to the further binding of `V` in `Q`.

A.1 Structure Values, and Pattern Variables

In the following program, the pattern variable `X` is declared and initialized first with the structure value denoting the pattern `P2`, and then with the structure value denoting `P3`.[5] The first call to `new(X)` will create a `P2` instance and the second a `P3` instance.

[5]The syntax `##P1` implies *reference to pattern* as opposed to *reference to instance of pattern.* In the declaration, `X` is restricted to refer to `P1` or its sub-patterns.
The syntax `P2##` implies *get the structure value of the pattern* as opposed to *execute the pattern.*
The syntax `X##` implies *store a structure value in the variable* as opposed to *execute the pattern denoted by the variable.*

Listing 16.

```
P : (# P1 : (# ... #);
       P2 : P1 (# ... #);
       P3 : P1 (# ... #);
       (* pattern var decl *)
       X : ##P1;
     do
       (* store P2 struc-val in X *)
       P2## -> X##;
       (* use pattern var as pattern *)
       new(X);
       (* store P3 struc-val in X *)
       P3## -> X##;
       new(X);
    #)
```

The structure value for `P2` created by `P2##` encapsulates the prototype for `P2` along with the instance of `P`. Explaining the need for static contexts is beyond the scope of this report. Refer to (Madsen, 1993) for more information on this. Every time an instance is created using the structure value, the saved static context is made the static parent of the instance.

References

Agesen, O., & Frølund, S. 1989 (December). *Dynamic Link and Load as a Basis for Implementing Extensibility.* Tech. rept. Aarhus University.

Bendix, B. G., & Østerbye, K. 1986. *Using Active Entities for Debugging and Monitoring of BETA Programs.* Tech. rept. Aarhus University.

Chiba, S., & Masuda, T. 1993 (July). Designing an Extensible Distributed Language with a Meta-Level Architecture. *In: Proceedings of the European Conference on Object-Oriented Programming (ECOOP).*

Dahl, O. J., Myrhaug, B., & Nygaard, K. 1968. *SIMULA 67 Common Base.* Tech. rept. Norwegian Computing Center, Oslo.

Ellis, M. A., & Stroustrup, B. 1990. *C++ Reference Manual.* Addison-Wesley Publishing Company.

Goldberg, A., & Robson, D. 1983. *Smalltalk-80. The Language and its Implementation.* Addison-Wesley Publishing Company.

Jensen, K., Wirth, N., Mickel, A. B., & Miner, J. F. 1985. *Pascal User Manual and Report: Revised for the ISO Pascal Standard.* Springer-Verlag.

Johnson, J. A., Nardi, B. A., Zarmer, C. L., & Miller, J. R. 1993. ACE: Building Interactive Graphical Applications. *Communications of the ACM*, **36**(4), 41–55.

Keene, S. E. 1989. *Object-Oriented Programming in Common Lisp: A Programmer's Guide to CLOS.* Addison-Wesley Publishing Company.

Kernighan, B. W., & Ritchie, D. M. 1988. *The C Programming Language.* Prentice Hall.

Kiczales, G., des Rivières, J., & Bobrow, D. G. 1991. *The Art of the Metaobject Protocol.* Cambridge, MA: MIT Press.

Kristensen, B. B., Madsen, O. L., Møller-Pedersen, B., & Nygaard, K. 1987. The BETA Programming Language. *In:* Shriver, B. D., & Wegner, P. (eds), *Research Directions in Object Oriented Programming.* MIT Press.

Madsen, O. L. 1993. The Implementation of BETA. *In: Object-Oriented Environments: The Mjølner Approach.* Prentice Hall International. ISBN 0-13-009291-6.

Madsen, O. L., Møller-Pedersen, B., & Nygaard, K. 1993. *Object Oriented Programming in the BETA Programming Language.* Addison-Wesley Publishing Company.

Magnusson, B. 1993. The Mjølner Orm System. *In: Object-Oriented Software Development Environments.* Prentice Hall International. ISBN 0-13-009291-6.

Malhotra, J. 1993 (November). Dynamic Extensibility in a Statically-compiled Object-oriented Language. *In: Proceedings of the International Symposium on Object Technologies for Advanced Software (ISOTAS'93).*

Meyer, B. 1988. *Object-oriented Software Construction.* Prentice Hall International. Series in Computer Science. ISBN 0-13-629031-0.

Mørch, A. 1993 (August). Designing for Tailorability: Coupling Artifact and Rationale. *In: Proceedings of the 16th Information Systems Research Seminar in Scandinavia (16th IRIS).*

Nørgaard, C., & Sandvad, E. 1990 (January). *Reusability and Tailorability in the Mjølner BETA System.* Tech. rept. DAIMI PB-300. Aarhus University.

Nørmark, K. 1992 (March). *From Hooks to Open Points and back again.* Tech. rept. Aalborg University.

Notkin, D., & Griswold, W. G. 1987 (June). Enhancement through Extension: The Extension Interpreter. *In: Proceedings of the SIGPLAN '87 Symposium on Interpreters and Interpretive Techniques.*

Ossher, H., & Harrison, W. 1992 (October). Combination of Inheritance Hierarchies. *Pages 25–40 of: Proceedings of the conference on Object-Oriented Programming Systems, Languages, and Applications (OOPSLA).* ACM, Vancouver.

Ossher, H. L. 1987. A Mechanism for Specifying the Structure of Large, Layered Systems. *Pages 219–252 of: Research Directions in Object-Oriented Programming.* MIT Press.

Pedersen, C. H., Sørensen, L. B., & Sørensen, P. F. 1987 (November). *The BETA Shadow Language — a basis for high level debugging.* Tech. rept. DAIMI IR-77. Aarhus University.

Stallman, R. M. 1984. Emacs: The Extensible, Customizable, Self-documenting Display Editor. *In: Interactive Programming Environments.* McGraw-Hill.

Trigg, R. H., Moran, T. P., & Halasz, F. G. 1987 (September). Adaptability and Tailorability in Notecards. *In: INTERACT 87, Stuttgart, Germany.*

Zarmer, C. L., & Chew, C. 1992 (November). Frameworks for Interactive, Extensible, Information-Intensive Applications. *Pages 33–41 of: Proceedings of UIST'92.*

Object-Oriented Type Evolution Using Reflection

Manicka Surendhar
Booz, Allen & Hamilton Inc.
8283 Greensboro Drive, McLean, VA 22102, USA

Suad Alagić
Department of Computer Science, Wichita State University
Wichita, KS 67260-0083, USA, e-mail: alagic@cs.twsu.edu

Abstract

We present a mechanism for supporting type evolution in large scale software systems. It applies to a typed object-oriented language and offers type extensions and type deletions. Type extension is the operation by which the type of an object can be extended to that of one of the derived types of its current type. Type deletion enables one to perform the reverse action of type extensions namely, changing the type of an object from its current type to one of its parent/ancestor types. These operations are particularly relevant to database and persistent programming languages but are typically not supported by their type systems. The vehicle used for implementing this technique is reflection of both the computational and linguistic kinds. The operations are type safe, retain the object identity and are incorporated within the object-oriented paradigm. The approach adopted has the ability to incorporate the persistence mechanism (if supported by the underlying language) and works for both the inheritance and subtyping relationships among object types.

Keywords : Object-oriented programming languages, Computational reflection, Linguistic reflection, Type evolution, Persistence, Object-oriented databases.

From TOOLS EUROPE '94 (Technology of Object-Oriented Languages and Systems).

1 Introduction

Any large scale software system must be able to support evolution and change. A particularly delicate problem is providing mechanisms for supporting evolution in database and persistent systems. Two kinds of evolution propounded in ([Skarra 87a], [Skarra 87b]) are *class or type modification* and *type evolution* which can further be classified into *type extensions* and *type deletions*. This type of evolution is particularly relevant to database systems and persistent object systems. Such systems are concerned with data which last for a long time. These data would have been created with one set of assumptions and, as the system develops, these assumptions would shift. *Class modification* is meant to support such a shift in the initial assumptions. [Skarra 87a], [Skarra 87b], [Penney 87] and [Banerjee 87] deal with systems that support class modifications. *Type extensions* are required to support natural changes taking place in the real world with time. The simplified paradigm in which a persistent object maintains its type during its lifetime is unrealistic. Consider, for example, a simple database which is used to maintain employee records in an organization. To begin with, all employees start off at entry level positions. Eventually, an employee might be promoted to a manager. Basically, the type of an object representing a real world entity is extended to its subtype. The identity of the object has not changed. *Type deletions* cause the opposite action. The current type of an object is restricted to that of one of its parent/ancestor types. Although such an evolution is common in the real world, current type systems do not permit this modification. Systems that support class modification recognize the importance of type evolution but still do not attempt to provide this facility. In [Albano 90], an object-oriented database programming language is presented that provides a type safe implementation of type extensions. However, the operation is stand-alone with respect to the object-oriented paradigm, even though the underlying system is object-oriented. Also, an explicit mechanism for type deletions does not seem to be supported. Moreover, the solution in [Albano 90] is applicable only to the subtype relationships among object types. Because of the generality of the reflective technology that we are using, our techniques are more general and more widely applicable and easier to implement.

We propose a method to support type safe type extensions within the object-oriented framework. The method uses *reflection* of both the computational ([Maes 87a], [Maes 87b] and [Maes 88]) and the linguistic kind [Stemple 92] to achieve type extensions. The method is a generic one, in that it can be applied to any object-oriented language. The resulting system can then support type extensions. In addition, if the underlying language supports persistence, the resulting system will be able to support persistence i.e., the mechanism employed for providing persistence will not be affected by this method. The results are thus applicable to the techniques of handling persistence such as those in Eiffel [Meyer 90] or in C++ based persistent languages ([Agrawal 89a], [Agrawal 89b]). Our illustrations and our prototype implementation are based on a C++ environment.

There are two well known relationships among object types ([Snyder 86], [Cook 89]). One corresponds to inheritance [Meyer 90] and the other to object subtyping ([Canning 89], [Cook 90] and [Snyder 86], [Alagic 93]). The object subtyping is based on the contravariant subtyping of methods in the argument types and it is type safe [Albano 90]. The object inheritance is based on the intuitively natural covariant extension of both the argument and the result types of methods ([Meyer 88], [Meyer 90] and [Lecluse 88]) and it does not allow substitutability or else run-time errors of programs that satisfy the static type check may occur [Cook 89]. In type extensions, the type of an object is extended from its current type to that of one of its derived types. The derived types may conform to either of the two relationships mentioned above. The method that we have developed is applicable to both relationships.

The paper is organized as follows. In section 2 we describe the problems associated with supporting type extensions. Section 3 briefly reviews the concept of *reflection*. In section 4 we outline our solutions to the problems defined in section 2. We explain in section 5 how type deletions are achieved using our approach and discuss in section 6 how our solution can be applied to both subtyping and inheritance. Section 7 outlines the method's ability to incorporate the persistence mechanism (if supported) of the underlying language. In section 8 we present our conclusions.

2 Type Extensions : The Problems

There are three important criteria that any system that proposes to support type extensions must take into consideration. Firstly, the identity of the object that is extended must be retained. It is always possible to create an instance of the subtype and somehow copy the information from the old object to the new object. The pitfall with this simplistic approach is that the identity of the old object is lost ([Skarra 87a], [Skarra 87b]). Retaining the identity of the object is important because object identity allows modeling of object sharing and provides a natural semantics for object updates ([Lecluse 88] and [Khoshafian 86]). Also, only by retaining the identity of objects is it possible to model the dynamic nature of real world entities.

Secondly, the operation must be type safe. In a database environment type safety is a very important factor. This is due to the fact that run-time type errors may result in very expensive recovery procedures. By supporting type extensions there should be no degradation in the type safety of the system.

Lastly, the operation should be provided within the object framework. This requirement is obvious as the system implemented is itself object-oriented. The *extend* operator proposed in [Albano 90] satisfies the first two of the afore mentioned criteria. By making the operator stand alone, however, they have failed to satisfy the last condition. The result of this approach is that the principle of encapsulation as dictated by the object-oriented paradigm is violated. The state of an object should be accessed or modified only by the methods defined in or inherited by the type of the object. The *extend* operator outlined in [Albano 90] provides an object with additional state by extending its type, but is not defined in the type of the object, nor is it inherited by that type.

In this paper we are proposing a method to support type extensions such that all the above conditions are satisfied.

3 Reflection

Reflection has been used to control the production and evolution of data and programs in database and persistent programming language systems [Stemple 92]. A reflective system basically allows its own structure to be altered from within. There are two kinds of reflection

- *Computational reflection* ([Maes 87a], [Maes 87b], [Maes 88] and [Feber 89]) in which a program alters its own interpretation. This is common in untyped object-oriented systems. We shall be using this technique in a typed framework.

- *Linguistic reflection* [Stemple 92] in which a program changes itself. Here we are interested only in type-safe compile-time linguistic reflection.

In this section we shall discuss briefly both kinds of reflection.

3.1 Computational Reflection

Computational reflection is defined as the behavior exhibited by a reflective system, where a reflective system is a computational system which is about itself in a causally connected way [Maes 87a], [Maes 87b].

A computational system is said to be causally connected to its domain if a change in one causes a corresponding change in the other and vice versa. Consider a system steering a robot arm [Maes 87b]. The system must contain data structures representing the position of the arm. The system is said to be causally connected to its domain (the robot arm) only if

- a change in the position of the robot-arm due to some external force causes a change in the data representing the position of the arm in the system and

- a change in the data in the system must effect a corresponding change in the position of the arm.

A *reflective system* is a causally connected computational system that has as object-system, itself [Maes 87b]. What this means is that a reflective system contains two domains. One domain is the one for which the system is designed to solve problems in and the other domain happens to be the system itself. By modifying the data that the system has to represent itself, it can modify its own behavior.

In an object-oriented language that supports a reflective architecture, every object in the language is given a meta-object. A meta-object also has a pointer to its referent object. The structures contained in an object exclusively represent information about the domain entity (i.e., the real world entity) that is represented by the object. The structures contained in the meta-object of the object hold all the reflective information that is available to the object. The meta-object holds information about the implementation and interpretation of the object ([Maes 87a]). By modifying the information contained in the meta-object, it is possible to modify the behavior of the system.

3.2 Linguistic Reflection

Linguistic reflection occurs whenever an expression in a language is being evaluated, and the result of the evaluation is itself evaluated as an expression in the language, in the ongoing computation [Stemple 92]. A reflective language has a subset called the *reflective sub-language.* Evaluation of expressions in this sub-language results in the generation of code which is in the same syntax as the original language. This new code is then evaluated in the ongoing computation. Thus a program is able to change itself.

4 Type Extensions: The Solution

We first outline our solution to achieving type extensions. The reason for [Albano 90] to adopt the approach mentioned in the previous section is the generic quality of the *extend* operator. The operation can have any type as the target, provided it is a valid derived type of the current type of the instance invoking the operation. In order to incorporate the operation into the object framework, *extend* must be defined in, or inherited by, every user defined type (*classes* in typed object-oriented programming languages). One way of accomplishing this would be for the system to define a class, and make every user defined class a derived class of this class, thus making it the root of the class hierarchy. This root class would have the *extend* operation as its only attribute thus enabling all user defined classes to inherit this attribute. However, the disadvantage with this approach is that the generic nature of the *extend* operation forces the class itself to be generic, thus requiring all user defined classes themselves to be generic, which leads to additional complications. In order to make this approach viable, a method must be identified by which the generic *extend* operation can be defined in a root class, so that the user defined classes do not have to be generic. We show in this section that using *reflection* we can achieve this.

In the solution that we are proposing we divide the system into levels

- the basic level or the level of the compiler,
- and the reflective or the meta-level.

In the reflective level we define a class which has only two attributes, namely the *extend* and the *delete* functions. *Extend* is therefore a reflective operation. This class is made the root of the class hierarchy by the system. Every user defined class is therefore automatically made a derived class of this class and therefore inherits the *extend* function. The structure of the reflective root class in C++ type pseudo code is shown below.

```
class ref_root{
public:  extend[T: ClassType](...);
         delete[T: ClassType];
               };
```

Although *extend* in the figure above has a generic *kind* [1] [Cardelli 88] parameter - *T* of type *ClassType* [2], this parameter is a reflective one, i.e. a parameter for the reflective computation. As *extend* is a call to the reflective level and is handled by linguistic reflection, its call results in code generated in the syntax of the underlying language, which is then evaluated in the ongoing computation. In the generated code *T* does not appear. Therefore, the generic parameter does not directly affect the compiler level and hence we do not have to parameterize the class itself. Therefore, the underlying language does not necessarily have to support higher-order notions such as types of types (kinds) [Cardelli 88]. The ellipsis represent the parameters that are used to initialize the additional data attributes of the derived class.

4.1 Inheritance Mechanism

An important feature of this solution is that it replaces the standard inheritance mechanism provided by the underlying language with an alternative technique using reflection. The reason for this decision is as follows. In order to be able to extend the type of an object to that of (one of) its derived type(s) memory must be provided to accommodate the additional attributes of the derived type. This memory required can be provided by creating an instance of the type that happens to be the type difference of the source and target types of the *extend* operation. This type difference therefore must be computed. However, as derived classes in all programming languages are defined incrementally (i.e., their definitions contain only the new and redefined attributes), they (the derived classes) automatically become the required type difference if they are viewed as base classes rather than as the derived classes that they actually are [3]. Therefore, by converting all derived classes into base classes we avoid the computation of the type difference between the source and target types of an invocation to *extend*.

Although the default inheritance mechanism is removed, the relationship that the designer of the classes intended between them must be maintained. This is achieved by the introduction of what we call *reflective data attributes* in the definition of the classes and in the symbol table. Using these data attributes it is possible to achieve inheritance and type extensions. The compiler, while parsing the definitions of the various classes, adds these data to the classes. The reflective data are different for base and derived classes. The example given below shows the reflective data that are to be added to a base class.

[1] type of types

[2] type of all class types

[3] base classes and derived classes are the terminology used in C++ to denote parent and subclasses respectively

```
class student{
      ...
      *ANY *meta_obj;
      *ANY *sibling;
      public:
        ....
       };
 class employee{
      ...
    *ANY *meta_obj;
    *ANY *sibling;
     public:
     ...
     };
```

The reflective data that are added to a derived class are illustrated by the following example:

```
class work_study:student, employee {
      ....
      public:
      ....
       };
```

The above code obtains the following form:

```
class work_study {
      ....
      *student     *ref
      *ANY         *meta_obj;
      *ANY         *sibling;
      public:
      ....
      };
```

The asterisks in the figures indicate reflective data. *ANY* stands for the root of the hierarchy at the compiler level. Every user defined class is a derived class of *ANY* [4]. For every base class we are defining a pointer to an instances' (of the class) meta-object (the pointer called *meta_obj*) which will be created if the instance requests for an *extend*. These meta-objects are therefore created lazily. They are used to model the behavior of the object as that of a derived type which happens to be the target type of the *extend* operation. The meta-object is an instance of the difference between the target type and the source type. The *sibling* pointer is used in the implementation of multiple inheritance. If an object wishes to be extended to a type that happens to be a derived type of more than one type, not only must an object of the target type be created, but also instances of the other parent types of the target type must be created. These objects are linked using the *sibling* pointer and they are created in the order in which they are stated in the definition. For example, *workstudy* inherits from both *student* and *employee*. However, as *student* appears first in the list, a *student* object appears in the link list before an *employee* object. For a derived class, in addition to the reflective data mentioned above, we have a pointer to an instance of the immediate parent of the class that appears first in the inheritance list. This happens to be *student* and therefore we have a pointer (called *ref*) to *student*. The purpose of this pointer will be explained in the next section. The alternative technique for achieving inheritance using reflection is implemented only for the user defined class hierarchy. System defined classes and their relationships with user defined classes are unaffected. This is because in some languages [Agrawal 89b], persistence is implemented using multiple inheritance and a root of persistence. In these systems, all types which the designer wishes to be persistent are made derived classes of this system defined root of persistence. These relationships are not affected by the modified inheritance mechanism.

[4] something similar to but not exactly the same as *void** in C++.

4.2 Reflective Computation

Reflection, though a very powerful tool, is used here for the sole purpose of achieving type extensions. The *reflective sublanguage* (see section 3.2) consists of the *extend* and *delete* operations only. The meta-objects referred to in section 3.1 are used here to model the behavior of objects that invoke *extend* as instances of the target type. These meta-objects are themselves only objects and actually happen to be the instances of the type difference between the current type of the object and the target type of the *extend* operation, which (the type difference) here happens to be the modified derived class. The original object is the *referent* of the meta-object. The system shifts to the meta-level and performs reflective computation when it comes across one of the following:

- an invocation of the *extend* method,
- an instance of a derived class [5],

[5] By derived class, we are referring to the derived class in the original program i.e. before a derived class is converted to a base class.

- and an extended instance.

In each case the reflective level generates code to produce the required effect.

For the first case code is generated to perform the following. To begin with an instance of the target type (meta-object) must be created. This is then linked to the object calling *extend* via the *meta-obj* pointer. The object is also linked to the meta-object through the latter's *ref* pointer. If the target type happens to inherit from more than one type, instances of these additional types are created and linked to the original object through the *sibling* pointer. This is shown in the following example where *student, employee* and *workstudy* were previously defined . The type information in the symbol table is modified to reflect these changes. Also, the appropriate reflective data used to support extensions are updated. Computation now returns to the basic level.

```
student x;
 ...;
x.extend[work_study](....);
```

The above code becomes

```
student x;
 ...;
x.meta_obj = new work_study(...);
x.meta_obj->ref = &x;
x.sibling = new employee(...);
```

In order to handle the construction of an instance of a derived class, the meta-level generates code to take care of the following. In an ordinary object-oriented language, i.e., one that does not support type extensions, construction of an instance of a derived class automatically initializes that part of the instance that corresponds to the parent class. In our system, as the default inheritance mechanism is being replaced, the initialization of the parent part(s) is performed by having the reflective computation generate code for the same. To begin with an instance of the parent class that appears first in the inheritance list (in the case of multiple inheritance) is created and assigned to the *ref* pointer of the instance of the derived class. In the case of multiple inheritance, instances of the other parent types are created and linked to the parent part using the *sibling* pointers. An example is given below.

```
work_study y(...);
```

The above code becomes

```
work_study y(...);
y.ref = new student(...);
y.ref -> sibling = new employee(...);
```

For other instances of the second case and for the last case, the reflective computation generates code so that the correct instance is being referred to in that particular situation. The search for attributes always starts from the most recent type upwards like in [Albano 90]. Type checking is performed simultaneously and, in most cases of assignments and normal procedure invocations that have class parameters, reflective computation is performed as a part of type checking. Examples of these two cases are given below. These examples must be considered under the scope of the previously given definitions.

```
x = y;
```

becomes

```
x = y.ref;
```

For the following example an instance of *student* originally, is assumed to have invoked *extend* with *workstudy* as the target type.

```
count << x.display;
```

The above code becomes

```
count<< x.meta_object -> display();
```

4.3 Type Safety

We conclude this section by stating that our system is as type safe as the underlying language that it enhances. This is due to the fact that the code generated by the meta-level satisfies the syntax and type rules of the base language. The only change in the syntax is the addition of the *extend* and *delete* operators. However, this is a reflective function and results in its replacement by syntactic and type safe code generated by the reflective computation. Therefore, the type safety of the resulting system is not affected.

5 Type Deletions

Type deletions involve changing the type of an object to that of one of the objects super or parent types.

The difficulty with type deletions is that programs using objects expecting them to be of the previous type will encounter problems. However, the approach mentioned above will be able to provide a type safe environment for executing type deletions. This is possible because of the fact that an object is basically composed of smaller objects corresponding to the supertypes and the modified derived type. For example, if *student* is a derived type of *person* then an instance of *student* will consist of two smaller instances : one corresponding to the base type *person* and the other to the modified (modified by our method as explained in section 4.1) derived type. Therefore, in order to move an object up the type lattice all we have to do is to delete the objects corresponding to the type difference between the source and target types. *delete* would also have to be declared in the reflective root class explained above so that it becomes a reflective operation.

Rather than simply deleting the objects corresponding to the type difference, which would result in a loss of the object identity, we can use the *ref* pointers defined by the system in derived classes. This can be seen from the example given below.

```
person x                          person x
student y                         student y
 ...                               ....
y.delete[person]                  x.delete[person];
y.getname()                       x.getname();
 ...                               ...
```

The above code becomes

```
person x;                         person x;
student y;                         ...
   ...;
y.ref=new person();
y.ref -> getname(                 x.meta_obj ->
                                  ref->getname();
 ...                               ...
```

Here we assume that *student* is a derived type of *person*. The code fragment on the left corresponds to the case in which an instance of *student* moves up the type lattice, so that it becomes an instance of the base type *person*. Reflective computation results in the type information being changed in the symbol table and in the search for attributes beginning at the correct type. This results in the generation of the code shown in addition to the original code fragment. The *ref* pointer is used to dereference the object of the appropriate type. In the code fragment shown on the right, x is an instance of type *person*, and is assumed to have invoked *extend* with *student* as the target type and then invoke *delete*. The code that is generated is obvious from the above explanation and from the previous example. Since type checking is performed by the reflective computation, programs that use objects expecting them to be instances of a different (a subtype) type would result only in compile time errors, therefore guaranteeing prevention of run time type errors. Of course, this does not solve the problems of those programs that have been compiled before type deletion.

6 Inheritance and Subtyping

If the underlying language supports subtyping, then the extended object will be an instance of the subtype. If the language supports inheritance, then the extended object will conform to the inheritance ordering.

As the inheritance mechanism is replaced by an alternative technique using reflection, the reflective computation can be designed so that the resulting collection of base classes conform to the behavior exhibited by either inheritance or subtyping. Objects extended by the *extend* operator will also obey the ordering followed by the underlying language. It should be emphasized here that inheritance is not type safe for the object substitution operation [Cook 89]. However, the objective of this paper is not to analyze the properties of object-oriented type systems, but to achieve type extensions without any degradation of the existing level of type safety offered by the underlying language.

Consider the following example:

```
class product {
  char* name;
  product* parts;
 public:
   product(char*);
   int equal(product*);
   product* get_parts();
   };
```

A covariant extension (in the Eiffel style [Meyer 90]) would have the following form:

```
class commercialproduct :: product{
  float price;
  commercialproduct* parts;
 public:
   commercialproduct(char*,float);
   int equal(commercialproduct*);
   commercialproduct* get_parts();
   };
```

A contravariant extension which results in a subtype is given below:

```
class commercialproduct :: product{
  float price;
  commercialproduct* parts;
 public:
   commercialproduct(char*,float);
   int equal(product*);
   commercialproduct* get_parts();
   };
```

7 Persistence

As mentioned earlier, the method can incorporate the persistence mechanism provided by the underlying language [6]. If the language uses a root of persistence as is done in O++ ([Agrawal 89a], [Agrawal 89b]), where generic base classes and multiple inheritance are used to achieve persistence, then the same mechanism would be used in the enhanced language as well. This is because the modification of the inheritance mechanism explained in section 4.1 is valid only for the user defined class hierarchy. Therefore, classes that derive from this root of persistence in the original language would continue to do so even in the enhanced language, thereby supporting persistence. The ability of this method to integrate a persistence mechanism can be shown with the following example adapted from [Agrawal 89a].

```
class item {
  Name: nm;
  double wt; /*in kg*/
public:
  item(Name xname, double xwt);
  Name name();
  double weight_lbs();
  double weight_kg();  };
```

[6] this statement is valid only if the language does support persistence

```
class stockitem {
  int consumption
 /*qty consumed per year*/
  int leadtime;
  /*lead time in days*/
  dual ANY *sibling;
public:
  int qty;
  double price;
  stockitem(Name iname, double iwt,
           int xqty, xconsumption,
       doublexprice, int xleadtime);
  int eoq();
/*economic order quality*/};
```

The above code becomes

```
class item {
  Name nm;
  double wt; /* in kg */
  dual ANY *meta-obj;
  dual ANY *sibling;
public:
  item(Name xname, double xwt);
  Name name();
  double weight_lbs();
  double weight_kg();
  };

class stockitem: public item {
  int consumption;
  int leadtime;
  dual item *ref;
  dual ANY *meta_obj;
public:
  int qty;
  double price;
  stockitem(Name iname, double iwt,
       int xqty,  int consumption,
     double xprice, intxleadtime);
  int eoq();
  /*economic order quality*/
  };
```

A sample code using the above class definitions would be:

```
persistent item *pip;
pip = pnew item("1m dram", 0.05);
pip->extend[stockitem]
(5000, 10000, 7.50, 15);
```

The above code becomes:

```
persistent item *pip;
pip = pnew item("1m dram", 0.05);
pip->meta-obj = pnew stockitem
(5000, 10000, 7.50, 15);
pip->meta_obj->ref = pip
```

The reflective data are qualified by the O++ keyword *dual*. This is necessary, as it is not possible at this stage of compilation to determine whether an instance of the class is to be made persistent or not. By classifying them as *dual*, it is possible to assign either a volatile or persistent object to them. The code fragment shown at the bottom of the figure creates an object of type *item* and extends it to *stockitem*. As the original object is declared to be persistent, the meta-object created is also created using *pnew*, the constructor of persistent objects. If the original object had been declared to be volatile, then *new* would have been used. This decision is made by the reflective computation. Using *dual* reflective pointers in the classes facilitates the management of persistent and volatile data.

8 Conclusions

We have proposed a method using reflection of both the computational and the linguistic kinds to enhance a strongly and mostly statically typed object-oriented language with type extensions and type deletions. The method ensures that the operation retains object identity even after the operation (either extension or deletion). Reflective technology has been used to accomplish type safety. The proposed solution can support both inheritance and subtyping and fits strictly within the object-oriented paradigm. It also has the ability of incorporating the persistence mechanism of the underlying language. The results are particularly relevant to object-oriented persistent and database programming languages. The technique has been implemented in a C++ based environment.

References

[Alagić 89] Alagić S., *Object-Oriented Database Programming*, Springer-Verlag, New York, 1989.

[Alagić 91] Alagić S., "Persistent Metaobjects", in *Implementing Persistent Object Bases : Principles and Practice. Proceedings of the fourth International Symposium on Persistent Object Systems*, Dearle A., Shaw G.M., and S.B. Zdonik (eds), Walter Kaufman Publishers, 1991.

[Alagić 93] Alagić S., Sunderraman R. and Bagai R., "Declarative Object-Oriented Programming: Inheritance, Subtyping and Prototyping, *submitted to a conference* , 1993.

[Atkinson 89] Atkinson M., Bancilhon F., DeWitt D., Maier D. and S. Zdonik, "The Object-Oriented Database System Manifesto", *Proceedings of the First Deductive and Object-Oriented Database Conference*, Kyoto, Japan, 1989.

[Albano 85] Albano A., Cardelli L. and R. Orsini, "Galileo: A Strongly Typed, Interactive Conceptual Language", *ACM Transactions on Programming Languages and Systems 10 (2)*, 1985, pp. 230-260.

[Agrawal 89a] Agrawal R. and Gehani N.H., "ODE (Object Database and Environment) : The Language and the Data Model", *Proc. ACM - SIGMOD International Conference on Management of Data*, Portland, Oregon, June 1989, pp. 36-45.

[Agrawal 89b] Agrawal R. and N.H. Gehani, "Rationale for the Design of Persistence and Query Processing Facilities in the Database Programming Language O++", *2nd International Workshop on Database Programming Languages*, Portland, Oregon, 1989.

[Albano 90] Albano A., Ghelli G. and R. Orsini, "Objects for a Database Programming Language", *Proceedings of the Workshop on Database Programming Languages*, P. Kanelakis and J. Schmidt (eds), Morgan Kaufman Publishers, 1991, pp. 236-253

[Banerjee 87] Banerjee J,. Kim W., Kim H. and H. Korth, "Semantic Enhancement and Implementation of Schema Evolution in Object-Oriented Databases", *Proc. ACM - SIGMOD Annual Conference on Management of Data*, San Francisco, California, May 1987.

[Cardelli 88] Cardelli L., "Types for Data Oriented Languages", in *Advances in Database Technology - EDBT '88, Lecture Notes in Computer Science, 303*, Schmidt J.W., Ceri S. and M. Missikoff (eds), Springer-Verlag, Berlin, 1988, pp. 1-15.

[Canning 89] Canning P., Cook W., Hill W. and W. Olthoff, "Interfaces for Strongly Typed Object-Oriented Programming", *Proceedings of OOPSLA Conference*, 1989, pp. 457-467.

[Cook 90] Cook W.R., W. L. Hill and P. S. Canning, "Inheritance Is Not Subtyping", *Principles of Programming Languages*, ACM Press, 1990, pp. 125-135.

[Cook 89] Cook W.R., "A Proposal for Making Eiffel Type Safe", *The Computer Journal*, Vol. 32, no. 4, 1989, pp.305-311.

[Cardelli 89] Cardelli L., Donahue J., Jordan M., Kalsow B. and G. Nelson, "The Modula - 3 Type System", *Conference Record, ACM Symposium on Principles of Programming Languages*, 1989, pp. 202-212.

[Feber 89] Feber J., "Computational Reflection in Class Based Object-Oriented Languages", *OOPSLA 1989*, pp. 317-326.

[Grogono 91] Grogono P., "Issues in the Design of an Object-Oriented Programming Language", *Structured Programming 12*, 1991, pp. 1-15.

[Khoshafian 86] Khoshafian S.N. and G.P. Copeland, "Object Identity", *Proceedings OOPSLA '86*, Portland, Oregon, September 1986, pp. 406-416.

[Lecluse 88] Lecluse C., Richard P. and F. Velez, "O_2, an Object-Oriented Data Model", *Proc. ACM - SIGMOD International Conference on Management of Data*, Chicago, Illinois, June 1988, pp. 424-433.

[Maes 87a] Maes P., "Concepts and Experiments in Computational Reflection", *OOPSLA 1987*, Florida, pp. 147-155.

[Maes 87b] Maes P., "The Use of Computational Reflection", 1st *International Symposium on Artificial Intelligence and Expert Systems, Vol. 1*, AMK Berlin, Berlin, West Germany, May 1987, pp. 289-307.

[Maes 88] Maes P., "Issues in Computational Reflection", in *Meta-Level Architectures and Reflection*, P. Maes and D. Nardi (eds), Elsevier Science Publishers B.V., North Holland, 1988, pp. 21-35.

[Meyer 88] Meyer B., *Object-oriented Software Construction*, Prentice Hall, 1988.

[Meyer 90] Meyer B., *Eiffel: The Language*, Prentice Hall, 1990.

[Penney 87] Penney D.J. and J. Stein, "Class Modification in the GemStone Object-Oriented DBMS", *Proc. ACM Conference on Object-Oriented Programming Systems, Languages and Applications*, Florida, October 1987, pp. 111-117.

[Sheard 91] Tim Sheard, "Automatic Generation and Use of Abstract Structure Operators", *ACM Transactions on Programming Languages and Systems, Vol 13*, 1991, pp. 531-587.

[Snyder 86] Alan Snyder, "Encapsulation and Inheritance in Object-Oriented Programming Languages", *Proceedings of OOPSLA Conference*, 1986, pp. 38-45.

[Stroustrup 86] Bjarne Stroustrup, *The C++ Programming Language*, Addison - Wesley, 1986.

[Stemple 90] Stemple D., Fegaras L., Sheard T. and A. Socorro, "Exceeding the Limits of Polymorphism in Database Programming Languages", *Advances in Database Technology - EDBT '90, Lecture Notes in Computer Science, 461*, Springer-Verlag, 1990, pp. 269-285.

[Stemple 92] Stemple D., Stanton R.B., Sheard T., Philbrow P., Morrison R., Kirby G.N.C., Fegaras L., Cooper R.L., Connor R.C.H., Atkinson M.D. and S.Alagić, "Type Safe Linguistic Reflection : A Generator Technology", *Research Report CS/92/6*, Department of Mathematical Sciences, University of St. Andrews, 1992.

[Skarra 87a] Skarra, A.H. and S.B. Zdonik, "The Management of Changing Types in an Object-Oriented Databases", *Proc. ACM Conference on Object-Oriented Programming Systems, Languages and Applications*, Portland, Oregon, September 1986, pp. 483-495.

[Skarra 87b] Skarra, A.H. and S.B. Zdonik, "Type Evolution in an Object-Oriented Database", in *Research in Object-Oriented Databases*, Shriver B. and P. Wegner (eds), Reading, Mass., Addison-Wesley, 1987.

METHODOLOGY (PART 2)

Capturing Object Interactions

Greg Adams
Object Technology International, Ottawa
greg@oti.on.ca

Jean-Pierre Corriveau
School of Computer Science, Carleton University, Ottawa CANADA K1S 5B6
jeanpier@scs.carleton.ca

Abstract
We propose a notation for describing the behavior of groups of interacting objects within an object-oriented system. Interactions among objects are described using *path expressions*, a notation based on regular expressions. Interacting objects can be assembled into *groups*, which in turn can be organized into abstraction hierarchies or combined to form more complex interaction groups.

This approach has several advantages over existing notations. First, it allows any number of sequences of interactions to be described using a single path expression. Second, since path expressions are based on regular expressions, they are both simple in form and easy to comprehend. Also, path expressions, like regular expressions, can be expressed as finite state machines, thus simplifying the task of writing automated tools for manipulating them.

1. Introduction

1.1 The Problem

The behavior of an object-oriented system (Budd, 1991) is characterized by its objects and their interactions. More specifically, objects within such a system communicate through the exchange of messages. The result is a cooperative effort to accomplish a set of tasks. Consequently, as Beck and Cunningham (1989) observe, "...no object is an island. All objects stand in relationship to others on whom they rely for services".

From TOOLS EUROPE '94 (Technology of Object-Oriented Languages and Systems).

Capturing object interactions is one of the main difficulties with describing object-oriented systems (e.g., Pernici, 1989, p.90; Bear *et al.*, 1990, p.28; Rumbaugh *et al.*, 1991, p.24). And, as Helm *et al.* (1990) note, although the object-oriented design literature contains numerous notations for describing the relationships among objects (see de Champeaux, 1993, for a summary), these notations typically do not adequately describe the behavior of the executing system that results from the interactions of its objects. The problem of describing the interactions of objects is compounded by the fact that, generally, an object can exchange messages with any other object in the system. Fortunately however, although an object can communicate with any other object, typically only a few **patterns** of communication are observed (Shlaer and Mellor, 1992) between objects. Therefore, it is important to identify these typical interactions (Lalonde *et al.*, 1991), which constitute the essence of the system (Lalonde *et al.*, 1992).

In this paper, we overview a novel descriptive notation for object interactions, called PEGs (for **P**ath **E**xpression **G**roups), which is discussed at length elsewhere (Adams, 1992). The PEGs notation allows the identification of *groups* of interacting objects. A group is defined to be a collection of objects and other groups that interact to accomplish a specific task. Path expressions (Campbell and Habermann, 1973) are used to describe the interactions within a group. They provide an abstract representation of the externally visible behavior of an object-oriented system, as typically depicted through its event traces[1]. Furthermore, systems of arbitrary complexity can be described because groups

[1] An *event trace* (Rumbaugh, *et al.*, 1991), or equivalently, an *interaction diagram*, (Jacobson *et al.*, 1992) captures a single, specific, sequence of messages. Conversely, because path expressions are based on regular expressions, a single path expression can capture several exchanges of messages.

(and their associated path expressions) are themselves treated as objects and can be organized into abstraction hierarchies.

1.2 Scope

Before presenting PEGs, it is important to delineate its relevance. The PEGs notation is not intended to be a formal (provable) specification such as those of Helm *et al.* (1990), Holland (1992), and Wills (1991, 1992). Instead, it provides a descriptive common ground between the loose informalisms of object-oriented analysis and the rigor of formal specifications. Let us elaborate. On the one hand, unconstrained natural language is too error prone to semantic confusion. On the other hand, formal notations are typically non-trivial to learn and of limited practical value. Conversely, PEGs captures the complexities that arise in an object-oriented using a simple notation that is both easy to understand and sufficiently structured to avoid ambiguities.

This work is motivated by the suggestions of Thomas (1992) and is based on the ideas presented Helm *et al.* (1990), Holland (1992) and Campbell and Habermann (1973). In the next section, we will briefly examine existing work. Then, we will introduce path expressions and the PEGs notation proper. A short example will be discussed. The paper concludes with a discussion of future directions for this work.

2. Existing notations

Several existing notations, such as those of Shlaer and Mellor (1992), Rumbaugh *et al.* (1991, pp. 85-96), Bear *et al.* (1990), and Pernici (1989) use variations on state diagrams or statecharts (Harel, 1987), as well as event traces, to describe the behavior of an object-oriented system.

State diagrams focus on the individual objects and their responses to specific events while in a particular state. As such, these diagrams do not directly address the problem of object interaction. Possible interactions must be reconstructed from the analysis of groups of state diagrams; a complex, error-prone task for the least.

Conversely, event traces, as mentioned earlier, explicitly depict a specific sequence of messages exchanged between objects. Any variation in the messages exchanged between these objects, even for the same task, requires a separate event trace. This observation also holds if the same messages are used with the same objects, but in a slightly different order. And arbitrary timing of messages remains quite problematic to represent. In essence, it is the set of all event traces for a system that gives a static description of all possible exchanges of messages in this system: patterns of interactions are not directly modeled. For this reason, event traces appear to be too fine-grained to be useful when working with complex object-oriented systems[2]. Instead, in our opinion, it is essential to have a notation that allows for the capturing of generic patterns of message exchanges: notational genericity offers an elegant solution to the problem of scaling up an approach to object interaction to the complexities of large object-oriented systems.

As an alternative to state diagrams and event traces, Wirfs-Brock *et al.* (1990) uses subsystem diagrams and collaboration graphs to describe the behavior of an object-oriented system. A subsystem diagram represents the system in terms of nested contours with each contour representing an object and the contracts it supports. A contract is a cohesive set of responsibilities that one object agrees to provide to another object. A collaboration graph describes collaborations between objects. Thus, Wirfs-Brock's strategy does provide the ability to describe groups of objects cooperating to accomplish a task. However, the resulting diagrams show the system in the event all interactions were to be triggered at once: the actual patterns of interactions that arise cannot be readily determined. In other words, these diagrams are too coarse-grained to capture typical patterns.

Finally, Helm *et al.* (1990) and Holland (1992) organize an object-oriented system into *groups* of interacting objects called contracts (see example in appendix). The notion of groups of interacting objects, which is central to PEGs, is generally acknowledged to be quite important in the object-oriented programming paradigm. For example, Gibbs *et al.* (1990) as well as Wirfs-Brock and Johnson (1990) have observed that reuse typically occurs either through the reuse of groups of objects interacting to accomplish tasks

[2] This observation has been confirmed in the work of the second author on capturing large industrial telecommunication systems using object-oriented technologies (Corriveau, 1994). More specifically, we have noticed that the complex behavior of such systems could lead to an unmanageable proliferation of use-cases (Jacobson *et al.*, 1992) and event traces.

or through the specialization of frameworks (i.e., hierarchies of classes to be reused through specialization).

For Helm and Holland, contracts can be arranged into inheritance hierarchies and composed of other contracts. A contract defines each participating object, the invariants maintained by the contract, and a specification of how the contract is instantiated. A contract also specifies any other contracts that are being refined (i.e., specialized) or included by the given contract. Contracts are orthogonal to classes and place the emphasis on capturing groups of interacting objects. The object interactions are embedded within the specification (using a formal style) of the operations of an individual object. Consequently, the thread of interactions can be difficult to determine, requiring a detailed examination of the specifications of each operation. This task is further complicated by the inheritance and refinement properties supported by contracts.

In this paper we build on the notion of groups of interacting objects as described by Helm *et al.* and Holland. In addition, path expressions (Campbell and Habermann, 1973) are used to explicitly describe the patterns of object interactions. This approach, presented in the next section, allows the expected threads of execution to be defined between groups of interacting objects or within a group of objects.

3. PEGs

3.1 Path Expressions

Path expressions are an integral part of the PEGs notation. We will briefly review path expressions and then describe how PEGs uses them. Path expressions were first introduced by Campbell and Habermann (1973) and subsequently generalized by Lauer and Campbell (1975) and Bruegge and Hibbard (1983). Campbell and Habermann use path expressions to synchronize concurrent processes. A path defines a set of permissible sequences of operations on a known set of objects. In other words, a path expression defines a set of possible traces. More formally, a path expression can be viewed as a grammatical object generating a trace language (Shields, 1979) and reducible to a finite state machine. As Campbell and Habermann (1973, pp. 91) remark, this notation is based on regular expressions, and thus provides a familiar conceptual framework, as well as allowing for reduction to finite state machines.

Campbell and Habermann's path expression notation consists of the following operators:

A,B	- Either A or B is performed.
A;B	- A is performed and then B.
{A}	- Any number of processes can perform A.
()	- Parenthesis enclose parts of an expression that are treated as a single item.

The path PATH P1,(P2;P3) END specifies that either P1 is performed by at most one process or P2 and then P3 are performed by at most one process. The expression between PATH and END is repeatedly executed. The path PATH P1;{P2;P3};P4 END specifies P1 is performed by one process and then the sequence of performing P2 and then P3 is performed by any number of processes. When no more processes are performing the sequence P2;P3 then P4 is performed by at most one process.

Path expressions have been applied to object-oriented systems as a mechanism for describing the ordering of operations within an individual object. Goldsack and Moreton (1982) use path expressions in a manner comparable to Campbell and Habermann: A path expression is associated with each Ada package. The path expression specifies the synchronization of the operations described in the package and the number of processes which may simultaneously perform a given path expression. Although the notation is different from Campbell and Habermann's, the intent is fundamentally the same. In the same vein, Procol (Van Den Bos and Laffra, 1989) uses path expressions to define a protocol for each object. But Procol does not directly capture the patterns of interaction of the system and inter-object communication is limited to specifying which object can perform an operation.

3.2 The PEGs Notation

PEGs describes an object-oriented system using two primary mechanisms:

- path expressions and,
- groups of cooperating objects

Path expressions are used to describe the patterns of interaction exhibited by the system. More specifically, these expressions are to capture the *typical* behavior of a system, that is, its important interactions (Lalonde *et al.*, 1991, 1992).

Path expressions offer several advantages over existing notations. First, a single path expression can describe any number of interaction sequences. Second, as mentioned earlier, path expressions are based on regular expressions, and thus are simple in form and easy to comprehend. Also, because these expressions are reducible to finite state machines, the task of writing automated tools for manipulating them is quite simplified (as suggested later).

The PEGs notation supports the inheritance and composition of paths: Paths can be composed of other paths, and interacting objects are formed into *groups*, which can be arranged into inheritance hierarchies or combined to form more complex groups. Interactions within a group are represented using path expressions. A group inherits its path expressions from its 'supergroup'. The terms 'subgroup' and 'supergroup' are used to convey the subclass-superclass nature of the relationship. Furthermore, a group's path expressions can reference inherited paths in a manner comparable to the **super** notation provided for Smalltalk methods. Also, groups can add to or override an inherited path. Finally, groups, their participating objects and the operations supported by those objects can either be abstract (in the object-oriented sense of the word) or concrete.

As mentioned above, in addition to containing objects, a group can also be composed of other groups. The process of reusing other groups is essentially a part-of relationship, with the composite group using other groups as parts. In PEGs, the use of one group within another group implies the use of all of its constituent elements. In other words, groups are treated as a single unit when used by another group.

Let us now turn to PEGs' path expression operators. The notation is similar to Bruegge and Hibbard's (1983) with the addition of some new operations. These added operators are provided as convenience mechanisms and can be expressed in terms of the basic path operators:

Operation	Meaning
A ; B	- A is followed by B.
A | B	- Either A or B is performed.
A*	- A is repeated zero or more times.
A+	- A is repeated one or more times.
[A]	- A occurs zero or once.
A & B	- Either A is performed and then B or vice versa.
()	- Parenthesis enclose parts of an expression that are treated as a single item.

In traditional path terminology A and B of refer to procedures. In PEGs, A and B specify a target object and the operation performed by it. For example, a partial PEGs path describing the behavior of a window viewing a file follows:

```
( (aFile read; aWindow updateText)
 | (aWindow saveText ; aFile write)
)*
```

This path expression specifies either the file is read (i.e., the object aFile has its operation **read** performed) and the window's text updated or the contents of the window are saved and written to the file. The entire path can be repeated any number of times (as indicated by *).

Unlike Procol (Van Den Bos and Laffra, 1989), path expressions in PEGs do not specify the arguments passed to operations. This stems from the difference in what each notation is trying to capture. Procol focuses on the operations *within* a given object, the ordering of invocations of its methods and, the types and restrictions on its arguments. PEGs' path expressions focus on the system at a higher level, capturing the patterns of interaction between objects. But, it is trivial for PEGs to provide this additional parametric information. However, the latter should typically be omitted when viewing the high level behavior of the system, and only shown when considering the details of a particular set of interactions. We did not include such information in our notation because we feel presenting the user with the arguments (their types, etc.) for each message would distract from the crucial task at hand, namely identifying the interactions between objects.

Let us now overview the notation for groups[3]. A group defines a collection of objects and groups that interact to accomplish a task. Groups are first class objects and have classes associated with them. Among other attributes, a group's declaration consists of::

[3] Adams (1992) presents a formal syntax for PEGS.

name
The name of the group.
description
A textual description of the group.
inheritsFrom
The supergroup the group is inheriting from.
participants
A collection of objects whose definition are specified by the group. This collection may also contain other groups used by the group.
invariants
Specifies, in a high level form, the invariant maintained by the group and the path expressions causing their satisfaction.
A group also comprises the following path expressions describing its behavior:
behavior
A path expression describing the high level behavior of the group. This path expression typically references other path expressions.
paths
A collection of path expressions providing a more detailed view of specific interactions. A name is associated with each path.

3.3 An Example

Here is an integral example of PEGs notation in order to illustrate path expressions and groups. It describes the relation between a Pane and a Dispatcher in Smalltalk/V[4]. It is assumed the reader is familiar with this example. Also, we have included several additional details which are explained at length in Adams (1992).

```
name:
   PaneDispatcher

descriptiveName:
   Pane/Dispatcher Framework

description:
A Pane and Dispatcher cooperate to control a
particular region of a window. Dispatchers are
responsible for processing I/O. Panes are
responsible for presenting the data to the user.
Panes communicate with a controlling model
from which their data is obtained.

abstract:
   yes

inheritsFrom:
   none

defines participants:
   dispatcher IS a Dispatcher.
   pane IS a Pane.

uses:
        none

secondary participants:
   scheduler IS LIKE a DispatchManager.
   topPane IS LIKE a TopPane.
   topDispatcher IS LIKE a TopDispatcher.
   model.
"the model controlling the pane/dispatcher"

 synonyms:
   pane = dispatcher pane.
"the dispatcher's pane is the pane participant"
   dispatcher = pane dispatcher.
"the pane's dispatcher is"
"the dispatcher participant"
   topPane = pane topPane
   model = pane model.

invariants:
   (pane contents REFLECTS model contents)
USING update.
 "the pane should reflect the data known by the
model"

behaviour:
   create ;
   open ;
   (windowActivating;
      (update*;
       cursorEntersPane;
         (update | userInput)*;
       cursorLeavesPane
      )*;
    windowDeactivating
   )*
   terminate.

 paths:
   create:
"path to create the group"
      model  >>
         pane model:;
"specifies the model"
         [pane name:];
"specifies the pane's name"
         [pane paneMenuSelector:].
"specifies a message that can be sent to the
model to obtain the menu"

   terminate:
"path to terminate the group"
      close.
```

[4] Smalltalk/V is a trademark of Digitalk Inc., CA.

```
   open:
      topPane >>
         pane reframe:;
"determine rectangle for the pane's area"
         pane open.

   close:
      topPane >>
         pane close ;
         model release.
"break connections between the model and the
pane"



update:
      model >>
"update the displayed information"
         refresh
         | (pane update: ; refresh)
         | (pane update:with: ; pane perform:)
         | (pane update:with:with: ;
                  pane perform:with:).
   cursorLeavesPane:
      USER >>
         dispatcher processInput ;
         dispatcher deactivate .
   cursorEntersPane:
      topDispatcher >>
         dispatcher processInput ; dispatcher
activate .
   windowActivating:
      topPane >>
         pane displayWindow .
   windowDeactivating:
      topPane >>
         pane graySelection .
   userInput:
"handle user input"
      USER >>
         dispatcher processInput ; dispatcher
processKey ;
         (menuRequest | keyInput | ctrlKeyInput |
            functionKeyInput).
   menuRequest:
         dispatcher processFunctionKey ;
         (topPane performMenu
          | (pane performMenu;
                  (topPane performMenu
            | model perform:))).
   functionKeyInput:
         (dispatcher select
          | (dispatcher processKey: ;
               dispatcher processFunctionKey:)).

 exception paths:
    none
```

The first section of a group's declaration specifies the name of the group and a description for the group. Two separate name fields, *name* and *descriptiveName*, are provided so that tools such as compilers can work with a formal syntax for PEGs, while still allowing the flexibility to provide a verbose descriptive name. The *abstract* field indicates whether or not the group is an abstract group. Abstract groups are intended to be specialized much in the same manner as abstract classes. Abstraction and inheritance are essential elements in promoting reuse of groups. The Pane/Dispatcher group shown below is an abstract group. An example of inheritance in groups is given in Adams (1992).

The second section of a group's declaration specifies the members of the group. Group members are one of the following:

- singleton objects declared by the group (*participants*)
- objects providing services to the group but not explicitly part of the group (*second participants*, which will not be explained further here)
- other groups

The Pane/Dispatcher group in the example defines two participants, *dispatcher* and *pane*, which are instances of the classes Dispatcher and Pane respectively. The Pane/Dispatcher group does not use any other groups, but does specify four secondary participants scheduler, topPane, topDispatcher and model. Comments are contained within double quotes (").

In addition, a collection of synonyms is specified. Synonyms provide a mechanism for attaching alternative names to objects. Synonyms are helpful when an object is being considered from different perspectives. In the Pane/Dispatcher group, the synonym definition,

pane = dispatcher pane.

specifies that *pane* and *dispatcher pane* represent the same object. Synonyms help clarify alternative ways of describing an object and allow convenient short forms.

The third section of a group's declaration specifies the *invariants*. Invariants are an important aspect of a group because they identify information the group's members cooperate to maintain. In other words, invariants identify dependencies between the objects. When specifying an invariant it is necessary to be able to specify the objects maintaining the invariant, and the mechanism through which the invariant condition is satisfied. Without both pieces of information it is difficult to ascertain the purpose and behavior of the invariant. PEGs identifies the invariant condition in high level terms, and specifies the path expression which causes its satisfaction. The form of an invariant is:

predicateCondition USING pathExpression

The Pane/Dispatcher invariant, demonstrates several aspects of the PEGs notation. The **REFLECTS** operator, adopted from Helm *et al.* (1990), specifies the existence of a relationship between the objects. The exact nature of the relationship is not relevant at this level of description. The invariant declaration of the example specifies that the pane's contents can be made to reflect the model's contents through the use of the path whose name is *update.* In PEGs, a path name can be substituted wherever a path expression is expected (see Adams, 1992).

The fourth and final section of a group's declaration specifies the group's behavior in two parts:

- high level behavior (*behavior field*)
- detailed behavior consisting of:
  - typical interaction patterns (*paths field*)
  - atypical interaction patterns (*exception paths field*)

Paths within PEGs are not intended to be a formal definition of all possible interactions; instead, we repeat, they are used to capture the essential and typical patterns of interaction.

The *behavior* path expression field captures the high level view, with subsequent *named paths* providing a more detailed view of the interactions. The behavior path expression usually contains references to other paths described in the *paths* field of the group's declaration. Consequently, PEGs not only supports the decomposition of the system into groups, but also supports the decomposition of the interactions within a group. This feature allows the client to quickly grasp the typical behavior while at the same time providing specific details about the behavior in the event they are required.

The behavior path of the Pane/Dispatcher group specifies that the *create* path typically occurs first, followed by the *open* path. This is eventually followed by a sequence of window activations and deactivations with intervening updates and user interactions occurring repeatedly. Ultimately the Pane/Dispatcher group terminates.

The *paths* field contains detailed path expressions whose form is:

pathName:
typicalInitiator >> pathExpression

or

pathName: pathExpression

The term typicalInitiator (>>) specifies the path is typically initiated by the object *typicalInitiator*. In the event several objects typically initiate the path, the following form is used:

(A | B) >>

This specifies **A** or **B** typically initiates the path. To indicate paths typically initiated by a user action, the keyword USER gives the typical initiator. *pathName* is a brief label describing the path and hence the set of interactions the path describes. The above named paths have several advantages: First, the ability to specify the originator allows the identification of the 'typical' case. Second, associating a descriptive label with a path expression has the effect of attaching meaning to the important sets of interactions exhibited by the group. This effectively does for interactions what Pernici's (1989) roles do for states, that is, to partition the behavior into meaningful named parts. Third, associating a label with a path allows the path to be referenced by other paths. This prevents unnecessary repetition of path expressions and improves readability.

As mentioned above, paths can reference other paths by referencing their name. In the Pane/Dispatcher example, *update* path typically occurs once the window has been activated (as indicated by the behavior path). The path is typically initiated by the *model* and results in either the *refresh* path or one of the other three paths occurring. Closing the window (the *close* path), is typically initiated by the topPane (which *IS LIKE* a TopPane). The associated path shows the set of interactions include *close* being sent to pane; followed at some point by *release* being sent to the model.

The *exception paths* field contains detailed path expressions describing the interaction patterns associated with the occurrence of an exception. PEGs maintains exception paths separately in order to distinguish typical behavior from atypical behavior. The Pane/Dispatcher group does not define any exception paths.

3.4 Future Directions

PEGs has been used for about two years at Object Technology International for documenting the interactions among groups of objects. Though useful in this respect, we envision a wider scope of application for this work. In this subsection, we briefly overview four areas we are currently investigating in the hope they will further enhance the usefulness of the PEGs notation.

First, PEGs is currently a text based notation. A graphical version of the notation may also be desirable. Path expressions can be visualized either by looking at 1) the behavior described by the path expression or 2) at the structure of the path expression. The former approach, which implies understanding the notation, remains an open question. Conversely, viewing the structure of a path expression can be accomplished by converting the path to a finite state machine. Unfortunately, such an approach may not be ideal. As Zave (1985) observes, the primary problem with finite state machines is the difficulty human readers have in comprehending them. An attractive alternative is to use Zave's own sequence diagrams, which build a tree structure to break up a sequence into subsequences. These tree-like diagrams are simpler to display than finite state machines. But more importantly, sequence diagrams are equivalent to regular expressions and so are path expressions. Therefore, path expressions can be represented as sequence diagrams without loss of information.

Second, Lalonde *et al.* (1992) proposes the development of tools for the regeneration of an object-oriented system's specification from its implementation. A potential starting point for the regeneration of a system could consist in a set of event traces produced by this system. Tools could then be used to generate path expressions from these traces. These paths would serve as the basis for reconstructing an analysis model of the system. In other words, they would constitute an intermediate step towards a comprehensive description of the system.

Third, by comparing an event trace for a particular execution of a system against the path expressions describing the system, PEGs can facilitate object-oriented verification and testing. If the trace cannot be generated from the path expressions, then either the path expressions are incorrect (which may, in turn, imply the system is not sufficiently understood) or an error in the implementation has been identified.

Finally, Janicki (1985) describes the notion of *equivalence* for path expressions. The extent to which this idea can be incorporated into PEGs is still unknown. Minimally, it is hoped that PEGs could use equivalences to determine whether two groups are *interaction-equivalent*, that is, whether they exhibit the same patterns of interaction. This ability would be extremely useful, specially for determining equivalence classes in object-oriented testing. In general however, establishing the equivalence of programs is an extremely difficult problem.

4. Conclusion

Existing approaches to capturing the behavior of an object-oriented system either focus solely on individual objects or lack the genericity required to handle a large number of possible interactions between objects. To address this problem, we have presented the PEGs notation, a method for describing the behavior of interacting objects using path expressions. More specifically, PEGs provides a mechanism to describe the typical patterns of interactions that form of the essence of the system's behavior.

PEGs provides only one view of a system of objects. Understanding and developing object-oriented systems often requires several different views (Rumbaugh *et al.*, 1991). Static views depicting the structure of objects and their relationships to each other at a single moment in time are a useful starting point when trying to understand a system (Ibid., pp. 84). The combination of a static view with the interaction view provided by PEGs appears to provide a better understanding of the system and its behavior.

Acknowledgments

The authors would like to thank Object Technology International and the School of Computer Science of Carleton University for their support of the original master's thesis on which this paper was based. The authors would also like to thank Dave Thomas for his suggestions to investigate the use of path expression for describing object interactions.

References

Adams, G. (1992) *Describing Groups of Interacting Objects using Path Expressions.* Masters Thesis, School of Computer Science, Carleton University, 1992.

Bear, S. *et al.* (1990) "Graphical Specification of Object Oriented Systems", *ECOOP/OOPSLA'90 Conference Proceedings*, Ottawa, Canada, pp. 28-37.

Beck, K., and Cunningham, W. (1989) "A Laboratory for Teaching Object-Oriented Thinking, *OOPSLA'89 Conference Proceedings*, New Orleans, Louisiana, pp. 1-10.

Bruegge, B. and Hibbard, P. (1983) "Generalized Path Expressions: A High-Level Debugging Mechanism", *Journal of Systems and Software*, vol. 3, pp. 265-276.

Budd, T. (1991) *Object-Oriented Programming*, Addison-Wesley.

Campbell, R. and Habermann, A. (1973) *The Specification of Process Synchronization by Path Expressions*, Lecture Notes in Computer Science, vol. 16, Springer Verlag, pp. 89-102.

Corriveau, J.-P. (1994) "On Object-Oriented Testing", technical report, School of Computer Science, Carleton University.

Gibbs S. *et al.* (1990) "Class Management for Software Communities", *Communications of the ACM*, Vol. 33 No. 9, pp. 90-103.

de Champeaux, D., Faure, P., and Lea, D. (1993) *Object-Oriented System Development,* Addison-Wesley.

Goldsack, S. and Moreton, T. (1982) "Ada package specifications: path expressions and monitors", *IEEE Proceedings* vol. 129, No. 9, pp. 49-54.

Harel, D. (1987)*On Visual Formalisms*, Technical Report, CMU-CS-87-126, Carnegie-Mellon University, Pittsburgh.

Helm, R., Holland, I. and Gangopadhyay, D. (1990) "Contracts: Specifying Behavioral Compositions in Object-Oriented Systems", *ECOOP/OOPSLA'90 Conference Proceedings*, Ottawa, Canada, pp. 169-180.

Holland, I. (1992) "Specifying reusable components using Contracts", Personal communication of work in progress, College of Computer Science, Northeastern University.

Jacobson, I. *et al.* (1992) *Object-Oriented Software Enginnering*, Addison-Wesley.

Janicki, R. (1985) "An Equivalence Notion for Path Expressions Systems", *Journal of Information Processing and Cybernetics*, pp. 283-295.

Lalonde, W., White, P. and McGuire, K. (1991) "Coordinators: A Mechanism for Monitoring and Controlling Interactions Between Groups of Objects", technical Report, School of Computer Science, Carleton University.

Lalonde, W., Pugh, J., Corriveau, J.-P., and White, P. (1992) "A Design Regeneration Tool for Object-Oriented Systems", to appear in the IBM journal of object-oriented technology.

Lauer, P., and Campbell, R. (1975) "Formal semantics for a class of high level primitives for coordinating concurrent processes", *Acta Information* pp. 247-332.

Pernici, B. (1989) "Objects with Roles, Object-Oriented Development", Université de Genève, pp. 75-100.

Rumbaugh, J. et al. (1991) *Object-Oriented Modeling and Design*, Prentice Hall, 1991.

Shlaer, S. and Mellor, S. (1992) *Object Lifecycles Modeling the World in States*, Yourdon Press.

Shields, M. (1979) "Adequate Path Expressions", *Proceedings of the Symposium on the Semantics of Concurrent Computation*, Evian-les-Bains, Lecture Notes in Computer Science, vol. 70, Springer Verlag, 1979, pp. 249-265.

Thomas, D. (1992) Personal Communication.

Van Den Bos, J. and Laffra, C. (1989) PROCOL: A Parallel Object Language with Protocols, OOPSLA'89 Conference Proceedings, New Orleans, Louisiana, pp. 95-102.

Wills, A. (1991) "Capsules and types in Fresco", *ECOOP'91 Conference Proceedings*, Geneva, Switzerland, pp. 59-76.

Wills, A. (1992) "Specification in Fresco, Personal communication of work in progress, University of Manchester.

Wirfs-Brock, R. and Johnson R. (1990) "*Surveying Current Research in Object-Oriented Design*} Communications of the ACM, vol. 33 No. 9, pp. 104-141.

Wirfs-Brock R., Wilkerson, B. and Wiener, L. (1990) *Designing Object-Oriented Software*, Prentice Hall, 1990.

Zave, P. (1985) A Distributed Alternative to Finite-State-Machine Specifications, *ACM Transactions on Programming Languages and Systems*, wol. 7, No. 1, pp. 10-36.

Appendix: An example of Helm *et al.*

```
contract SubjectView
Subject supports[
        value: Value
        SetValue(val: aValue) ->
          Dvalue{value = value}; Notify{}
        GetValue(): Value -> return value
        Notify() ->
          < ||v : v:eViews: v -> Update() >

        AttachView(v : View) -> {v eViews}
        DetachView (v : View) -> {v eViews}
]

Views: Set(View) where each View supports[
        Update -> Draw()
        Draw -> Subject ->
         GetValue()
          {Views reflects Subject.Value}
        SetSubject(s : Subject) -> {Subject = s}
]

invariant
        Subject.SetValue(val) ->
                < v: v eViews :
                  v reflects Subject.Value >

instantiation
        < ||v :  v:eViews: < Subject
          -> AttachView(v)||
                v -> SetSubject(Subject) >>

endContract
```

Traceability in the Object-Oriented Software Life Cycle

Franck Barbier †
La Chantrerie — CP 3003
44087 Nantes CEDEX 03 — France
Phone: (33) 40 68 32 01 — Fax: (33) 40 68 30 66
E-mail: fbarbier@ireste.ireste.fr

Abstract

Traceability is a fundamental aspect of object-oriented software development. In particular, traceability of transition between analysis and design has to be highlighted to bring out the understandability of the object-oriented software life cycle. In a classical approach, transition process and design activity are often considered as model restructuring activities where traceability is hard to manage. In another approach, called OSM in this article, transition process and design activity are considered as model combination activities. Not only the relationships between objects depicted in the same model type (analysis model, underlying configuration model and design model) are important. The relationships relative to the process of adapting an analysis model to design constraints for example, are important too and have to be built and highlighted. In such a context, traceability becomes easier to describe, and thus to manage.

Introduction

This article deals with "Object Select and Merge", or OSM, which is a general and rigorous framework for designing in an object-oriented way. Most efforts concerning object-oriented software development have been concentrated on representation techniques rather than on the software life cycle, which is, in our opinion, very different when using object-oriented technology. In the distinction between Object-Oriented Analysis (OOA) and Object-Oriented Design (OOD), many problems arise from the lack of a clear definition of the transition process between analysis and design and, more generally, from a lack of a precise definition of the object-oriented software life cycle itself.

This article tries to develop this point of view through the concept of traceability. The following is a definition of this concept by E.V.Berard [Berard 93]: "Traceability is the degree of ease with which a concept, idea, or other item may be followed from one point in a process to either a succeeding, or preceding, point in the same process. For example, one may wish to trace a requirement through the software engineering process to identify the delivered source code which specifically addresses that requirement". In OSM, this definition leads us to consider the transition process between analysis and design, not as, classically, a model restructuring activity, but as a junction of object flows and a model combination activity. This is the heart of OSM which is first discussed in this article. Then, the applicability of OSM is illustrated through an example of a programmable thermostat. This example permits us, in particular, to investigate briefly some points of detail of OSM when used with a given object-oriented environment, here based on C++.

I. From OOA models to OOD models

Analysis is known as a representation technique and a process for problem domain modeling whereas design is dedicated to solution domain modeling. However, in practice, many difficulties exist as Monarchi and Puhr observe [Monarchi 92]: "It is, however, difficult to find a clear distinction in the OOAD research. In particular, it is difficult to determine where OOA ends and OOD begins". Let us have a deeper look at these difficulties.

From TOOLS EUROPE '94 (Technology of Object-Oriented Languages and Systems).

† ERTO/IRIN/Université de Nantes

Since OOAD methods have existed, the authors of these methods have provided a strategy to transform OOA models into OOD models. The term "strategy" is more acceptable than the term "technique" because, as we know, no rigorous and flexible framework has been really defined for this transformation, except perhaps [Shlaer 91] with "recursive design". More generally, if present OOAD methods can be considered as good and efficient representation techniques, they do not propose a clear and strong approach of the object-oriented software life cycle (see [Edwards 90] for a complete study of the object-oriented software life cycle). As a consequence, when using these methods, design appears as a very hard task in comparison with analysis: how to use OOA models to build OOD models while taking into account all the constraints associated with design like software architecture definition, data managment strategy, software control implementation, user interface construction, etc?

During analysis, many constraints are put aside, in particular those linked to deep software nature (real-time, graphics, business...). Complexity is inherent to problem space, namely the real world, and representation techniques (entity/relationship modeling, state transition modeling...), which are by nature free from implementation considerations, lead clearly and rigorously, in fact in a <u>technical way</u>, to OOA models. During design, complexity is inherent to solution space, namely the software built, and, in our opinion, is greater than complexity linked to analysis. In real-time software for example, software control is probably the most important problem while in business software, data managment is. While solving such problems, sometimes simultaneously, OOA models often appear as constraints instead of aids. In other words, OOA models tend to be transformed or restructured, in fact adapted and unlike analysis, often <u>in a non technical way</u>, to obtain OOD models. Traceability managment becomes difficult, indeed even impossible. The aim of OSM is to avoid this. For that, let us list three invariants of object-oriented software development.

The first invariant is that one of the main aims of analysis is comprehension, more precisely, problem domain comprehension. Thus, OOA models, in most cases, cannot guide software implementation in place of OOD models. If so, what is the utility of OOD models? This remark seems obvious but many studies on OOAD methods show OOA models translated into pseudocode or into programming language (object-oriented or not).

The second invariant is that one of the main aims of design is traceability, more precisely traceability associated with the object-oriented software life cycle. Thus, OOD models have to express and to explain how code — OOI models for Object-Oriented Implementation models — is obtained from OOA models while taking into account all the fundamental decisions which are made during design.

Finally, the third and final invariant is that the transition process from OOA models to OOD models is an activity of model adapting as long as there is an aim switching from problem domain definition to solution domain definition. While an analyst is trying to understand the problem, he cannot add to a class appropriate attributes and/or operations to implement software control, he cannot know class libraries to address efficiently software reuse, etc. So, model adapting appears as a natural part of the object-oriented software life cycle as Aksit & Bergmans observe [Aksit 92]: "In the design phase, the software engineer <u>revises</u> and extends the analysis model (...)" (our underlining), as Shlaer & Mellor observe [Shlaer 91]: "(...) it represents a basic synchronous design that can be extended, elaborated, and <u>adjusted</u> to accommodate size and performance constraints as required." (our underlining), as Rumbaugh & al. observe [Rumbaugh 91]: "(...) the analysis models are elaborated, <u>refined</u>, and then optimized to produce a practical design." (our underlining), etc.

<u>The problem is in the very nature of the model adapting activity</u>. Generally, model adapting means model restructuring, in other words, OOA models are modified to meet the constraints linked to the decisions made during design. In such a context, a first important question arises: shall we spend time on analysis rather than on design, if OOA models are modified so that, in some cases, the model restructuring activity is more sizeable than the analysis activity itself? In the same way a secondly important, even fundamental,

question arises: how to manage traceability if OOA models are broken?

To answer the first question, our opinion is that even if OOA models are adapted, OOA cannot be considered as a subordinate activity. Precise specification can be obtained with OOA in a well suited approach like in [Barbier 92] for example. To answer the second question, our opinion is that tangible benefits can be obtained if OOA models are broken according to a rigorous and flexible way, in other words, if OOD models are expressed as functions of OOA models, like in OSM.

II. OSM as an object-oriented design process

Shlaer & Mellor have proposed in [Shlaer 93] a simplified typology of object-oriented design processes: designing by elaboration and designing by transformation. In this article, another, even complementary, process of design is proposed: designing by selection and merging [Barbier 93].

Because design is a solution-centered activity, the machine's underlying configuration plays a main role in the sense that the solution cannot be specified without considering the machine's capabilities. During detailed design, the underlying configuration is used like a "real" machine (the machine's capabilities are viewed as low-level constraints, portability cannot be addressed). During preliminary design, the underlying configuration is used like an "abstract" machine, especially an object-oriented "abstract" machine which is called in OSM, the Basic Class Library (BCL): each of the machine's capabilities can be viewed as a service of a BCL object. This hypothesis is realistic. Most object-oriented environments have a BCL often integrated as part of the whole library of classes: Smalltalk-80 with for example, the classes "Process", "Semaphore"... Eiffel with for example, the classes "MEMORY", "EXCEPTION"...

Thus, in OSM, design is considered as the junction of two main object flows: the OOA models object flow and the BCL object flow. In OSM, two important flows take part in design too: the object flow of tool class libraries and the "functional requirements" flow.

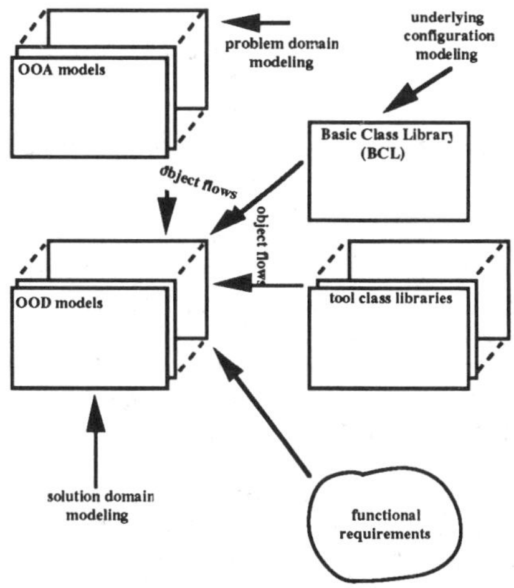

figure 1: OSM flows

III. The OOA models object flow and the BCL object flow

The meaning of an object flow is simple: if O is an object of the OOA models, O is or is not selected to become an object of the OOD models. In the same way, if O is an object of the BCL, O is or is not selected to become an object of the OOD models. For a given piece of software, an object of the OOA models or of the BCL participates directly (selected), indirectly (not selected but "used") or not at all in design: it is obvious that an object of the BCL participates or does not participate at all in design (for example, the class "Semaphore" in Smalltalk-80 can be without interest for a given piece of software), it is less obvious that an object of the OOA models does not participate at all in design. Let us take an example (Shlaer & Mellor formalism):

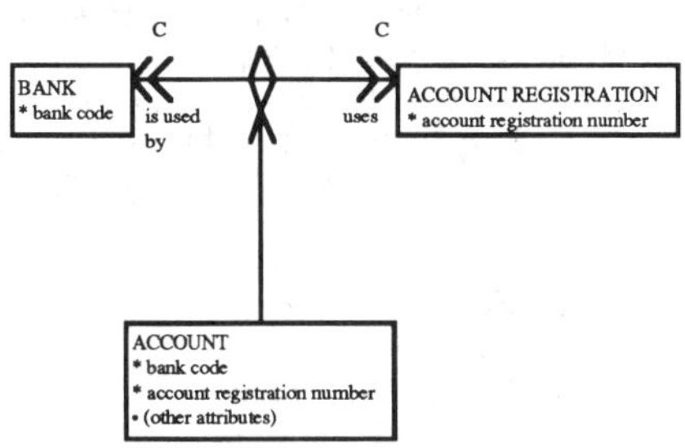

figure 2: an OOA model (Shlaer & Mellor "information model")

In figure 2, an analyst has specified that in a consortium of banks, an account from a bank must be distinguishable from an account from another bank. In fact, an account is completely identified by concatenation of two of its attributes: the bank code and the account registration number (asterisks in figure 2). However, the process of creating an account can bring about different solutions. Account registration numbers can be predefined (first case), and as a consequence, instances of the "Account registration" class are predefined too, so that the "Account registration" class will be selected in the OOD models. In this first case, the "Account registration" class participates directly in design. On the other hand, account registration numbers can be obtained from any computation (second case), so that the "Account registration" class will not be selected in the OOD models. In this second case, the "Account registration" class does not participate, even indirectly, in design. In the OOD models, the service that will make the computation of account registration numbers will probably be assigned to the "selected" (in OSM jargon) "Bank" class.

So T, traceability in OSM, is: for O_D which belongs to the OOD models, $O_D=T(O_A{}^1, ..., O_A{}^n, O_{BCL}{}^1, ..., O_{BCL}{}^m)$ where $O_A{}^1, ..., O_A{}^n$ belong to the OOA models and $O_{BCL}{}^1, ..., O_{BCL}{}^m$ belong to the BCL. This definition of T is incomplete. Let us study the remainder of OSM.

II2. The tool class libraries object flow and the "functional requirements" flow

Naturally, if O is an object of the OOD models, O can be obtained from objects of class libraries other than the BCL, like dedicated libraries ("GeneralParser" in Smalltalk-80 for example is typically a dedicated class). Thus, the tool class libraries object flow is a natural flow in the object-oriented software life cycle.

The "functional requirements" flow is more interesting. The idea of "functional requirements" comes from the Jackson System Development (JSD) method [Jackson 83], more precisely, from the "function step" of the specification process of this method. In OSM, functional requirements complete models to meet design constraints. For example, if a given piece of software has to be embedded, memory constraints may require specific functions to avoid memory overflow. At least one object from the BCL (e.g. the class "MEMORY" in Eiffel) has to be composed with at least one object from the OOA models (e.g. a class of the OOA models selected to become a class of the OOD models) to address the functional requirement of avoiding memory overflow. When we have underlined the terms "revises", "adjusted" or "refined" in paragraph I., we have emphasized a main issue of design. Model adapting does not come from anywhere but from the "functional requirements". In fact, these terms hide the very nature of adapting, and thus the understandability of the object-oriented software life cycle itself. Let us expand on this idea with another example.

A typical functional requirement linked to the model in figure 2, could be for the process of creating an account (second case):

> What: ensure the understandability of a new account registration number (short and explicit code, quick and easy interpretation: account type? bank agency? ...).
>
> When: each time a new account is created.

This example of functional requirement shows that an object of the OOD models has its origin traced with objects not only from the OOA models and the BCL but also from design constraints. In this sense, an object has to be defined so that appropriate operations achieve this functional requirement: here, a "hierarchical code" class for example which has to be stored in a tool class library for later reuse. So, traceability is a central concept of the object-oriented software life cycle: revisions, adjustments and refinements come from nowhere else but from the "functional requirements".

Finally T, traceability in OSM, is: for O_D which belongs to the OOD models, $O_D=T(O_A{}^1, ..., O_A{}^n, O_{BCL}{}^1, ..., O_{BCL}{}^m, O_{TCL}{}^1, ..., O_{TCL}{}^p, FR^1, ..., FR^q)$ where $O_A{}^1, ..., O_A{}^n$ belong to the OOA models, $O_{BCL}{}^1, ..., O_{BCL}{}^m$ belong to the BCL, $O_{TCL}{}^1, ..., O_{TCL}{}^p$ belong to the tool class libraries and FR^1, ..., FR^q are the "functional requirements".

II3. From selection to merging

Selection is the first activity of OSM as far as objects from different origins have to be selected or "used" to obtain objects of the OOD models. Merging is the second activity of OSM and leads to the defining of combination (another suitable term is "fusion") of an object O_D of the OOD models: it is equivalent to study the term "used". In this definition of traceability, $O_D=T(O_A{}^1, ..., O_A{}^n, O_{BCL}{}^1, ..., O_{BCL}{}^m, O_{TCL}{}^1, ..., O_{TCL}{}^p, FR^1, ..., FR^q)$, the nature of the relationships between O_D and $O_A{}^1, ..., O_A{}^n, O_{BCL}{}^1, ...$ does not appear. The most frequently encountered nature of these relationships is aggregation, inheritance or client/supplier like in Eiffel [Meyer 88]. The purpose of OSM is to develop a flexible approach to the merging activity and, in this sense, to develop a typology of the relationships between O_D and $O_A{}^1, ..., O_A{}^n, O_{BCL}{}^1$, etc. This issue is not developed formally in this article. However, some examples of these relationships will be shown now.

III. Applying OSM

Because OSM is not a method but a rigorous and flexible framework for designing, we develop here an example based on an OMT analysis (see [Rumbaugh 91] from p.105 to p.110). This example deals with a programmable thermostat. Although this article does not address the OMT method, it is necessary to state that analysis in the OMT method produces an "object model", a "dynamic model" and a "functional model". For the example retained here, the "dynamic model" is the most significant model whereas the "functional model" is the least. Since the aim of this article is not to develop analysis itself, we simply depict a part of the "object model" and the "dynamic model" as a synthesis of analysis results — as it has already been exposed, see [Rumbaugh 91] for the complete "dynamic model".

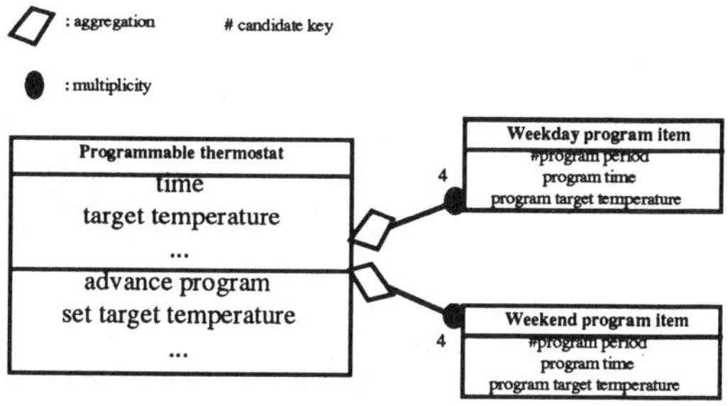

figure 3: an OOA model (OMT "object model")

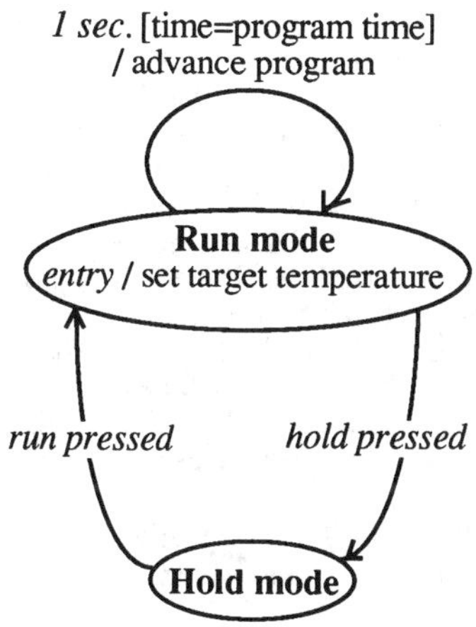

figure 4: an OOA model (OMT "dynamic model")

In the "object model" of figure 3, a "Programmable thermostat" class has a "time" attribute which indicates the current time and a "target temperature" attribute which indicates the current target temperature to maintain. The "Programmable thermostat" class is made up of 4 weekday program items and 4 weekend program items.

In the "dynamic model" of figure 4, when the event "1 sec." occurs for the "Programmable thermostat" class, the "advance program" operation is activated as far as the condition "[time=program time]" is true. In this case, the "Programmable thermostat" class leaves the "Run mode" state and reaches again this state ("entry" keyword). The "set target temperature" is also activated taking into account if it is a weekday or a weekend. In the "Hold mode" state, the weekday program and the weekend program are ignored as far as the event "Run pressed" occurs for the "Programmable thermostat" class.

As already explained, the main objective of analysis is comprehension. From this point of view, the OOA models of figures 3 and 4 are satisfactory ones. However, the OOD model adapted from the OOA models is quite different in the sense that some quite important modifications have occurred. Why? The designer (who, in this example, is not the same person as the analyst) applies the locality principle as defined by Liskov [Liskov 87]: "Locality allows a program to be implemented, understood, or modified one module at a time: (...) 3. Only local reasoning is needed to determine what a program does and whether it does the right thing." (our underlining). According to this logic, the designer builds a class called "Time data" in which he groups time data and computations so that locality increases. Note that in the OOA models, time data does not permit local reasoning insofar as time attributes are distributed among 3 classes. This is a typical decision made during preliminary design which can not and must not occur during analysis. Consequently, model adapting occurs so that the OOD model appears as follows (in a classical approach):

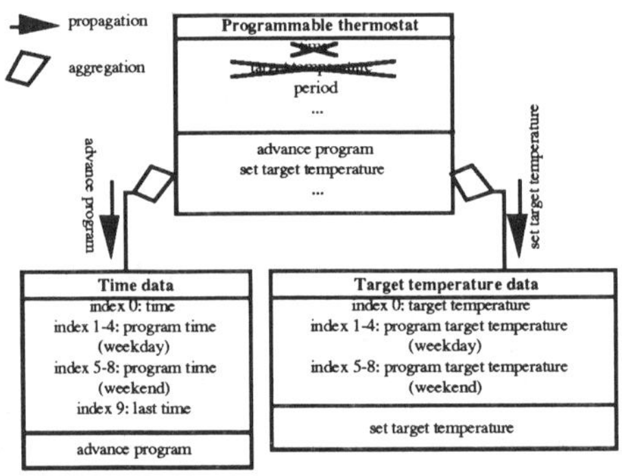

figure 5: an OOD model in a model restructuring approach

In the OOD model of figure 5, the OMT notation has been kept. In such a model, model restructuring leads us to ignore in particular the relationships between the OOA models and the OOD model. Traceability is not highlighted because the deep origin of restructuration does not appear. Thus, the "time" and "target temperature" attributes have been deleted and the "period" attribute has been added from the "Programmable thermostat" class. Design details have been shown in figure 5 so that the "Time data" class and the "Target temperature data" class appear to have the form of an indexed collection. Finally, detailed design leads to this pseudocode for the "advance program" operation which computes the "period" attribute of the "Programmable thermostat" class:

```
refresh time (index 0) from machine clock
if time (index 0) - last time (index 9) >= 1 sec. then
        if change from weekday to weekend or
          from weekend to weekday then
                compute new period value
        else
                if time (index 0) = time (index period)
                then
                        compute new period value
                end if
        end if
end if
refresh last time (index 9) from time (index 0)
```

Model adapting occurs in OSM in a different way and leads to the expression of traceability as follows:

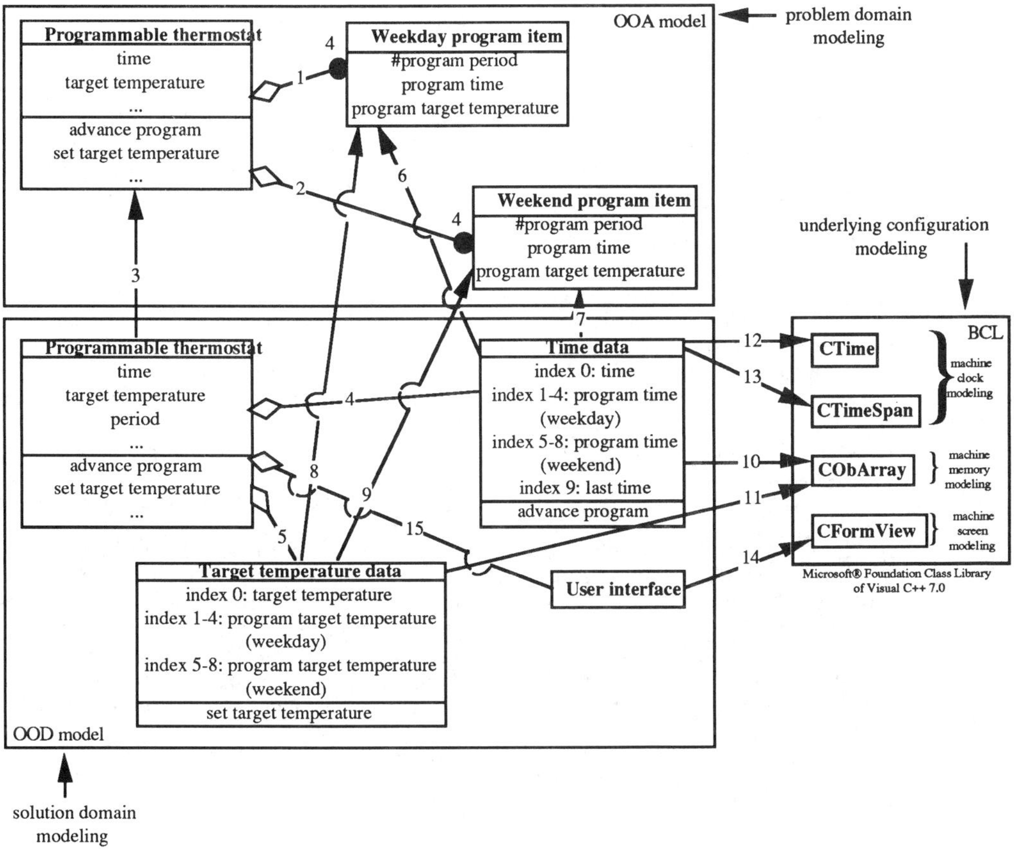

figure 6: an OOD model in a model combination approach

Some comments on figure 6:

— 1, 2, 4, 5 and 15 are five aggregation relationships relative not to the process of model adapting but to the object-oriented models themselves.

— 3 is an inheritance relationship relative to the selection of the "Programmable thermostat" class and its adaptation to design constraints (the "time", the "target temperature", the "advance program" and the "set target temperature" are inherited unlike the "period" which is added when designing).

— 6, 7, 8 and 9 are four relationships which trace the application of the locality principle with the following meaning: "is specified by".

— 10 and 11 are two inheritance relationships relative to the use of a BCL object. 12 and 13 are two client/supplier relationships relative to the use of two other BCL objects.

— 14 is an inheritance relationship relative to a functional requirement at the origin of a specific "User interface" object.

An important remark: in this example, is it possible to consider that the OOA models of figures 3 and 4 are bad ones? In other words, the OOD model of figure 5 may have played the role of an OOA model in place of those of figures 3 and 4, and thus no transition problem between analysis and design should have existed? Do not forget that large object-oriented software development involves many people and it cannot be realistic to consider the object-oriented software life cycle as an iterative and progressive aim switching: what a person does with precise objectives has to be modified (adjusted, refined, revised... or better: traced) by someone else with other precise objectives. In OSM, through the concept of traceability, the hypothesis of aim switching is made early on and facilitates object-oriented software development.

Conclusion

In the object-oriented software life cycle, traceability is, in our opinion, not a subordinate aspect but a natural part of the process of analyzing and designing. The software development process must depend on such a hypothesis in order to facilitate software maintenance.

The idea of stable objects like those from the BCL and the OOA models, and less stable ones like those which come from the "functional requirements" facilitates, in OSM, the iterative and progressive development of objects as combination or fusion of other objects. Object flows depict combination or fusion as a junction area. If the selection activity in OSM seems natural and obvious, the merging activity is more difficult in the software development process: many constraints have to be satisfied and many decisions have to be made while taking into account all the possible kinds of relationships between the objects. Through our experience, object-oriented environments are at the moment quite heterogeneous and do not always facilitate the merging activity viewed in OSM as free from implementation considerations.

Bibliography

[Aksit 92] M.Aksit, L.Bergmans. Obstacles in object-oriented software development, OOPSLA'92 proceedings, p.341-358, 1992.

[Barbier 92] F.Barbier. Object-oriented analysis of systems through their dynamical aspects, JOOP, p.45-51, May 1992.

[Barbier 93] F.Barbier, J.Bézivin. Object-oriented design: the OSM scheme, TOOLS USA'93 proceedings, August 1993.

[Berard 93] E.V.Berard. Essays on object-oriented software engineering, volume 1, Prentice Hall, 1993.

[Edwards 90] J.M.Edwards, B.Henderson-Sellers. The object-oriented systems life cycle, Communications of the ACM, p.143-159, September 1990.

[Jackson 83] M.Jackson. System development, Prentice Hall, CAR Hoare Series Editor, 1983.

[Monarchi 92] D.E.Monarchi, G.I.Puhr. A research typology for object-oriented analysis and design, Communications of the ACM, p.35-47, September 1992.

[Liskov 87] B.Liskov. Data abstraction and hierarchy, OOPSLA'87 addendum to the proceedings, October 1987.

[Meyer 88] B.Meyer. Object-oriented software construction, Prentice-Hall International Editions, 1988.

[Rumbaugh 91] J.Rumbaugh, M.Blaha, W.Premerlani, F.Eddy, W.Lorensen. Object-oriented modeling and design, Prentice-Hall International Editions, 1991.

[Shlaer 91] S.Shlaer, S.J.Mellor. Object lifecycles, modeling the world in states, Yourdon Press Computing Series, 1991.

[Shlaer 93] S.Shlaer, S.J.Mellor. A deeper look at the transition from analysis to design, JOOP, p.16-21, February 1993.

Selected Results from an Empirical Study on Problem Areas and Trends of Object-Oriented Programming

Hermann Sikora
GRZ-Linz, Genossenschafts-Rechenzentrum, Inc.
Goethestr. 80, A-4020 Linz, Austria

Abstract

Selected results are presented from an extensive empirical study conducted as a user survey entitled "Problem Areas and Trends in Object-Oriented System Development". The primary goal of the study was to determine the position of object-oriented programming as seen by practitioners, by means of an extensive picture of their experience and opinions. For this purpose we deliberately handled some questions that might appear trivial because they have—ostensibly—been exhaustively treated elsewhere. The results can serve as the basis for an evaluation of how large the gap is between science and products on the one hand and practical development work on the other hand.

The analyses presented deal with project management, development tools, and the use of inheritance mechanisms. The selection was based on the core statement of the original study, which showed that—despite advanced research results and continuously improved products—the major problems still were in the following areas: (a) development tools that only partially do justice to the paradigm and so inadequately support the exploitation of the potential advantages of object-oriented programming (e.g., reuse); (b) mastering the complexity of class libraries (familiarization and navigation) and (c) the correct use of inheritance mechanisms.

Keywords

object-oriented programming, user survey, project management, tools, class library, application framework, inheritance

1 Motivation and Methodology

There have been relatively few studies to date that (empirically) approach problem areas associated with object-oriented programming (OOP), among them [Fang 93], [Henderson-Sellers 92], [Henderson-Sellers 93], [Henry 90], [Li 93], and [Mancl 90]. The primary goal of this study was to determine the position of OOP as seen by practitioners, by means of an extensive picture of their experience and opinions.

For this purpose, interviews were conducted with 35 OOP developers. The confidential interviews averaged 90 minutes. The 35 questions, designed for free response, were grouped as follows: characteristics and concepts of object-oriented programming languages (OOPLs), class libraries/application frameworks, project management, and trends.

1.1 The Gap between Theory and Practice

Some of the questions and results that we present seem trivial at first glance. This is not because the author intends to rehash topics that have long since been treated exhaustively in the scientific arena. We cannot be satisfied with crossing off topics simply because a multitude of articles have appeared in papers in conference proceedings. Only real solutions that are later proven in practice permit us to consider such topics depleted.

The goal of this study was thus to establish a basis for the evaluation of the extent to which practitioners can profit from scientific findings in the area of OOP by means of corresponding development environments, or whether the general opinion is that—despite advanced research results and continuously improved products—the potential advantages of OOP cannot (yet) be realized adequately and/or with sufficient comfort.

For this reason we chose interviewees who were directly involved in practice: Half of the candidates were from industry; the rest were from the academic sector, although even these were active on the practical end of development (see Section 1.2, "Characteristics of the Sample").

Therefore the study can be seen as a determination of the position of OOP with a strong relationship to practice. Another goal of the study was to substitute concrete empirical results for speculation about the opinions of practitioners. (In the realm of this paper, only a small excerpt from the complete study can be presented.)

1.2 Characteristics of the Sample

In selecting the practitioners, we were careful to assure that they had solid education in software engineering in general and OOP in particular. Furthermore, we selected practitioners who continuously kept themselves informed on the most important scientific publications on the subject of OOP.

We defined goals for the characteristics of the interviewees in the sample according to the following considerations:

- We strove for a balance between practitioners from industry and those from academia.
- An individual interviewee must have at least six months of experience in OOP, whereby a maximum of ca. 20% may have less than one year of experience.
- Approximately 30% of the total sample should have more than three years of experience in OOP.
- The sample is not to be selected according to the OOPL used.
- At least one third of the sample should be persons unfamiliar to the interviewer before the start of the study. These persons are to be reached via contacts at conferences, references by third persons, etc.
- The OOP projects under development by the interviewees should have industrial dimensions (i.e., large projects).

In order to be able to reflect the background of the interviewees, a classification scheme was defined as depicted in Fig. 1. This table includes the absolute and relative numbers for the respective categories.

Furthermore, the participants were differentiated according to additional categories, depending on whether they were from the academic or the corporate sector. In addition, the category *"Mixed"* was defined to cover those persons who were primarily in the academic sector, but were involved in projects under practical conditions for commercial applications.

Figure 2 shows this classification (with absolute and relative numbers). Figure 3 indicates which OOPLs were used by the interviewees. A single respondent was permitted *multiple responses.* As Fig. 3 shows, C++ is the OOPL most used by the interviewees. We emphasize, however, that the sample was not selected according to this criterion.

The industrial OOP projects of the interviewees covered areas such as: development of domain-specific application frameworks (e.g., for the automation of industrial control tasks), CIM applications (e.g., production control station), bank applications, object-oriented development environments, and various tools.

Category	*Developer Experience*	*Typical Characteristics*	*Number*	*%*
A	6 months to 1 year	Familiar/experienced with one OOP-environment	7	20,0
B	1 to 3 years	Experienced with one OOP-environment, familiar with other environments	17	48,6
C	3 years and more	Experienced with more than one OOP-environment, experienced in the design and implementation of class libraries/application frameworks and/or OO programming environments	11	31,4
		Totals:	35	100,0

Fig. 1: Classification scheme for interviewees

Background	*Num.*	*A*	*B*	*C*	*%*	*%(A)*	*%(B)*	*%(C)*
Academic	14	6	4	4	40,0	17,1	11,4	11,4
Corporate	15	1	11	3	42,9	2,9	31,4	8,6
Mixed	6	0	2	4	17,1	0,0	5,7	11,4
Totals:	35	7	17	11	100,0	20,0	48,6	31,4

Fig. 2: Distribution of Interviewees in "Academic", "Corporate" and "Mixed"

Number of Interviewees = 35

Absolute Numbers:

Language/Environment	*Σ*	*A*	*B*	*C*	*Acad.*	*Corp.*	*Mixed*
C++	30	7	15	8	13	12	5
Smalltalk	24	3	10	11	9	8	4
Objective-C	2	0	1	1	0	1	1
Eiffel	6	0	2	4	4	2	0
OO Pascal Dialects	7	2	1	4	3	2	0
Others	12	0	6	6	5	5	2

Relative Numbers:

Language/Environment	*%(Σ)*	*%(A)*	*%(B)*	*%(C)*	*%(Ac.)*	*%(Co.)*	*%(Mix.)*
C++	85,7	20,0	42,9	22,9	37,1	34,3	14,3
Smalltalk	68,6	8,6	28,6	31,4	25,7	22,9	11,4
Objective-C	5,7	0,0	2,9	2,9	0,0	2,9	2,9
Eiffel	17,1	0,0	5,7	11,4	11,4	5,7	0,0
OO Pascal Dialects	20,0	5,7	2,9	11,4	8,6	5,7	0,0
Others	34,3	0,0	17,1	17,1	14,3	14,3	5,7

Fig. 3: OOP languages and environments used by the interviewees (each respondent can have multiple responses)

1.3 Analysis of Results

The survey results were analyzed qualitatively. In the following we present in concise form selected evaluation results related to project management, development tools, and the use of inheritance mechanisms. The complete study results (ca. 100 pages) can be found in [Sikora 93]. Here we selected from this study only the subjects that reflected consensus among the interviewees, with the exception of passages that begin with "individual remarks/opinions".

We employ the following acronyms: AF (application framework), CL (class library), MI (multiple inheritance), OO (object-oriented), OOP (object-oriented programming), OOPL (object-oriented programming language), SI (single inheritance), and CASE (computer aided software engineering). For object-oriented analysis and object-oriented design, we use OOA and OOD, respectively (without intended reference to any product).

2 Selected Analyses

The following questions were selected:

- *What management differences exist between conventional and object-oriented projects?*
- *Which criteria do you use to evaluate a CL/AF product?*
- *What future developments do you see in the area of application frameworks?*
- *What is your opinion of tools for OOA and OOD, and what do you expect of these tools?*

Three questions on multiple inheritance were analyzed collectively under the title

- *Pro and contra multiple inheritance*:
  - *Do you consider multiple inheritance to be problematic?*
  - *Are there problems that can be solved more elegantly with multiple inheritance than with single inheritance?*
  - *Is there a danger of producing bad designs due to multiple inheritance?*

Responses were collated according to content criteria that are listed below with the respective question. The results do not necessarily reflect the opinion of the author.

What management differences exist between conventional and object-oriented projects?

◊ *Life-cycle phase orientation differs from conventional software development*

The process of object-oriented software development also includes phases, but it is characterized more by phases of reuse and rapid prototyping, which produces an incremental working model with more iterations than in conventional development.

◊ *Design quality varies*

The design phase differs considerably from that of conventional programming because the available software building blocks so central to the object-oriented paradigm induce a primarily bottom-up development approach.
The degree of reusability of CLs depends on the quality of their design. Object orientation cannot compensate for poor design decisions. In OOP, design decisions tend to be propagated more than in conventional systems: a designer profits from good design or suffers due to poor design that is imposed by the CL.

◊ *Prototyping is more in the foreground, and redesign is more frequent and easier*

Ideally, a designer should predict all future applications and user requirements in terms of inheritance, which is impossible. In order to still achieve a well-designed CL, proven design principles must be applied and there must be a readiness to constantly (actively) improve the CL. Multiple redesigns of the inheritance hierarchy are the rule rather than the exception. Redesign activities dominate over design activities.

The analysis, design, coding and test phases are significantly shorter than in traditional programming, overlap a great deal, and thus establish a cycle. Naturally, turnaround times must be short.

◊ *Implementation is faster*
The goal of the implementation phase is the reuse of existing building blocks. Design and implementation begin to blend together and the border between them is dynamic.

◊ *Maintenance is simpler and more flexible*
Maintenance activities in the usual sense (contrary to redesign) are easier to carry out because all applications based on a given AF have the same basic structure. Future extensions in the realm of maintenance can never be predicted exactly. OOP offers a flexible approach because the designer can leave many details open for later modification, without encumbering the target application.

◊ *Consistent document structure is accompanied by more complex archiving*
In contrast to conventional programming, OOP offers structural consistency through all documents created in the course of a project, from analysis to design to code documentation. Another difference is the archiving of all resulting documents, especially the code files. System functionality is usually more distributed over significantly more files than in conventional programming.

◊ *The object system and application development are interwoven*
OOP project management covers two areas: the maintenance of the object system (e.g., CL/AF) and the development and maintenance of target applications. CL/AF and application developers must remain in close contact, since both sides can profit from the suggestions of the other group. There are more dependencies between project teams and subprojects and less independent parts than in conventional programming.

◊ *OOP impacts on the division of labor in software development*
Little experience is available in the organization of divided-labor object-oriented system development. The goal is always the design of a class hierarchy, which requires many agreements and a significant flow of information among teams, and to a greater extent than in conventional programming. Agreement on interfaces proves harder to reach because the hierarchy adds another dimension that must be considered.

◊ *Designers must depart from strictly project-oriented thinking*
A new system of incentives needs to be introduced that promotes active striving for not just specific, short- and medium-range project goals, but also long-range goals in the sense of the continuing development of the CL/AF. Projects come and go, but CLs/AFs have greater longevity, which makes appropriate maintenance essential. Strictly project-oriented thinking must be replaced by company-oriented thinking with reuse as a prime goal.

◊ *OOP has implications for cost calculations*
The key question is: "What is the monetary value of a class?" The effects on cost calculation must be considered because classical cost analysis no longer applies.

Which criteria do you use to evaluate a CL/AF product?

◊ *Theoretical and practical evaluation*
The evaluation should be carried out in two parts. First, the theoretical part encompasses the evaluation of the simplicity, completeness, machine independence, and extensibility. The second part consists of a practical trial of how easily an application can be created. Simply working through the documentation is not adequate since, e.g., hundreds of classes prove analytically intangible. We provide the following evaluation criteria:

Product policy

- Supported platforms and standards (hardware, operating systems, window systems, style guides, compilers)
- Maintenance and product support provided by the software manufacturer
- Availability of the source code and the implementation language
- Compatibility with other CLs/AFs
- Interfaces to other systems (e.g., conventional environments, databases)

Available features and concepts

- Available classes and functionality

- Availability of de facto standard classes for general purposes (e.g., collection, string, window classes; basic building blocks)

Design quality of CL/AF
- Plausibility, comprehensibility and general usability of the available concepts (e.g., abstract classes that are used)
- Size and complexity in relation to the functionality
- Depth of class hierarchy and its structural clarity
- Homogeneity (consistently object-oriented or hybrid)
- Logical grouping within the CL/AF (availability of mini-CLs/AFs)
- Concepts to solve basic problems in each application
- Portability via abstract interfaces to operating systems, window systems, and style guides
- Flexibility and simplicity of (re)use
- Power of the abstraction primitives (e.g., the position of the implemented concepts within the hierarchy allowing them to be used and modified simply from anywhere)
- Power of application primitives (e.g., the position of classes that implement visual objects)

Software engineering viewpoint
- Design of the class interface
- Applied programming conventions
- How the features of the underlying language are employed (correct/intended use of specific language features)
- Status of development (new or mature, stable)

Usability (simplicity and efficiency of applications)
- Basic characteristics (generally applicable or problem-specific)
- Learning effort
- Average number of subclasses that need to be defined to achieve an executable application for a given problem domain
- Similarity to other CLs/AFs (extent to which existing know-how can be reused)

Restrictions in relation to
- Object-oriented modeling
- Predefined control flows in the AF

Metrics
- Size of typical target applications after linking
- Run-time efficiency
- RAM and disc storage requirements

Programming environment
- Presence of (graphical) tools (and their integration) for
    - Prototyping-oriented incremental software development (e.g., with a visual component for application painting at the highest level)
    - Navigation (i.e., graphical class browser with hypertext features as a general, central navigation instrument)
    - Archiving and retrieval of class definitions and documentation (i.e., access to the distributed interface of a class with all inherited attributes)
    - Filter mechanisms (e.g., access to hooks with selective blending-out of currently irrelevant details)
    - Debugging and instrumentation (i.e., a dynamic, high-level source code debugger for stepwise execution of methods to become familiar with the existing protocols between objects)
    - Access to meta-information at run time
- Turnaround times (presence of an interpreter with an intelligent incremental linker)
- Source code management (with accommodation of the special aspects of object-oriented programming, e.g., the high degree of scatter of the code)

Documentation
- Source code
- Description of central, abstract concepts
- Cookbook with sample applications of varying levels of complexity
- Tutorials for learning under system supervision (e.g., animation components

for dynamic visualization of the control flow logic)

- Context-sensitive explanatory components to answer questions like
  - What are typical application domains for this class?
  - How is this class used correctly?
  - What relationships exist?

What future developments do you see in the area of application frameworks?

◊ *Slow development*

Development to date has been slower than anticipated. Products are available on the market for very few problem domains (above all, standard data types and user interfaces), and for industrial applications there is practically nothing available. AFs are usually handled in-house by companies, since proliferation out of house would counteract the competitive edge that was achieved by developing the AF and/or no compensation would be made for development costs. There is no sign that this trend will change.

◊ *Domain-specific versus universal application frameworks*

Both domain-specific AFs, which are planned and optimized for a certain application domain, and large, universal AFs can be anticipated, although domain-specific AFs will take the lion's share of future research and development resources.

Examples of application domains include: (network) communication, compiler construction, operating systems, commercial applications (with connections to relational and OO database management systems), object persistence, hypertext, multimedia, and mathematics (e.g., symbolic computation). AFs are also imaginable for docking with domain-specific parts, e.g., for banking or automation. This would be a framework in a framework.

If domain-specific AFs are to work together, then this will be possible only via a very small common denominator, e.g., a common root class `Object`, which only provides fundamental functionality.

Universal AFs will be ones that cover functionality that is not uniquely ascribed to an individual domain. These large AFs have the advantage that no communications problems need to be solved as in multiple smaller AFs. Its features could be compared to an extensive operating system in which only one subset is in active use.

What is your opinion of tools for OOA and OOD, and what do you expect of these tools?

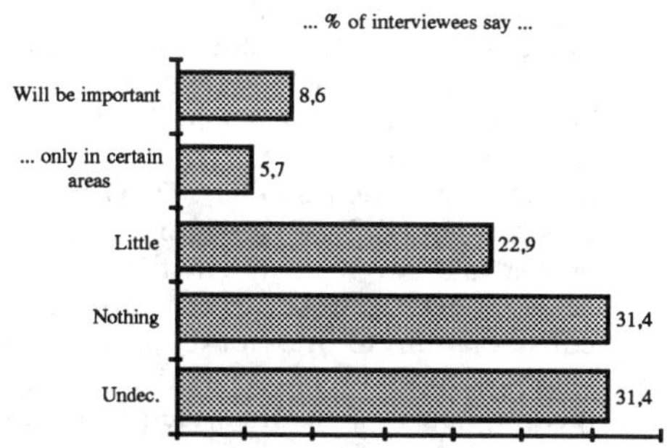

Fig. 4: "What is your opinion of tools for OOA and OOD, and what do you expect of these tools?"

◊ *Wish list*

- Support of various views so that not each user can see everything (inheritance, composition)
- Support for reuse of existing code (CLs)
- Automatic code generation
- Handling of modifications in all directions
- Harmonic, seamless phase transitions
- Integration in a development environment

◊ *Criticism*

- These tools are usually not more than specialized graphic editors that often base on classical methods and show discontinuities. So far there are very few real OOA/OOD methods that can serve as a basis for corresponding tools.
- Analysis and design are rather intangible processes and can hardly be represented graphically; thus expectations and hopes are modest. Nevertheless, as with the buzzword CASE, a corresponding boom

is to be anticipated (especially if object-oriented projects fail). But more experience is necessary in order to be able to develop tools for the practitioner.

- OOA/OOD tools conceal the danger of overdesign (and resulting lost time): Diagrams are drawn to the smallest detail without any real usefulness.
- OOA/OOD tools demand that the designer clearly understands the problem. This means that the use of such tools is destined to fail when requirements are unclear. Good knowledge of the application domain and experience will prove to have more positive effects than the use of an OOA/OOD tool. If a developer is thoroughly familiar with an AF and has a good development environment, then an OOA/OOD tool is superfluous. OOA/OOD tools will disappear into development environments.
- Many OOD tools give too little consideration to the reuse of existing code and primarily support the development of new systems from the ground up.

Pro and contra multiple inheritance

Three questions regarding multiple inheritance are combined for evaluation purposes. First we present questions with short, quantitative answers (Figs. 5 to 7); then we do a qualitative analysis. The *"Undec." (undecided)* in the quantitative analyses covers responses such as *"Cannot be answered in this form"* and *"That depends."* The associated explanations are contained in the subsequent qualitative evaluation, found under the titles "Pro MI" and "Contra MI" below.

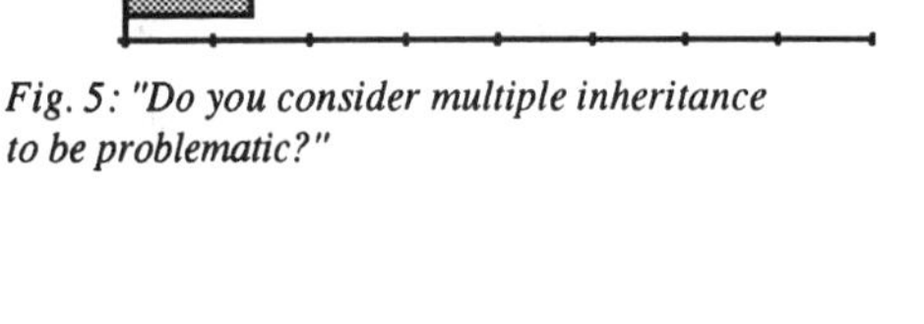

Fig. 5: "Do you consider multiple inheritance to be problematic?"

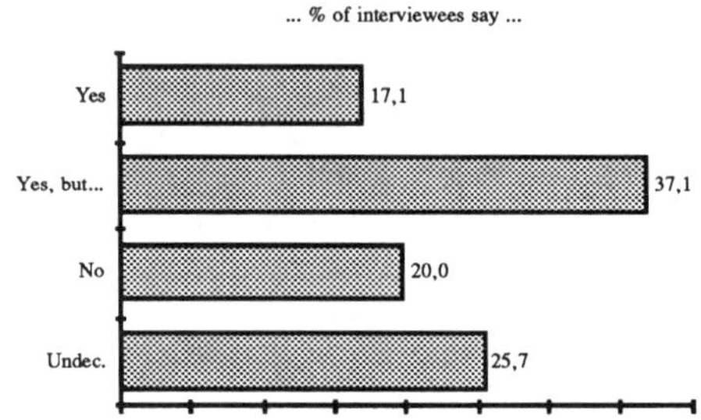

Fig. 6: "Are there problems that can be solved more elegantly with multiple inheritance than with single inheritance?"

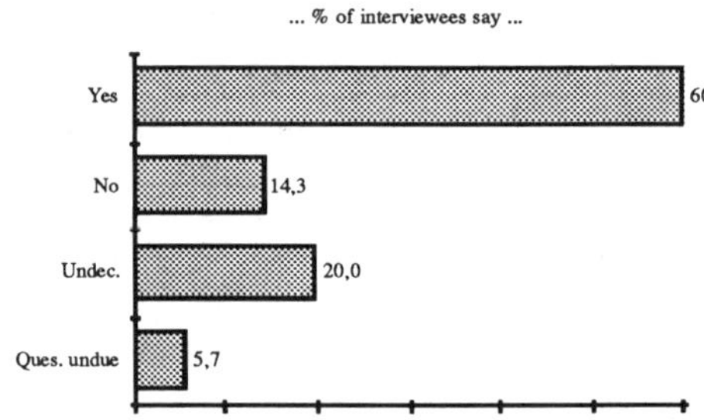

Fig. 7: Is there a danger of producing bad designs due to multiple inheritance?

Pro MI:

◊ *Prerequisites for the useful application of MI*
MI is a powerful concept that can be very useful if the developer has a wealth of experience and works with extreme discipline. The developer must be aware that the elegance of an MI solution is generally accompanied by greater structural complexity.

If this experience prerequisite is fulfilled, MI affords more advantages than drawbacks, particularly if it is important to achieve a 1:1 representation of the analysis phase and MI principles were applied during analysis. MI does not necessarily produce a more elegant solution, but a more logical one with respect to the mental model if this model cannot be expressed naturally with SI. Despite the availability of appropriate technologies (e.g., wrapping, object composition) certain, unambiguous, generally applicable guidelines are lacking for converting MI solutions to SI.

◊ *Application examples*
Plausible MI applications seldom exist, but they do exist:

- *Linking of class libraries:* Given the task of having to link two or more CLs, MI generally provides the only feasible (although admittedly difficult) approach.
- *Support of multiple views:* In working with graphic objects, it is often necessary to support multiple views of them. Although such tasks can also be handled with SI, there are situations in which MI designs represent the more elegant design decision.
- *Support of portable applications:* A hardware-independent CL, for example, encapsulates hardware-dependent protocols. These are combined via MI with hardware-independent classes in order to achieve a hardware-specific version.

Contra MI:

◊ *Various views and mixing them*
Two perspectives have to be considered in viewing an MI application, the *expression* and the *code levels*. The former involves the formulation of meaningful semantics (data modeling). Many MI applications lack clear semantics; it is often only a case of wanting to comfortably handle various kinds of classes in the class library at some location. The use of (multiple) inheritance in today's systems mixes these two views. MI networks are simpler to build than SI hierarchies, but in many cases a confusing of the *"has-a"* and *"is-a"* relations is evident. This indicates a lack of understanding of the problem.

◊ *Complexity*
MI is simple only in the syntactic sense; its semantics are highly complex. A CL with MI represents a network structure, which is much less comprehensible than a tree structure that results from SI. If MI is used frequently, a number of difficult design problems are generated, and reuse and maintenance are complicated because they require a deeper knowledge of the class network. It proves nearly impossible to follow control flow paths in AFs that base primarily on MI.

◊ *Few plausible applications*
Many MI examples cited in the literature are trivial, incorrect and/or far fetched. These examples usually base on disjunct sets, which are easy to realize in MI, yet they do not actually profit from MI. One of the few examples in which the application of MI eases comprehension is the special case of the mixing of protocols that are represented by classes that differ significantly in their inheritance structure.

◊ *Wanton application of MI*
MI—more than other concepts of OOP—incorporates the temptation to abuse. With sufficient, thorough thought, an SI solution can be found that makes the MI solution and its associated problems superfluous. An initial feeling that MI should be used is insufficient justification. Wanton application of MI generates the problem of maintaining ever growing classes that contain extraneous components.

◊ *Conflict resolution*
The mechanisms for conflict resolution (when identical names are inherited) naturally present a further dimension of complexity. In order to avoid losing an overview, only small MI classes should be designed, and these should ideally be located near the root of a treelike network. The mechanisms offered in today's languages are insufficiently transparent: It is often not easy to answer questions ad hoc with certainty. In fact, MI permits differing semantics in various languages.

◊ *Restricted flexibility*
Combining various protocols is a static process. Flexibility is limited, and the compiler requires more information at compile time compared to an SI solution with the wrapping concept. The dynamic SI variant consists of distributing the protocol over several classes, which leads to an object composition: one object is in the foreground, while other objects are written to it. This is not visible at the interface, but control is more precise and fine tuning is possible. The drawback of this SI solution is the additional effort, since the target object must delegate

certain tasks. This drawback is relativized, however, because the MI solution also demands additional effort in that conflicts must be resolved.

◊ *Individual remarks/opinions (pro and contra)*

- Normally only certain thought patterns, rather than a concept itself, lead to poor design. If MI is used as a fetish, this will obviously lead to poor design, even if solid intellectual achievement is available. MI demands a high degree of discipline, yet it would be incorrect to forbid MI.
- The use of MI depends on the level. On the design level MI is essential, but this does not apply at the implementation level. If MI is used in implementation, it must be tamed to avoid *spaghetti-inheritance*. The question "When should which be applied?" must always have an answer.
- It is already a challenge to coordinate a team that is to work together on a CL that is based on SI. MI dramatically intensifies this problem. MI is contrary to the motto "Keep it simple!".

3 Final Remarks and Summary

All interviewees showed very positive attitudes about OOP. They considered their time at developing with OOP to be more efficient and more satisfying than previous development work.

Despite the multitude and quality of theoretical work in recent years and the continuing enrichment and improvement of products on the market, there was consensus on certain important problem areas of OOP that are not considered as solved or adequately solved. The primary problem areas are:

- *Mastering the complexity of CLs/AFs:*
  Much of the complexity that is avoided during development by using a CL/AF naturally does not disappear, but is only dislocated to other time-demanding areas, such as the processes of familiarization with and navigation through a CL/AF.
- *Documentation of design decisions and patterns:*
  To enable an application developer to use a CL/AF correctly and efficiently, it is necessary to understand certain central design decisions and patterns. To motivate the CL/AF designers to keep their documentation thereof complete, current and consistent, (better) tools are needed to support this process.
- *Class retrieval:*
  Archiving classes and later retrieving them on the basis of specific requirements remains an unsolved problem. Currently a developer can usually do no more than a simple search for suitable classes in the realm of navigation through the CL/AF.
- *Debugging:*
  In the case of hybrid languages, debuggers that accommodate the specialties of OOP are rare. Debuggers from integrated object-oriented development environments can serve as models, but even they need more attention.
- *Project Management:*
  Practical approaches to project management that incorporate the peculiarities of OOP are lacking. Company-wide development environments must actively support the view that a CL/AF represents the know-how and thus the fundamental capital of a software firm that vests in OOP. Reuse-programming must supplant the conventional project-oriented approach in order to actually exploit the potential advantages of OOP.

Considering the positive experiences and attitudes of the interviewees with respect to OOP in general, it is surprising to hear their sober prognosis for developments in the area of AFs and their generally negative acceptance of tools for OOA and OOD.

References

[Fang 93] Fang, Z., Lowther, B., Oman, P., Hagemeister, J.: Constructing and Testing Software Maintainability Assessment Models. In: Proceedings of the IEEE-CS International Software Metrics Symposium, May 21-22, Baltimore, MD, 1993

[Henderson-Sellers 92] Henderson-Sellers, B.: Some Metrics for Object-Oriented Software Engineering. In: Proceedings of Tools 6, Sydney 1992

[Henderson-Sellers 93] Henderson-Sellers, B.: The Economics of Reusing Library Classes. Journal of Object Oriented Programming, Vol. 6, No. 4, 1993

[Henry 90] Henry, S. M., Humphrey, M.: A Controlled Experiment to Evaluate Maintainability of Object-Oriented Software. In: Proceedings of the IEEE Conference on Software Maintenance, San Diego/Los Alamitos, CA, 1990, 258-265

[Li 93] Li, W., Henry, S.: Maintenance Metrics for the Object Oriented Paradigm. In: Proceedings of the IEEE-CS International Software Metrics Symposium, May 21-22, Baltimore, MD, 1993

[Mancl 90] Mancl, D., Havanas, W.: A Study of the Impact of C++ on Software Maintenance. In: Proceedings of the IEEE Conference on Software Maintenance, Los Alamitos, CA, 1990, 63-69

[Sikora 93] Sikora, H.: Problem Areas and Trends of Object Oriented System Development: An Empirical Study (in German). Upper Austrian Chapter of the Austrian Chamber of Commerce, Linz, Austria, 1993

Embedding of rule-based expert system capabilities in object-oriented applications by using or simulating active behaviour.

Ray Fernández Rupérez, ray@euskom.spritel.es
Dpto. de Lenguajes y Sistemas Informáticos, Facultad de Informática San Sebastián, Spain.
Ados Soluciones Software, Mugako Ibilbidea 1, of.4, Lasarte, Spain.

Craig Jones, Department of Computer Science, Univ. of Aberdeen, Scotland, UK

José Ramón Zubizarreta, jipzuaij@si.ehu.es
Dpto. de Lenguajes y Sistemas Informáticos, Facultad de Informática de San Sebastián, Spain.

1 Abstract

This paper explores the embedding of deductive and reactive capability, in the form of rule support, in applications developed in an object-oriented language.

The presented design shows how this capability can be attached with minimum -and deterministic-change to an existing system, using a mix between the active rule approach and the traditional production rule system approach, so that a compromise can be achieved between space use and efficiency.

We focus in the reuse of existing rule sets, with minimum or no change. These are usually expressed in knowledge-base or expert system languages (in our case, an OPS5-like one).

Inference engines usually monitor working memory changes by polling on a change set. We revise this by considering the start of an inferencing period as the action of an active rule. Active rules are attached to the class definition of objects to monitor certain change events. The premises of the rules are then evaluated by each affected object, under the control of an inference engine adapted for this, which eventually fires the actions expressed in the rules, in a conventional manner.

From TOOLS EUROPE '94 (Technology of Object-Oriented Languages and Systems).

2 Overview

2.1 Introduction.

Rules can be used for performing different types of tasks such as production of facts, integrity constraint declaration, deductive concept definition, etc. Active rules are those evaluated when a certain event happens.

Expert systems are one of the main use of rule sets and apply them to a dynamic set of entities (known as 'working memory' in this context). Also commonly, rules are added to database systems (relational or object-oriented) as an extension or in a database programming language. In the latter case, the rules are the application; in the former, the environment (that is the database's behaviour) is altered so that applications based on rules can be written. One can see tasks where rules would be interesting if only we did not need to change the environment to use them: input validation, semantic consistency on an invoicing application, optimum landing path determination for the next plane arrival. These tasks are usually accomplished by adding interpreted subsystems (e.g., input validation masks, or external binding to the landing path determination) with an expert system tool and by manual hard-coding to provide semantic consistency.

We present a system for adding rules to any object-oriented application. If the final objective is the development of an expert system, then such original application would be nothing more than passive "working memory", together with the user interface. If the final objective is an invoicing application, then the original does not need to have any restriction checking mechanism, as all of them can be added as rules.

The result of this project has been an Expert System Library ('ESL' from here on) designed and implemented in Eiffel [Meyer92]. The design is not dependent on this host-language, though, and maintaining a type system is possible with it (although few languages are as type safe as Eiffel).

The classes designed allow knowledge about the entities of the application to be represented, and provides knowledge representations for premises, actions, meta-actions, rules and modules. The entities of the application are used as structured facts by the knowledge base. Expert system inferencing with rule priorities is provided, with support for uncertainty. Modules are used to group rules into semantically linked knowledge chunks. Multiple rule sets and one truth maintenance system can be active simultaneously.

Many rule sets exist in the many expert systems already developed. The embedding schema and the ESL presented below, have been developed with its reuse in mind. These rules are written in several languages. We focus on OPS5-like ones [Forgy82], as the rule sets we need to reuse are written using members of this family [Pikaza92]. Completely new rule expression languages, suited for typed OO, can be created. But by keeping mainly the old syntax as a front-end, then translating to the host language (Eiffel for the ESL), existing rule sets are simply '*dropped*', and the experts need not be retrained in a new knowledge representation language. On the other hand, the power of the host language will be retained for the action part and the condition of the premises.

The inference engine of the expert system, as described in [Fernández93, after Pikaza92], has been specified to perform inferencing using forward and backward chaining, with support for rule priorities, uncertainty, and truth maintenance systems. The ESL allows multiple expert systems to be integrated with the application, with each one operating independently upon it.

Many related or similar applications to our can be cited, both on the activity side (KEE's *gauges*, LOOPS' *active values*, ADAM's *active rules* [Diaz 91]) and the rule-set side (OPS5, NEXPERT, Prolog). MAMUR [Pikaza92], and the PIDA proyect (to be published) were the main motivations for this project; KEE and ADAM and have been taken into account in different moments of the development.

The Sather language [Omohundro93] has been taken into account at certain design moments (the 'hook' mechanism described below is patterned after Sather's attribute access hiding).

2.2 Outline of the embedding process and its outcome.

The process for the embedding is the following:

- A base application exists. The objects of this application represent the domain of the knowledge to be expressed.

- A structured set of knowledge to enforce on the application exists, expressed as rules. The knowledge is structured into families (rules that must always be true (truth maintenance set), validity rules (invariants of classes), etc.) and each family can be a hierarchy of modules. The rule expression language can be as expressive as the language in which the application is written (*host* language), as they will be finally translated into such code. This paper uses a an OPS5-like rule expression language, that keeps the host's syntax for certain parts.

- The original application is changed in the following ways:

    - Events: any attribute used in any rule has its change monitored by 'hooking' on the change method (or procedure, member function, ...). Sather [Omohundro93] offers a single change method for each attribute, with the name of the attribute, making 'hooking' easy, as any read and write on an attribute can be monitored by hiding the original one under a layer. ADAM [Díaz91] also defines a access and modification method for each attribute. C++ allows the redefinition of the assignment operator. The Sather and ADAM approach is used in Eiffel by enforcing attribute change to be encapsulated in a single method. This represents a slight enforcement on the original application, on the other hand, it is also a good software engineering practice.

- Conditions: Each class with monitored attributes is given functions to evaluate the conditions expressed in the rules; one function per different premise in the rule set. The monitoring 'hook' will test these premises. Premises are owned by the type class on which they pose a test. This allows the rule base to use the type hierarchy of the application: premises on abstract types -those with no instances- can be defined, because the object will dispatch the evaluation of those premises to the parent abstract type.

- New elements added to the original application:
  - Actions: A class is defined for each rule, inheriting the behaviour of a class and providing effective implementation of the execution method (matching the rule' s action part). Each time that rule's action is to be executed, an instance of this class is created with properly instantiated parameters (i.e., the results of the unification process on the unbound variables of the rule).
  - Inference engine: Any inferencing mechanism whose interface with working memory (through premises and actions) is well defined, can be used. We chose the RETE procedure [Forgy82], and adapted it to a safe object-oriented language such as Eiffel and redesigned it for this kind of interface [Fernández93].
- Dynamic behaviour: From each part's viewpoint (application and inference engine) they are an application and an expert system. The application is stopped each time a monitored event happens, and an iteration of the inferencing process is run.

2.3 Object-Oriented Programming as the Knowledge Representation.

High-level languages such as production rule languages, object-oriented programming languages, and procedural deduction systems provide the expert system builder with more degrees of freedom than an expert system shell. The rule-based approaches are well suited to the expression of knowledge of the 'if ... then' form, but are less well suited to describing complex objects and the relationships between them. Object-oriented programming languages provide programmers with an alternative framework for organising knowledge in terms of declarative representations of domain objects. The procedural side of the problem solver is factored into the classes of these objects, which contain their own procedures and which can communicate with each other.

Another advantage of object-oriented programming is that it is a more analogical style of knowledge representation than that found in systems based on predicate calculus or production rules. Instead of knowledge about a domain object being scattered among the many rules or axioms that reference it, the knowledge is collected into one place, which is a representation of the object itself. This chunking is virtual, in the sense that not all of the information about an object will necessarily be stored in the corresponding computational object, but it still holds that, to issue a request to an object, the representation is dealt with directly by sending a message to it.

3 Analysis.

Given the previous work to this project [Pikaza92], the RETE matching algorithm [Forgy82] was chosen for the inference engine. The analysis overview must start with the main functionality modules of resulting applications (figure 1).

Figure 1. Main modules and their relationship.

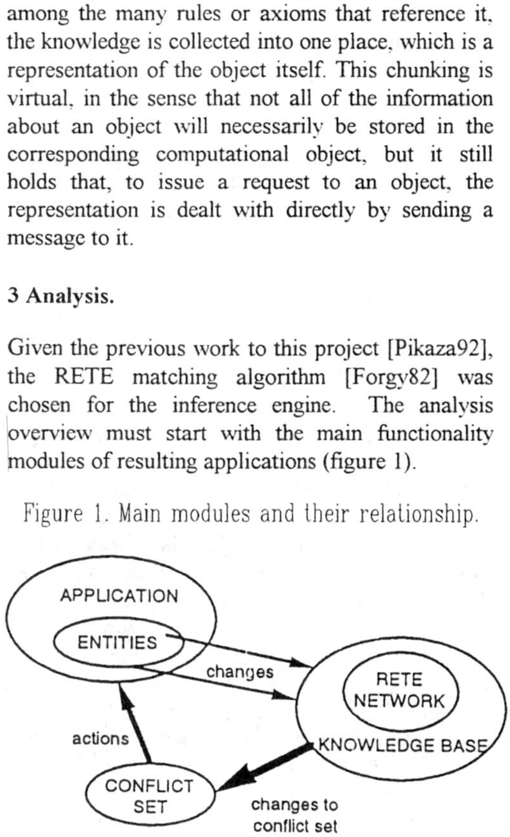

The RETE algorithm is well known; detailed explanation of its adaptation to an environment such as that enforced by figure 1 is described in [Fernández93]. References to RETE details have been avoided in this paper.

The expert system needs to monitor those entities of the application involved in the knowledge base: this could be done by regular inspections of the entities or by altering the entities so that they inform the expert system of all changes to themselves - specialisation of entities can be done neatly in object-oriented designs by the specialisation of classes. The former method has the disadvantage that it needs to scan all entities of the application and then compare them with those of the previous state to determine which ones have changed, whilst the second method is much more efficient as only entities which have changed are considered by the expert system. Care needs to be taken that all changes to an entity are detected.

We want our system to have safety, to keep the typing of the implementation language, and the minimum interpretative functionality and code duplication.

3.1 Knowledge Representation.

The expert system is to use the entities of the application as the 'facts' of the expert system. We wish to avoid rewriting the application in order to incorporate the expert system, and so the structure of the assertions and facts of the knowledge base is constrained to the structure of the application - as the application can be any Eiffel program, the structure of the facts will be Eiffel objects, their attributes and the values of these attributes. Assertions, then, and patterns upon assertions will have three levels: the object level (*frame*, in the usual Artificial Intelligence terminology), the attribute level and the value level. Entities of the object level and value level are actual Eiffel objects, whereas attributes are merely a method of accessing the values of an object.

The knowledge base this project was designed to deal with is written in an OPS5-like language, used in a LISP-based expert system (MAMUR, a diabetes diagnosis system [Pikaza92]).

A detailed explanation of the structure of rules as used in Artificial Intelligence, of the rootings of OPS5-like languages to this, and the adaptation needed for the linking of such structure and syntax to a pure object oriented language is beyond the scope of this conference, and will be presented elsewhere.

3.2 Knowledge Representation and the inferencing mechanisms.

The RETE interface to the 'world' (that is, its working memory) as specified in the references has been slightly changed, following fig.1, so that it can be substituted by other inference engine, and linked with an application without large disruptions. The image of the application the inferencing mechanism will perceive is a collection of premises (in RETE, each path linking its internal structures to the objects it is inferencing on, corresponds to a premise; premises can then be used to provide the link to an application, given they perform as defined by the algorithm: this fits perfectly the encapsulation and modelling support of the object oriented languages).

3.3 Premises.

A premise will extract the values from the attribute upon which it is defined and if necessary perform a test at the value level. In this way, the functionality of the top part of the RETE network is provided by the knowledge representation.

When unification is needed (unbound values are present in the premise), the inference system needs only the object and the value of the attribute to perform the unification; so that, the object is known by the moment it is asked for a value, which can be supplied as the evaluation value of the premise (normally, losing its type information until it is 'returned' to the application in the form of an instance of the unbound value to the rule' s action, where the type information can be retrieved, because the dynamic type of the value object is known, as it is the type of the attribute inspected).

The consequence of Eiffel not representing attributes as slots (so that they can be retrieved by inspection on the class) is that to extract an attribute's value the attribute needs to be explicitly named, which implies that premises will have to be represented as Eiffel code. The production of internal knowledge representation is harder now as it requires generation of Eiffel code. Strictly speaking, it is possible to cheat with the languages internal constructs to access the attributes by name, but this requires going beyond the standard Eiffel.

3.4 Actions.

For the same reason as premises, actions will need to use Eiffel code to express its actions upon the attributes of the application's entities. The representation will have to include a method for the actions to instantiate the variables contained within themselves with values bound to the variables by the unification mechanisms. The use of Eiffel code in the representation of actions will be a large advantage allowing almost any action upon the object to be performed, yet with the safety of object-orientedness to restrict actions to those features exported by the data class.

3.5 Rules.

A rule is a structure of premises and actions. The rules are used by the expert system to provide a structure on the knowledge so that inferencing can be performed. The RETE procedure will also need to use the rules to construct its network. A procedure in the rule's class could perform this on the current rule - then as the knowledge base creates its rule objects each rule can invoke the RETE constructor.

For the RETE constructor, the rule needs to provide the premises in a sequential manner and in a manner that allows access to the premise's truthness value, to link to the working memory. To create actions, the RETE constructor will need to be able to determine which variables are involved in the right-hand side of the rule; this information can be provided by the rule. In addition, this terminal node will need to communicate its results, in order for rule instantiation to be performed, to the rule that created it. The rule, then, needs to be able to produce instantiations of its actions for a particular set of variable bindings produced by unification while inferencing.

3.6 The output.

The inference engine will normally obtain a set of instantiated rules to be executed (their premises fulfilled). This is the conflict set. The final part of the expert system engine chooses one of them -priorities (static and dynamic), certainty and other mechanisms exist. The output of the expert system functionality is ... nothing!; from the application' s point of view, objects change by themselves, and actions have been executed.

4 The example application.

Throughout the rest of this document, the examples presented will refer to a simple example application, that allows the user to define the national costumes of the countries of the world.

We will assume that some experts exist know the arcane relationships between the colours of the HATs of these costumes and the FLAGs of the represented country. The knowledge presented in the rules tries to reflect part of these experts' knowledge.

So that, the application has objects of type HAT and FLAG, and these have one or several attributes to reflect its colour. The rules link the colours of the flags between them (to allow or forbid certain combinations, ...) and with the hats' ones.

5 Design.

Following Monarchi's typology [Monarchi92], OMT [Rumbaugh91] was chosen as the analysis and design methodology instead of the Eiffel-based methodology B.O.N. It turned out though that abstract Eiffel was used primarily for the design stage. This was mostly due to Eiffel's powerful facility of deferred functions and assertions that allow models to be built relatively easily. This has been a very pleasant, and productive, surprise.

Where needed, GOOD diagrams (Graphics for Object-Oriented Design), produced by a tool supplied with Eiffel to document designs, are used to illustrate the designs. The nodes represent classes, single arrows show inheritance relations between classes, while double arrows show client-supplier relations. Deferred classes (those not includint implementation for some specified feature) are marked with an asterisk. Section 6 will present an example.

5.1 Expert System Connection.

How do we connect an expert system to an application? There exists a spectrum of solutions:

one extreme being that a programmer is forced to rewrite the entire application, the other is a compiler that is able to smoothly perform the changes to the application in order to connect it. There are many solutions between these, most involving the programmer to alter the application code to some degree. If this has to be done then we wish it to be done safely; this implies having clear procedures that the programmer is to follow and ideally forcing changes with the use of the compiler's error-checking as a 'stick' to drive the programmer along the correct path to expert system connection.

The main problem with expert system connection is the addition of code to detect changes in the application's entities - code segments like these are lately referred to as *hooks* (*gauges*, *active values*, ...). We can use a solution without hooks, but this involves the programmer extending the application to record all changes to its attributes involved in the expert system and then passing this to the expert system. In addition, for the truth maintenance system we will require hooks to implicitly fire the expert system.

These *hooks* clearly remind us of active behaviour on the application's entities, and in fact, that is the approach taken: the applications objects will have active rules on them, having as the only action the firing of the inferencing mechanisms. For the moment, only change is monitored, although the mechanism described can allow extensions. The bibliographical references on active behaviour explain the semantics of these *hooks*.

Application classes will connect to the ESL by having their name changed (and so hidden to the original clients and heirs), and a new class with the original name will inherit from it, and then add the functionality needed (hooks, ...).

In Eiffel, this will involve renaming attributes and showing features with the old attribute name that access and change it, so that the change can be monitored. The more a language offers towards data hiding, the more it will help us to implement this approach: we have already mentioned how Sather and ADAM are more supportive to this approach, as both disallow the direct access to a variable (or 'slot', 'attribute', ...); KEE has *gauges* that can be activated on every change to an attribute's value (usually linked to visual controls or displays); CLOS and C++ will allow to redefine the assignment operator (:=), thus making the addition of the mechanism easier.

The obvious disadvantage to this approach is the extra overhead of a function call on a read access to an attribute involved in the knowledge base. To compensate for this we could record those attributes used by the expert system which are very volatile and remove the hooks upon them. The expert system can assume instead that on every invocation of the expert system that these attributes have changed and process them accordingly.

It can be seen that normally the premises of the knowledge base are not highly volatile or even if they are we can use another attribute that is updated (i.e., *copied*) on expert system invocation from the volatile attribute - providing a kind of sampling function.

5.2 Attribute monitoring.

The input to the inference mechanism is defined to be the set of premises, instantiable on objects to acquire their truth values. Hooks in the application generate actions to indicate changes in the application's state.

We will use the term '*token*' to refer to a change in the application's state, relevant to the rule set (i.e., a change of the value of an attibute inspected by the premises of a rule). The tokens need to be routed to the correct premise items (see 3.2) to enter the inference mechanism. Each token can affect several premises (each with a different test).

We make the premises actual objects, connected to the inference mechanisms and the class (here considered as the family of objects of same type) of which the premise inspects an attribute. Tokens are routed to the premises directly from the object, as part of the active behavior implemented by the *hooks*. Making premises entities in their own right seemed necessary as they will need to be embedded in the rules of the knowledge base as well as the object'sclass.

5.3 Representing Premises.

We wish to represent the premises using code with a simple deterministic structure if the code is eventually to be produced automatically. Conceptually too, we would perhaps wish the premises functionality to be self-contained. With these ideas in mind, we come to the conclusion of representing each premise as an individual class. The general functionality can be provided by generalised premise classes, whilst the code specific to the premise is implemented in the premise's class.

The use of a generic type parameter in the general premise class, will allows the premise's object's type to be passed, though when we wish to access a specific feature of the type we need to inherit from a specific version, for example: PREMISE[FLAG]. In addition, other classes can be inherited from to access constants (with which the tests are done).

What does the inference mechanism actually require from the premises? Either those tokens that have successfully passed the premise's tests or the ability to answer a query from the inference engine as to whether a token is acceptable or not. The former approach prevents the need for the inference engine to carry the object's type (as no further object-specific operations are required to do the inference), so that direction was chosen. In addition, the RETE algorithm will require the variable names used in the premise for unification. As these are static they can be passed to the RETE system on its creation (i.e., at the start of the application run).

As one premise object will now perform the necessary extraction and value comparison tests, the routing information in the object's class just needs to pass the application object to the correct premise object, and which change has just occurred. Each premise is specific to just one attribute of the object, so the invocations of the relevant premises can be placed in the hooks of the attribute's change function.

5.4 Representation of Actions.

As discussed in the analysis section, actions will need to use Eiffel code as their representation - the question is as to whether to express each action separately in its own class or not however, as actions are not shared this seems unnecessary, unless we were going to require actions as separate units for backward chaining.

The actions will use a set of variable bindings produced by unification, to produce instantiations of themselves. Developing this idea leads to the design of having the actions of a particular rule expressed in a class with their instantiations as instances of this class. As an instantiation of a rule really only requires the actions with their variables instantiated, it will be these instances of the actions' class that will be used by the conflict set. This is similar to the approach of having command classes defining arguments for the command, and command instances when the argumentes are supplied, as suggested in [Meyer88].

A method needs to be found of allowing actions to be expressed using the unbound variables of the premises. On reflection, it can be seen that a reference to the appropriate object is needed so that we can perform actions upon it. These references can be provided by the functions in the class, which extract the appropriate object from the variable bindings. However, this design is inefficient as each action that uses a variable will cause the function to search the variable bindings again. Instead of using functions, we can perform the extraction of the objects from the variable bindings at the creation of an instantiation and assign them to the value of the attributes of the class.

A flaw with these designs is that the instances of the unbound variable will be of type ANY as the object types are discarded on entry to the inference mechanism (so that it can be written to handle any type of data). To re-instantiate the type, an assignment attempt can be performed - we know the type of the object we are expecting (unless, of course, there is an error in the implementation), so it is just a matter of telling the compiler what we believe; appropriate assertions (supported by Eiffel) can be used to check for errors. The mechanism used (called *reverse assignment* in Eiffel), is not considered good engineering practice in general. In this case, its use is correct as no *fail* possibility exists -except, as said, an implementation fault-.

The design is illustrated by an example set of actions of a rule in figure 2. The system supports actions to be executed taking the certainty of the action (as it is the conclusion of a rule that can have certainty-weighted premises), as shown by the figure. The action shown does inspection or modification of the HAT and FLAG objects, that fulfill the premises or the rule; these objects are passed to the action in a VARIABLE_BINDINGS object (thus a variable lenght argument).

Figure 2. GOOD diagram for actions.

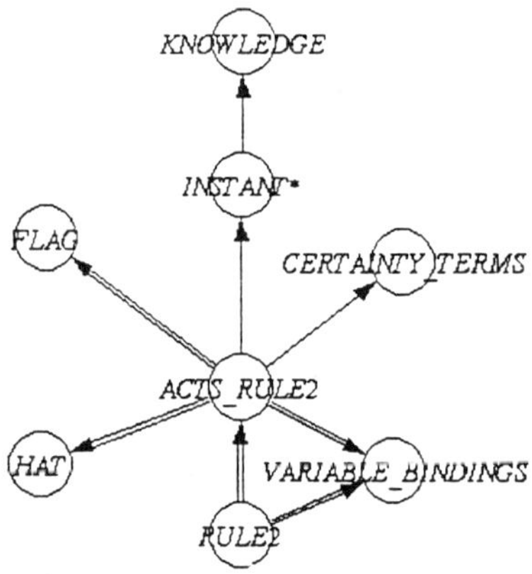

5.5 Representation of Rules.

Rules need to contain a collection of premises and actions and a method of producing instantiations of itself. Rules must also be registered with the inferencing mechanism (so that they create its data structures accordingly).

The premises will need to be accessed sequentially, so this implies a list representation. Further, we will know how many premises a rule has at compile time, plus the premises of a rule will not need to change their order, so the most efficient representation could be used (Eiffel provides an appropriate structure, FIXED_LIST, combining the properties of lists and arrays).

The subscription mechanism can then easily use this representation to obtain the first premise, the next premise and to see if the current premise is the last one of the rule.

The actions of the rule will consist of actions objects that have been instantiated with a set of variable bindings. The rule does not need to be connected to these actions but it does require a mechanism for creating them. To create an instantiation of the actions, the rule will have to ask the correct actions class to create an instance of itself and then use a set of variable bindings to instantiate the actions.

The functionality of the rules that is not specific to a particular rule is collected into a general rule class.

To create a rule, we need to store references to its premises in its premise list. These references are obtained using the method of inheriting the reference from a class. The references are produced by 'once' functions -explained below- that create the premise objects on their first invocation and thereafter return a reference to it. Any other object wishing to access it just needs to inherit the function - as we have multiple inheritance in Eiffel the use of inheritance in this manner does not constrain the class at all. This method is the standard method of sharing objects in Eiffel, and provides a neat solution to this general object-oriented problem.

Figure 3. GOOD diagram for a rule set

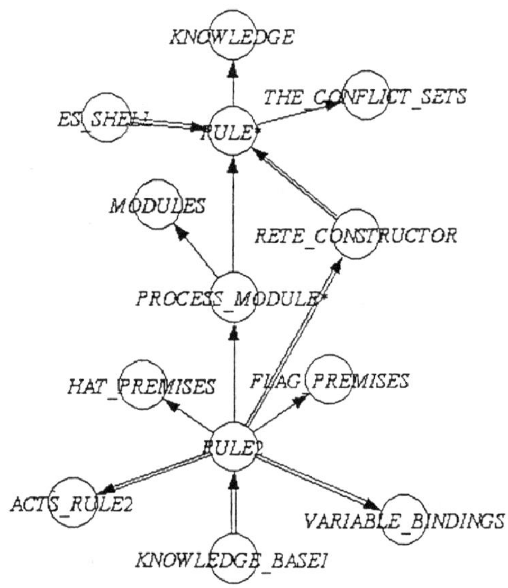

Each rule stores a list of which unbound variables are used by the actions, so that the variable bindings are passed to the instantiation of a rule. The rule also contains behaviour to join the conflict set and execute its action. The design is illustrated by figure 3, which also illustrates how rules can be grouped into modules (*PROCESS_MODULE* and *TMS_MODULE* in the example). The use of the modules for structuring the knowledge will be presented elsewhere.

5.6 The Expert System.

So far we have seen how the individual objects of the expert system have been designed and sketches of their implementation. Now it is time to reinforce how they all connect and work together to produce an expert system.

The first step is how all the objects are created and connected. To start this the expert system is referenced. The reference is done using the standard Eiffel method of using 'once' objects -explained below-:

```
class EXPERT_SYSTEM_1
...
expert_system_1: KNOWLEDGE_BASE1 is
once Result.Create end;
```

The first invocation causes the object to be created, while subsequent invocations will return the same reference to the object. Those classes wishing to use the reference simply inherit from it.

The expert system has been written so that it is connected to an application; during the initialisation of this application it needs to ask the expert system to build itself by creating it. All the knowledge base's rules are then be created and stored into two lists - one for normal rules and one for truth-maintenance rules. Each rule builds a list of its premises causing the creation of those that have not already been created (as the premises can be shared, a rule's premise may have already been referenced and hence created).

Each premise on its creation, registers with the inferencing mechanism. The same holds for rules as well as their actions.

5.7 Dynamics.

The message for a rule to instantiate itself, however, will not come until tokens are flowing through the RETE network, which only happens once the application starts altering objects involved in the knowledge base's premises. If the application calls the change function of a hooked attribute, tokens are generated and passed to the appropriate premises which extract the values and filter out those tokens that fail a value test. The premises then pass the tokens to the alpha nodes. This causes the inference mechanism to activate and cause various rules to instantiate themselves; these instantiations are added to or removed from a conflict set.

Eventually, the application will invoke the expert system, at which point all premise buffers are flushed and as long as the conflict set is not empty an instantiation is selected and fired by the conflict set. The execution of these actions will alter objects of the application (or if meta-actions, objects of the expert system) which if hooked will cause tokens to be added to the expert system. Once this is done, we repeat the cycle: flush the premise buffers, check to see if the conflict set is not empty and fire a rule instantiation. This continues until the conflict set is empty and then control returns back to the application.

The truth maintenance system differs slightly in that its hooks in the application invoke the expert system directly with 'fire_tms'. Tokens are not buffered, but pass into the RETE network and possibly cause instantiations to be added to the conflict sets. When a hook invokes the expert system, an instantiation is chosen from the TMS's conflict set, if it is not empty, and executed, presumably restoring truth in the application. Once the actions have executed, the cycle is repeated: check conflict set, fire best TMS instantiation, until the TMS's conflict set is empty. A complication arises if the restoration of truth alters the same hooked attribute that caused the original invocation of the TMS (this is quite likely); however, if truth is being restored, then there will be no infinite looping because the recursive invocation will be removing the offending instantiation from the conflict set so preventing the recursion going further.

6 An example.

The first step of defining the knowledge base using this library is to translate the abstract rules into the internal representation. To perform this we need to write representations of the premises and actions involved using code templates. We will use as example the rule:

```
if FLAG(x) main_colour   (c)
  & HAT(y)   colour   (c)
  & HAT(y)   size   = large
then HAT(y) flag   (x)
  & FLAG(x)  worn_on   (y)
```

6.1 Representing Premises.

One class is created for each different premise, inheriting from a *_PREMISE abstract class (and code template, or generic class) according to the premise type, and then defining what this abstract class forces us to. The name of each class reflects the class, attribute and indexing number of the premise.

- Premises with a variable in the value position. Structure pattern **<object> <attribute> <unbound>**
  Like our first and second premises, with an unbound value to be unified. These premises' classes inherit from VARIABLE_PREMISE[<object>], and supply the implementation for the abstract features:
    - to know the name of the inspected attribute (the feature 'frame_variable', a text equal to <attribute>).
    - to obtain the value of <attribute>, given the appropriate method (the feature 'get_value', that receives an object of type <frame> and returns the value of the <attribute>.
    - to know the name of the unbound value (the feature 'data_variable', a text equal to <unbound>).
- Premises with a test. Structure pattern: **<frame> <attribute> <test>**
  Like our third premise, with a test to be evaluated. This premise's class will inherit from the type of the value used in the test and from TEST_PREMISE[<frame>], and supply the implementation for the abstract features, :
    - to know the name of the inspected attribute (the feature 'frame_variable', a text equal to <attribute>).
    - to know whether or not the test is true or false (the feature 'test_satisfied', that receives an object of type <frame> and returns the Boolean result of the test).

Mechanism to provide references to these premises are needed

A class to store as features all the premises defined on one application's class is created. The store is a class function that creates the premise objects once and keeps them ('once' methods in Eiffel). The premise objects are created with the first created object of that class (or even before, in some languages), and the reference is shared by every instance.

6.2 Representing Actions.

Actions of a rule are represented in one class per rule, inheriting from an abstract action class. When an instance of the rule is created, it is passed the values resulting from the unification of the unbound variables of its rule - and also a certainty and priority factor, of interest for inherited methods to resolve certainty in truth maintenance system issues.

At creation time the instantiated action saves the passed values in variables of the right type (declared in the class). The Eiffel mechanism "reverse assignment" is used: an untyped assignment, that fails if the dynamic type of the assigned object is not compatible with the declared type of the receiving variable. That will not be the case, as the received value will be the value of an attribute of the same kind. This is done mainly for allowing an untyped inference engine to be used.

The class must also implement the action execution feature 'perform_actions', using the previously saved values for anything the underlying language allows us to do on the application. Some actions, however, may want to inform the inference engine to keep on inferencing, or be meta-rules that change the environment of inferencing.

6.3 Representing Rules.

A class is defined for each rule, inheriting from the premise store classes and owning its action object as a feature. At creation time, the rule registers with the inference engine (this can then build the necessary structures for the RETE algorithm [Fernández93]). It also stores its premises at creation time in an indexed way, so that the inference engine can ask for its values to be evaluated without knowing the name of the premise class (thus not being linked to a defined rule set). The class functionality will create the instances of the actions when they have to be executed.

If rules are to be organised into modules, they register to a module by inheriting from a module-definition class. These classes inherit from the MODULES abstract class, and define the module name.

- **Creating a Knowledge Base class**. The knowledge base is the class that creates all the rules as class variables (using the 'once' mechanism previously mentioned) so that it can be shared between application modules, and keep them. As many knowledge bases as needed can be created (as they are registered to an instance of the inference engine, they are full expert systems) .

- **Connecting the Knowledge Base**. To connect the knowledge bases to an application the original frame classes (in our example FLAG and HAT) have to be renamed (to, for example, FLAG_ORG and HAT_ORG). We then need to write classes (using the original names), which specialise these renamed classes by adding the hooks for the expert system. So in our new FLAG class we need to add the hooks for the attribute 'main_colour'.

- **Invoking the Expert System**. To invoke the expert system we inherit our reference to the expert system and invoke the 'fire' procedure on the inherited attribute (the expert system object).

7 Conclusion and further work.

The aim of this paper was to explain a development of a object-oriented libray that enabled expert system facilities to be embedded in an application, and the reuse of knowledge already reflected in OPS5-like languages.

The library provides facilities to represent knowledge about the entities of the application and an expert system structure and run-time facility to perform inferencing upon the application using this knowledge. Thus, automatic transformation can be done of the existing rule sets into a form supported by the host OO language and aplication.

A number of issues have arisen that are not solved yet, or can be further investigated:

- Scalability and the performance on a real-world problem must be faced correctly by the working system. It has been designed mainly for rewriting an expert system application (MAMUR [Pikaza92]; medium number of rules and objects); but it **has** been designed at every stage to face a database-order number of objects, with medium-small number of rules (for the PIDA [to be published] system). The idea behind this approach has been to exchange some of the space gained by using a pure-active approach for the speed gained by using an inferencing mechanism. RETE based algorithms are of the fastest many-object many-pattern matchers available.
- The possibility of a failure in an attribute change due to a rule in the knowledge base has to be dealt with more detail, trying to maintain the non-disruptive approach. The same applies to the Truth Maintenance approach, available by having an independent set of rules active and attached to the originator class of the application (the "main" one).
- Efficiency / memory occupation balancing at the time of rule-compile, and at runtime.
- Certainty has to be obtained from external experts. [Pikaza92] presents a certainty mechanism fully internal to the inference engine, where expert knowledge is reflected in matrices.
- The same applies to rule priorities.
- Creation of the compiler from the rule set and application classes to the extended application (with expert system functionality attached).

8 Acknowledgments

The funds for the development of the part of the project described in this document were supplied by Ados Soluciones Software S.A.

One personal grant was supplied by Iberdrola S.A., through the Asociación de Industrias Electrónicas del Pais Vasco: and another EEC grant allowed for the stay of the British member of our group.

9 References

[Anwar93] Anwar.E, Maugis.L, Chakravarthy.S, 'A new perspective on Rule Support for Object-Oriented Databases'. SIGMOD 5/93. ACM.

[Diaz92] Díaz.O. 'Deriving Active Rules for Constraint Maintenance in an Object-oriented Database'. In A M Tjoa and I Ramos, editors. Proc. Database and Expert systems Applications (DEXA) pages 332-337. Springer Verlag. 1992.

[Diaz91] Díaz.O, Paton.N, Gray.P. 'Rule Management in object-oriented databases: a unified approach'. Proc. of VLDB, Barcelona, Sept. 1991.

[Fernández93] Fernández.R, Martin.S, Zubizarreta, J.R.'Development of a RETE Matching Algorithm class set using the Eiffel language'. To be published. Computer Science School of the Basque Country University, Spain. Sept. 1993.

[Forgy82] Forgy. C. 'RETE algorithm: A fast algorithm for the Many Pattern/Many object matching problem'. Artificial Intelligence, 19. 1982.

[Jackson90] Jackson.P. 'Introduction to Expert Systems'. Addison-Wesley.1990.

[Meyer92] Meyer.B, 'Eiffel - The Language', Prentice Hall. 1992.

[Monarchi92] Monarchi. D. E. & Puhr, G. I., 'A Research Typology for Object-Oriented Analysis and Design'. Communications of the ACM, Vol 35, No 9. 1992.

[Nerson92] Nerson, J.M. 'Applying Object-Oriented Analysis and Design'. Communications of the ACM, Vol 35 No 9.1992.

[Omohundro93] Omohundro.S, 'The Sather 1.0 Specification'. International Computer Science Institute internal document. March 1993.

[Pikaza92] Pikaza Acha.J.M, 'MAMUR: Una herramienta modular multinivel basada en la satisfacción de restricciones' (MAMUR: A modular multilevel tool based on restriction satisfaction). Ph.D. Thesis. Computer Science School of the University of Deusto, Bilbao, Spain. 1992.

[Rumbaugh91] Rumbaugh.J et al. 'Object-Oriented Modeling and Design'. Prentice-Hall.1991.

10 Appendix. Sample language code for the example (Eiffel code)

We use one knowledge base with one rule on a two-class application (HAT and FLAG, as described in section 4). The rule is the following:

```
if     FLAG(x)    main_colour  (c)
     & HAT(y)     colour   (c)
     & HAT(y)     size   = large
then   HAT(y)     flag (x)
     & FLAG(x)    worn_on (y)
```

Expressing that a *flag* **x** with *main colour* equal to the *colour* of a large *hat* **y**, **IS** the flag corresponding to the *hat* **y**, and it is *worn on* that hat, and no other.

We show simplified code (only for illustration purpose). Hooks on monitored attributes of classes are also needed, as described previously:

```
-- Premise 1 on colour attrib
class PREM_HAT_C_1 export
repeat VARIABLE_PREMISE
inherit
  VARIABLE_PREMISE[ FLAG ]
  define frame_variable,
         data_variable, get_value;
feature
   Create is do make_premise
   end;
   frame_variable: CHARACTER is 'y';
   data_variable: CHARACTER is 'c';
   get_value (frame: FLAG ): ANY is
      do Result := frame.colour
   end;
end


-- Premise 1 on size attribute
class PREM_HAT_SZ_1 export
   repeat TEST_PREMISE
inherit
   TEST_PREMISE[HAT]
   define frame_variable,
          test_satisfied;
```

```
   SIZE
feature
   Create is do make_premise end;
   frame_variable: CHARACTER is 'y';
   test_satisfied (frame: HAT):
BOOLEAN is
   do Result := (frame.size = Large
) end;
end


-- Premise 1 on m_c attribute
class PREM_FLAG_MC_1 export
   repeat VARIABLE_PREMISE
inherit
   VARIABLE_PREMISE[ FLAG ]
   define frame_variable,
          data_variable, get_value
feature
   Create is do make_premise end;
   frame_variable: CHARACTER is 'x';
   data_variable: CHARACTER is 'c';
   get_value (frame: FLAG ): ANY is
      do Result := frame.main_colour
      end;
end


-- Premises defined on flag objects
class FLAG_PREMISES
   PREM_FLAG_MC_1: PREM_FLAG_MC_1 is
       once Result.Create end;
end


-- Premises defined on hat objects
class HAT_PREMISES
   PREM_HAT_C_1: PREM_HAT_C_1 is
       once Result.Create end;
   PREM_HAT_SZ_1: PREM_HAT_SZ_1 is
       once Result.Create end;
end


-- Actions of rule HAT_MATCH
class OUR_ACTIONS inherit
   INSTANT define perform_actions
   CERTAINTY_TERMS
feature
   y: HAT;
   x: FLAG;
Create(vars:VARIABLE_BINDINGS,
rule_priority:INTEGER):INTEGER
   is do
   priority := rule_priority;
   module_tag := rule_module;
   certainty_value := Certain;
   -- They are of type HAT & FLAG
   y ?= vars.value ('y');
   x ?= vars.value ('x');
   end;
perform_actions is
   do
   x.change_worn_on ( y );
   y.change_flag( x );
   end;
end


-- One rule
class HAT_MATCH inherit
   MODULE_1 redefine
current_instant;
   HAT_PREMISES
   FLAG_PREMISES
feature
   current_instant: OUR_ACTIONS;
   Create is
   do
   premises.Create (3);
   premises.put_i_th
               (PREM_FLAG_MC_1, 1);
   premises.put_i_th
               (PREM_HAT_C_1, 2);
   premises.put_i_th
               (PREM_HAT_SZ_1, 3);
   priority := 15;
   engine_constructor.build;
   end
end


-- One module of rules
deferred class MODULE_1 inherit
   MODULES;
   RULE define module_tag
feature
   module_tag: INTEGER is
      do Result := 'MODULE_1' end;
end


-- One knowledge base
class KB_1 export
   repeat ES_SHELL
inherit
   ES_SHELL
feature
   Create is
     do rules.Create;
        rules.add_right (RULE_1)
        end;
   RULE_1: HAT_MATCH is
     once Result.Create end;
end


-- The expert system
class EXPERT_1
feature
   COSTUME_ES: KB_1 is
      once Result.Create end;
end
```

EIFFEL IN ACTION

EIFFEL ESSENTIALS

Eiffel Essentials Presentation

by:

James McKim, Hartford Graduate Center, USA

EIFFEL PRINCIPLES AND APPLICATIONS

Expressing and Processing Constraints in Eiffel

Asokan Suppiah, Ted Lawson, Andrew Jones

Department of Computing Mathematics
University of Wales College of Cardiff
PO Box 916, CARDIFF CF2 4YN, Wales, UK
{Ashokltedlandrew}@uk.ac.cf.cm

Abstract

In this paper we describe a technique to express general constraints in Eiffel code. The constraint expressions are converted into parse trees at run time. These structure can then be used in computations involving the constraints. We describe a set of Eiffel classes supporting the expression of such constraints in Eiffel code. These classes represent binary relations and conjunctions in general. The potential of these classes is demonstrated by describing a system that accepts temporal constraint expressions and produces corresponding parse trees which can then be converted into a critical path network of events. Extracting the critical path from this structure is shown to illustrate the usefulness of this system.

1 INTRODUCTION

Conditions and constraints such as:

salary > 2000 or salary < 2000 and status = "manager",

or:

point inside circle or point outside square

occur in all kinds of computing applications. In order to process a constraint - in order to, say, search for the set of values that a constrained variable may take - its textual representation first has to be converted into some kind of internal data structure. Typically this will be some kind of parse tree.

From TOOLS EUROPE '94 (Technology of Object-Oriented Languages and Systems).

In this paper we describe a cluster of Eiffel classes which define such a structure. More significantly we describe how such constraints can be expressed textually as Eiffel code. Such code will typically appear in clients of our classes. When this code is compiled and executed an internal representation of each constraint is created as a structure of Eiffel objects forming a parse tree. This structure can then be used in computations involving the composite constraint. The classes are applicable to a wide range of constraints and are independent of the constraints' semantics, although appropriate semantics can be introduced in descendants inheriting from the cluster.

In devising a format for coding constraint expressions in Eiffel code we decided that the code

1) should be easily intelligible,

2) must uphold normal Eiffel programming conventions,

3) must be pure Eiffel code and must not have expressions embedded in it couched in some specialised "little language" or 4GL. In this respect our approach differs from other attempts to use Eiffel in constraint processing such as [Beauchesne et al. 93].

It is worth noting that these aims could not have been achieved with a conventional procedural language, although some other object-oriented languages such as Smalltalk would have supported an approach similar to ours.

We said that the classes are applicable to a wide range of constraints. More specifically they are applicable to any constraint which takes the form prescribed by this grammar:

relational_expression ::
item binary_relation item

conjunction ::
and | or

conjunction_expression ::
relational_expression *conjunction* *constraint*

constraint ::
relational_expression
| *conjunction_expression*
| "(" *constraint* ")"

The two examples of constraints given at the beginning of this section fit this grammar.

To demonstrate the use of the classes and the potential for including constraint semantics in descendants of the classes, we will concentrate on a particular kind of constraint namely *temporal* constraints. These are constraints on the timing of events. Typically they contain temporal binary relations such as "before", "after", etc., and conjunctions such as "and", "or", etc. For example, suppose the notice for an annual general meeting (AGM) has to be sent out after a planning meeting but before the AGM. This could be expressed more formally as the constraint:

AGM_notice after committee_meeting and
AGM_notice before AGM

Once coded formally such a constraint could be interpreted by computer so that, for example, appropriate reminders for the events were triggered to appear in real time. Alternatively a set of such constraints might be used to generate a critical path network for the events.

The next section of the paper describes how binary relations between temporal events can be expressed in Eiffel. It also demonstrates how a set of Eiffel-coded temporal binary constraints can be converted into a parse tree of objects. The third section shows how binary relational expressions can be joined using temporal conjunctions such as "and" and "or". It also describes the cluster of Eiffel classes that represents constraint expressions. The fourth section explores some alternative approaches to the one we have taken in order to highlight the advantages of our approach. Finally, in the last section we demonstrate how parse trees of objects representing a set of temporal constraints can be converted into a set of objects forming a network structure. This structure is essentially a critical flow network of constrained events. The section also shows how a critical path can be extracted from the structure.

2 BINARY RELATIONS

In this section we will look at how we can express relational expressions in Eiffel. We first look at how binary relations (e.g. "salary > 2000") can be expressed in pure Eiffel code in such a way that when executed, a corresponding parse tree structure is created. For illustrations we will use binary relations between temporal events, and initially we will concentrate on just one relation, "before".

Examples of the "before" relation occur in constraint expressions such as

AGM_notice before AGM,

etc. One way to express this in Eiffel is as follows:

AGM_notice.before (AGM)

In our system parse trees for "before" relations are represented by objects of the class BEFORE_RELATION. They are created by a corresponding function in a class called TEMPORAL_EVENT:

before (like Current): BEFORE_RELATION

A "before" relation object can be created very naturally by applying the *before* function to temporal event objects, as shown in the code below:

```
class SOME_CLIENT

feature
    AGM_notice,
    AGM: TEMPORAL_EVENT;

    aBefore_Relation:
            BEFORE_RELATION;

    some_routine is
    do
        ...
        aBefore_Relation :=
                AGM_notice.before (AGM)
        ...
    end

end -- class SOME_CLIENT
```

Typically one would not assign the result of the function to an entity, as we have done here, but pass it as an argument to another function. We will illustrate this in detail later.

The class BEFORE_RELATION contains two main attributes

left, right: TEMPORAL_EVENT

which simply refer to the left and right events - *AGM_notice* and *AGM* in this example. Figure 2.1 illustrates the parse tree that would be created at run time for the above code example.

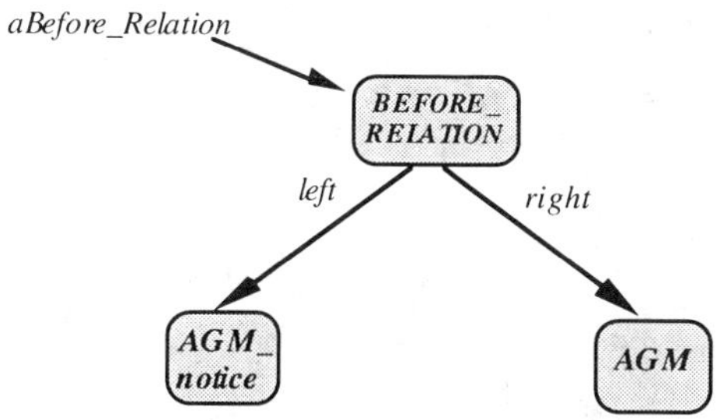

Figure 2.1 Parse tree structure that represents *"AGM_notice.before (AGM)"*

There are of course other possible temporal binary relations. Obvious examples are "after" and "equals", and if we consider events to have durations then there are relations such as "during", "includes", "overlaps", and so on. A full list is given in section 6. Any such relation can be provided for simply by building the appropriate class (e.g. AFTER_RELATION) and including the corresponding function (*after*) in TEMPORAL_EVENT.

To make all binary relation classes consistent, there is a common parent TEMPORAL_RELATION from which they inherit the features *left* and *right*. This class represents temporal relations in general, i.e. binary relations between temporal events. This class in turn inherits a more abstract class BINARY_RELATION which represents binary relations in general, i.e. binary relations between arbitrary items. It is a parameterised class and the type of item, e.g. TEMPORAL_EVENT, is supplied as an actual type parameter.

The classes are displayed in the diagram in figure 2.2. Circles or ellipses represent classes and uninterrupted arrows represent inheritance. A deferred class is marked with an asterisk.

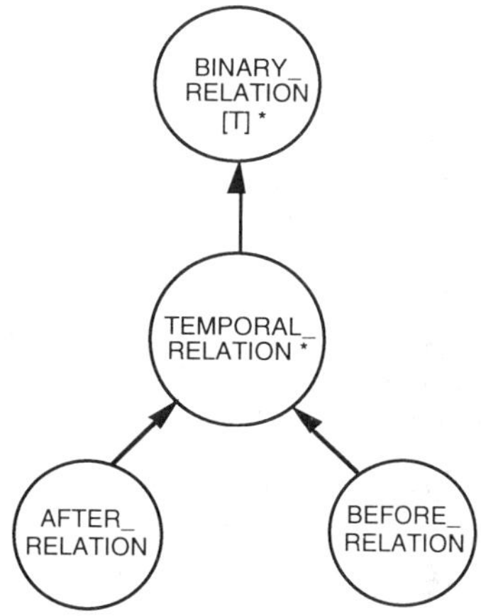

Figure 2.2 Temporal binary relation classes

3 CONJUNCTIONS

We will now look at how full constraints can be expressed. As presented in the grammar, a constraint can be either a binary relational expression (such as the examples in the last section), or a conjunction expression where several relational expressions are connected using conjunctions. e.g.

```
AGM_notice after committee_meeting and
AGM_notice before AGM
```

As in the previous section we will use temporal constraints as illustrations. In our system, the above constraint can be expressed in Eiffel as

AGM_notice.after (committee_meeting)
and *AGM_notice.before (AGM)*

Once coded in Eiffel, such an expression will produce a suitable parse tree when executed. Parse trees for "and" conjunctions between temporal binary relations are represented by objects of the class TEMPORAL_AND. They are created by the function

infix *"and" (other: CONSTRAINT):*
TEMPORAL_AND

which appears in all temporal binary relation classes such as BEFORE_RELATION, AFTER_RELATION, etc., and also in temporal conjunction classes such as TEMPORAL_AND. (The class CONSTRAINT which appears here will be described later. For the moment we will simply state that binary relation classes such as BEFORE_RELATION and conjunction classes such as TEMPORAL_AND conform to the deferred class CONSTRAINT).

The following code illustrates the use of the *and* function and the classes.

```
class SOME_CLIENT

feature
   AGM_notice, AGM,
   committee_meeting:
            TEMPORAL_EVENT;
   aTemporal_And:
            TEMPORAL_AND;

   some_routine is
   do
      ...
      aTemporal_And :=
          AGM_notice.after
            (committee_meeting) and
            AGM_notice.before (AGM);
      ...
   end

end -- class SOME_CLIENT
```

In the above code, *and* function is applied to the object created by the first temporal relational expression (*AGM_notice.after (committee_meeting)*) with the object created by the next expression (*AGM_notice.before (AGM)*) as the argument.

The class TEMPORAL_AND has two main attributes

left, right: CONSTRAINT

which hold the references to constraints which are joined - instances of the binary relation classes AFTER_RELATION and BEFORE_ RELATION in this example.

Our system also supports "or" conjunctions between temporal events. These are represented by objects of the class TEMPORAL_OR.

There are more general classes AND_ CONJUNCTION and OR_ CONJUNCTION which represent conjunctions in general. Specific conjunctions such as TEMPORAL_ AND inherit the features *and* and *or* from these classes. AND_CONJUNCTION and OR_ CONJUNCTION in turn inherit these features from a deferred parent CONJUNCTION.

To make BINARY_RELATION and CONJUNCTION interchangeable in arguments to *and* and *or* functions, they have a common parent CONSTRAINT. This class represents constraint expressions in general. These can be "and-ed" together and "or-ed" together so it introduces the *and* and *or* functions. More specifically, this class provides the type conformance for the left and right items of CONJUNCTION.

The classes described so far allow constraints which follow the grammar shown in figure 3.3 to be expressed in Eiffel code, and suitable parse trees to be created when that code is executed.

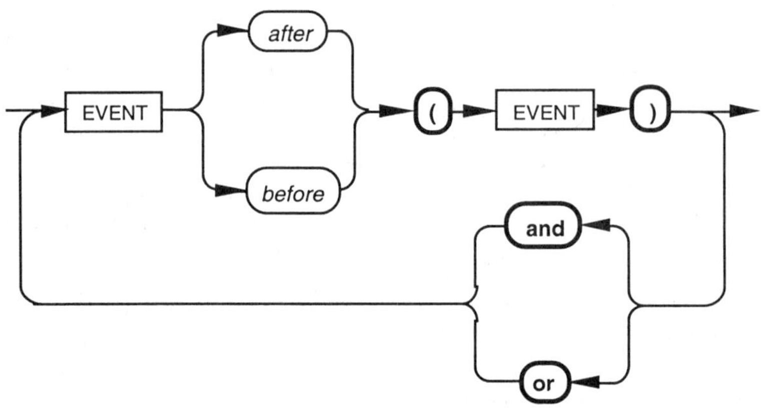

Figure 3.3 Constraint grammar supported

Figure 3.4 summarises the inheritance hierarchy of the cluster of classes described so far.

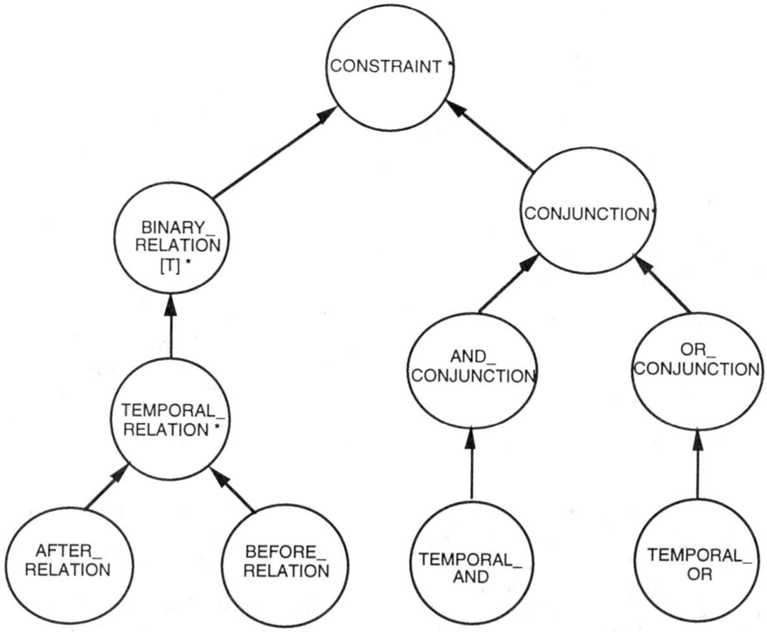

Figure 3.4 Eiffel classes of our system

4 OTHER WAYS TO EXPRESS CONSTRAINTS IN EIFFEL

The technique presented in sections 2 and 3 for expressing constraints in Eiffel is only one of a number of possible ways of doing this. In this section, we look at some different ways to express constraints.

For illustration, the following temporal constraint is used throughout.

> "event5 is after event2 and event5 is after event3 or event5 is after event4"

We will discuss the following four ways of expressing this constraint:

- coding the expression in a little language,
- arranging relational expressions so that they are evaluated sequentially,
- grouping items with similar relations,
- amalgamating simple relational expressions in a multi-dot statement.

4.1 Coding in a little Language

A constraint can be expressed as a string in some specially-devised little language. This can contain tokens such as "after", "before", etc., and place holders for items in the relation. The string can then be parsed at run time and the appropriate structure of objects created. For example,

> *parse ("(%e after %e and %e after %e) or %e after %e", <<event5, event2, event5, event3, event5, event4>>)*

where *%e* is the place holder. The second argument to the parse operation here is a manifest array. Using it allows us to pass varying numbers of events to the *parse* operation.

This technique is similar to that used in, for example, certain C Library routines such as *printf()* for formatting output. It has several disadvantages though. Firstly we are forced to implement our own versions of facilities that the Eiffel compiler already provides, such as the mechanism to parse nested expressions. Secondly, extending the little language's expressive power so that different kinds of constraint could be expressed would mean altering the potentially quite complicated code inside the *parse* routine. Also, difficulties arise when trying to mesh the little language's code with Eiffel code. For example, having to use place holders such as *%e* rather than the events themselves in the expression, can make the expression somewhat obscure. Finally, we feel that code which incorporates complicated expressions in another language is often inelegant and difficult to maintain.

4.2 Arranging relational expressions to be evaluated sequentially

Perhaps the simplest way to implement a system for accepting constraints in Eiffel is to require each binary relation expression to be a separate Eiffel instruction. For example,

"event5 after event2 and event5 after event3"

could be expressed in Eiffel as

event5.after (event2)
event5.after (event3)

However, unless we allow only one type of conjunction (e.g. "and"), expressing complicated constraints becomes quite cumbersome. For example, it would follow that to express "event5 after event2 and event5 after event3 or event5 after event4" we would have to write:

event5.after (event2)
event5.and
event5.after (event3)
event5.or
event5.after (event4)

This assumes that an event effectively treats each new instruction as if it is the next input token, requiring the object to maintain a kind of state machine. Also, providing control over the precedence of conjunctions is awkward. We can do this by providing features such as *open_bracket* and *close_bracket* to group the relations. For example.

event5.open_bracket
event5.after (event2)
event5.and
event5.after (event3)
event5.close_bracket
event5.or
event5.after (event4)

but the notation is clumsy.

Alternatively, relational expressions and the conjunctions can be arranged in a Reverse Polish Notation. For example, the above expression can be rearranged as

event5.after (event2)
event5.after (event3)
event5.and
event5.after (event4)
event5.or

Here a conjunction will be applied to the preceding two expressions. This eliminates the worry about precedence but reverse polish notation is not a natural way to express constraints - it is not in common use.

4.3 Grouping items with relations

A disadvantage of the approach in the previous sub-section was that the sequence of instructions could be long and cumbersome. This approach can be tidied using the manifest arrays provided in Eiffel version 3. In such a case, all the events referring to the same relation could be grouped and passed to the binary relation as an *ARRAY* structure. For example,

event5.after (<<event2,event3>>)
event5.or
event5.after (<<event4>>)

One drawback of this approach is the explicit use of "<<..>>" even for a single event. Another less obvious, but more serious drawback that applies to the techniques described in this section and in section 4.2 is that the set of instructions forming a constraint can be distributed across in a large block of code and mixed in with other statements. This will significantly obscure the semantics of the constraint. Also, there is the danger that a constraint could be used in some instruction before it had been fully formed.

4.4 Multi-dot notation

A complex structure such as the one presented in the previous section can be compacted by amalgamating a sequence of expressions in a multi-dot statement [Meyer 92, p340]. For example

event5.after(event2).and.after(event3).or.
after(event4)

This is quite readable as a constraint. However there are two disadvantages. There must be a feature on the right of each dot, so an event referred to by an entity can only appear at the left of the statement. This means that we can only adopt a system where the left hand side of each binary relation is understood to be the same item (in this case *event5*). It would not be possible to represent e.g.

event5.after(event2).and.event3.before
(event7)

using this technique. Secondly the precedence is fixed to be from left to right. The above expression will always be evaluated as

(*event2* and *event3*) **or** *event4*

and not otherwise. i.e. it is impossible to use brackets to denote the precedence.

5 PROCESSING TEMPORAL CONSTRAINTS

We will now demonstrate how Eiffel coded temporal constraints which have been transformed into parse trees can be processed further. In particular we will show how we can derive a critical path network (represented as a structure of Eiffel objects) from them. We will also show how this network can be analysed to generate the critical path.

e1 before e2 by 10 days and
e1 before e3 by 11 days,
(e6 after e2 by 8 days or
e6 after e3 by 8 days) and
e6 after e4 by 6 days,
e1 before e4 by 10 days,
e5 after e2 by 6 days and
e5 before e7 by 2 days,
e7 after e6 by 5 days and
e7 after e4 by 8 days.

The critical path network for the above set of constraints is displayed in figure 5.1. The arrows indicate the chronological order of events with the durations between them. An "or" conjunction is turned into a special event which occurs whenever any one of the preceding events completes.

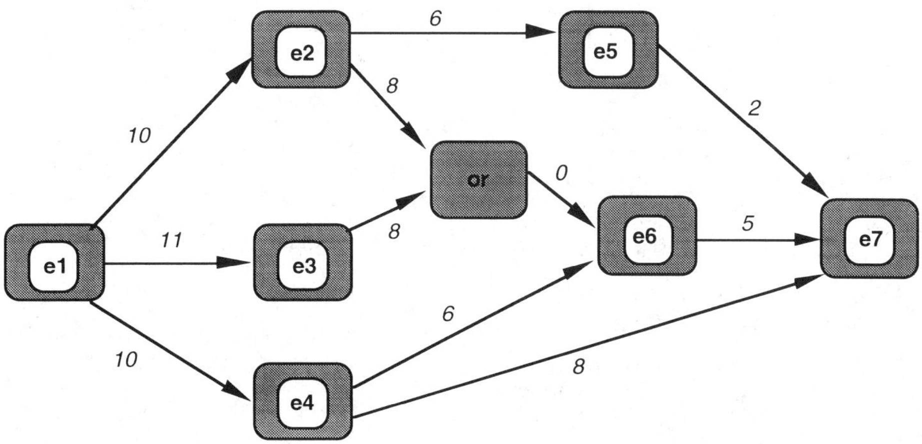

Figure 5.1 Critical path network with conjunctions

A critical path network illustrates numerous interconnected events, such as those in a large project such as constructing a house or a dam. In a critical path network related events are separated by a duration, such as "2 days". This could be because each event takes a certain amount of time for completion or simply because events have to be spaced apart for some reason.

The following example lists a set of temporal constraints which can be converted into a critical path network. There is an implied "and" between all of these.

As we mentioned earlier, these constraints when coded in Eiffel can be converted at run time into a set of parse trees. These can in turn be translated into a network of events, where each is linked to others according to its relations.

In order to allow for durations in "after" and "before" relations we have to create different versions of the event and relation classes we described in section 2. Specifically, events are now represented by the class DUR_TEMPORAL_EVENT. This contains different versions of the *after* and *before* functions which include the duration argument.

after (like Current; d: DURATION): DURATION_AFTER

before (like Current; d: DURATION): DURATION_BEFORE

These temporal binary relation features create objects of the type DURATION_AFTER and DURATION_BEFORE which (like AFTER_RELATION and BEFORE_RELATION) inherit from TEMPORAL_RELATION. The class DURATION represents some time unit or possibly a combination of units such as days, hours, months, etc. in some calendar system. A pair of DURATIONs can be compared with one another and arithmetic operators such as add, subtract, etc., can be performed on them (see [Balthazaar et al. 91, Lawson et al. 93]).

Using these classes the set of constraints given above can be written as:

```
e1.before(e2,ten) and e1.before(e3,eleven)
(e6.after(e2, eight) or e6.after(e3, eight))
    and e6.after(e4, six)
...
```

We will now show how these can be used to form a critical path network and how the critical path is extracted. For this we need a class CPN *[T -> DUR_TEMPORAL_EVENT, D-> DURATION]*. This represents critical path networks. A network can consist of arbitrary events which have features *after* and *before* (inherited from DUR_TEMPORAL_EVENT) which take arbitrary durations as arguments.

The critical path network is assembled by repeated applications of a feature *set* which takes a constraint as an argument. There is also a procedure *calculate_cp* which computes the critical path for the network. The critical path is then available as an array of events in the attribute *critical_path*. The use of these features is demonstrated in the following code:

```
class SOME_CLIENT

feature

    c: CPN   [DUR_TEMPORAL_EVENT,
                DAYS];
    p:ARRAY[DUR_TEMPORAL_EVENT];
    e1,..,e7:    DUR_TEMPORAL_EVENT;
    one,...,eleven: DAYS;
                -- inherits from DURATION

    some_routine is
        do
            ...
            c.set (e1.before (e2, ten) and
                    e1.before (e3, eleven));
            c.set ((e6.after(e2, eight) or
                    e6.after(e3, eight)) and
                    e6.after(e4, six));
            c.set (e1.before (e4, ten));
            c.set (e5.after (e2, six) and
                    e5.before (e7, two));
            c.set (e7.after (e6, five) and
                    e7.after (e4, eight));
            c.calculate_cp;
            p:= c.critical_path;
            ...
        end

end -- class SOME_CLIENT
```

When this code is executed the entity *p* will refer to an array of events corresponding to the critical path through the network. *Set* interprets its argument, which is a parse tree, and converts it into a network. This is done using a feature called *extract* which appears as a deferred feature in class CONSTRAINT. *Extract* is defined in classes DURATION_AFTER, DURATION_BEFORE, TEMPORAL_AND and TEMPORAL_OR to carry out operations which cause the parse trees represented by each of these kinds of objects to be converted into an appropriate part of the critical path network. The operations work in a recursive descent fashion with the *extract* operation in TEMPORAL_AND calling the same operation in its *left* and *right* features.

A critical path network (such as figure 5.1) is represented by a structure of two types of objects: CP_EVENT_NODE and CP_OR_NODE.

The CP_EVENT_NODE represents a temporal event node in the critical path network. As we mentioned earlier, the network can have a special event CP_OR_NODE which represents an "or" conjunction. To make them compatible, they both inherit a deferred parent CP_NODE. This class contains two main attributes

```
succeeding: LINKED_LIST[CP_NODE[T]]
preceding: LINKED_LIST [CP_NODE[T]]
```

that are used to hold the references of the succeeding and preceding nodes in the network. For example, e1 before e4 by ten days

would require a link from *e1* to *e4* (add to *succeeding*) and the reverse from *e4* to *e1* (add to *preceding*).

Now that we have seen how a critical path network is formed from a set of temporal constraints we will show how the critical path is extracted from this network of objects.

In order to extract the critical path, we need to compute the *earliest occurrence time* (EOT) and *latest occurrence time* (LOT) of each event of the network.

The EOT of an event is the time in which it can begin after all its preceding events complete. The length of the longest path from the first event to the last event is the EOT of the whole network. The LOT for each of the events is the time in which it can finish without causing any delay to the final completion time.

In order to extract the critical path, the network must be acyclic [Weiss 92, Minieka 78]. Also there should be one starting event (*e1*) and one terminating event (*e7*), and all the others must be linked to one or more events. To compute EOT and LOT for each of the events, we used the algorithm in [Weiss 92] modified to deal with "or" conjunctions.

The EOT of an "or" node is the minimum of all the preceding node's EOT's plus the corresponding durations between them and the "or" node. The LOT of an event which precedes an "or" node (e.g. *e3*) does not depend on the LOT of the "or" node if the EOT of the event and the duration is later than the EOT of the "or" node.

Figure 5.2 shows the critical path network with the critical path marked.

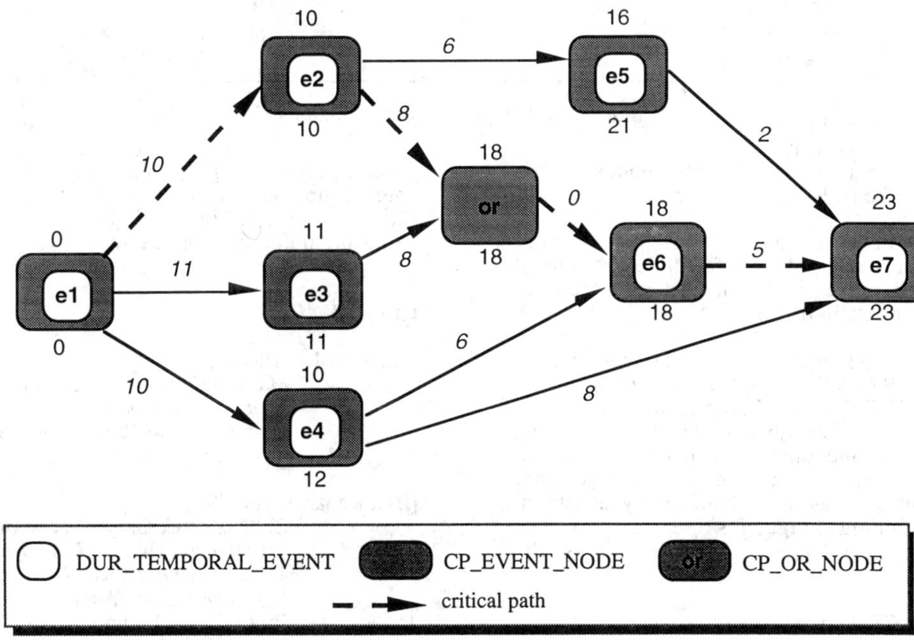

Figure 5.2 Earliest occurrence time (above each event) and latest occurrence time (below). Critical path is highlighted.

6 FUTURE WORK

There is a good scope to extend the general cluster of constraint classes and also to add features to the system that was mentioned. The following are considered worth investigating:

- other temporal binary relations,
- accommodating the 'not' operator,
- time-dependent event triggering,
- deriving further classes for dealing with other kinds of constraints.

In section 2 we mentioned that the "before" relation is only one of several possible temporal binary relations. We hope to try to support other possible relations. These are listed in figure 6.1 (introduced in [Allen 83]).

Relation	Inverse Relation
A before B	B after A
A meets B	B is_met_by A
A overlaps B	B is_overlaped_by A
A equal_to	B equal_to A
A includes B	B is_included_by A

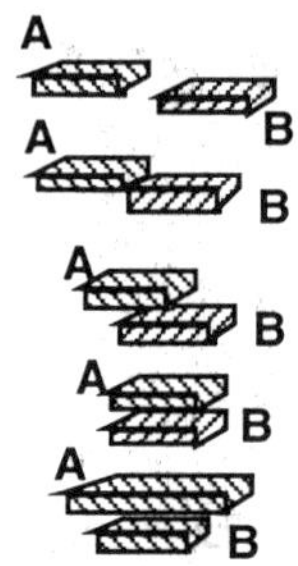

Figure 6.1 Temporal binary relations

These relationships can be provided for simply by building the appropriate class (e.g. EQUAL_RELATION) and then adding the function (*equal*) to the event class.

In section 3 we mentioned that the class CONSTRAINT represents constraint expressions that can be "and-ed" together and "or-ed" together. In addition it would be possible to include the 'not' constraint in constraint expressions. A class embodying this type will be added to the cluster.

Instead of deriving a critical path network from a set of Eiffel-coded temporal constraints, we could instead use them to trigger events in real time.

From the general constraint classes such as CONSTRAINT, CONJUNCTION and BINARY_RELATION described in this paper we could derive further classes for dealing with constraints other than temporal ones. In this way we could support various other domains such as those handled by constraint programming languages (see e.g. [Cohen 90]).

7 CONCLUSION

We have described a cluster of Eiffel classes which offers useful services for applications which require an elegant way to express and process temporal constraints. These are derived from more general classes which can support the expression of constraints in general, provided that they follow a particular abstract syntax.

We have also shown that such constraints can be expressed naturally in pure Eiffel code without the need for a specially-devised "little language".

The cluster could be extended to cater for a larger set of temporal binary relations and operators, and time-dependent event triggering.

From the general constraint classes, we could derive further specialised classes for dealing with other kinds of constraint. In this way, we could support various other domains such as those handled by constraint programming languages. This is encouraging because although some more specialised languages would clearly provide powerful facilities for implementing our ideas (e.g. the operators and metaprogramming facilities of Prolog [Clocksin et al. 81]), we have been using what is intended to be very much a general purpose language to this end. We have opened up the exiting possibility of using Eiffel, on its own, in all kinds of constraint-based programming applications.

REFERENCES

[Allen 83] Allen J F,
Maintaining Knowledge about Temporal Intervals,
Comms. ACM 26(11), pp509-521, 1983

[Balthazaar et al. 1991]
Balthazaar C, Gray A, Lawson T,
An Object-Oriented Temporal Model Embodied as Eiffel Software Components,
Proc. Conf. Technology of Object-Oriented Languages and Systems (TOOLS), pp 249 - 257, Prentice Hall International, 1991

[Beauchesne et al. 93]
Beauchesne T, Caminel T, Dupont S, Druile L,
Semantic and logical object tool, in *Object-oriented Applications*, Meyer B, Nerson J-M, eds, Prentice Hall International, 1993

[Clocksin et al. 1981]
Clocksin W F, Mellish C S,
Programming in Prolog,
Springer Verlag, Berlin, 1981

[Cohen 1990] Cohen J,
Constraint Programming Languages,
Comms. ACM 33(7), pp 52 - 68, 1990

[Lawson et al. 93]
Lawson T, Balthazaar C, Gray A,
Temporal Software Components in *Object-oriented Applications*,
Meyer B, Nerson J-M, eds,
Prentice Hall International, 1993

[Meyer 92] Meyer B,
Eiffel: The Language,
Prentice Hall International, 1992

[Minieka 78] Minieka E,
Optimisation Algorithms for Networks & Graphs,
Marcel Dekker Inc, 1978

[Weiss 92] Weiss M A,
Data Structures and Algorithms Analysis,
Benjamin/Cummings, pp 289-302, 1992

The Potential For Reverse Type Inheritance in Eiffel

Ted Lawson[1], Christine Hollinshead[1], Munib Qutaishat[2]

[1] *Department of Computing Mathematics, University of Wales College of Cardiff, PO Box 916, CARDIFF CF2 4YN, Wales, UK {ted|scmch}@cm.cf.ac.uk*

[2] *Department of Computer Science, University of Jordan, Amman, Jordan*

Abstract

The desire for correctness in Eiffel code through static typing sometimes works against software reusability as promoted by polymorphism. Specifically, the Eiffel typing system only recognises that two classes have semantically equivalent features in common if they inherit declarations of those features from a common ancestor. Only then can instances of the classes be treated polymorphically as being instances of the same supertype. But classes often have features in common which are not derived from a common ancestor, particularly if they have been developed independently for the same kinds of application. In order to turn this commonality into polymorphism, it must be factored out to form a new parent, and then the classes must be modified to inherit from this parent. But modifying the classes may be impossible, typically because their source code is not available; or such action may be undesirable because it may invalidate their maintenance warranty. The only other way to reuse the classes together is to create a new heir or client of each class, but this approach is uneconomic for hierarchies of classes. In this paper we explore a more radical solution. We imagine introducing a "reverse type inheritance" operator into the Eiffel language. The facility can be seen as the dual of ordinary Eiffel inheritance as it applies to typing, and will allow a common parent class to be created for a set of existing classes without affecting the existing classes in any way. It will allow us to define a supertype by generalising a set of existing types. We discuss the need for such an operator (which we call "adopt") and explore its potential interaction with the Eiffel typing system. We broadly discuss a way of implementing it, and its practical limitations as a solution to the identified problem.

From TOOLS EUROPE '94 (Technology of Object-Oriented Languages and Systems).

1. Introduction

Suppose we have two Eiffel classes, BOX and CIRCLE which are not related to one another:

```
class BOX
feature
    draw is        --- draw the box
        do ...
    end;

    height, width, area, boundary: REAL;
    set_dimensions( h, w : REAL) is
    do ...
    end
end
```

```
class CIRCLE
feature
    draw is        --- draw the circle
        do ...
    end;

    radius, circumference: REAL;
    set_radius( r : REAL) is
    do ...
    end
end
```

Now suppose that we want to include instances of both classes in, say, drawing objects defined by this class:

(An earlier version of this paper was presented at the 13th International Eiffel Users Conference, Santa Barbara, August 1993).

```
class DRAWING
inherit LINKED_LIST[ SHAPE]
feature
    ...
    draw_it is        --- traverse the list
                      --and draw each shape
    do
        from start
        until off
        loop
            item.draw;
            forth
        end
    end
end
```

From this code we can see that any object that is to be included in a drawing object must have a suitable *draw* operation defined in its class. (Both BOX and CIRCLE have such a feature.) Also, the Eiffel type checking system dictates that the declaration of that feature must be inherited from the class SHAPE. So before we can put boxes and circles into drawings, we have to modify the classes BOX and CIRCLE so that they inherit from SHAPE (figure 1).

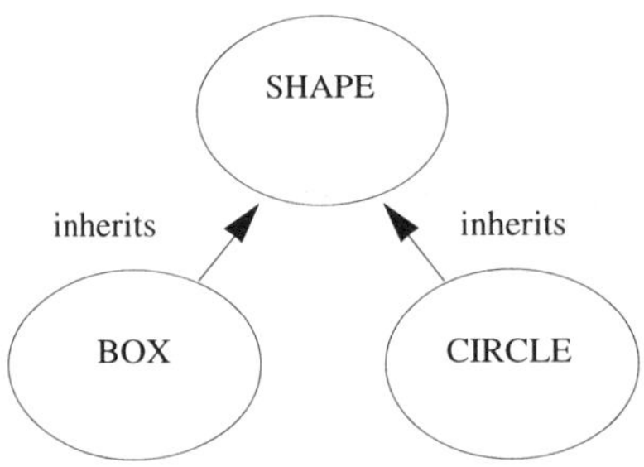

Figure 1

But we can only modify BOX and CIRCLE if we are their *manager*. By that we mean two things in this context:

(1) we have access to their source code,

and

(2) we accept responsibility for maintaining them.

Obviously, to modify a class we need its source code - and furthermore, once we have modified it, any warranty on the class or any obligation on a third party (e.g. a software vendor) to maintain it will almost certainly be invalidated; hence (2) above. As soon as we modify a class, we must accept responsibility for its subsequent maintenance.

This example illustrates a situation where the desire for correctness in Eiffel code through the rigorous application of static type checking works against reusability as promoted by polymorphism. We want to reuse the classes BOX, CIRCLE with our class DRAWING, but Eiffel's typing system will not let us do this unless we manage these classes.

There is of course another way that the classes can be reused in this situation, although it may not be economic. Instead of modifying BOX and CIRCLE, we can define heirs to them, BOX_SHAPE and CIRCLE_SHAPE say. These heirs can also inherit from SHAPE, so allowing us to put instances of these classes into drawing objects. However, suppose that BOX and CIRCLE already have several heirs and descendants, e.g. COLORED_BOX, HATCHED_BOX, SCALEABLE_CIRCLE, and so on. The type system will not allow their instances to be included in drawing objects because they are not descendants of SHAPE. To overcome this, we must create a new heir for each of them, e.g. COLORED_BOX_SHAPE, HATCHED_BOX_SHAPE, etc. (figure 2).

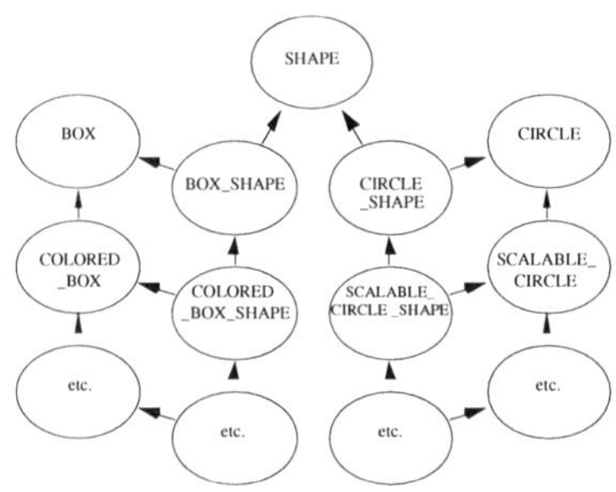

Figure 2

We end up having to duplicate both hierarchies, producing an unwieldy proliferation of new classes.

There is another alternative method but it is less economic still. We can create descendants of SHAPE which are clients of BOX, CIRCLE, etc. rather than heirs. We duplicate the features of BOX, etc. in each corresponding client, and have each feature call the corresponding feature in the supplier. Clearly this approach is even more labour intensive and less attractive.

So we are back to the problem that the typing system will not let us reuse the classes BOX and

CIRCLE together unless we are their manager - unless we have their souce code, and take on the responsibility for maintaining them.

Now, there may be many occasions when we wish to reuse classes that we do not manage - classes which are supplied by third parties and which continue to be maintained by them. Provided that such classes exist as part of a single hierarchy, with sets of common features "factored out" into more general ancestors in a way that anticipates their subsequent reuse, situations such as the one illustrated above should not arise. It depends on how effective the factoring out process has been.

There are essentially two different approaches to making the factoring out process effective. The first [Meyer 1990a 1990b] requires a deep understanding of the application domain and an ability to recognise the abstract data types that will be most useful in that domain. Such understanding and recognition can be achieved by carrying out generalisation phases during the development process.

The second approach [Johnson 92], [Casais 92], involves factoring out in a fine-grained way so that users of the resulting class hierarchy have a wide choice of classes and of ways to combine them in order to meet particular requirements.

However, neither approach deals with the problem of having two or more *separate* class hierarchies, as in the BOX and CIRCLE example, which we do not manage. Two such hierarchies may have many semantically equivalent features in common, but this commonality may not have been factored out into common parents, typically because the hierarchies have been developed independently. We need a way to factor out the commonality *retroactively* - after the classes have been developed. In the next section we explore the possibility of adding a mechanism to Eiffel which will help us do just that.

2. Reverse Type Inheritance

Proposals for extending an existing programming language should always be treated with extreme skepticism:

> 'If today you decide against a language extension, you can always change your mind tomorrow. But the reverse does not work: once the construct is there your are stuck with it *in saecula saeculorum.*' [Meyer 91].

Lets not be daunted though. Let us imagine an extension to the Eiffel programming language in the form of a "reverse type inheritance" facility, which will allow the commonality between unrelated classes to be factored out retroactively. Such a facility will solve the problem illustrated in the previous section by the BOX and CIRCLE classes.

This facility will take the form of two extra keywords added to the language: ***adopt*** and ***foster***. (The term "adopt" was suggested by [Lebedev 93].) To explain what they will do, let us use them to define the class SHAPE that we required in the drawing example:

```
-- (Not Eiffel 3)
deferred foster class SHAPE
    adopt
        BOX;
        CIRCLE
    feature
        draw is
            deferred
    end
end
```

The semantics of the ***adopt*** operator will be such that the following two rules will apply:

(1) the types of class BOX and CIRCLE will directly conform to the type of class SHAPE;

(2) class SHAPE will directly depend on classes BOX and CIRCLE.

In other words BOX and CIRCLE (and all their descendants) will conform to SHAPE but will not depend on SHAPE. They will be made to conform to SHAPE without being modified or affected in any way. The conformance and dependency relations between the adopting and the adopted classes, which in normal inheritance run in the same direction, will run in opposite directions (figure 3).

Certain restrictions must be placed on classes defined in this way in order to maintain the level of type-safety that Eiffel programmers have come to expect. In particular, a class such as SHAPE may only contain features which are common to all the classes it adopts. In this context we define a feature to be common to a set of classes if

(1) the feature has the same name in each class (subject to renaming - see below),

and

(2) it is possible to define a signature to which the signature of the feature in each class conforms.

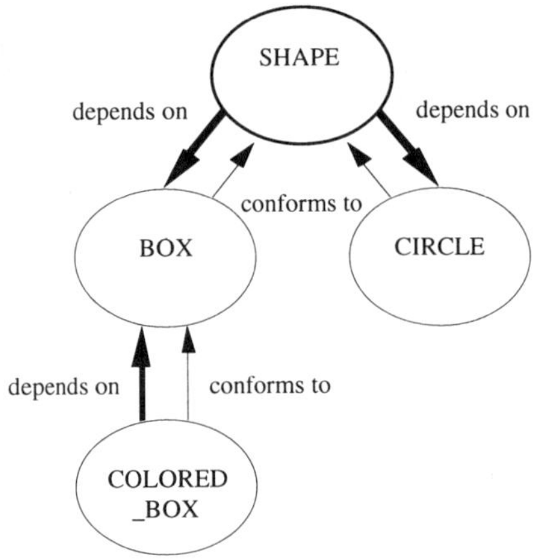

Figure 3
COLORED_BOX inherits BOX.
SHAPE adopts BOX, CIRCLE.

An additional constraint is necessary if assertions are to be considered. This is discussed in section 4.

Common features could include ones that adopted classes inherit.

These restrictions ensure that a statement such as *s.draw* , where *s* is of type SHAPE, is type correct.

Restricting the features that may appear in a class such as SHAPE sets it apart from conventional Eiffel classes. To highlight its extraordinary nature, we declare it to be a "foster" class.

The signature of every feature in a foster class must be such that the signature of the corresponding feature in every class that the class adopts conforms to it. So in SHAPE, for example, the signature of feature *draw* must be such that the *draw* feature in both BOX and CIRCLE conform to it.

A further restriction is that a foster class may not inherit from any class that is not also inherited by all the classes it adopts. This is necessary to allow efficient dynamic binding to be implemented. We will discuss this later.

The class type of a foster class can be seen as a generalisation of the types of the classes it adopts. More precisely, it can be seen as involving either the intersection of the types of the classes it adopts, or the union, depending on how we define the notion of type. A type can be thought of either as a set of features or as a set of objects with those features. (These views correspond to the notions of *intension* and *extension*. [Pedersen 89]). If we think of a type as a set of features then a foster class type will be at most the intersection of the types of the classes it adopts. Alternatively, if we think of a type as a set of objects then a foster class type will be at least the union of the types of the classes it adopts.

One name for this kind of relationship between types is "generalisation" [Pedersen 89], but that term is also applied in several other contexts associated with object-orientation (see e.g. [Meyer 90]). Less overloaded terms are "reverse" or "upwards" inheritance [Schrefl 88]. We will call the facility described here "reverse type inheritance", because only type information will be reverse inherited.

To be useful, a foster class must be able to have clients, and from their point of view it should be indistinguishable from a conventional class. However, achieving this transparency will mean solving some awkward implementation problems. We will examine these shortly.

3. Adopting and Renaming

In our example, the feature *draw* which was common to both BOX and CIRCLE happened to have the same name in both classes. This would be unlikely in reality. It is quite probable that semantically equivalent features in different classes developed by different programmers will have been given different names. To address this, reversely inherited features will be allowed to be renamed in the foster class. This facility can be used to map together differently named features from different adopted classes. For example, if classes BOX and CIRCLE had semantically identical features called *boundary* and *circumference* respectively, they could be mapped together in foster class SHAPE like this:

```
-- (Not Eiffel 3)
deferred foster class SHAPE
    adopt
        BOX
            rename
                boundary as perimeter;
        CIRCLE
            rename
                circumfernce as perimeter;
    feature
        perimeter : REAL;
end
```

Here Eiffel's renaming facility, conventionally used to circumvent name clashes in multiple inheritance, will be used to cause a name clash deliberately!

Unfortunately a difficulty may arise if the adopted classes are common ancestors of another class. Lets suppose that there is a class CIRCULAR_BOX which inherits from BOX and CIRCLE (figure 4).

CIRCULAR_BOX will conform to foster class SHAPE and so a statement such as *s:=cb* in the code below will be type correct.

```
-- (Not Eiffel 3)
class SOME_CLIENT
feature
    s : SHAPE         ---adopts BOX
                      --and CIRCLE
    cb: CIRCULAR_BOX  -- inherits BOX
                      --and CIRCLE
    r : REAL

    some_routine is
    do
        !!cb ;        -- create a circular box
        s := cb;
        r := s.perimeter;
    end
end
```

However, an ambiguity arises when a statement such as *r:=s.perimeter* is executed because this is mapped to two features *boundary* and *circumference* in classes BOX and CIRCLE respectively, which are inherited by CIRCULAR_BOX as two separate features. Now, should the call *s.perimeter* be dynamically bound to *circumference* or to *boundary* ? There is no way of deciding. The same problem occurs with ordinary inheritance when a feature is doubly inherited, renamed and redefined (see [Meyer 91 p191]).

A simple, though incomplete, solution will be to use the order that classes are specified in the foster class and the order in which features are renamed in each **adopt** clause to designate a priority for features. Then, where there is ambiguity in dynamic binding, binding can be made to the feature with the highest priority. So in the example above the feature call *s.perimiter* will bind to the feature *boundary* in class CIRCULAR_BOX because *boundary* appears first in SHAPE.

To see why this solution is incomplete, suppose that we have three adopted classes A, B, C with features *x*, *y* and *z* respectively all of which are mapped to one feature *f* in a foster class. And suppose there are three descendents AB, BC and

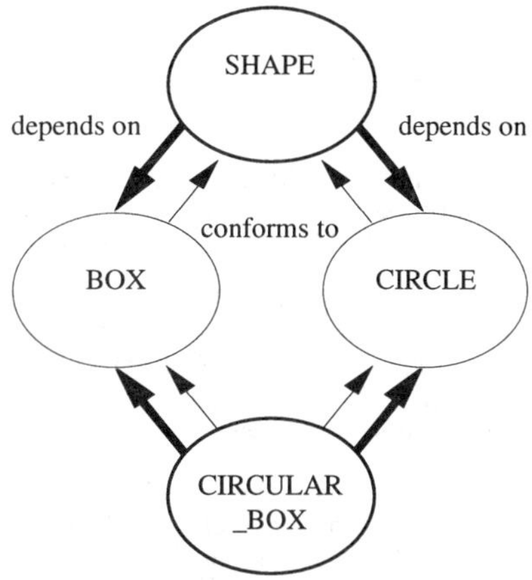

Figure 4
SHAPE adopts BOX, CIRCLE.
CIRCULAR_BOX inherits BOX, CIRCLE

AC which multiply inherit from A and B, B and C, and A and C respectively. In such a case the desired binding from *f* might be to x in AB, y in BC but z in AC. Our proposed solution would not allow this to be specified. We could, however, reasonably assume that such cases will be rare.

The solution employed in the case of repeated ordinary inheritance (see [Meyer 91 p191]), which is to introduce a ***select*** clause to mark one of a set of renamed features as being the one that is dynamically bound, cannot be adapted for this problem for the following reason. If features from three or more classes are mapped together but only a subset of those classes are repeatedly inherited by some descendent, then that descendent might not inherit the feature that has been selected.

4. Adopted Assertions

A vital part of Eiffel's support for software correctness is its assertion mechanism. Lets explore the impact of reverse type inheritance on assertions.

For assertions, the rules for reverse inheritance will be the reverse of the rules for conventional inheritance as described in [Meyer 88 pp256-259, Meyer 91 pp152-154]. Specifically:

> the precondition of a feature in a foster class must be no weaker than the precondition of each corresponding feature in the classes it adopts.

And conversely:

the post condition of a feature in a foster class must be no stronger than the post condition of each corresponding feature in the classes it adopts.

Class invariants, which are essentially postconditions that apply to all features in the class, will have a similar rule to postconditions.

The rule for preconditions can be enforced by defining the precondition of a feature in the foster class to be a composite one made by ANDing together the precondition of all the corresponding features in the adopted classes.

Conversely, the rule for postconditions can be enforced by defining the postcondition of a feature in the foster class to be a composite postcondition made by ORing together the postcondition of all the corresponding features in the adopted classes.

There is a complication though. A clause in an assertion in an adopted class could refer to some feature which does not appear in its foster class.

For postconditions the offending clause can simply be replaced in the composite postcondition by the logical constant True. Since True is the weakest of all assertions the rule for postconditions will still be upheld.

For preconditions though the situation is more complicated. Naively we could replace the offending clause by the logical constant False, which is the strongest of all assertions. But since all the clauses of all the preconditions will be ANDed together, the composite precondition will also be False, so any calls to the foster class's feature will be rejected as having failed the precondition.

Instead we must refine our definition of what constitutes a common feature among a set of classes. Specifically we must add a third rule to the two commonality rules mentioned in section 2 above:

A feature is defined to be common to a set of classes if

(1) the feature has the same name in each class, subject to renaming,

(2) it is possible to define a signature to which the signature of the feature in each class conforms,

(3) it is possible to define a precondition, other than False, which is no weaker than the precondition of the feature in each class.

Enforcing the third rule will mean that if the precondition of a feature in a class refers to some other feature that is not common to a set of classes then the first feature cannot itself be common to that set of classes. It cannot appear in any foster class which adopts the whole set. Features with elaborate preconditions will be less likely to be candidates for factoring out into foster classes.

5. Implementing Reverse Inheritance

Implementing reverse type inheritance will mean solving some awkward problems at compile time. The main difficulty is how to achieve efficient dynamic binding when the target entity is of a foster class type.

Efficient dynamic binding in languages such as Eiffel is usually achieved by resolving feature names to feature table indices at compile time, and then at runtime, indexing the feature tables rather than searching them. With conventional Eiffel inheritance, it is possible to arrange that a particular feature has the same table index for every class that inherits it. The value of the index is fixed by the most senior ancestor containing the feature. (For simplicity, we will ignore the case of multiple inheritance, where efficient dynamic binding requires an extra level of indirection involving information about the static type of the target entity.) So in the following Eiffel code:

```
class SOME_CLIENT
feature
    f : FIGURE      -- defines draw
    b : BOX         -- inherits FIGURE
    c: CIRCLE       -- inherits FIGURE
    some_routine is
    do
        !!b;        -- create a box
        !!c;        -- create a circle

        f:= b;
        f.draw;     -- draw a figure

        f:= c;
        f.draw;     -- draw a figure
    end
end
```

the *draw* feature can be resolved to a single fixed index value at compile time. (Figure 5 illustrates this.)

The index value is then used to index either

BOX's feature table or CIRCLE's feature table at runtime depending on the dynamic type of the object that entity *f* refers to.

The problem imposed by reverse type inheritance is this. Consider the following code:

```
class SOME_CLIENT
feature
    s : SHAPE         ---adopts BOX
                      --and CIRCLE
    b : BOX           --- defines draw
    cb : COLORED_BOX; ---inherits BOX
    c: CIRCLE         --- defines draw

    some_routine is
    do
        !!c ;         -- create a circle
        s := c;
        s.draw;       -- draw a shape

        !!cb ;        -- create a coloured box
        s := cb;
        s.draw;       -- draw a shape
    end
end
```

As before, SHAPE is a foster class adopting BOX and CIRCLE, and so these two classes will then conform to SHAPE, according to the reverse type inheritance rules that we proposed above. So too will their descendants such as COLORED_BOX, and therefore statements such as *s := cb* will be type correct.

The problem is that because BOX and CIRCLE do not inherit the *draw* feature from a common ancestor, the feature table index for *draw* will not necessarily be the same in both classes. In fact typically it will be different.

To address this problem, a feature call on a target entity of a foster class type, such as the statement *s.draw*, must be implemented differently from a feature call on an ordinary entity. More precisely, at compile time we will have to compute a dynamic class set (DCS) for all entities of foster class types in the system. The notion of dynamic class sets is described in [Meyer 91 pp364-367]. The DCS is the set of classes of all the objects that that entity may refer to at runtime within a particular system. In the example above the DCS of entity *s* is the set {CIRCLE, COLORED_BOX}.

Once the DCSs have been found, a two dimensional feature table will be constructed for each foster class in the system. This will have a row for every feature in the foster class and a

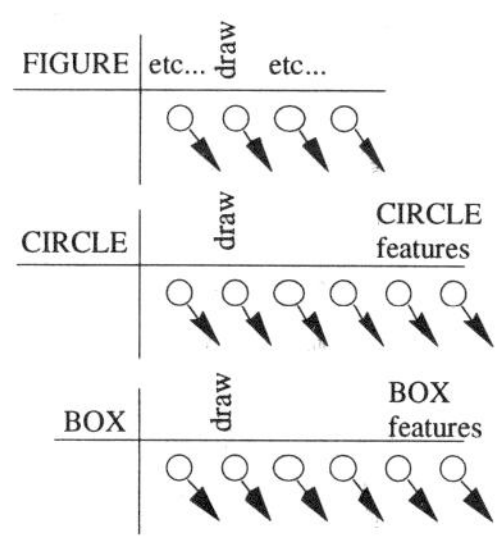

Figure 5
Simplified feature tables for FIGURE, CIRCLE and BOX

column for every class in the union of all the DCSs for entities of that class type (figure 6).

Each entry in the table will point to the feature implementation for the corresponding class. Indices to rows of the table will be computed at compile time. Therefore in a statement such *s.draw* , the *draw* feature will be resolved at compile time to a fixed row index value. The column index into the table must be extracted at runtime either from the object that the entity refers to or from its dynamic class. For this, a column index unique to each class in the system must be computed at compile time and made available to objects of that class. (Conventional Eiffel environments typically assign a similar kind of index to each class for use in handling dynamic binding involving multiple inheritance.)

To summarise, the compiler will compute a DCS for all foster class type entities in the system, and use these to build a feature table in each foster class. Feature calls involving such entities must be treated specially, so that instead of the feature implementation being found from the feature table in the object's dynamic class, it will be found from the two-dimensional feature table in the foster class. Note that feature calls on functions returning foster type entities must be treated likewise; as must formal generic type entities or functions, (such as *item* in LINKED_LIST which was used in the DRAWING class) if the generic parameter is actualised to a foster class type.

We can see now why it will be difficult to allow a foster class to inherit from an ordinary class, unless that class is inherited by all the classes that the foster class adopts. Consider the following code:

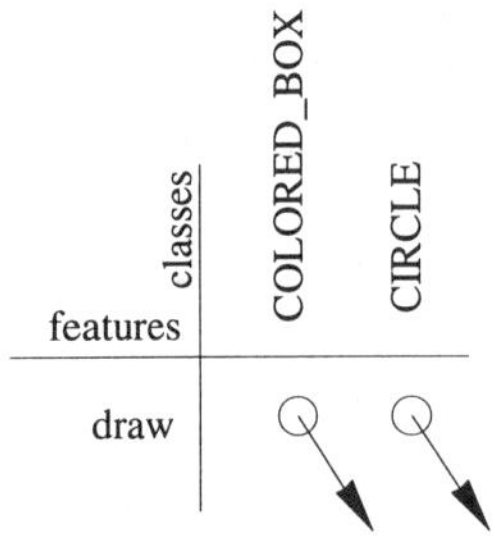

Figure 6

```
class SOME_CLIENT
feature
    d: DRAWABLE    -- defines draw
    s : SHAPE      -- adopts BOX, CIRCLE
                   -- & inherits DRAWABLE
    cb : COLORED_BOX; --inherits BOX

    some_routine is
    do
        !!cb ;   -- create a coloured box
        d:= cb;
        d.draw;      -- draw a drawable
    end
end
```

Suppose that SHAPE inherits the feature *draw* from DRAWABLE as well as adopting BOX and CIRCLE. Class BOX then conforms to SHAPE which conforms to DRAWABLE, and therefore the statement *d := b* is type correct. However, DRAWABLE is not a foster class and so compiler will treat the feature call *d.draw* conventionally. It will assume that the index for *draw* is dictated by DRAWABLE and that it is fixed for all classes which conform to DRAWABLE. But BOX does not depend on DRAWABLE and so the feature table index for *draw* could quite easily be different in the two classes, so the feature call would probably fail.

Note however that a foster class such as SHAPE could inherit from a class that all its adopted classes also inherit because the inherited class will establish common indices for the features in the adopted classes. This means, for example, that SHAPE could inherit from class ANY, without causing any difficulties.

6. Shortcomings and limitations

There are several sources of inefficiency in the mechanism described above and there are practical limits to the extent to which we can factor out commonality retroactively between classes.

Firstly, determining each foster class's DCS may involve repeatedly accessing many classes at compile time, and this could significantly increase the turnaround time for large systems. Also the DCS of each entity will change from one system to another, and so the feature table for each foster class will have to be recomputed for each different system that uses it.

Secondly, because there must be a column index unique to each class in the system, a foster class's feature table will probably contain many empty columns, corresponding to classes that are not in its DCS. The table will be sparse in other words.

Finally, unrelated sets of classes could well have semantically equivalent routines in common but the arguments to those routines could be in a different order, so their signatures would not conform. It is easy to picture a naive language extension which would allow differently placed arguments to be mapped together. For example, suppose that class BOX had a feature *zoom(centre : POINT, factor : REAL)* which we wanted to map to a feature *scale(factor : REAL, centre : POINT)* in foster class SHAPE. The mapping could be specified like this:

```
-- (Not Eiffel 3)
deferred foster class SHAPE
    adopt
        BOX rename
            zoom( centre :POINT,
                factor : REAL) as
            scale( factor : REAL,
                centre:POINT);
        CIRCLE

    feature
    scale( factor : REAL,centre:POINT) is
            deferred;
        end
end
```

However, to implement such a facility we would need a mechanism for binding arguments dynamically. Designing an efficient one and incorporating it into Eiffel would not be at all easy.

7. Conclusion

We have explored the possibility of extending the Eiffel programming language with a facility that will allow common features among classes that we cannot or should not modify to be factored out retroactively. This will allow different class hierarchies that have been developed separately to be reused together in an economic way. Such a facility is compatible with the stringent Eiffel typing rules and with Eiffel's assertion mechanism, although the classes created by it must have restricted semantics compared with ordinary classes. Such a facility is also compatible with Eiffel's fast dynamic binding system although it will most likely entail a disproportionate increase in turnaround time because dynamic class sets will have to be computed at compile time.

Acknowledgements

We would like to thank James McKim and Tom Wicklund for their contributions to some of the ideas presented here.

References

[Casais 92] Casais E., "An Incremental Class Reorganization Approach", Proc. ECOOP 92, Madsen O.L. ed., Springer-Verlag Berlin, 1992

[Johnson 92] Johnson P.,"Reusability Through Fine-grain Inheritance", Software - Practice and Experience, 22(12), 1049 - 1068, December 1992

[Lebedev 93] Lebedev V., "Re: Reverse Inheritance in Eiffel ??" Message i.d. memo.101551@cix.compulink.co.uk on Usenet group: comp.lang.eiffel, 29 March 1993

[Meyer 88] Meyer B., "Object-Oriented Software Construction, Prentice-Hall, 1988

[Meyer 90a] Meyer B, "Lessons from the Design of the Eiffel Libraries", Comms. ACM, 33(9), pp69-88, 1990

[Meyer 90b] Meyer B, "The New Culture of Software Development", Journal of Object-Oriented Programming, November/December 1990

[Meyer 91] Meyer B., " Eiffel: The Language", Version 3, Prentice Hall, 1991

[Pedersen 89] Pedersen C.H., "Extending Ordinary Inheritance Schemes to Include Generalisation", Proc. OOPSLA '89, pp407-417, 1989.

[Schrefl 88] Schrefl M., Neuhold E., "Object Class Definition by Generalisation Using Upward Inheritance", Proceedings of 4th Intl. Conf. on Data Engineering, 1988

C++ AND OBJETS

C++ EXPERIENCES

Automatic Transformation of Hybrid Object and Logic Specifications to C++ Code

V. Karakostas & L. Pourkashani
Department of Computation
UMIST, PO Box 88
Manchester M60 1QD
UK

ABSTRACT

This paper argues that a combined use of languages is needed for object-oriented software construction, since no single language can be ideal for all the phases of prototyping, design and implementation. The approach discussed in this paper is based on the combined use of two object-oriented languages. The first of them (*Amore*), a hybrid object and logic-based language, is used for specifications prototyping, whilst the second one, (C++) is used for the final system construction. An automatic tool transforms Amore specifications to C++ code templates which can be manually modified by the programmer. This approach shortens the time consuming and error prone activity of manual translation of specifications into code, whilst at the same time improves the quality of the delivered system.

1 Introduction

This paper argues that a multiplicity of languages is needed for the construction of object-oriented software, since no single language is ideal for all the different activities (specification, design, coding) taking place in the software lifecycle.

During the system specification phase, for example, important decisions have to be made by the analyst regarding the modelling of the application domain. It has to be decided which domain concepts are of interest and how they will be modelled so as to guide the implementation of the target system.

From TOOLS EUROPE '94 (Technology of Object-Oriented Languages and Systems).

At the same time the concepts have to be understandable by the future users, so that the specification can be validated before the implementation begins. The specification must be concerned only with information relevant to the description of the domain and disregard other (e.g. data structure selection) that is to be used later in the implementation stage. Provision of exceptional conditions and memory management strategies are also amongst the things that should be considered in the final stages of the software development.
In order to satisfy the above requirements there is a need for methods, techniques and tools which rapidly generate executable systems, possibly inefficienct ones, but which nevertheless exhibit (a subset of) the desired functionality. Such methods, techniques and tools come generally under the name of *prototyping*. Robust and efficient production systems can be obtained from prototype using the method of *transformational* programming. Transformational programming is a method of program construction by successive application of *transformational rules*, i.e. mappings from one program scheme to another.A hybrid logic and object-oriented language called AMORE is used for generating prototypes of a software system. These protoypes are subsequently transformed automatically into C++ code templates which can be manually completed by the programmer at a later stage. In this way the approach proposed in this paper speeds up the software development process, while at the same time enhance the quality of the software by delivering error free code The approach is summarised in Figure 1

The structure of the paper is as follows. Section 2 discusses the object and logic oriented features of Amore. Section 3 presents a set of strategies for transforming Amore constructs into corresponding

C++ code. Section 4 discusses experiences with applying the approach to implement a graphical rail network simulation system. We conculde with plans for enhancements to the approach and further research.

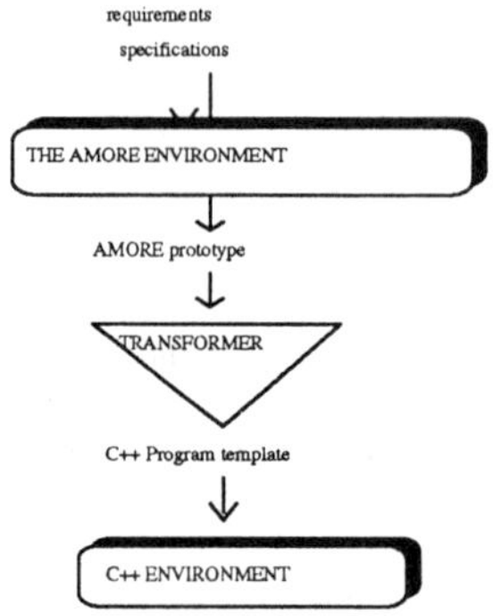

Figure 1: Amore to C++ Transformer System Architecture

2 THE OBJECT-ORIENTED LANGUAGE - AMORE

AMORE, (A Method, Object, Rule Environment), is a programming language that provides object-oriented extensions to Prolog [Palaskas 89]. The integration of the two approaches offers a flexible environment for the development of advanced information systems applications, in which Logic Programming (Prolog) is used for reasoning and Object-orientation provides facilities for structuring the domain, maintaining consistency of the modelled concepts and activating general reasoning mechanisms. [Iline 87] AMORE objects are defined in terms of *slots* and *methods.*Type definitions are supported in the form of *constraints* attached to slots. *Slot constraints* can be checked during run-time when the contents of one object's slot are modified. AMORE does not support data abstractions and encapsulation. The slots of one object can be directly accessed. An object can sensor modification of its slots by attaching to it *daemons* and *constraints.* In AMORE, objects can be either classes or instances.. A Class object defines the properties of instance objects which belong to that class. Object definitions in AMORE are symmetric. The language exploits the concept of *metaclass* (the class of a class) for the definition of class methods and slots. Class objects are instances of their metaclass.

Three types of objects are distinguished in AMORE:

Class Objects **:** The term *class* in AMORE has a similar meaning to the one used in other object-oriented languages such as Smalltalk and EIFEL [Meyer 88] Classes can be organised in hierarchies forming lattice inheritance networks.

Instance Objects **:** Instance manipulation methods, such as persistent storage and retrieval of instances, deletion and creation, are defined in the class *class* and all of the AMORE classes inherit them.

Metaclass Objects **:** A class is itself an instance of a metaclass. The definitions of the class methods and slots of a class are declared in the metaclass of that class. Classes inherit slots and methods via the metaclass network. This approach allows uniformity in the treatment of messages to classes. The metaclass network is maintained by the system automatically.

Figure 2 shows the definition of the classes *employee* and *company* in Amore. *Employee* is a subclass of *person* whilst company is a subclass of *amore_object* (a system class).

```
defclass employee.
    supers person.
slots.
        works_for,
        type instance_of ( company
endclass.
defclass company.
supers amore_object.
slots.
        employs,
          type instance_of ( employee),
          cardinality ( 0, many ),
          default [],
          inverse_of works_for.
endclass.
```

Figure 2: definitions of classes *employee* and *company*. (words in bold are reserved)

Slots and methods of objects are accessed by the use of *messages*. Messages that refer to slots, can be *queries* or *assertions*. Queries usually return the values of the addressed slot which in turn can be stored or derived. Slot value assertions are under the control of the run-time AMORE constraint management system, which performs controlled constraint evaluation whenever a slot value is changed. Slots can also have associated *daemons* which are activated during updates of slot values. When messages refer to methods the object performs the actions as specified by the *code* for these methods. Valid messages to an instance of an object, must refer to properties which have been given as slots or methods in the class definitions.

The descriptive power of slots in AMORE is further enhanced by the use of *facets*. Facets put more functionality into slots and can be used to constrain, invoke actions and derivations when one slot of an object is accessed. Different kinds of facets can be defined for one slot. Facets associated with slots describe *type, cardinality, inverse relationships, default values, general constraints* and *daemons*. These facets can be grouped into three categories according to their functionality: *constraint checking facets*, the *default value facets* and the *daemon type facets*.

Methods in AMORE are used to describe the behaviour of an object in response to a message received by that object. A method definition is equivalent to a clause definition in Prolog and can have a variable number of arguments, and also it can be distributed to more than one clause. Within the context of a class, methods can backtrack. The special variable ***self*** is unified with the instance of the class which receives the message.

3 THE AMORE TO C++ TRANSFORMATION SYSTEM

The transformation strategies that are proposed in this section, enable system developers to quickly transform an Amore prototype into C++ code templates. In the remaining of this section we outline the strategies that we adopted for the transformation of class declarations, type definitions, inheritance, daemon and method definitions from Amore to C++.

Strategies for Class Transformations

The slots and methods declared in AMORE are all supposed to be *public*. Therefore after the classes are transformed to C++, the developer should change the scope of the members according to preference to accomplish data-protection and information hiding. Before a name (identifier) can be used in a C++ programme, it must be declared; that is, its type must be specified to inform the compiler what kind of entity the name refers to. Declarations can also be definitions; that is, they can also define memory addresses (storage allocation) for the name to refer to. The strategy that has been chosen for class definitions is that the member variables are defined in the class definition body, whilst the member functions are just declared in the class, and their definition follows the class definition, accompanied by the *scope resolution operator*. The concept of metaclass in AMORE, is supported by C++ as well. In a class definition, one can define **static** data members for those attributes of which only one copy should exist for the whole class rather than an individual copy for each instance. Functions can also be declared static. Static members reduce the number of global variable and function declarations. In AMORE the metaclass concept is syntactically supported by the **common** and **private** keywords, of which the former refers to all instances of the class and the latter to the class itself.

In our transformation strategy, we first declare static members variables and then instance variables. The same rule applies for definitions of class member functions. An example of definition of class employee in both AMORE and C++ is given in figure 3.

```
defclass employee.
    superclasses person.
    private.
    slots.
        total_employees,
            type integer,
    slots.
        works_for,
            type instance_of ( company),
            cardinality ( 0, 1 ),
        age,
            type integer ( 18, 60 ),
            inheritance append,
        salary,
            type integer ( 20000, 100000).

        method primary.
        take_job ( _employer, _salary ) :-
            self<-works_for := _employer,
            self<-salary := _salary.
endclass.
```

a) AMORE class

```
class employee : public person
begin
    static int total_employees;
    int salary ;
    int age ;
    company works_for ;

    boolean ChangeSalary ( int _newValue );
    boolean ChangeAge ( int _newValue );
    void take_job ( _employer,_salary );
end /* employee */

boolean employee :: ChangeSalary ( int _newValue )
begin
  if ( _newValue < 20000 ) return false;
  if ( _newValue > 100000 ) return false;
/* Exception handler can be defined and invoked */
end /* ChangeSalary */

boolean employee :: ChangeAge ( int _newValue )
begin
  if ( ! person :: ChangeAge (_newValue) ) return false;
  if ( _newValue < 18 ) return false;
  if ( _newValue > 60 ) return false;
/* Exception handler can be defined and invoked */
end /* ChangeAge */

void employee :: take_job ( _employer,_salary )
begin
  works_for = _employer;
/* For slot ** salary ** a call to ChangeSalary is necessary. */
  salary = _salary;
end /* take_job */
```

b) C++ transformed class

Figure 3 Correspondence between AMORE and C++ class definition

Strategies for Inheritance

Single and multiple inheritance is supported by both languages. In order to transform the inheritance in C++, the inheritance information of the desired class is retrieved from the Prolog internal database and the list of superclasses are declared as *public* superclasses of the equivalent C++ class. The reason that the inheritance is *public*, is that AMORE does not support *private* or *protected* modes. Therefore as presented before, this modification is left for the developer.

Strategies for Slot Constraints

Since AMORE is not a strongly typed language, it is possible to come across slots that their type is not defined, although it is assumed that by the end of the design stage, the type of all the slots are known. If a slot is found that its type is unknown, the transformer generates a warning message in the C++ code template file.

For each slot, the **defaults** record of the class is retrieved, and if a value is found for the slot, this value is extracted from the list of default values, and it is assigned to the variable after its declaration.

Since slots' cardinalities constraint the population of the slot values, they are interpreted as the array boundaries in C++. In other words, if a slot has any cardinality except one to one, it is defined as an array, the size of which is the upper value of the cardinality description. To clarify the definition of arrays, a comment is placed in front of the variable definition stating the actual cardinality definition in AMORE code. The basic types in AMORE are *integer, real, atom* and *boolean*, which are transformed to *int, float, char** and *boolean* respectively.

Two other non-basic types which are used in AMORE, are *instance_of* and *member.* Instance_of is used in order to constraint ***part-of*** relationships. This type is actually used when the content of a slot is consist of an object of another type (instance_of (*classname*)). In this case the equivalent form will be a member variable, which is of type *classname.*
If the constraint imposed on the slot is in the format,
constraint (member (it, [male, female])
then an enumeration type is defined and placed in an enumeration file, with the enumerated values being the set of listed values (in this case male and female). The name of the enumerated type is automatically derived by adding *'Type'* at the end of slot's name. Figure 4 shows some AMORE slot definitions and the equivalent C++ member variable definitions.

```
defclass person.
    superclasses amore_object.
    slots.
        sex,
         constraint ( member ( it, [male, female] ) ),
        age,
          type integer ( 0, 120 ),
        names,
          type string ( 20 ),
          default [undef],
          cardinality ( 1, 3 ).
endclass.
```

a) AMORE class

```
class person : public amore_object
begin
    sexType sex ;
    int age ;
    char names [ 20 ] [ 3 ] = [undef] ;
        /* Cardinality is 1 : 3 */

    boolean ChangeAge ( int  _newValue );
end /* person */
```

b) C++ class

Figure 4: Slot type definitions.

Strategies for demons

Daemon facets on slots define activities which are triggered when the contents of the object's slot are accessed. There may be two categories of daemons associated with slots. Daemons which operate when the contents of slots are *queried* (**if_needed**) and daemons which operate when the values of the slots are *updated* (**before_changed, when_changed** and **after_changed**).

Daemons of the 'query' category, associate a derivation rule with a slot; the slot value is calculated and returned when the contents of a slot are queried.

type of the slot. Therefore, now it becomes clear why we inserted a fact, in the definition phase of the slot, when it had an *if_needed* daemon.

Figure 5 shows a sample *if_needed* daemon which returns the instances of *clerk* managed by some specific instance of *manager*. The right side of the figure shows the equivalent C++ member function. In the class body only the name and the return type of the function is specified, while in the function definition section, in addition to the daemon body, an extra statement which returns the derived value, is added at the end of the function.

a) AMORE class

```
defclass manager.
    superclasses employee.

    slots.
        manages,
          if_needed ( it := self<-works_for<-clerks ).

endclass.
```

b) C++ class

```
class manager : public employee
begin

    /* WARNING : Static type declaration missing */
    /* Type of variable * manages * is not defined. */

      void* GiveManages ();
end /* manager */

void* manager :: GiveManages ( )
begin
   manages = (works_for -> clerks);
   return manages ;
end /* GiveManages */
```

Figure 5 A sample of *if_needed* daemon

Strategies for Update demons

The second category of daemons, which operate during changing of the value of a slot are *before_changed, when_changed* and *after_changed.* The difference between these two types of daemons, is that the *before_changed* daemon operates before the slot value has been changed, while the *after* and *when_changed* daemons operate after the value of the slot has been changed. Thus, these two set of daemons are transformed to two types of member functions; *ChangeSlotname* and *CheckSlotname.* According to the type of daemon defined for a slot, whenever the value of a slot is being changed, one or both of these functions is invoked.

Figure 6 shows a sample class which has a *before_changed* daemon constraining the sale price of a product. The daemon specifies that the sale price can only be changed between 17:00 and 8:00 hours.

```
defclass product.
    superclasses amore_object.
    slots.
    name,
    stock_on_hand,
       type integer,
    cheapest_supplier,
       type instance_of ( supplier ),
    salesprice,
       type integer ( 0, 2000 ),
       default 0,
       before_changed ( hour ( _time, _hour ),
                        ( _hour > 17; _hour < 8 ) ).
endclass.
```

a) AMORE class

```
class product : public amore_object
begin

    int salesprice = 0 ;
    supplier cheapest_supplier ;

    /* WARNING : Static type declaration missing
    */
    /*  Type of variable ** name ** is not defined. */

    boolean ChangeSalesprice ( int _newValue );
end /* product */

boolean product :: ChangeSalesprice ( int
_newValue );
begin
  if ( _newValue < 0 ) return false;
  if ( _newValue > 2000 ) return false;
 /* Exception handler can be defined and invoked */
  hour(_time,_hour);
  if (_hour > 17 )
  begin
  end
  else begin
    _hour < 8;
  end
end /* ChangeSalesprice */
```

b) C++ class

Figure 6: Transformation of *before_changed* daemon

Strategies for methods

Unlike most object-oriented languages, AMORE supports, *before, primary* and *after* methods. The primary method overrides inherited primary methods, while all before and after methods are executed in an order determined by the precedence list of the class. Messages sent to methods have the effect of firing these methods in a three-phase sequence. First the before methods are executed, these methods are retrieved by classes in the precedence list, which is searched upwards from the most to the least specific class. Second the primary method is fired and finally all the after methods, traversing the precedence list in the *reverse* order are fired The policy which was used to transform the methods is as follows:

a) the before, primary and after methods are transformed to *BeforeMethodname, AfterMethodname* and *PrimaryMethodname.*

b) a *chief function* is defined with the same name as the AMORE method, which is responsible for calling the methods in the precedence lists hierarchy.

c) If a primary method is defined in a class, which does not have any before or after method definitions, neither in the class nor in the superclasses, this method would be the chief method, and instead of being called

PrimaryMethodname, it will be called *methodname.*

d) If a class has a definition for either of before or after methods, but no definition for a primary method, a chief function is declared for that class, which is responsible for calling the pre/post condition methods and the primary method, which should have been defined somewhere in the class precedence list.

e) The body of the chief function (except in case ***c)***) is a series of function calls, while the body of the rest of member functions is the equivalent C++ pseudo-code.

```
defclass employee.
superclasses person.
 slots.
   works_for,
      type instance_of ( company),
      cardinality ( 0, 1 ),
   age,
      type integer ,
   salary,
      type integer .

method primary.
take_job ( _employer, _salary ) :-
   self<-works_for := _employer,
   self<-salary := _salary.
endclass.

defclass clerk.
superclasses employee.
 slots.
   salary,
      type integer ,
   reports_to,

method before.
take_job ( _employer, _salary ) :-
  (
    _managerSalary :=
          _employer<-manager<-salary,
     _salary*2 > _managerSalary, !,
      fail; !
  ).

method after.
take_job ( _employer, _ ):-
   _prevclerks := _employer<-clerks,
   _employer<-clerks := [self | _prevclerks].
endclass.
```

Figure 7. Before and after method definitions.

```
class employee : public person
begin
   int salary ;
   int age ;
   company works_for ;

   void take_job ( _employer,_salary );
end /* employee */

void employee :: take_job ( _employer,_salary )
begin
  works_for = _employer;
/* For slot ** salary ** a call to ChangeSalary
is necessary.  */
  salary = _salary;
end /* take_job */

class clerk : public employee
begin
   int salary ;

   void BeforeTake_job ( _employer,_salary );
   void AfterTake_job ( _employer,_temp );
   void take_job ( _employer,_salary );
end /* clerk */

void clerk :: BeforeTake_job (
_employer,_salary )
begin
  if (_managerSalary = (_employer -> manager -
> salary) )
  begin
    _salary * 2 > _managerSalary; !;
    return false;
  end
  else begin
    !;
  end
end /* take_job */

void clerk :: AfterTake_job ( _employer,_temp )
begin  ...
```

Figure 7 shows a sample class with before and after method definitions.

Strategies for demon and method bodies

Methods and daemons are expressed in terms of Prolog predicates. Because of the declarative level of programming, backtracking, and lack of a strong typing system for parameter declaration and local variable names, it is impossible to generate exact C++ code, and at the final stage some modifications should be done by the programmer. The desired modifications are proposed to the programmer with comments in the transformed file.

4 Experimentations with the Transformational System

The Amore to C++ transformation approach was validated by applying it to the construction of a graphical rail network simulation package. The main purpose of the package was to simulate the usage of the network and identify areas of traffic conjestion, estimate delays etc. A prototype exhibiting the basic functionality of the package was built within one week, using Amore and was subsequently transformed into C++ templates. Figure 8 shows an Amore class and the corresponding C++ class template. A working system was created by adding the following features to the C++ templates:

- Dijkstra's algorithm for finding the shortest path was implemented and replaced the dummy ones used in protoype
- error recovery routines were placed in the code
- Appropriate C++ procedures were placed, so instances of the classes *stations, tracks* and *trains* were created dynamically

The above feasibility study revealed the advantages of the transformtional approach over conventional ones. By comparing the execution speed of these two systems (AMORE and C++) it became clear that the C++ version run much faster than the prototype.. As an example, the prototype algorithm which animated the trains, had to be modelled by the backtracking mechanism of Prolog, which ran 10 times slower than the equivalent C++ implementation which was programmed using the *switch* [Stroustrup 91] construct.

Similar arguments prove the importance of transforming prototypes written in high-level design languages such as Prolog and its derivations, to lower-level more efficient implementational languages. Other reasons for prototype transformation include the implementation of memory management and error recovery routines in the target system, features which are not supported by the high level languages.

5 Conclusions

The research described in this paper combines the concept of prototyping with object-orientation methods in order to construct software systems. The experience from programming languages shows that there is no such thing as a universal language capable of satisfactorily supporting all requirements of applications. Therefore it has been proven that a multi-paradigm approach is inherently better for extending a language's applicability than adding features to a coherent single paradigm language [Zave 91]. AMORE as an object-oriented extension to Prolog, combines reasoning and object structuring capabilities. The language inherits the semantics of Prolog which is not a strongly typed language and therefore makes it suitable for prototyping and coping with incompleteness of information during the early stages of software development. order to use effectively and efficiently the feedbacks of the prototyping stage in a short amount of time, we developed a transformer.

```
class station : public amore_object
begin

    static void drawStations ( );
    station neighbours [ 2000 ] ;
       /* Cardinality is 1 : many */
    int noPlatform ;
    int noSiding = 10 ;
    int xcoo ;
    int ycoo ;

    boolean ChangeXcoo ( int _newValue );
    boolean ChangeYcoo ( int _newValue );
    void init ( );
    void drawSelf ( );
    void occupyPlatform ( );
    void freePlatform ( );
    void occupySiding ( );
    void freeSiding ( );
end /* station */

static void station :: drawStations ( )
begin
  forall(instance_of(station,_instance),(_instance ->
drawSelf( )));
end /* drawStations */

boolean station :: ChangeXcoo ( int _newValue );
begin
  if ( _newValue < 0 ) return false;
  if ( _newValue > 999 ) return false;
/* Exception handler can be defined and invoked */
end /* ChangeXcoo */

void station :: drawSelf ( )
begin
  _W = (graphic -> Win);
  _Dpy = (graphic -> Dpy);
  _Gc = (graphic -> Gc);
  _x = xcoo;
  _y = ycoo;
  _x1 = _x - 15;
  _y1 = _y - 15;
  XFillArc(_Dpy,_W,_Gc,_x1,_y1,30,30,0,23040);
  _x2 = _x + 17;
  _y2 = _y - 5;

constructor_of(station,object(station,_name,_temp));
  atomlength(_name,_length);

XDrawString(_Dpy,_W,_Gc,_x2,_y2,_name,_lengt
h);
end /* drawSelf */

void station :: occupyPlatform ( )
begin
  _noPlatform = noPlatform;
  if (_noPlatform > 0 )
  begin
    !;
    _noPlatform1 = _noPlatform - 1;
    noPlatform = _noPlatform1;
  end
  else begin
    return false;
  end
end /* occupyPlatform */
```

Figure 8: C++ class template for station

Results from the raiil network simulation study used for validating the approach, have shown that approximately 85% of the C++ code was automatically derived from the prototype, whilst the rest 15% had to be coded manually. Such figures indicate the significant impact of our approach on software productivity and quality.

Future enhancements to this work can be achieved in two different areas:

- Improving the automation of the transformation process.
- Developing a software environment with two major components i.e. tools for generating prototypes and tools for deriving the production code from the final prototype.

In order to improve the automation of the transformation process, it is suggested that the capability of learning should be added to the transformer. That is specially useful for transformation of invocation of daemon function calls. At the moment this transformation is based on an one to one mapping. We suggest that in complex expressions which more than two slots are accessed per a message, and at least two of them have daemon facets, user advice should be requested. The user solution is then added to a knowledge base, so that whenever similar patterns are found, the transformation could be done automatically and in case of ambiguous patterns, user assistance will be asked.

References

AMORE- A METHOD, OBJECT, RULE ENVIRONMENT (1989)
The RUBRIC Implentation Manual, Information Systems Research Group, Department of Computation, UMIST, UK.

Clocksin, W.F.; Mellish, C.S. (1981)
Programming in Prolog, Springer-Verlag, 1981.

Goldberg, A.; Robson, P. (1983)
Smalltalk-80 : The Language and its implementation, Addison-Weseley, Reading, Massachusetts, 1983.

Iline, H.; Kanoui, H. (1987)
Extending Logic Programming to Object Programming, The system LAP, IJCAI 1987, Milano, pp. 34-39, 1987.

Leibrandt, V.; Schnupp, P. (1984)
An evaluation of Prolog as a Prototyping System, in Budde, R. (ed.) Approaches to Prototyping, Springer-Verlag, 1984

Palaskas, Z.; Loucopoulos, P. (1989) *AMORE-Object-Oriented Extensions to Prolog,* Proceedings of TOOLS '89, Paris-France, 1989.

Stroustrup, B. (1991) *The C++ Programming Language,* 2nd edition, Addison-Wesley, 1991

SPATIO2 : An object oriented approach for a generalized spatial information system

Mohamed EL ADNANI, Michel SCHNEIDER

Laboratoire d'Informatique
Université Blaise Pascal Clermont-Ferrand II
Complexe Scientifique des Cézeaux
63177 Aubière CEDEX
Tél: 73.40.77.70 Fax: (33) 73.26.88.29
Email: eladnani@libd1.univ-bpclermont.fr

Abstract
This paper concerns the spatial information system, SPATIO2, the main objectives of which are the simultaneous management of several geometrical representations, the possibility to be extented to new geometrical types and the ability to permit access to all kinds of users. We present the object model and the architecture of the system. We also illustrate the possibility of applications through an example.

1) Introduction

Spatial information systems (SIS) are complex systems resulting from the development and the integration of many techniques coming from various domains such as database, computer assisted drawing, geometrical data computing. Indeed, data involved in these systems are complex and large. They have a geometrical part which necessitates specific representations and specific processings.

SIS have come to light during the 1960 decade and have evoluate very quickly [Smith 87]. Most commercialized SIS are based on the relational model, which has proved its efficiency for classical applications. However, this model appears not enough flexible for spatial applications and many extensions have been proposed [Mohan 88, Voisard 92].

From TOOLS EUROPE '94 (Technology of Object-Oriented Languages and Systems).

Development of new SIS are now based on the object oriented model. This model offers many facilities for spatial applications. The more significatives are the following [Choi 90, Mohan 88]:

• Abstraction of data at different levels

This concept permits the definition of a set of classes linked through composition relationships and generalization/specialization relationships. It is very important for SIS, since SIS manage complex objects linked through geometrical and semantical relationships.

• Identity of objects

In the object model, each object received a unique identifier at its creation, before any affectation of a value. This identifier cannot be changed nor reused. This feature is also important for SIS. For example a geographical area can be defined and can receive an identifier independantly of the values of its properties or of the objects composing it.

• Extensibility

The object model facilitates the design of extensible systems thanks to the dynamical creation of types. This feature is particularly interesting for spatial applications. In fact, a majority of applications can be initialized with a limited number of object types and can then evoluate as and when required. Extensions are made through the schema of the database at different levels [Chrisment 92]:

-adding/deleting classes
-adding/deleting attributes
-insertion of methods
-management of versions.

• High level query langages

Object oriented languages take better into consideration the nature of spatial queries which are often object oriented and rarely tuple oriented. In fact, in applications such as planification and management of natural ressources, queries are concerned with precise geographical areas and not with a set of geographical entities.

Due to these facilities, the object oriented model is suited both for the design and the development of SIS. Numerous prototypes of SIS have adopted it. There are roughly three categories of systems. First, there are systems based on some aspects of the object approach like SYSTEM 9 [Van Eck 90] and TIGRIS [Herring 89]. In these systems, data are managed through a server of objects and graphical interfaces are implemented through graphical objects. Second, there are systems which are based on a specific object model. PROBE [Orenstein 88] is an example of such a system. Its main objective is the elaboration of an extensible OODBMS for managing spatial data and also temporal data. Third, there are systems based on existing OODBMS. Example of such systems are SIRO-SPOT [Haldstead 90] based on ONTOS and GOODS [Voisard 92] based on O2.

In this paper we propose a SIS called SPATIO2 which can be placed in the third category. Compared with existing systems, SPATIO2 presents two originalities.
First, it permits the integration of several data representations and is thus able to cover a broad range of spatial applications. Such an integration allows the user to choice the best representation for his (her) application [Laurini 92]. It permits also to modelize with a same system, applications requiring simultaneously different representations.
Second, it offers a set of operations independant of the internal represention of the spatial data. Indeed, the concept of abstraction in the object model permits the definition of a class hierarchy at different levels of abstraction and the affectation of a set of operations at each level. These operations are virtual at the upper level. They are defined only at the lower level, the one of the concrete objects.

This paper is organized as follows. In section 2 we present quickly the data model of the system. More details about this model can be found in [El Adnani 93]. Spatial analysis and spatial operations are described in section 3. Section 4 is a discussion about the extensibility of the system. In section 5 we present the graphical interface and its functionnalitites. An example of application is given in section 6.

2) The data model of SPATIO2

The data model of SPATIO2 is object oriented. It offers an integrated management of the spatial informations in avoiding the separate management of the descriptive part and the geometrical part. Geometrical classes are defined through a hierarchy divided in two parts: the abstract classes and the concrete classes.

Abstract classes are superclasses wich modelize only the geometrical part of a spatial object. Their internal representation is hidden to the user. Theses classes are the following : ObjPonctual for ponctual objects, ObjLinear for linear objects and ObjSurf for surfacical objects. Geometrical operations are attached to these classes. These operations are methods sharing by all the representations (figure 1).
Concrete classes modelize the geometry of spatial objects by taking into account their internal representation. In our model, three internal representations are available: the spaghetti representation, the topological representation and the raster representation [Laurini 92, El Adnani 93].

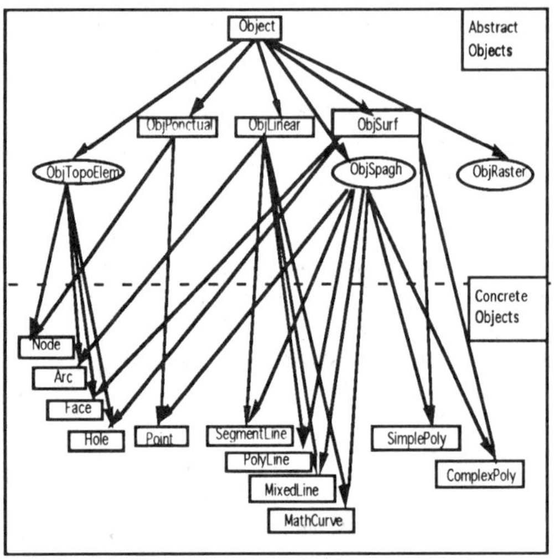

Figure 1: Hierarchy of predefined geometrical classes

The object approach permits to classify the geometrical objects according to two criteria : the dimension and the geometrical

representation. For example, the geometrical class MixedLine is used to modelize a linear real entity (it is thus a sub-class of the class ObjLinear) and is represented through the spaghetti representation (it is thus a sub-class of the class ObjSpagh).
This choice of modelization permits to group the geometrical operations on two levels. The first level groups the operations specific to a particular representation. These operations are implemented by methods attached to the class ObjSpagh (for the spaghetti representation), the class ObjTopoElem (for the topological representation), the class ObjRaster (for the raster representation). The second level groups the operations which are shared by all the geometrical representations. For example, the display or the rotation of a line is a shared operation which applies to a line, independantly of its representation.

3) Spatial analysis and spatial operations

These is no precise definition of the term "spatial analysis" and the different activities involved by the spatial analysis are sources of confusion both for the designers of softwares and for the users. This analysis can be seen as a cognitive process wich needs different operations (there is at least one geometrical operation) for deriving descriptive and spatial characteristics of a spatial phenomena [Openshaw 92, Champoux 92].
Several proposals for classifying these operations appear in the literature [Champoux 92, Laurini 92]. For the SPATIO2 system, we have naturally grouped it into two catagories : the factual operations and the spatial operations.
Factual operations are those offer by traditional systems. They are logical operations (<, >, =, ≠, for exemple) and arithmetical operations (Max, Min, Avg, Sum). They do not induce any problem for their implementation.
Spatial operations involve at least one spatial object as operands. They depend on the geometrical part of the operands. Usually, a geometrical information comprises metrical data (coordinate, length, area,...) and topological data (membership, proximity,...). So we distinguish two kinds of spatial operations: metrical operations and topological operations.
Metrical operations depend on the geometry, the dimension and the scale of the representation. topological operations modelize the different topological realationships which exist between the spatial objects.
Another category groups all the spatial predicates having two spatial objects as operands. These objects can belong to the same type or to different types. A spatial predicate is used to verify if a spatial property is satisfied. "inside" and "outside" are example of spatial predicates. In the SPATIO2 system, all these operations are considered as basical operations. They are implemented as global methods at the level of the abstract classes. Thanks to the concept of method overloading, these operations are redefined at the level of the concrete classes.
With the object approach, the problem of reusing results of spatial operations as operands forf other operations is simply solved. In fact, spatial operations can produce results under the form of a set of objects of different types. For example, intersection of two lines can produce a set of segments and a set of points. With classical models, it is not possible to apply an operation to an heterogeneous set of types. In the object model, it is possible to define an abstract super-class (ObjSpagh for example) with instances of different types.

4) Extensibility of SPATIO2

The architecture of SPATIO2 comprises three layers [El Adnani 93]. The first layer is the graphical interface, the second is the geometrical layer and the third is the physical layer.
The graphical interface permits interactions with different kinds of users. It is explicited in the next section.
The geometrical classes (abstract and concrete classes) are defined with their methods in the geometrical layer.
The physical layer takes charge of the storage of the data on the physical devices and their protection. This layer uses the functionnalities of an OODBMS.
The user or the designer can define new specific classes through the graphical interface. A new class can be added to existing classes either as a subclass or either as a class with an attribute having a type of an existing geometrical class. In either case, the new class reuses the predefined geometrical methods.
It is also possible to add new geometrical types. A new geometrical type defines in fact a new class for which the designer has to define the attributes and the methods. This class can be

inserted in the hierarchy of the predefined classes. This insertion can only takes place at the level of the concrete classes.
The new geometrical classes are seen by the system like the predefined geometrical classes. This is made possible thanks to a library of geometrical methods. The system manages this library as a separate class. It is recognized by all the other classes, through the mechanism of the "friendly classes".
In the library, the methods having two geometrical objects of different types as operands are grouped together. This grouping is valid both for the predefined classes and the new classes. In fact, in a class, only the specific behavior of the objects of this clas must be defined. For example, for the intersection operation of the class MixedLine, only the intersection between a mixed line and another mixed line is defined. The intersection with a mixed line of another type is defined elsewhere in the library. Thus, if a new class A is inserted in the hierarchy, the designer adds to the library all the methods having as operand an object of type A and an object of a predefined type. The class A is viewed by a predefined class B like a basic class.
This mechanism ensures the extensibility of the system to new geometrical types. This extensibility is very important for general purpose systems (not dedicated to a specific application).

5) The graphical interface

The SPATIO2 graphical interface is one of the most important part of the system. Thereby, its design has received a particular attention. The graphical interface of any spatial information systems (SIS) must be designed and implemented with the whole system and must not appear as "something to be done after the design and the implementation (of the system) has been completed" [Egenhofer 90]. It is, for a naïve user, the unique way to communicate with the system. The success and effectiveness of any system is function of both the mode for querying data and the mode for displaying the data.

The graphical sub-system of SPATIO2 is composed of two layers: the application layer and the translation layer (figure 2).

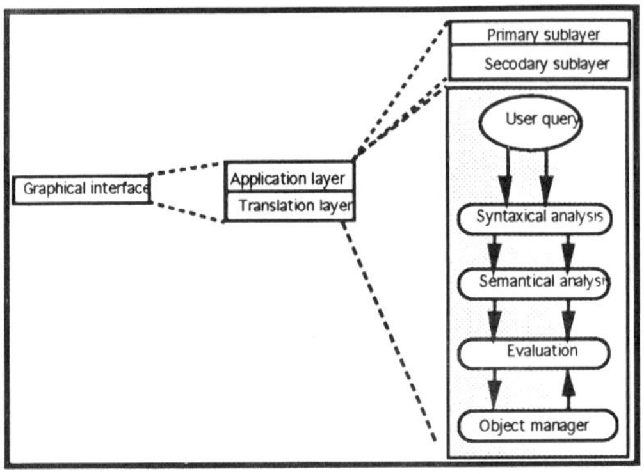

figure 2: The SPATIO2 graphical interface

The application layer

The application layer permits the interaction between the system and the user. There are two sublayers: the primary and the secondary sublayers.

The primary sublayer is dedicated to novice users for querying or modifying the database through specific applications. This sublayer manages windows, menus and queries.
Windows are specific to an application and can be implemented by using general graphical tools or by programming directly with the X11 primitives.
Menus visualize the actions that can be made on the objects. These menus are dynamic in the sense that they depend on the type of the selected objects. For example, a map is an entity on which operations such as zooming and browsing can be executed. The spatial entities of this map may have some operations wich are visualised if the user select one of these entities. To facilitate the manipulations, operations are grouped within classes [Abel 92].

Queries can be graphical or textual. But at this level, graphical queries are more often used. All graphical queries have an textual equivalent form, but the reverse is not true. Indeed, with the textual mode, it is possible to expressed complex queries which have several levels of imbrication. Textual mode is more often used in the secondary sublayer.

The secondary sublayer is dedicated to designers of spatial applications. These users are more familiarized with the system and they know all the predefined geometrical classes.

Designers can use an object oriented design method for specifying a hierarchy of classes specific to an application. These classes are spatial classes which have factual attributes and spatial/geometrical attributes. Factual attributes are specific to an application, while spatial attributes are instances of geometrical predefined classes.

We have seen that spatial applications are primarily concerned by two kinds of relationships: the ISA relationship used to hierarchize classes, and the Part-of relationship used to aggregate objects [Choi 90].
Internal representations of spatial objects are transparent at this level. The user can choice the internal representation of his application. The adequate instanciations and calls of methods are made transparently by the system.
At this level, the user may also indicate to the system the type of the spatial indexes for each class. Indeed, the system may support several spatial indexes, the management of which is transparent.
Textual queries can be expressed directly by using an extension of the SQL language (Object-SQL) or by programming in C++. This last query style allows navigation from object to object using links. Researches over trees and graphs are then more easier.

The translation layer

The main fonctionnalities of this layer are:

- Translation of graphical queries,
- Processing of queries,
- Optimisation of disk accesses.

The translator transforms graphical queries into SQL queries.
Graphical interrogation process starts by loading the workspace of the user. This space is either a direct representation of a partial database (a map for example) or a schema of classes representing the database conceptual schema.
Members of the From clause are the classes chosen by the user for his (her) query. Members of the Select clause are the selected attributes and the methods which are necessary to manipulate these attributes. Conditions are expressed in an interactive way: the system displays for each attribute or class a set of operations which are available, and the users select one or several operations. The translator can thus derives the corresponding SQL conditions. After this stage, a SQL query, equivalent to the graphical query, is produced.
Processing of textual queries is composed of a syntactical analysis, a semantical analysis and an evaluation. The semantical analysis has in charge the checking of coherence between classes, objects, and functions or methods [Damier 91]:

- Existence of manipulated classes,
- Existence and origin of attributes involved in the query,
- Path validity of the object graph,
- Existence of functions and validity of types.

The evaluation is made in two stages: the first one evaluates the factual/semantical part of the query. The second one evaluates the spatial/geometrical part if necessary. Spatial methods attached to predefined classes are called during this last stage.

As in traditional systems, a query optimizer is called during the evaluation stage. The optimizer recognises the existence of spatial/factual indexes and uses them to optimize queries.

6) Example of an application

Our system is able to implement different types of applications such as spatial applications and connecting applications such as hyperdocument and hyperconcept applications [Agosti 93].
We suggest in this section, a brief description of this kind of applications with our system.

An hyperdocument permits representation and management of a collection of multimedia documents (maps, texts, images). An hyperconcept permits a representation of concepts that are used to semantically characterize the documents of the collection.

The implementation, in our system, of hyperdocuments and hyperconcept have as purpose to interrogate the database by content, but not by values of attributes. This means that it is possible, for the user, to retrieve informations from the database without knowing in details all attributes and all relations. For example, the user has the possibility to formulate a query like "Retrieve all French cities whose degree of pollution is critic" although an attribute "Pollution" is not attached to the "Cities" of the database.

The design approach for systems supporting semantical queries two levels of modelization.
In the first level, the hyperdocument is defined. An hyperdocument is a set of complex objects and a network of links between them. Each complex object is a combination of several simple objects (for example, maps are made of points, lines, polygones texts, images).

In the example of figure 3, the object Obj1 is composed of sub-objects {SObj11, SObj12, SObj13, SObj14}. This object is linked to another object Obj2 by a reference link via the sub-object SObj14.

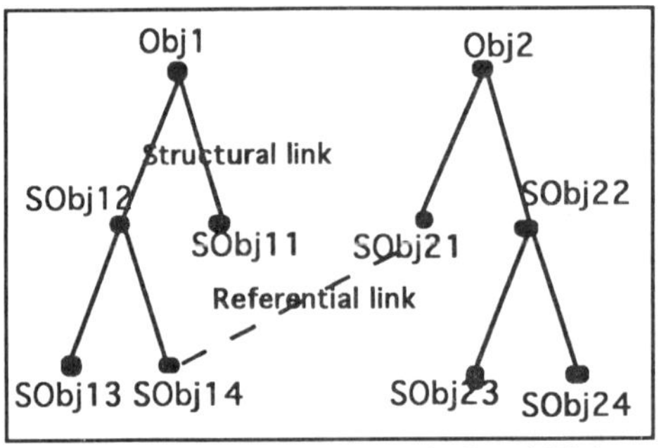

Figure 3: Example of structural and referential links

The implementation of this hyperdocument with SPATIO2, is possible by using concrete class wich are predefined by the system or added by the user. Structural links are modelled by the Part-of relationship, and referential links are modelled by object identifiers.
So, two networks are constructed: a network of structural links witch permits creation of complex objects, and a network of referential links wich permits the modelization of the links between complex objects. It is possible to navigate between objects through these two networks.

The second level creates an hyperconcept which is defined by a set of semantical terms. Each semantical term is assumed to describe semantically the content of objects of the first level. This description is neither complete nor unique. Indeed, one object of the first level may have various descriptions which reflect different user requirements. So, an object have different semantical terms associated to it. On the opposite, one semantical term may be associated to several objects.

With the SPATIO2 system, these semantical terms are implemented as classes. Each class has one or more synonym names which describe various concepts (pollution, tourism, industry). The relation between a class which associates a semantical term and the objects of the first level is modelized by the inheritance relationship. For example in figure 4, the designer establishes an inheritance relationship between the map MapX and the classes Pollution, Tourism, Industry and Demography, in order to describe the contents of this map. So, one instance of this map, will have as properties all synonyms of the terms Pollution, Tourism, Industry and Demography. Consequently, the user can retrieve this map, through one of these concepts.

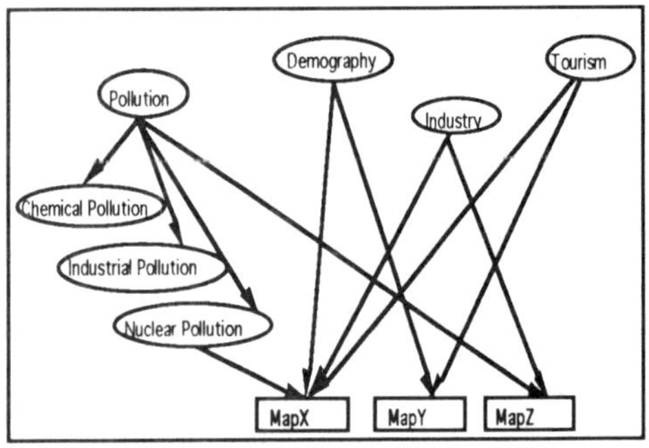

Figure 4: Example of hyperconcept

Several specialization/generalisation links can exist between classes (concepts) of the second level. The Pollution class for example, can be specialized in three sub-classes: ChemicalPollution, NuclearPollution and IndustrialPollution.
If two classes of the second level are related by a specialization relationship, the two corresponding sets of objects at the first level are associated by the sub-set relationship. In our example, the set of objects corresponding to the concept chemical-Pollution is a sub-set of the set of objects corresponding to the concept Pollution.

Conclusion

We have presented in this paper the main functionnalities of the spatial information system SPATIO2. SPATIO2 permits the integration of several internal geometrical representations. Its data model ensures the management of the two parts of spatial informations. It is designed as an upper layer of an OODBMS (O2, ONTOS, ...). It can thus reuse all the functionnalities of such a system : persistance of objects, error recovery, concurrent accesses, ...

The object model of SPATIO2 permits the definition of geometrical operations which can be applied to sets of objects of different types. This feature is rarely present in existing systems.

The implementation of SPATIO2 is currently in progress on a SUN station. The definition of the classes of the geometrical layer and their methods is coded in C++. The implementation of the graphical interface is achieved through a graphical interface generator.

Different kinds of applications can be developped by using SPATIO2 thanks to its extensibility. Among these applications, we can quote management of hyperdocuments and hyperconcepts, cartographic management, urban management.

BIBLIOGRAPHIE

[Abel 92] D. J. Abel, S. K. Yap, R. Ackland, M. A. Cameron, D. F. Smith, G. Walker, "Environmental decision support system project: an exploration of alternative architectures for geographical information systems", Int. J. Geographical information systems, Vol. 6, No. 3, pp. 193-204, 1992.

[Agosti 93] M. Agosti, F. Crivellari, G. Deambrosis, G. Gradenigo, "An object-oriented approach for the conceptual modelling of geographical, structured and textual data", Revue de géomatique, Vol. 3, N°. 1-2, pg. 149-165, 1993.

[Champoux 92] P. Champoux, Y. Bédard, "Notions fondamentales d'analyse spatiale et opérateurs spatiaux", Volume 2, N° 2, pp. 187-208, 1992.

[Choi 90] A. Choi, W. S. Luk, "A Bi-Level Object-Oriented Data Model for GIS Applications", Compsac 90, Chicago, Oct.29-Nov.2 1990.

[Chrisment 92] C. Chrisment, G. Pujolle, G. Zurfluh, "Base de Données Orientées Objets", Technique de l'Ingénieur, Traité Informatique H 3840, 1992.

[Damier 91] C. Damier, B. Defude, "Le prototype OMEGA: un SGBD extensible pour les applications géographiques", Revue SEGA, Vol. 1, Num. 1, 1991.

[David 91] B. David, "Modélisation, représentation et gestion d'informations géographiques: une approche en relationnel étendu", Thèse de Doctorat, Paris 6, Juillet 1991.

[Van Eck 90] J. W. Van Eck, M. Uffer, "A presentation of System 9", in [Davi91], pp. 26.

[Egenhofer 90] Max J. Egenhofer, "Interaction with geographic information systems via spatial queries", Journal of Visual Languages and Computing, N°. 1, pp 389-413, 1990.

[El Adnani 93] M. El Adnani, M. Schneider, "Un modèle orienté objet pour les informations spatiales", RPO'93, la Grande Motte, France, 1993.

[Herring 89] J. R. Herring, "A fully interacted geographic information system", in [Davi91], pp. 26.

[Halstead 90] M. Halstead, H. Mackenzie, P. Milue, S. Milton, J. Smith, "A spatial object toolkit", URPIS 18, Canberra, Nov. 21-23, 1990.

[Laurini 92] R. Laurini, D. Thompson: "Fundamental of spatial information systems", The APIC series, Number 37, Academic Press, 1992.

[Mohan 88] L. Mohan, R. L. Kashyap: "An Object-Oriented Knowledge Representation for Spatial Information", IEEE Transaction on Software Engineering, Vol. 14, No. 5, May 1988.

[Openshaw 92] S. Openshaw, C. Brunsdon: "An introduction to spatial analysis in GIS", International GIS Sourcebook, 1991-1992.

[Orenstein 88] J. A. Orenstein, F. A. Manola: "PROBE: Spatial Data Modeling and Query Processing in an Image Database Application", IEEE Transaction on Software Engineering, Vol. 14, No. 5, May 1988.

[Smith 87] T. R. Smith, S. Menon, J. L. Star, J. E. Estes: "Requirements and principles of large-scale geographic information systems", Int. J. Geographic Information Systems, Vol. 1, No. 1, pp 13-31, 1987.

[Voisard 92] A. Voisard, "Base de données géographiques: du modèle de données à l'interface graphique", Thèse de Doctorat, Paris-Sud, Centre d'Orsay, 1992.

Interobject Communication Mechanisms

Adelino da Silva
Universidade Nova de Lisboa
2825 Monte de Caparica, Portugal

Abstract

In this paper a concurrent object-oriented model is introduced. The model relies on the fundamental notions of active objects, passive objects, and interobject communication mechanisms. Active objects are conceived as anthropomorphic processing agents using resources and communicating with other agents. Passive objects are regarded as resources used by the agents operating in a shared memory architecture. A set of classes dealing with mutual exclusion and synchronization mechanisms are presented. The reutilization of sequential object-oriented structures in the definition of interobject communication mechanisms is emphasized. Several examples illustrate how the model achieves an effective integration of concurrent principles and techniques into the object-oriented methodology.

1. Introduction

Purely sequential programming languages tend to view an object as a record of functions together with a hidden state representation. The member functions provide an encapsulation of the object's behavior. However, since these functions are usually statically defined, objects are not allowed to dynamically change behavior. Other problems are the servicing of requests in class hierarchies and the synchronization constraints between requests. Some authors have extended the basic object oriented model in order to account for patterns of communications. The Eiffel methodology [Meyer 92a], for instance, introduced the notion of Design by Contract [Meyer 92b]. According to this view, classes communicate on the basis of contracts, which are documented as assertions in the text of the software itself. A contract governs the relation between client objects requesting services and supplier objects providing services. This notion closely follows the fundamental tenets of Hoare's CSP [Hoare 78] and Milner's CCP [Milner 89], in which input and output are basic primitives and that parallel composition of communicating sequential processes is a fundamental program structuring method. However, implementing contracts in a purely sequential language barely augments the complexity without the benefits of effective behavior separation.

From TOOLS EUROPE '94 (Technology of Object-Oriented Languages and Systems).

In this paper a concurrent object-oriented model is introduced. The model relies on the fundamental notions of active objects, passive objects, and interobject communication mechanisms. Active objects are conceived as anthropomorphic processing agents using resources and communicating with other agents. Passive objects are regarded as resources used by the agents operating in a shared memory architecture. The concepts of class and lightweight process are unified in the Thread class. An active object is an instance of *Thread* executing a prescribed behavior, which may be redefined by inheritance or substitution. Concurrency abstractions for the C++ language are encapsulated in class libraries. A set of classes dealing with mutual exclusion and synchronization mechanisms are presented. The reutilization of sequential object-oriented structures in the definition of interobject communication mechanisms is emphasized. Several examples illustrate how the model achieves an effective integration of concurrent principles and techniques into the object-oriented methodology.

2. A Concurrent Object-Oriented Model

In line with several concurrency methodologies [Agha 90, Caromel 93, Milner 89, Nierstrasz 93], we view an object as a process, meaning an abstract machine that communicates by passing messages. It is then possible to characterize the service types associated with an object in terms of request and reply messages. As expressed in [Nierstrasz 93] "services represent contracts or `promises´ over the message-passing behavior of the object". On the other hand, an object may change its abstract state to alter the availability of selected services. In our approach we have adopted the notion of active objects, in which each object has a script associated with a local thread that runs concurrently with all the other active objects in the system. The distinction between active and passive objects has been followed in many concurrent object-oriented languages. Usually, a local thread is scheduled for execution as soon as the object is created. In our implementation the thread enters the ready sate at creation time. It enters the running state after being scheduled for execution according to its priority and the scheduling policy. However, the scheduler begins operation only after the execution of an initial command is issued to start the thread system. This means that threads created before this initial command may enter the running state only after it has been issued. In contrast with the view expressed in [Meyer 93] we regard the active-passive distinction beneficial, since it is semantically closer to the the real situations we want to model. From our perspective, the evolution of programming towards higher-level constructs has been oriented by the need of friendlier conceptual tools. This means, in general, to draw closer the semantic gap between real and conceptual tools. Certainly, we can conceive forks that behave like philosophers, but fortunately we can easily dispense with them in the real world (more seems to be less).

Passive objects are then basically regarded as resources, and active objects as agents using resources and communicating with other agents. An active object or agent is not allowed to directly use the services of other agents. The only way agents can interact is through message passing. On the other hand, we don't have to limit ourselves to just one script per object as stated in [Meyer 93]. There are mechanisms available in the framework of strongly-typed, object-oriented languages enabling dynamic behavioral substitution. One such mechanism involving external functions was proposed in [Silva 92]. Other mechanisms involve dynamic, member-function replacement. A thread, in this scheme, is an instance of a thread class with a characteristic default behavior, which can be overridden at construction time or at later stages. This permits the customization of instance behaviors, and points towards the incorporation of object orientation within the object-oriented framework [Silva 92]. Specialization through inheritance and polymorphism continue to be available as fundamental tools. Hiding mechanisms throughout the inheritance graph remain valid.

In order to introduce concurrency in a object-oriented system three main approaches have been followed. First, a new concurrent object-oriented language may be conceived. Second, an existing object-oriented language may be extended, namely by modifying the compiler or by introducing new keywords that are resolved by a pre-processor. Third, a library may be designed. In this case, concurrency abstractions are provided by external libraries. The first approach is the most time-consuming and difficult to implement. Apart from the fact of being not fully debugged, most of these new languages lack proper development tools and have restricted circulation. However, they permit to rethink anew the concurrency problem without the restrictions of a host sequential language. The second approach, as followed in [Bershad 88], has proved an affordable compromise between conception and implementation of new concurrency constructs. The library approach has been followed in more recent proposals. It comes from the realization that an object-oriented language does not require modification, or its compiler for that matter, in order to support concurrency in a fully integrated manner [Loer 93]. A concurrent model following this orientation was recently proposed [Karaorman 93].

3. Library Design

The problem of how to organize class libraries has been influenced by the Smalltalk class hierarchy where a single object class was defined at the top. This organization has been followed in many libraries for the C++ language [Stroustrup 91], namely in the NIH class library [Gorlen 90]. However, the closed architecture of the Smalltalk environment does not suit the openness admissible in C++ and other recent object-oriented languages. The problem of library design has recently been given renewed attention [Stroustrup 93, Ellis 93]. An important design issue in library design is reutilization support. There are trade-offs associated with both reusing libraries and designing self-contained libraries [Ellis 93]. In order to evaluate the code reutilization capabilities provided by class libraries one should ask how ease would it be to reuse coded class hierarchies from different libraries. A Smalltalk like hierarchy is poorly suited for this purpose since it relies on a single "universal" root class for each library, providing different basic services according to the application they serve. Library diversity reflects the diversity of applications. A library supporting interactive graphics has different constraints than a library supporting concurrency. Nevertheless, low-level data structures with similar features tend to be supported by all self-contained libraries. But even these features are difficult to factor out. A library organized as a forest of multiple hierarchic trees with a loosely coupled graph of interactions between classes and objects is expected to facilitate library coexistance and reutilization.

In many C++ class libraries it is common practice to derive classes from one top element class defining the characteristics of objects that can be placed in lists, when the objects are intended to be linked. This practice pushes the definition of more application oriented classes down the inheritance tree. In NIH, for instance, the Process class inherits from the linked list class. The hierarchic path, from the root is: Object - Link - Process. The linked list class is a general purpose class for singly-linked list links and, in our perspective, should not be incorporated in the special-purpose hierarchy of the process class. In [Iactors 92] the following (partial) top-down hierarchy was defined: ORDINAL - ELEMENT - THREAD - PROCESS. *ORDINAL* refers to objects that can be ordered. *ELEMENT* refers to objects that can be placed in lists. *THREAD* refers to objects defining a thread of execution. *PROCESS* refers to threads with real-time support. In this class hierarchy the purpose of the ORDINAL class is to enable objects to be compared using comparison operators. The class includes a virtual member function, Compare(ORDINAL &), which must be defined in derived classes. The ELEMENT class typically contains at least two pointers, for implementing a double-linked list. It is apparent that the classes of interest for the definition of processes were supplemented with two classes (ORDINAL and ELEMENT) dealing with the queuing of processes. This approach tends to hinder code reutilization for two reasons. First, modifications or substitutions made in the thread derived classes have to take into account the top classes. This occurs in spite of the fact that the classes dealing with processes constitute a coherent hierarchy by themselves. If someone for instance intends to modify the PROCESS class subtree, knowledge of how the ORDINAL and ELEMENT classes are defined is in general required. Second, common libraries usually support the services provided by those top classes. In the above classification, it would be difficult to join the services provided by one library for linking elements with the services provided by another for thread management. Therefore, from our point of view, the THREAD class should be promoted to the top of the hierarchy. The problem of linking objects should be handled by classes grouped in an orthogonal hierarchy, enabling the linkage of different object types. The application of multiple inheritance or even HAS-A relationships would then better suit the purpose of library reutilization.

4. Designing a Library Supporting Concurrency

Following the above considerations a C++ class library supporting concurrency has been designed. The library uses some of the atomic primitives incorporated in the concurrent programming toolkit Interwork™ [Iwork 91]. The toolkit is a C program library for building concurrent programs, and it is available for DOS™ and Unix™ environments. Processes are implemented as lightweight processes or threads. The class dealing with thread management is illustrated in figure 1.

```
class Thread {
private:
  char *tname;              // thread's name
  int tnum;                 // thread's id
  int priority;             // thread's priority
protected:
  virtual void Task() = 0; // thread's active behavior
// set current thread's priority
  void AdjustCurrentPrior(int p);
// thread suspends itself for a specified amount of time
  void Sleep(TIME it);
  void End(int code); // end currently running thread
  void Preempt();       // preempt running thread
public:
  int Read() { return tnum; }
  char *Name() { return tname; }
  Thread(char *nm, int i, int prio);
  ~Thread() { Ctrl_Thread::KillThread(tid[tnum]); }
};
```

Figure 1. Introducing concurrency: the Thread abstract class

All processes inherit from the Thread abstract class with a single active thread per object named Task. The Thread constructor is responsible for creating the thread with its specific name, identification, and priority. The class incorporates features that control its own running behaviour. A thread may adjust its priority, put itself to sleep or decide to be preempted. The thread is killed if the object ceases to exist. It is worth noting that we regard the object's behavior, as well as other services that may be provided by the object as protected. As referred to before, the active object is considered an independent agent whose services can only be used by other agents if previously requested and accepted. Nevertheless, derived agents are allowed to inherit the expertise of the parent. Processes inheriting from the thread class are responsible for the definition of the specific communication mechanism they want to follow. In [Silva 92] we have used asynchronous shared message passing as the main communication mechanism among agents.

Features enabling a thread to control other threads are grouped in the Ctrl_Thread class (figure 2). The Stack class deals with the stack management. Threads have their own stacks so that they can be suspended and later resumed. A predetermined amount of memory is assigned to each stack. Operations for stack management are grouped in the Stack class. The Mode class controls the three scheduling modes considered: non-preemptive, preemptive and time-sliced. Non-preemptive scheduling ensures that a running thread remains in execution until it gives up control. Preemptive scheduling allows preemption whenever a thread of higher priority is made runnable. Time-sliced scheduling gives each process a time slice in which it is allowed to run before being preempted by another thread of the same or higher priority. Thus, the processor is shared between multiple runnable threads with the highest priority.

5. Mutual Exclusion and Synchronization

5.1 Mutual Exclusion

In a shared memory architecture mutual exclusion between competing threads must be considered. Mutual exclusion allows a thread to temporarily prevent all others from using a shared resource. The exclusion mechanisms must consider not only the serialization of concurrent accesses to a resource but also the problem of interrupt handling and preemptive scheduling. Interrupts asynchronously preempt the execution of a thread. It is often necessary to ensure that certain sections of code execute atomically, i.e. without interruption by an interrupt handler or another thread. This situation usually arises when multiple threads and/or interrupt handlers access shared data structures. On the other hand, preemptive scheduling requires synchronized accesses to shared data structures to make sure that all functions shared by multiple threads are designed in a reentrant manner. A reentrant function allows multiple, simultaneous invocations by threads and/or interrupt handlers. Most C library functions are not reentrant. Reentrant calls to non-reentrant functions can be prevented by temporarily disabling thread preemption.

```
class Stack { // threads have their own stacks
  int stack;
public:
  Stack() { stack = 1024;}  // default stack's size
  static int Currentsz();
  static void Stacksz(int sz); // modify stack's size
  static void Check();
// the main stack can be used instead of the thread's
stack
  static int MainStack();
  static int ThreadStack();
};

class Ctrl_Thread {
public:
// threads are accessed through their ids
  static void KillThread(ID id); // kill thread
  static void WakeupThread(ID id);
// modify thread's priority
  static void SetThreadPrio(ID id, int p);
  static int ThreadPrio(ID id); // query thread's priority
  static void SetThreadTmSlice(ID id, TIME timesz);
  static TIME ThreadTmSlice(ID id);
  static void Run(); // run the thread system
  static void Stop();
  static void SetTmSlice(TIME sz);
// get id of currently running thread
  static ID RunningThread();
};

class Mode {
// initializes the thread system and manages the
// scheduler's mode
  short mode;
public:
// modes are: non-preemptive, preemptive, and
// time-sliced
  enum runmode { nonpreempt = 0, preempt = 1,
                 timeslice = 2 };
  void Init(runmode = 2);
  void Chgmode(runmode ); // change running mode
  Mode() : mode(2) {} // timesliced mode by default
  ~Mode();
};
```

Figure 2. Classes for stack management, thread control, and scheduling mode definition.

Three basic exclusion mechanisms are in general considered: interrupt locks, preemption locks and semaphores. In object-oriented implementations an interrupt lock object provides a structured access to disabling and enabling interrupts. The interrupt lock constructor disables interrupts and its destructor re-establishes the condition which existed prior to locking. Therefore, interrupt disabling and enabling are always paired and generated in a correct order. Since construction and destruction are the only operations considered, an interrupt lock object does not need to be named. Analogously, a preemption lock has only a constructor to disable preemptive interrupts and a destructor to re-enable them (see figure 3). Semaphores provide a more selective access to a resource. Disabling preemption and/or interrupts affects the real-time responsiveness of the application by increasing preemption and/or interrupt latency, and should be avoided wherever possible. Semaphores only blocks threads that request usage of the resource protected by the semaphore. This assures that only the subset of threads competing for a shared resource need delay their execution.

5.2 Semaphores

In order to deal with the problems of mutual exclusion and thread syncronization it is useful to redesign some low level primitives such as semaphores, locks, critical sections and monitors [Ben_Ari 91] in object-oriented terms. Semaphores serialize concurrent access to a resource without having to disable interrupt-driven preemption. The semaphore only blocks processes that request usage of the resource protected by the semaphore. The semaphore class typically contains a queue, for processes waiting to acquire the semaphore, a pointer to the process which acquired the semaphore or NULL when the semaphore is free, a count variable, the semaphore's name or identification, and the Wait and Signal member functions for semaphore acquisition and release. The count variable is initialized by the constructor. Initializing the semaphore to zero enables the semaphore to be used to exchange signals between threads. A thread awaits a signal by executing Wait and blocks if the signal has not occurred. When another thread signals by executing Signal the blocked task resumes execution. Initializing the semaphore to some positive integer i permits i threads to concurrently access shared data. If a semaphore is free, the first thread issuing a Wait request on that semaphore obtains it without waiting and the semaphore becomes busy. A process waiting on a busy semaphore which it does not own is enqueued into the semaphore's waiting queue. Other operations may be defined. In particular, it is often useful to allow a time-out interval to be passed to the Wait primitive. It unblocks the calling task if the interval expires before a signal arrives. Signalling a semaphore and suspending the running thread must be performed as an atomic action or single uninterruptible operation in order to guarantee that the Wait/Signal primitives correctly update the data within the semaphores. Figure 3 presents the Semaphore class declarations.

```
class Semaphore {
private:
// semaphore's structure as declared in [Iwork 91]
   TASKSEM sem;
// waiting time interval; ( TIME -1) refers to an infinite
// time-out
   TIME interval;
public:
// semaphore's initialization as defined in [Iwork 91]
   Semaphore(int val, TIME interv) : interval(interv)
      { Init_sem(&sem,val); }
   Semaphore() : interval((TIME) -1)
      { Init_sem(&sem,1);}
// initialization of semaphore's value (mainly for arrays)
   void Isem(int i) { sem.tasksem1[1] = i; }
   int Semv(); // return semaphore's value
// atomic primitives as defined in [Iwork 91]]
   void Wait() { P_sem(&sem,interval); }
   void Signal() { V_sem(&sem); }
};

class Plock { // Preemption Lock
public:
   Plock()  { Disable_preemption(); }
   ~Plock() { Enable_preemption(); }
};
```

Figure 3. Definition of semaphores and preemption locks.

5.3 Regions and Monitors

A commonly observed problem with semaphores is the unstructured way applications must use the Wait and Signal operations. Another problem is that semaphores are used for mutual exclusion as well as for condition synchronization. Regions [Andrews 91] provide a more structured approach than semaphores for specifying mutual exclusion. Resources are grouped together and encapsulated in a region. Mutual exclusion is automatically provided by the constructor and destructor of the region. Synchronization may be obtained by programming boolean condition explicitly within the region. However, in the current implementation these synchronization mechanisms have not been incorporated in the region class. As declared in figure 4, a (simplified) region consists of a pointer to a semaphore, which is initialized by the constructor. The semaphore is awaited during construction and signalled by the destructor.

```
class Region {
private:
  Semaphore *semaph;
public:
  Region(Semaphore& aSemaph)
    { semaph= &aSemaph; semaph->Wait(); }
  ~Region() { semaph->Signal(); }
};

class Monitor {
private:
// (one) entry semaphore for monitor exclusion
  Semaphore e;
// array of monitor conditions (defined as integers)
  Array<int> condition;
// array of semaphores for monitor's condition variables
// (initialized to zero)
  Array<Semaphore> c;
  int nc;
public:
  Monitor(int sz) :
    e(1, (TIME) -1), condition(0,sz-1),c(0,sz-1), nc(sz)
      { for(int i = 0 ; i< sz; i++) c[i].Isem(0); }
//  initialization to "0" of semaphores'array
  void Begin() { e.Wait();  }
  void End()   { e.Signal(); }
// 'mWait' delays executing process on condition
// variable-index cond
  void mWait(int cond)
    {++condition[cond];
     e.Signal(); c[cond].Wait(); e.Wait(); }
// One process delayed on condition variable (index
// cond) is awakened. No efect if no process is waiting
  void mSignal(int cond) {
    if(condition[cond])
      { --condition[cond]; c[cond].Signal(); }}
};
```

Figure 4. Region and Monitor classes

A region object does not need to be named. For automatic region objects, destruction is carried out when its scope is deleted. In its simpler implementation, when executing in a nested region a process retains exclusive access to the outer resource. Deadlock may occur if processes are allowed to wait. In order to obviate the need to guarantee that processes do not interfere, regions are better used when there is a single region for each shared resource. Moreover, delays within regions should be avoided. Regions may be nested as long as they access different resources. When using regions in a class that encapsulates a resource, it is often of convenience to insure mutual exclusion in all public member-functions. This may lead to a self-deadlock of the running process. The problem can be avoided by implementing the following scheme: if a process already owns a semaphore it can still issue additional wait requests on this semaphore without blocking. This enables nested calls of the process's member-functions which as a rule acquire the semaphore to guarantee exclusive access to common resources.

In order to encapsulate higher-level mutual-exclusion and synchronization operations, monitors [Andrews 91] can be used. A monitor class contains data and access methods to manipulate the data. Member functions serialize the access to the data which is kept private. Public member functions are executed in a mutually exclusive manner as in regions. However, unlike in regions, condition synchronization in monitors is provided by condition variables. A condition variable is used to delay a thread that cannot safely continue executing until the monitor's state satisfies some condition. It is also used to awaken a delayed thread when the condition becomes true. The monitor's member-functions mWait and mSignal in figure 4, provide for this kind of synchronization. They have been implemented using semaphores, following the approach outlined in [Andrews 91]. Execution of `mWait´ delays the executing thread and temporarily releases monitor exclusion. Execution of `mSignal´ awakens one delayed thread, if there is one, maintaining exclusive access to the monitor. The monitor class allows for the definition of an array of condition variables. Figure 8 presents an example illustrating the application of monitor objects.

5.4 Asynchronous Interobject Communication

As we have seen a monitor encapsulates the operations performed on a shared object. Shared objects are used as passive objects. They are mainly used for communication and synchronization between threads. A shared object may be used for transferring data between interacting threads. Read and write access to shared objects are granted to the interacting threads in a mutual exclusive manner. To increase concurrency in a system a shared object can allow parallel accesses whenever the integrity of the data is preserved. A shared object can allow several threads to read concurrently shared data. However, writing data must be exclusive with any other reading or writing thread. Asynchronous data transfer requires some form of buffering between threads. Objects may be passed between threads by placing them in queues. Usually queues are used to pass objects by reference, i.e. without copying the objects into the queue. Instead, the queue maintains references to the enqueued items. Nevertheless, in order to allow queues to be safely called by multiple threads and/or interrupt handlers queues must provide mutual exclusion. Starting with the sequential code of some singly-linked list data structure as provided in many libraries, it is possible to configure a queue supporting mutual exclusion. This is accomplished by specializing the queue operations through inheritance from the singly-linked list class, and encapsulating the queue in a monitor-like data structure.

Queues are a commonly used structure used for synchronization purposes. In its most simple form, a thread synchronizes when it attempts to obtain an item from a queue enqueued by another thread. However, in this form, the waiting thread is busy, repeatedly checking for the arrival of the item, therefore wasting computer time. A better technique of inter-thread synchronization is to signal the waiting thread when an object becomes available. If a thread attempts to dequeue an object from an empty queue the thread will suspend execution awaiting the arrival of the object. When another thread places an object into an empty queue, it unblocks the waiting thread which resumes execution after dequeuing the enqueued object. This way of synchronization is often referred to as non-busy-waiting and can be implemented with semaphores. The declarations in figure 5 exemplify the use of this technique in the design of a concurrent non-busy waiting queue class. The Queue class is publicly derived from a circular singly linked list. The Slist class provides all the functionality for appending and detaching the relevant object from the list. *Enqueue* takes a pointer to the object to be added to the back of the queue. If the operation is successfully, *enqueue* returns a pointer to the object inserted, otherwise zero. *Dequeue* detaches the object at the front of the queue and returns a pointer to it. If the queue is empty it returns zero. The cs semaphore is used for mutual exclusion and *Qsem* for synchronization. The semaphores' waiting times are set to infinite. Hidden features in the declaration of figure 5 are memory allocation and deallocation. The Slist::append member-function allocates memory. However, *cs* does not ensures mutual-exclusion as far as memory allocation is concerned. Other concurrent threads not executing queue operations may request memory as well. Therefore, mutual exclusion for dynamic memory allocation must be insured separately, namely by redefining the allocation operator. Likewise for memory deallocation.

```
template <class T> class Queue : public SList {
public:
  Queue(T *a = 0) :
    SList((dtorf_t) dtf,a),
    Qsem(0,(TIME) -1),
    cs(1,(TIME) -1) {}
  T *enqueue(T *a) {
    Region(cs);
    T *p = (T *) SList::append(a);
    Qsem.Signal();
    return p; }
  T *dequeue() {
    Qsem.Wait();
    Region(cs);
    return (T *) SList::gethead(); }
private:
  Semaphore Qsem, cs;
  static void dtf(T *);
  Queue(const Queue<T> &);
  Queue<T> &operator=(const Queue<T> &);
};

template<class T> void Queue<T>::dtf(T *p)
    { p->T::~T(); }
```

Figure 5. Concurrent non-busy-waiting queues

6. Examples

In order to illustrate the application of the concurrent object-oriented model described above we present three examples: the dining philosophers and the multiple producers-consumers using a bounded queue and a bounded buffer with monitors.

Dining Philosophers. For a description of the ubiquitous dining philosopher's problem please refer to, e.g. [Andrews 91, Ben_Ari 91]. To avoid deadlock, the solution presented in figure 6 assumes asymmetric behavior of one of the philosophers when picking up the forks. A philosopher eats only if he has two forks. The right fork has the same number as the philosopher's id. The left fork is equal to the philosopher's id plus one, modulo five.

Multiple Producers and Consumers. Figure 7 presents the multiple producers and consumers problem [Andrews 91, Ben_Ari 91] using a bounded integer queue limited to ten elements. Two (static) producers and three consumers were defined. Each producer attaches a serial number to each product taken from a shared number dispenser before enqueuing it. The Serial_Number class enforces mutual-exclusive access by the producers.

Multiple Producers and Consumers with Monitors. The C++ language code in figure 8 illustrates the application of monitor objects to the implementation of a circular buffer class with concurrent access. The buffer object could be used in the synchronization of the activities of multiple producers and consumers as in figure 7. The producers and consumers objects would be similarly defined. Alternatively, the Buffer class could be defined by inheritance from the Monitor class.

7. Conclusion

In this paper a concurrent object-oriented model for shared memory architectures has been presented. The model relies on the basic notions of active objects, passive objects, and interobject communication mechanisms. A class library supporting concurrency mechanisms has been designed. Reutilization of sequential constructs and concurrent mechanisms were especially emphasized. An active object is an instance derived from the Thread abstract class. A single active thread per object is considered. In order to deal with the problems of mutual exclusion and thread syncronization, low level primitives were implemented in object-oriented terms. These new constructs provide an effective encapsulation of interobject communication and synchronization operations. Queues were used as the main higher-level mechanisms used in synchronization. Through examples, it was shown that different types of concurrent queue semantics integrate well into the object-oriented model. The proposed library provides the building blocks for the development of higher-level communication and synchronization mechanisms. Their standardization and integration into the agent model of computation are expected to facilitate concurrent programming.

References

[Agha 90] Agha, G. Concurrent object-oriented programming. *Comm. ACM* 33, 9, Sept. 1990.

[Andrews 91] Andrews G. R. *Concurrent Programming: Principles and Practice*. The Benjamin/Cummings Pub. Comp., Inc. 1991.

[Ben-Ari 91] Ben-Ari, M. *Principles of Concurrent and Distributed Programming*. Prentice-Hall International, 1991.

[Bershad 88] Bershad, B. N., Lazowska, E. D., and Levy, H. M. PRESTO: A system for object-oriented parallel programming. *Software - Practice and Experience* 18, 8, Aug.1988.

[Caromel 93] Caromel D. Toward a method of object-oriented concurrent programming. *Comm. ACM* 36, 9, Sept. 1993.

[Ellis 93] Ellis, M.A., and Carrol M. D. Trade-offs of self-contained libraries. *C++ Report* 18-41, 5, 6, July-Aug. 1993.

[Gorlen 90] Gorlen K. E., Orlow S. M., and Plexico P. S. *Data Abstraction and Object-Oriented Programming in C++*. John Wiley & Sons, 1990.

[Hoare 78] Hoare, C.A.R. Communicating sequential processes. *Comm. ACM* 21, 8, Aug. 1978.

[Iactors 92] *Interactors™ - User Manual and Design Guide*. Objective: Systems, Canada, 1992.

[Iwork 91] *Interwork™ - Concurrent Programming Toolkit v3.1: User's Manual*. Block Island Technologies, Beaverton, Oregon, USA, 1991.

[Karaorman 93] Karaorman M., and Bruno J. Introducing concurrency to a sequential language. *Comm. ACM* 36, 9, Sept. 1993.

[Loer 93] Loer, K-L Concurrency annotations for reusable software. *Comm. ACM* 36, 9, Sept. 1993.

[Meyer 92a] Meyer B. *Eiffel, the Language*. Prentice-Hall, Englewood Cliffs, N.J., 1992.

[Meyer 92b] Meyer B. Applying design by contract. *IEEE Comput.* 40-51, 10, Oct. 1992.

[Meyer 93] Meyer B. Systematic concurrent object-oriented programming. *Comm. ACM* 36, 9, Sept. 1993.

[Milner 89] Milner R. *Communication and Concurrency*, Prentice-Hall, 1989.

[Nierstrasz 93] Nierstrasz O. Regular types for active objects. In *Visual Objects* (D.Tsichritzis ed.), Centre Universitaire d'Informatique, Université de Genève, 1993

[Silva 92] Silva, A. Acting on inheritance hierarchies. Proc. of the 3rd Eurographics Workshop on Object-Oriented Graphics, Champèri, Switzerland, 1992.

[Stroustrup 91] Stroustrup B. *The C++ Programming Language* (2d ed), Addison-Wesley, Reading, MA, 1991.

[Stroustrup 93] Stroustrup B. Library design using C++. *C++ Report* 14-22, 5, 5, June 1993.

```
class Forks {
private:
  Array<Semaphore> fork; // to be initialized to "1"
  int nf;
public:
  Forks(int sz) : fork(0,sz-1), nf(sz) { Isem(); }
  void Isem() { for(int i =0 ; i < nf; i++) fork[i].Isem(1); }
  void Get_forks(int);
  void Return_forks(int);
  friend Philosopher;
};

void Forks::Get_forks(int i)
{
  if(i) { fork[i].Wait(); fork[(i+1)%nf].Wait();}
  else  { fork[(i+1)%nf].Wait(); fork[i].Wait();}
}

void Forks::Return_forks(int i) { fork[i].Signal(); fork[(i+1)%nf].Signal(); }

Forks fks(5);

Semaphore Psem(1, (TIME ) -1);

class Philosopher : public Thread {
private:
  int id, count;
public:
  Philosopher(char *name, int pi, int prio, int n, int c) : Thread(name,pi,prio), id(n), count(c) {}
  ~Philosopher() {}
  void Task();
  void Think();
  void Eat();
  void Print(char *);
  void Count() { ++count; }
};

void Philosopher::Task() { while(TRUE) { Think(); fks.Get_forks(id); Eat(); fks.Return_forks(id); } }
void Philosopher::Think() { Sleep((TIME) 5); }
void Philosopher::Eat() { Count(); Print("Eats"); Sleep((TIME) 3); }
void Philosopher::Print(char *s)
   { Region(Psem); cout << "Philosopher " << id << " " << s << "\n"; cout.flush(); }

int  main()
{
  Mode smd = Mode(); smd.Init(Mode::timeslice); Ctrl_Thread::SetTmSlice(5);
  char *s[5] = {"PHI0" , "PHI1" , "PHI2" , "PHI3" , "PHI4" };
  Philosopher *ph[5];
  for(int i=0 ; i< 5 ; i++) ph[i] = new Philosopher(s[i],i+1,0,i,0);
  Ctrl_Thread::Run();
  for(i=0 ; i< 5 ; i++)  delete ph[i];
  return 0;
}
```

Figure 6. Dining philosophers

```
class Serial_Number {  // serial number dispenser
  Semaphore sk;
  Array<int> pick;      // array of serial numbers
  int current, size;
public:
  Serial_Number(int sz) : sk(1, (TIME) -1), pick(0,sz-1), current(0), size(sz)
     { for (int i = 0; i < sz; ++i) pick[i] = i+1;}
  int Current() { Region(sk); return pick[current]; }
  int Pick() { Region(sk); int x =pick[current++]; current %= size; return x; }
};

class IQueue : public SList {
private:
  Semaphore Qempty, Qfull, Qmutex;
  IQueue(const IQueue &);
  IQueue &operator=(const IQueue &);
  int count;
public:
  IQueue(int sz) : count(0), SList(dtf), Qempty(0,(TIME) -1), Qfull(sz, (TIME) -1), Qmutex(1, (TIME) -1) {}
  void enqueue(int n) {
    Qfull.Wait(); Qmutex.Wait();
    ++_count; SList::append((void _near *) n);
    Qmutex.Signal(); Qempty.Signal(); }
  int dequeue() {
    Qempty.Wait(); Qmutex.Wait();
    count = count? count-1: 0;
    int x = (int) SList::gethead();
    Qmutex.Signal(); Qfull.Signal();
    return x; }
};

class Producers : public Thread {
   void Task();
public:
   Producers(char *name, int pi, int prio) : Thread(name,pi, prio) {}
};

class Consumers : public Thread {
   void Task();
public:
   Consumers(char *name, int pi, int prio) :  Thread(name,pi, prio) {}
};

Serial_Number tk(10); IQueue myQ(10);
void Producers::Task() { while(TRUE){ myQ.enqueue(tk.Pick()); Sleep((TIME) 2);}}
void Consumers::Task() { while(TRUE){ myQ.dequeue(); Sleep((TIME) 5);}}

int main() {
  Mode smd = Mode();  smd.Init(Mode::timeslice);
  Producers P1("Task P1",1,0); Producers P2("Task P2",2,0);
  Consumers C1("Task C1",3,0); Consumers C2("Task C2",4,0); Consumers C3("Task C3",5,0);
  Ctrl_Thread::Run();
  myQ.clear();
  return 0;
}
```

Figure 7. The multiple producers and consumers problem using a bounded queue.

```
class Buffer {                 // circular buffer with concurrent access
  Array<int> buf;
  Monitor m1;                  // shared buffer`s monitor
  int front, rear;             // index variables
  int count;                   // number of full buffer locations
  int not_full, not_empty; // used as monitor`s conditions "0" and "1" respectively
  int bsize;                   // buffer size
public:
  Buffer(int sz) : buf(0,sz-1), m1(2), front(0), rear(0), count(0), not_full(0), not_empty(1), bsize(sz) {}
  void Deposit(int);
  int Fetch();
};

void Buffer::Deposit(int data)
{
  m1.Begin();
  while(count == bsize) m1.mWait(not_full);
  buf[rear++]=data;
  rear %= bsize;
  count++;
  m1.mSignal(not_empty);
  m1.End();
}

int Buffer::Fetch()
{
  m1.Begin();
  while (!count) m1.mWait(not_empty);
  int result = buf[front++];
  front %= bsize;
  count--;
  m1.mSignal(not_full);
  m1.End();
  return result;
}

Buffer buf(10);               // ten elements´ buffer

Serial_Number tk(10);         // defined as in figure 7.
```

Figure 8. Illustrating the application of monitor objects

Experiences in Object Oriented Software Redesign

D.Dabbene, F.Luise, E.Valfre

Alenia - Defence Aircraft Division.
Artificial Intelligence Laboratory.
C.Marche 41 - 10146 Torino
Italy
Tel. +39-11-7180890
Fax. +39-11-7181003
E-Mail LIAT@liat.alenia.polito.it

1. Abstract.

The paper addresses topics related to the object oriented redesign of a diagnostic expert system called ADAM which has been developed, first, with GoldWorks, a Lisp based tool, and then using C++. Problems and solutions regarding the architecture redesign of its graphic interface are specially highlighted. The paper contains a brief description of how the system was and a wider one of how it is now, including technical considerations.

1.1. A brief description of the ADAM Project.

The ADAM project [3] has begun with the purpose of developing a system to support technicians in the unscheduled maintenance of the AMX military aircraft during the fault search phase. Since the system domain has to cover all aircraft systems and subsystems it has to manage a great amount of knowledge.

The development of the project led to the creation of a shell for the diagnostic system composed of a specialized graphic interface for knowledge acquisition and a consultation module (which can be used alone like a run-time system version).

From TOOLS EUROPE '94 (Technology of Object-Oriented Languages and Systems).

Both the shell and the applications developed with it have to be used directly by the end users, who are required to be familiar only with the basic interface facilities of the system.

1.2. The Project's phases and organization.

We organized the system development [3] in two main phases:

. in the first phase we addressed the problem of knowledge representation developing a complete prototype aimed at solving the problems related to:

- where and how to acquire the knowledge
- how to represent the knowledge (and how to implement it)
- which are the system's requirements from the user's point of view, i.e. how the user expects to interact with the system, which are the features he needs, which information is better to display during the use of the system.

In this phase exploratory programming allowed us to interact rapidly with users and experts, changing and modifying rapidly the system according with their requirements and suggestions, maintaining the development focus on the knowledge level. For these reasons we chose a lisp based AI tool: GoldWorks.

. in the second phase, starting from the first prototype, we are actually developing the final version using a more conventional waterfall model. The prototype coming from the previous phase was used to extract the system's requirements and the knowledge representation formalism. The goal of this phase is to develop a well engineered, efficient, portable and easy to maintain system, using state of the art software engineering methodologies. The focus of this phase is therefore on design and architectural issues. The prototype developed in this phase is written in C++.

2. The first system version.

The first phase was devoted to solve problems about the way to represent the knowledge and to work with the end users to define the system's requirements through rapid prototyping.

2.1. The Knowledge Representation and Reasoning Mechanism.

The formalism chosen to represent diagnostic knowledge is the "Decision Tree", which represents the reasoning process in the application domain (aircraft) very well and is general enough to represent the diagnostic reasoning in many applications.

A decision tree is a typical sequence of tests that starts from the detected symptoms and leads to the fault location. Symptoms are the roots of the decision trees, Tests are the intermediate nodes and Faults are the leaves. Each test has two or more associated answers that represent the links to other objects (tests or faults). Decision trees have a great advantage: They are a direct and explicit representation of the mental process of the expert. Thus they are immediate, easy to read, understand and modify.

The reasoning mechanism consists mainly in a search algorithm which explores the decision trees. In order to make the consultation more flexible and interactive and to optimize the fault search, some features have been added.

2.2. The Knowledge Object Design.

The decision trees described in the former chapter have a direct and simple object implementation (Figure 1). *Symptoms, Tests* and *Faults* are directly linked together by dependency lists contained in instance variables. The class *DiagnosticObjects* is used to set up a further difference among *DecisionNet* objects: In fact *Symptoms* are simple objects that belong to the decision nets only as starting points of the diagnostic reasoning while *Tests* and *Faults* have more characteristics, i.e. associated lists of multiple symptoms, job guides (that explain how to perform the test or fix the faults), explanatory images, etc.

One of the system modules to be developed was the graphic editor to allow the interactive creation of the objects of the decision tree. It became thus necessary for the decision tree objects to be able to display themselves on the screen, recognize when the mouse was on them and so on. This is the reason why we added the graphic capabilities directly into the diagnostic objects, implementing the *DISPLAY* class, that was inherited by the object taxonomy root. Even though this solution worked quite well, it was clear that the class taxonomy was simple because all objects had the same graphic aspect, so the *DISPLAY* class implemented a unique graphic face. The diagnostic objects, in fact, were displayed as a graph of boxes (with a text inside), linked by lines. The objects themselves took care of displaying the links, by keeping inside them a list of the objects which they were linked to.

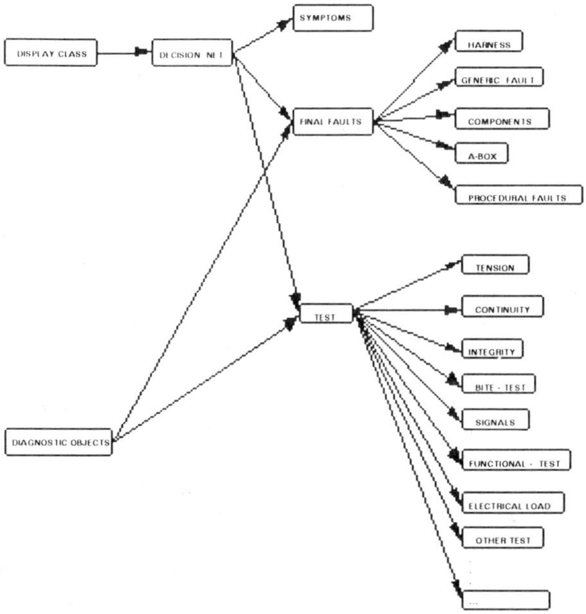

Figure 1.

3. The second version of ADAM.

In the second phase, that is currently in progress, we have to cope with two main problems: The change of technology from a Lisp based tool to C++ (we had no previous experience in C++) and the change of focus from knowledge representation problems to design and architectural ones.

3.1. The new architecture.

In the second version of the system, class hierarchy and the system design were considerably changed and refined. The main impact was on the design of the overall architecture, especially as far as the graphic system interface was concerned.

During the first phase we found the necessity to represent the knowledge using not only decision trees, but also other kinds of graphs (with a greater complexity) i.e. cause/effect diagrams modeled through finite state automata, Petri Nets etc. Obviously this fact led to expand and to make more flexible and generalizable the architecture of the graphic editor.

It was clear, in fact, that the complexity of this module would be highly incremented and that it would be necessary to give a great care to its redesign.

The AI tool used in the first phase did not commit to a particular architectural approach or design paradigm and the system design coming from this phase revealed its limits in the transition to a less flexible environment (C++). For instance the choice to make the domain objects drawing themselves coupled the domain structure with the particular window system and with a lot of implementation details that obviously are not concerned with the diagnostic knowledge.

We had also the necessity to have objects with different "faces" (not only boxes) . With the previous taxonomy the solution to this problem could not be very nice because we had just one class for the display and we judged that developing a method with a case statement to choose the face of the object was neither an object oriented solution nor a good idea.

Moreover the control structure was too implicit in the interface and menu structures and thus difficult to modify. The implicit links among diagnostic objects (that can be of different types), via a dependency list in an instance variable, collided with the strong type checking, the lack of a RTTI (Run Time Type Identification) and the need of casting everything.

For all these reasons we took two main design decisions:

- to totally separate the graphic aspects from the domain objects, generating a library of independent graphic objects that can be owned by the domain objects

- to implement the control structure through a set of finite state automata.

3.2. The classes taxonomy.

Class hierarchy was modified as in Figure 2 and the results were quite surprising: Despite the language limits, the system design was cleaner, more flexible and generalizable than the first one.

At the top of the hierarchy there are four classes: *Schema, GraphicContext, GraphicObj,* and *ModelObj*. The overall interface architecture is based on relationships among these classes.

ModelObj is the top of the model objects' taxonomy: Each model object has characteristics related only with its semantics.

GraphicObj is the top of the graphic objects' taxonomy: Graphic objects have characteristics related to their display on the screen as coordinates, dimensions etc. They are owned by the model objects and are the "pure face" of them.

GraphicContext contains all the graphic objects created by the user: It is a kind of database of the objects on the screen used to find the objects selected with the mouse, the objects to redisplay after a scroll or a zoom operation and so on. During a system run, several instances of *GraphicContext* can be built according to the graph structure that the user inserts. In fact a special kind of *ModelObj*, the *ComplexObj*, allows users to organize their objects in different levels (a *ComplexObj* can contain any number of *ModelObj*) and each level is represented with a different *GraphicContext*. This feature is very useful to cope with graph complexities: For instance a network of objects can be considered as a set of objects representing simpler sub networks linked in some way, whose details can be seen descending in deeper levels.

The *Schema* class plays the role of a metaclass (metaclasses are not available in C++, so it was necessary to emulate them) giving the general behavioral rules of the objects according to the different kind of graph the user is building (Decision Tree, Petri Net etc.). For instance the *Schema* knows what kind of *GraphicObj* must be created when the user creates a *ModelObj*, if a particular type of object is linkable with another type (for example in a Petri Net, places cannot be linked together), what to do when an object is deleted (do other objects to delete exist ?). Moreover each "schema" contains all the graphic contexts created. Obviously during an application is possible to have simultaneously different "schemas".

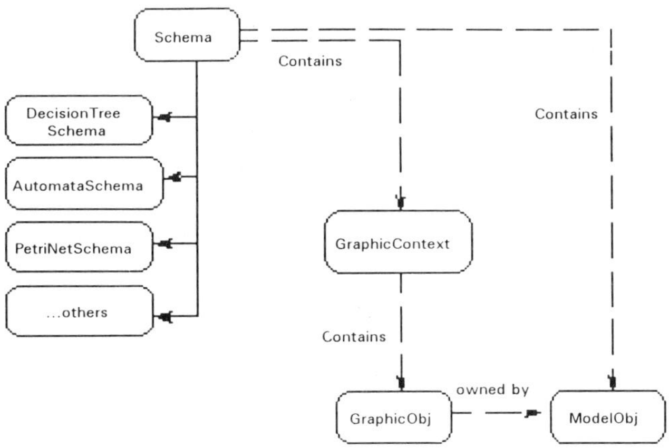

Figure 2.

Graphic objects know how to display themselves, interfacing with the system virtual device (called *Drawer*) that can be linked to the screen or to a printer: They have a pointer to the domain object they represent but they have no idea of the owner behavior and semantic. The taxonomy of *GraphicObj,* that can be seen in Figure 3 constitutes a library that can be easily incremented without affecting the rest of the system implementation.

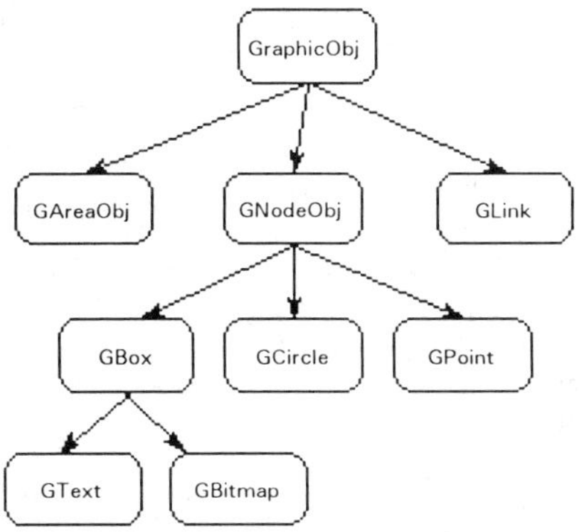

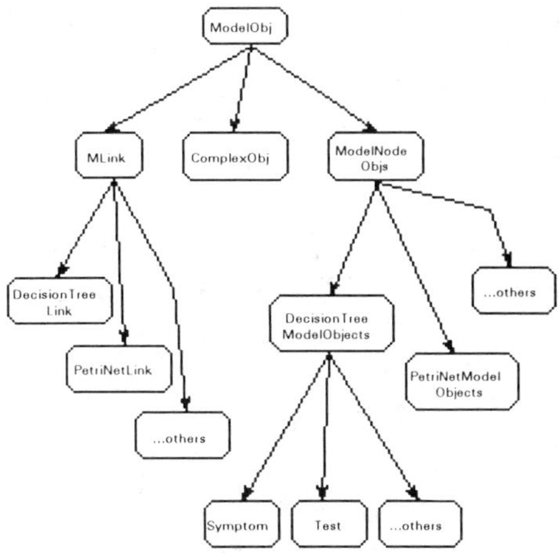

Figure 3.

On the other hand, the model objects do not know how they are represented on the screen (they have no pointer to the owned object) and are independent from the specific window system utilized: They implement exclusively the model semantic and can be used even without interface. Thus, in our system, a model object IS NOT a graphic object, but an object that can be

REPRESENTED BY a graphic object. Moreover there is not a 1 to 1 correspondence between a model object and a graphic object: For instance a link between two objects can be graphically composed by more than one segment, while in the model there is only one instance of link. Each graphic segment of the link will be owned by the same instance of the model link.

The taxonomy of the model objects (*ModelObj*) in Figure 4 has been partitioned into three classes: *ModelNodeObjs*, *MLink*, and *ComplexObj* whose role has already been illustrated inside the *GraphicContext* explanation.

Class *ModelNodeObjs* contains the nodes of the various models, partitioned in the different kinds of "schemas" (*DecisionTreeModelObjects*, *PetriNetModelObjects*, ...).

MLink contains the links among the *ModelNodeObjs*: We chose in fact to represent the links directly through explicit objects, avoiding the use of adjacency list of the first version. They also are partitioned in the same way of the *ModelNodeObjs*. We could have put the different links under the respective classes of model objects (*PetriNetLink* directly under *PetriNetModelObjects*) and use multiple inheritance but we wanted to simplify the

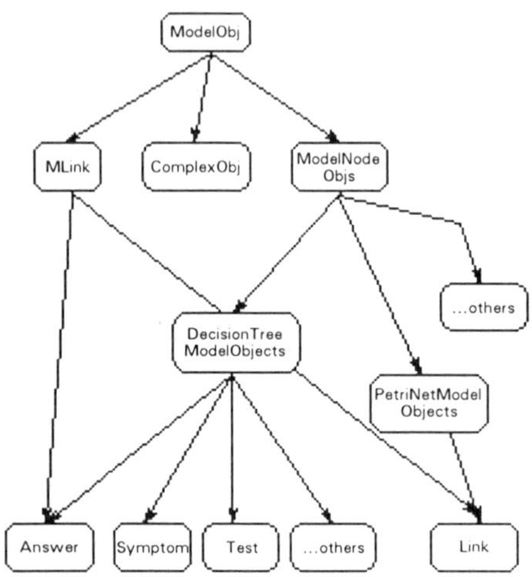

Figure 4.

inheritance lattice every time it was possible.

The partition of the overall architecture in *GraphicObj* and *ModelObj* makes use of delegation instead of inheritance unlike the first version of the system. We think that this approach presents some advantages:

1) First of all, from the semantic point of view, it is more correct compared to the solution of the first release of the system (a diagnostic object is not a geometric object and has not display properties)

2) Simplicity in the inheritance chain (single inheritance)

3) Greater modularity and then greater easiness to software reuse through delegation. It is possible to reuse software simply asking an instance to supply a service

4) Greater flexibility (independence from Window System etc.)

We found delegation a powerful tool for the design. Another example of delegation is in the object display mechanism. The graphic objects, in fact ,do not use directly the Windows functions to display themselves but call the methods defined by a virtual display called *Drawer* that is specialized in two subclasses: *CanvasDrawer* and *PrinterDrawer*. In this way graphic objects do not take care of the device in use in a particular moment (it would be possible, for instance, to send the display on a Sun Workstation) but simply ask the *Drawer* to perform certain generic graphic operations (drawing a line, for example). Moreover the class *Drawer* takes care of zooming and shifting that are therefore transparent to the graphic objects.

3.3. The Control Structure

The system control structure was heavily modified as well. Instead of a set of functions distributed in the interface objects, the control structure has been explicitly represented by a set of finite state automata: It is one of the possible approaches for object oriented systems [5], [6]. Each user operation generates an event that is caught by an event handler that dispatches the event to the current state of the current finite state automaton. It is quite simple to implement finite state automata in C++. It is only necessary to generate a class for each automaton's state, with a virtual member function for each state transition. All the automaton's classes must be derived from a base class in which all the virtual functions (especially the IsA methods) must be declared. The automata generated in this way are very simple to control and modify. The reduction of the complexity of the program decreases the number of bugs and of side effects and permits an easy tuning of the system behavior.

The finite state automata for the knowledge acquisition module (the module we are working on) are general enough to be used not only for decision tree editing but also for every kind of graph: It is only necessary that the automaton has some behavioral rule related to the type of graph. For example an editor for finite state automata can create a link from each node (that is each state) to another, while an editor for Petri nets can create a link only between a node owned by a place and a node owned by a transition (and vice versa). These rules are few and are related to the object creation, deletion and linking. The problem is then solved using the special class *Schema*. This class defines the graph characteristics, that is, the rules of objects behavior for a particular kind of graph (i.e. there is a method that takes two nodes and returns a Boolean that specifies if they can be linked together). We have different "Schemas" : One to edit a Petri net, one for finite state automata, one for decision trees and so on.

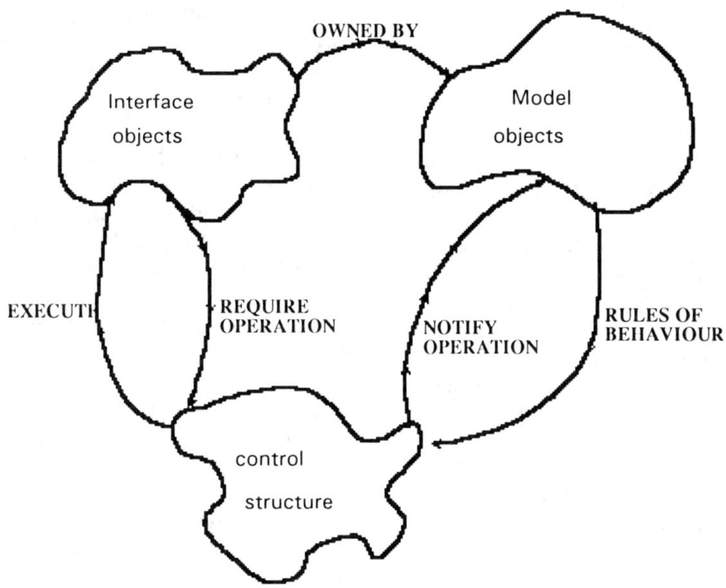

Figure 5.

The overall architecture achieved in this way (see Figure 5) is very close to the idea of the Model-View-Control paradigm of Smalltalk [4]. In Smalltalk "model" refers to a representation of the application domain as an information model, while view is a specification of how aspects of a model are displayed to a user. The "controller" is the specification of how the user can communicate or interact with the applications in order to request changes in the view or in the underlying model. There is a taxonomy of classes for each of these components that permits to build an application choosing the appropriate classes, and the paradigm allows a high degree of software reuse.

In our application the model objects implement the Model, the interface objects the View and the automata the Controller. The three modules are decoupled enough to be used for other purposes.

4. Final Remarks.

Even if the reengineering work described above is still in progress, it gives us some insight for future developments:

. Even if inheritance is a powerful tool, attention must be paid to avoid its excessive use, that can cause a lot of problems, especially in strong typed languages. In particular one should not inherit, if his goal is just to include or reuse software/code (like we did in the Lisp version of the system); one should use inheritance only when the relation IS-A between the class from which one inherits and the inherited class is really satisfied. Delegation revealed itself to be a powerful tool to reuse software: from one side it generates fewer problems (for example less casting problems) and from the other side allows a more semantically correct design of the class structure. Using delegation, software reuse means to ask instances to supply a service (for which they are developed) and not to add a service to instances that need it.

. Object oriented programming skill is a good starting point, but it is not sufficient to achieve the capability to design a good object oriented system. Some methodologies for object oriented design can be found in literature [5]: They can be helpful even though they must be interpreted considering the designer's skills and needs.

. The M-V-C paradigm is extremely useful for building systems with complex user interfaces, allowing a clean way for interaction structure design and code reuse.

The ADAM project proved that object oriented programming can be successfully used to develop knowledge based systems in which the knowledge representation formalism is a graph. Object oriented programming turned out to be a very powerful tool for developing software systems: The overall system design is the critical bottleneck to utilize all its power.

The project revealed the necessity to use all the state of the art tools for the development of object oriented systems. We are investigating the available CASE tools that support object oriented design, not only to improve our code productivity but also to support and maintain the system documentation: An important issue of systems that will have a long life cycle. Object Oriented Database Management Systems are also under study: They can be a good way to store object knowledge bases.

5. Acknowledgment

Thanks to Mr.Ricci, Mr Damiani, Mr Alessio (members of the Adam project) and Mrs. Totaro for their precious contribution.

6. Bibliography.

[1] [Coplien 92] ADVANCED C++ PROGRAMMING STYLES AND IDIOMS. Addison Wesley, 1992.

[2] [Dabbene et al. 93] E. BUILDING OBJECT ORIENTED EXPERT SYSTEMS: EXPERIENCES AND LESSONS LEARNED ON THE WAY. Proceedings of C++World, 1993

[3] [Damiani et al. 93] ADAM. AIRCRAFT DIAGNOSTIC AND MAINTENANCE.

Proceedings of the 3rd Congress of the Italian Association for Artificial Intelligence, 1993

[4] [Goldberg 90] INFORMATIONS MODELS, VIEWS, AND CONTROLLERS. Dr.Dobb's Journal, July 1990.

[5] [Rumbaugh et al. 91] OBJECT ORIENTED MODELLING AND DESIGN. Prentice Hall, Inc. 1991.

[6] [Rumbaugh 93] CONTROLLING CODE. HOW TO IMPLEMENT DYNAMIC MODELS. Journal of Object Oriented Programming, May 1993.

C++ PRINCIPLES

Safe Iterators

Hans Albrecht Schmid
FB Informatik, FH Konstanz

Abstract

In general, both active and passive iterators do not work correctly if during the time span, in which an iterator iterates over the elements of a container, the state of the container is modified by intermitting operations as e.g. adding or removing of elements. However, in modern object-oriented event-driven applications, inter-
mitting operations cannot be avoided.

This paper categorizes the problems that may occur in the presence of intermitting operations in three categories. It defines the correct behaviour of a safe active iterator for this case.

Different approaches to implement safe iterators are analysed. An implementation is described in detail that shows excellent performance characteristics, since it causes practically no overhead except for potential problem cases.

1. Introduction

An iterator object allows to access all elements of a container object or of an instance of an abstract data type without knowledge of its internal structure. (In the following we will speak of an iterator or of a container, respectively, when we mean an iterator object or, respectively, a container object or an abstract data type instance.) Thus, an iterator represents a generalized, abstract loop over all elements of a container, which has one and the same form for different container classes, and which is also applicable to container classes like sets for which no ordering relationship among the elements is defined and, as a consequence, no "next element" service is available.

From TOOLS EUROPE '94 (Technology of Object-Oriented Languages and Systems).

Two kinds of iterators are distinguished, active ones and passive ones [Booch87]. A passive iterator is defined in the form of a single service (called e.g. "Iterate") that executes a given operation for all elements of a container. This form is typical for Ada libraries of abstract data types, which use a generic procedure as iterator and pass the given operation as a generic package parameter. Different kinds of passive iterators are distinguished in [Uhl90], and constructs to control the iteration flow, i.e. to visit only a subset of all container elements, are provided.

The advantage of the passive form of iterators is its inherent safety, both against erroneous use and intermitting execution of other operations on the same container. In a sequential execution thread or process, the execution of a passive iterator cannot be intermitted by any other operation and be affected by it. Even when parallel execution threads or processes access the same container (object), no problems can occur if a mutual or a reader/writer kind of exclusion of a complete iteration operation is provided. This can be easily done by locking.

The disadvantage of the passive form of iterators is the missing granularity. An iterator must have visited all (or a selected subset of) elements of a container before another access to an element is possible. This disadvantage is a particular problem for object oriented event controlled systems. It cannot be tolerated there, in many cases [Baeumer92], since the control flow and the sequencing of operations should be controlled by the user and not by the system (desktop paradigm).

The active form of iterator provides the elementary loop control constructs "access of the current element", "advancing to the next element", and "check if more elements are available", by which a visiting sequence or, respectively, a generalized loop over the elements of a container is to be composed.

Active iterators are quite common in C++ class libraries.

The advantage of active iterators is the greater granularity and flexibility. The disadvantage is their missing safety against two kinds of erroneous use:

- wrong composition of the iteration loop control constructs , and
- state changing operations that intermit with the execution of an iteration loop.

Every user of a container library should understand the potential safety problems with active iterators such that he or she can avoid them. We will distinguish and explain three classes of problems that may occur when inserting or removing elements from a container during the time span of the iteration (shortly called "intermitting state changing operations").

No precautions against the first kind of erroneous use do seem possible, except for integrating the iteration control constructs into the programming language. However, safety in presence of intermitting state changing operations can be achieved, as this paper will show. We will define the correct behaviour of a safe iterator, as we will call it, in the presence of intermitting state changing operations. Then, it will be shown how to realize and implement safe iterators.

2. Example Iterator

As an example, an active iterator from [Schmid93] is used:

```
class ADT { /* ...*/ }; //some container class

class Iterator {
    ADT* TheADTptr;
    Index TheCurrentElement;
       // represents implicitly the state
public:
    Iterator( ADT* L);
       //start at first node
    Boolean IsValid();
       // returns False if no more element is to be
       // visited
//following services are only applicable
//if Iterator.IsValid()
    Index Get();
       //returns index of the current element
    void Next();
       //advances current element to next element
};
```

The services Get, Next and IsValid provide the elementary loop control constructs "access of the current element", "advancing to the next element", and "check if more elements are available".

An Index object (called also cursor), which is returned from the service Get, gives an external reference to an element of a container. It can have a Nil-value when no element is referenced. Services of the class Index like

Elementtype Index::GetElem(void)

allow to access the value of an element that is referenced by the index object. (Note that this requires no operation on the container once an index is obtained!)

This definition of an index makes disappear two problems which, according to Booch [Booch87, p.160], make the definition of active iterators more complex than that of passive ones. First, an active iterator needs to have a state, which indicates in the simplest case only if the iterator references an element or not. This state information is stored implicitly with the Index "TheCurrentElement", since the Nil-value of the index represents the state "done" of the iterator. The second problem is how to get the value of an element that is referenced by the iterator without having to pass the container as a further parameter (argument). In the class library that is used as an example, iterators do not have to cope with this problem, because it is provided for by the class Index.

3. The Problem

During the span of time in which an active iterator iterates over the elements of a container, the state of the container may be changed by intermitting calls of container services. Services that change the structure of the container by e.g. adding or removing elements are to be distinguished from services that modify only the values of elements, but do not change their relationship to other elements and leave the structure of the container unchanged. Intermitting calls to services of the latter category do not affect an iterator.

However note that modifying the value of an element or of its key in a sorted representation might change its position in the sort and its relationships to the other elements, so we have to include this service into the first category (besides services that add or remove elements). For containers as, e.g. lists or trees, for which the user has control over the position of an element, services like moving an element to another position will also change the structure and belong to the first category.

Intermitting calls to services of the first category may cause different classes of problems. One class of problems occurs when the element being currently referenced by the iterator (we will call it the "current element") is removed from the container. Another class of problems is caused by the current element being shifted to another entry of the data structure (that represents the container), as a consequence of inserting or removing elements. Then, the iterator references a wrong element since the reference is bound to the entry, and not to the element.

Altogether, three classes of problems affecting an iterator were identified that are described in detail in the following sections, as they may occur in a sequential process. Additionally, these problems show up when one container (object) is accessed from different parallel tasks or parallel threads at a time.

3.1 Removing the Current Element.

The first problem case occurs when removing the current element as illustrated in the following example 1 and fig.1.

```
//Example 1
ADT A=...;          // AbstractDataType (Container)
                    // with elements of Elementtype
Iterator Current( A);
while ( Current.IsValid() )
{   if ( Current.Get().GetElem() == "CC" )
        A.Remove( Current.Get() );
    Elementtype E = Current.Get().GetElem();
    Current.Next();
}
```

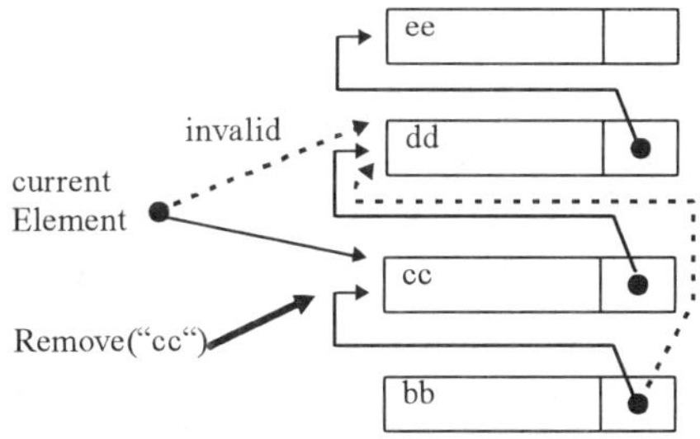

Fig.1 Removing the current element

The iterator Current is attached to the container A and iterates over all elements of it. The statement A.Remove(...) removes the current element of the iterator via its index. The problem is what the following statement Current.Get().GetElem() means, which tries to access the removed element. What is the meaning of the statement Current.Next() that tries to advance the iterator, i.e. which element is the next one to a removed element? This semantics is not welldefined for "unsafe" iterators.

The problem demonstrated is based on a logical level. Therefore, it is found with every container class, independent on its functionality, its representation, and ist implementation.

3.2 Implicit Shifting of the Current Element

The second problem case is illustrated by example program 2 and fig.2; it may be found only with certain representations of a container.

```
//Example 2
ADT A=...;          // AbstractDataType (Container)
                    // with elements of Elementtype
Iterator Current( A);
Index    Second = ...;
Elementtype Element = ...;

while ( Current.IsValid() )
{   if ( Current.Get().GetElem() == "GG" )
    A.Insert( Element, After( Second));
      //insert as third List element
    Current.Next();
}
```

The iterator Current is attached to the container A. Suppose the data representation of the container A is an array (as shown in fig. 2), where the sequence of the elements is represented by physical adjacency, and the reference to the current element of the iterator is kept in some form of an array index. During the iteration, an element is inserted (which needs not be adjoining to the current element) inmidst of existing elements.

A part of the existing elements must be shifted to other entries in order to create an empty entry for the new element, as fig. 2 shows. Shifting of elements is required as well when an element is (physically) removed (i.e. no valid bit is used to indicate that it is removed logically).

If the current element is one of the elements to be shifted, the iterator will not reference, after the shifting, the current element, but one of its adjacent elements. That means, the shifting causes an implicit change of the current element, resulting in either an element being visited twice or being stepped over during the iteration.

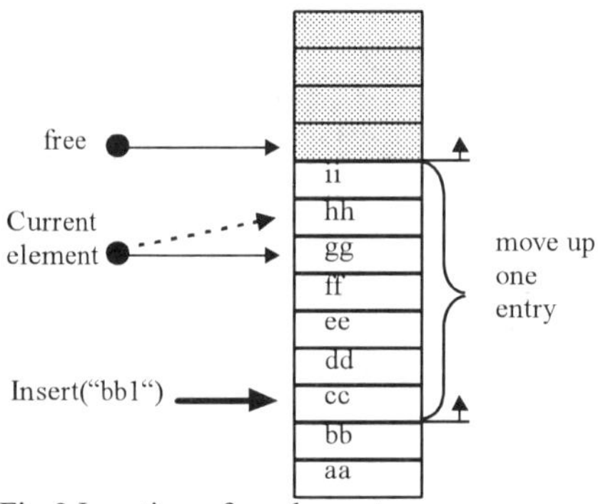

Fig.2 Insertion of an element

This problem will not be found with linked data representations inclusive hash chaining methods. The reason is that they use pointers to represent the logical neighbourship relation, such that no shifting of elements is required when an element is inserted or removed. Here, an element remains in its entry or at its storage space, from its insertion up to its removal, as long as it is part of the data structure. Data representations with this property are called "**entry invariant**".

Open addressing hash representations as, for example, quadratic probing, use a logical chaining to represent the relations among different elements. All of these representations which do no reorganisation of elements are entry invariant, too. However, when a reorganisation is done as, e.g., with Brent's open hashing, the elements are moved among different entries, such that the representation is not entry invariant. Problems similar to those shown arise.

3.3 Invalidation of the Iterator

When iterating over trees, it may be approriate for efficiency reasons (if the are no parent pointers kept in the tree nodes), to keep the whole path from the root to the current element in the iterator. An iterator that contains not only a reference to the current element, but also to other elements, is said to have a "**spanned representation**" and is called "**spanned**". Even with entry invariant data representation, problems similar to case 2 arise, if, for example, a node on the path is removed, or if a tree may be reorganised with insert or remove services as, e.g., an AVL tree. (A. Hasler [Hasler93] observed this problem when testing the library [Schmid93].) In both cases, the reference to the current node remains correct. However, the path from the root to this node is not correct any longer after the operation. Since the path is used to advance to the next element, the iterator does not work correctly; it may visit elements of the tree twice or leave them out.

4. Definition of Safe Iterators

Iterators are called safe if the problem cases illustrated in section 3 do not occur. In this section we will define the notion of a safe iterator precisely, before we will show in the following sections in which way safe iterators can be realized.

The definition of a safe iterator distinguishes the cases 1 and 2, 3 from section 3:

An iterator is called safe when during an iteration:
(case 1)
Some service that removes the current element of the iterator is executed, and if after the execution of this service:

(1) the access to the current element returns as a result a value indicating that the current element is not valid and cannot be accessed

(2) visiting of the following elements delivers access to exactly the same set of elements as in the case no remove service had been called,

or

(case 2 and 3)

some service is executed that inserts (a) new element(s) or removes element(s) that are different from the current element of the iterator, and if after the execution of this service

(3) the reference to the current element delivers the same element as before, even if its physical position may have changed

(4) visiting of the following elements delivers, apart from the elements inserted or removed with the respective service, access to exactly the same set of elements as in the case the respective service had not been called.

(5) if an element/elements was/were removed by the respective service it/they are not visited during the remainder of the iteration

(6) if an element/elements was/were inserted by the respective service it is undefined if it/they are visited during the remainder of the iteration or not.

Please note that condition (6) leaves a degree of freedom to an implementation that allows to insert elements according to the structure of the respective data representation. It depends on the data representation and the details of the parameters of the respective service (as e.g. the value(s) of the respective element(s)), if the element(s) are inserted in the part of the structure that was already visited or in the other part still to be visited.

Repetitions and combinations of the cases discussed above can be found, too. For instance (see fig.3) may, during the time an iteration is stopped, the current element be removed, then the element that follows it (in the visiting sense of the iteration), and a new element is inserted in its place. According to the definition, the access to the current element, when taking up the iteration again, must deliver invalid as result. The element visited as next may, but needs not be the newly inserted element. Visiting of the following elements delivers access to exactly the same set of elements minus the second removed one as in the case the two remove services and the insert service had not been executed.

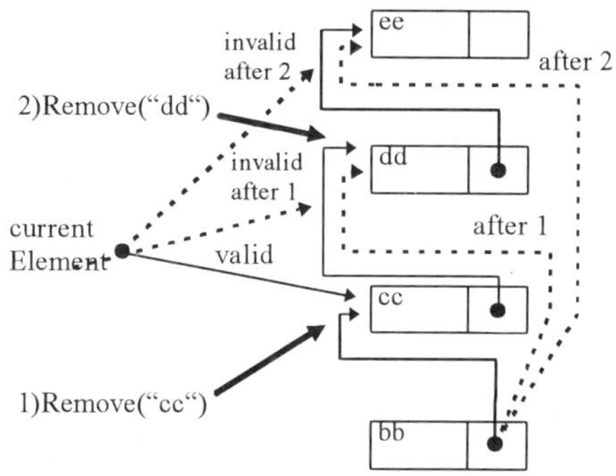

Fig.3 Removing of current element and adjacent one

Furthermore, there are services like the move service, which is provided by a list, that removes an element from one position of the list and inserts it at a different position of a list. Such services are considered as a combination of the elementary insert and remove services discussed above.

5. Realizing Safe Iterators in Particular Cases

An approach to realize safe iterators is to extend the data structures, which represent the container, such that the iterator has sufficient information, after the modification of the data structure, that it can resume correctly the iteration. The idea is that the container needs not to know the iterators that are attached to it, at a given point of time. We will demonstrate that this approach delivers only special solutions for restricted cases.

5.1 Entry Invariant Data Representations with Physical Adjacency

As a simple case, we consider entry invariant data representations with non-spanned iterators. Then, problem case 2 and 3 do not occur, as we have shown. A safe iterator must avoid problem case 1; that is it must determine from the information contained in the data structure

- if the current element was removed during the time span in which the iteration stopped
- the next element to be visited according to the visiting sequence.

At a first glance, these requirements seem to be satisfied without additional effort for entry invariant data representations where the neighbouring relation is based on physical adjacency, as for example open addressing hashing methods without reorganisation. They have a valid bit (and a deleted bit), anyhow, which shows if an hash table entry contains a valid element or if it is empty. When accessing the current element (with a Get() or similar service) the iterator uses the valid bit to check if the referenced element is still valid. If it was removed in the meantime the iterator returns invalid as a result, otherwise, it returns the reference to the current element. Visiting of the next element is done by accessing the physical adjacent entry and checking, if it is empty or contains an element, as long until an entry with a valid element is found.

However, there is a case, where condition (1) is not fulfilled: A new element is inserted in place of the removed element during the time span in which the iterator is still referencing this entry. Then the valid bit is set to valid again. Now, the iterator cannot find out any longer that the current element has been removed and is invalid.

One might try to solve this problem by introducing a second flag that is set after an insert service call, and reset when an iterator visits (i.e. advances to) the element. However, this fails to work when several iterators are attached to the same container. As a consequence, safe iterators can only be realized in this way with the limitation to one iterator for entry invariant data representations with physical neighbourship.

5.2 Chained Entry Invariant Data Representations

A problem similar to the one described is found for chained entry invariant representations as e.g. chained lists or trees. With unsafe iterators, a removed element is chained out and its entry or storage space is returned to the storage management. With safe iterators, the space or entry cannot be returned since an iterator may reference the entry of the removed element. Therefore, a valid bit (as above) is introduced and, in addition, the removed element is chained out and the other elements, for example in the list, are rechained as fig.4 illustrates. Note that the chaining of the removed element to its neighbours is kept.

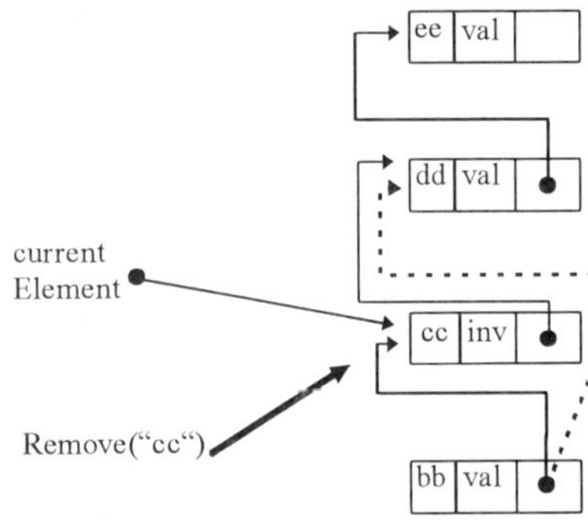

Fig.4 Preserving of the removed current element

Thus, we have achieved that the iterator works correctly when elements are removed: it references the chained out element as current element and finds out from the valid bit that it has been removed. If the next element (in iteration sequence) is removed, too, as shown in fig.4, there is no problem: the iterator, when advanced to the next element, follows the chain as long until it finds a valid element.

As long as a removed element remains in its entry, there are no problems. If the entry, however, is returned to storage management which, let us suppose, allocates it only to new elements of the same container (object), the same problem as identified above is found and, in addition, a new one: the newly inserted element may have a different position in the list or tree such that advancing the iterator to the next element might deliver a wrong result.

This means that the storage deallocation of the removed element must only be done when no iterator references it any longer. The consequence is that an iterator would have to notify the container when it has advanced, and, in addition, each iterator (object) must register with a container when it is created and attached to it. The reason is that, if several iterators are active at the same time, the returning of the storage of the removed element can only be done when all iterators have notified the container about advancing to the next element.

As a conclusion we have found out for entry invariant data representations that storing of additional information in the data structure is not sufficient, but that communication among the container and the iterators is required. In the next section we will show that, presupposing the possibility of communication, simpler solutions are feasible.

5.3 Non-Entry Invariant Data Representations

If one would try to follow the discussed approach for non entry invariant data representations one would encounter much more difficulties, due to the fact that information about the shifting of elements had to be stored in the data structure.

The difficult problem is arising again when more than one iterator is attached to a container. One of these may have reacted (when executing a service Next) already to the shifting information and have set up correctly its reference to the current element, others may not yet have done this. The difficulty is now that the shifting information is not any longer relevant to the first iterator, but still relevant to the the others. And another insert or remove service call neccessitating shifting may occur in this situation! Keeping book on this, if at all possible, would certainly be too expensive.

6. The General Solution

The idea behind this approach is that when a container modifies its data structure it checks if an iterator is affected by this modification. If so, the container sets up the iterator correctly again. To do this, the container must know all iterators attached to it.

An iterator (object) registers itself with a container (object) when it is created and attached to it. This means that the container knows, at any point of time, all iterators attached to it. When the container executes an method that might affect an iterator (as e.g. removing an element) it can check directly if any of these iterators is actually affected by comparing the position of the iterator with the position of the removed or shifted elements. If this is the case, the container modifies the reference to the current element such that it is correct again. This modification may consist of different actions depending on the problem case (see section 3) concerned:

6.1 Removing the Current Element

The actions required when removing the current element are demonstrated by an (entry invariant) chained list representation of a container, as illustrated in fig.1. Please note that the container itself might be a list, sort, or set without making any difference. Suppose an iterator attached to the container has as current element the one with value cc.

If an element is removed, the container has to check if an iterator is attached to it and, if so, if the iterator is affected by the removal of the element. Both is the case when the element with value cc is removed. Therefore, the iterator has to be changed to reference the next element (in the sense of the iteration sequence). The entry of the removed element is returned to storage management.

In addition, the information must be stored that the iterator is invalid and that it references, already, the next element and not the current one. Otherwise, accessing the current element would deliver the next element instead of invalid as a result. To this purpose, an explicit iterator state is introduced. In addition to the two (implicit) states "valid" and "done", a third state named "invalid" is introduced, which indicates that the current element is invalid and that the iterator references already the next element.

To summarize, the container changes not only the reference of the iterator to the next element, but also sets the iterator state to invalid. In the invalid state, the Get service of an iterator will return invalid as result, and the Next service will not modify the reference to the current element, but will just set the iterator state to valid.

6.2 Implicit Shifting of the Current Element

The actions required when the current element is shifted to a different entry are demonstrated by an (non entry invariant) tabular list representation (where entries are kept in an array and physical adjacency represent logical neighbourship) of a container, as illustrated in fig.2. Suppose an iterator attached to the container has as current element the one with value gg, and suppose that an element is inserted between the elements with value bb and cc.

The container will find out that an iterator is attached since it has registered with it. It checks if the iterator is affected by comparing the index range of the elements to be shifted (in the example, this is 3 to 9) with the index of the current element of the iterator. If the latter one is in the range to be shifted, it must be modified, otherwise it remains unchanged. In our example, the reference to the current element is to be incremented by one entry.

The iterator itself needs not to know that it references, after the execution of the insertion or removal method, a different entry (but the same element). It performs its services as usually.

6.3 Invalidation of a Spanned Iterator

A spanned iterator may be invalidated by all methods that might modify the path from the root of the tree to the current element, that is with methods removing elements, or with methods inserting elements when this is connected with a tree reorganisation.

A container has to check, after a remove method or a tree reorganisation, if a (spanned) iterator is attached, and, if so, if the path kept in the iterator is identical to the path in the tree. This is easily done by following the path kept in the iterator from the root to the current element, and checking with each step, if the next node in the path is a son of the node in the tree. If no divergence is found, the iterator is still correct. Otherwise, it has to be corrected according to the actual path through the tree.

7. Extensions for Safe Iterators and Containers

7.1 Safe Iterator User Interface

The user interface of the class SafeIterator is presented and related to that of a "normal" unsafe iterator (compare section 2).

The Get-service of a safe iterator

```
Index SafeIterator::Get( void);
```

may return invalid as a result when the iterator state is invalid. If exceptions are used the syntax of this service requires no change. The semantic difference is that the exception InvalidCurrentElement may be thrown. If no exceptions are used an additional parameter is required:

```
Boolean SafeIterator::Get( Index& Current);
   //returns Index of current element and True
   //if current element valid
   //returns False, if current element invalid
```

The function IsValid is renamed to IsNotDone since it delivers the result True if the current element is invalid, but the end of the iteration loop is not yet reached.

Now, a typical iteration loop will have the following form:

```
ADT          AnADT;
SafeIterator AnIterator( AnADT);

while ( AnIterator.IsNotDone() )
{  Index Current;
   //...
   if ( AnIterator.Get( Current) )
     {/*process element with Index
                        "Current"*/; }
   else
     {/* action for case that current
                element was removed */; }
   AnIterator.Next();
}
```

7.2 Container Extensions

In the following, the modifications are considered that are not visible to a user. Each container is extended by the services Register and Deregister. An iterator uses them to notify a container about its creation and about the end of its lifetime.

```
class ADT
{
//
IteratorList TheIteratorList;

void Register( const SafeIterator& I);
  //adds I to TheIteratorList
void Deregister( const SafeIterator& I);
  //removes I from TheIteratorList
friend class SafeIterator;
  //for access to Register/Deregister
public:
//...other functions
};
```

Further, each container method that modifies the data representation is to be extended by an implementation of the actions, which were presented in section 6. This will be discussed in section 8.

7.3 Safe Iterator Extensions

Iterators are modified with regard to three aspects. First, they have to notify the attached container about their start and end of lifetime. This is done by extending the constructor and the destructor as shown below.

Second, an iterator must allow its container to find out which element of the container is referenced by it. The existing Get service cannot be used since it does not return the reference if the iterator state is invalid. However, the container has also to get the reference, if the state is invalid (for the reason that the container has to modify this reference in the case that current element is invalid and the next element is shifted or removed). The service

```
Index SafeIterator::GetCurrent( );
```

is provided and declared private since it should not be used by a user. The container is declared as a friend of the class SafeIterator.

Third, the private service

```
void SafeIterator::Modify( const Index& I,
                           IteratorState S = Valid);
```

is offered to allow a container to change the reference to the current element and the state, if an iterator is affected by a modification of the data structure.

Summarizing, the element data and functions of the class SafeIterator are presented:

```
class SafeIterator
{
    enum IteratorState {Valid, Done, Invalid};
    ADT* TheADTptr;
    Index CurrentElement;
    IteratorState TheState;

    Index GetCurrent( )
      //returns Index of current element
      //or, if invalid, of next element
    { return CurrentElement; }

    void Modify( const Index& I,
                 IteratorState S = Valid)
      //sets current element to I and denotes if it is
      //valid or not, i.e. refers to next element
    {  CurrentElement = I;
       TheState = S;
    }

    friend class ADT;
public:

    SafeIterator( ADT& A
                 /*further parameters*/ )
    {  //existing code
       TheADTptr = &A;
       CurrentElement = ...;
       //notifies ADT A about its existence
       A.Register( *this);
       //indicates current element as valid
       TheState = Valid;
    };

    ~SafeIterator( )
    {  //existing code
       //notifies ADT A that existence is finished
       TheADTptr->Deregister( *this);
    };

    Boolean Get( Index& Current)
      //returns Boolean if current is valid
      //if yes Current is set to the current element
    {  if ( TheState == Valid)
         {Current = CurrentElement;
          return True;
         }
       else
         return False;
    }
```

```
    void Next( void)
    {  if ( TheState == Valid)
          //set CurrentElement to next element
       else if ( TheState == Invalid )
          TheState = Valid;
    }

    Boolean IsNotDone( void)
    {return (TheState != Done) ? True : False; }

};
```

8. Data Representation Specific Container Extensions

Now, the base is set to describe in detail how the container methods, which modify the structure of the data representation, have to be extended for the handling of safe iterators. All other container methods remain unchanged.

8.1 Methods Removing Elements

Let us consider a method Remove. The actions required concern case 1, removing of the current element (where they are the same for entry invariant and non entry invariant data representations), and case 2 and 3 (where they are required only for non entry invariant data representations and spanned iterators).

```
    class List: public ADT { /*...*/ };

    void List::Remove( const Elemtype& E)
    {normal actions:
       determine entry TheEntry of E
       deconstruct E
       with tabular list representation
                          -non entry invariant
         determine From which entry To which
                 entry shifting by By is required
         shift entries from From to To
         adjust administration information
       or, alternatively, with linked representation
                                  -entry invariant
         deallocate TheEntry
    actions required to make iterators safe
       foreach (AnIterator from TheIteratorList)
                                            do
         { is current element AnIterator removed?
           case 1- for all representations
             if ( AnIterator.GetCurrent() ==
                           index of TheEntry )
               AnIterator.Modify(Next(
                   AnIterator.GetCurrent()), False);
           case 2 - only for non entry invariant
                                   representations
           is current element of AnIterator
                                   shifted?
           if ( From <= AnIterator.GetCurrent()
                                   <= To )
             AnIterator.Modify(
                 AnIterator.GetCurrent() + By);
                 case3 - not included
         }
}
```

As normally (i.e. without safe iterators) the element to be removed is searched for. It is deconstructed and deallocated, either by returning it to storage management or by shifting other entries of a tabular representation to fill up the hole.

Then, the actions specific to make iterators safe are performed. It is checked if iterators are attached to the container. If no, no more actions are required. If yes, for each iterator the following is done:

1. First, for any data representation, it is checked if the current element is removed. That means, the index or the reference, respectively, of the element to be removed is compared with that of the current element. If they are identical, the current element is removed. The iterator needs to be modified; it is advanced to the next element and its state is set to invalid. Otherwise, no action in this regard is required.
2. Second, for non entry invariant data representations only, it is checked if the current element is shifted to another entry. This is done by comparing its index with the index range of the elements to be shifted. If the index of the current element is in the range, it needs to be adjusted such that it references the new entry of the current element. The state remains as it was, either valid or invalid.
3. If the data representations has a spanned iterator it needs to be checked, additionally, if a e.g. tree reorganisation was done and, if yes, if the spanned path from e.g. the tree root to the node that is the current element is affected by the reorganisation. If so, the spanned iterator is reconstructed; the new path from the root to the current element is determined and the iterator is modified to contain this path.

8.2 Methods Inserting Elements

Let us consider a method Insert using example 2 (see fig.2). Actions are required only for non entry invariant data representations and spanned iterators (case 2 and 3).

```
class TabularList: public ADT { /*...*/ };

Index TabularList::Insert(const Elemtype& E,
                                  Position P)
{ normal actions:
    determine entry TheEntry at which new
                          element is to be inserted
  with tabular list representation
                          -non entry invariant
    determine From which entry To which
        entry shifting by By is required
    shift entries from From to To
    adjust administration information
  or, alternatively, with linked representation
                                  entry invariant
    allocate entry TheEntry for E
    insert E in TheEntry
  actions required to make iterators safe
  foreach (AnIterator from TheIteratorList)
                                          do
    case 2 -only for non entry invariant
                                  representations
    is current element of AnIterator shifted??
      if ( From <= AnIterator.GetCurrent()
                                          <= To
          AnIterator.Modify(
            AnIterator.GetCurrent() + By);
      case3 - not considered
}
```

As normally (i.e. without safe iterators) the entry at which the new element is to be inserted is determined. If it is ocupied by another element the entry is made free by shifting a range of entries of. After the new element is inserted at the - now empty - entry, the actions specific to make iterators safe are done.

It is checked if iterators are attached to the container. If no, no more actions are required. If yes, for each iterator the same actions as described for the Remove method under 2) and 3) are done.

9. Conclusions

Safe active iterators, as introduced in this paper, provide the flexibility and the fine granularity of active iterators, and same as passive iterators, they guarantee a correct visiting sequence even in the presence of intermitting operations that change the structure of the container state. We have defined what is understood to be a correct visiting sequence.

The disadvantage of safe active iterators is that they provide no protection from erroneous use by a user.

A great advantage of the realisation and implementation of safe iterators, which was introduced, are its performance characteristics, which are summarized as follows: If no safe iterator is attached to a container (object) the overhead of the solution is negligible. Only when safe iterators are attached to a container, container methods that modify the structure of the elements of the container cause an overhead, which is proportional to the number of attached iterator objects.

When safe iterators are used from parallel threads or processes, locking is required.

10. Acknowledgements

My thanks are due to Mrs.Buerkle und Mr. Baeumer from RWG Stuttgart, who made me aware of the requirement for safe iterators [Baeumer92] in modern object oriented banking applications [Buerkle92], and to Achill Hasler who identified a problem situation for active iterators.

11. References

[Baeumer92]
H.Baeumer, U.Buerkle:
Private communication, 1992

[Buerkle92]
U.Buerkle, G.Gryczan, H.Zuellighoven:
Erfahrungen mit der objektorientierten Vorgehensweise bei einem Bankenprojekt; Informatik Spektrum 15, p.273-281, 1992

[Booch87]
G.Booch:
Software Components with Ada;
Benjamin Cummmings, Menlo Park, 1987

[Hasler93]
A.Hasler:
Private communication, 1993

[Schmid93]
H.A.Schmid:
An extremely generic C++ collection library;
prepared for publication

[Stroustrup92]
B.Stroustrup:
Die C++ Programmiersprache;
Addison-Wesley, Bonn, 1992

[Uhl90]
J.Uhl and H.A.Schmid:
A Systematic Catalogue of Reusable Abstract Data Types;
Lecture Notes in Computer Science 460,
Springer, Berlin, 1990

Using Inheritance to Provide Subschema Views in a Shared Persistent Object Database

Colin Charlton, Paul Leng and Mark Rivers
Department of Computer Science, University of Liverpool
PO Box 147, Brownlow Hill, Liverpool L69 3BX, United Kingdom.

Abstract

Object-oriented persistent programming reduces the 'impedance mismatch' between application programs and the stored data which they need to manipulate. This reduction is especially beneficial in applications such as CAD data management, where the data concerned has a complex and dynamic structure. The authors are using an implementation of persistent **C++** to write multiple CAD applications sharing a single persistent store. One problem that has arisen from compile-time class definition in **C++** is that not all classes may be compiled into all applications; this leads to problems because programs may access objects of unrecognised classes through polymorphic references.

Other persistent **C++** implementations require that an application program be recompiled with the appropriate class definition before objects of that class may be accessed. This is inconvenient when there are many programs and the global schema is frequently extended. This paper presents a mechanism by which objects of unrecognised classes may be loaded and treated as instances of a recognised superclass, allowing easy addition of new classes to the global schema without requiring recompilation of any existing application programs.

From TOOLS EUROPE '94 (Technology of Object-Oriented Languages and Systems).

1 Introduction

Recently, research into electronic and VLSI CAD data management has tended towards an integrated approach in which design tools are used within a single uniform framework, and function as separate application programs over a single shared design database. This removes the need for the designers to manage independent tools, numerous files of associated data in (perhaps) incompatible formats, and translator programs to resolve such incompatibilities [Mülle 87].

An integrated design database must be capable of representing all the information used in every aspect and phase of the design process. This information has many inter-related dimensions; in the case of circuit design data, these include the hierarchical partitioning of designs, reuse and configuration of such partitions, the representation of designs in different forms (such as functional descriptions, schematic diagrams and physical layouts) and the relationships between these, and so on. The data increases in quantity continuously with advances in technology, and new forms of data need to be added frequently to support new applications. The required information model is very complex, and this complexity is growing. Much CAD database research effort has been directed at searching for data models that can deal with this complexity.

One popular direction of this research centres on *object-oriented* data models [Heiler 87]. These are particularly attractive because the basic philosophy of object-orientation is the management of complexity through abstraction mechanisms. Database objects can be created which correspond to identifiable entities in the real-world domain, and relationships and classifications among these objects/entities can also be expressed. Objects can be constructed as encapsulations of implementational details with a well-defined external interface, thereby concealing the complexity of object internals behind a simplified abstract view.

Another benefit of object-oriented data models within CAD databases concerns the *impedance mismatch* problem [Zaniolo 84]. Impedance mismatch refers to conflicts between the application programming model and the data model. Data structures manipulated by application programs in one form may be stored in the database in a very different form, resulting in obfuscated schemata and traversal overheads. A good example is the traditional relational model; typical design data contains a large number of structures involving repeating groups and polymorphic treatment of record types. Both lead to fragmentation of a relational representation into many small relations, with a very different organisation to that of the application program data structures [Kent 79]. The object-oriented approach can provide a unifying paradigm which spans both the application model and the data model; objects stored in the database can be retrieved and represented as similarly-structured objects in an object-oriented application programming language.

For this reason, we have been exploring the benefits of using object-oriented persistent programming for managing and sharing CAD data. Persistent programming languages allow programs to create values (objects) that outlive the execution time of their creator programs and can be shared between programs [Atkinson 87]. Persistent objects created by CAD applications constitute a database shared between those applications. This approach helps to further reduce impedance mismatch in two ways: the programmer need not be aware of how program structures are stored in the database; and the method of access becomes part of the programming model, since an interface via a declarative query language is not necessary. We have chosen **C++** as our implementation language, and have extended it with data persistence and sharing facilities.

The Problem

A conventional **C++** application cannot deal with new classes of object without recompilation, because **C++** data type definitions (classes) are expressed statically and compiled into each application program. In a system that involves many application programs and frequent introduction of new classes, such recompilation is likely to be a serious inconvenience.

As an example to illustrate the importance of this, consider an application that organises generic design objects. It should not refuse to handle new unrecognised kinds of design object, such as `VHDLdesign`, just because class `VHDLdesign` had not been written at the time the tool was compiled. Nor should the tool require recompilation in order to install the means to deal with `VHDLdesign` objects as generic designs.

This paper presents a technique that allows persistent **C++** programs to manipulate objects of classes which are unknown at compile time. A class provides a view of its instances, defining the ways in which they can be manipulated. The technique presented allows an inherited superclass to be used as a *restricted view* if the actual class of the object is not recognised.

2 An Implementation of Persistent C++

Several implementations of persistent **C++** are described in the literature. These fall into two main groups: those that provide **C++** interfaces to general object-oriented database systems, for example GemStone [Butterworth 91] and O_2 [Deux 91], and those that extend **C++** with specialised storage facilities for persistent objects, for example E [Richardson 89] and Avalon/C++ [Detlefs 88]. A hybrid approach has become more popular recently with the advent of general purpose persistent object managers designed to be able to support a number of persistent object languages, for example Mneme [Moss 90] and ObServer [Hornick 87]. These tend to handle objects as uninterpreted chunks of bytes, so that the complexity and overhead of interpreting object contents is deferred to the clients.

The systems described in the literature all require class definitions to be compiled into each **C++** application before it can manipulate objects of that class. Database systems such as GemStone and O_2 offer powerful multi-client, multi-server architectures with support for distribution, concurrency control and object clustering. However, because they have their own data models, interfacing via **C++** classes must also involve a mapping procedure by which the class is either imported to the database or exported from it. In order for a client to use an object, its class must be defined within both the database and the application program. We therefore chose to base our implementation on a simple storage manager that deals with uninterpreted blocks of bytes. There is no need to interpret data according to a global database schema before passing it to the application program, since the application program makes its own interpretation, and new classes of object can be stored without having to import a class definition to the storage system.

Apart from meeting functional requirements, there are two major issues in the design of a persistent **C++**, concerning the static and the dynamic aspects of persistence extensions. Firstly, the effect on the programming model should be minimised. Syntax extensions to express persistence should be clean and simple, and objects should be manipulable in the same way whether they are persistent or volatile, affording *transparency*; transparency is an important factor in minimising impedance mismatch between application programs and the persistent database. In particular, the transfer of objects between primary and secondary store should occur transparently. Secondly, performance must not be adversely affected by any necessary run-time support.

A clean implementation of persistent **C++** would require integrated extensions to **C++** syntax, processed by a translator or compiler which fully parses the language. Such a translator would be a complex and time-consuming piece of work, and so elegance of implementation has been compromised for the prototype. A more sophisticated implementation is planned for future work.

The organisation of the system described is shown in Fig. 1. Two new keywords and some associated syntax have been added to the **C++** language, and a sophisticated macro preprocessor is used to generate standard **C++** from persistent **C++** source. The preprocessor is an extension of the Texas Instruments COOL preprocessor [Fontana 91]. The program code added during preprocessing provides the facilities by which the compiled program interacts with the object storage system. The persistent object layer manages objects locally, and shared storage and synchronisation is supported by the raw data service which comprises local and remote processes and required communications.

Persistent Objects and Smart Pointers

A class can be given persistent capabilities by replacing the keyword `class` with the keyword `persistent`, as shown in Fig. 2. This allows (but does not force) objects of the class to become persistent. Persistent classes can inherit one or more base classes provided these bases are persistent too. The persistence properties are given by `virtual` inheritance of a common root class, `_POB`, although this is hidden from the programmer by the preprocessor.

A different kind of pointer, the *smart pointer*, is provided for referencing persistent objects. Four smart pointer classes are defined by the preprocessor for every persistent class. Smart pointers are objects that can be dereferenced using the usual **C++** syntax—the `->` operator. For a class `Gate`, the provided smart pointer classes are `P_Gate`, `PC_Gate`, `AP_Gate` and `APC_Gate`. The differences between these are described later. The use of named classes (`P_Gate`) instead of pointer types (`Gate*`) is another compromise of transparency due to the preprocessor-based implementation. Once again, the parser-based implementation will alleviate this problem by introducing a more natural `persistent Gate*` syntax for declarations.

Volatile objects are created on the free store using `new`, and can be made persistent by assigning the returned volatile pointer to a smart pointer. This assignment allocates an object identifier (OID) unique within the database, and causes the object to become managed within the persistent object layer. When a persistent object is accessed via a smart pointer at some point in a program, it may or may not be memory-resident; if not, the smart pointer loads it. There is no way to derive a volatile pointer from a persistent pointer, since the duration of the object's

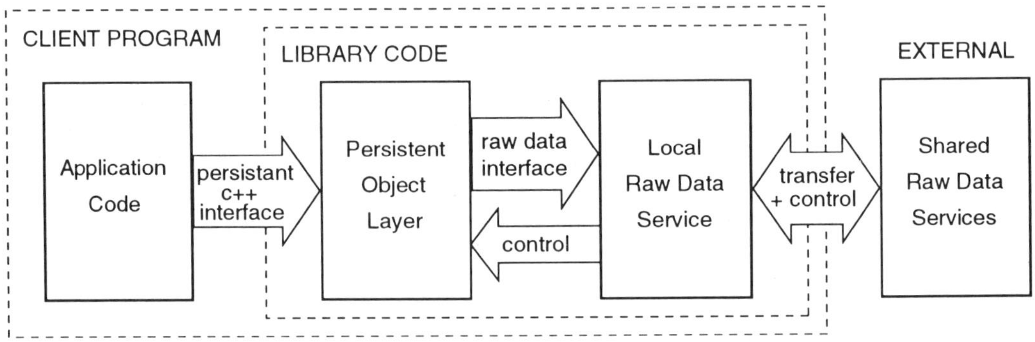

Figure 1: The organisation of the client/database interfaces

residence in memory cannot be guaranteed. The recommended way of creating a persistent object is to assign the result of a `new` call directly to a smart pointer.

Preserving Polymorphism

Each persistent class has two special member functions which handle conversion of its instances between their internal format and their storage format. In an ideal system, and in the planned second implementation, these will be automatically generated, but in the prototype they are defined by the programmer with the member names `in` and `out`. In Fig. 2, `SchemGate` objects contain just a set of pins and a name. The pins are persistent objects and so are referenced through smart pointers (held in a `Set`). The `SchemGate::in` function defines how the elements of a `SchemGate` object are retrieved from the special input stream `in`, which provides a number of operations to retrieve input—for example, `in.getch()` to get the next character. Similarly, `SchemGate::out` defines how an object is translated into storage format on the `out` stream, in such a way that it is suitable input for `SchemGate::in`.

When an object is loaded from persistent store by dereferencing a smart pointer, a new local copy is created and the `in` function for the appropriate persistent class is called to read in the storage representation and restore the contents of the allocated copy accordingly. The `in` functions for base classes are called automatically. However, because objects may be loaded through smart-pointers to base classes, the class of the pointer cannot be used to determine the class of the object copy to be created.

Each class is therefore given a unique identifier, and stored objects contain the identifier for their class. Class identifiers are stored in a table in the database, along with the name of the class. When a client declares a persistent class, the preprocessor defines a static registration object which, on program start, searches for the name of the class in this table and assigns the correct identifier within the client. If the name is not in the table, it allocates a new identifier and creates an appropriate entry in the table. New classes of persistent object can therefore be added to the database 'on the fly'.

The preprocessor also defines one function for each class, which allocates memory and calls the appropriate `in` function. The registration object inserts a pointer to this function into a table indexed by the class identifier. When an object of any class is loaded, its stored identifier is used to select the correct loader function from the table. Objects are therefore loaded correctly by base class smart pointer dereferences.

Constant Objects and Concurrency Control

If a **C++** object is declared or referenced as `const`, the compiler will not allow any of its data members to be modified. Member function calls are also forbidden on `const` objects unless the function has been declared `const`, in which case the compiler guarantees that it cannot modify any data members.

The **C++** notion of a constant object therefore of-

```
persistent SchemGate {                      // SchemGate objects may be persistent
    char* name;                             // name of gate is not embedded
    Set<AP_Pin> pins;                       // Pins are clustered with Gate
};

persistent SchemGate::in {                  // convert SchemGate from store format
    name = hardcopy(in.getln());            // load name and copy to free store
    while (in.getch() == 'P') {             // each pin pointer has a preceding 'P'
        pins.add(AP_Pin(in));               // load pin pointers and add to set
    }
}

persistent SchemGate::out {                 // convert SchemGate to store format
    out.putln(name);                        // output the name
    if (pins.iterate()) {                   // if there's any pins
        do {                                // then for each one
            out.putch('P');                 // output a 'P'
            out.putptr(pins.member);        // and the Pin pointer (i.e. Pin OID)
        } while (pins.next());              // (note: because these are aggregate
    }                                       // ptrs, the Pins will be output next)
    out.putch('=');                         // finally, terminate list with non-'P'
}

persistent SchemGate::body {}               // static data concerned with SchemGate
```

Figure 2: The persistent class declaration syntax

fers an attractive mechanism by which concurrent access control can be implemented for multiple copies of shared data objects. `P_Gate` and `PC_Gate` smart pointers point to mutable and constant `Gate` objects respectively. When a `PC_Gate` is dereferenced, the compiler will protect the `Gate`'s members from alteration; if the object is not resident, it is sufficient to retrieve a read-only copy. When a `P_Gate` is dereferenced, changes to data members are possible so if the object is not resident, a writable copy is retrieved. If a `P_Gate` is dereferenced and a read-only copy is resident, it is replaced with a writable copy.

Whenever a member function is called for an object, the object is locked into memory so that uncaching or relocation does not invalidate the volatile `this` pointer (implicit in many member accesses). In the case of non-`const` member functions, this also prevents the write-lock being surrendered until the function returns, making all the object changes effected by the function appear to other clients as if they were applied atomically. A similar locking scheme is implemented by '`uMutex`' classes in the concurrent **C++** extension μ**C++**[Buhr 92], but this provides total mutual exclusion, failing to exploit the `const` property to determine read or write locks.

Concurrent access control and a simple atomic update mechanism are therefore implemented completely transparently to the programmer, since access and locking requirements are deduced from standard **C++** program constructs. Although this simple scheme lacks the power of more sophisticated systems, extension is possible whilst retaining the simple transparent default. The preprocessor-based implementation relies on the use of a new keyword `locking` to apply locks on member functions; the planned parser-based implementation will eliminate this.

Careful design is of increased importance with respect to the use of constant objects. It is important that `const` objects and pointers are employed wherever possible to avoid acquiring unnecessary write-locks. This maximal use of `const` is regarded as good **C++** programming practice anyway.

Aggregate Pointers and Clustering

To support efficient retrieval from store, objects can be clustered together. A cluster contains one or more objects which are stored in one chunk and retrieved by one request, but loaded independently. When one object in a cluster is requested, the whole group is retrieved; likewise, the group is written together.

Clustering is controlled in the prototype by the use of *aggregate* pointers. An aggregate smart pointer behaves similarly to other kinds of smart pointer, except that when an aggregate pointer is saved as a member of an object, it causes the object to which it points to be saved subsequently, in the same cluster block. Two kinds of aggregate smart pointers are provided, for constant and changeable objects.

Note that read/write locks apply to whole clusters, not just individual objects. When a write-lock is requested on one object in a cluster, the whole cluster is loaded and write-locked. A scheme to load and lock sub-clusters will be an important enhancement in the next implementation.

Implicit Smart Pointer Conversion

C++ pointers undergo a number of implicit type conversions when passed as parameters or used in assignments. In order to be used transparently, smart pointers ought to allow the same conversions. It is for this reason that the smart pointer class system as presented has replaced the earlier template-based implementation described in [Charlton 91].

A **C++** pointer to a class object can be implicitly converted to a pointer to an object of an accessible base class, provided that this conversion is unambiguous. Ambiguity occurs if the base is inherited more than once along different paths in a multiple inheritance graph, and the restriction of conversion to accessible base classes ensures that inherited members which are inaccessible in the derived class are not made accessible by the conversion, thereby breaking encapsulation.

These conversions are implemented for smart pointers by organising each kind of smart pointer into an inheritance graph that mirrors that of the persistent classes. Any derived-to-base conversion that is applicable to ordinary pointers to these classes is therefore also applicable to smart pointers provided they are passed by reference. In the preprocessor implementation, pointers may only be converted to pointers to public base classes. The inheritance of members between smart pointers is not an issue, as each pointer redefines its own set of public inline member functions.

C++ pointers can also be implicitly converted from pointers to changeable objects to pointers to `const` objects. The converse is not true, because object constancy would be violated. This kind of conversion is implemented for smart pointers using constructors—a `PC_Gate` can be constructed from a `P_Gate`. Note that these two kinds of conversion can operate together, since the constructor argument can be implicitly converted from a smart pointer to a publicly derived class. Implicit smart pointer conversion is illustrated in Fig. 3. The pointer types `AP_` and `APC_` interact similarly; an `APC_Gate` can be converted to a `PC_Gate`, and an `AP_Gate` can be converted to any other kind of smart pointer to a `Gate`.

3 Partial Interpretation

Earlier it was seen that clients can load objects of a particular class `D` through a pointer to a base class `B`, provided that a pointer conversion from `D*` to `B*` is legal and unambiguous. The `D` object would be loaded as a `D` despite being referenced as a `B` object. However, the possibility exists that, since the database is shared by multiple client programs, class `D` may not be defined within the loading client even though class `B` obviously is. The client should still be able to load the object and work with it as an instance of `B`, or some intermediate derived class of `B`, without recompilation to recognise `D`. This is essential for dynamic extensibility of the system as explained in the introduction.

In this treatment of database classes, client schemata constitute *logical subschemata* [Geppert 93], and the global data schema is the union of all of these. In a logical schema, a base class can be seen as a restricted view of those classes derived from it—including those that are not part of the logical schema. In database terminology, confusingly, the base class is a *derived type*. An approach such as that described by Wiederhold [Wiederhold 86], where objects are extracted from a relational database via relational views, could be used to restrict object views to that of base classes, but would require the expression of the view as a query over the global schema. The *partial interpretation* method presented

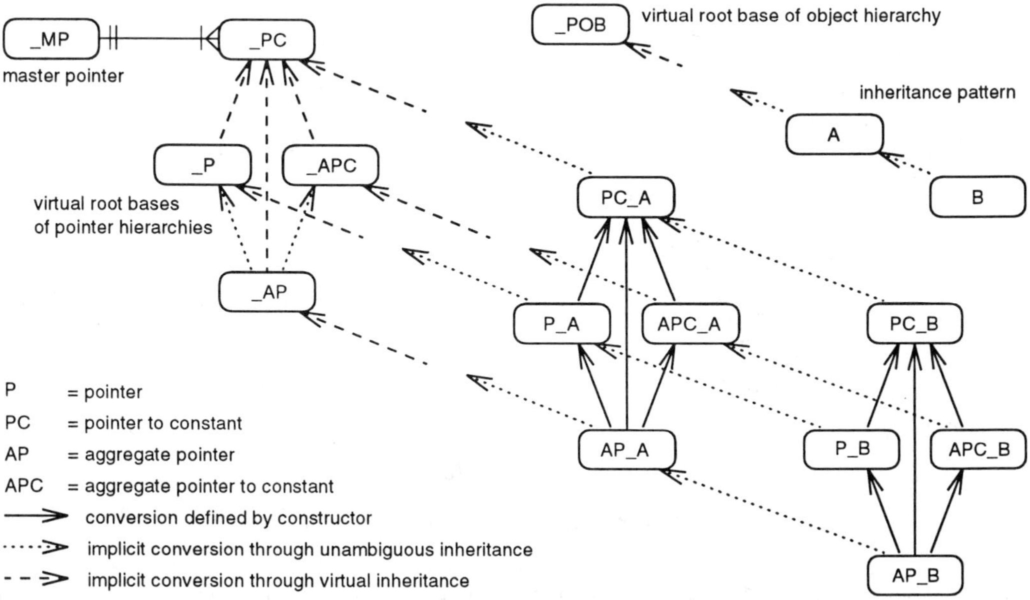

Figure 3: Implicit smart-pointer conversion paths

here can automatically extract the data relevant to a view because this is easily determined from the rules and implementation of **C++** inheritance.

Sub-Objects and Slices

In the **C++** inheritance model, an object of a class contains a *sub-object* for each of its direct base classes (if any), and a *slice* containing the data members defined by that class. Sub-objects may be nested, if the base classes have base classes. If an indirect base class is inherited more than once, through different direct bases, one sub-object exists for each of these occurrences. A single sub-object can be shared by sub-objects if the inheritance is specified to be `virtual`.

For example, consider Fig. 4(a). Because `E` inherits `B` twice, each instance of `E` has two `B` sub-objects, embedded within the `C` and `D` sub-objects. However, because `A` and `B` are both derived from `_POB` by `virtual` inheritance, a single `_POB` sub-object is shared by all `A` and `B` sub-objects—of which there are three within an `E` instance.

Class pointer conversion from a derived class to a base involves adjusting the pointer to point to the appropriate base sub-object within the derived class object. Partial interpretation of an object is another form of class pointer conversion. When a `D` is to be loaded through a pointer to a `B`, a legal and unambiguous conversion from a `D*` to a `B*` must be possible. If type information for `D` is unavailable to the compiler, the persistent object system must provide it at run-time so that the legality of the conversion can be guaranteed. An illegal conversion results in an exception, but can only happen as a result of a bad explicit conversion in some other client program.

When a new persistent class is added to the database registry, information on the base classes is also stored. This comprises a list of the base class identifiers in declaration order, each with a flag indicating whether the base is publically inherited. To ensure that a partial interpretation conversion from `D*` to `B*` is unambiguous, the persistent object system establishes that `B` is only inherited once by `D`. To establish that the conversion is legal, it checks that all the inheritance steps on the path from `B` to `D` are public. The nearest client-recognised class to

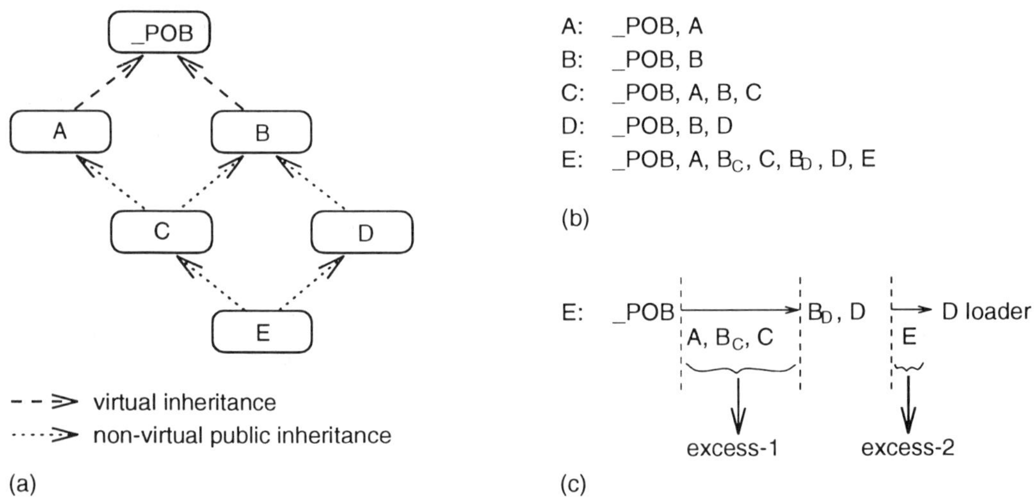

Figure 4: Partial interpretation of object construction data

D on this path is selected as the one which gives the most complete view of the partially interpreted object. The sub-object corresponding to this class is loaded and the pointer points to this.

In Fig. 4(a), if E is the only class missing from the client schema, an E object may still be loaded through a pointer to an A; the C sub-object within it is loaded and the pointer points to this. However, an attempt to load an E through a pointer to a B would raise an exception since the conversion is ambiguous.

Implementation

Ultimately, an object is stored as a sequence of slices. Each slice corresponds to the data written by the `out` function for that class. The sequences are nested in the same way that sub-objects are nested; the sequence for a particular class of object is the same regardless of whether it is an outer object or a sub-object.

The preprocessor-based prototype uses **C++** constructors to implement the `in` functions, and the order of slices is determined by the order of construction of sub-objects as specified by the **C++** language: for each object or sub-object, its own sub-objects are constructed first, in order of class declaration, followed by its slice. The `out` functions guarantee that the same order is adhered to when storing objects. Virtual base classes are a special case; these are constructed before any other sub-objects, in a language-specified order. The prototype does not support virtual inheritance of persistent classes, because the **C++** compiler employed seems not to adhere to any predictable construction order for virtual bases.

The construction orders for the classes in Fig. 4(a) are shown in Fig. 4(b). Class `_POB` provides persistence-related internals for each persistent class object; the preprocessor ensures that it is virtually inherited by any persistent class declared without bases. Every persistent object therefore has a `_POB` slice stored first.

Loading a partially interpreted object involves searching through the stored data for the required sub-object. First the `_POB` slice is loaded, then the data is skipped up to the start of the sub-object. After loading the sub-object, any remaining data is skipped. If the loaded copy is writable, these two sections of skipped data are inserted uninterpreted into two buffers (`excess1` and `excess2`) and are re-inserted in the appropriate places when updating the stored object. Fig. 4(c) shows how an E object is loaded as a D, skipping both the C sub-object (`excess1`) and the E slice (`excess2`).

Fig. 5 shows the storage format used in the prototype. The slices are separated by `SLISEP` character

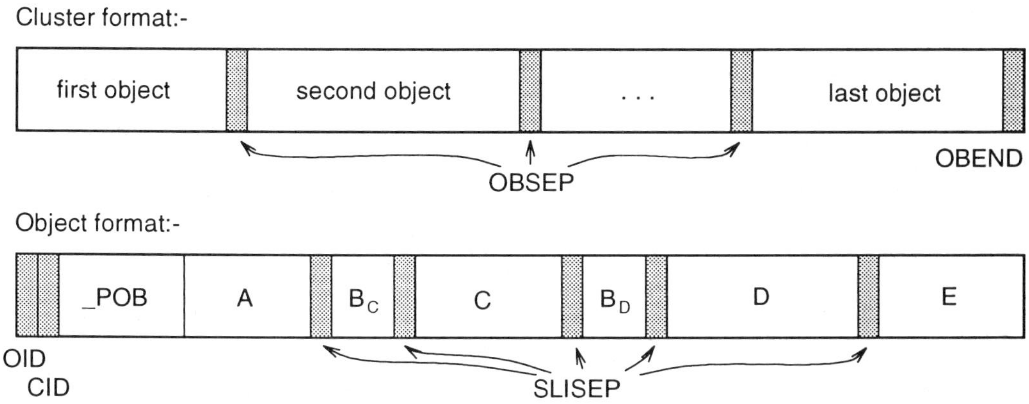

Figure 5: The storage format of objects and clusters

codes; the inheritance lattice is used to determine the number of slices that need to be skipped after constructing _POB, and this is given as a construction argument to the object, so that skipping is performed by the _POB constructor. In the example in Fig. 4(c), three slices are skipped. After loading the sub-object, all remaining slices are skipped up to the next OBSEP or OBEND character code; these delimit objects within a cluster.

Implications for Program Design

In **C++** there is only one way in which objects of different classes can provide derived-class-specific behaviour when accessed through a pointer to a base class: via virtual functions. The derived-class-specific parts of an object are not otherwise accessible through a base class pointer, and so apart from calls to virtual functions, the fact that these parts may not be loaded and recognised is irrelevant to the use of the object. Virtual functions are therefore the only language mechanism for which the semantics are affected by partial interpretation.

A call to a virtual function on an object of class X may not resolve to the implementation attached to X as would be guaranteed in plain **C++**, since the calling client may not recognise X nor consequently the X-specific definition of the virtual function. Instead, the call resolves to the definition appropriate for the class of the loaded sub-object. The meaning of virtual function calls is changed from 'use the implementation appropriate for the actual class' to 'use the most appropriate implementation available'. Shared persistent classes must be designed with this in mind.

4 Conclusion

This paper has presented a mechanism by which base classes within a persistent **C++** application are used as subschema views onto unrecognised derived classes defined elsewhere in the global schema. This allows applications to resolve polymorphic references to stored objects of unrecognised classes without necessitating recompilation. In an environment where many applications share a common persistent store, such as a CAD data management system, this facilitates easier and more flexible extension of the system.

A novel use of the **C++** concept of constant objects to implement simple, transparent concurrent access control and locking has also been described.

The prototype implementation makes a number of concessions to its experimental nature. Future work on this project involves the development of a more transparent and robust implementation of persistent **C++** that incorporates the ideas explored in the prototype.

Acknowledgements

This work has received support through an equipment donation from Hewlett Packard, and a research studentship from the UK Science and Engineering Research Council.

References

[Atkinson 87] Malcolm P. Atkinson and O. Peter Buneman. Types and persistence in database programming languages. *ACM Computing Surveys*, 19(2):105–190, June 1987.

[Buhr 92] P. A. Buhr, Glen Ditchfield, R. A. Stroobosscher, and B. M. Younger. μC++: Concurrency in the object-oriented language C++. *Software Practice and Experience*, 22(2):137–172, February 1992.

[Butterworth 91] Paul Butterworth, Allen Otis, and Jacob Stein. The GemStone object database management system. *Communications of the ACM*, 34(10):64–77, October 1991.

[Charlton 91] Colin Charlton, Paul Leng, and Mark Rivers. Using C++ to model digital circuit design data. In *Short Paper Proceedings of East EurOOPe Conference*, Bratislava, September 1991.

[Deux 91] O. Deux et al. The O_2 system. *Communications of the ACM*, 34(10):34–48, October 1991.

[Detlefs 88] D. D. Detlefs, M. P. Herlihy, and J. M. Wing. Inheritance of synchronization and recovery properties in Avalon/C++. *IEEE Computer*, 21(12):57–69, December 1988.

[Fontana 91] Mary Fontana, LaMott Oren, and Martin Neath. A portable implementation of parameterized templates using a sophisticated C++ macro facility. Distributed with the Texas Instruments COOL preprocessor, 1991.

[Geppert 93] Andreas Geppert, Stefan Scherrer, and Klaus R. Dittrich. Derived types and subschemas: Towards better support for logical data independence in object-oriented data models. Technical Report IFI-TR 93.27, Institut für Informatik der Universität Zürich, June 1993.

[Heiler 87] Sandra Heiler, Umeshwar Dayal, Jack Orenstein, and Susan Radka-Sproull. An object-oriented approach to data management: Why design databases need it. In *Proceedings of 24th ACM/IEEE Design Automation Conference*, pages 335–340, 1987.

[Hornick 87] M. F. Hornick and S. B. Zdonik. A shared, segmented memory system for an object-oriented database. *ACM Transactions on Office Information Systems*, 5(1):70–95, January 1987.

[Kent 79] William Kent. Limitations of record-based information models. *ACM Transactions on Database Systems*, 4(1):107–131, March 1979.

[Mülle 87] Jutta A. Mülle, Klaus R. Dittrich, and Angelika M. Kotz. Design management support by advanced database facilities. In *Proceedings of IFIP WG 10.2 Workshop on Tool Integration and Design Environments*, pages 23–49, 1987.

[Moss 90] J. Eliot B. Moss. Design of the Mneme persistent object store. *ACM Transactions on Information Systems*, 8(2):103–139, April 1990.

[Richardson 89] Joel E. Richardson and Michael J. Carey. Persistence in the E language: Issues and implementation. *Software Practice and Experience*, 19(12):1115–1150, December 1989.

[Wiederhold 86] Gio Wiederhold. Views, objects and databases. *IEEE Computer*, 19(12):37–44, December 1986.

[Zaniolo 84] Carlo Zaniolo et al. Object-oriented database systems and knowledge systems. In Larry Kerschberg, editor, *Proceedings of 1st International Workshop on Expert Database Systems*, pages 50–65, 1984.

C++: Attacks and Defenses

Juan Alvarez-Rubio

Depto. de Ciencias de la Computación - U. de Chile
Blanco 2120, Santiago, Chile - jalvarez@dcc.uchile.cl

Depto. de Ingeniería Telemática - U. Politécnica de Madrid
Ciudad Universitaria, Madrid 28040, Spain - jalvarez@dit.upm.es

Abstract

C++ is the most popular object oriented language. Its wide spreading is explained by the C++ bandwagon inertial effect, mainly due to the upward compatibility with the C language. However, developers and teachers need to know studies of the language in order to evaluate their strengths and weaknesses.

The literature provides two kinds of documents. First, there are papers that discourage the use of C++, criticizing the features of the language. On the other hand, the C++ books present all the features of the language enthusiastically, without any criticisms, to a "captive" audience that already decided the use of the language. This work shows a balanced and objective view, analyzing the most significant features of the language, contrasting attacks and criticisms against strengths and defenses.

1 Introduction

Undoubtedly, C++ is the most used object oriented language. This situation is mainly explained because of many software developers did the transition from C to C++. The technical strength of the language have been secondary.

Like other languages in the past, C++ has raised controversy. Many criticisms address the compatibility with C and the complexity of the language:

From TOOLS EUROPE '94 (Technology of Object-Oriented Languages and Systems).

- "Incrementing C by 1 is not enough to make a good object oriented language" [Sakkinen88]
- "C is an elegant language; it is small and simple. The syntax of C++ is similar to that of C, but its semantics are neither small nor simple" [Edelson89]
- "I will be deeply disappointed if the bandwagon effect indeed makes C++ the object-oriented language of the 1990s" [Sakkinen92].
- "C++ is overly complex" [Joyner92]
- "C++ is a difficult language in which there may be a very fine line between a feature and a bug" [Ellemtel92]
- "C programmers often solve bugs by adding extra ()s, *s and &s, without understanding the problem" [Joyner92]
- "C++ programmers often solve bugs by adding extra references, virtual functions, copy-constructors and assignment operators without understanding the problem" [personal adaptation to the previous quotation]
- "If C++ is the answer, what's the question?" [Plauger93]

The C++ defense is mainly found in the books and papers introducing the language:

- "C++ is a general purpose programming language designed to make programming more enjoyable for the serious programmer" [Stroustrup91]

- "I thank Bjarne Stroustrup for inventing such an elegant language and encouraging others to help develop and teach it" [Pohl89]

- "The C++ language provides the key capabilities and benefits offered by object-oriented programming, without including features that would constrain its use to a limited set of application domains and environments" [Jordan90]

- "Special thanks go to Bjarne Stroustrup for the wonderful language he has given us" [Lippman92]

- "C++ has been a language at the right time and the right place" [Coplien92]

- "Where C was permissive and error prone, C++ is restrictive and safe" [Martin92]

In order to evaluate the suitability of C++ in teaching and production, we will offer a general and balanced view of the most significant features of the C++ language, without excessive technicality.

2 Discussion

The C++ language comprises many features and concepts. We will analyze the attacks and defenses gathered in the following aspects:

- base language C
- C improvements
- C++ culture
- classes
- inheritance
- operator overloading
- other aspects

2.1 Base language C

The C programming language, base of C++, deserves a detailed and independent analysis. We will sum up the main criticisms appeared in previous papers [Sakkinen92,Joyner92].

- *Syntax.* In general, the syntax is considered overly terse. The use of upper and lower case encourages name overloading, causing confusion and errors. The shortage of delimiters for control statements is considered negative with respect to other modern languages like Ada. The multiple meanings of some keywords (static, virtual) and symbols (& * ::) is also criticized. C++ keeps the antimathematical notation for octal constants (07 = 7, but 070 = 56).

- *Pointers.* One of the more important source of program errors, the pointers admit arithmetic operations with strict rules that can not be controlled. Many pointer idioms (for example `*p++ += *q++`) can be replaced by more readable and likewise efficient code (`a[i] += b[i]; i++;`). Finally, the syntax of pointer declarations is confused:

```
int* p, q; // int *p, q;
           //not int *p, *q;
```

- *Arrays.* They concentrate the greater amount of attacks. The indexes begin always from zero and theirs values are not controlled in execution time. There are not operations for complete arrays. Functions can not receive arrays by value and can not return an array. C++ allows to define a class to overcome the restrictions [Lippman92, Stroustrup91].

- *Strings.* Additionally to the problems of arrays, the strings mix data with metadata (\0) generating dangers, inconveniences and inefficiencies. Like arrays, a suitable C++ class can be defined.

- *Other data types.* It lacks sets, a boolean or logical type, true multidimensional and dynamic arrays. On the other hand, the enumerations are considered integers by the arithmetic operators. At present, there is a proposal to add the boolean data type to C++ [Bruck93]. Like arrays and strings, sets can be implemented with a C++ class [Alvarez94].

- *Operators.* The following are the main attacks: too many operators (C: 44 [Kernighan88a], C++: 57 [Stroustrup91]), some operators are superfluous (++, +=), too much operator precedences (C: 15 [Kernighan88a], C++: 18 [Stroustrup91]), the order of operand evaluation is undefined (`f(x)+g(x)`), they produce some paradoxical situations (`1<2<3 == 3<2<1`, `matrix[i,j]` ≡ `matrix[j]`).

- *Control statements.* Break and continue are applied only to the inner loop. The for instruction is considered too much powerful and superfluous (because it can be expressed through a while loop). Finally, switch concentrates the greater amount of attacks: there is no automatic exit after each branch, the case clause accepts only constants values and it does not admits ranges of values, it is not mandatory that all the possible values be considered, an efficient implementation is not guaranteed.

- *Assignment.* The symbol = is debated because of it corresponds to the mathematical equality. Also, due to the assignment is an operator (and not a statement), it is strange that the side effect is more important that the result.

- *Preprocessor.* It is not integrated to the language and it is applied only in a lexical level. Fortunately, C++ provides alternatives to some uses of the preprocessor: constant definition, inline functions.

A general evaluation [Kernighan88] enumerates the following strengths of the C language: compact, efficient, expressive, small, portable, absence of restrictions, relative "low level", good target language. The weaknesses consider: some poor choices of operator precedences, the switch statement, complicated declarations are often hard to read, portability problems on undefined or implementation-defined properties.

2.2 C improvements

This section deals with the criticisms to the new C++ facilities not related to classes, inheritance and operator overloading. Therefore, they can be simply considered as an improvement to the base language C.

- *Functions.* The new facilities for functions upgrade the language, but some details present weaknesses. First, because of a prototype can omit formal parameter names, the purpose of a function is less readable. On the other hand, default parameters are restricted to the last parameters. The function overloading is solved through the types of the arguments (signature), without consideration of the result type. Finally, the inline specifier does not guarantee an in-line expansion and it is only a hint to the compiler.

- *Declarations.* C++ allows that declarations can be intermixed with executable statements. However, one of the most popular application can produce problems:

```
for(int i=0; i < n; ++i)
...
for(int i=0; i < n; ++i)
//error: i already declared
...
```

- *References.* The usefulness of a reference is recognized, but it is simply considered as syntactic sugar over constant pointers.

```
void swap(int& x, int& y)
{int t=x; x=y; y=t;}
swap(a,b);

void swap(int const *px,
          int const *py)
{int t=*px; *px=*py; *py=t;}
swap(&a,&b);
```

A reference can also be applied to define synonyms, but this use is hardly criticized.

```
int& j = i; j++; //i++
```

2.3 C++ "Culture"

One of the most hard criticism to the language [Sakkinen92] says that the self-sufficiency is an irritating feature of some developers of programming languages. This situation produces a peculiar terminology as shown in the following table adapted from [Sakkinen92]:

C++ literature	Conventional terminology
class	class
object	object, instance
data member	data component
function member	function component
static data member	common data comp
static function memb	common function
base class	base/super class
derived class	derived/sub class
virtual class	sharable
non-virtual class	duplicatable

A sketch of defense recognizes the collective progress with Simula 67, Ada and Clu influences [Stroustrup91].

2.4 Classes

. The class is the original and fundamental C++ concept. It is the mechanism designed to implement abstract (user defined) data types. The goal is to hide the representation and to offer operations, following the same ideas of the basic built-in types. Thus, a user program will not depend on ADT implementation.

The feature is useful and powerful but it is not exempt of attacks:

- *Syntax and Interface.* The redundant equivalence with a structure (except that the default specifier is private) is defended with the compatibility with the C language. The class text must contain public (interface) and private (representation) members. The advantage is that the compiler knows the size of the objects, so these can be directly handled without using pointers [Ellis90]. Consequently, changes in the private members also require the recompilation of the programs.

- *Constructors.* These novels member functions are executed during an object definition. They do not accept names others than the class name and their signature must to be unique. On the other hand, the default copy-constructor (and the default assignment operator) produces problems when objects need dynamic storage.

- *Destructor.* Member function designed to be implicitly invoked just before an object be deleted, unfortunately it also admits explicit calls.

- *Friends.* These functions, that can access the private members of a class, present three problems [Joyner92]: they change the object state from class outside, they add extra coupling, and they access, without restriction, all the private members (not only the interesting ones).

  Efficiency is the main justification of the friends functions. The product between a matrix and a vector is a classical example. If the function is a friend of the classes matrix and vector, then it can know and access both internal representations, avoiding intensive member functions calls.

2.5 Inheritance

An object-oriented (and not an object-based) language must provide inheritance. The C++ facilities are very powerful, however, the following are some weaknesses:

- *Function redefinition.* A function in a derived class hides, and it does not overloads, a function with the same name in the base class. The rationality is to avoid surprises to a class user. Unfortunately, this spirit can be violated using the function through a pointer to a base class. In order to prevent the problem, some people proposes that the non-virtual functions can not be redefined in a derived class, or, at least, that the compilers write a warning message.

- *Virtual functions.* This mechanism was designed to implement dynamic binding. A function, declared as virtual in the base class, can be redefined in a derived class. A proper function is selected at execution time according to the type of the object pointed by a base class reference (or pointer).

  Specifically, the virtual specification in the base class is criticized, because of the derived class decides their use. Also, the curious syntax for a pure virtual function (that requires the redefinition in the derived class) is debated: `virtual void f(int) = 0;`.

- *Multiple inheritance.* The possibility to derive a class from several base classes is discussed. In fact, some languages (like Ada-9x) do not include the feature. However, in some situations the availability of multiple inheritance facilitates the modeling.

  The virtual inheritance (needed in fork-join hierarchies to avoid the duplication of members) is attacked because it requires the specification in the intermediate classes, and not at the last level.

  ```
  class A { ... };
  class B: public virtual A {};
  class C: public virtual A {};
  class D: public B, public C {};
  ```

- *Class of an object* . [Sakkinen92] writes that the fundamental defect is the type (class) loss. In other words, C++ does not provide a mechanism to retrieve the class of an object. Two arguments are presented in [Ellis90]. First, this requires that the internal representation of an object be changed, generating an incompatibility with C. Second, this could change the programming style from virtual functions to decisions taken from class examination.

2.6 Operator overloading

The purpose of this powerful facility is to apply the predefined operators to abstract (user defined) data types. But, some aspects have suffered attacks.

- *Syntactic sugar.* The invocation of an operator is a notational simplification. In fact, `x+y` is equivalent to `x.operator+(y)` (in case of a class member) or `operator+(x,y)` (for a friend function).

- *Only for classes.* It is not possible to overload the operators for basic (built-in) types. The defense says "the intent is to make C++ extensible, but not mutable". Thus, the usual meanings of the operators can not be changed.

- *Semantic relation between operators.* The user, and not the language, has the responsibility to define the proper meanings for related operators. Examples: == and !=; < and >; =, + and +=.

- *Operators can not be added nor changed.* For example, for exponentiation, it is not possible to add the operator **. Neither it is allowed to change the associativity and the precedence of the operator ^. The aim is not to confuse the user nor to complicate the syntax analysis.

- *Operands evaluation.* Given that the class operators are special member functions, then the operands (arguments) are evaluated before the execution. Thus, the effect of the logical operators (`&&, ||`) can not be achieved. Remember that these operators evaluate the second operand only if it is necessary.

- *Postfix operators.* In order to distinguish the meanings of some unary operators, the postfix increment and decrement must be defined with an integer parameter (for example operator++(int)).

  The defenses are that the feature was vigorously requested by users, and all other unary operators are prefix. In any case, the normal use of the operators is kept (for example, X++), although the alternative notation is allowed (X.operator++(n)).

- *Prohibitions.* Some operators cannot be overloaded (`. .* :: ?: sizeof`). "The reason for disallowing the overloading of . and .* is that they already have a predefined meaning for objects of any class as their first operand. Overloading of ?: simply did not seem worthwhile" [Ellis90].

- *Defaults.* The assignment, address, and comma operators have sensible predefined meanings. If problems are produced, they can be redefined or hidden. As a matter of fact, the assignment operator is normally redefined when dynamic storage is demanded.

A general defense to the observations related to the operator overloading is that the philosophy was to mimic the behavior of the operators on the basic types.

2.7 Other aspects

This section will sum up criticisms to some not related aspects.

- *Portability*. The lack of a standard version of the language causes many problems. A draft standard is scheduled for September 1994 [Stroustrup93]. Unlike C, neither exists a classic C++. On the contrary, there are different releases of AT&T and GNU compilers. Also, it is debated that C++ is not exactly a superset of the language C. The defense would be that the situation has allowed the evolution of the language.

- *I/O*. The shift operators (<< `and` >>), overloaded in the streams classes, present some problems with expressions that contain operators with lower precedence. Thus, the expression `cout<<a=b` needs to add parenthesis to the assignment. Also, it is uncomfortable to define friend functions in order to read/write class objects.

- *Garbage collection.* There is not automatic garbage collection. The programmer has the responsibility to free unused storage. However, it is possible to write good storage managers, but it will not be in the standard [Stroustrup93].

3 Conclusions

Like other languages in the past, the C++ language has raised controversy. The attacks, often slanted, have an excessive emphasis in language details. Some criticisms are reasonable, however they are not contrasted with the advantages and strengths.

The implicit "defenses", in books of the language, consider the compatibility with C as a strength. Also, the fact that C++ is the most used object-oriented language is a positive evaluation of the technical features. Many of the "obscure" aspects of the language mainly affect to the libraries developers instead of "final" programmers.

In sum, like other languages, C++ presents strengths and weaknesses. Many deficiencies can be overcome through rules and style recommendations ([Ellemtel92]). The next standard, and the supporting tools and libraries, will considerably assist the job of the C++ programmers.

Acknowledgements

The research for this paper was partially supported by the Scientific Cooperation with Iberoamerica Program of the Spain Education and Science Ministry.

References

[Alvarez94] Alvarez-Rubio,J.; *Sets for C++*; To appear in TaTTOO94 (Teaching and Training in the Technology of Objects) Proceedings; Leicester, U.K.; January 1994

[Bruck93] Bruck,D.; Koening,A.; *Extension proposal: Boolean data type*; ANSI Doc No: X3J16/93-0143; September 1993

[Coplien92] Coplien,J.; *Advanced C++*; Addison-Wesley; 1992

[Edelson89] Edelson,D.; Pohl,I.; *C++: Solving C Shortcomings?*; Computer Languages Vol. 14, No.3; 1989

[Ellemtel92] Ellemtel Telecommunication Systems Laboratories, Sweden; *Programming in C++: Rules and Recommendations*; 1992

[Ellis90] Ellis,M.; Stroustrup,B.; The Annotated C++ Reference Manual; Addison-Wesley; 1990

[Jordan90] Jordan,D.; *Implementation Benefits of C++ Language Mechanisms*; Communications of the ACM; Vol.33, No.9; 1990

[Joyner92] Joyner,I.; *C++?? A critique of C++ (2nd ed)*; comp.lang.c++ newsgroup; November 1992

[Kernighan88] Kernighan, B.; Ritchie,D.; *The state of C*; Byte; August 1988

[Kernighan88a] Kernighan,B.; Ritchie,D.; *The C Programming Language (2nd ed)*; Prentice-Hall; 1988

[Lippman92] Lippman,S.; *A C++ Primer (2nd ed)*; Addison-Wesley; 1992

[Martin92] Martin,R.; *A response to Joyner Critique of C++*; comp.lang.c++ newsgroup; June 1992

[Plauger93] Plauger,P.J.; *Programming Language Guessing Games*; Dr.Dobb's Journal; October 1993

[Pohl89] Pohl,I.; *C++ for C Programmers*; Benjamin/Cummings; 1989

[Stroustrup91] Stroustrup,B.; *The C++ Programming Language*; Addison-Wesley; 1991

[Stroustrup93] Stroustrup,B.; *Comments on garbage collection, C compatibility, standards, etc.*; comp.std.c++ newsgroup; may 1993

[Sakkinen88] Sakkinen,M.; *On the Darker Side of C++*; ECOOP'88 Proceedings, Springer-Verlag; 1988

[Sakkinen92] Sakkinen,M.; *The Darker Side of C++ Revisited*; Structured Programming, Vol. 13; 1992

SMALLTALK WORLD

SMALLTALK ESSENTIALS

Smalltalk Essentials Presentation

by:

Trevor Hopkins, University of Manchester, UK

SMALLTALK APPLICATIONS

Creating Tools in HotDraw by Composition

John Brant **Ralph E. Johnson**
University of Illinois at Urbana-Champaign
Department of Computer Science
1304 W. Springfield Ave.
Urbana IL 61801, USA.
e-mail: {brant,johnson}@cs.uiuc.edu

Abstract

As frameworks evolve, it is common for reuse by inheritance to be replaced by reuse by composition. This has happened recently to HotDraw, a structured drawing editor framework for Smalltalk. Class Tool, which once was frequently subclassed, has been broken into several smaller components, and new tools can now be defined entirely by composing other objects. Although creating a new tool might require creating a new component, the amount of code necessary to create a new tool has decreased significantly, and it is easier to learn how to create a new tool. This is not only important for users of HotDraw, but illustrates a design technique that can be used in other programs.

From TOOLS EUROPE '94 (Technology of Object-Oriented Languages and Systems).

1 Introduction

As frameworks evolve, it is common for reuse by inheritance to be replaced by reuse by composition. One reason that inheritance is used first might be that Smalltalk offers better support for inheritance than it does for composition. Another reason might be that it is easier to think about incrementally modifying an object than about breaking it into orthogonal parts. Whatever the reason, the first thought of designers seems to be to reuse behavior by inheritance, and designs based on composition evolve from ones that are based on inheritance.

For example, the original Model-View-Controller reused scrolling behavior by inheritance. A controller would reuse scrolling by being a subclass of ScrollController. In ObjectWorks\Smalltalk 4.1, a view is scrolled by wrapping it in a ScrollWrapper. This makes it easy to have both scrolling and non scrolling forms of a view, which was hard to achieve in the original version of MVC.

This paper describes how part of HotDraw has been redesigned to make it more reusable. The redesigned part is class Tool, which represents a user interface mode that can be selected from a palette. Originally the only components of Tool were an icon and cursor. We gave it two additional components. The result is that each tool can be described by a table, and we have a simple direct-manipulation "Tool Builder" application for defining new tools. Moreover, it is simpler and requires less code to define a new tool in the current version of HotDraw than in the original version.

2 HotDraw

HotDraw is a framework for structured drawing editors [Johnson 92]. It can be used to build editors for specialized two-dimensional drawings such as schematic diagrams, blueprints, music, or program designs. The elements of these drawings can have constraints between them, they can react to commands by the user, and they can be animated. The editors can be a complete application, or they can be a small part of a larger system.

HotDraw was originally designed by Kent Beck and Ward Cunningham when they were at Tektronix. Patrick McClaughry reimplemented HotDraw to work with ObjectWorks\Smalltalk R 4.0, and we have since modified it to work with R 4.1 and VisualWorks.

The basic HotDraw framework is made up of Drawing, Figure, Tool, Handle, and DrawingEditor. A drawing is a complete picture, while a Figure is a component of a Drawing. A Tool represents a mode of the drawing editor. Selecting a figure (with the SelectionTool, for example) causes the figure to present a set of handles that can be manipulated with a tool to change the figure. Finally, the DrawingEditor specifies the drawing being edited and the set of tools that are available to edit it. It acts as the "main program" of HotDraw, though it usually does little once the application starts. Figure 1 shows a drawing containing a RectangleFigure which is selected, an ArrowFigure, a TextFigure, a BezierFigure, and a SplineFigure. The palette of tools is on the left. The selected RectangleFigure has eight handles. The DrawingEditor is the model of the window.

Drawing and Figure are similar to CompositePart and VisualPart of ObjectWorks\Smalltalk R4.1. The only difference between Drawing and CompositePart is that drawings cache the underlying image to improve performance and they provide a step method to support animation. The only difference between Figure and VisualPart is that figures provide a handles method to access their handles, they are responsible for knowing their location in the drawing, and they notify dependents when any of their attributes change. DrawingEditor is a typical model, responsible only for providing a Drawing (i.e., acting like a ValueHolder of a Drawing) and for providing a palette of tools.

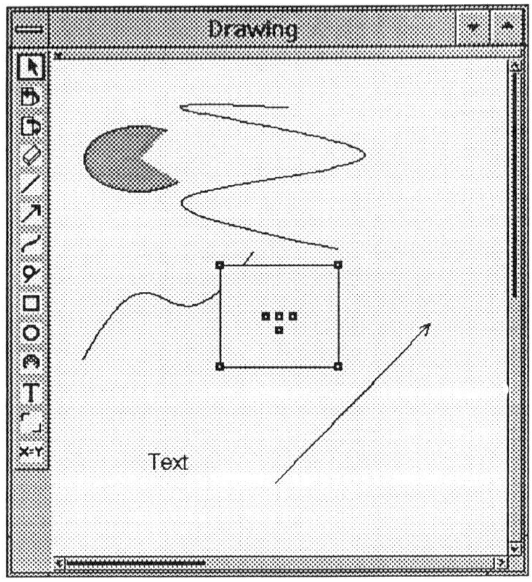

Figure 1: Default drawing editor

Tool and Handle are the classes in HotDraw that are most different from anything provided in ObjectWorks\Smalltalk. Tools are responsible for modifying the drawing based on a user gesture, such as a mouse drag or a keyboard press. A tool converts user actions into operations on a drawing, and so is similar to a controller. In fact, the DrawingController class delegates many of its operations to the current tool, and so tools could be thought of as an extension of the controller. However, a tool also has an icon that it displays in the tool palette and it has a cursor that it uses to let the user know which tool is selected. Thus, it is better to think about it as a user interface mode.

Handles represent attributes of the selected figures that the user can edit. Manipulating a handle changes the corresponding attribute in the selected figure. For example, manipulating a corner handle changes the size of a figure, and there can be handles that change the interior color of a figure or the border width and color.

A handle is a figure, so it is displayed just like any other figure. The SelectionTool is normally the only tool that is aware of handles. It requests handles from figures that it selects, and it manipulates handles.

3 Tools

After figures, new tools are the parts that developers using HotDraw need to create most often. Tools are responsible for interpreting a user action, such as a mouse drag or a keyboard press, by performing some action on the drawing such as moving a figure, creating a new figure, etc. Most new tools are made because the drawing needs to be changed in a new way. The next most common reason for new tools is to create a more refined version of some other existing tool. Still other times that new tools are created result from the need to combine actions from a few different existing tools into one new tool.

All tools implement both the press and processKeyboard methods. These methods are invoked by the DrawingController when the user presses the red (left) mouse button or a key on the keyboard, respectively. Within these methods the tool is responsible for modifying the drawing, and after all user manipulation actions are complete, the tool will then return control back to the drawing controller.

All tools in the original version of HotDraw handled user input in one of two ways. A tool could perform the operation itself, or it could delegate the responsibility to some other object such as a handle or a figure class.

One example of the tool handling the responsibility itself is when the selection tool selects a group of figures by drawing a bounding box around them. When the selection tool, receives control, it first checks to see what figure was pressed by the user. If the user didn't press any figure then the selection tool performs the multi-selection action. This is done in the marqueeFromUser method shown in Figure 2. The control loop moves the bounding box to the current mouse position. When the mouse button is released, the loop will terminate, and then all figures in the bounding area will be selected.

The other way that a tool handles user actions is to delegate them to some other objects such as a handle or a figure class to create a figure. An example of this occurs when the user uses a handle to modify an attribute of a figure. When the tool detects that the mouse is over a handle when the button is pressed, it sends the handle the invoke: message, and the handle keeps control until the button is released. An example invoke: method is given in the code segment in Figure 3. The invoke: method contains a control loop that is very similar to the one given above, in that it will read the current mouse position and perform some action based on this new position. It also breaks out of the loop when the user quits manipulating the handle (i.e., when the user releases the red mouse button). After this is done, the handle will perform any finalizing action that is needed and return control back to the selection tool.

4 Problems

Although this is an obvious way to implement user interactions, it has many problems. One problem is that code is often duplicated. These examples are typical because the most of the duplicate code is reading the sensor for either keyboard or mouse input. For example, in the sample applications that came with the original version of HotDraw, there were 11 instances of a control loop that read the mouse input. Clearly, this is not optimal code reuse. This duplicate code is more difficult to maintain, since

```
marqueeFromUser
  | gc startPoint stopPoint rectangle |
  gc := self view graphicsContext.
  gc lineWidth: 1.
  gc paint: MarqueeImage.
  stopPoint := startPoint := self sensor cursorPoint.
  rectangle := startPoint corner: stopPoint.
  [self sensor redButtonPressed]
    whileTrue:
      [self drawing damageRegion: rectangle.
      self view repairDamage.
      stopPoint := self sensor cursorPoint.
      rectangle := Rectangle vertex: startPoint vertex: stopPoint.
      gc displayRectangularBorder: rectangle at: Point zero].
  self drawing damageRegion: rectangle.
  self view repairDamage.
  self view selections: (self drawing figuresIn: rectangle)
```

Figure 2: Original Code from SelectionTool

```
invoke: aView
  | anObject sensor newPoint oldPoint |
  sensor := aView controller sensor.
  oldPoint := sensor cursorPoint.
  aView hideHandlesWhile: [
    [sensor redButtonPressed]
      whileTrue:
        [newPoint := sensor cursorPoint.
        anObject := self sense: newPoint - oldPoint.
        anObject notNil ifTrue: [self change: self owner by: anObject]].
        oldPoint := newPoint.
        aView repairDamage]]
```

Figure 3: Original Code from Handle

if the sensors change protocol, then many different code fragments must be updated. This problem of duplicate code can also be seen to a lesser extent with the code that performs the changes to the drawing.

Another problem is that the code that performs changes to the drawing is distributed over many classes, tools, handles, and figure classes. This makes HotDraw more difficult to learn and debug since it may be hard to tell which code is being executed. In addition to this code being distributed over many classes, in most cases it is also entwined with the code that reads the sensors. This also makes it harder to debug.

Other problems are more related to how tools are created. Tools in the original version of HotDraw are monolithic, encompassing the displaying of their cursors and icons as well as manipulating the drawing. As a result, it is difficult to make a new tool by composing properties of two different, existing tools. For example, suppose that you wanted a tool that created a new figure when the user clicked on the background, but allowed the user to manipulate an existing figure in the same manner as a selection tool. In order to make such a tool, you would have to subclass either a figure creation tool or the selection tool, and then copy methods from the other into the newly created class. For this example, you would probably subclass the selection tool and then copy three other methods from the creation tool into the new class. You would still need to modify the **press** method in the new tool so that it will act properly when pressed on the background. In addition to duplicating code, this is more work than should be required to make a tool out of existing tools, since it requires you to read code and decide which methods should be copied or changed.

5 A Solution

One way to eliminate the problems listed above without losing any functionality is to create two new types of objects and to modify the roles of tools, handles, and figure creation.

Readers and commands are new objects that help eliminate the duplicate code that appeared in many of the tools, handles, and figure creation methods. These are similar to the manipulators and commands of Unidraw, which inspired our solution [Vlissides 90]. Readers read the sensor values, and the commands perform the actual changes to the drawing. Both of these objects work together to carry out the user manipulation. Readers get the current value of the sensors and pass it onto the commands, which perform an action based on the new sensor value. This method reduces the 11 instances of a control loop that checked the mouse sensor to one. If the sensor protocol for checking the mouse changes, we will only have to change our code in a few places. Moreover, this method makes debugging new commands easier since all code for changing the drawing is located only in these command objects, and the command that is being executed is easily found from the tool being used.

Readers must implement three methods, **initialize:command:**, **readSensor:**, and **effect**, while commands implement methods that correspond to a particular reader. An example command for a DragReader is listed in Figure 4. This command performs the same multi- selection actions as was seen earlier. Readers rarely need to be subclassed, and in fact in the new system, there are only three readers, two for the mouse and one for the keyboard.

Splitting commands and readers from the tools, handles, and figure creation methods makes it easy to create tools. Tools contain their icon and cursors as before, but now they also contain a table that maps a given figure and a reader to a command. With this scheme when the user performs some operation, the current tool creates a reader for that operation. After creating the reader, the tool finds the figure that the user is manipulating, and looks up the command in the table that matches the reader and figure. After the command is found, the tool will clone it and initialize the reader with the command. The reader will then ini-

```
initialize: aPoint
  originalStartPoint := aPoint.
  lastPoint := aPoint

moveTo: currentPoint
  | gc rectangle |
  lastPoint := currentPoint.
  rectangle := Rectangle vertex: originalStartPoint vertex: lastPoint.
  gc := self graphicsContext.
  gc paint: MarqueeImage.
  gc displayRectangularBorder: rectangle at: Point zero.
  self drawing damageRegion: rectangle

effect
  self drawing selections: (self drawing figuresIn:
      (Rectangle vertex: originalStartPoint vertex: lastPoint))
```

Figure 4: New Code for MultiSelectionCommand

	DragReader	ClickReader
default	Multi-selectionCommand	←
ConstraintHandle	Constraint command	←
CommandHandle	Figure command	←
Figure	Selection and Constraint command	Selection command
RectangleFigure	↑	↑
... all other subclasses of Figure	↑	↑

Table 1: Command table for the SelectionTool

tialize the command with the current mouse point. After the initialization phase is finished, the tool begins looping over the reader. The reader will update the command with the current mouse position, and return true when the user manipulation action is not finished. When the reader returns false, the tool will tell the reader that the user action is finished and the command to produce its effect and clean up.

Command lookup is performed by the tool trying to find a match in the table for the given figure. An example of the SelectionTool's table is shown in Table 1. If no match if found the tool climbs up the figure's inheritance hierarchy until a match is found. Once a match is found then the tool will find the closest reader for the figure that is in the table, and return its command. From the SelectionTool's table below, we can see that given a ClickReader and a RectangleFigure, the command that is selected is the selection command, since Figure is the first class in the RectangleFigure's hierarchy which has an entry in the table. On the other hand, if the reader is a ClickReader and the figure is a ConstraintHandle, then the command will be a constraint command. Since ConstraintHandle is in the table, we take the command for the closest reader in the table which is the constraint command corresponding to the DragReader. If the tool was not able to find a match for the figure after climbing the inheritance hierarchy, then the default command for the tool is chosen. For example, if the user clicked on the background of the drawing, then the SelectionTool will try to find an entry in the table for a ClickReader and a figure which is nil. Since the figure, nil, and its superclasses are not in the table, the SelectionTool will pick the multi- selection command.

By using tables to represent the tool and the possible actions that it can take, we can now create tools by just filling out a table, and also supplying it with two cursors and the icon for the tool. Furthermore, there is rarely any need to make a subclass of tool, since most information that describes a tool is given in this table. In fact the only subclass of tool in the entire HotDraw system and all of its applications is the TextTool. This tool is able to edit and create text in the drawing. A subclass was needed since the tool needed to remember the text figure being edited from one manipulation action to another. Even special figures like handles don't need any special care in processing. All we need to do is place them in our table with their respective commands.

Since defining a new tool is just filling out a table, we created the Tool Builder to facilitate this entry. An example is shown in Figure 5. There are two main parts to the tool builder. The first is the browser located on the left, which is used for create new tools and define their actions. The other part is the icon and cursor editor. This is a normal HotDraw application that is used to edit either the icon or cursor when one of the icon, cursor, or manipulating cursor buttons is selected. There are five parts to the browser. The top left pane lists the tools that are currently in the system. The middle pane of the browser lists the kinds of figures that the tool will perform actions on, and the top right pane contains the readers for the selected figure and tool. In the middle there are a set of buttons which let the user switch from editing cursors or icons to editing the command tables for the mouse and keyboard part of the tools. The bottom pane shows the command that will be invoked when this tool is invoked on the specified figure. The example given in Figure 5 shows the command that is performed when the SelectionTool is pressed on some figure besides a handle, and when the user is performing a drag action with the mouse. This command is a composite command called a GroupCommand which when executed will select (SelectionCommand) and allow the user to move the figure (ConstraintCommand).

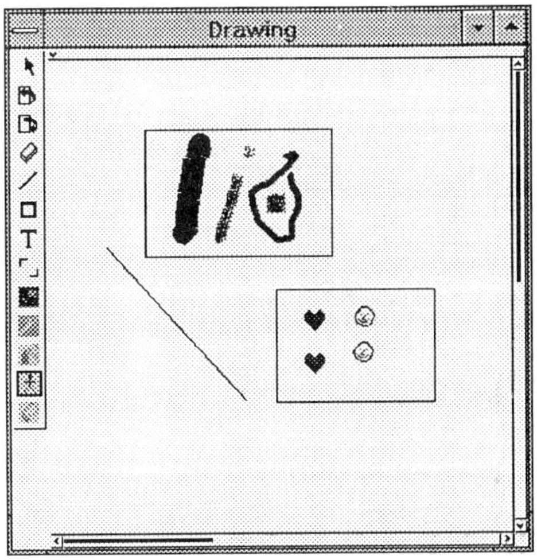

Figure 6: HotPaint drawing

6 Example

One of the example applications for HotDraw is the HotPaintEditor. This application is similar to painting programs like the Paintbrush program that comes with Microsoft Windows. An example screen is shown in Figure 6. The original implementation of this editor contained four new tool classes in addition to a new figure called CanvasFigure and a new drawing editor class.

All of the new tool classes dealt in some way with changing the CanvasFigure. They performed actions such as drawing lines, spray painting, erasing, and drawing special decals such as hearts or happy faces on the CanvasFigure. All of these tools needed to redefine the press method in order to perform their special action. An example of the line drawing tool's press method is given in Figure 7. As can be seen from this method, it contains the usual control loop that reads the current mouse location and then draws a line in the CanvasFigure. Furthermore, you can see that this tool checks that the type of the figure that is being manipulated is actually a CanvasFigure.

The PaintbrushTool class was replaced by a

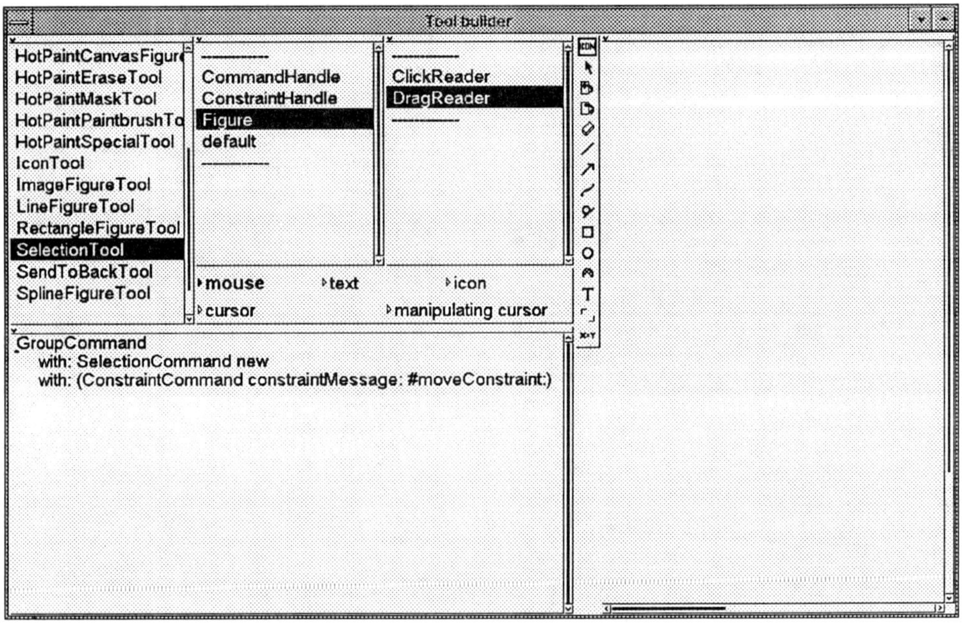

Figure 5: Tool builder

```
press
  "Paint stuff on canvas object."
  | figure aPoint lastPoint |
  lastPoint := nil.
  [self sensor redButtonPressed]
    whileTrue:
      [aPoint := self sensor cursorPoint.
      figure := self figureAtPoint: aPoint.
      figure class = CanvasFigure
        ifTrue:
          [self brushWidth: figure width ** 2.
          lastPoint isNil
            ifTrue: [figure paintAt: aPoint brushWidth: brushWidth]
            ifFalse: [figure paintFrom: lastPoint to: aPoint brushWidth: brushWidth].
          lastPoint := aPoint]
        ifFalse: [lastPoint := nil]]
```

Figure 7: Original Code for PaintbrushTool

```
initialize: aPoint
  lastPoint := aPoint.
  figure paintAt: lastPoint brushWidth: figure width ** 2

moveTo: currentPoint
  figure
    paintFrom: lastPoint
    to: currentPoint
    brushWidth: figure width ** 2.
  lastPoint := currentPoint

effect
  figure paintAt: lastPoint brushWidth: figure width ** 2
```

Figure 8: New Code for PaintbrushCommand

PaintbrushCommand class. This class replaces the press method of PaintbrushTool. The temporary variables figure and lastPoint become instance variables. This resulted in a considerable savings since much of the code was needed for these two common tasks. The resulting code for the new command is listed in Figure 8.

After converting these four tools to the new version of HotDraw, additional savings were noticed. Instead of there being a separate command for each tool, two tools were able to consolidate their commands into one. Additionally, the erase command was able to become a subclass of the line drawing command. The separation of tools into three parts resulted in smaller, more reusable objects being created.

7 Conclusion

Inheritance is not the only reuse technique offered by object-oriented programming. Often the most reusable designs are those where the primary reuse technique is instance composition.

Conventional programmers who are trying to write reusable software often make their programs table driven. This is a good technique for object-oriented programs too. The difference is that the elements stored in the table can be other complex objects like figure classes or readers, and it is easy to use the built-in inheritance relationships to make the tables smaller, as we did with the figure classes. Thus it is easier and more efficient to make table-driven object-oriented programs. A design reaches a new level of reuse when it becomes so composable that new kinds of objects can be designed entirely by filling in tables. Then you can provide a tool so that people can customize and extend your system without programming. Even when new code must be written, such as new commands, a design style leading to small, composable objects will tend to make them simple and easy to write.

HotDraw is available by anonymous ftp from st.cs.uiuc.edu.

8 Acknowledgments

Many thanks to Gordon Davis, Brian Foote, Paul Keefer, Dan LaLiberte, Don Roberts, and Bill Walker for providing many helpful comments.

References

[Johnson 92] Ralph E. Johnson. Documenting frameworks using patterns. In *Proceedings of Conference on Object-Oriented Programming, Systems, and Applications*, pages 63–76. ACM, 1992.

[Vlissides 90] John M. Vlissides. *Generalized Graphical Object Editing*. PhD thesis, Stanford University, June 1990.

A Dossier Server: an independent service bus between object applications and relational data bases.

M. Migeon
INGENIA & GICR 2000
Tel: 91 05 50 20
Fax: 91 66 35 99
email: Migeon@ingenia.fr

Abstract: Object oriented technology is increasingly the reference in software engineering. However, an application analysis in terms of objects should be distinct from that of functional analysis, and also relational data base models.

This paper shows how we have developed an application *Dossier Server*[1], one of two logical servers at the center of the GICR information system, which is properly oriented object. Conceiving this application in terms of objects, we have kept it from an approach too functional or too "polluted" by the relational organisation of data.

As well, this approach has permitted the development of an "open" application by employing the concept of a software service bus. In particular, we can add or respecify a client application, or add a data base without modifying the server (or other client applications). Our "contractual" approach is inspired by the model Object Management Architecture (OMA) of Object Management Group [OMG 92].

Lastly, we wanted the automatic generation of that part of the *Dossier Server* which handles the connection and conversion of information between the data bases and the client applications.

Keywords: client/server architecture, object oriented programming, Smalltalk, automatic code generation.

From TOOLS EUROPE '94 (Technology of Object-Oriented Languages and Systems).

1. Introduction

The GICR 2000 is a group of a dozen retirement funds whose object is to realise a new administrative system. Typical of many administrative projects, the GICR adopted both object oriented applications and relational data bases. Object oriented bases are still not fully accepted in this domain. Relational bases may be an advance on previous types of data storage and access, but a fundamental problem remains. How to prevent models associated with non-object bases - in our case relational - from polluting the object oriented applications.

The conception of systems in terms of objects requires preliminary analysis which is not only functional, but also oriented object. This means that the objects realise concepts analysing their domain, and are not only a means of structured programming. For this reason we have employed tools for a conception oriented object. The specification employed the method Shlaer & Mellor [Shlaer 92] available as the tool System Architect [Popkin 92]. The conception used the method Booch [Booch 92] in the form of Rose/Rational [Rational 92]. The realisation of the applications is in Smalltalk/V [Goldberg 83] [Digitalk 91].

Between the client applications and the data bases, the GICR developed two servers.
The *Dossier Server* allows the client to treat data at the conceptual level of dossier and document. A dossier is like a classic paper file. To constitute a dossier means to organise all the documents necessary for a particular administrative activity. Dossiers and documents correspond more closely to the idea of an administrative activity than do relational tables.
The *Activity Server* distributes the administrative activities between agents, and controls the suspension and then the resumption of these activities

(by other agents if necessary). The creation and resumption of activities is generated by external events (reception of an information, verification by a superior).

Our conception of these servers is such that our applications plugs onto a software bus, conforming to the model OMA of OMG. Since CORBA [OMG 91] products implementing this model are still unavailable, the services offered to clients follows a protocol as close as possible to CORBA so that future products can be integrated.

2. The issues

The fundamental problem for us is to mitigate the influence of models of data management (usually relational), and also that of functional treatment. To code in an object language is not sufficient. Anyone can write a program of 1000 unstructured lines of code, even in ADA. It is too easy to create classes which simply translate functions, add attributes and adopt methods which are bijective with sub-functions. It is also easy to create classes resembling relational tables, giving them read/write methods, which are called by those "functional classes". What happened to the object oriented approach? This type of application can be developed without any gain in productivity, reusability or evolution.

Proper object oriented conception should lead developers out of a strictly functional approach. This, however, is not the subject of our exposé. Our contribution aims to help programmers avoid being mentally structured by pre-existing relational data models. We want strictly object oriented information structures and related services without any relation to their physical organisation. The objects should conceptualise the administrative activities, while the base should be organised in parallel, independently of these objects. In this way, we develop services in the spirit of OMA/CORBA: the services exist somewhere, somehow on the software bus. The client applications, structured in their own way, just call these services.

Finally, there is the automatic generation of the code for the *Dossier Server* from the formal description of the object structures, relational structures and the mapping which links them.

3. Principles of the *Dossier Server*

The principle tasks of the *Dossier Server* include the following:

- Offer an object oriented conception of information, justifying the introduction of the concepts of dossier and documents.
- Insure the persistence of dossier information. This is for reasons of security. During the treatment of a dossier, the information entered or calculated can pass into incoherent or incomplete states. Such information should not be inserted immediately into the data base.
- Insure the independence of storage, localisation and management of data bases by a unique interface of services offered.
- Permit the sharing of information and control of the resulting conflict through logical locking devices.

4. Architecture of the system

Before developing the "how" of the *Dossier Server*, it is important to present the general architecture of the system. The system is distributed between different machines. The *Dossier Server* integrates the system, by offering. services to clients. These services are, for example, creation of a dossier, closure of a dossier, reading a document etc. The applications can't access data except via the services and this data is necessarily in the form of dossiers and documents. We illustrate this situation in the following diagram:

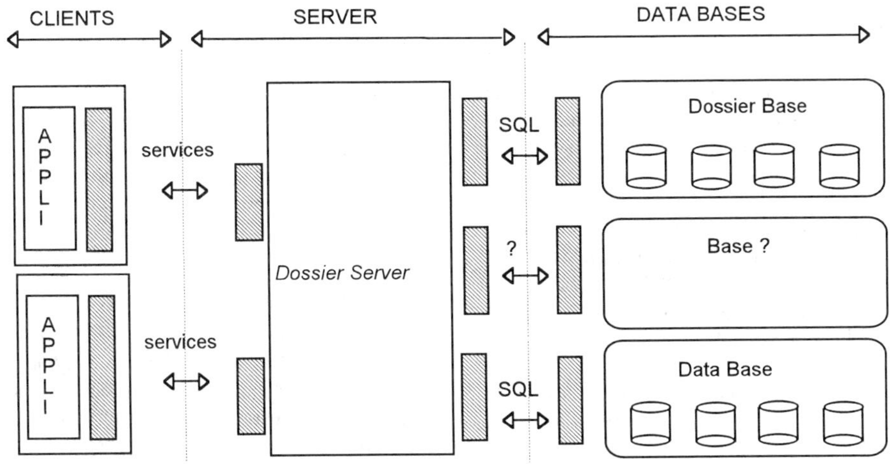

The shaded boxes represent the interfaces.

Fig1: System architecture

Here client/server architecture implies the management of multi-threads and implies the use of an information carrier (Object Request Broker) in a heterogeneous environment. We use CORBA (OMG) to normalise the communication protocol between application objects .

Initially, we've limited ourselves to connecting a single application to the *Dossier Server*. This avoids the implementation of a communication protocol with multiple flows. As well, the *Dossier Server* is implemented as an independent extension of the client application to eliminate the communication between the application and the *Dossier Server*. The independence between application and Server still exists, we only need to incorporate CORBA products to realise the desired architecture. The architecture simplified is:

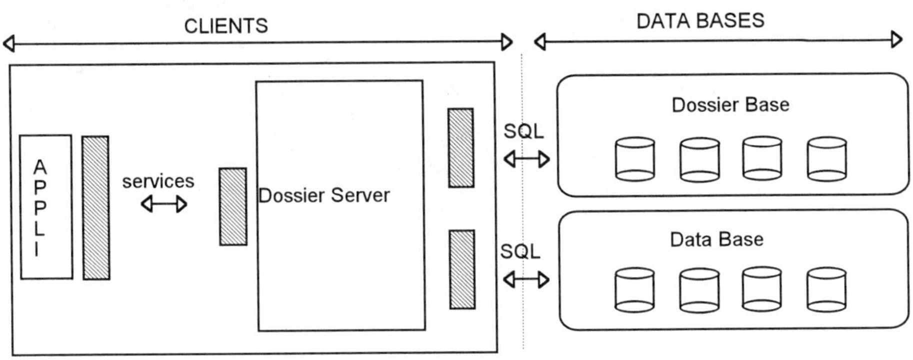

Fig2: Temporary system architecture

5. Relation between the object model et the relational model

The client applications are written in the object language (Smalltalk/V). Since we want to interrupt and resume these application, their objects must be persistent.

The data is presently stored and distributed by a RDBS. Our task would be easier with an object data base. We are obliged to construct a gateway between the data situated in the relational world and the application objects.

The two problems are not of the same order. The first is a question of writing and reading the attributes of objects known by a unique identifier. In the second case, the data isn't related bijectively to the object attributes and isn't necessarily accessible via an unique identifier.

So we are interested by two different object/relational models:

- The first is a relational representation of data associated with the objects of an application in view of their being read or written.
- The second is a representation of objects as relational data in view of their storage by the *Dossier Server*.

6. Access to data by SQL requests

Starting from the description of classes (and the attributes) of an activity and specifying the relational representation for associated data, it is possible to construct automatically the reading and writing services (generating for each object its SQL requests). The following scheme is an example of the relations between an object application and relational tables via the SQL requests:

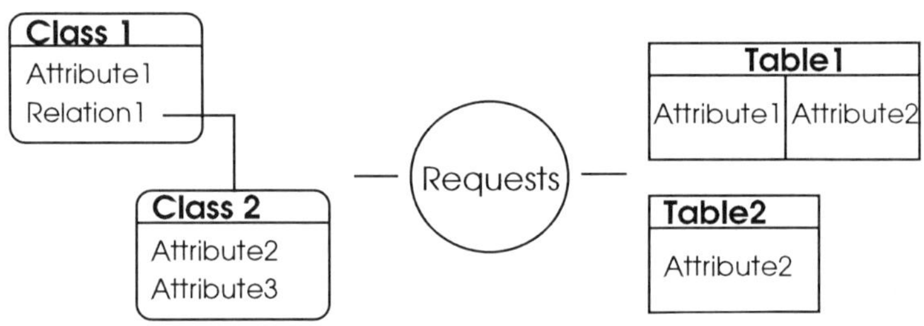

Fig3. Data access

In general, storage of data (the value of an object attribute) is identified in the relational model by a key to a table. For data D associated with an attribute A of an object O there is a table T containing the data in a column C. The data is accessible by criteria (k_i) $1<i<m$ and if need be the joints (j_i) $1<i<p$. The criteria and joints constitute the access key to the data.

A column x of the table A is noted:

$$T_A.C_x$$

A joint is the comparison between two columns from two different tables:

$j(P) = P(T_A.C_x\,,\ T_B.C_y)$ where P is a predicate.

A criterion is the comparison between value v and those stored in the column of a table:

$k(P,v) = P(T_A.C_x\,,\ v)$ where P is a predicate.

The data is accessible either by object, or by table. One has the equation:

$$D = ReadObjectData(O,A)$$

$$D = ReadTableData(T,C,k_1...k_m, j_1...j_p)$$

In the relational model, a read is defined which furnishes the data as a function of the values of criteria (c_i) $1<i<m$. This function can only be used when the data is unique and accessible by a single key.

We define $\leftarrow$ as assignation. The tables and columns of joints are accessible, respectively, by the functions *Tables* and *Columns*. The table and the column of a criterion are obtained respectively by the functions *Table* and *Column*.
The function,

$D \leftarrow ReadObjectData(O,A)$ is equivalent to

$D \leftarrow$ Read$(c_1...c_m)$ with

Read: ***select*** *C*

from *T, Table(k*$_1$*), ... Table(k*$_m$*),*

Tables(j$_1$*), ... Tables(j*$_p$*)*

where *k*$_1$*(=,c*$_1$*)* ***and*** *... k*$_m$*(=,c*$_m$*)*

and *j*$_1$*(=)* ***and*** *... j*$_p$*(=)*

The function of multiple selection,

$\{ D_1 ... D_n \} \leftarrow \{ ReadObjectData(O_1,A) ... ReadObjectData(O_n,A) \}$ is equivalent to

$\{ D_1 ... D_n \} \leftarrow$ Load$(c_1...c_m)$ with

Load: ***select*** *C*

from *T, Table(k*$_1$*), ... Table(k*$_m$*),*

Tables(j$_1$*), ... Tables(j*$_p$*)*

where *k*$_1$*(P,c*$_1$*)* ***and*** *... k*$_m$*(P',c*$_m$*)*

and *j*$_1$*(P'')* ***and*** *... j*$_p$*(P''')*

The function to update the data,

WriteObjectData(O,A,D) is equivalent to

Save$(D,\ c_1...c_m)$ with

Save: ***update*** *T* ***set*** *(T.C = D)*

from *T, Table(k*$_1$*), ... Table(k*$_m$*),*

Tables(j$_1$*), ... Tables(j*$_p$*)*

where *k*$_1$*(=,c*$_1$*)* ***and*** *... k*$_m$*(=,c*$_m$*)*

and *j*$_1$*(=)* ***and*** *... j*$_p$*(=)*

Another function allowing the insertion of a new data,

WriteObjectData(O,A,D) is equivalent to

Insert$(D,c_1...c_m)$ with

Insert: ***insert into***

T (Column(k$_1$*), ... Column(k*$_m$*) , C)*

values *(c*$_1$*...c*$_m$ *, D)*

The selection or writing of different informations for the same object is made by generalising the previous expressions.

The requests Read, Load, Save and Insert are registered in the data base storing the data in the form of procedures[2].

7. Storage of objects in a relational data base

The storage of objects in the *Dossier Server* data base is made by SQL requests[3]. The following scheme gives a relational representation of the application objects:

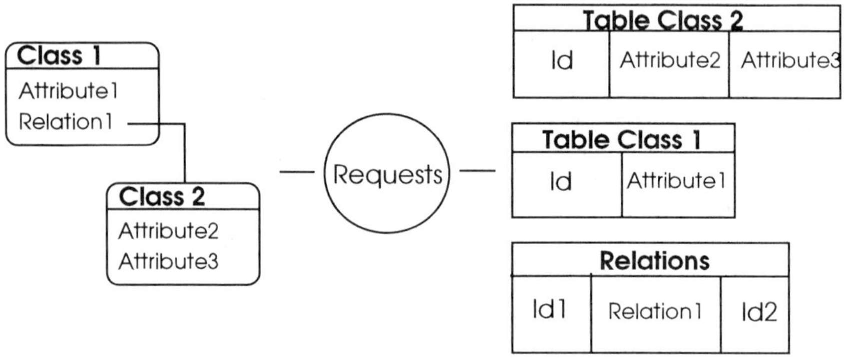

Fig4. Object Storage

We define the function *Id* which gives the unique identifier for an object.
We distinguish two types of attributes for an object. We call *relations* the attributes for which the value is an instance or a sequence of instances of a class.

The storage of a class instance is made in a table reserved for the objects of this class. We name O_X the instance of the class X and T_X the corresponding table. We make a bijection between the attributes $(A_1, ..., A_n)$ of the object and the columns $(C_1, ..., C_n)$ of the table:

$(v_1, ... v_n) = Attributes(O_X, A_1, ..., A_n)$

is equivalent to

$(v_1, ... v_n) = Columns(T_X, Id(O_X), C_1, ..., C_n)$

The read function of attributes of an object from its relational description is:

Values: ***select * from*** T_X ***where Id*** $= Id(O_X)$

The relations are stored in the table $T_{relations}$. A relation R is defined by:

$R(O,A) = O'$ for a unique object or

$R(O,A) = \{ O', O'', O''' ... \}$ for a list of objects.

Each relation of an object is an occurrence in the table $T_{relations}$:

$R(O,A) = O'$ is equivalent to

$Relation(T_{relations}, Id(O), A, Id(O'))$

The relations of an object are obtained from the following function:

Relations: ***select * from*** $T_{relations}$
where Id $= Id(O_X)$

Saving an object O_X in the data base is:

Write: ***update*** T_X ***set*** $(C_1 = v_1 .... C_n = v_n)$
where Id $= Id(O_X)$
delete $T_{relations}$ ***where Id*** $= Id(O_X)$
insert into $T_{relations}$
values $(Id(O_X), R_1, R(O_X, A_1))$
where Id $= Id(O_X)$
insert into $T_{relations}$
values *(...)*
where Id $= Id(O_X)$
insert into $T_{relations}$
values $(Id(O_X), R_q, R(O_X, A_q))$
where Id $= Id(O_X)$

The requests Values, Relations, and Write are registered in the data base storing the dossiers in the form of procedures.

8. Architecture of the *Dossier Server*

The *Dossier Server* is an application of the system. Naturally, we have specified it by the method Shlaer & Mellor, conceived it by the method Booch and realised it in Smalltalk/V. The actors of the *Dossier Server* are the objects of type dossier and document. These objects are the only interface between the client application and the *Dossier Server*. The client communicates with the *Dossier Server* via the services implemented in the dossiers and documents classes. By definition:

- There is a bijection between an activity and a type of dossier;
- A type of dossier is composed of documents whose types are known at the defining of that dossier;
- A document is composed of attributes and relations whose types are known at the definition of that document.

The *Dossier Server* is architectured around four objects apart from the document and dossiers. They are:

- A data server which interfaces between the documents and the data stored in the relational data base;
- A server of dossiers and documents handling the persistence of dossiers and documents;
- A dossier manager handling the relations between object instances and the occurrences of dossiers and documents;
- An access to a RDBS managing the relational tables.

All objects and constants necessary to the application are stored in an object environment:

```
Smalltalk at: #SDEnvironment put: Dictionary new.
```

These objects are directly accessible by the objects coming from the class `SDObject`.

```
Object subclass: #SDObject
   instanceVariablesNames: ''
   classVariablesNames: ''
   poolDictionaries: 'SDEnvironnement'
```

The following scheme produced with Rose/Rational, shows the object architecture of the *Dossier Server*.

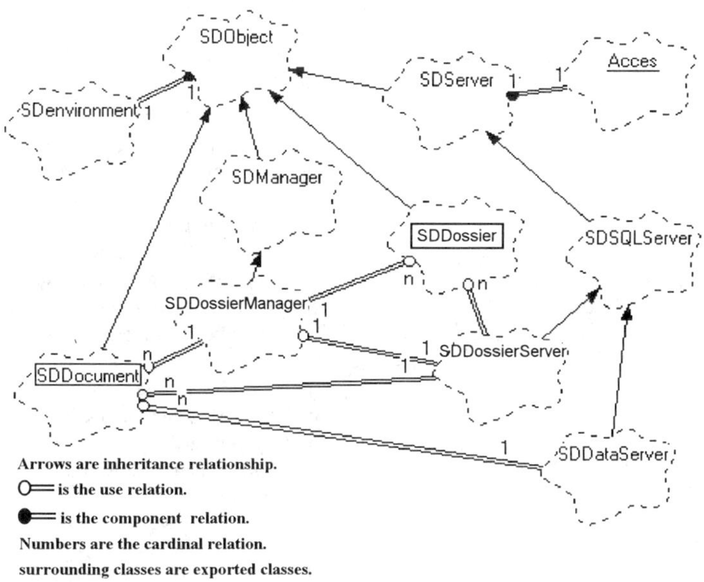

Fig5: System components

The services are methods implemented in the classes `SDDossier` et `SDDocument`. A service call means either:

- The creation, modification or destruction of a dossier or document, with it being registered or effaced in the Dossier base (accessible via the server `SDDossierServer`) and in the dossier manager (`SDDossierManager`).
- The insertion, destruction or update of data if the document contains an interface with the data base (accessible via the server `SD-DataServer`).

The services are defined independently of dossiers, documents, data base and network adopted. For example, the service **updateDocument** is for saving the image of a document in the dossier base. Its definition is:

```
updateDocument: dossier
"dossier containing the documents"
 | fid did |
"catch all errors"
 SDError do:
 [ "find dossier ID"
   fid := SDDossierManager searchFid: dossier.
   "find document ID"
   did := SDDossierManager searchDid: self.
   "use transactional mode"
   SDDossierServer withTransaction:
   [    "update method is specific"
      self update: fid did: did]
   "automatic rollback and exit"
   ifError: [:error | ^error]]
"exit"
handle: [:error | ^error].
```

The service **ReadDocument** is for reading the data associated with a document. Its definition is:

```
readDocument: dossier status: status
   selector: selector criteria: criteria
 | fid |
 SDError do:
 [ fid := SDDossierManager searchFid: dossier.
   SDDataServer withTransaction:
    [ SDDataServer
       readDocument: self class name
       lock: fid status: status
       selector: selector criteria: criteria.
"generated method"
       self
        updateAttributesAndAccessor: selector
        status: status.]
   ifError: [:error | ^error]]
 handle: [:error | ^error].
```

For the object `SDDataServer`, we define the method for calling the read operation.

```
readDocument: type lock: lock status: status
   selector: selector criteria: criteria
"procedure are string"
 status
  case: DocumentFree do:
   [self callProcedure:
        'readdocumentfree',type,selector,
        criteria asLastArguments]
  case: DocumentLock do:
   [self callProcedure:
        'readdocumentlock',type,selector,
        lock asArgument,
        criteria asLastArguments].
```

9. Generation of *Dossier Server*

We have seen that the services are implemented as the methods of objects `SDDocument` et `SD-Dossier`. We know that the contents of a document and its interface with the information that it manipulates is specified by the client application. We still need to define a program to generate automatically the Smalltalk methods (access to services ≈ Stub CORBA) and to SQL procedures or others (access to data ≈ BOA + Object Services CORBA) specific to each type of document and dossier.
From descriptions contained in a source dossier we produce (via a parser) the abstract syntax of which the items are the descriptions (objects). From these descriptions are generated the methods necessary for the Dossier Manager, for the servers, for the dossiers and documents as well as the procedures to access and store the data. The code obtained is added to the *Dossier Server* by intermediary of the object `CodeSmalltalk` for the code Smalltalk and by object `CodeSQL` for the SQL orders. The following scheme shows these steps:

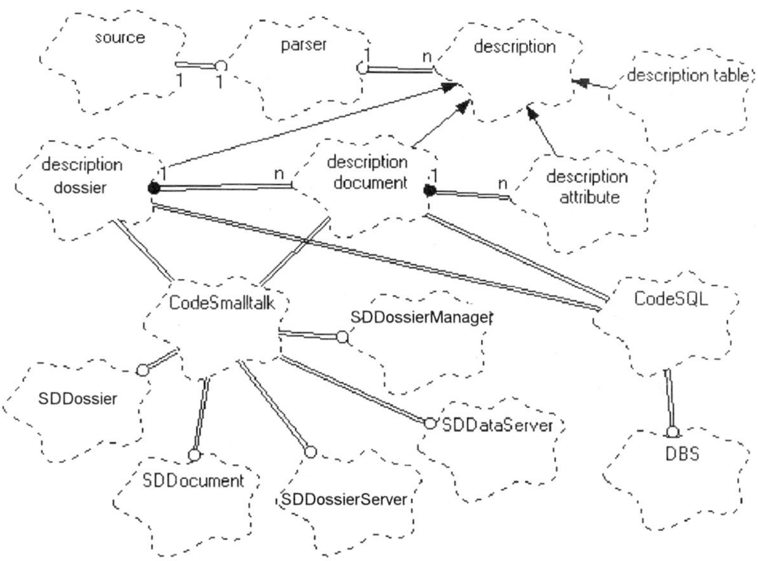

Fig6: Sytem generator

For example, let's define a document **A** having an attribute **x** of which the value is stored in a relational table **T**. This definition by the application and its interface with the *Dossier Server* is:

```
SDDocument subclass: #A
 instanceVariablesNames: 'x'
 classVariablesNames: ''
 poolDictionaries: ''

Type Number
   smalltalk integer;
   sql int;
EndType

Document A
 attributes (x : Number) ;;
 readers readX (n : Number) ;
   (m) = select x from T where x=@n ;
   x = m ;;
EndDocument
```

For the service **updateDocument** we generate from the objects `DescriptionDocument` and `DescriptionAttribute` for each type of document the following code:

```
update: fid did: did
 SDDossierServer updateDocumentA: fid
   did: did status: status
   selector: selector accessor: accessor
   x: x.
```

For the object `SDDossierServer` we generate access to the procedure:

```
updateDocumentA: fid did: did status: status
   selector: selector accessor: accessor
   x: x
 self callProcedure: 'updatedocumentA ',
   fid asArgument, did asArgument,
   status asArgument,
   selector asArgument, accessor asArgument,
   x asLastArgument.
```

The SQL procedure is:

```
updateDocumentA @fid int @did int @status int
 @selector char(200) @accessor (200) @x int
   update A set
    (status = @status, selector = @selector,
     accessor = @accessor,
     x = @x)
   where fid = @fid and did= @did
```

For the service **readDocument** and for each type of document we generate the following code:

```
updateAttributesAndAccessor: aSelector
 status: aStatus
   SDDataServer decodeDocumentA: [:access :v1 |
       x := v1.
       accessor := access.
       status := aStatus.
       selector := aSelector].
```

For the object `SDDataServer` we describe a decoder which transforms the result and the access into Smalltalk objects.

```
decodeDocumentA: bloc
"accessor is computing during the request"
   bloc value: accessor
"result is translated"
       value: result isInteger.
```

The SQL procedure is:

```
readdocumentfreeAreadX @n int
   select x from T where x = @n
```

10. Interface between *Dossier Server* and the applications

We'll end this article by a simple example. Consider the following activity (part of an application):

"The activity consists in reading the address of an individual whose social security number is known or/and the address of all the individuals having the same name. The activity searches its information in a relational table called NamesAndTowns"

NamesAndTowns				
lastname	**firstname**	**ssn**	**town**	**code**
Migeon	Maurice	null	Arcachon	33
Migeon	Maurice	1234	Ollioules	83
Migeon	Maurice	null	Paris	75

The result for the name Migeon Maurice and the social security number 1234 is:

- IndividualSSN is Migeon Maurice Ollioules 83
- IndividualsNames is the collection of 3 individuals of the same name living in Arcachon, Ollioules et Paris.

We need to specify the definition of an application before proposing a solution to the problem posed by the example. An application is composed of activities. These activities are independent of each other. An activity is analysable into tasks. An activity relates bijectively to a type of dossier and manipulates the documents associated with this dossier. The choice of activity and the tasks is under the control of the *Activity Server*. The life-cycle of an activity is shown in the following scheme:

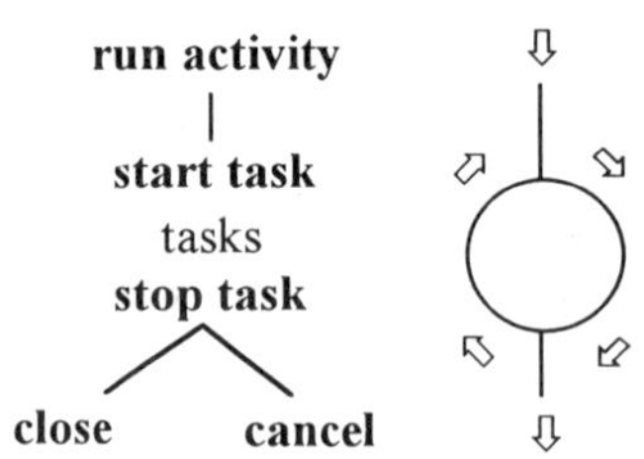

Fig7: Activity livecycle

To interface an activity with the *Dossier Server* means to describe the type of dossier associated with it, to number the types of attributes and the types of documents manipulated, giving their interface with the data base. The objects [of the activity] either persistent or needing access to data are the documents. They need to be defined as sub-classes of the class `SDDocument`.

We supply the interface of the dossier and associated documents with the *Dossier Server*:

```
//dossier description
Dossier DossierReadAdress
//this dossier contents Individual
//and Address documents
 contents Individual Address ;;
//Individuals are roots documents
 roots Individual ;;
EndDossier

//types mapping
Type DataString
 smalltalk string;;
 sql char(100);;
EndType

Type Number
 smalltalk integer;;
 sql int;;
EndType

//Individual interface
Document Individual
//persistent attributes are
 attributes
  (lastname : DataString)
  (firstname: DataString)
  (ssn : Number) ;

//relations are
 relations
  (address : Address) ;;

//readers are
 readers
//sql access, ssn is argument
 sql readBySSN (ssn : Number) ;
//left part is the result of request
//right part is the request,
//args are prefixed by @ (sql notation)
   (last first c z) =
    SELECT lastname, firstname, city, zipcode
     FROM NamesAndTowns
     WHERE ssn=@ssn ;
//firstname is first and lastname is last
   lastname = last;
   firstname = first;
//address relation is build with c and z infos
   address = (city : c) (zipcode : z) ;;

//loaders are
 loaders
//last and first are arguments
 sql readByNames (last : DataString)
        (first : DataString) ;
  (c z) =
   SELECT city, zipcode
    FROM NamesAndTowns
    WHERE lastname=@last AND firstname=@first;
//only address is build, names are known
   address = (city : c) (zipcode : z);;
EndDocument
```

```
//Address interface
Document Address
 attributes
        (city : DataString)
        (zipcode : Number);;
//no direct loaders, readers or writers
EndDocument
```

We resume: The application is written completely in Smalltalk. It uses the services of the *Dossier Server* and the *Activity Server*. It is independent of the organisation of data.

11. Conclusion

The combination of an object oriented conception and an object language such as Smalltalk has enabled us to attain the following objectives: satisfy the needs of users by offering open services, while following an iterative development allowing the rapid prototyping of a satisfactory solution. The use of object technology is more and more adopted in the case of client/server architecture. An evolution in the culture of administrative computing is taking place. The realisation of an important information system including the *Dossier Server* which we have just presented is a noteworthy example. Finally, in order to take advantage of an real industrial approach, we should remain as close as possible to the normalisation work of the OMG. Our own systemic analysis relating to this kind of computing architecture could be considered as an another practical justification of the pertinence of the international movement around CORBA.

12. Acknowledgements

I thank Joel Loubière for his participation in the development, Mark Booth coordinator of GICR 2000 for the translation, as well as Michel Lai and Philippe Le Blé for their remarks and advice in the writing of this article.

13. References

[Booch 92] Grady Booch, *Conception orientée objects et applications*, Addison-Wesley, 1992

[Digitalk 91] Digitalk, Inc., *Smalltalk/V Windows tutorial and Programming Handbook*, Los Angeles CA, 1991.

[Goldberg 83] A. Goldberg and D. Robson. *Smalltalk 80: The language and its implementation.* Addison-Wesley, 1983.

[OMG 91] The Common Object Request broker: *Architecture and Specification* Ref: OMG 91.12.1 Revision 1.1

[OMG 92] The Object Management Architecture Guide Ref: OMG 92.11.1 Revision 2.0

[OTI 93] Envy *Product Development tools For Smalltalk* Object technology International Ottawa, Ontario Canada 1993

[Popkin 92] Popkin inc., *System Architect*, New York NY, 1992

[Rational 92] Rational Inc, *Rational Rose for Window version 1.0.7*, Santa Clara CA, 1992

[Shlaer 92] Sally Shlaer and Stephen J. Mellor *Object Life Cycles Modelling the World in States* YourDon Press Prentice Hall Building EngleWood Cliffs 1992

---

1 We use Dossier in the sense of a Folder containing documents.

2 Requests are compiled and not interpreted.

3 Defined automatically from existing classes.

Testing Smalltalk Code in Multi-person Projects

Trevor P. Hopkins
Computer Science Department, University of Manchester
Oxford Road, Manchester, M13 9PL, UK
Email: tph@cs.man.ac.uk

Abstract

The testing of application fragments during development can be tedious and time-consuming, especially when dependent parts of the application are not available: perhaps they have not be developed yet, or are being constructed simultaneously by other team members. For object-oriented development, this issue is even more important, since it will often be desirable to develop software components which are for use in many different applications.

This paper considers some of the issues of testing software in large developments using the Smalltalk language and programming environment, where many individuals may be involved in the design and coding of parts of a system. In particular, specific support for '*test harnesses*' is discussed, together with the details of a general-purpose class to support the testing of application fragments.

1 Introduction

Very often, during multi-person software development in Smalltalk [Goldberg 84], informal testing procedures which are adequate for small projects are found to be quite unsuitable. Since, in larger projects, it is essential to divide the development effort into many pieces, which are undertaken by different individuals, at least some testing will have to be performed in isolation. In particular, when the development of general-purpose re-usable classes is encouraged, and kept in a managed library, the testing of these classes is very important.

This paper considers techniques which can be applied to the testing of Smalltalk code in large developments. Suitable units for development and test are considered, together with points in the development process where testing can be applied. The construction of '*test harness*' classes is considered, and the management problems involved are identified. Finally, a special class to aid in the construction of test harnesses, without excessive proliferation and duplication of classes is described in detail.

In more, detail, the focus of this paper is on the testing of individual components or units of an object-oriented design, before incorporation into a complete application. Since it is naive to assume that classes or other components can in general operate in isolation from other units, it is vitally important to be able to test a particular component before all other components that it relies on are available. To do this, some form of 'framework' or 'test harness' will be required, where the as-yet unimplemented objects required by the component under test can be temporarily replaced, so that the component under test can be evaluated in a structure as close as possible to the 'real' usage.

Other work on testing frameworks (such as [Smith 92]) tend to assume separable independent components, which can be tested in isolation; this approach is unlikely to be generally applicable. This is particularly true in a Smalltalk system, with notoriously high levels of interaction between objects. This paper does not consider aspects such as the difficulties which encapsulation and inher-

From TOOLS EUROPE '94 (Technology of Object-Oriented Languages and Systems).

itance add to testing; see for example [Berard 91] for more information on these issues.

Unless otherwise noted, the techniques discussed in this paper are likely to be suitable for all versions of Smalltalk. However, they have only been tested using ObjectWorks\Smalltalk version 4.1 [ParcPlace 92]; the code examples given are specific to ObjectWorks, but can readily be reworked for other Smalltalk versions. A working knowledge of Smalltalk is assumed throughout this paper.

1.1 Units of Development

When many software engineers are developing a Smalltalk application, it is of course necessary to divide up the work into suitably sized and reasonably independent units. These same units might also be used for testing purposes, as well as re-usable components in a library.

1.1.1 Classes as Development Units

In object-oriented development, it is sometimes naively assumed that individual classes can be developed quite independently. Of course, in practice this is unlikely to be the case. Firstly, classes are often strongly related by inheritance to existing classes, either from the 'base' system, or from additional library items or applications. Equally, classes are strongly related to other classes with which it has 'use' or 'part-whole' relationships. In either case, a new class is not independent of existing ones.

Secondly, the nature of typical Smalltalk development is such that an individual developer is likely to be simultaneously constructing several classes intended to work together, which may or may not be related by inheritance. A developer may design and implement a hierarchy of classes, perhaps refining a general abstraction in several different but related subclasses, or may develop classes intended to be used together in a compositional [Helm 90] style. It is also likely that an individual's work will require methods to be added to other classes.

As an example of the tight coupling between classes unrelated by inheritiance , consider the development of applications with a significant graphical user interface (GUI) component, using the Model-View-Controller (MVC) approach (for ObjectWorks\Smalltalk), or ViewManagers and Windows (in Smalltalk/V for Presentation Manager [Digitalk 91]). Developers will add new concrete subclasses to existing abstract superclasses, as well as devise specific ways in which instances are used together.

1.1.2 Development Components

In practice, therefore, a more comprehensive and less class-centric view of development units is widely used. A *component* (sometimes called a *package* or *capsule* [Wills 91, Wills 92]) will consist of a group of classes with their own methods, together with methods for other classes, initialization code and (perhaps) documentation. A component of this form is a more general unit for development, as well as for re-use (in libraries, for use in many delivered applications), and for testing. Such components will clearly depend on the existence and operation of other components; for any particular delivered application, the dependencies between components must form a directed acyclic graph.

Another important kind of unit of development which is worth identifying separately are *frameworks* [Johnson 92]. A framework is a set of standardized abstractions for addressing a range of applications (or application parts) in a given domain. Frequently, frameworks are represented as a collection of classes, intended to be used in a particular way. Abstract classes will be specialized for new requirements, while instances of concrete classes will be assembled in new and different ways. The MVC and ViewManager-Window systems are examples of such design frameworks.

In this paper, it will be assumed for simplicity that the unit of development is a single new class, using many existing classes, and perhaps adding a few new methods to those classes. However, the techniques considered are readily extended to the testing of components where many classes are developed together.

1.2 Testing in the Development Process

In small-scale Smalltalk developments, testing is often treated in a very ad-hoc fashion. For example, this can be as simple as checks that a class behaves according to the developer's informal understanding of the requirements; this is very common where the requirements, as well as the design and implementation, are being evolved together in an iterative style. Another 'test' is that a new class apparently 'works' without generating errors, in the particular cases used in the application.

Clearly, this ad-hoc approach is inadequate for larger and more carefully managed developments, where the overall operation of a system is dependent on the correct behaviour of many parts, developed separately. Amongst other problems, it would be undesirable to have to wait until the complete system was assembled before having a chance of finding many of the errors. Furthermore, it is not really suitable for use where classes are expected to be reusable in many applications.

Instead, we require tests which check for correct behaviour against a detailed predetermined specification, perhaps even a formal (mathematical) specification. The tests themselves can be designed using detailed design interface information ('black-box' testing), or in conjunction with the actual implementation used ('white-box' testing). The tests can be created by a developer implementing a class, or (better) by an independent software engineer, or perhaps generated automatically from a design support (CASE) tool.

In this section, we consider the way in which testing can be integrated throughout the development process. Not that this has the desirable side-effect of getting all developers directly involved with the quality management process.

1.2.1 Testing during Development

The first opportunity for testing is during initial development of a new class. Tests will be designed and applied, in order to satisfy the developer that the new class behaves as expected, and so that all the features and capabilities can be tried out as they are added. Conventionally, a developer will write code to test and/or illustrate the use of a new class; this code is sometimes included in 'example' class methods.

In a large development, there will often be different developers for classes which rely on one another; for example, there may be separate developers for the 'model' and 'view' parts of an application. This is different from a small development, where a single developer can produce both model and view aspects, as a single package. Nevertheless, there are separate skills involved: model developers are likely to be more familiar with the general behaviour of the objects in the application domain, while those constructing graphical user interfaces will probably be HCI specialists. One requirement, therefore, is the ability to develop and test a 'view' without a 'model' being available, or vice versa. An example of testing a view class in the absence of the corresponding model is given in section 2.3.2.

1.2.2 Component Delivery Testing

Once completed, components will be submitted for integration into a complete application (see section 1.2.4, or considered for inclusion in a re-use library. Increasingly, re-use libraries are being regarded as company assets [Hopkins 90], and valued and managed as such. Libraries are therefore often the focus of significant management and quality assurance activity, in order to keep the value of the software assets high. This is therefore an appropriate point for the application of tests generated independently of detailed code development, as well as other 'quality checks', such as design and code quality metrics, and documentation quality,

1.2.3 Testing after Component Change

We rarely find that reusable software components are 'right first time': genuinely general-purpose software is usually the result of an extensive process of review and redevelopment. It is important that the testing of classes is kept in line with revisions and extensions to those classes; any special testing code must be re-worked together with the class itself. It is important to be able to test both the new features of a class, as well as reassurance that old capabilities work exactly as before. Clearly, it is necessary to keep the testing code in the library with the associated component. This kind of 'regression testing' is very important, as part of the version control task in the management of the re-use library.

1.2.4 Integration Testing

In organizations with a well-managed re-use library, there are often separate roles (or individuals) for different parts of the development process. In particular, there is often a clear distinction between those developers who design and construct (potentially) re-usable components and frameworks, and thus expand the library, and those developers who assemble end-user applications from the library components and frameworks. Effective re-use depends on being able to write very little new code specific to an application; instead, applications consist almost entirely of existing components, assembled differently. Hitherto, we have been considering testing activities for the first kind of developer; here, we consider integration (and 'end-product') testing.

Clearly, each new application will have to be tested both during construction, as well as once completed. The testing of the complete application, although very important for quality reasons, is fairly straightforward to carry out, since the entire application is indeed there to be tested. Nevertheless, it is desirable to keep test code with the application, and to ensure that this test code is kept up-to-date when new versions of the application are produced.

Testing during assembly is more difficult, since there may be new (but still potentially re-usable) components being developed by other developers, which are not yet available; this means that 'temporary' classes and other code may be needed, which only approximates to the behaviour of the real thing. However, these classes may be discarded once the application is completed.

1.3 Constructing Testing Classes

We have seen the need for special classes, and other code fragments, for testing only in several cases: during the independent construction and re-development of re-usable components; when potentially re-usable components are included into a library, and when components are assembled into the complete application. In the same way in which Cox [Cox 91] uses a hardware metaphor for object-oriented development ('Software ICs'), here such code is referred to as a '*test harness*'.

1.3.1 Test Harness Classes

The requirements for individual 'test harness' classes is often rather simple: they have to conform to (usually part of) the public interface specification of the 'real' class they are replacing. This specification is often available either from detailed design information, or from the documentation of the 'real' class under development.

The interface requirements for a test harness class are frequently straightforward: certain messages require standard objects to be returned, such as numbers, boolean values or strings, or perhaps nothing useful is returned. The objects returned may always be the same, or they may be generated or selected sequentially (or even at random) from a collection of candidate objects. Sometimes, a test harness class is expected to store objects (in instance variables, for example), which can later be retrieved by accessing messages.

Of course, there may be more sophisticated test cases required: a suitable instance of application-specific classes may be created and returned, for example. Although many more test cases are possible, in practice most of the interface requirements are rather simple.

1.3.2 Problems

Clearly, test harness classes need to be developed together with the components they test, and may need to be kept with those components when they are added to the library. Note that there may be separate test harness classes for independent tests for library quality assurance and/or integration reasons. Here we have a potential management problem, with large numbers of classes being added to the library which are not of themselves useful, but merely to support testing. There is even the potential for confusion with the 'real' classes, which the test harness is intended to mimic. It would be desirable to keep the number of test harness classes to a minimum, to ease this problem.

A perhaps more serious problem, from an object-oriented viewpoint, is that there is often lots of behaviour common to many test harness classes, which is duplicated unnecessarily. We would like to have a single place where common behaviour for all test harness classes can be kept. One possibility is to devise an abstract class, and to add subclasses for test- and application-specific behaviour. While this avoids the code duplication problem, a large number of different classes are created, which have to be managed.

2 A TestObject Class

This section describes the design and implementation of a 'generic' test harness class, many instances of which can be combined with the component under test; section 2.3 considers how this can be used in practice.

To avoid the proliferation of 'test harness' classes, we require a *single* class, instances of which can be created with *any* desired behaviour. In this section, a class called TestObject is described, *individual instances* of which can have both *state* (corresponding to 'instance variables') and *behaviour* ('methods'). In fact, the individual responses to messages are specified using a *block*, which is supplied as the argument to an 'installation' method. Starting with an instance of TestObject called tester, blocks of code are installed using the do: on: method:

```
| tester |
tester := TestObject new.
tester
   do: [ "some expressions" ]
   on: #message1.
tester
   do: [ "more expressions" ]
   on: #message2.
```

When the tester subsequently receives message1, the corresponding block will be executed. The mechanism for adding state 'variables' is discussed in section 2.1.1.

2.1 Basic Structure and Operation

In the current implementation[1], class TestObject is a subclass of Model, to provide an efficient implementation of the dependency mechanism. Methods which signal changes using this mechanism are described in the next section. In some cases, however, the dependency mechanism might not be used extensively, so an alternative approach would be to make class TestObject a subclass of Object.

```
Model subclass: #TestObject
  instanceVariableNames: 'name monitor
          messages states '
  classVariableNames: 'RandomGen '
  poolDictionaries: ''
  category: 'Testing-Support'
```

Four instance variables are defined. The name variable (a String) and the monitor variable (a Boolean are used to control the displaying of trace information (see section 2.1.2). The messages variable references a Dictionary which maps Symbols representing the names of messages to blocks. Finally, the states variable refers to a Dictionary of Symbols representing state variables (see section 2.1.1). The class variable RandomGen is initialized to an instance of Random[2] and is used for generating random objects and selecting at random from collections (see section 2.2.2).

The key to the operation of the TestObject class is the doesNotUnderstand: method. In Smalltalk, this message is sent to an object when the method lookup for the previous message send has failed: i.e. there was no corresponding method in the class of the receiver object, or any of the superclasses. The argument to this message is an instance of class Message, representing the failed message. A default implementation of doesNotUnderstand: is in class Object, which suspends the current process and opens a 'notifier' signalling the error to the user.

In class TestObject, the doesNotUnderstand: method is redefined. The Message name (selector) is extracted, and the corresponding block is extracted from the messages Dictionary; if none is found, then the default implementation of doesNotUnderstand: is executed. The block is executed, with the arguments taken from the Message. A simplified version of the doesNotUnderstand: method in class TestObject is shown below.

[1]The code for class TestObject is now available from the Manchester Smalltalk Goodies Library. For more information on the Library, and how to access it, send email to "goodies-lib@cs.man.ac.uk" with the subject line "help; index".

[2]Class Random is a standard class in Smalltalk-80 and ObjectWorks\Smalltalk, but can easily be added to other versions.

```
doesNotUnderstand: aMessage
    | block args |
      "...code elided..."
    block := messages
      at: aMessage selector
      ifAbsent: [
          ↑super doesNotUnderstand: aMessage].
    block isNil ifTrue: [↑nil].
    args := aMessage arguments.
      "...more code elided..."
    ↑block valueWithArguments: args
```

The blocks in the messages Dictionary can be added directly, using the do: on: method, or indirectly using methods described later in this section.

It can be seen that the normal method lookup mechanism (i.e. finding the appropriate method in a class-specific Dictionary[3] has been replaced with finding the appropriate code in an instance-specific Dictionary.

2.1.1 Storing and Accessing State

A typical requirement of a 'test harness' class is to retain an object supplied as an argument to a message, and return that object when requested by another message. (In a real class, the object would typically be retained by an instance variable.) This kind of behaviour is so common that a special mechanism in TestObject is provided to support it. The instance variables states references a Dictionary which maps Symbols (representing instance variables) to arbitrary objects. Note that this approach means that we can have any number of instance variables, and that they can even be declared dynamically.

As a very simple example, consider the following use of TestObject:

```
| tester |
tester := TestObject new.
tester set: #var1 on: #var1: .
tester get: #var1 on: #var1.
```

This code effectively declares a variable called var1 with methods to return (var1) and set (var1:) its value. So, the messages var1 and var1: can now be used in a conventional-looking way to set and answer instance-specific variables.

[3]Actually, a MethodDictionary.

```
tester var1: 3@4.
tester var1.
```

The result of the last expression is to answer with the Point supplied as an argument to the previous message.

Since it is often desired to signal some kind of change (using the *dependency* mechanism) when a 'variable' is set, an additional method set: changed: on: is available in class TestObject. This allows a 'variable' to be set from the argument of a message as before, but associates a third Symbol which is used as the first argument to the changed: with: message.

2.1.2 Monitoring Messages

Often, it will be useful to be able to see the sequence of messages received by a TestObject, in order to determine whether the operation is indeed as expected. A simple-minded approach is taken here: monitoring information is (optionally) displayed in the Transcript. In the present version, the name of the message is displayed; arguments and return values are not printed. An instance variable called monitor is provided, together with suitable accessing and instance creation methods, to allow Transcript output to be selectively enabled and disabled.

Of course, we will often have more than one instance of TestObject in a test harness, so it is important that we can tell which particular instance is receiving a message. One simple way of achieving this to generate a unique identifier for each instance, and prepend the monitoring output with this identifier. A suitable numeric identifier can be generated by sending messages such as asOop or hash to the instance. This is barely adequate, as identifying TestObjects using (apparently) random integers, which are different each time the test harness is created, rapidly gets very confusing.

The current implementation uses a further instance variable name, which can either be a String or nil. An instance can optionally be 'named' at instance creation time; is unnamed, then a synthetic name (using asOop) is used instead.

More sophisticated tracing mechanisms could be provided is required. For example, each message received, together with the arguments, as well as the object returned, could be recorded in a suitable data structure retained by a further instance variable in class TestObject. This would allow for very detailed analysis of the behaviour of the class under test, and would even permit a comparison of the results of different 'runs' of the test[4]. This would allow a fairly simple regression-test mechanism to be implemented.

Alternatively, or perhaps as well, a textual record of the sequence of message sends, with argument and return values, could be written onto an external file, using a suitable FileStream. This approach might be appropriate if the amount of information generated during testing is very large.

2.1.3 Matching Block Arguments

When building test harnesses using TestObject, it frequently occurs that not all of the arguments to messages generated by the class under test are actually required – at least, for test purposes. In particular, when using the sequential and random selection methods described in section 2.2, it is very convenient to be able to ignore the message arguments.

However, in Smalltalk, attempting to evaluate a block with the wrong number of arguments results in an error. For convenience, and to reduce the risk of a trivial error occurring during testing, the arguments supplied by a message are matched to the actual arguments in the corresponding block. When a message is sent to a TestObject, the doesNotUnderstand: method compares the number of message arguments with the number of block arguments. If there are more message arguments, the argument list is truncated; if there are more block arguments, then additional arguments (initialized to nil) are appended. A full version of the doesNotUnderstand: method, including the monitoring and block argument matching code, is shown below.

```
doesNotUnderstand: aMessage
    | block args |
    monitor ifTrue: [
      Transcript
        cr;
        show: self name, ': ',
            aMessage selector; space].
    block := messages
      at: aMessage selector
      ifAbsent: [
        ↑super doesNotUnderstand: aMessage].
    block isNil ifTrue: [↑nil].
    args := aMessage arguments.
    args size > block numArgs ifTrue: [
     args := args copyFrom: 1 to: block numArgs].
    block numArgs > args size ifTrue: [
      args := args, (Array new:
              (block numArgs - args size))].
    ↑block valueWithArguments: args
```

[4]Random selections could be used only if the generator seed was reset for each run.

2.2 Sequential and Random Selection

One useful capability widely required by a test harness class is to return a suitable object, selected from some collection of such objects. The objects might all be of the same class, or could be any mixture. The selection might be made sequentially, so that the same sequence of objects will be answered given the same test conditions, or they might be selected at random. A further, related capability is to answer randomly-generated objects; numbers and strings are particularly useful here.

Note that all of these behaviours will work when associated with messages with any number of arguments, including zero, because of the matching of block arguments described in section 2.1.3

2.2.1 Sequential Selections

To select from a collection of objects, the selectFrom: on: method is provided. On each send of the associated message, the next item from a collection of objects is returned. For example:

```
| tester |
tester := TestObject newMonitoring: true.
tester
  selectFrom: #(101 102 103 104 105)
  on: #getNumber.
```

On the first send of the getNumber message, the SmallInteger '101' will be returned; on subsequent sends, the numbers '102', '103' and so on will be returned. Of course, any kind of collection of any object can be used; for example:

```
tester
   selectFrom: (OrderedCollection
      with: 3@4
      with: Compiler new
      with: Dictionary new)
   on: #getObject.
```

Note that the selectFrom: on: method also provides a convenient way of selecting from a sequence of numbers (of any kind), by supplying an Interval to represent the desired sequence. For example:

```
tester
   selectFrom: (-10 to: 10)
   on: #getInteger: .
tester
   selectFrom: (0 to: 1 by: 1/32)
   on: #getFraction.
```

Once the end of the collection of objects is reached, the current implementation 'wraps around' to start again from the beginning of the collection; thus the same sequence of objects will be used for as long as necessary.

Two special sequential selection methods are also provided. One method (selectBooleanOn:) simply answers first true and then false repeatedly. The method selectInstanceFrom: on: answers with a newly created instance of a class, where the first argument gives a collection of classes. The classes to be used can be given either as a collection of classes directly, or as a collection of Symbols which are the names of classes. This is so that the following two expressions give the same effect:

```
tester
   selectInstanceFrom:
        #(Set Bag OrderedCollection)
   on: #getCollection.
tester
   selectInstanceFrom: (Array
      with: Set
      with: Bag
      with: OrderedCollection)
   on: #getCollection.
```

Currently, the classes are instantiated by sending the message new; of course, this is not always appropriate. A better mechanism would allow for a class-specific instance creation method to be used; at present, this has to be done 'by hand', using the do:on: method.

Finally, it should be noted that current implementation uses list processing techniques, using class OrderedCollection. From a runtime performance point of view, perhaps a better implementation would be to use Streams.

2.2.2 Random Selections

As well as methods which select sequentially from a collection of objects, further methods are provided which select at random. By analogy with those methods described in section 2.2.1, methods called randomSelectFrom: on:, randomSelectBooleanOn: and randomSelectInstanceFrom: on: are provided. These methods use the RandomGen class variable. Note that random selections cannot be used if we are attempting to provide repeatable tests, such as the regression tests outlined in section 1.2.3,

A further commonplace requirement for testing classes are messages which return a number, character or string, but the exact value is not important. To facilitate this, additional methods are provided which return random values, as illustrated below.

```
tester randomSmallIntegerOn: #getInteger.
tester randomPositiveIntegerOn: #getPositiveInt.
tester randomFloatOn: #getFloat.
tester randomCharacterOn: #getChar.
tester randomPrintableCharacterOn:
                    #getPrintableChar.
tester randomLowerCaseLetterOn: #getLetter.
tester randomStringOn: #getString.
tester
  randomLowerCaseStringLength: 20
  on: #getWord.
```

2.3 Class TestObject in Use

In this section, a few larger examples of the use of class TestObject are given, which illustrate the use of the methods described previously.

2.3.1 Simple Usage

In typical use, a TestObject will make extensive use of the get: on: and set: on: methods, since many classes allow fairly direct access to their instance variables. Also, there will be many methods which are effectively ignored by the TestObject, since they are not intended to have externally-visible effects, and methods which return simple values, such as Booleans. This usage is illustrated by the example below:

```
| tester res1 res2 |
tester := TestObject newName: 'a Customer'.
tester monitor: true.
tester set: #name on: #name: .
tester get: #name on: #name.
    "Variable name used."
tester set: #address on: #address: .
tester get: #address on: #address.
    "Variable address used."
tester selectBooleanOn: #isCreditWorthy.
tester on: #open.

tester name: 'Manchester University'.
tester address: 'Oxford Road, Manchester, UK'.
res1 := tester name.
res2 := tester address.
tester isCreditWorthy.
tester open.
```

Another typical use of class TestObject is to mimic, for test purposes, a collection of objects of a specific class. For example, the following code creates a TestObject which partially imitates an OrderedCollection containing Strings.

```
| tester |
tester := TestObject newName:
        'an OrderedCollection'.
tester randomStringOn: #add: .
tester randomStringOn: #addLast: .
tester randomStringOn: #first.
tester randomStringOn: #last.
tester randomStringOn: #removeFirst.
tester randomStringOn: #removeLast.

tester randomPositiveIntegerOn:
        #occurrencesOf: .
tester randomSelectBooleanOn: #isEmpty.
tester randomSelectBooleanOn: #includes:.
[tester isEmpty] whileTrue: [
   Transcript cr; show: (tester removeFirst)].
```

This example illustrates some of the random selection methods discussed in section 2.2.2.

2.3.2 Testing Views without Models

A frequent requirement when developing Smalltalk applications is to be able to test a sophisticated *view* and *controller* structure[5], without the corresponding *model* being available. Class TestObject can often be made to stand in for as-yet unimplemented model objects.

As a simple example, consider an application which implements a 'dice':[6] a window (view) displays 'spots' in the conventional way, with a model which can answer with a randomly selected value between one and six. A controller allows user input (e.g. a mouse click) to change the model. In this example, it is likely that the view and controller between them represent a significant part the complexity of the code, and might be implemented and tested before the model is available.

The following example uses an instance of TestObject to act like a model for a dice application. Note the use of the set: changed: on: message to signal changes to the view.

```
| tester |
tester := TestObject newName: 'a Dice'.
tester monitor: true.
tester set: #unused changed: #unused on: #roll.
tester randomSelectFrom: (1 to: 6) on: #value.
DiceView openOn: tester.
```

As a more sophisticated example, consider an application which monitors and displays important aspects of a running Smalltalk system, such as the number of Processes, input/output activity and so on. The model for such an application has to contain a Process which run periodically, and collects appropriate statistics. The view structure is likely to be complex, with different combinations of views and display styles used.

The following example uses a TestObject to stand in for the model in a system monitor application, and makes use of many of the TestObject features. Some messages are ignored (using on:); some use do: on: to return various objects (PopUpMenus, OrderedCollections, etc.); random selection from In-

[5]It is assumed in this paper that the Model-View-Controller (MVC) mechanism from ParcPlace's Smalltalk-80 or ObjectWorks\Smalltalk is being used. However, similar principles apply to the Window-ViewManager or Model-Pane-Dispatcher mechanisms in Digitalk's Smalltalk/V.

[6]Strictly, the singular should be 'die', not 'dice'.

tervals and the random generation of Strings is utilized. There is even an example of the use of randomSelectInstanceFrom: on:; the application dynamically reconstructs the view structure, using different display classes, depending on whether the information is to be displayed using a line graph, bar chart or strip chart.

```
| tester topView monitorView |
tester := TestObject newName: 'a MonitorModel'.
tester monitor: true.
tester on: #currentDisplayCount:.
tester on: #currentResource: .
tester on: #buildScaleFactors.
tester on: #displayPoints: .
tester
  do: [(10 to: 100) asOrderedCollection]
  on: #currentCollection.
tester
  do: [PopUpMenu labels: 'test' values: #(test)]
  on: #resourceMenu.
tester
  do: [10]
  on: #currentLower.
tester
  set: #currentStyle
  changed: #currentStyle
  on: #currentStyle: .
tester
  set: #displayInterval
  changed: #displayInterval
  on: #displayInterval: .
tester
  get: #displayInterval
  on: #displayInterval.
tester
  randomSelectFrom: (100 to: 300 by: 25)
  on: #scale.
tester
  randomSelectFrom: (10 to: 100 by: 10)
  on: #displayPoints.
tester
  randomMixedCaseStringLength: 12
  on: #label.
tester
  randomSelectInstanceFrom:
    #(LineGraphView HistogramView
      DifferenceHistogramView BarStripView)
  on: #currentStyleView.
```

3 Concluding Remarks

Class TestObject is a general-purpose test support class which can be used throughout the development process, and which avoids the proliferation of 'dummy' classes created specifically for testing purposes. In practice, most testing requirements can be met by using this technique.

Note that the 'instance specialization' approach used in class TestObject can be useful in many other cases. For example, it can be conveniently used to develop 'finite state machines' [Hopkins 93] in Smalltalk.

3.1 Problems and Restrictions

Of course, there are some aspects of a 'real' system which cannot be adequately captured by the TestObject approach suggested here. For example, the replication of 'enumeration' methods (such as do:) in collection classes is difficult, although some simple cases can be written straightforwardly enough. Other more sophisticated cases where blocks are passed around as arguments to methods, and manipulated in a general fashion, are also difficult to mimic. However, most straightforward testing requirements can be met using this class, although some problems remain.

3.1.1 Method Name Clashes

One problem which can occur is a clash between the names of messages defined in classes Object and Model, with message names defined for instances of TestObject. Messages which can sometimes cause problems in this way include at:, at: put: and size. Of course, since the normal method lookup always happens before the doesNotUnderstand: message is sent, it is not possible to special implementations for these methods.

One possible solution would be for TestObject not to inherit from Object at all, but to be a standalone class. This is readily achieved by assigning to nil the superclass field of TestObject class. This approach is widely used for general 'encapsulators' [Pascoe 86], concurrent control constructs [Hopkins 89, Foote 89] and object distribution [Dollimore 93]; however, in this case, it introduces rather more problems than it solves. Class Object contains many useful methods which will almost certainly be required; these include printOn:, inspect. yourself and class. There would be considerable extra work required to duplicate these methods. Furthermore, some special action would be required to open a notifier, in the event of a TestObject being sent a message it really cannot understand.

An alternative (and rather simpler) solution is to provide new implementations of the troublesome methods, in class TestObject. These explicitly send doesNotUnderstand: to self, to force the dynamic lookup using the messages Dictionary. For example, the implementation of at: put: is:

```
at: index put: value
    ↑self doesNotUnderstand: (Message
      selector: #at:put:
      arguments: (Array with: index with: value))
```

Although diminished, the method name clash problem still remains, and users of class TestObject need to be aware of potential problems. Also, similar problems can occur with method names directly implemented in class TestObject, although this is less likely to be a problem in practice.

3.1.2 Concurrency

The current TestObject test harness cannot very easily stand in for real classes which generate concurrent activity; i.e. classes which make use of Processes. Furthermore, no attempt is made to make class TestObject safe when messages are sent within more than one Process. Although it has not been tried, previous experience with using instances of Dictionary accessed concurrently suggest that the operation would give unexpected and inconsistent results.

Class TestObject can be made concurrency-safe by including an additional instance variable (perhaps called accessProtect), which is initialized to a Semaphore; the doesNotUnderstand: method could be rewritten to operate entirely within a critical region, using the critical: method. This would ensure that only one Process could execute the doesNotUnderstand: method, and consequently the messages and states Dictionarys, at a time. A better solution, but suitable for ObjectWorks\Smalltalk version 4.1 only, would be to use a RecursionLock[7] rather than a Semaphore; this prevents deadlocking if the same critical region is re-entered. Perhaps a better solution would be to construct a subclass of TestObject (ThreadedTestObject), which reimplemented the doesNotUnderstand: method appropriately.

[7]Class RecursionLock supports critical regions in a similar fashion to Semaphore. However, RecursionLock does *not* attempt to suspend an active Process if the critical region is used re-entrantly.

3.1.3 Performance

The runtime performance of TestObject is likely to be rather poor. Typical Smalltalk implementations take many milliseconds to generate the doesNotUnderstand: message, which is followed by a lookup in a Dictionary and the execution of a block. If monitoring is enabled, further time is taken to display information in the Transcript. The total time taken is likely to be very much larger than the normal binding of message to method, which is of course heavily optimised by the Smalltalk virtual machine.

For testing purposes, however, this low performance is unlikely to be a problem, as TestObjects will undoubtedly be replaced by 'real' objects when the final application is assembled. After all, it is the 'correctness' of the application component, not its runtime performance, which is an issue here. However, the user should be aware that TestObjects are slow, particularly in applications where there is significant real-time or concurrent behaviour.

3.2 Further Work

There is certainly plenty more possibilities for extending the approach to testing in multi-person Smalltalk developments. For example, regression tests could be run automatically and the results comparison every time a new version of a class was added to a library. It might also be possible to generate tests automatically from interface specifications, as part of a CASE tool.

One aspect not considered at all in this paper is the testing of 'subclass' or 'protected' interfaces. This is likely to be more difficult, since adding subclasses can extend or change the behaviour in a very general way. However, carefully specifying and testing a subclass interface might lead to an ability to test design frameworks, independently from any particular application using that framework.

Acknowledgements

The author would like to thank Richard Puttick (IBM UK) for simulating discussions which led to the ideas discussed in this paper. The author would also like to thank Mario Wolczko (Sun Microsystems Labs, Inc.) and the anonymous referees for detailed comments materially affecting the presentation and structure of this paper.

References

[Berard 91] Edward V. Berard, *Essays on Object-oriented Software Engineering*, Prentice-Hall, 1991.

[Cox 91] Brad J. Cox and Andrew J. Novobilski, *Object-Oriented Programming: An Evolutionary Approach* (second edition), Addison-Wesley, 1991.

[Digitalk 91] *Smalltalk/V for Presentation Manager: Tutorial and Reference Manual*, Digitalk Inc., 1991.

[Dollimore 93] Jean Dollimore and Wang Xu, *The Private Access Channel: a Security Mechanism for Shared Distributed Objects*, in *Proceedings of Technology of Object-Oriented Languages and Systems* conference (TOOLS 10), pp. 211–222, Prentice-Hall, 1993.

[Foote 89] Brian Foote and Ralph Johnson, *Reflective Facilities in Smalltalk-80*, in *Proceedings of Object-Oriented Programming: Systems, Languages and Applications* conference (OOPSLA'89), pp. 327–335, 1989.

[Goldberg 84] Adele Goldberg and David Robson, *Smalltalk-80: the Language and its Implementation*, Addison-Wesley, 1984.

[Helm 90] Richard Helm, Ian M. Holland and Dipayan Gangopadhyay, *Contracts: Specifying Behavioral Compositions in Object-Oriented Systems*, in *Proceedings of Object-Oriented Programming: Systems, Languages and Applications* conference (OOPSLA'90), pp. 169–180, 1990.

[Hopkins 89] Trevor P. Hopkins and Mario I. Wolczko, *Writing Concurrent Object-Oriented Programs using Smalltalk-80*, BCS Computer Journal, vol. 32, no. 4, pp. 341–350, 1989.

[Hopkins 90] Trevor P. Hopkins and Brian C. Warboys, *Asset Management and Object-Oriented Technology*, in *Hotline on Object-Oriented Technology* (HOOT), vol. 1, no. 11, September 1990.

[Hopkins 93] Trevor P. Hopkins, *Implementing State Machines in Smalltalk*, Technical Report UMCS-93-3-1, Computer Science Department, University of Manchester, 1993.

[Johnson 92] Ralph E. Johnson, *Documenting Frameworks using Patterns*, in *Proceedings of Object-Oriented Programming: Systems, Languages and Applications* conference (OOPSLA'92), pp. 63–76, 1992.

[ParcPlace 92] *ObjectWorks\Smalltalk Version 4.1 Reference Manual*, ParcPlace Systems, 1992.

[Pascoe 86] G. A. Pascoe, *Encapsulators: A New Software Paradigm in Smalltalk-80*, in *Proceedings of Object-Oriented Programming: Systems, Languages and Applications* conference (OOPSLA'86), pp. 341–346, 1986.

[Smith 92] M. D. Smith and D. J. Robson, *A Framework for Testing Object-oriented Programs*, Journal of Object-Oriented Programming, Vol. 5, no. 3, pp. 45-53, June 1992.

[Wills 91] Alan C. Wills, *Capsules and Types in Fresco*, in *Proceedings of the European Conference on Object-Oriented Programming* (ECOOP'91), Pierre America (ed.), LNCS 512, Springer-Verlag, 1991.

[Wills 92] Alan C. Wills, *Formal Methods Applied to Object-oriented Programming*, Ph.D thesis, University of Manchester, 1992.

Eiffel-like assertions and private methods in Smalltalk

Manuela Carrillo-Castellón Jesús García-Molina *
Dpto. de Informática y Automática. Univ. de Murcia
Santo Cristo,1. Murcia 30001. Spain
e-mail: molina@dia.um.es

Ernesto Pimentel
Dpto. de Lenguajes y Ciencias de la Computación. Univ. de Málaga
Pza. El Ejido, s/n. Málaga 29014. Spain
e-mail: pimentel@ctima.uma.es

Abstract

In this paper, we describe the current state of a project whose aim is the extension of the Smalltalk environment by incorporating mechanisms and tools promoting the development of quality software. We have included in the Smalltalk context a number of possibilities, which were not available in the original definition of the language. In this sense, assertions can be specified in our extension, in an Eiffel-like style, so gaining all benefits that the use of assertions bring with them. We also propose an approach to declare private methods, so that the information hiding capability of Smalltalk is improved. These mechanisms are integrated with a new browser and documentation tools increasing the understanding of the class behaviour. The extension has been made by maintaining the Smalltalk philosophy; that is, all elements incorporated to get the new characteristics are defined only using Smalltalk components.

*The work of Jesús García was partially supported by a grant PCT91/04 from "Consejería de Cultura, Educación y Turismo de la Comunidad Autonóma de la Región de Murcia"

From TOOLS EUROPE '94 (Technology of Object-Oriented Languages and Systems).

1 Introduction

Smalltalk [Goldberg 83] was designed with the purpose of defining a language and an associated programming environment which acted as an interface between the models of the mind and those of the computer, based on the model of communicating objects [Ingalls 81]. Its origins go back to the beginning of the seventies and for many years has been the principal reference to explain the meaning of object-oriented concepts. Smalltalk facilitates rapid prototyping of applications because it is a dynamically typed language with an interpreted environment that includes powerful and robust tools.

By the middle of the last decade object-oriented programming began to be considered as a very powerful technique to improve software quality, favoring reuse and extensibility. However, Eiffel [Meyer 88] could be the language that better illustrates this view. The same as Smalltalk, it is a pure object-oriented language, but it is strongly typed and combines object-oriented concepts with the characteristics of large-programming languages, such as assertions and exception mechanisms. Eiffel becomes an elegant notation for writing legible programs due to its simplicity of design. This language has been successfully accepted in the academic community but it has not spread through the industrial community yet, because it lacks quality programming environments.

We have attempted to improve the Smalltalk environment in the same way as Eiffel, by proposing mechanisms and building tools, improving several features such as: class understanding, class design, software components specification, debugging and testing programs and class documentation, among others. So, we have augmented Smalltalk with the following characteristics:

1. Assertions checking mechanisms.

2. Classes can include private operations.

3. A browser that improves the understanding of the code, alleviating the illegibility caused by the typeless style, and also including the application and specification concepts, as is quoted in [Wu 90].

4. Automatic generation of classes documentation.

It should be clear that we do not intend to construct a new Smalltalk system, but to enrich an existing one, as is the case of Smalltalk/V [Digital Inc. 91], though our work is portable on any Smalltalk system.

The fact of having quality environments available has promoted the expansion of the Smalltalk users community. We believe this community will be able to take advantage of the improvements offered by our project, having a more appropriate framework to develop software.

In the following section we will discuss the drawbacks of Smalltalk programming which motivate our work, and we outline the approaches that we have chosen to alleviate them. Next, we will describe the Eiffel-like assertion mechanism embedded in Smalltalk. Then, we will explain a modification of the Smalltalk/V environment for distinguishing between public and private operations. Finally, we will establish some conclusions and future work.

2 Drawbacks of Smalltalk

The Smalltalk language is simple due to the fact that it is based on very few concepts (object, class, method, message, polymorphism and inheritance) and to the uniformity provided by the model of communicating objects through messages. The environment supplies a WIMP interface style (windows, icons, menus and pointing device), offers a rich hierarchy of classes and the system tools enable access to the class text in run-time, since the classes are also objects.

But Smalltalk, unlike Eiffel, was not designed from the view point of the object-oriented paradigm as a software engineering technique, so it presents some drawbacks which make software construction more difficult. However, we think that it is possible to improve it, in the way exemplified by Eiffel, with extensions that attenuate these drawbacks. We started our project with this idea, trying to approach the following problems of Smalltalk: a) the typeless style, b) the non-separation between public and private features (method in the Smalltalk terminology), c) the non-supporting of the assertion concept, d) the lack of a methodology promoting the development of reliable classes.

The lack of types declaration makes the methods rather unreadable, so that it is very difficult to capture the meaning of a class only by reading it. We have built a new browser based on [Wu 90] to facilitate the understanding of the classes. As well as distinguishing among abstract vision (specification) and concrete vision (implementation) of a class, this browser also includes the concept of application (separating classes included in an application from classes of the system), and it also allows the addition to the class specification of information which cannot be deduced from the text of the class, such as variable type, object type returned by a method or if a class is abstract.

We have added some documentation tools which are similar to short and flat commands from Eiffel, as well as others intended to favour the sharing of classes among Smalltalk systems, having our extensions available or not.

In order to produce Smalltalk software components with a precise specification, we have enriched it with Eiffel-like assertions. As is quoted in [Meyer 92c], "without assertions it is not possible to produce truly industrial software components". The same as Eiffel, debugging and documentation tools are based on assertions. The debugging process especially takes advantage of the role played by the assertions as a methodical way to annotate the classes with debugging statements.

The assertions also allow the application of the "Design by Contract" methodology in the Smalltalk context. This methodology, described in detail in [Meyer 92a] using Eiffel, was devised in a parallel way to Smalltalk with the aim of building reliable software. It is based on the metaphor "Software by Contract" that proposes the inclusion of proper assertions into the classes. Assertions establish a contract among a class and its clients. This contract forces the client to fulfill certain conditions each time he makes use of a class service (the client has to check that the precondition, stating the requirements of any call to a routine, is satisfied); on the other hand, the class designer has to ensure that each routine will have the expected behaviour (stated as a postcondition expressing the effect of a such routine). The contract also need to take into account the concept of class invariant or property that must be satisfied by all instances of a class in every stable state.

In short, our assertion mechanism embedded in Smalltalk will help developers in the building of reliable classes and in the distribution of classes with a proper specification.

In Smalltalk, all methods defined in a class are considered part of its protocol or interface, and it is not possible to declare private methods. It implies a violation of the information hiding principle that all object-oriented languages should support. We have modified the way of storing the source code of the methods in order to implement a non-selective version of method privatization. This implementation permits the declaration of private methods, such that they can only be used within the class including them; that is, when they are sent to the current object (the *self* entity).

3 Including assertions in Smalltalk

By using assertions, the Smalltalk programmer will be able to include some elements of a specification at the class level (class invariant), at the message level (pre and postconditions) and at the method level (loop invariant, loop variant) in the same way as an Eiffel programmer. So, assertions provide a good mechanism to specify, debug and document a class, in a Smalltalk environment.

The "Design by Contract" methodology is fully applicable, except in handle exceptional cases in which the approaches *a priori* and *a posteriori* [Meyer 92a] are not valid, because we have not developed an exception mechanism yet. Assertions can be monitored in run-time, existing the same possibilities as in Eiffel. So, we have considered the following situations:

1. All the assertions are activated.

2. Only the preconditions are activated.

3. Preconditions and postconditions are activated.

4. All the assertions are deactivated.

For the same reasons presented in [Meyer 92a], by default, only the preconditions are activated.

Throughout this paper we will use the class *Account* as a simple example of class, whose instances represent banking accounts. The definition in Smalltalk of this class could be:

```
Object subclass: #Account
  instanceVariableNames:
    'balance owner personalCode'
  classVariableNames: ''
  poolDictionaries: ''
```

where the state of each instance is represented by the value of the instance variables: *balance*, *owner* and *personalCode*, storing the available money, the owner and the personal number of the account, respectively. Methods defined in this class could be *deposit:*, *withdrawal:*, *balance:* and *changeCode:*, whose meanings are easily deduced from their names.

We will describe below the assertion mechanism included in Smalltalk. This extension is meant to substantially modify the class *ClassHierarchyBrowser* which provides the interface with the programmer.

3.1 Class invariant

We have added to all the class creation methods, a new parameter specifying the invariant of the class. With respect to the storage of the invariant, since it is common to all the instances of a class, we outline two possibilities. The first one was to assign it to a class variable, and the other one to store it as a new field of the class descriptor. We chose the first one since we did not consider it appropriate to modify the structure of the class descriptor, though the implementation might have been simpler.

The class invariant is specified when the class is defined, and it is made by using a block which contains the boolean expression defining the invariant. The syntax used to express the conditions are fixed by the methods defined in the class *Boolean* and its subclasses. So, the definition of the class *Account* could be made in our proposal by sending a message to the root class *Object*, as follows:

```
Object subclass: #Account
  instanceVariableNames:
    'balance owner personalCode'
  classVariableNames: ''
  poolDictionaries: ''
  classInvariant:
    '[(balance>0) and:
    [owner nationality = 'Spanish']]'
```

The class invariant appears as a string containing a block, since a syntactic check must be made to assure that its structure is right, and that involves instance or class variables previously declared. The invariant checking is made by executing a convenient code when an instance of the class is created, and before and after a method is called.

In the example above the class invariant of *Account* establishes that the account balance will be greater than zero and that the nationality of the account owner has to be Spanish. It may seem strange that one of the conditions appears as block and the other does not, but this is necessary because of the implementation of the logical operators 'and' and 'or' in Smalltalk/V. The conjunct which appears as a block, includes the sending of the message *nationality* to an object which represents the account owner. Actually, it is not desirable that an assertion includes messages, for the obvious reasons explained in [Meyer 92a]: they must only involve methods of unimpeachable quality, that do not change the state of the current object or give rise to errors. However, in Smalltalk the interface of a class only contains methods, and the only way of consulting the value of an instance variable is defining a method that returns the object that it references. Supposing that the instance variable *owner* references to objects of the class *Person*, the method *nationality* included in this class could be:

```
nationality
  ↑nationality
```

Obviously, these kinds of methods do not cause problems since they are "safe functions", that is, they have not side effects.

We are also working on the possibility of expressing more complex conditions in the class invariant (e.g. by iterating on structures), but we are not developed it. It could be got by using enumerating messages in the class *Collection*, having as argument the block which defines the invariant. If this capability is achieved the assertion language of Eiffel will be improved.

3.2 Pre and postconditions

Assertions are composed by boolean expressions, including the same extensions that are provided in Eiffel: *old*, to refer the state of an object before executing the method; and *nochange*, to indicate that a given object has not changed its state, i.e. the *old* state coincides with the current state.

Pre and postconditions are used to specify the behaviour of a method. The new template that the system browser presents to the programmer, when he decides to add a new method, is the following one:

```
messagePattern
  ''comment''
  |temporaries|
  require: [..].
    < statements >
  ensure: [..].
```

In this template two new clauses appear, indicating the possibility of including pre and postconditions in the method. We have used the same keywords as in Eiffel: *require* and *ensure*, to specify the pre and postconditions of a method, respectively. This kind of assertion also must be included in the code as Smalltalk blocks. So, the aspect of a Smalltalk method containing pre and postconditions could be illustrated by the *withdrawal* operation on the class *Account*:

```
withdrawal:pesetas
  ''Withdraws the amount pesetas from
  the banking account''
  require:
    [balance>=pesetas and:
        [pesetas<10000]].
  balance ← balance-pesetas.
  ↑balance
  ensure:
    [(self old) balance
        = balance+pesetas]
```

The meaning of pre and postcondition appearing in *withdrawal* are evident from the text of the class. In the postcondition the extension *old* (appears as a message on the current object) is used to reference the state of the object before the method is executed. The *balance* message sent to the object returned by the expression *self old* has the same nature that the method *nationality* presents.

Really, the clauses *require:* and *ensure:* are not special sections in the method code. They are messages which are sent to the current object (i.e. *self*) when it is convenient. So, the Smalltalk philosophy (i.e. all actions are made by sending of messages to objects) is maintained. The system allows the using of these messages not refering the entity *self*, only as a syntactic sugar.

When the system saves a method, previous to its translation into bytecodes, a series of messages is added to the method code intended to check assertions in run- time. The aspect of these control messages depends on the assertions controlling the behaviour of the method, and also on the class invariant, since it must be also checked before and after the method is executed. So, for example, the *withdrawal* method will be really stored as:

```
withdrawal:pesetas
  ''Withdraws the amount pesetas from
  the banking account''
  self chekInvClass: [balance > 0].
  self require:
    [balance>=pesetas and:
        [pesetas<10000]].
  balance←balance-pesetas.
  self ensure:
    [(self old) balance
        = balance+pesetas].
  ↑self return: [balance]
```

In this case, the control messages check the precondition, the postcondition and the class invariant. The last one will be checked before and after the execution of the body of the method is executed. The message *checkInvClass* checks if the invariant is true and it pushes the object state in a stack, which is a global variable for the class *Stack*, named *StackAssertion*. The message *return:* checks the invariant and if this is true, it executes a pop operation on the stack, so removing the state of the current object. The messages *require:* and *ensure:* check the pre and postconditions, respectively. Obviously, the manipulation of these control messages is transparent for the programmer.

Assertions can be checked everywhere in the code by means of a *check* message applied to the *self* entity. So, we can use expressions as *self check: [cond]*, which will check if the assertion *cond*, which is passed as argument, is satisfied at that moment.

Loops specification is also possible by means of the invariant and variant loop, such that the *gcd* could be redefined in the class *Integer* by:

```
gcd:b
  ''Greatest common divisor of b and
  the receiver object''
  |x y|
  require: [self>0 and:[b>0]]
  x←self.
  y←b.
  [x=y] invariant: [x>0 and:[y>0]]
        variant: [x max: y]
        whileFalse:
             [(x>y)
                      ifTrue: [x ← x-y]
                      ifFalse: [y ← y-x]
             ].
  ↑x
```

In the instance creation methods it is necessary to verify that the invariant is fulfilled for the created object. In Smalltalk the creation methods are not declared explicitly, but they are a special case of class methods. Therefore each time a class method is stored the user is asked if it creates instances or not.

In the text of a class method which creates an instance the symbol "↑" must appear before the message creating the instance, to indicate that it is the object returned by the method. The class method *openAccount* of the class *Account* is an example of a method creating instances:

```
openAccount:pesetas owner:aString
  ''Creates a banking account with an
  initial balance given by pesetas,
  and an owner called aString''
  ↑((self new)
    initialize:
      (Array with:pesetas with:aString))
```

So, when a creation method is saved, the symbol "↑" is looked for, and the method *checkInvClass*, whose argument is a block, is applied on the returned object. In the example above, the argument is an empty block, since there is not any postcondition. Internally, the method *openAccount:owner:* will be stored as:

```
openAccount:pesetas owner:aString
  ''Creates a banking account with an
  initial balance given by pesetas,
  and an owner called aString''
  ↑((self new)
    initialize:
      (Array with:pesetas with:aString))
    chekcInvClass:[].
```

Note the *Account* class invariant, namely *balance* is positive, is not included in the block argument of *checkInvClass:*. This is because Smalltalk is not statically typed, and it does include a default initialization for instance variables. So, the value checking for the *balance* variable could imply a run-time error when it has not been previously initialized by an instance method. Nevertheless, it does not mean that the class invariant can be violated when an object is created, because any instance variable initialization must be made by using an instance method, which will contain its corresponding class invariant checking.

It is worth noting the special messages *require*, *ensure:*, or *check:*, cannot be directly emulated by an *ifTrue:* or similar messages. The differences are not only syntactical. In fact, the new predefined methods do not only check boolean expressions; they also make some other actions, as: storing the old state of objects, raising error messages related with the assertion violation, ...; and we think they can provide a good approach to construct fault-tolerant software (e.g. by supporting an exception handler.)

3.3 Assertions and methods redefinition

The "design by contract" methodology promotes a better use and understanding of inheritance and dynamic binding. We have taken into account the redefinition rule [Meyer 92b] which regulates the combination of the assertions with method redefinition: the precondition must be weaker than the original one, and the postcondition stronger. In this sense, we provide similar mechanisms as in the last version of Eiffel, by considering the new methods: *requirelse:* and *ensurethen:*; such that its arguments are added (by the appropriate logic operators) to the assertions corresponding to the redefined method.

3.4 Assertions and Debugging

As is quoted in [Meyer 92b], assertions provide a debugging and testing mechanism more appropriate than the traditional techniques, since it is based on the software component specifications (pre and postconditions).

In our case, when the execution of a message produces an error, because of assertion failure, the initial state of the receiver object is restored, and the user is shown a window indicating the kind of error produced. After this, the user can run the Smalltalk system debugger in order to act conveniently and to continue the execution. To restore the state of an object the *StackObject* stack is used. Since at a given instant, one or more methods will be in an intermediate point of its execution, this stack will store the states of the objects to which has been applied some message, maintaining the order in which they have been executed. *StackObject* stores objects of the class *ObjectContext* which has three instance variables: one of them stores a deep copy of the current object, allowing the restoring of the state, the second one stores a reference to the current object, and the last one stores the block containing the postcondition.

The class *ClassHierarchyBrowser* has also been modified so that a) the option of saving a method adds the control messages corresponding to the assertions checking, and b) the visualization of a method is done with the format shown by the template seen above, eliminating the auxiliary code. In a parallel way, all classes implementing the rest of tools of the environment have also been modified. Basically, these classes have been: *ClassBrowser*, *Debugger*, and *MethodBrowser*. It has also been necessary to add new methods to the class *Behaviour* and to its subclasses *Class* and *MetaClass*.

We must emphasize that our system is portable to other ones not including this assertions mechanism. On the one hand, communication from our system to a non-extended environment is guaranteed, since the exporting process of the source code from a class text to a file includes the possibility of using a filter which removes the control messages, and all the auxiliary information generated by our environment. On the other hand, the extended system can also import classes developed by other systems. All this has been made possible by modifying the protocol for the class *ClassReader*. In addition, some tools are also supplied in order to simulate the functional character of *short* and *flat* commands of Eiffel, automatically generating documentation intended for the clients of a class.

4 Privatization of methods in Smalltalk

An object-oriented language must be able to establish in an explicit way the interface of a class, that will be composed by the operations and attributes considered visible by the class designer. In Eiffel, it is possible to decide if an attribute or an operation is visible only for a group of classes (in an extreme case, to the whole system). Out of the attributes exported by a class, the clients can only consult its state, that is, they cannot modify it directly.

In Smalltalk, the interface of a class is considered to be composed by all the methods of the class, and it is not possible to restrict the accessing to them; that is, every method is considered public. If we take into account that in Smalltalk the only way to give a value to an instance variable is by using an instance method, then the limitation in relation with the information hiding becomes obvious. It is a common practice in this language to associate two methods to each instance variable: one for consulting its value, and another one for changing it.

We have modified Smalltalk/V so that it allows the declaration of private methods and public attributes in consulting mode. Each time the programmer adds a new class to the system, a method is generated for each instance variable with the same name, and returning its value (if the instance variable is declared private the corresponding method is not created).

In a similar way, when a new method is defined in a class it is possible to decide if it will be public or private by means of a pair of buttons. If the method is stored as private, then the prefix "private" is added, automatically, to its name in order to differentiate it from the public protocol, but this handling is totally transparent to the programmer.

We have considered a non-selective version of the privatization mechanism so that a private method is considered as such for all the class clients, including itself, because of the lack of typing in Smalltalk; so, it is not possible to establish statically a selective privatization.

The selectors of the methods belonging to the private protocol are stored internally with a different name to the one given by the user (e.g. by adding the prefix "private"), so the clients of a class can only use the public protocol. In this way, when they are used from a client class a typical error message will be produced: "message not understood". However, private methods can also be applied on the entity *self*, and these situations must not be considered erroneous. To avoid the generation of an error when messages are sent to *self*, the system has to recognize if the corresponding method is public or private. But, when a method is created, the entities and methods used in its definition may be unknown. To solve this problem the prefix "private" is added to all selectors applied on *self*, and each time a public method is defined a method with the same selector, but preceded by the prefix, is automatically created, whose body only contains a message invoking the public version on the entity *self*.

The privatization of methods has been made possible by modifying a number of classes. So, the class *ClassHierarchyBrowser* was modified to change the interface aspect, as well as the storage process. On the other hand, the class *Behaviour* provides a new protocol to separate public methods from private ones. In a similar way, the tools *ClassBrowser*, *Debugger* and *MethodBrowser* have been conveniently updated to present the new functional character.

5 Conclusions and future work

Our main aim has been extending Smalltalk with new mechanisms and tools, in order to increase programmer productivity. In this paper, part of our project has been described, that is, a way to incorporate assertions in the class and method definition, and an approach to hide components have been proposed. Different mechanisms to specify assertions have been included to apply the "design by contract" methodology in the context of Smalltalk. We believe this methodology can substantially help Smalltalk programmers to develop reliable software. Moreover, assertions are very useful in debugging and automatic documentation. In this sense, we are now interested in the inclusion of an exception handling mechanism to also exploit the usefulness of assertions in relation with the construction of fault-tolerant software.

We think our assertion mechanism can be also applied to the object-oriented databases management system, GemStone, since it uses Smalltalk as a data model. We are studying the way we could adapt our work to such a database system.

It has not been possible to include a selective version of the method privatization, because of Smalltalk is not statically typed. Actually, our mechanism facilitates the privatization but it does not prevent it, since the user of a Smalltalk system could easily verify the prefix of the private methods, so avoiding this privatization approach.

Our environment also has an educational interest since it allows the use of Smalltalk in problem solving courses, such as is described in [Wiener 93], and where the object-oriented paradigm is introduced as a software engineering technique.

References

[Goldberg 83] A. Goldberg and D. Robson. *Smalltalk-80: The language and its implementation*, Addisson-Wesley, 1983.

[Ingalls 81] D.H. Ingalls. "Design Principles behind Smalltalk", in *Byte*, August, 1981.

[Meyer 88] B. Meyer. *Object-Oriented Software Construction*, Prentice- Hall, 1988.

[Meyer 92a] B. Meyer. *Eiffel: The Language*, Prentice-Hall, 1992.

[Meyer 92b] B. Meyer. "Design by Contract", in D. Mandrioli and B.Meyer (eds), *Advances in Object-Oriented Software Engineering*, Prentice-Hall, 1992.

[Meyer 92c] B. Meyer, "The New Culture of Software Development: Reflections on the Practice in Object-Oriented Design", in D. Mandrioli and B.Meyer (eds), *Advances in Object-Oriented Software Engineering*, Prentice-Hall, 1992.

[Digital Inc. 91] Digital Inc. *Smalltalk/V Windows Tutorial and Programming Handbook*, 1991.

[Wiener 93] R. Wiener and L. Pinson. "OOP: An academic Perspective", in *Journal of Object-Oriented Programming (Education and Training Supplement)*, May 1993.

[Wu 90] T. Wu. "A better browser for object-oriented programming", in *Journal of Object-Oriented Programming*, November 1990.

Three tools for Smalltalk programmers: task oriented views, information cards, and SCRC card

Ivan Tomek
Jodrey School of Computer Science
Acadia University
Wolfville, Nova Scotia, Canada
ivan.tomek@acadiau.ca

Abstract: At the time of its inception, the programming environment of Smalltalk-80 provided Smalltalk programmers with unparalleled tools for program development. From our experience, however, we found that productivity of Smalltalk program development can be greatly enhanced by adding tools that provide alternative views of the class library and support program development. We developed several such facilities and used them both in program development and to help students learning Smalltalk. Two such tools - the Task Oriented View and the Info Card are outlined at the beginning of this paper. We also describe a simple tool based on the well known concept of CRC cards (SCRC cards) that can make systematic program design easier. We use SCRC cards in teaching object oriented program development (OOPD) and as a part of a more complete set of OOPD tools now under development.

From TOOLS EUROPE '94 (Technology of Object-Oriented Languages and Systems).

1. Introduction

When Smalltalk [Goldberg1983, ParcPlace1992, Digitalk 1992] was introduced, its environment represented a major step forward for program developers. The System Browser is an excellent tool for the development of code,and the debugger and inspector continue to provide powerful support for testing. However, in our experience, a developer needs more support than access to source code in the library of existing classes and methods.

We found the System Browser (Figure 1) lacking for a fundamental reason directly related to object oriented programming with a large library of predefined classes and methods. The advantage of programming in such an environment is that previously declared and tested modules can be reused and this advantage grows as the size of the library grows. At the same time, however, programming becomes more difficult because it is increasingly difficult to find which predefined modules solve the problems at hand, and once they are found, it may not be obvious how they should be used. Although this problem is well known and has been attacked by several researchers, it has not been successfully resolved in any existing environment to the best of our knowledge.

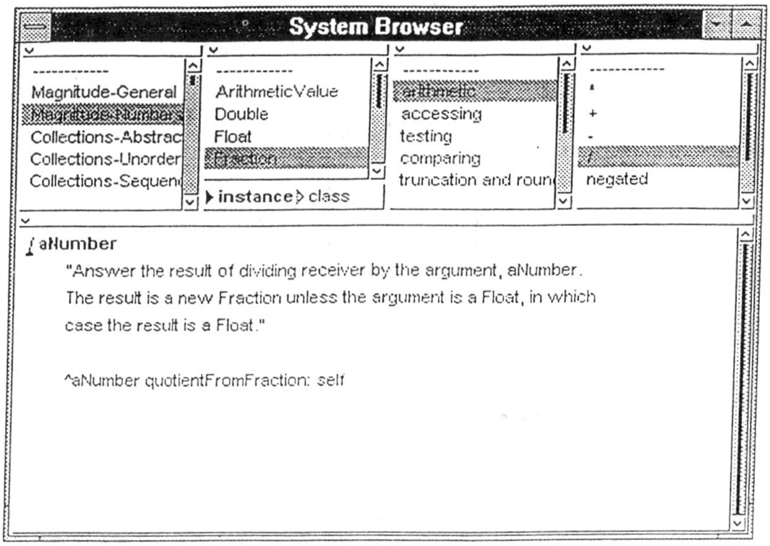

Figure 1. Smalltalk System Browser.

For the sake of completeness, before we start our analysis, we must note that the System Browser in Smalltalk-80 provides a tool that somewhat alleviates the problem by forcing the programmer to group classes into categories. Unfortunately, this help is minimal and even experienced programmers may have difficulty identifying the category containing the desired class[1]. Besides, even when one gets hold of the desired class, the browser has other limitations including the following:

- Class listing provides access to methods grouped in protocols. Although the User Guide encourages programmers to separate 'private' methods from 'public interface' methods, browsing the library shows that even the system classes do not follow this advice. Since the browser opens an undiscriminating window on all methods, it is often very difficult to decide which ones are the appropriate ones, often simply because of the sheer size of the method library. In other words, the browser shows too much.
- While showing too much, the browser also shows too little. In particular, the most appropriate method for a given task may be a method inherited from a superclass rather than declared in the current class. Since the hierarchy tree may be quite deep and since the System Browser does not provide information on inherited methods, it may be difficult to find the appropriate method by browsing the superclasses, particularly when one does not know exactly what one is looking for. For this reason, tools have been developed to provide this information.
- While the browser provides access to all methods and their declarations, it rarely shows examples of their proper use. One can, of course, browse all the senders of the method but this is of limited value because it is time consuming and possibly misleading; besides, this kind of browsing often leads to methods that have nothing to do with the desired use because of heavy use of polymorphism. The browser also often opens on methods that contain the desired symbol in the heading of its declaration rather and do not really send it as a

[1]To overcome this problem, the browser allows the user to search for the desired class and bypass the categories.

message. Moreover, there are situations in which one could use one of several methods but only one is the most appropriate and the browser does not provide any hints as to which one it is.

- Another difficulty with the access to methods via the System Browser is that the source code or usage patterns does not always reveal what is the expected nature of a method's arguments and what kind of object it returns.

After identifying the above drawbacks, we have concluded that the problem is that the Smalltalk environment provides only one out of several possible views of the class and method library and that several alternative views are needed including the view of Smalltalk from the perspective of programming tasks rather than available classes, and the view of classes from the point of view of their usage rather than their declaration. We have implemented these two views in the form of the task Oriented View (TOV) and InfoCards, both described in the following sections.

2. Task Oriented View (TOV)

When a programmer needs to implement an unfamiliar task, he may not know where to start looking, which class to use, and how[2]. In fact, more complicated tasks often require the use of several different classes. The purpose of the Task Oriented View or TOV is to provide easy access to this type of information.

TOV is a depository of information about tasks and topics. Its purpose is to provide information on topics ranging from general such as the use of the mouse or programming of graphical user interfaces, to quite specific such as the use of popup windows or data structures or control of flow of execution in Smalltalk. An important role of TOV is to allow the user to record new experience with Smalltalk for future use.

The following are some of the consideration that guided our design of TOV:

- As the class library gets bigger and as the programmer's experience with it grows, new information needs to be added. Similarly, mistakes in information stored in TOV must be corrected. Consequently, TOV must make it possible to add new information and edit existing information.
- Most tasks encompass a variety of subtasks or perspectives and it should thus be possible to categorize tasks further into several levels of subtasks. Our implementation provides three levels of depth called Topics, Keywords, and Descriptions but all levels do not have to be used for each topic.
- Different users or even the same user at different times may think of the same topic or task in different terms and may use different terminology to describe it. Consequently, the mapping between topics and information should be many-to-many. In other words, it should be possible to access the same information using various alternative terms. Since our approach is not based on queries but uses selection lists, the user should thus be able to define synonyms, allowing him to view the information in his own perspective.
- In some cases, information provided for a given Topic at a lower level, for example all information associated with a certain keyword, may be useful as a sub category in another Topic. This means, that not only the mapping Topic $\rightarrow$ information should be many-to-many, but that even mapping between the individual levels should be many-to-many. This will make it possible, for example, to link a selected subtopic with several different topics without duplication.

---

[2]We use the masculine pronoun to represent both male and female programmers.

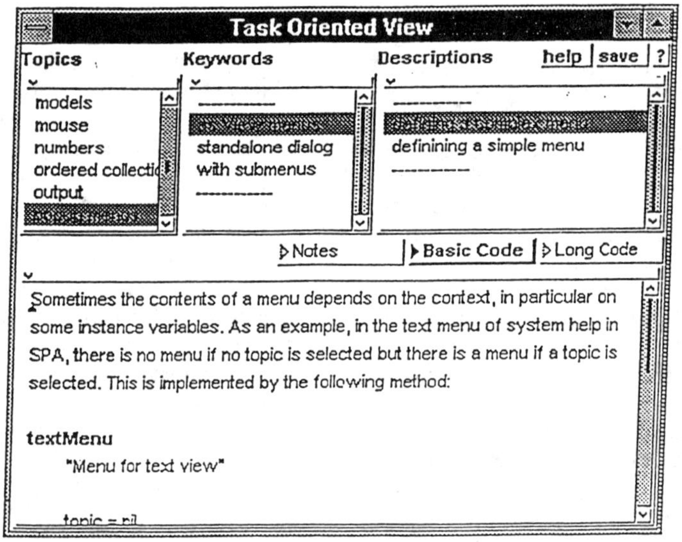

Figure 2. Task Oriented View showing topic **popup menus**, subtopic **as View menus**, and keyword **defining a complex menu**. The text in the bottom view is information about the selected Topic-Keyword-Description combination.

In our illustration of TOV in Figure 2, the top three selection-in-list views provide access to Topics, Keywords, and Descriptions. When TOV is first opened, the initial display shows only the list of existing Topics. Once a Topic is selected from the scrollable list, the comment associated with the topic appears in the bottom view and the keywords are displayed in the middle selection list. When a Keyword is then selected, the text in the bottom view is replaced with information about the subtopic, and the list of Descriptions corresponding to the subtopic is displayed in the rightmost top view[3]. Finally, when a Description is selected, the corresponding text is shown in the bottom view.

In addition to hierarchical selection based on topics, keywords, and descriptions, textual search over the whole body of the TOV information and other forms of access are available. On a stylistic note, we recommend that the comment displayed in the bottom view include Smalltalk code fragments that can be executed on the spot and transported and reused in new applications.

[3]Note that the widths of the three lists are not the same because the length of terms describing Topics, keywords, and Descriptions are usually different.

3. Info Cards

When a user finds how to perform a certain task, possibly via TOV, he may need to look up some details about the usage of a particular class. Alternatively, he may not have used the TOV at all and knows what he needs to do but does not remember all the details and the System Browser does not provide this information in a convenient form. As an example, we have already mentioned that the user often needs to know not only which methods are declared in the class's external interface, but also which inherited methods are appropriate and how they should be used. To provide this information is the purpose of InfoCards.

To access an existing InfoCard, the user selects from an InfoCard directory (Figure 3). Once an InfoCard for a particular class is displayed, it can stay on the screen and the user can thus view as many InfoCards at the same time as he wants. An InfoCard is labeled with the name of the class and its contents is organized hierarchically as in the TOV. When the card is first displayed, the text view on the left displays general comments about the class, the Tasks selection list shows a list of tasks that the class can perform, and the Methods view is empty. The Tasks list usually parallels protocols declared for the class in the System Browser but its contents is under the control of the programmer who created the card and can be changed at any time. This has two reasons - the creator may not like the organization in the browser, and some of the protocols or tasks may not actually be available in the declaration of the class because they are inherited.

Once the user of the card selects a task in the Tasks view, the Methods view displays the names of methods included in this group, and the text view on the left displays the comment created for this particular task. Finally, when the user selects a method in the Methods view, the text view changes again and shows the text associated with the method. In creating the information for a class, the author should again think about possible reuse and give examples of code that can be directly transported into new applications and reused after minor modification.

The **hierarchy** button in the bottom right corner of the card shows the place of the current class in the Smalltalk class hierarchy in the text view, the **class** button opens a regular Smalltalk browser on the current class, and the **methods** button displays a popup menu with all methods documented on this card and the selection of an item on the menu opens a view on its comment. Since all information on the card is editable, the user can add new tasks and methods and their comments, modify the existing comments, or move individual components around.

At present, InfoCards for existing classes must be created manually and we have done this for over 50 built-in Smalltalk classes so far. Initial information for InfoCards for new classes can be derived automatically from SCRC cards introduced in the next section. We are also considering the idea of obtaining initial information about existing classes from the Smalltalk library on the basis of class and method comments as is done, for example, in Synopsis [Synopsis].

Since the TOV and InfoCards are constantly at the user's fingertips, the library of InfoCards and the richness of the TOV and the quality of their contents should keep growing with the use of the system and should eventually contain a large amount of expert, personalized, and easily accessible information.

4. SCRC -Smalltalk CRC cards

SCRC cards are complementary to InfoCards. While InfoCards provide information about existing classes, SCRC cards are designed for the development of new classes. In effect, TOV and InfoCards are support tools for SCRC cards since a programmer would typically use them to obtain information about existing classes and methods when designing new code via SCRC cards.

An SCRC card (Figure 3) is organized in much the same way as an InfoCard card and this makes the two of them easier to use. Moreover, since the nature of most of the information on an SCRC card is the same as the information displayed on an InfoCard, an SCRC can be 'engineered' into an InfoCard by copying relevant information from an existing SCRC card (automatically) and editing it to a form better suited for the InfoCard purpose since an SCRC card is essentially the developer's view of a class and contains some information irrelevant for a potential user of the class when the class becomes a part of the library.

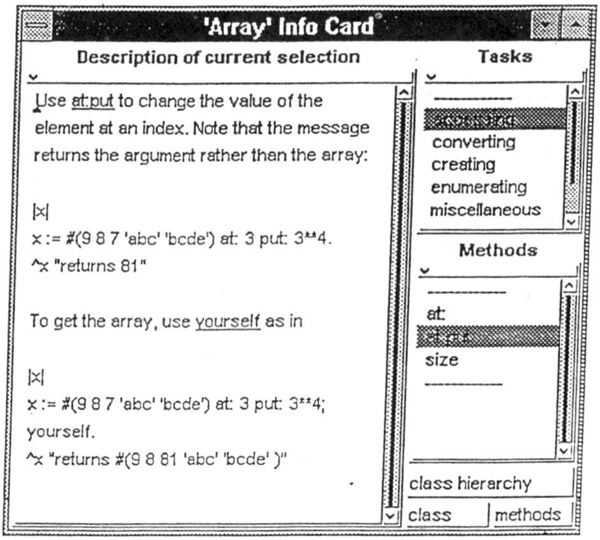

Figure 3. InfoCard for class Array with selections Task = **accessing**, Method = **at:put:**, displaying the description of method at:put: with information about the purpose of the method, examples of its use with arrays, and information about the returned object. All code is executable allowing the user to examine the exact behavior of the method.

SCRC cards are an extension of the idea of Class-Responsibility-Collaborator cards, better known as CRC cards [Beck 1989]. In their original implementation, CRC cards are 3x6 inch paper cards used to capture information about classes needed to implement an application, as the classes emerge during the analysis of the problem and take shape. Each card contains the class's name, a brief description of its purpose, a list of phrases describing its responsibilities, and a list of its collaborators (Figure 4).

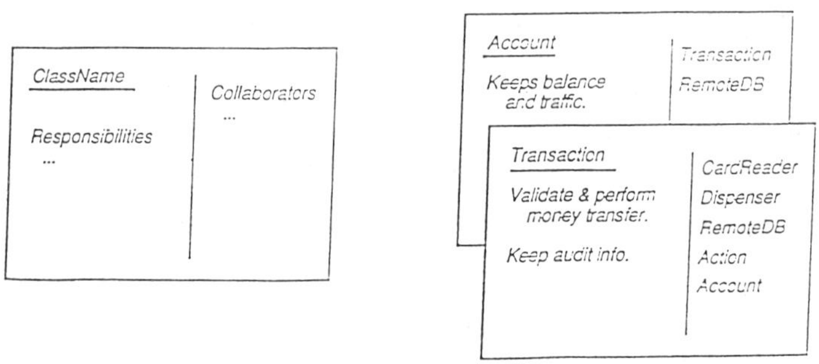

Figure 4. A CRC card [Beck 1989].

The idea of a CRC card has been used extensively in introducing object oriented thinking, and occasionally even as a part of formal analysis and design [Wirfs-Brock 1990]. As far as we know, however, an implementation of the concept as a computer tool has not been described in the literature it is well suited as a low level tool for object-oriented CASE (Computer Aided Software Engineering) systems, bridging the gap between high level description and its source code implementation.

The possible role of CRC cards in object oriented program development (OOPD) [Booch 1991, Coad 1991a, b, Rubin 1992, Rumbaugh 1991, Wirfs-Brock 1990] can be described in terms of the following context: At the high level of abstraction, object oriented analysis and design result in the creation of complex diagrams (Figure 5) showing

- the structure of the class hierarchy - subclassing,
- the structure of modules (subsystems) formed by grouping related classes,
- the aggregation of classes showing how more complicated classes use less complicated classes as their components,
- communication between classes and, at a higher level, communication between modules.

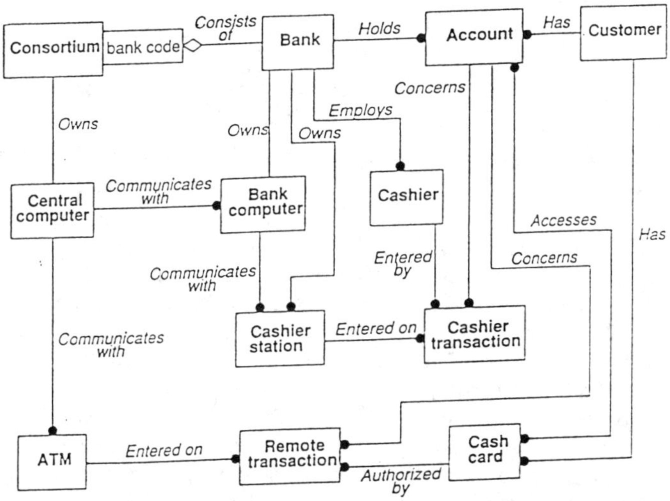

Figure 5. A typical object diagram showing dependencies and relationships between classes needed to implement an application [Rumbaugh 1991].

Progressively, this high level description must be converted into detailed descriptions of individual classes and their methods, and then into their implementation. Since class descriptions created during analysis and design directly map into classes in the implementation, and since responsibilities map into class protocols, the CRC concept provides a natural bridge between analysis, design, and implementation. It thus allows **incremental transformation** of analysis (abstract breakdown of the problem into classes and their general responsibilities) into design (identification of responsibilities and description of methods implementing them, specification of major internal variables) and implementation (declaration of classes and their methods). SCRC cards are a computer tool that implements this principle and allows this incremental development.

An SCRC card (Figure 6) is labeled with the name of the class that it describes and provides selection lists allowing access to information about the class. When an SCRC window is first opened to start a new class, all subviews are empty and the user can begin entering the class's description and its responsibilities in the topmost list on the right hand side of the window and their descriptions using short phrases capturing the essence of their functions.

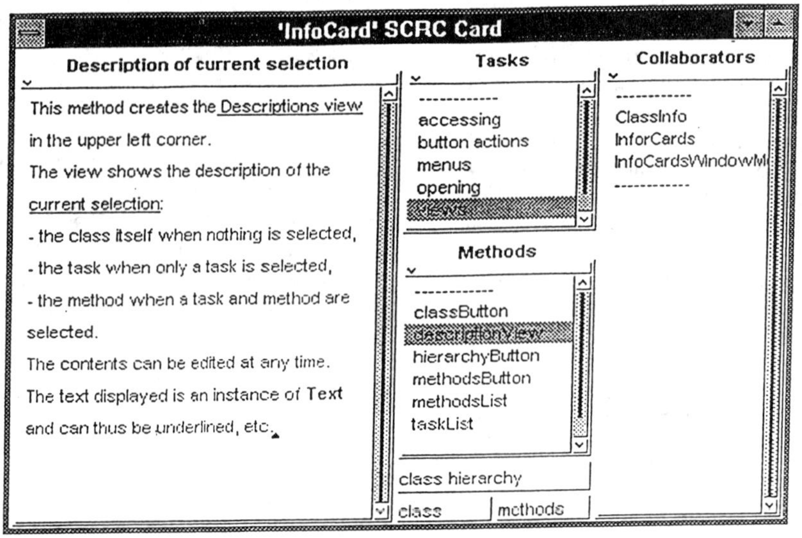

Figure 6. SCRC card.

The purpose of the other views on an SCRC card is similar to that of Infocards and this consistency makes both tools easier to use. When the user selects an existing responsibility entry (called Task for consistency with InfoCards), the contents of the Description view changes and displays the description of the responsibility. At the same time, the Methods selection list displays the list of methods implementing the selected responsibility, and the Collaborators view shows the names of classes needed to implement the responsibility.

When the user selects a method in the Methods list, its description appears in the Description view, replacing the previously shown description of the responsibility. The Collaborators view also changes accordingly. A method description initially contains a brief explanation of the purpose of the method but as the development progresses it will eventually acquire a description of the arguments of the method and of the object that its execution returns.

In the development process, SCRC cards are created during problem analysis and their use continues during the design phase. Initially, only the class description and responsibilities are entered, then responsibility descriptions are added and used to name and describe the required methods, and collaborators and variables are defined. As this is being done, the user may automatically commit the SCRC card-defined classes and their descriptions, variables, responsibilities (protocols), and methods to source code. In other words, class declarations and stumps of method declarations can be produced as a background result of the definition of cards. Eventually, the user declares the code of the stump methods and this can be done in the description window using the same style as in the regular Smalltalk browser. In this way, SCRC cards thus support a smooth seamless transition from initial specification to programming implementation. All code created during this process may, of course, be immediately tested within the SCRC card itself. Since the contents of a card may be archived at any point, descriptions and fragments of test code entered into the card during the analysis and design stages may be used as the class's 'formal' specification and eventually executed when the code is implemented, providing a direct link between specification and testing.

Although SCRC cards are used to create classes whereas InfoCards are used to obtain information about the purpose and the external interface of existing classes, much of the information on an SCRC card is similar to the information on an Infocard. This makes it possible to create InfoCards from SCRC cards by automatically transmitting the shared information from SCRC to the corresponding InfoCard and then editing the information to fit its different purpose.

5. Conclusion and future work

While TOV and InfoCards are, to the best of our knowledge, tools that have not yet been used in any Smalltalk environments, SCRC cards are an extension of an idea proposed several years ago but still arousing interest,. Our experience with all three is that even though they are 'dumb' tools with no pretense at intelligence other than the user's, they greatly improve programming productivity and make Smalltalk much easier to learn. Their usefulness is enhanced by the built-in internal relationships between the information associated with them and their links to the Smalltalk environment which allows automatic commiting of design decisions to Smalltalk code.

TOV and InfoCards are just two of several tools that we have prototyped and intend to integrate into a single system wide help facility. Other help tools existing at the time of writing include Method InfoCards, on line Glossary, and on line Environment help. As with the facilities described in the previous sections, the information provided by these tools to some extent overlaps. As an example, comments and examples of the use of a particular method may be accessed both via Class InforCards and Method InfoCards. All tools are designed to take advantage of this and access a single database of data so that updates via one tool are automatically reflected in other views.

The Help system, in turn, should become a part of a program development environment to include SCRC cards, an interactive user interface builder, a prototype interface mockup generator, and a state interface engine. Their prototypes have already been implemented, and work on their more definitive implementation is underway. Design of other tools to progressively include functions found in CASE systems is under consideration.

Acknowledgements

Initial work on prototypes of the tools described or mentioned in this paper was carried out in collaboration with Ravi Palepu, Oliver Oey, Michelle Bellgrave, Roger Lewis - all students at Acadia University.

References

[Beck 1989] Beck K., Cunningham W.: A laboratory for teaching object-oriented thinking, OOPSLA'89 Proceedings, 1989, pp. 1-6.

[Booch 1991] Booch G.: Object oriented design with applications, Benjamin-Cummings Publishing, 1991.

[Coad 1991a] Coad P., Yourdon E.: Object oriented analysis, Yourdon Press, 1991.

[Coad 1991b] Coad P., Yourdon E.: Object oriented design, Yourdon Press, 1991.

[Digitalk 1992] Smalltalk/v tutorial and programming handbook, Digitalk Inc., Los Angeles, 1992.

[Goldberg 1983] Goldberg A., Robson D.: Smalltalk-80. The language and its implementation, Addison-Wesley, 1983.

[ParcPlace 1992] ParcPlace Systems: Objectworks\Smalltalk User's Guide, Release 4.1, Sunnyvale, California, 1992.

[Rubin 1992] Rubin K.S., Goldberg A.: Object behavior analysis, Communications of ACM, pp. 48-62, September 1992.

[Rumbaugh 1991] Rambaugh J., et al.: Designing object oriented software, Prentice-Hall, 1991.

[Synopsis] Synopsis - The Team Documentation Tool for Smalltalk/V, Synopsis Software, 8609 Wellsley Way, Raleigh, NC 27613, USA.

[Wirfs-Brock 1990] Wirfs-Brock R., Wilkerson B., Wiener L.: Designing object-oriented software, Prentice-Hall, 1990.

PANELS AND DEBATES

The Managers' Forum

The Great Language Users' Debate

TUTORIALS

Comparison of O-O languages

Richard Wiener
Journal of Object-Oriented Programming
135 Rugely Court
Colorado Springs, CO 80906
USA
e-mail: rswiener@elbert.uccs.edu

Abstract: The major features of C++, Smalltalk, and Eiffel will be compared from the perspective of object-oriented software development. Carefully crafted code segments in C++, Smalltalk, and Eiffel that focus on key issues associated with object-oriented software construction will form the basis for comparing the languages. It is recommended that the attendee have some working knowledge of either C++, Smalltalk, or Eiffel.

Richard Wiener is the editor-in-chief of the *Journal of Object-Oriented Programming* and associate professor of computer science at the University of Colorado at Colorado Springs. He has written 16 books on the subjects of Software Engineering, Data Structures, C, C++, Pascal, Modula-2, Smalltalk, and Objective-C.

The Eiffel Method

Christine Mingins
Object Technology Group
Dept. of Software Development
Monash University
Caulfield Campus
PO Box 197, Caulfied Campus
Australia 3145
e-mail: cmingins@fcit.monash.edu.au

Abstract: Object-Oriented software developers should no longer need to view programming languages as mere coding notations. It should be possible to view a language at once as a design, specification, and implementation formalism. The Eiffel language has been designed with the single purpose of providing mechanisms for dealing with the significant problems of creating truly reusable components and class hierarchies. This tutorial will demonstrate how the Eiffel language and the associated BON notation combine to provide an effective and elegant method for Object-Oriented design. Participants will be led through a case study which highlights the problems faced in designing for reuse, regardless of language, and the solutions which Eiffel provides.

Christine Mingins is a Senior Lecturer at Monash University, specialising in Object-Oriented Software Engineering. She is on the editorial board of the Journal of Object-Oriented Systems, and a member of the NICE Libraries Standards Committee. She is also extensively involved on a consulting basis, introducing Object technology into business organizations.

Ada 9X

Alfred Strohmeier
Swiss Fed Inst of Technology
EPFL-DI-LGL
CH-1015 Lausanne
Switzerland
e-mail: alfred.strohmeier@di.epfl.ch

Abstract: This tutorial is intended to present the object- oriented extensions of Ada 9X and to teach their methodological use. It demonstrates how Ada 9X supports the creation and use of reusable software components. It is designed to give a complete understanding of the basics of object-oriented programming with Ada 9X as well as the new mechanisms of the language and their relationship to classical object-oriented programming techniques.

Alfred Strohmeier is a Professor of Computer Science at the Swiss Federal Institute of Technology in Switzerland where he leads the Software Engineering Laboratory. He has been teaching object-oriented design and Ada since 1981 in academic and industrial settings. He is a Distinguished Reviewer of Ada 9X and head of the Swiss delegation to the Ada working group of ISO.

O-O Requirements Analysis and Logical Design

Donald Firesmith
Advanced Software
Technology Specialists
17124 Lutz Road
Ossian, Indiana 46777-9406
USA

Abstract: This tutorial provides an in-depth introduction into the software requirements and logical design activity of ADM4, a fourth generation object-oriented systems and software development method designed for use on large, complex, and even real-time applications. Three static architecture and three dynamic behaviour models are presented. These six models will be captured using associated diagramming techniques and OOSDL a concurrent, object-oriented specification and design language based on Eiffel, Dragoon, ADA and ADM4. The material in this tutorial significantly updates the information in the book *Object-Oriented Requirements Analysis and Logical Design: A Software Engineering Approach*, published by John Wiley & Sons (1993).

Donald Firesmith is the President of Advanced Software Technology Specialists (ASTS), an object-oriented training and consulting company and the author of *Object-Oriented Methods, Standards and Procedures* (Prentice Hall, 1993). He is the developer and maintainer of the ADM development method and the OOSDL specification and design language.

Rigorous Development of Concurrent O-O Systems

Eugène Dürr and Stephen Goldsack
Utrecht University
Dept. Computers and Physics
Buys Ballot Laboratory
P.O.Box 80.000
3508 TV Utrecht
The Netherlands
email:durr@fys.ruu.nl

Abstract: This tutorial will present an approach to system development using an Object Oriented specification language based on VDM called VDM++. The language uses object structures derived from classes and supporting inheritance and polymorphism, is strongly typed, uses structures (sets, sequences and maps) and provides high level specifications. VDM++ objects may be concurrently active, and mechanisms are provided for specifying synchronisation constraints. Features are provided to handle the development of systems controlling or modelling dynamic, systems with real-time requirements, often given mathematical descriptions in differential equations. An approach will be presented for specifying such objects at a high level using continuous variables, supported by a development method to transform them to the discrete form used in programs.

Eugène Dürr is technical manager for CAP Gemini Innovation in The Netherlands and assistant professor at Utrecht University. He is project manager of the Esprit project Afrodite and the Drive project CombiCom.

Stephen Goldsack is Emeritus Professor of Computing Science at The Imperial College of Science, Technology and Medicine in London; he has published 2 books on Ada, and participated in the DRAGON and FOREST projects.

Comparison of Analysis and Design Methods

Martin Fowler
Martin Fowler
29 Milford #2
Boston, MA 02118
USA
e-mail: 100031.3311@CompuServe.COM

Abstract: This tutorial shows how to look inside methods to see how they differ, and more importantly, how they are the same. It examines several of the most well-known methods, including Booch, Coad/Yourdon, Jacobson (OOSE), Odell/Martin (Ptech), Rumbaugh (OMT), Shlaer/Mellor, and Wirfs-Brock (RDD, CRC). This tutorial shows the techniques each method uses and how different methods use different dialects of the same techniques, varying the notation and introducing new concepts. It uses examples to show how the same system is expressed in different ways by the various methods. The tutorial also compares the design approach advocated by each method.

Martin Fowler is an independent consultant providing education and training in analysis and design, object technology, and clinical health care systems to a range of clients in Europe and the US, in particular the UK National Health Service.

Library Design

Bertrand Meyer
Interactive Software Engineering, Inc.
270 Storke Road, Suite 7
Goleta, CA 93117
USA
e-mail: bertrand@eiffel.com

Abstract: Object-orientation holds the promise of reuse. But the design of a high-quality library is an exacting process, almost a profession in itself. This presentation, drawing from the experience of developing thousands of successful reusable classes, will introduce a set of principles for constructing libraries.

Bertrand Meyer is the author of several books including *Object-Oriented Software Construction, Introduction to the Theory of Programming Languages* and *Eiffel: The Language (Prentice Hall).* He is the Series Editor for Prentice Hall's Object-Oriented Series. The material for this presentation will be largely drawn from his newest book, *Reusable Software: The Base Object-Oriented Libraries.*

O-O Modeling for Flexible Manufacturing Systems

David Hill
Laboratoire d'Informatique
l'Université Blaise Pascal
Clermont FD II
Campus du Cézeaux
63177 Aubière
France
e-mail: benny@glm.univ-bpclermont.fr

Abstract: This tutorial will show how object-oriented techniques are used in the industry to model flexible manufacturing systems and automatic material handling systems. It will set model validation and verification problems and explain major existing tools and modelling environments. The second part introduces the key concepts of the object model which can be directly applied to model manufacturing systems. Each concept is presented with a concrete example of manufacturing system modelling. The third part will present how the O-O technology is used and applied in the industry to model and evaluate existing systems and how to design future systems. The methodology presented has been supported by the French Ministry of Research and is now being used in large companies and international groups. A set of real case studies are presented in increasing order of complexity.

David Hill is associate professor at the IEI (European Institute of Computer Science) in Clermont-Ferrand, France. He authored a book on OOA modeling and simulation (Addison Wesley, 1993).

Project Management for Object-Oriented Systems

George–Pierre Reich and Franck Barbier
Reich & Cie
27 rue Jules Vernes
44700 Orvault France

IRESTE
Atlanpole
la Chantrerie CP 3003
44087 Nantes Cedex 03
France
e-mail: fbarbier@ireste.fr

Abstract:
One rationale for using OO systems is getting quality. To enforce quality, we need a project management designed with this aim. We also have to know what is quality software, i.e. we have to know how to validate a product. The tutorial will explore the following topics: What issues are specific to object-orientation?; forecasting the size and effort; evaluating the results; checking and testing; packaging; types of troubles with types of typing; special treatment for inheritance; building a single common process for all OOPL; ability to follow standard OO methods. It will conclude with a forecast of future trends. The presentation will be based on numerous examples drawn from the authors' experience.

Georges-Pierre Reich is manager of a company dedicated to Smalltalk development products and components.

Franck Barbier is a Doctor in Computer Science, Associate professor at University of Nantes. Author of the book *Techniques orientées objets et CIM* and numerous journal publications in JOOP, IEEE, Genie Logiciel. He has given training sessions for OMT, OOA (Coad/Yourdon), Shlaer/Mellor and Eiffel.

The Role of Prototyping in Software Development

Gustav Pomberger and Rainer Weinreich
Johannes Kepler Universitat Linz
Institut fur Wirtschaftsinformatik
und Organisationsforschung
Software Engineering
Altenbergerstrasse 69
A-4040 Linz-Auhof
AUSTRIA
e-mail: pomberger@swe.uni-linz.ac.at

Abstract: It is often assumed that prototyping can provide support in achieving some of the major goals of software engineering: exact fulfillment of user requirements; increased reliability and robustness; modularity of both the development process and the product; simple and adequate usability; easy maintenance and extensibility; reusability of software components in various projects; reduction of costs of production, operation and maintenance. The goal of the tutorial is to give the participants a broad overview of the possibilities and the limits of prototyping-oriented software development, to demonstrate a prototyping-oriented software development environment that was implemented with object-oriented means, and to inform participants of the potential for success of prototyping based on experience in several large projects.

Gustav Pomberger was previoulsy professor of computer science at the University of Zurich. Since 1987 he has been a professor of computer science at the University of Linz and since 1992 he has served as the leader of the C. Doppler Research Laboratory for Software Engineering.

Rainer Weinreich is research assistant at the University of Linz and a staff member of the C. Doppler Laboratory.

Essential Techniques for O-O Development

Steve Cook
Object Designers Ltd.
Glebe House
Great Hallingbury
Bishops Stortford
Herts CM22 7TY
United Kingdom
e-mail: scook@cix.compulink.co.uk

Abstract: This tutorial is aimed at software developers using object-oriented analysis and design methods. It is divided into four sections, each discussing a problematic aspect of the development process and offering a technique to solve the problem. You will learn (1) to distinguish between essential, specification and implementation models, each having a different purpose and a different set of related modelling techniques; (2) how to use simple statements in formal logic to express the properties and behaviour of objects accurately; (3) how to divide your software systems into architecturally-coherent parts, giving flexibility, simplicity and re-use; and (4) how to introduce concurrent processes into an object-oriented design, and how to synchronise concurrent access to objects, with special emphasis on the principle of "design by contract".

Steve Cook is founder and Managing Director of Object Designers Ltd, a UK-based consultancy practice specializing in object-oriented methods. He has practiced object-oriented software development for more than ten years. He has written many articles on object-oriented techniques and is writing a book with John Daniels, called *Designing Object Systems*, to be published by Prentice-Hall during 1994.

Metrics for Object-Oriented Design

Brian Henderson-Sellers
School of Information Sciences
University of New South Wales
P.O. Box 1
Kensington 2033
New South Wales
Australia
e-mail: brian@socs.uts.EDU.AU

Abstract: The use of metrics in project management of software systems development is an essential component of developing a competitive advantage based on quality products. In this tutorial the need for both process and product metrics will be explored at all phases in the life cycle. Traditional metrics will be evaluated as candidates for use in managing software developments based on the object paradigm and the need for new metrics to describe the iterative development process and the new structures (e.g. inheritance, services) unique to object technology will be highlighted. Reuse within the object-oriented framework will be evaluated using a cost-benefit approach.

Brian Henderson-Sellers is Professor of Information Systems in the School of Computing Sciences at the University of Technology, Sydney and author of *A Book of Object-Oriented Knowledge* (Prentice Hall, 1992).

Object-Oriented Analysis and Design with C++

Marc Goldberg
Rational
3320 Scott Blvd.
Santa Clara, CA 95054-3197
USA
e-mail: marc@rational.com

Abstract: This tutorial presents the concepts, techniques and processes of object analysis and design. It introduces the new unifying Booch's notation published in the reference book *O-O Analysis and Design with Applications*, Benjamin Cummings, 1993. This notation unifies the best of Booch 91, Rumbaugh, Coad, Jacobson and Schaeler-Mellor approaches in a complete and consistent framework. The notation is also used to describe the process of analysis and design. A real life European case study is offered to illustrate the different aspects of project management related to an object oriented development.

Marc Goldberg is manager of O-O product line at Rational in Santa Clara (USA). He has been actively involved in developing object-oriented systems in Europe and in the US for the past several years. He also speaks as the Rational representative at the OMG Consortium.

Teaching Object-Oriented Techniques

James McKim
Hartford Graduate Center
275 Windsor Street
Hartford, CT 06120-2991
USA
e-mail: jcm@mstr.hgc.edu

Abstract: An O-O course should address the claims of high quality made on behalf of the O-O paradigm. One way (perhaps the only way) for students to test such claims is to build a small but high quality product as part of the course. This tutorial will address such issues as: picking a reasonable and appropriate project to build; whether and how students should work in teams; keeping students from dropping too far behind or getting dangerously far ahead; dividing a project into a sequence of reasonable deliverables within the context of a one semester course; just what the deliverables should be. The presentation will also discuss how such an approach can be scaled down so that students in short industry courses can get maximum benefit in the limited time allowed.

James McKim, Jr is professor of computer science at Hartford Graduate Center and has more than twenty year's experience teaching mathematics and computer science. He has authored, coauthored and reviewed a number of textbooks and articles in both areas.

Multimedia and Object-Oriented Development

Peter Ward, Colin Parrot and Farath Arshad
University of Leeds
IMP School of Geography
University of Leeds
Leeds LS2 9JT
Great Britain
e-mail: peter@geog.leeds.ac.uk

Abstract: The evolution of a set of Eiffel-based tools will be presented with reference to the GPE (graphical programming language, based on C++), the 'Media Language' and 'Garden' (based on Eiffel and a new set of Class Libraries). These tools will be illustrated with reference to a number of application projects and working prototypes. Then the use of Eiffel in the construction of classes encapsulating some of the key features of UNIX and the X11 imaging model will be covered. Some of the key issues involved in the construction of systems and interfaces for educational and training applications will be described. Finally, some of the key practical and pragmatic issues for designers, programmers and developers of object-oriented multimedia applications will be summarized followed by an open discussion, question and answers.

Peter Ward is Director of the Information Modelling Programme (IMP) Group at the University of Leeds and a Consultant to CleverWare, a software house in Leeds.

Colin Parrot is a Consultant to Cleverware.

Farath Arshad is a Senior Research Scientist and Consultant to IMP.

Introduction to Object-Oriented Database Management Systems

Klaus Dittrich
Institut fuer Informatik
Universitaet Zuerich
Winterthurerstr. 190
CH-8057 Zuerich
Switzerland
e-mail: dittrich@ifi.unizh.ch

Abstract: Object-oriented database systems try to blend object- oriented concepts as they first emerged in programming languages with concepts from traditional (e.g network and relational) database management. In this tutorial, we will first discuss some shortcomings of existing DBMS and their data models and thus motivate why there is a need for further progress in this area. We will then explain the salient features of object-oriented data base systems and demonstrate how they extend previously known concepts. Finally, we point out their relationship to existing (i.e. relational) database technology and speculate on future developments.

Klaus Dittrich is professor for informatics at the University of Zurich, Switzerland where he heads the database technology research group. Prior affiliations include Forschungszentrum Informatik (FZI) at the University of Karlsruhe, Germany and IBM Almaden Research Center, San Jose, USA. He is a consultant for various companies and government agencies and is co-chairing VLDB 1995.

Object-Oriented Software Engineering

Ivar Jacobson
Objective Systems SF AB
Box 1128
S-164 22 KISTA
Sweden
e-mail: ivar@os.se

Abstract: This tutorial defines a process concept for object- oriented software development which covers the whole life cycle for software products (including embedded system software). The objective is furthermore to understand the need for several models in system building, how use cases help the development process to design the requested system, to find the right objects, to work as the glue between different models and to structure each model of a large system, and how the real world, naive objects found during the analysis activities should be implemented by other objects robust against future changes of the system. The following topics are covered: the process concept, different scenarios for the process, the model concept and the use case concept.

Ivar Jacobson is founder and VP of Technology at Objective Systems in Sweden, a software company that develops and markets the object-oriented development method ObjectOry. He has over 20 year's experience in the telecommunications industry. He developed an early object-based design technique, a major portion of which has evolved into the international standard CCITT/SDL.

A Critical Comparison of C++ and Eiffel – A Clash of Cultures

Richard Wiener
Journal of Object-Oriented Programming
135 Rugely Court
Colorado Springs, CO 80906
USA
e-mail: rswiener@elbert.uccs.edu

Abstract: This course presents a detailed and critical technical examination and comparison of object-oriented software development using C++ and Eiffel 3. The cultural differences between the "C++ mindset" and the "Eiffel mindset" are explored and illustrated with many examples. The Eiffel notion of "Programming by Contract" is compared to the C++ approach. Other technical issues that form the basis for comparing C++ and Eiffel are: (1) Software reuse - myth or reality in each language, (2) The scourge of memory leakage, (3) Mapping object-oriented design to implementation, (4) Genericity and inheritance, and (5) "What you see is what you get" or perhaps not! This intermediate level course assumes that the attendee has some experience with either C++ or Eiffel.

Richard Wiener is the editor-in-chief of the *Journal of Object-Oriented Programming* and associate professor of computer science at the University of Colorado at Colorado Springs. He has written 16 books on the subjects of Software Engineering, Data Structures, C, C++, Pascal, Modula-2, Smalltalk, and Objective-C.

Distributed Programming in C++, from sockets to CORBA

Michael Klug, Michael Stal
SIEMENS AG Corporate R & D
Dept. ZFE BT SE 32
Otto-Hahn-Ring 6
D-81739 Munich
P/O box D-81730 Munich
Germany
e-mail: Michael.Stal@zfe.siemens.de
e-mail: Michael.Klug@zfe.siemens.de

Abstract: The first part of this tutorial will present the basic concepts of interprocess communication. A class library will be presented which allows embedding basic communication patterns into Object-oriented programming. The second part will present distributed programming using a CORBA platform. A distributed system, Scalable Personal Object-oriented Network, will be used as an example to give an introduction to distributed O-O programming at high-level.

Michael Stal is a software engineer at Siemens Corporate Research and Development. He is a member of the C++ standards committee X3J16 as well as a member of the OMG.

Michael Klug is software engineer at Siemens Corporate Research and Development. Previously he was involved in the automatic transformation of existing source code to C++. He is currently working on the design and implementation of an O-O distributed system.

Frameworks: A Programmer's View of Developing Reusable Software

Ralph Johnson
Dept. of Computer Science
U. of Illinois at
Urbana-Champaign
1304 W. Springfield Ave.
Urbana IL 61801
e-mail: johnson@cs.uiuc.edu

Abstract: The key to reusable software is not the design of individual components, but the design of a framework for the components. Frameworks are reusable designs for an application or a subsystem expressed as a set of classes and the way that instances of these classes collaborate. A framework describes not only how to partition the responsibilities of a system among its components, but also how to think about a problem. It is therefore not only a way to reuse code, but also a way to reuse design and analysis information. This tutorial will describe frameworks and give a couple of examples. It will describe and illustrate the difference between a black-box and a white-box framework, will describe how frameworks evolve, and will teach some techniques for making a framework more reusable.

Ralph Johnson has been involved with building frameworks for operating systems, structured graphics editors, visual programming environments, code optimization, and accounting. He is on the faculty of the University of Illinois at Urbana-Champaign and has helped organize several OOPSLA's, including OOPSLA '93 as program chair.

AUTHOR INDEX

ABOUT THE TOOLS CONFERENCE SERIES

We hope you enjoy this TOOLS volume, reflecting the contributions to one of the conferences in the TOOLS series.

The conference series was started in 1989 to provide an international forum for the dissemination and advancement of object-oriented technology. The conference emphasizes the applications and practical aspects of the object-oriented methods; it also accepts theoretical and conceptual contributions provided they have a strong relevance to practitioners.

The conferences provide an opportunity for managers, developers and researchers interested in the progress of the field to meet, review the state of the art and exchange experiences. Each conference consists of the following elements:

- Invited lectures by leading international experts.
- In-depth tutorials on elementary, intermediate and advanced aspects of object-oriented technology.
- Submitted contributions, selected by the TOOLS program committee through a rigorous refereeing process.
- Exhibition of commercial and academic tools, products and services in the O-O field.
- Workshops providing experts with a setting to discuss advanced aspects of the technology.
- User group and standards meetings (normally on the day following the conference proper) held in conjunction with TOOLS to take advantage of the presence at the conference of many potential participants.

Reflecting the international nature of interest in and contributions to object-oriented development, the conference is held three times a year on three different continents: TOOLS EUROPE, TOOLS USA and TOOLS PACIFIC.

The following table gives a rough schedule for each event, and of the corresponding deadlines for submitting papers. Please note that this information is only approximate and that the actual dates may vary; check check the details with the conference organization at one of the addresses below, especially if you wish to submit a paper.

Event	Location	Date	Deadline for submissions
TOOLS EUROPE	Western Europe	March	September of previous year
TOOLS USA	California	Early August	March of same year
TOOLS PACIFIC	Pacific region	Late November or early December	August of same year

Proceedings of all TOOLS conferences starting with TOOLS 4 are available from Prentice Hall worldwide. Proceedings for earlier conferences are available from the conference organization at one of the addresses below.

For information about any of the conferences please send electronic mail to **tools@tools.com** or contact either of the two addresses below:

TOOLS Conferences
P.O. Box 6863
Santa Barbara, CA 93160
USA
Phone: (805) 685-1006, Fax: (805) 685-6869

TOOLS EUROPE
104 rue Castagnary
75015 Paris
France
Phone: +33/1-45 32 58 80, Fax +33/1-45 32 58 81

Prospective authors should also contact the TOOLS organization to get a copy of the *Guidelines for TOOLS authors* and maximize the likelihood of having their paper accepted. The Guidelines are available both in paper form and by electronic mail.